NICHOL'S SERIES OF STANDARD DIVINES.

PURITAN PERIOD.

With General Preface

BY JOHN C. MILLER, D.D.,

LINCOLN COLLEGE ; HONORARY CANON OF WORCESTER ; RECTOR OF ST MARTIN'S, BIRMINGHAM.

THE

WORKS OF HENRY SMITH.

VOL. II.

COUNCIL OF PUBLICATION.

W. LINDSAY ALEXANDER, D.D., Professor of Theology, Congregational Union, Edinburgh.

JAMES BEGG, D.D., Minister of Newington Free Church, Edinburgh.

THOMAS J. CRAWFORD, D.D., S.T.P., Professor of Divinity, University, Edinburgh.

D. T. K. DRUMMOND, M.A., Minister of St Thomas's Episcopal Church, Edinburgh.

WILLIAM H. GOOLD, D.D., Professor of Biblical Literature and Church History, Reformed Presbyterian Church, Edinburgh.

ANDREW THOMSON, D.D., Minister of Broughton Place United Presbyterian Church, Edinburgh.

General Editor.
REV. THOMAS SMITH, M.A., EDINBURGH.

THE WORKS

OF

HENRY SMITH;

INCLUDING

SERMONS, TREATISES, PRAYERS, AND POEMS.

WITH LIFE OF THE AUTHOR,
BY THOMAS FULLER, B.D.
AND OTHER BIOGRAPHICAL NOTES.

VOL. II.

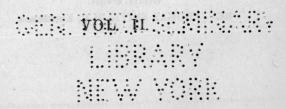

EDINBURGH: JAMES NICHOL.
LONDON: JAMES NISBET AND CO.   DUBLIN: G. HERBERT.

M.DCCC.LXVII.

EDINBURGH :

PRINTED BY JOHN GREIG AND SON,

OLD PHYSIC GARDENS.

CONTENTS.

SERMONS, &c.

THE BANQUET OF JOB'S CHILDREN.

THE BANQUET OF JOB'S CHILDREN.

And his sons went and banqueted in their houses, every one his day; and sent and called their three sisters, to eat and drink with them. And when the days of their banqueting were gone about, Job sent and sanctified them, and rose up early in the morning, and offered burnt-offerings, according to the number of them all: for Job thought, It may be that my sons have sinned and blasphemed God in their hearts. Thus did Job every day.—JOB I. 4, 5.

THIS book is a story of patient Job, and shews how God can deal with all, and how they should receive all things at his hand; seeing the most innocent man in the world, when God would try him, was brought so low, that the devil had power to lay upon him what torment he would, death only excepted, and yet he stood to it with such constancy, that he saith, 'Though the Lord kill me, yet will I trust in him.' Such power was given unto his faith, and love, and patience, that they overcame the devil, which said, that if he might have leave to plague him, he would make him 'blaspheme God to his face,' ver. 11. Therefore God would have this victory to be recorded of all such as are sick, or sore, or needy, or oppressed; that whatsoever pain we suffer, we may remember that Job's pain was sharper than this, and yet could not make him so impatient, but when like a man he was offended with his torments, like an holy man he was more offended with himself, and angry with his anger. Therefore at last God returned to him, and removed his troubles, and made his end more honourable than his beginning; as if he should say, Thus it shall be done to the man which is not offended with my chastisements.

Now to our purpose. In the first verse of this chapter the Holy

Ghost sheweth what a good man Job was, saying, that he was 'an upright and just man, one that feared God, and eschewed evil.' In the second verse he sheweth what store of children Job had, saying, 'he had seven sons and three daughters.' In the third verse he sheweth what store of riches Job had, saying, 'His substance was seven thousand sheep, and three thousand camels, and five hundred yoke of oxen, and five hundred asses,' &c. In the fourth verse he returneth again to his children, shewing how they were occupied before the wind came, and blew the house upon their head, saying, 'His sons went and banqueted in their houses, every one his day, and called their three sisters to eat and drink with them.' In the fifth verse he cometh again to Job, and shews a proof of his virtues, which he commended him for before, saying, 'That when his sons had banqueted, he sent for them, and sanctified them, and rose up early,' &c.

So if ye ask what his sons did; the Holy Ghost saith, that *they banqueted.* If ye ask where? he saith, *in their own houses.* If ye ask when? he saith, *every one kept his day.* If ye ask who were the guests? he saith, that one invited another, and the other invited him again, *and they called their sisters to them,* and so made merry together. If ye ask what farther Job did? the story saith, that after every feast, first *he sent for his sons,* and then *he sanctified them,* and then *he sacrificed for them;* the reason is added, because Job thought, 'It may be that my sons have sinned and blasphemed God in their hearts.' His zeal in this action is declared by three circumstances: first, that 'he rose up early in the morning;' secondly, that 'he offered so many acrifices as he had sons;' thirdly, that he performed this offering 'every day' while the feast lasted. Of every circumstance a little, because some had rather hear many things than learn one.

First, here is to be noted, that amongst the blessings of Job, his children are reckoned first. So soon as the Holy Ghost was past his spiritual blessings, which he mentioneth in the first verse of all, before all his other blessings, lands, and houses, and goods, and cattle, and friends, and servants, he speaks of his children as the chiefest treasure which Job had, next unto his virtues; although he was counted the greatest man for riches, and cattle, and all things else, in all the east parts, ver. 3. Therefore the devil, when he had taken away all his other riches, took away his children last of all, trying him as it were by degrees; as if he should say, I have a greater plague for him yet; if the losing of his goods, and stealing of his cattle, and burning of his houses, and slaying of his servants, will not move him, yet I know what will rouse him: when his children are all feasting together, I will raise a mighty wind, and blow down the house upon their heads, and kill every son and daughter which he hath at a clap. Indeed, this news frighted him sorest, as appeareth in the twentieth verse. His patience was so great, that when they brought him word of his oxen, and camels, and asses, and sheep, he never shrunk; we do not read that he made any answer, as though he cared not for them; but when he had heard that his dear children, seven sons and three daughters, after he had brought them up to ripe years, were slain all at once, then the story saith, that 'he rose up from his seat, and rent his garments, and shaved his head, and fell down to the ground, and cried, Naked came I out of my mother's womb, and naked shall I return again.' So even the devil knoweth what a man loveth, and what a blessing it is to have children. Therefore, when God commanded the man and the woman to 'increase and multiply,' it is said before that 'God blessed them,' Gen. i. 28, which was the first blessing that was given to man which is called a blessing, the blessing of children. Again, when God spake the same words to Noah and his sons, it is said before, that 'God blessed Noah and his sons,' Gen. ix. 1. So children came still under the name of *blessing.* Thus God himself sheweth that children are his gifts, to make you thankful for them, and careful of them, as Job was. And therefore some men have more riches, and some less, and some none, because it is 'the blessing of God,' as Solomon saith, 'which maketh men rich,' Prov. x. 22. So some men have many children, and some few, and some none, because it is 'the blessing of God,' as David saith, 'which sendeth children,' Ps. cxxvii. 3, and cxxviii. 3, 4. But this is the difference between temporal blessings and spiritual blessings, that spiritual blessings are simply good, and therefore do all men good that enjoy them; as faith, and love, and patience, can never hurt a man, but better him; and temporal blessings are as he which hath them. To a good man riches are good, honours are good, health is good, liberty is good, because he doeth good with them; but to an evil man they are evil, because they make him worse, and he doeth evil with them; as Jeroboam had not done so much hurt if he had not been in such honour. Therefore we pray for health, and wealth, and honour, and rest, and liberty, and life, with a caution, *If it be God's will;* as Christ prayed for the removing of his cross; because we know not whether they be good or evil, whether they will make us better or worse, or whether we shall do good with them or hurt. Thus when Job had his cattle, and his houses, and his friends, and his servants, and his childreu about him, he was like a man of whom David speaks, 'The righteous man shall flourish like a palm-tree,' Ps. xcii. 12. Therefore the devil said, that 'God had made a hedge about Job,' Job. i. 10. As an hedge goeth round about a garden, so God's blessings went round about Job; according to that Ps. xxxii. 10, 'Him which trusteth in the Lord, mercy shall embrace on every side.'

Thus Job was endowed with children; but how his children were affected, we cannot define so well as of their father, because the Holy Ghost saith nothing of them but that they banqueted, which doth sound as though he noted a disparity between Job and his sons, as there was between Eli and his sons; for oftentimes a godly father hath untoward children, which make him watch, and fast, and pray, and weep, when they little think, while they themselves ruffle, and swear, and banquet, and game, till poverty falls on their purses, as the house fell upon their heads. So it seems that Job's sons were secure upon their father's holiness, as many are upon their father's husbandry, which think, The old man hath enough for us; we need not care to get or save. So they might think, Our Father sacrificeth for us; we may feast and be merry; his devotion will serve for us; he is an old man, let him pray, and God will hear him. One Lot is enough in an house. But if Job had bred up his sons so, God would not have commended him, but rebuked him, as he did Eli. Therefore, this is not spoken against Job's sons, that they banqueted, as it is spoken against the Israelites, that they 'sat down to eat, and rose up to play.'

For, first, it is not like that he which was so commended of God that he said, 'No man was like him upon the earth,' ver. 8, would not teach his children in their youth, as he prayed for them after. Again, if they had been epicures, and libertines, and bezzlers, God would not have heard his prayer for them, no more than he would hear Samuel's prayer for Saul. Again, if they had despised that God which their father worshipped, he would never have said as he saith, 'It may be that my sons have blasphemed God,' as though some fault might escape them by ignorance or rashness; but he would have said, My sons are blasphemers, and therefore I must punish them; for that which the law said against blasphemers after, that Job understood by the law of conscience, written in his heart, as Paul saith, Rom. ii. 15.

Again, if they had used their feasts for their lusts, like them which say, 'Let us eat and drink, for to-morrow we shall die,' it had been vain for Job to speak to them of sanctification, for they would not have sanctified themselves at his bidding. But it is said that before Job offered sacrifice for them, they were sanctified; that is, they considered the faults which they had committed, and repented for them, and reconciled themselves, and then Job sacrificed for them. Again, if their feasts had been surfeiting and disorders, like our wakes and revels, Job should have forbidden their feasts, and not prayed God to pardon their sins which they committed in feasting, and suffer them to sin still; for that were to mock God, as though he desired not pardon for their sins past, but rather leave for them to sin still.

Lastly, we do not see by any circumstance of the story that they abused their feasts either in suspected houses, or profane company, or corrupt speeches, or impure gestures, or wanton dancings, or unlawful dalliances, or vain superfluities, but that our feasts might be allowed if they were like unto theirs. For, first, they did feast in their own houses; they did not run to ordinaries, or alehouses, or taverns, as they which seek for the strongest wine, or hunt after news, or worse purposes; but, like good neighbours, they invited one another home, and kept their hospitality in their own houses, as our gentlemen should do that lie about London, which are a kind of non-residents from their poor neighbours. Secondly, they did not feast every day, like the rich glutton in Luke xvi., but every one kept his day in the year when their feastings came. So it is not meant that the sons did nothing but feast, and the father nothing but pray; but, as the feasts of the Jews came at certain times of the year to celebrate some blessings of God, so they observed their feasting times, to celebrate their good wills one to another. Lastly, they did not join themselves with ruffians, and swearers, and tipplers, as all are wont to meet together at a feast; neither did they invite the rich to their tables, as James saith, which are feasts of flattery; but they were all one kin and one heart, brethren and sisters, like the disciples, which sat down together.

All this doth shew that their meetings tended to nourish amity, and that they had respect to the continuance of their peace, and increase of their love one towards another, which was the first cause that feasts were instituted in the primitive church, and therefore called the 'Feasts of Charity,' only that friends, and kinsmen, and neighbours might meet one with another to receive the blessings of God, and rejoice together like Joseph and his brethren, lest Christian familiarity should wear out of use and be forgotten. For ye may see in Eccles. ii. 24, and iii. 12, and v. 18, where Solomon speaketh of the joy, and pleasure, and delight which we may take in God's creatures ; and again in Ps. civ. 15, where David saith, that as bread was made to strengthen, so wine was made to comfort the heart, that God would not only have us fed, but of his exceeding goodness he would have us cheered and comforted beside, as he sheweth by this abundance of his creatures, in that he hath ordained so many things more than we need. Why did God create more things than we need, but to shew that he alloweth us needful and comfortable things ? For all the good things which were not created for need, were created for delight. Therefore even the Scriptures have commended solemn feasts, in Lev. xxiii., Num. xxviii. 29, Exod. xiii., where ye may read of sundry feasts commanded by God himself ; as the feasts of gathering fruits, the feasts of trumpets, the feasts of tabernacles, the feasts of new moons, the feasts of reconciliation, the feasts of dedication of the temple, &c. Beside, it is said that ' Abraham made a great feast the same day that Isaac was weaned,' Gen. xxi. 8 ; so it is said of Samson, that he made a feast when he was married, Judges xiv. 10. And at a feast in Cana, Christ shewed the first miracle that ever he wrought, turning water into wine, John ii. If feasts had been unlawful, Christ would not have been there ; therefore the wise man saith, 'There is a time to laugh,' as well as he saith, 'There is a time to weep,' Eccles. iii. 4. When he saith there is a time both to laugh and weep, he implieth that the time to laugh is not every day ; as it is said of Dives, that ' he fared deliciously every day,' Luke xvi., for then there were a time to laugh, but no time to weep. Therefore, if ye will know the time when to laugh, and when to weep, God hath set Uriah for an example. When the church was quiet, and his country safe, Uriah could rejoice as well as others ; but when the church was troubled, and his country in danger, though the king bade him go home, and eat, and drink, and solace with his wife, he would not do so, but said, ' The ark of Israel and Judah dwelleth in tents, and my lord Joab and the servants of my lord abide in the open field ; and shall I go to my house, and eat, and drink, and be merry with my wife ? By thy life, and by the life of thy soul, I will not do this thing.' See what a sin he counted it to feast then, which at another time he counted no sin. Therefore, if ye ask when it is time to feast, and when to fast, learn of Uriah ; he forbade not to feast, but if he should see your feasting now, he would say, as Elisha said to Gehazi, 'Is this a time to take a reward?' Is this a time to make feasts ? Nay, the father and the sons both had need to arise early now, and sacrifice together ; for if ever the house were falling upon our heads, as it did upon theirs, now the devil hath sent forth his winds, now the pope hath laid his ordnance, nay, our own hands, which should prop it, are digging as busily as the enemies, with reproaches, and slanders, and suggestions, to undermine the church, which is falling already, that we might die like the Philistines, with the temple upon our heads. Is this a time to feast, Uriah, when the house of God is beset like the house of Lot; when the armies of antichrist are preparing against God's people? As the voice asked Zechariah, and Amos, and Jeremiah, what they did see; so if you ask your prophets what they do see, they may say, they do see the wolf devouring the lambs. We see a dark ignorance running over the land, like the blackness of Egypt; we see the Romans coming in again, as they came to Jerusalem, and sacking the temple; we see the papist carving of images, and the people kneeling before them; we see the professors of the gospel shrink away, as the disciples fled from their Master when he was taken. Is this a time to feast, Uriah? is this a time to flatter? is this a time to dissemble? is this a time to loiter? is this a time to keep silence? is this a time to gather riches? is this a time to revenge wrongs? is this a time to set forth pageants? No, saith Hezekiah, 2 Kings xix. 3, 'This is a time of tribulation,' in which the prince, and nobles, and people should humble themselves, as the citizens of Nineveh, lest the ark be taken from England, as the ark was taken from Israel, which God grant that our eyes never see!

Thus much of Job's children, how every one had his several house; which sheweth how God blessed them with riches, as he did their father, and what care Job had, like a father, to provide for them; then how they feasted together, which sheweth 'how sweet and pleasant a thing it is for brethren to dwell together in unity,' Ps. cxxxiii. 1.

Now you shall see what the old man doeth, which was so commended in the first verse; the story saith, that 'he sent for his sons, and sanctified them, and sacrificed for them.' In which words the Holy Ghost sheweth the pattern of an holy man and good father, which kept the rule that God gave unto Abraham, to 'bring up his children in the fear of the Lord.' Job doeth not as some, which when they have passed their bounds, set all at random, and say with Cain in Gen. iv., 'My sin is greater than can be forgiven;' but he goeth to the remedy, as the Jews when they were stinged went to the brazen serpent: albeit my children have not done their duties in all points, but offended in their feastings, yet am I sure that God will have mercy upon them and upon me, if we ask him forgiveness. Therefore, he sent for his sons like a father, and then he taught them like a preacher to sanctify themselves, and then he offered sacrifice for them. First, we will speak of the cause which moved Job to sacrifice for his sons, set down in these words, Job thought, 'It may be that my sons have blasphemed God in their hearts.' He was glad, good man, to see his children agree so well together; but he would have them merry, and not sin, and, therefore, he puts them in mind every day while they feasted, to sanctify themselves. He condemneth not honest mirth and sober feasts, to maintain amity and peace; but, being thoroughly acquainted with man's infirmity, he shewed that he never had observed any feasts so duly celebrated, but some disorder or other hath crept in, whereby God hath been dishonoured at his own table, either for superfluity of meat, or excess of drink, or unchaste songs, or corrupt speeches, or wanton dancings, or unseemly dalliances. The devil hath been still at one end, and is lightly the master of the feast. Therefore Job thought with himself, It may be that my sons have committed some scape like other men: I cannot tell, they are but men; it is easy to slip when occasion is ready, though they think not to offend. He had no apparent cause to suspect them, and therefore he speaks in the doubting phrase, 'It may be that they have sinned.' It is better to be fearful than too secure; that which happeneth often in the like case, he might well doubt it, though he had warned them before; therefore his heart was not quiet, but still this ran in his mind all the while they feasted, 'It may be that my sons sin.' How wary was Job over himself, which was so jealous over his sons, lest one sin should slip from them! Nay, if ye mark, he speaketh not of any open or gross sins which he feared; but he speaketh of a sin in the thought, 'It may be that my sons have blasphemed God *in their hearts.*'

Blasphemy is properly in the mouth, when a man speaks against God, as Rabshakeh did; but Job had a farther respect to a blasphemy of the heart, counting every sinister affection of the heart as it were a kind of blasphemy, or petty treason. Thus the penitent man doth aggravate his sins, and stretch them as it were upon the rack, to make his small sins seem great sins, that he might beware as well of small as great. Contrariwise, the profane and carnal-minded man doth mince, and flatter, and extenuate his sins, as though they were no sins, because they should not trouble him. For this sin, which Job calleth blasphemy, which is the highest name of sin, the papists call but a venial sin, that is, but a slight sin, because it is in the thought: so Job and they differ in judgment.

Now concerning this speech of Job, 'It may be that my sons have sinned,' or, It may be that myself have sinned, which I may properly and rightly term the jealousy of a holy man; herein Job sheweth in what fear he stood of his sons so long as their feast lasted, even as a merchant doth till his ship come home. First, we may see this, that the best things may soon be corrupted by the wickedness of men; such is our nature, ever since Adam chose evil before good, good hath been turned into evil, Gen. iii., notwithstanding that our intent and meaning be good. As for example, when an husband loveth his wife, or a father loveth his children, these are good and holy and commendable things; yet there is no man can be found that doth love his wife or his children with that evenness, as I may call it, or just proportion, but that there is some odds in the balance when his affection is weighed, which may crave pardon, like the feasts of Job's children. If this odds be in all our measures, then it is no strange case, that Job thought with himself, that his children might offend God in the thing that of itself offendeth not. Therefore it is good for man, so long as he liveth in this world, to remember still that he is amongst temptations, and sits at a feast like Job's children, where he may soon take too much. If the fish did know the hook, and the bird had seen the net, though they have but the understanding of fishes and birds, yet they would let the hook alone, and fly over the net, and let the fowler whistle to himself. So we must look upon our riches as we look upon snares, and behold our meats as we behold baits, and handle our pleasures as we handle bees, that is, pick out the sting before we take the honey; for in God's gifts Satan hath hid his snares, and made God's benefits his baits; that, as Adam said, 'The woman which thou hast given me tempted me to sin,' so they may say, The riches, or the honours, or the liberty, or the wife, or the servants, or the children, or the meats, or the wit, or the beauty which thou hast given me, tempted me to sin. So many sins lie in wait for us about our meats, and drinks, and beds, and ways, that, unless we watch, pray, and look about us at every time, 'It may be,' as Job saith, 'that we may sin,' in our doings, or in our sayings, or at least in our hearts, as he thought of his sons. Therefore, no doubt, but as Job thought that his sons might offend in their feastings, so he taught them even when they were feasting, and when they sat at the table, and when they drank one to another, to think oftentimes, We may sin, as our father told us which bridled their mirth, and stopped many words at the door, even when sin was at the tongue's end. You are not Job's sons, but you are come to be Job's scholars ; therefore, learn that which his children learned. If a man did but carry this watchword with him, whensoever he eateth, or speaketh, or bargaineth, it would cut off a thousand idle words and wicked acts in one year, for which he shall give account.

The second lesson which Job seems to point us unto is, to prepare ourselves before we eat the communion ; that is, to sanctify ourselves and meats, as Christ did : when they had nothing but a few fishes and bare bread, yet there was prayer before they did eat. For, as Paul saith, 'All the creatures of God are sanctified unto us by prayer and thanksgiving.' He which doth not pray to God for his daily bread, nor thank him for it, doth not receive the creatures of God, but steal them from him, as a man which taketh a thing without asking or thanking. There is a kind of men which I speak of, which hold it too sad a matter to say a short grace before they fall to meat, lest it should fore-speak their mirth, and keep them in a sober mind till they rise again. I have heard many say, that they cannot be merry unless they swear, and whoop, and carouse, and dally, and gibe ; therefore, if they can choose, they will never be a guest where any godly man is present, lest his countenance or word shall dash their sport ; and if any matter of God happen to come in while they are in the vein, it is like a damp which puts out their lights, and turns their mirth into heaviness, as the hideous hand which wrote upon the wall cast Belshazzar into a dump. These men had need to leave their feasting, and go to praying ; for they desire to die, like the Jews, with the quails in their mouths. It may be, thought Job, that my sons have a spice of this vanity. If it be so with the godly sort, as Job's children were, that they may forget themselves at such a time, and step too far, and slip a sin ; what shall we say of them that drive God out of their company when they banquet, and say that Scripture doth not become the table ? as though we should forget God while we receive his benefits. We need not say as Job said, 'It may be that they blaspheme God in their hearts ;' for they blaspheme him with their mouths : we need not say, 'It may be that they do sin ;' for they do nothing but sin, and their feast is a feast of sins, as if the devils should banquet together. But they which feast as Job would have his children, sanctify themselves before, and eat as in the presence of God, and are merry as it were with the angels ; when they take their bread, they think with themselves, What a goodness is this, that God giveth such virtue to bread to sustain life, which hath no life in itself! and when they see so many things before them prepared for the flesh, they consider with themselves, What care God hath of my soul, which careth so much for my body, which shall go to dust!

There is yet another lesson which will stand you in great stead, if ye mark it. When Job here saith, 'It may be that my sons have sinned;' hereby he teacheth us to suspect the worst of the flesh, and to live in a kind of jealousy of ourselves, as he saith that his manner was, Job ix. 28, 'I feared all my works;' that is, he did mistrust himself, and washed[1] his hands, and his feet, and his eyes, and his ears, and his tongue, lest they should sin; as a mercer mistrusts his prentice lest he should filch, so he thought not only whether his sons sinned, but he thought of his own sins too. When thou seest some selling in their shops, some tippling in the taverns, some playing in theatres, then think of this with thyself: It is very like that these men swallow many sins, for God is never so forgotten as in feasting, and sporting, and bargaining; then turn to thy compassion, and pray for them, that God would keep them from sin when temptation is at hand, and that he would not impute their sins to their charge; so we should do for our brethren, as Job did for his children. Again, so we ought to think when we ourselves come from places of temptation, which infect like a corrupt air, It may be that I have sinned. Have I seen and heard all this, and not slipped my foot with them? come I home sound and whole? have I drawn none of the infected air? doth none of the dust stick upon my garments? Look about, my soul, and if thou rememberest any sin which slipped from thee, then pray for thyself, as Job did for his children. If thou wilt not pray for thyself, who shall pray for thee? If thou wilt not repent thyself, who shall repent for thee? Look not for Job to sacrifice for thee. Job cannot sacrifice for thee, but thou mayest sacrifice thyself, and none but thee. This should be the thought of every Christian, not whether we have pleased, not whether we have revenged, but whether we have sinned; for if Job was so jealous of his children, how should we be of ourselves!

[1] Qu. 'watched'?—ED.

SATAN'S COMPASSING THE EARTH.

SATAN'S COMPASSING THE EARTH.

Then the Lord saith unto Satan, Whence comest thou ? And Satan answered the Lord, saying, From compassing the earth to and fro, and from walking in it. And the Lord said unto Satan, Hast thou not considered my servant Job, how none is like him in the earth, an upright man, one that feareth God, and escheweth evil ?—Job I. 7, 8.

I HAVE spoken of the question already, now of the answer. *Compassing* here doth signify tempting, and the *earth* doth signify all the people of the earth ; as if he should say, I come from tempting all men. It is some vantage unto us to hear that the Spaniards are coming, before they come ; and what number they have, and how they are appointed, that we may levy our forces accordingly. But, beloved, there is a greater adversary than the Spaniard, which brings in the Spaniard, 'your adversary the devil.' It is good for us to hear whence he comes, that we may be in a readiness against him, as we prepare against them. Therefore this scripture and this time accord well. In Rev. xii. 10, the devil is called 'an accuser,' and now I am an accuser of the accuser ; he accuseth us to God, and God accuseth him to us, that when he comes like an angel, yet we may say to him like Christ, 'Avoid, Satan !' First, give me leave to say unto you, as Christ said unto his disciples, 'Take heed how you hear ;' for that which I am to speak unto you of the devil, the devil would not have you hear. And therefore, as he is here called a compasser, so he will compass your eyes with shows, and your ears with sounds, and your senses with sleep, and your thoughts with fancies, and all to hinder you from hearing while the articles are against him ; and after I have spoken, he will compass you again with business, and cares, and pleasures, and quarrels, to make you forget that which you have heard, as he hath made you forget that which you have heard before ; or else to contemn it, as though you might do well without it, as he hath compassed them which do walk in the streets while the voice of God soundeth in the churches as they pass by. Therefore, before every sermon ye had need to remember Christ's lesson, ' Take heed how ye hear.'

Now to the matter, ' Satan, from whence comest thou ?' ' I come from compassing the earth.' Here the devil is called in like a jailer, which keeps some in perpetual prison, and some are bailed, and some return to prison again, and some are executed. They which sin fearfully stay as it were about the prison, but are not bound ; they which sin wittingly are under lock ; they which sin greedily are under lock and bolts ; they which die in their sin are like them which are condemned : this is the bondage which we have brought ourselves unto for a fair apple. When the tempter overcame us, we were removed out of paradise, where we were seated ; when we have overcome the tempter, we shall be translated into heaven, where he was seated. Heaven-door was wide, and the way was broad, before the rebellion ; but when we knocked at the cannel door,[1] then the good door was shut. Heaven is large, but the way to heaven must be narrow ; therefore God hath set our enemies in the gate to fight with us before we enter, that this saying might be verified, ' The kingdom of heaven is caught by violence.' So soon as we rise in the morning, we go forth to fight with two mighty giants, the world and the devil ; and whom do we take with us but a traitor, this brittle flesh, which is ready to yield up to the enemy at every assault ? Only he which suffereth Satan to compass us doth stay him from destroying us. When God asked Cain, ' Where is thy brother ?' Cain lied, and said, ' I cannot tell' ; when God asked Sarah why she laughed, Sarah lied, and said, ' I laughed not ;' but when God asked the devil from whence he came, he answered truly, ' I come from compassing the earth.' And yet he which speaketh truth himself taught them to lie, as he is called the father of liars, because he teacheth all others to lie. How then ? Was Cain worse than the devil because he lied and the other told truth ? By this you may see that carnal men do not know so much of God as the very devil knoweth ; for he knew that God could tell where he had been, but Cain doubted whether God could tell what he had done, and therefore he made a lie. Thus the devil teacheth his scholars to do worse sometimes than he

---

[1] Qu. ' kennel-door' ?—ED.

will do himself; even as he would bring them, if it were possible, into a worse plight than he is in himself. The devil's faith cannot save us, no more than it can save him; the devil's knowledge cannot convert us, no more than it doth convert him; and yet he would not have men believe that which he believeth himself, nor have us understand so much as he understandeth himself. For if Cain had understood so much as he, that God knew whether he lied or no, he would have answered God truly, as Satan did. But the devil knew that there was no dissembling with God, who knows what he asks before he asks; therefore he told truth to God, though he lie to man; for to lie unto him which knoweth, is as if one should lie to himself. But Cain was not so well learned; he thought peradventure God might understand his murder, as a thief suspecteth in his heart that the judge may know his theft, but he doubted whether God did know it, and therefore he denied it, like one which is guilty, but thinks that if he confess he shall be hanged; and therefore though evidence and witness accuse them, yet you see many will not accuse themselves.

From compassing the earth. He which was called *Satan* before, which signifieth *an adversary*, is here said to 'compass the earth;' which is to say, being put together, an adversary compassing the earth; and therefore let the earth beware, like a city which is besieged with the adversaries. The devil hath more names than any prince hath titles; some God hath given to him, and some he hath given to himself. But this is to be noted in the devil's names, that he never calleth himself a liar, nor a tempter, nor an accuser, nor a slanderer, nor a deceiver, nor a devourer, nor a murderer, nor a master, nor an adversary, nor a viper, nor a lion, nor a dragon, nor a wolf, nor a cockatrice, nor a serpent. But when Christ asked him his name, he called himself Legion, which imports a multitude, as if he should brag of his number; and here he calls himself in effect the compasser of the earth, as if he should brag of his power. And in Luke iv. 6, he calleth himself the possessor of the earth, as if he should brag of his possessions; and in the same he calleth himself the giver of the earth, as if he should brag of his liberality. Thus he which is evil itself doth shun the name, because he would not be hated; and therefore no marvel if men 'call evil good,' and would be counted honest, though they be never so lewd, for so will the devil. But as God never called the devil but by those names which the devil hated, so he never calleth sinners by those names which they call themselves. For if you observe the scripture, there is no name of the devil, but in some place of Scripture or other the wicked are called by the same name. He is called a liar, and they are called liars; he is called a tempter, and they are called tempters; he is called a murderer, and they are called murderers; he is called a slanderer, and they are called slanderers; he is called a viper, and they are called vipers; he is called a lion, and they are called lions; he is called a wolf, and they are called wolves; he is called a serpent, and they are called serpents. Thus God would they that shall be damned should have the name of him which is damned, to put him in mind. Now, none of the devil's names are in the book of life, and therefore liars, and tempters, and slanderers, and murderers, and defamers, are not; therefore these are devil's names. This I note, to shew you how deadly God doth hate sin, that neither the devil nor his followers could ever get a good name of him; for all this compassing, he could never compass this, to shuffle any praise of himself into this book of life; for he doth not compass heaven, but earth, though he would compass both. The devil himself doth tell us here that he compasseth, and he telleth us not why he compasseth; but his name Satan, that went before, which he spake not of, doth tell us why he compasseth. Because it signifies *an adversary*, it gives us to understand that he compasseth the earth like an adversary. God doth compass the earth like a wall to defend it; the devil compasseth the earth like an enemy to besiege it. For *enemy* is his name; he is envy, even to the name.

Three things I note wherefore the devil may be said to compass the earth: first, because he tempteth all men; secondly, because he tempteth all to sin; thirdly, because he tempteth by all means. So whosoever sinneth, wherein soever he offendeth, whereby soever he is allured, the sin, the sinner, and the bait, are compassed and contrived by the arch-politic, which calls himself a compasser. Many have their names for nought, because they do nothing for them; like Laban's images, which were called gods, though they were but blocks; but the devil deserves his names. He is not called a tempter, a liar, a slanderer, and an accuser, and a deceiver, and a murderer, and a compasser, in vain; like St George, which is always on horseback, and never rides; but he would do more than by his office he is bound to. Others are called officers, because they have an office; but he is called an enemy, because he shews his envy. Others are called justicers, because they *should* do justice; but he is called a tempter, because he practiseth temptations. Others are called pastors, because they *should* feed; but he is called a devourer, because he doth devour; and we call him a compasser, because that he doth compass. Ever since he fell from heaven he hath lived like Cain, which cannot rest in a place, but is a runagate over the earth, from door to door, from man to man, begging for sins as the starved soul begs for bread. He should have dwelt in heaven, and not been compassing the earth; he should have sung with the angels, and not been quarrelling with men; but he hath changed his calling, and is become a compasser, that is, to lay fetters upon men, as God hath fettered him, lest they should ascend to the place from whence he is fallen. Therefore in this the liar spake truth when he said, 'I come from compassing the earth;' as if he should say to God, I come from the slaughter of thy servants; not to ask forgiveness for all the souls which he hath slain already, but to get a commission that God would make him knight-marshal over the world, to slay and kill as many as he hated; like the bramble which set itself on fire first, and then fired all the wood. Peter, describing the devil's walk, saith, that 'he goeth about;' the devil saith, that 'he goeth a-compassing.' Peter put in, 'seeking whom he may devour;' the devil leaves out *devour*, and saith no more but that he 'compasseth.' This circular walk is peculiar to the devil, and therefore may be called the devil's circuit. All other creatures go forward, but the devil goeth about; which may well be applied to the crafty devil, because to go about is commonly taken to undermine; when any meaneth to destroy you, then we say, he will compass you; so when the devil compasseth, then beware lest he devour. For the devil goeth about men as the fowler goeth about the lark to snare her, as the thief goeth about the house to rob it, as the ivy goeth about the oak to kill it. The devil's walk is a siege, which goeth about but to find an issue to go in; for he goeth about until he can get in to be a possessor. He is content to be a compasser. The first name the devil hath in Scripture is a serpent; he is a serpent, and so are his ways like a serpent, which windeth himself like a circle. As God is said to make an hedge about men, so here the devil is said to make an hedge about men; but this is an hedge of temptations, and that is an hedge against temptations. As David saith, the angels compass us, so might he say, the devils compass us. Satan compasseth, and man is compassed. Satan is like the circumference, and man is as it were the centre; that is, temptations go round about him, and he dwelleth in the midst of them. Thus much of compassing; now what he doth compass.

I come from compassing the earth. This is the devil's pilgrimage, from one end of the earth to the other, and then to the other again, and then back again; like a wandering merchant, which seeketh his traffic where he can speed cheapest. I have heard of some travellers which have gone about the earth. but I never heard of any that had seen all parts of the earth ; but this old pilgrim Satan, which hath been in heaven, and in paradise, and in the earth, and in the sea, and in hell, and yet hath not done his walk ; but, like the sun, which courseth about the earth every day, so there is not one day but Satan seeth every man upon earth. As a compass hath no end, so he makes no end of compassing. Because he is such a compasser of the world, therefore Paul calleth him ' the god of this world ;' not a piece of the world, as England, or Ireland, or France, or Germany, or Spain ; but of the world, that is, of all the countries, and cities, and towns, and villages, and houses. The pope talks of his kingdom, how many provinces are under his dominion ; but the devil's circuit is greater than the pope's. One would think that he could never tend half his flock, because he is vicar of so great a monarchy, and yet he is never non-resident. You may see his steps everywhere, so brim and fresh, as though they were printed in ashes. If God make you see your country naked, your temples desolate, your cities ruinated, your houses spoiled, you will say the Spaniards have been here ; so when you see your minds corrupted, your hearts hardened, your wills perverted, your charity cooled, your judges bribers, your rulers persecutors, your lawyers brabblers, your merchants usurers, your landlords extortioners, your patrons simonists, your pastors loiterers, you may say the devil hath been here. Seeing then these weeds grow in every ground, you may bear the devil witness, that he doth compass all the earth. If a man love his friend, he will say, I will go an hundred miles to do him good ; but if the devil hate a man, he will go a thousand miles to do him hurt. The devil doth not go his progress like a king, only for delight ; but all the way he goeth, Peter saith, ' he seeketh whom he may devour.' The devil goeth a-visiting, he will teach the sick how they shall recover their health, he will whisper the poor how they shall come by riches, he will tell the captives how they shall redeem their liberty ; but to devour is the end of his visitation. Therefore Peter called him a lion, and said, that he ' went about,' and told us that he 'sought' as he went ; at last he saith, ' to devour,' and there he ends ; shewing, that devouring is his end.

Now you shall hear whom he compasseth, and to what he compasseth, and how he compasseth. When it is said, that the devil compasseth the earth, it is meant that he compasseth the men of the earth ; out of which I gather, first, of all creatures he compass-

eth men; secondly, that he compasseth all men, and by conse-
quence that he compasseth good men. The devil is like an archer,
and man is his mark, and temptations are his arrows. As Peter is
called 'a fisher of men,' so the devil may be called a hunter of
men; for of all creatures his envy is only to men, because man was
made to serve God, and inherit the joys which he hath lost; therefore he is called no slayer, but a man-slayer. When there are no
men upon earth, then the devil will compass the earth no more.

Secondly, he assaulteth all men, like Ishmael, which was against
all. It is said of Saul and David, 'Saul hath slain his thousand,
and David his ten thousand;' but if you put in Satan, you may set
up the number, and say, Satan hath slain his hundred thousand. As
there is a legion of men, so there is a legion of devils; that
as they say Peter's angel, so they might say Peter's devil. For
Christ would not have called Peter *Satan*, if Satan had not backed
him. As death killeth all, so the devil tempteth all; when he hath
Eve, he hunteth for Adam; when he hath Adam, he hunteth for
Cain; as the father was tempted, so was the son; as the mother
was tempted, so must her daughters. Every man but Christ may
say, I have been overcome; but Christ himself cannot say, I have
not been tempted. In the Spanish inquisition the protestants are
examined, but the papists slip by; but in the devil's inquisition
papist and protestant, and atheist and puritan, and all are examined.
He is not a captain of forties, nor of fifties, nor of sixties, nor of
hundreds; but he is general over all which fight not under Christ's
banner; he possessed the two Gergesites, which were men; he possessed Mary, which was a woman; he possessed the man's son,
which was a child. Nimrod is called 'a mighty hunter,' which
killed beasts; but this is a mighty hunter, which killed Nimrod
himself. God keep us out of his chase!

Thirdly, he warreth against the righteous, even because they are
righteous. As God makes the barren fruitful, and the fruitful to
bear more fruit, so the devil would have them serve him which
serve him not; and they which serve him, to serve him more; and
therefore, as the giant encountered with David, so the devil encountered with David and with David's Lord. He which gave him leave
here to tempt Job, was after tempted himself, although the net
brake, and the bird escaped. Yet as he tempted Christ thrice together, and as he desired to sift Peter more than others, so they
that follow Christ, and are like Peter, are sifted more than others.
For this viper is like the viper which seized upon Paul. Among
many which stood by the fire, the viper chose out Paul, and lighted

upon him before all the rest ; so if one be holier than another, this viper will battle with him. And there is great reason why the godly are tempted more than the wicked ; because the wicked are his servants, and do tempt others.

As he tempteth all men, so he tempteth to all sins ; for hell and the devil are alike ; therefore, as hell is never filled with sinners, so the devil is never filled with sins; and therefore when he had made Peter deny his Master once, he made him deny him twice ; and when he made him deny him twice, he made him deny him thrice. For this cause our sins are counted amongst those things which are infinite, because the devil and our flesh meet together every day to engender new sins. All the devil's riches are in baits ; he hath a pack full of oaths for every one which will swear ; a pack full of lies for every one which will deceive ; a pack full of excuses for every one which will dissemble. As he doth go through the streets, into every shop he casts a short measure, or a false balance ; as he passeth by the taverns, he sets dissension betwixt friends ; as he passeth by every inn, he casts a pair of cards, and a pair of dice, and a pair of tables ; as he passeth by the courts, and finds the lawyers at the bar, he casts amongst them false evidences, forged writings, and counterfeit seals. Thus in every place where he comes (like a foggy mist), he leaves an evil savour behind him. The murmuring of Moses, the dissimulation of Abraham, the idolatry of Aaron, the incest of Lot, the drunkenness of Noah, the adultery of David, the flight of Jonah, the denial of Peter ; name Satan, and thou hast named the very spawn of all sins, which with his tail plucked down the stars from heaven. How many hate their enemies and friends too, and yet embrace this enemy, because he kisseth when he betrayeth, as though he would not betray ! Avarice saith, I will make thee amiable ; tyranny saith, I will make thee dreadful ; sloth saith, I will make thee beautiful ; vanity saith, I will make thee merry; prodigality saith, I will make thee beloved. So the poor sinner stands distract how he may follow all sins at once ; seeking grapes of thistles, and roses of thorns.

As he tempteth to all sins, so he tempteth by all means ; for the name of a compasser doth import a cunning tempter. There is craft in compassing. The hunter maketh a rail about the deer, as though he would guard them, when he meaneth to take some of them ; the fowler goeth about the bird as if he did not see her, when he comes to snare her. If men have so many sleights to compass their matters, how can the compasser himself hold his fingers ? If the serpent's seed be so subtle, what do you think of the old serpent, who hath been learning his trade ever since the creation? If men's trades may be called crafts, the devil's trade may be called craft. Herod is called a fox, but this fox taught him his subtlety. This is he that prepared flatterers for Rehoboam, which prepared liars for Ahab, which prepared concubines for Solomon, which prepared sorcerers for Pharaoh, which prepared witches for Saul, which prepared wine for Benhadad, which prepared gold for Achan, which prepared a ship for Jonah, which prepared a rope for Haman. He goeth not about for nothing. But this is the first trick of his compassing, he marks how every man is inclined, what he loves, what he hates, what he fears, what he wants; and when he hath the measure of his foot, then he fits him. Ask what you will, here is he which offered the whole world. What? Shall Jonah stay for want of a ship? Nay, here is a ship, go and fly from the Lord. Shall Esau stay for want of broth? Nay, here is a mess of broth, go and sell thy birthright. Shall Judas stay for want of thirty pence? Nay, here is thirty pence, go and betray thy Master. Shall Pilate stay for want of an halter? Nay, here is an halter, go and hang thyself. The tyrant shall not want a flatterer, the wanton shall not want a mate, the usurer shall not want a broker, the thief shall not want a receiver. He is a factor between the merchant and the mercer, and the gentleman and the tenant; he is a make-bate between the man and his wife; he is a tale-bearer between neighbour and neighbour. Thus if you ask me what is the devil's trade or occupation, all the day long he is making nets, and gins, and snares to catch thee and me, which gape for the worm.

If then the devil be such a busybody, which meddleth in every man's matter, let us remember what the wise man saith, ' A busybody is hated ;' the devil is to be hated, because he is a busybody. The Jews could not abide the publicans, because they were like sumners and takers, which carried toll out of their country into another; how then can we abide this great publican, which taketh toll over all the world? nay, not toll of men, but men themselves? He which compasseth the earth, compasseth us, even us that stand here. Therefore, what shall I say, but as Christ said, When the thief compasseth the house, shall not the owner guard the house? If the city be compassed and not defended, how shall it stand? As the devil runneth round about, so the armour must go round about us; and then, though he compass us, yet he shall not overcome us; but as the Israelites were safe, though the water compassed about them, as the three children were safe, though the flames compassed about them, as Daniel was safe, though the lions compassed about him, so they which have Christ's armour are safe, although the devil compass about them. 'I will not fear, saith David, 'what man can do unto me;' nay, I will not fear what the devil can do unto me, for he which is with me is greater than he which is against me. Thus much of the devil and his compassing.

As the serpent compasseth, so doth his seed; and, therefore, Solomon calls the ways of the wicked crooked ways. This is the great compasser, there be little compassers beside; like the pharisees, of whom it is said, that 'they compassed sea and land to make one like themselves.' Instead of these compassers we have seminary priests, which compass from Rome to Tyburn, to draw one from Christ to antichrist. I will not name all compassers beside, lest I be compassed myself; but this I speak within compass, that there is a craft of compassing, and Satan is the craft-master, and the rest are his prentices, or factors under him. When he compasseth some men, he sets them to compass other men; and so he hath his compassers and spies in every country, like continual liegers to follow his business for him, which will do it as faithfully as himself. If he appoint them to lie, they will lie as fast as he; if he appoint them to deceive, they will deceive as cunningly as he; if he appoint them to slander, they will slander as falsely as he; if he appoint them to flatter, they will flatter as smoothly as he; if he appoint them to mock, they will mock as scornfully as he; if he appoint them to revenge, they will revenge as spitefully as he; if he appoint them to persecute, they will persecute as fully as he. So if he do but say, Let there be an oath, straight there is an oath; let there be a lie, straight there is a lie; let there be a flout, straight there is a flout; let there be a bribe, straight there is a bribe; let there be a quarrel, straight there is a quarrel. Therefore in this the liar told the truth, for he hath compassed the earth indeed.

Thus you see what the devil answered, when God asked him from whence he came. Now if God should ask you, as he asked the devil, from whence you came before you came hither to him, or rather, whither you will go when ye depart from him? I do verily think that some here did come from as bad exercises as the devil himself, and that when they do depart from this place, they will return to as bad exercises again as the devil did; some unto the taverns, and some unto the alehouses, and some unto stages, and some unto brothels, and some unto dicing, and some unto quarrelling, and some unto cozening. I would fain know this, If the devil came from tempting, and you from sinning, who was better occupied? he in commanding you, or you in obeying him? They which come to the church, and return to their sins, come to the Lord as the devil came, not to be reformed of his evil, but to have a passport to do more evil. If any such be here, he hath learned nothing, but goeth empty away; for they which come like Satan, go like Satan. A little water is sprinkled upon them, which falls off again to the ground so soon as they are out of the church door; all which they learned is forgotten, like a perfume which savoureth no longer than they abide in the house where it burneth. Therefore, as I warned you at first, 'Take heed how ye hear,' so I warn you now, Take heed lest this compasser come and steal that which you have heard. For when Judas had received the sacrament, the devil entering into him, after that could never be driven out again; so if the devil enter into you after you have received this warning, he will possess you like Judas, stronger than he did before, and every word shall condemn you. As 'he which eateth' the sacrament 'unworthily, eateth his own damnation;' so he which heareth the word unfruitfully, heareth his own damnation, for 'the word which I have spoken,' saith Christ, 'shall judge you in the last day.'

A CAVEAT FOR CHRISTIANS.

A CAVEAT FOR CHRISTIANS.

Let him that thinketh he stands take heed lest he fall.—1 COR.
X. 12.

WHEN you have examined yourselves by the touchstone which I
gave you, ' Whether you be in the faith or no;' if you find that you
stand in the faith, ' Let him which thinketh he standeth take heed
lest he fall.' Three sentences we borrowed of Paul: In the first, he
exhorted us to be Christians; in the second, he taught us to know
whether we be Christians or no; in the last, he warneth us, if we
be, to persevere, and take heed lest we fall. St Paul doth not
teach us these phrases to doubt of our salvation, or of the mercy of
God, as the papists say, but of our constancy in his service; not,
lest we fall from our election; but, lest we fall from our righteousness. This is a godly fear, and ' blessed is he,' saith Solomon,—
not, which standeth in fear of God's mercy, but—' which standeth in fear' of his own frailty, Prov. xxviii. 14, as Job did, which
' feared all his works,' Job ix. 28. We must have confidence towards God, but diffidence towards ourselves; for God will be true
to us if we be true to him. This fear is not contrary to faith, but
cannot stand without it; therefore ' take heed lest ye fall,' is, take
heed lest ye sin, as the Israelites sinned: an admonition gathered
from the fall of the Jews, to them which stand, or to them which
think they stand, to take heed lest they fall. As a chronicler in a
story gives a watchword by the way, to admonish the reader of
some special things to be marked; so the apostle, teaching us to
make use of all that we hear or read, after he had shewed how the
Israelites stood sometime, and how they fell after again, which
were the elect people of God, the beacon of the world, and glory
of nations, until they crucified him who would have saved them,

ends with a sigh, as if he should say, It grieves me to record their folly, and to discover the nakedness of my countrymen! What should I rehearse any more? If they fell thus, take them for a warning, and 'Let him that thinketh he standeth take heed lest he fall.' Here we are set to the sinner's school, to see what we can learn of the wicked; as the bee doth gather honey of weeds; for 'all which is written, is written for our instruction,' Rom. xv. 4. 'These things,' saith Paul, 'are written to admonish us, upon whom the end of the world is come,' 1 Cor. x. 11; as if he should say, We have need to take more heed than they under the law, because we live in the last and worst days, when the dragon is let loose, and 'hath great wrath, because his time is short,' Rev. xii. 12. Now if you would know how the Israelites fell, read but from the sixth verse, and you shall see how they flitted from sin to sin, like a fly which shifteth from sore to sore. They 'tempted' the Lord (saith Paul), they 'murmured,' they 'lusted,' they 'committed idolatry,' they served the flesh, they 'sat down to eat, and rose up to play.' Take heed (saith Paul), O ye Corinthians, lest ye live so too. You shall not do evil because others do so; but these things are written for your learning: therefore first you shall learn, that as they fell away, so you may; and then by their fall you may learn to stand.

Thus the apostle warneth us, that we are all in a house ready to fall, all in a ship ready to sink, and all in a body ready to sin. Who can say what he will do when he is tried? Therefore Paul saith not, Let him that standeth take heed lest he fall, but 'Let him that *thinketh* he standeth take heed lest he fall:' warning us before that we take heed of falling, and to examine how we stand, whether we stand or no. For when he makes his speech of them which 'think they stand,' not of them which stand, he intends that few stand in comparison of them which think they stand. Many think themselves wise, that are fools like others; as many think themselves pure, which are profane like others. Solomon noteth, Prov. xxx. 12, 'There is a generation which are pure in their own conceit, and yet are not washed from their filthiness;' as though there were a generation or sect of such men. And again, Prov. xx. 6, 'Many men will boast of their goodness, but who can find a faithful man?' So, many seem to stand, which stand not; many think they believe, which know not what faith meaneth; many look to be saved, which cannot tell who shall save them, no more than Nicodemus knew what it was to be born again. The reason is, many are afraid to sound too deep, and examine their conscience, lest it should upbraid them with the noisomeness of their sins.

Therefore, as a favourable judge, which would save the malefactor, will ask him so cunningly, that he will answer for him too ; and then he will say, I find no fault in this man, let him pay his fees and be gone ; so will such a man say, I find no fault in this faith ; methinks it is a sound faith, methinks it is a good faith, methinks it is religion enough, when I come to the church, and love my neighbour, and obey my prince, and give every man his own, and pay my tithes, and fast twice a-week, as the pharisee did; methinks this is well, what would you have more ? Have I not kept all the commandments ? Luke xviii. 21. No, saith Christ ; 'there is one thing behind ;' examine thyself, and still thou shalt find something behind, like a cobweb in the top of an house when the floor is swept. Therefore well does Paul say, ' he that thinketh that he stands,' not he which stands ; for he which stands in Christ falleth not ; but he which thinketh he stands falleth suddenly, and may finally, unless he stand upon his watch. *Take heed* is a good staff to stay upon, and so often a man sins as he casts it from him ; all go astray.

But this is the difference between the sins of them which have faith, and them which have no faith. They which have no faith fall like an elephant, which, when he is down, riseth not again ; they which have faith do but trip and stumble, fall and rise again. Their falls do teach them to stand, their weakness doth teach them strength, their sins do teach them repentance, their frailness teacheth them constancy, as Peter was better after his denial than he was before. Judas did never stand, but seemed to stand ; the disciples knew not that he was a thief, for they asked, 'Is it I ? Is it I ?' Christ knew, as it appeareth, when he gave him the sop, and said, 'That which thou doest, do quickly.' If ever he had stood, he could not have been termed 'the son of perdition.' Many did seem to the world to go out of the church, but John saith they were never of the church ; meaning, that if they had been of the church, they could not have gone out of it ; for the true vine could not leave her grapes, nor the olive her fatness, nor the fig-tree her sweetness ;—so they which stand in the faith do not fall away, but seem to fall, as hypocrites seem to stand. The best men have had their slips, but always they rose again, as though they had sinned to teach us repentance ; therefore their sins are written, which else should have been concealed for their honour. For they were not registered in spite to disgrace them, but to admonish us, that, when we see such a field of blood, like carcases which the dragon hath slain, we may fear to set upon him unarmed, lest we be slain like others. As Solomon 'beheld the field of the slothful, which was full of thistles and weeds,' Prov. xxiv. 30, so we must behold the sins of others, to learn by them. 'I passed by,' saith Solomon, 'and considered it well; I looked upon it, and received instruction.' This note is in the margin of your Bibles, 'That I might learn by another man's faults;' so Solomon sheweth how we should look upon other men's faults. If we behold and consider them, and look upon them to receive instruction, as Solomon did, then do we behold and consider and look upon them well; or else, as Abraham might see the smoke of Sodom, but Lot might not see it, so they which can make use of sin, may hear, and see, and speak of errors of men, yet it is not lawful for others, because they are as a spider which gathereth notning but poison. Did not many pervert the sins of the patriarchs, and apply them to themselves, as they should apply their doctrines? But these things, saith Paul, are not written for our imitation, but for our admonition, that is, for a caveat, lest we do the like; for they repented that which they did, and shall we do that which they repented? Christ saith, 'Follow me,' without limits; but Paul saith, 'Be ye followers of me, as I follow Christ.' So we must follow the patriarchs, and prophets, and apostles, as they followed Christ, lest, following that which they repented, we sustain or suffer that which they escaped. This is the lesson for all but Christ, 'Let him which thinketh he stands take heed lest he fall.' When Paul had distilled the capital sins of the Israelites, this is the quintessence, that is, all the profit which he could wring out of them, 'Let them that think they stand, take heed lest they fall.'

Who would have said that Jerusalem would have become an harlot? that the chosen people should become the cursedest upon the earth? Yet so it is, saith Paul, thus and thus they have done, and thus hath God forsaken them, that all the world may take heed how they stir up the lion of Judah, which devours the wicked like bread. Who would have thought, when Lot was grieved with the sins of Sodom, that he would have committed a worse sin himself: first to drink till he was drunken, then to lie with his own daughters? Yet he did so. Who would have thought that Noah, when he builded the ark, because he believed in God, and gave example to all the world how they should save themselves, when the flood was past, would have given the first example of sin to his own sons? Who would have thought that David, when he was persecuted for his godliness in the desert, would have slain the husband for the lust of the wife, when the blessings of God did call him to thankfulness ? Who would have thought that Solomon, when he prayed in the temple, and was termed by God the wisest man in the world, would have taken more concubines unto him than any heathen in the world ? 'How are the mighty overthrown,' saith David, 2 Sam. i. 25. Like Peter, which said he would never forsake Christ, and forsook him first. The strong men are fallen, even Solomon himself, and David, and Noah, and Lot, and Samson, and Peter, the lights of the world, fell like stars of heaven. These tall cedars, strong oaks, fair pillars, lie in the dust, whose tops glittered in the air, that they which think they stand, may take heed lest they fall.

Can I look upon these ruins without compassion, or remember them without fear, unless I be a reprobate, and my heart of flint ? Who am I that I should stand like a shrub, when these cedars are blown down to the ground, and shewed themselves but men ? The best man is but a man, the worst are worse than beasts ; no man is untainted but Christ. They which had greater gifts than we, they which had deeper roots than we, they which had stronger hearts than we, they which had more props than we, are fallen like a bird which is weary of her flight, and turned back like the wind in the twinkling of an eye. Who would not have mocked him that should have said sometime as Elisha said to Hazael, what wickedness he should do in time to come, that he should slay and trample men, women and children ? Hazael blushed to hear thus of him, and said, 'Am I a dog, that I should do this ?' 2 Kings viii. 13, as if he would never do it while he were a man, but count him a dog when he comes to that. So they which are charged like Hazael blush to hear thus of themselves, and would have scorned sometime at him which should once have said, when they were zealous and studious preachers, and persecuted for their preaching, that the time would come when they should be loiterers, time-servers, lovers of the world, and greedy wolves, devourers of their flocks, and persecutors ; they would have said, Am I a dog ? am I a beast ? am I a reprobate, that I should do this ? They would never believe this till it came to pass ; and being fallen, they say they have sinned ; like Hazael, which blushed before he sinned, and was impudent after. Therefore, let no man say what he will be, before he have examined what he is, but run his course with a trembling fear, always looking down to the rubs which lie before him, and the worthies which are slain already ; and remember, when any spectacle of frailty is in thine eye, this is my warning ; for no man hath more privilege than

another.   This is the profit we should make of other men's faults,
like a pearl which is taken out of the serpent ; when we see our
brother's nakedness, it should move us to compassion of him, and
a fear of ourselves.   For when we rejoice at another's fall, like Ham,
as the leprosy went from Naaman to Gehazi, so God 'turneth his
wrath from them,' and it lighteth upon us, Prov. xxiv. 17, 18, and
such as have despised others without remorse, have fallen in the
like, or more shamefully, themselves, and never rose again.   What
shall we do then when we hear of other men's faults ?   Not talk as
we do, but beware by them, and think, Am I better than he ? am
I stronger than Samson ? am I wiser than Solomon ? am I chaster
than David ? am I soberer than Noah ? am I firmer than Peter, if
God should leave me to myself, if he should withdraw his hand
which holds me ?   Into how many gulfs have I been falling, when
God hath prevented me of occasion, or delayed the temptation, or
wonderfully kept me from it, I know not how ? for he delivereth
me from evil, as he delivered David from the blood of Nabal by
Abigail, which came unlooked for.   So he hath prevented many
wonderfully, when they were assaulted so hardly, that they thought
to have yielded to the enemy.   Sometime I may say there wanted
a tempter, sometime I may say there wanted time, sometime I may
say there wanted place ; sometime the tempter was present, and
there wanted neither time nor place, but God held me back that I
should not consent : so near we have glided by sin, like a ship which
rides upon a rock, and slips away, or a bird which scapes from the
fowler when the net is upon her.   There is no salt but may lose
his saltness, no wine but may lose his strength, no flower but may
lose his scent, no light but may be eclipsed, no beauty but may be
stained, no fruit but may be blasted, nor soul but may be corrupted.
We stand all in a slippery place, where it is easy to slide, and hard
to get up ; like little children, which overthrow themselves with
their clothes, now up, now down at a straw, so soon we fall from
God, and slide from his word, and forget our resolutions, as though
we had never resolved.   Man goeth forth in the morning, weak,
naked, and unarmed, to fight with powers and principalities, the
devil, the world, and all their adherents ; and whom doth he take
with him but his flesh, a traitor, ready to yield up at every assault
unto the enemy ?   Thus man is set upon the side of a hill, always
declining and slipping ; the flesh muffleth him to make him stumble,
the world catcheth at him to make him fall, the devil undermineth
him to make him sink, and crieth still, Cast thyself down ; and
when he falleth, he goeth apace, as Peter, who denieth thrice to-

gether; and when he is fallen, is like a stumbling-stone in the way for others, that they may fall too. Therefore, 'Let him that thinketh he standeth, take heed lest he fall.'

So earnestly must we call upon our souls, that we be not weary of well-doing; for happier are the children that never began, than Judas, whose end was worse than his beginning. Wisdom and righteousness are angry with him that leaveth his goodness to become worse. If thy spouse hath committed fornication, thou mightest have divorced her; but he which leaveth his righteousness to live in wickedness, forsakes his spouse to commit fornication, and is divorced from Christ himself. If thou wert like the vine, or the olive, or the fig-tree, they would not leave their grapes, or their fatness, or their sweetness, to get a kingdom, but the bramble did. If thou be like the bramble, what wilt thou do when the fire comes? As this is a memorandum to all, so especially let him that ruleth, and him that teacheth, take heed lest he fall; for if the pillars shrink, the temple shakes. As when a great tree is hewn down, which is a shadow to the beasts, and a nest to the birds, many leaves, and boughs, and twigs fall with it; so many stand and fall with them whose lamps give light to others, even as Jeroboam's sin made Israel to sin. Therefore Paul hath given you a watchword, which every one should write upon his table, upon his bed, and upon his nails, lest he forget in one hour; for he which stands now may fall before night. Sin is not long in coming, nor quickly gone, unless God stop us, as he met Balaam in his way, and stay us, as he stayed the woman's son, when he was a-bearing to his grave. We run over reason, and tread upon conscience, and fling by counsel, and go by the word, and post to death, as though we ran for a kingdom. Like a lark, that falls to the ground sooner than she mounted up; at first she retires as it were by steps, but when she cometh nearer the ground, she falls down with a jump; so we decline at first, and waver lower and lower, till we be almost at the worst, and then we run headlong, as though we were sent post to hell: from hot to lukewarm, from lukewarm to key-cold, from key-cold to stark dead; so the languishing soul bleeds to death, and seeth not his life go, till he be at the very last gasp. Woe be unto him that is guilty of this murder! If the blood of Abel cried for vengeance against his brother Cain, which slew his body, shall not God be revenged for the death of his soul? 'Where is thy brother?' saith God. Nay, where is thy soul? hast thou slain it, which was my spouse, my temple, mine own image? If the servant which hid his talent was cast into darkness, what shall be done unto thee

which hath lost thy talent ?   For he which falls from his righteousness doth not hide his talent, but more, he doth lose it.

Thus, if you never knew what good to make of evil, this you
may learn in the sinner's school, 'Let them which think they stand
take heed lest they fall;' and let them which are down care to rise ;
and the Lord so direct our steps, that we may rise again !

THE POOR MAN'S TEARS.

THE POOR MAN'S TEARS.

He that shall give to one of the least of these a cup of cold water in my name, he shall not lose his reward.—MATT. X. 42.

THE argument I have to entreat of is only of giving alms to the poor, and when and in what sort we ought to relieve the poor. Herein, for your better instruction, I will shew what alms is, how and to whom alms must be given, and wherefore we are to give alms. I know in these days, and in this iron age, it is as hard a thing to persuade men to part with money, as to pull out their eyes, and cast them away; or to cut off their hands, and give them away; or to cut off their legs, and throw them away. Nevertheless, I cannot but wonder that men are so slow in giving of alms, and so hard-hearted towards the relief of the poor, when the promises of God warrant them not to lose their reward. St John saith, 'He that hath the substance of this world, and seeth his brother want, how can the love of God be in him?' 1 John iii. 17. This is a question which can hardly be answered of a great number; no, it will not be considered of a number, nor regarded of a number. And yet the evangelist hereby layeth open unto all persons, that he which hath wealth, seeing his brother in want, and will not relieve him, he loseth the love of God: which love is so great as is the love of a natural mother unto her own child; nay, more than that, it is a love so firmly settled, that it is impossible to be removed.

There are many rich persons that think scorn to relieve the poor, of whose hard dealing we have a precedent in Luke xvi. The rich man in his lifetime would not relieve Lazarus, but despised him; yea, he forgot God, and thought there was no God (but his gold) that could in justice punish him for despising the poor. Lazarus died for want, and so did Dives for all his wealth, who soon after, being in hell, beheld Lazarus in heaven, triumphing in Abraham's bosom, while he was tormented in hell-fire. This fire burneth, scaldeth, scorcheth, and tormenteth; of which, when the rich man felt the smart, though all too late, he sorrowed and repented, and would fain have sent word thereof unto his friends. But he could have no messenger for all his lordly livings, nor no releasement of his torments for all his bags of gold. Now, to whom would he have sent word? Forsooth, to a number of his friends, that indeed think there is no God nor devil, no heaven, no hell, nor torments in hell-fire after this life. This example of Dives may admonish such hard-hearted persons to be mollified with the tears of the poor, that they may, when Dives hath dined, let Lazarus have the crumbs.

We read in Matthew, that when Christ cometh to judgment, he 'will say to them on the left hand, Go from me, ye cursed, into hell-fire, which was prepared from the beginning,' &c.; by which appeareth, that hell-fire is not only hot, but it is everlastingly hot, and never hath end. Let therefore hell-fire, and the eternal torments thereof, admonish you to be merciful to the poor. To this also may be added, what he will say to the righteous, 'Go ye into everlasting joys,' which never shall have end. 'When I came among you as a stranger, you received me; when I was naked, you clothed me; and when I was hungry, you fed and refreshed me.' Which proveth that the kingdom of heaven belongs unto him that harboureth strangers, clotheth the naked, feedeth the hungry, comforteth the sick, and doth perform such charitable acts of compassion. Yet we are not, as the papists, to account it meritorious, but to do it as a faithful Christian, in faith and true zeal of a Christian life; for 'every tree that bringeth not forth good fruit is hewn down, and cast into the fire.' It is not enough for us only to bear fair leaves, but we must also bring forth good fruit, otherwise let us be sure our Saviour Christ will forsake us.

The prophet Isaiah saith, 'If thou break thy bread unto the poor, and pour forth thy heart unto them, thy light shall rise in darkness, thy dimness shall be as the noontide, and God shall still guide thee,' Isa. lviii. 7, 10, 11. Whereby appeareth, that those deeds of charity are commonly performed by the righteous that still seek to enjoy the pleasures of heaven, which are so far beyond the common imagination of men, that no heart can think, no ear can hear, no tongue can speak, no pen can write the unspeakable pleasures thereof.

Christ saith, 'It is a deed more blessed to give to them than to

take from them,' Acts xx. 35 ; for the excellency of Christians consisteth in leading a godly life, and giving of alms, as the excellency
of all things is shewed in their giving. The sun giveth his light, the
moon her light, the stars their light, the clouds their water, the
trees their fruit, the earth her herbs, the herbs their flowers, the
flowers their seeds, and the seeds their increase ; yea, beasts and
birds, fowls and fishes, give naturally in their kind, and are more
careful and loving one to another than we, which made Job[1] say,
' Go to the beasts of the field, and they will teach thee,' Job
xxxv. 11. For man is most unnatural to man, and so far digressing
from nature in his kind, that let some ungodly rich cormorants see
a poor person beg, this is their present sentence of him, Whip the
rogues ! To bridewell with these rogues ! It is pity these rogues
be suffered to live ! Then if they fall sick, let them famish, starve,
and die ; all is one to them, for of them they shall receive no
comfort.

Augustus Cæsar, a heathenish emperor, thought that day to be
lost wherein he did not benefit some poor person, and with money
relieve him from penury. And I doubt not but some godly men
there be that take delight in relieving the poor with their continual
alms, not superstitiously to be seen of men, but secretly to be seen
of God. The Lord increase the number of them, and make their
example redound to the relief of thousands !

Alms is a charitable relief given by the godly to the sick, to the
lame, the blind, the impotent, the needy, the hungry, and poorest
persons, even such as are daily vexed with continual want ; to
whom, even of duty, and not of compulsion, we ought to impart
some part of that which God hath mercifully bestowed upon us.
For as we daily seek for benefits at God's hand, which he doth continually give us, so ought we therewith to relieve the poor, sith God
hath so commanded us. The performance whereof we ought not
to drive off from time to time, but to do it when they desire to
have it done. For the true obedience of God doth forbid us to
prolong or drive off the doing of good things, as appeareth in Noah,
who, when he was commanded, did enter the ark ; Abraham, when
he was commanded, did forthwith offer up his son Isaac, and did
circumcise his house upon the same day he was appointed. A
learned writer, called Nazianzen, saith of himself, that when in his
youth he had once lost the tenor of good life, grey hairs were got
about his head ere he recovered it again. Whereby I gather, that
when we are young, if we harden our hearts against the poor, if we

---

[1] Elihu.—ED.

do not willingly impart our bread to them, but drive their hungry stomachs stubbornly from our doors, that doubtless grey hairs will come upon our heads, before we can find the right way to pity and compassion. O let us take heed that our hearts be not hardened against the poor, nor that we give our alms to get glory of the world; but so let us give our alms that the one hand may not know what the other doth. Yea, we ought to give with such equality, that our poor neighbours may be relieved, to whom indeed we ought to become contributors, as Job was. All people have not one belly; for as one chimney may be hot, so another may be cold; one pot moist with liquor, when another may be dry; one's purse empty, when another's is full; so one poor man's belly full, and another's empty. That is a good commonwealth that looketh to every member in the commonwealth, and those men are worthy of riches that look daily to the feeding of their poor neighbours. Let therefore the tears of the poor admonish you to charity, that when Dives hath dined, Lazarus may have the crumbs.

Now let us proceed, and consider what we must give, and to whom we must give. In the text we are willed to give, though it be but a cup of cold water, or a piece of bread. This containeth matter both for the taker and the giver. Bread will serve beggars, and they must be no choosers; yet bread will not serve some beggars, that boldly upon Gad's Hill, Shooter's Hill, and such like places, take men's horses by the head, and bid them deliver their purses. For these fellows are of the opinion of the Anabaptists, that every man's goods must be common to them, or else they will force them to part them; but these are saucy beggars, which ought to be suppressed by godly policy. As for the other sort of beggars, and other poor persons, they must be content to take up their cross, endeavour themselves patiently to suffer their ordinary grievances, and remember that man's nature may be satisfied with a little.

As touching how much we should give, we are taught, that if we have much, we should give accordingly; if we have but little, give what we can spare. Saint Luke counselleth us, 'if we have two coats, we must give one to him that hath none; and of meat likewise,' Luke iii. 11. But as touching this question, little need to be spoken, when our own covetous hearts are ready enough to frame excuses.

Some will make a question of their alms, and say, they know not what the party is that demandeth relief, or beggeth alms of them. Oh, say some, I suspect he is an idle person, dishonest, or perhaps an unthrift; and therefore refuse to give any relief at all. To this

I answer, They are needless doubts; for we ought to relieve them, if we know them not for such persons, and let their bad deeds fall on their own necks; for if they perish for want, we are in danger of God's wrath for them; but to give unto such as we know of lewd behaviour, thereby to continue them in their wickedness, were very offensive. We are not still tied to one place for giving our charity, but it stretcheth far; for we are commanded not only to relieve our own countrymen, but also strangers, and such as dwell in foreign nations.

Again, here the giver may learn to give freely; for the thing he giveth is but bread or water. Bread is the fruit of the earth; and for that the earth gives it us, we may the better give it again. But bread in this place signifieth all things necessary; for the fare and cheer in old time was contained under the title of *bread*, and all manner of drink under the title of *water*. But in this, as in all other things, the simplicity of the old world is quite gone out, and new and corrupt things are lately crept in. In the old time Jacob desired he might have bread in his journey; but now the case is altered, for we must have sundry dishes of contrary devices, framed for the taste of the mouth, and pleasantness of the stomach, which is used with great superfluity, and far more cost than needeth. Better now to fill the belly than the eye; although to content the common multitude, the eye is the only thing which must be pleased. Yet, when you are in the midst of all your jollity and costly fare, let the tears of the poor admonish you to relieve them, that when Dives hath dined, Lazarus may have the crumbs.

The tears of men, women, and children are grievous and pitiful; and tears give cause of great compassion, especially the tears of such as therewith are constrained to beg for their relief. But if the tears of the rich for the loss of their goods, or the tears of parents for the death of their children, or the tears of kind-natured persons for the loss of friends, or other wrongs sustained, ought generally to be regarded and pitied; then much more should the tears of those breed great compassion in the hearts of Christians, whom beggary, want, and extremity of miserable hunger, constraineth to shed tears in most grievous and lamentable sort. Oh, what shall a man say unto those pitiful faces which are made moist through the extremity of hunger, wherein are most bitter and sharp effects, a thing above all extremes?

To a hungry body every bitter thing is sweet, and every foul thing seems clean. Hunger made the apostles glad to eat the ears of corn, David glad to eat the shew-bread, Lazarus desirous to eat crumbs, and Elias content with meal. In the destruction of Jerusalem, it made the mother eat her own child ; and in the wailings of Jeremiah, people to eat their own ordure. It made people cry to Pharaoh for bread ; it made an ass's head and the dung of pigeons to be eaten in Samaria, and others to swoon and lie dead in the streets. The affliction of hunger causes bitter tears, and brought all these things to pass. David saith that God 'numbered all his tears in a bottle,' Ps. lvi. 8. David's tears were worthy to be preserved; but if ever tears were worthy to be numbered, the tears that are shed for famine, howsoever men neglect to regard them, they are undoubtedly gathered together into God's bottle, and thence they rain as waters out of vials, in way of revengement of those that take no compassion of such a woful spectacle.

Tears are the last thing that man, woman, or child can move by; and where tears move not, nothing will move. I therefore exhort you, by the lamentable tears which the poor do daily shed through hunger and extreme misery, to be good unto them, to be charitable and merciful unto them, and to relieve those whom you see with misery distressed.

The Scripture saith, ' Give to every one that asketh,' Luke vi. 30. God gave herbs and other food unto every living thing. Every commonwealth that letteth any member in it to perish for hunger, is an unnatural and uncharitable commonwealth. But men are now-a-days so full of doubts, through a covetous desire to themselves, that they cannot abide to part with anything to the poor, notwithstanding that God hath promised he will not forget the work and love which you have shewed in his name to the poor and distressed.

Some will say for their excuse, that they are overcharged by giving to a number of persons, and therefore they cannot give to so many beggars ; for by so doing they might soon become beggars themselves. David answered this objection very well, and saith thus, 'I never saw the just man forsaken, nor his seed beg his bread,' Ps. xxxvii. 25 ; whereby he meant, that in all the time that he had lived (and the like for any man living the years of David), he scarcely ever saw that upon an upright heart in giving, a man was brought to beggary.

There are a number that will deny a poor body a penny, and plead poverty to them, though they seem to stand in never so great extremes ; when, in a far worser sort, they will not stick immediately to spend ten or twenty shillings. The rich worldling makes no conscience to have ten or twenty dishes of meat at his table, when in truth the one half might sufficiently satisfy nature, the rest run to the relief of the poor ; and yet in the end he might depart better refreshed with one dish than commonly he is with twenty. Some will not stick to have twenty coats, twenty houses, twenty farms, yea, twenty lordships, and yet go by a poor person whom they see in great distress, and never relieve him with one penny, but say, God help you ; I have not for you. There are lawyers that will not stick to undo twenty poor men, and merchants that make no conscience to eat out twenty others, that have their hundreds out at usury, their chests crammed full of crowns, and their coffers full of golden gods, or glistering angels, that will go by twenty poor, miserable, hungry, impotent, and distressed persons, and yet not bestow one penny on them ; and though they do most shamefully ask it, yet can they most shamefully deny it, and refuse to perform it.

The people of this world can very easily find a staff to beat a dog; they are never without excuses, but ready to find delays, and very pregnant to devise new shifts to keep in their alms. Now will I shew you reasons why we should give. God saith, ' Whoso giveth to the poor, lendeth to the Lord, and shall be sure to find it again,' Prov. xix. 17, and receive for the same an hundred fold. And again, ' Blessed is he that considereth of the poor and needy ; the Lord shall deliver him in the day of trouble,' Ps. xli. 1. Hereby appeareth that we shall receive our alms again, except we doubt whether God's word be true or no. For confirmation whereof the prophet David saith, ' The testimonies of God are true and righteous,' Ps. xix. 9. And God speaks by the mouth of the prophet Isaiah, saying, ' The word is gone out of my mouth, and it shall not return,' Isa. xlv. 23, and lv. 11. The promise which God made to Sarah was found true ; his promise made to the children of Israel was found true; his promise to Joshua in the overthrowing of his enemies was found true. God promiseth David his kingdom, to Solomon he promised wisdom, to Pharaoh he threatened destruction by water, to Saul the loss of his kingdom, and to Solomon the dividing of his kingdom : all which, and far more, proved true. Then let us not doubt of God's promises, but fear his judgments ; for from time to time they have been found true and just. Let us consider that we must die, and leave our goods we know not to whom ; then, while we are here, let us distribute thereof unto the poor, that we may receive our reward in the kingdom of heaven. God saith by St Luke, ' O fool, this night will I fetch away thy soul, and then that which thou hast got, who shall possess it ?' Here is a question worth the noting, and meet for rich men to consider, especially such as hoard up wealth, and have no regard to the relief of the poor.

Do they think that the wealth which they have gathered together
will come to good after their decease ? No ; it will melt and consume away like butter in the sun. The reason is, because they
would not do as God hath commanded them, in distributing part of
that to the poor which was lent them by the Lord.

The children of God, in the 6th of the Apocalypse, cry out, ' How
long, O Lord, thou that art holy and true, dost thou not judge and
revenge our blood upon those that dwell on the earth ?' Rev. vi. 10.
Whereby appeareth that God exerciseth good men, and those whom
he loveth, in the troubles of this world, which we account long ;
yet is their time but short, although their trouble makes it seem
long.   But these, I say, ought to be content ; and all those that do
trust in God must be content to relieve one another for a time,
since after a short time we shall doubtless find the fruits of our
alms again.   Short is man's life while we are in this world; David
compareth it to a vapour, to a bubble, to wind, to grass, to a shadow,
to smoke, and every fading thing that consumeth in a moment.
Isaiah compareth it to the removing of a tabernacle, and Job to an
eagle's wing or a weaver's shuttle.   So that our life is but short ;
and after a few days, though you think them many, whatsoever you
mercifully bestow upon the poor here on earth, you shall certainly
find the same again both in heaven and on earth.   Solomon, in the
21st of the Proverbs, saith, ' He that stoppeth his ear at the cry of
the poor, shall cry himself, and not be heard,' Prov. xxi. 13.   ' The
bread of the needy is the life of the poor : he that keepeth it from
them is a man of blood,' Ecclus. xxxiv. 21.   St Paul saith, No man
giveth but he that hath received, 1 Cor. xv. 3; and an ancient
father of the church doth charge the rich with waste, for which they
shall surely answer.   Art thou not, saith he, a robber, in keeping
another man's substance, and to reckon it as thine own ?   It is the
bread of the hungry which thou dost retain, the coat due to the
naked thou lockest in thy house, the shoes that appertain to the
barefoot lie drying in thy house, and the gold which should relieve
the poor lies cankering in thy coffers.   Which saying, as it teacheth
the liberality due unto the poor, so it blameth the careless rich,
that account all to be their own, and will part with nothing, keeping to themselves more than is sufficient.   But to such St James
saith, that at the latter day the mite in the crumbs, the moths in
the garments, and the rust in the gold, shall fret them like cankers,
James v. 2, 3.   Ambrose saith, It is no greater sin to take from
him that rightly possesseth, than, being able, not to give him that
wanteth.

The right rich man, that duly deserveth that name, is not known by his possession, by his costly fare, and costly building; by his sumptuous palace, by his plate, jewels, and substance; but by considering the poor and needy. Whereof Austin saith thus, The rich are proved by the poverty of others. So that still the Scriptures and fathers prescribe not an indifferency, but a necessity, not at pleasure, but upon duty, that the poor and needy should be considered and relieved.

Where is the large liberality become that in times past was rooted in our forefathers? They were content to be liberal, though they applied it to evil purposes. The successors of those which in times past gave liberally to maintain abbots, friars, monks, nuns, masses, dirges, trentals, and all idolatry, seeing the abuses thereof, may now bestow it to a better use, namely, to foster and feed the poor members of Christ.

The world is as great as it hath been, the people now are more rich than they have been, and more covetous than they have been, yea, they have more knowledge than ever they had; yet they want the desire they have had to become liberal, and seem therein most wilfully ignorant.

The extortioner can spare nought unto the poor, for joining house to house, and land to land, though he have the poor man's curse for it. The prophet Isaiah saith, The extortioner doeth no good to the poor, but daily seeketh to root them forth of doors. The pride of apparel maketh us forget the patches of the poor; our costly fare, their extreme hunger; and our soft lodging, their miserable lying.

Oh how liberal were people in times past to maintain superstition! and now how hard-hearted are they grown, not to keep the poor from famishing! Will ye make a scorn of the poor and needy? The poor now perisheth by the rich men, and no man considereth it. This is not the right duty of faithful Christians; this ought not to be the fruits of our profession; neither is this the mercy which we learn by the word.

Therefore, towards the relief of the poor, I say, Give, and give gladly; for the bread that is given with a stony heart is called stony bread, though necessary to be taken by the poor to slake hunger; yea, it is but sour bread. Such a giver, in my opinion, is next kinsman unto Satan, for he gave Christ stones instead of bread; but this man giveth Christians stony bread. The wise man saith, Lay up thy alms in the hands of the poor, and know that in the end what thou keepest thou shalt lose ; but that thou givest to the poor shall be as a purse about thy neck. For as this life waxeth old, and our days pass away, so shall this vain pelf pass away from us, neither shall riches help in the day of vengeance ; but the corruption abideth, which fretteth like a canker. Then what shall it profit to get all the world ? And when the world forsaketh us, that shall be most against us that best we loved while we were in the world. Let every man therefore persuade himself that his soul is better than those subtle riches, the possession whereof is variable and uncertain, for they pass from us much more swiftly than they came unto us ; and albeit we have the use of them even till the last day, yet at length we must leave them to others. Then, ere you die, lay them forth for the profit of your poor brethren. Learn to forsake the covetous world before it forsake you, and learn counsel of our Saviour Christ, who adviseth you to 'make friends of the wicked mammon,' Luke xvi. 9.

We see daily that every one is good to the poor (as we commonly say), but they will give them nought but words. Then, I say, great boast and small roast makes unsavoury mouths. Yet if words will do any good, the poor shall not want them ; for it doth cost nothing to say, Alas ! good soul, God help thee, God comfort thee, I would I were able to help thee ; and such commonly will say so that have store of wealth lying by them. Such still wish well unto themselves in wishing themselves able ; but of such wishing and such wishers I say, as a beggar said to a bishop who made the like answer, that if such wishes were worth but one halfpenny to the poor, I doubt they would not be so liberal. I wish you, good brethren, leave wishing, and fall to some doing. You lock up, and will not lose ; you gather together even the devil and all; and why ? Because you would fain hatch the cockatrice's egg ; you nurse up a canker for yourselves ; you keep the pack that shall trouble your voyage unto God, as Christ saith, ' Oh how hard shall it be for a rich man to be saved. It shall be easier for a camel to go through a needle's eye,' Mat. xix. 23, 24. This he saith not, because no rich man shall be preserved ; but because the merciless rich man shall be damned. We are admonished to liberality by sundry natural examples. The clouds, if they be full, do yield forth their rain ; much rain is a burden to clouds, and much riches are burdens to men. It is said of Abraham, Gen. xiii. 12, that he was burdened with gold ; yet Abraham was a good man, but it burdened his head to be busied with the cares of gold. Again, to eat much, to drink much, and to rest much, is a burden to the soul, though it be pleasant to the body ;

and in Luke xii. 19, it appeareth, that abundance of riches maketh one to eat much, drink much, and rest much ; then, were it not for the covetous minds of those that have much, they might impart to the poor one part of that which they daily spend in superfluity. If this be not amended, I let you to understand, that the poor must cry, and their voice shall be heard, their distress considered, and your vengeance shall be wrought. I tell you troth, even in Jesus Christ, that the poor have cried unto the Lord, and he hath heard them. With speed, therefore, open your ears ; if not to man, yet to Christ, who continually commandeth us to give and bestow upon the poor and needy. 'Give, and it shall be given you,' saith he by Luke, chap. vi. 38 ; and setteth before our eyes the example of the poor widow's mite ; as also the example of a covetous rich man, who, demanding how he might obtain eternal life, was answered thus by him, 'Go, sell all thou hast, and give to the poor,' Mat. xix. 21 ; not that it is necessary for every man so to do, or that a man cannot be saved without he do so ; but thereby teaching him particularly to loathe the world, and generally seek means for the daily cherishing and the refreshing of the poor. Do not continually feed your equals, for that is offensive ; but when you may spare to spend and banquet yourselves, then call the poor and impotent, and refresh your poor distressed neighbours and brethren ; and when Dives hath dined, let Lazarus have the crumbs. And still remember the saying of St Matthew, 'Blessed are the merciful, f r they shall obtain mercy,' Mat. v. 7.

To conclude. Beloved in the Lord, let me entreat you rich men to consider it is your duty to remember the poor, and their continual want ; you that eat till you blow, and feed till your eyes swell with fatness ; that taste first your coarse meats, and then fall to finer fare ; that have your several drinks for your stomach, and your sorts of wine for your appetite ; impart some of your superfluity unto the poorer, who, being comforted by you, will doubtless pray for you, that God will bless you and yours, and increase your store a thousand-fold ; which if they shall forget, yet the promises of God remain inviolable towards you for the same.

If the proud would leave their superfluity in apparel, their excess in embroidery, their vanity in cuts, guards, and pounces, their excess in spangling, their fantastical feathers, and needless bravery, the greater part would suffice towards the relief of the poor, and yet they have sufficient to suffice nature.

Let the glutton seek only to suffice nature, and leave his daily surfeiting in belly cheer ; then might the poor be fed with that which he oftentimes either loathsomely vomits forth, or which worketh as an instrument to shorten his own life.

Let the whoremonger leave off his dalliance, and his inordinate expenses for maintaining of his wickedness; and it shall be good for his body, and better for his soul, yea, his purse shall be the heavier, and he thereby better able to relieve the poor.

Let every artificer and tradesman live orderly, avoiding super-fluous expenses, not spending his money vainly at dice, tables, cards, bowling, betting, and such like, but live, as becometh civil Christians, in the fear of God; they may have sufficient for the maintenance of themselves and their family, and yet the poor may be by them sufficiently relieved.

Let us consider that we, who have our beginning from God, ought generally to bend our actions towards the pleasing of God; and doing as he commandeth us, we please him; for if we help the poor, we help him; and doing all charitable actions to the poor, he accounteth it as done unto himself.

Let us generally learn not to contemn or despise the poor, but according to our abilities help them, and consider of their extremes, and at any hand not disdain and upbraid them with the titles of base rogues, or such like; but in all godly Christian means cherish and comfort them with such charitable relief as we may in reason afford unto them, yea, and consider of their case as if it were our own.

Let us take example of good Cornelius the captain, of whom mention is made in the Acts of the Apostles, to whom the angel of God appearing in a vision, said thus, 'Cornelius, thy prayer and thine alms are come up before God,' Acts x. 4. Lo, here the reward, and also of whom thou shalt be rewarded.

Let us consider of their misery, that with hungry chops and lank bellies would willingly feed on that which you wastefully consume; the poor, I say, would find good comfort of that which commonly you fling to your dogs and on your dunghills; and let us have regard to their coldness, their nakedness, their misery and grievous necessity; think of this, and comfort them. And let us be mindful that poverty and want compelleth many an honest person to take in hand the performance of much vile and slavish business; and that therefore they deserve to be succoured with mercy and pity, rather than to be despised for their poor estate. Oh think, if some hard-hearted persons were in their miserable estate, how gladly would they be refreshed, that now scarcely yield one penny to their relief!

Lastly, let us call to mind the example of the widow of Sarepta, whose provision and store was little, and when the prophet of the Lord came to her to ask her bread, she answered, 'I have nothing but a little flour in a barrel, and a little oil in a cruse,' 1 Kings xvii. 12, which notwithstanding she willingly bestowed upon him ; for which a thing worthy memory followed ; for her barrel was again filled with flour, and her pot with oil. This was the Lord's doing, for fostering the poor prophet of the Lord. Sure the plenty that cometh by the poor is much ; for the field of the poor is fruitful, it surrendereth again the fruit to them that give aught; yea, if it be but a cup of cold water, as saith our Saviour Christ, Mark x. To whom be all honour, power and dominion, now and for ever. Amen !

AN ALARM FROM HEAVEN.

AN ALARM FROM HEAVEN,

SUMMONING ALL MEN UNTO THE HEARING OF THE TRUTH.

Go teach all nations, baptising them in the name, &c.—MAT. XXVIII. 19.

THE apostle Paul writing to Timotheus telleth him, that 'God would have all men come to the knowledge of the truth and be saved,' 1 Tim. ii. 4. In which words the apostle giveth him to understand, that there is none other way either for priest or people to come unto God, but by that ordinary means, which is the hearing of the word; the which the apostle calleth his truth, because it is not only true of itself, but also doth witness of his truth, who is truth itself. By the very same name doth our Saviour Christ call God's word, when, making his prayer to his heavenly Father, for the elect, he saith, 'Father, sanctify them in thy truth;' and immediately addeth, 'Thy word is the truth,' John xvii. 17. The next thing that the apostle advertiseth Timothy of is, that this truth, being rightly known, bringeth salvation to them that so know it. And this the apostle confirmeth by an argument taken from his own faith, when he saith, 'I am not ashamed of the gospel of Christ, for it is the power of God, able to save every believer,' Rom. i. 16. And last of all, the apostle hath set down the generality of this truth, both in saying to Timothy that God would have *all men* to be acquainted with it; and to the saints at Rome, that it is able to save *every* believer. Hereof it cometh that, writing to the Colossians, he exhorteth them not so much to the hearing of this truth taught them, as to an inward entertainment of the same, when he says, 'Let the word of Christ dwell in you plentifully in all wisdom, teaching and admonishing your own selves,' Col. iii. 16. *Teaching* themselves, because many of the Colossians seemed to be ignorant of that which they should know ; and *admonishing* themselves, because a number of them did know much but practised little.   So that such is the entertainment that God's word ought to find amongst us, as David promised thereunto, when he said, ' O Lord, teach me the way of thy statutes, and I shall keep it even unto the end,' Ps. cxix. 33.   And we are taught to entertain God's word by the example of John, who, receiving the little book at the hand of the angel, was commanded to eat that book, Rev. x. 9 ; partly to teach us that God's word must abide within us, and partly to signify that our bodily bread serveth not our soul's necessity, Mat. iv. 4.   Isaiah said that he had carefully carried God's message ; for ' I was found,' saith he, ' of those that sought me not, and have been made manifest to them that have not asked after me,' Isa. lxv. 1.   Howbeit he was not so careful in speaking, but the people were as careless in hearing ; for the which cause he uttereth this complaint, ' Lord, who hath believed our report ? or to whom is the arm of the Lord revealed?' Isa. liii. 1.   When Jeremiah had faithfully delivered the message of the Lord his God, in rebuking those Jews which burned incense to the idols of Egypt, he saith that all the men that knew that their wives had burned incense to strange gods, and a great many women which stood by, gave him this answer, ' The word which thou spakest unto us in the name of the Lord, we will not hear it of thee, but what we think good, that will we do,' Jer. xliv. 14, 15.   Such was the wickedness of the people so many years past, as appears in many places of God's word, among the which that of those in Babylon was not the least, which moved Jeremiah to send Seraiah unto them with the book, and with a strait charge, that when he had read it unto them, he should bind a stone unto it and cast it into the river Euphrates, Jer. li. 63 ; to teach the Babylonians and all men, that as the hard stone caused the good book to sink in the water, so hardness of our stony hearts is not only the depriving of us of many good blessings, but also a violent sinking of our souls in sin.

The just consideration whereof moved the apostle Paul to expostulate the matter with every hard-hearted sinner in this sort : ' Dost thou not know that the bountifulness of God leadeth thee to repentance ? But thou, after thy hard heart that cannot repent, dost heap up to thyself wrath against the day of wrath, and of the declaration of the just judgment of God,' Rom. ii. 4, 5.   And yet to see what small preparation there is unto repentance !   Every godly man wisheth, like zealous Jeremiah, 'Oh that mine head were a fountain, and that mine eyes were rivers of tears, that I might weep day and night for the slain of my people,' Jer. ix. 1. So grievous is the way of the ungodly unto the child of God, that he cannot account it any better thing than a race wherein they run, striving who shall come first to the devil, when they lead a life as void of repentance as if sin were seen and allowed, and hell-fire but an old wife's fable. What made Jeremiah so weary of his people, but that he saw them weary of well-doing ; for, sighing and sorrowing, thus he saith, ' Oh that I had a cottage in the wilderness of wayfaring men, that I might leave my people and go from them : for they are all adulterers, and an assembly of rebels,' Jer. ix. 2.

So long as Stephen the martyr talked to the Jews of their pedigree, they hearkened unto him diligently, Acts vii. ; but when he rebuked their sins, saying that they were ' a stiff-necked people, and of a hard heart, resisting the Holy Ghost,' in persecuting the prophets, and putting to death the Lord of life, then they stopped their ears, and gnashing their teeth, ran upon him, and stoned him to death. So fareth it at this day amongst men, that many are as well contented to hear pleasant things, as the Jews were to hearken to Stephen repeating their parentage ; but if a man shall hit all sorts of ill manners, as well as speak to all sorts of men, they hold it as a principle, that he forgetteth his text who remembereth their sins, notwithstanding they know that it is the minister's duty to ' tell the house of Jacob their sins, and to let Israel hear of their transgressions,' Isa. lviii. 1 ; and the people's part not only to be content, but also desirous to know their duties, and to shew their desire in the forwardness of their coming before him that ought to teach ; otherwise we might imagine that God spake in sport, when he said by his prophet, ' The priest's lips shall preserve knowledge, and the people shall seek it at his mouth,' Mal. ii. 7 ; for so thought the evil-disposed people in Ezekiel's time, who used to hear him preach with the like affections that many bring now-a-days, concerning whose fruitless hearing God informeth Ezekiel, by saying unto him, ' Son of man, the children of my people talk of thee by the walls, and in the doors of houses, and speak one to another, every one to his brother, saying, Come, I pray you, and hear what is the word that cometh from the Lord. They come unto thee as the people used to come, and my people sit before thee, and hear thy words, but they will not do them : for with their mouths they make jests, and their hearts go after their covetousness. And, lo, thou art unto them as a jesting song of one that hath a pleasant voice and can sing well : for they hear thy words, but they do them not,' Ezek. xxxiii. 30, &c.

These people, and the people which were in the time of Hosea the prophet, may meetly be matched with the men of our age, who were as ready to rail on the priest, as he was pressed to reprove their sins ; for, saith Hosea, 'these people are as those that rebuke the priest,' Hosea iv. 4. It is most true, that the want of salvation proceedeth both of the lack of teaching, and of the want of faith to believe rightly that which is taught. The first of these is approved by the words which the Holy Ghost spake by the mouth of this prophet last named, thus, 'My people are destroyed for lack of knowledge,' &c., Hosea iv. 6. The other by the testimony of our Saviour, Christ himself, who, sending his eleven to preach and baptize, saith, 'He that believeth and is baptized, shall be saved; he that believeth not, shall be damned,' Mark xvi. 16. Why went the rich man to hell, but either for one of these causes afore-named, or for them both ; that is to say, because he never frequented the word of God, whereby faith is begotten in the hearts of the hearers; or if he heard the same word, yet it was heard so carelessly, that it took no root at all. And, indeed, that answer which Abraham made to his request seemeth to aver the truth of that which I say; for when request was made by that hell-hound, that a messenger might go from the dead to his five brethren which were yet at his father's house, &c., Abraham replied thus, 'They have Moses and the prophets, let them hear them;' for as Abraham saith, if that which Moses hath set down of God's justice cannot batter our brazen faces and hearts of adamant, nor the unvaluable and most assured promises made by Christ to his elect, and recorded by his prophets, cannot drive us from sin, and draw us to himself ; then there is no more hope of us in hearing the word of God than was of Simon, Acts viii. 23, and Judas, Acts i. 18, though they heard the word, and received the sacraments ; for our life is no other way reformed by a careless kind of hearing, than Jeroboam redressed the religion in Israel when he set up two golden calves, the one in Dan, and the other in Bethel, that the Israelites might worship them, 1 Kings xii. 28 ; or Nebuchadnezzar in his kingdom, when he destroyed idols, that he might be worshipped as God. It is matter so true, that no man can so much as imagine, much less speak, the contrary without great offence, that God hath done so much for his vine as by any means might be, Isa. v. 4 ; insomuch that David the king of Israel never had greater cause than the prince and people of England have, to say of the goodness of God, 'He hath not dealt so lovingly with any nation as with us,' Ps. cxlvii. 20, in giving to us so long use of his laws; and yet he that compareth the pastors' painful preaching with the people's little profiting, in most places of this land, shall find just occasion to think that the Son of God hath pronounced that same curse upon this English vine, which he uttered against that fruitless fig-tree mentioned by Mark, in these words, 'Never fruit grow on thee henceforth,' Mark xi. 14. God grant that there be not some men who measure the meat by the man; like those proud citizens which said, 'We will not have this man reign over us,' Luke xix. 14, and loathe the message because they like not the messenger; like those scornful Jews that told Jeremiah to his face, 'The word which thou speakest to us in the name of the Lord, we will not hear it of thee; but whatsoever we think good, that will we do,' Jer. xliv. 14, 15; but that they may 'know those men which labour among them, and have the oversight of them in the Lord;' and not barely know them, but also 'love them for their good works' sake,' 1 Thes. v. 12, 13.

Thus having finished the former circumstances as compendiously as I promised, I proceed to the next words, the which contain in them the second part of a Christian minister's duty, which is, to minister the sacraments rightly, whereof one is set down in his due order by the instituter Christ himself when he saith, 'Baptizing them in the name of the Father, and the Son, and the Holy Ghost.'

Now, because the word *baptism* hath divers significations in the Scripture, I will here set down as many of them as my memory can record. First, the word *baptism*, according to the true meaning of the Greek word *baptisma*, doth not signify only a dipping, but such a dipping in the water as doth cleanse the party dipped; and for that the primitive church did use to put the party baptized quite under the water, therefore Paul, writing both to the Romans and Colossians, useth these words, 'We are buried, then, with him in baptism unto his death: that like as Christ was raised up from the dead by the glory of the Father, so we also should walk in newness of life,' Rom. vi. 4, Col. ii. 12; in which words the apostle sheweth what resemblance their baptism hath with Christ his death and resurrection. Secondly, *baptism* is used for a bare washing, in which sense our Saviour spake when he said to the pharisees, 'You lay apart the commandments of God, and observe the traditions of men, as the washing of pots and cups; and many such things ye do,' Mark vii. 8. And in the same sense we read in the epistle to the Hebrews, when the author saith that 'the old tabernacle consisted of many washings and ceremonial rites, until the day of reformation came,' Heb. ix. 10. Thirdly, by *baptism* we may understand affliction, as our Saviour Christ did, in saying to James and John, the sons of Zebedee, ' Can you be baptized with that baptism wherewith I must be baptized ?' Mark x. 38 ; and to his disciples, ' I must be baptized with a baptism ; but how am I pained until it be ended !' Luke xii. 50. Fourthly, *baptism* is a liberal distribution of the graces of God, as appeareth in these words, ' John baptized with water, but you shall be baptized with the Holy Ghost within these few days,' Acts i. 5. Fifthly, the word *baptism* is taken for doctrine only, as in that place wherein the Holy Ghost, having occasion to speak of Apollos, a Jew of Alexandria, saith that he was ' mighty in the Scriptures, and did know but the baptism of John only,' Acts xviii. 24, 25. And last of all, *baptism* is taken for a reverent order of ministering that sacrament in the church, and the whole sanctification of the parties baptized, as in the words of this present part of Scripture, ' baptizing,' &c.

But to speak of the sacrament itself. It hath been usual with almighty God from time to time to confirm his covenants with seals set to the same. For example, we see that there is a rainbow in the clouds, the reason whereof is, that God having in his justice destroyed the old world for sin (only Noah and his family being excepted), the same God in his mercy made a covenant with Noah, that he would never destroy it so again. For confirmation thereof, he set the rainbow in the clouds, as a seal to that covenant betwixt himself and Noah, Gen. ix. 12, &c. So was circumcision given to Abraham as a seal of confirmation in that promise, that ' in his seed all nations of the earth should be blessed,' Gen. xvii. 10, 11, so that as many as were circumcised were within compass of that covenant, instead whereof we have baptism, the which whosoever shall refuse, we account him as cut off from God's church. Christ Jesus gave invisible grace by visibly laying his hands upon children and other sick people, Mark x. 16. So he gave the gift of his Holy Spirit unto his disciples, when, ' having breathed upon them, he said, Receive ye the Holy Ghost,' John xx. 22.

The sacraments were ordained in the church of God for three uses: First, that we should acknowledge all those to be our fellow-servants whom we see to have put on the same livery with ourselves; and in this sense said the apostle Paul, ' All those that are baptized unto Christ have put on Christ,' Gal. iii. 27. Secondly, the sacraments do put a manifest difference betwixt the true church and the false, as Peter hath taught us in saying, ' Repent and be baptized, every one of you, in the name of Jesus Christ : for to you is the promise made, and unto your children, and all that are yet far off, even so many as God shall call,' Acts ii. 28, 39 ; and our Saviour saith, 'To such belongs the kingdom of God,' Mark x. 14 ; that is, to such as lead an innocent life. The third use of the sacraments is to seal up in the hearts of the elect all those promises which God hath made unto them in Jesus Christ, his Son and their Saviour ; in the which sense Paul spake when he said, that ' Abraham received the sign of circumcision as a seal of that righteousness which he had by faith,' Rom. iv. 11 ; and in the very same sense our Saviour saith, ' He that believeth, and is baptized, shall be saved,' Mark xvi. 16. But it is to be considered that the instituter setteth down the form of administering the sacrament, when he saith, ' Baptizing them in the name of the Father, and of the Son, and of the Holy Ghost.' He commandeth to baptize in the name of the Father, and of the Son, because the Holy Ghost proceedeth from the Father and the Son, and in the name of the Holy Ghost ; for ' except a man be born of water and the Spirit, he cannot see the kingdom of God,' John iii. 5. When our Saviour offered to wash Peter's feet, he imagined it to be needless work, for ' Thou shalt never wash my feet,' saith he, John xiii. 8 ; but when Christ answered that ' such as are not washed by him have no part with him,' that is, neither part of his Spirit, nor of his kingdom, Peter bethinking himself better, would not have ' his feet only, but also his hands and his head washed.' Howbeit it is not necessary to wash any more than is unclean. As Peter's feet, defiled with dirt and mire, so our souls, spotted with sins, must be cleansed by Christ his blood only. And after this manner it is necessary that every one of us should be washed, whereof the outward putting of water upon the party baptized is a lively figure. John Baptist was sanctified in his mother's womb, as the angel had foreshewed, Luke i. 15 ; but when our Saviour Christ came to him to be baptized, 'John put him back and said, I have need to be baptized of thee, and comest thou to me?' Mat. iii. 14. That kingly prophet, David, was ' a man after God's own heart ;' yet he saith of himself, ' I was born in iniquity, and in sin hath my mother conceived me,' Ps. li. 5. Job was called by God himself ' a just and upright man, fearing God, and eschewing evil,' Job i. 1 ; whose peer was not found upon the face of the earth ; notwithstanding all this, he saith of himself, ' Who can bring a clean thing out of filthiness ?' Job xiv. 4. The which question is all one with Paul's affirmation, who saith, ' Such as the root is, such are the branches,' Rom. xi. 16. As if he had said, if Adam, the father of us all, was undefiled, then are we his sons clean also ; but if he were once dead in sin, being our root, then how could we his imps have life of ourselves? And this was spoken of original sin; as for actual sins, namely, those sins which we continually commit, they are as palpable as the darkness of Egypt, the which, as Moses saith, was so gross that 'it might be felt,' Exod. x. 21, 22. Insomuch that David saith, 'When God looked down from heaven upon the children of men,' that is, when he considered man's conversation, 'they were all so far gone out of the way, that there was none that did good,' Ps. xiv. 2, 3; insomuch that the prophet repeateth it with an emphasis, and saith, 'no not one.' And the man of God, Moses, saith, When God beheld the boldness of the old world in sinning, 'it repented him that he made man,' Gen. vi. 5, 6; that is, he was sorry that man, whom he had made to live well, should live so ill. The continual sin of Sodom brought fire and brimstone from heaven to consume them in the same, Gen. xix. 24. David, feeling the burden of his sins, began to sink under them; for saith he, 'My sins are gone over mine head, and are like a sore burden, too heavy for me to bear,' Ps. xxxviii. 4. Paul having by the virtue of the law learned his sins, for he 'had not known sin, except the law had said, Thou shalt not sin,' Rom. vii. 7, fell to lamenting of them thus, 'O wretched man that I am! who shall deliver me from this body of death?' Rom. vii. 24. Where it is to be noted, that he calleth his body 'a body of death' in respect of sin, which giveth power to death over our bodies. And to conclude: of such force is sin in us, that if the goodness of God had not so pre-ordained, that 'the unbelieving husband is sanctified by the believing wife, and the unbelieving wife by the believing husband, our children should be very unclean,' 1 Cor. vii. 14.

Again, being washed or 'baptized in the name of the Father, Son, and Holy Ghost, we are advertised, that we must give godly, Christian, and holy names unto our children, in token of their sacred profession, for 'holy is he that hath called us.' And that we may be the more forward so to do, it will be worth our labour to consider of a few examples tending to the same purpose. As of Zacharias the father of John Baptist, who being dumb when that his son was born, 'his friends made signs unto him how he would have him called. And asking for a pair of writing tables, he wrote, saying, His name is John,' Luke i. 62, 63; which word *John* is as much as to say, *grace;* and thus was Zacharias commanded by the angel to name him, Luke i. 13. The Scripture affordeth plentiful examples of those that have given names to their children according to such occasions as have been offered in the time of their travail. As when Rachel went with her husband Jacob toward Bethel, to build an altar unto God, she travailed in childbirth, and in travailing died; but before she departed, 'she called his name Benoni,' that is, the son of her sorrow; ' but his father Jacob called him Benjamin,' that is, the son of his right hand, Gen. xxxv. 18. So Leah having borne to Jacob four sons, she said, ' Now will I praise God,' Gen xxix. 35, &c. And that she might the better bear in mind her promise, she named her last son *Judah*. When the man of Benjamin came from the Israelites with his clothes rent, and dust upon his head, in token of heaviness, and certified father Eli that God's ark was taken by the Philistines, and that his two sons were slain, the old father ' fell backward out of his seat, and broke his neck.' And his daughter-in-law, Phinehas's wife, being frighted with fear, fell in travail, and died in childbed; but before her death she called her son *Ichabod,* that is, Where is the glory of God? 1 Sam. iv. 18, &c., meaning thereby, that she accounted the glory of God to be taken from Israel, when God's ark, which was a figure of his church, wherein we glorify his name, was taken away by the enemy; and secondly, to admonish all parents so to nurture up their children, that they may seek to maintain the glory of God better than Eli did, for the wickedness of whose children, as also for the father's default in not correcting them, God had threatened before, that if he once began with him, he would make an end with him, 1 Sam. iii. 11–14. So that, as the prophet saith, ' Children, being the fruit of the womb,' as they come from God, are a good blessing, and 'an heritage that cometh from the Lord,' Ps. cxxvii. 3, because he it is from whom every good and perfect gift doth proceed; yet in respect of men, so may the matter be handled, that they shall find no such cross or curse as graceless or unruly children; such as Esau and his two wives, who were ' a grief of mind' and a heart-breaking unto Isaac their father, and Rebecca their mother, Gen. xxvi. 35.

It is true, that the very godliest men and women have rather desired sons than daughters at the hands of God; but they did it for good and godly purposes. As when Abraham desired a son, to the end that Eliezer, the steward of his house, being a stranger, namely, a man of Damascus, should not be the heir of his goods, Gen. xv. 2. So did Hannah pray to God for a son, when she said, ' O Lord of hosts, if thou wilt look on the trouble of thine handmaid, and remember me, &c., and give unto thy handmaid a man-child, then will I give him unto the Lord all the days of his life,

1 Sam. i. 11, &c.   And as the very name of a son is in price and preferred at this day, so hath it been heretofore; as when Phinehas's wife being near her death in travail, the midwife with the rest thinking to comfort her, said, ' Fear not, for thou hast borne a son,' 1 Sam. iv. 20.   When the angel said to Abraham, This time twelve-month Sarah thy wife shall bear a son, Sarah laughed, as partly doubting, and partly joying that so aged a woman as she should conceive a son by so aged a man as Abraham was, Gen. xviii. 10, 12. The same angel that certified Zacharias that Elizabeth his wife should bear John the Baptist, said, not only that it should be a son, but such a son as should bring joy unto him and many more, Luke i. 13, 14.   And that angel Gabriel that was sent of God to Mary, the mother of our Saviour, according to his humanity, saith, that instead of fear, ' she had found favour with God ;' and his reason is this, ' for thou shalt bear a Son, and shalt call his name Jesus,' Luke i. 30, 31.   As if he had said, It is a great bless-ing of God to bear a child, and a greater to bear a man-child ; but to be so far in God's favour as to bear such a son as shall be the Saviour of the world, it is the greatest grace which hath been heard of; in the which God make his church joyful, and for the which in special, and for all the rest of his blessings in general, God make us thankful.   Amen.

A MEMENTO FOR MAGISTRATES.

A MEMENTO FOR MAGISTRATES.

The sceptre of thy kingdom is a right sceptre. Thou lovest right-eousness, and hatest iniquity : therefore the Lord hath anointed thee with the oil of gladness above thy fellows.—Ps. XLV. 6, 7.

THE author of this 45th Psalm, speaking of the government of Solomon, avoucheth that he cannot rule rightly that loveth not to judge justly, and that he usurpeth authority that dealeth partially. For we must remember that he measureth Solomon's worthiness to reign by his well swaying of the sceptre ; the which Solomon could not have handled so commendably as he did, if he had not been carried away with an earnest desire to deal indifferently among men in causes of controversy. But most plainly appeareth his great desire of godly government in that hearty prayer which he uttered unto almighty God, when he saith, 1 Kings iii. 9, 'Give unto thy servant, O Lord, an understanding and a wise heart, to judge thy people ; that I may discern betwixt good and evil.' In this prayer it is plain that although he was a king, yet he calleth himself the servant of God ; for 'promotion cometh neither from the east, nor from the west, nor yet from the south, but from God, who plucketh down one, and setteth up another,' Ps. lxxv. 6, 7. And Solomon having prayed for wisdom and understanding, he sheweth where-unto he would apply those gifts of God, even unto the glory of him that gave them ; 'to judge thy people, that I may discern betwixt good and evil,' saith he ; for 'by him kings reign, and by him princes decree justice,' Prov. viii. 15.

When Jethro, the father-in-law of Moses, came out of the land of Midian to see Moses, Exod. xviii., being at the mount of God, which was mount Sinai, and beheld how the people flocked unto Moses their magistrate for justice and judgment ; by due consideration thereof, Jethro found these three inconveniences: first, that Moses wearied himself with sitting in judgment from morning until night ; secondly, that he was too tedious unto the people which attended upon him all that time ; and, thirdly, that notwithstanding his carefulness in judgment, and their earnest expectation of justice, he was not able to despatch so many matters as were brought before him, but with a light hearing, and a little regarding of many men's causes. Wherefore Jethro, being a man very desirous that justice might proceed, that no man's matters should slightly be slipped over, counselleth Moses to make more magistrates in Israel ; and to the end that this might be performed the better, Jethro doth point at the disposition of those men which should bear rule ; for, saith he, 'Thou shalt choose out among all the people men of courage, dealing truly, fearing God, and hating covetousness ; and them shalt thou make governors over the people,' Exod. xviii. 21.

By this you may perceive how Jethro in counselling, and Moses in practising, did both aim at justice and true judgment. For it is not a mean matter, or light labour, for men of years to sit from morning to night in judgment ; no, their years' antiquity, and consequently their bodies' imbecility, cannot easily endure it ; besides, the care of common causes heard at home, and that which is the biggest burden of all, the continual good of the commonwealth, which they meditate carefully when we sleep securely, is not to be forgotten. But herein are many magistrates greatly to be blamed, in that they cause the people to attend upon them from morning until night, with expenses great and continual, whilst they find no end of poor men's matters, because they wish no end of spending money. 'Are their minds set upon righteousness' which deal thus ? Ps. lviii. 1. No, no, they are the same that the prophet spake of, when he said, 'The ungodly seek occasions against the righteous, and gnasheth upon him with his teeth,' Ps. xxxvii. 12 ; for the crafty counsellor taketh occasion to hinder his client's just cause, that he might still feed upon the poor man's purse. The lawyer who careth not to deal unfaithfully, is like the crystal glass, which flatteringly sheweth unto every man a fair face, how evil-favoured soever he be. So can he persuade the simple swain that his cause will bear a strong action, be it never so weak.

Oh remember what God said unto Israel, 'You shall not do what seemeth good in your own eyes,' but what I command you, Deut. xii. 8. Then know that you do not that which he hath commanded, because you deal not with mercy and truth. For if ever the time required, and occasion was offered, to move that question to magistrates, which David did in his days, namely, ' How long will they proceed to give unjust judgment, and to accept the person of the ungodly ?' Ps. lxxxii. 2, now is the time and occasion present. For I do not doubt but it is too true that the prophet hath spoken, who saith that the ungodly are more set by than the righteous ; and this is the cause that wrong judgment doth proceed, Hab. i. 4. How can justice sit when there is no seat appointed for her ? You may be sure she will not have to do with ' the stool of wickedness,' where mischief standeth instead of justice, Ps. xciv. 20. It was a worthy commendation that David uttered in the praise of Jerusalem, when he said, ' There is the seat for judgment,' Ps. cxxii. 5 ; the which appointing of that seat for judgment was an argument that they loved justice. And, first, the place wherein it was set assureth us hereof, for it was set in the gate, where-through men might have passage to and from the judgment-seat. Secondly, the manner of framing the seat in the gate, namely, that the judges of force must sit with their faces towards the rising of the sun, in token that their judgment should be as pure from corruption, as the sun was clear in his chiefest brightness. Oh happy house of David, whose seat was set so conveniently, whose causes were heard so carefully, and matters judged so justly ! The Israelites thought themselves well apaid when they had the government of Deborah, that virtuous woman, for all was laid abed ' until she came up a mother in Israel,' Judges v. 7 ; and as she was a good governess in her time, so she loved those that were like unto herself, ' for,' saith she, ' my heart is set upon the governors of Israel,' ver. 9. David was a good king while he lived, as it did appear by the testimony of God himself, who said of him, ' I have found David my servant, with my holy oil have I anointed him,' Ps. lxxxix. 20. Secondly, by his appealing to God for judgment in this case, when he saith, ' Be thou my judge, O Lord, for I have walked innocently,' &c., Ps. xxvi. 1. And last of all, by that good counsel which he gave upon his deathbed unto Solomon his son, who was to succeed him in that kingdom : ' For,' saith he, ' thou shalt prosper and come to great honour, if thou keepest the commandments which God commanded Moses,' 1 Kings ii. 3.

When Philip, the king of Macedonia, did cast off the earnest suit of a poor widow with this slender answer, Go thy way, for I have no leisure to hear thee now ; she replied thus, And why hast thou leisure to be a king ? As if she should have said, God hath given thee time to reign, and power to govern, that thou mightest apply them both unto the end wherefor they are given thee, for ' Mercy and truth preserveth a king, and with loving-kindness his seat is upholden,' Prov. xx. 28. When Solomon prayed to God for 'an understanding heart,' 1 Kings iii. 9, that he might do justice among God's people, it is said, that his prayer pleased God passing well, because Solomon asked wisdom rather than wealth, and knowledge rather than honour; for thereby he gave evidence that his heart was set upon righteousness, for out of the abundance of the heart the mouth speaketh. It is a most excellent prayer which the prophet maketh when he saith, Ps. lxxii. 1, 'Give thy judgment unto the king, O Lord, and thy righteousness unto the king's son,' &c. 'Then shall he judge the people according unto right, and defend the poor;' wherein the prophet prayed for himself, while he governed the kingdom of Israel, and for his successors in the same, having relation unto that promise spoken of in the 132d Psalm, 'The Lord hath made a faithful oath unto David, and he will not shrink from it, saying, Of the fruit of thy body shall I set upon thy seat. If thy children keep my testimonies which I shall learn them,' &c. And the prophet proceeding to say, 'then shall he judge the people according unto right, and defend the poor,' by this word *then*, he insinuateth, that when God giveth grace to the magistrate, then he cannot choose but do right, and defend those which do sustain wrong. But when the prophet saith, ' and defend the poor,' some man would think that he had said enough before, and therefore might have cut off this speech. But it is to be remembered, that a sick man needeth not the physician, or the wayfaring man his weapon, at one time only ; but as often as the patient is sick, so often he must have the physician's counsel, and as often as the traveller is assaulted, so often he useth his weapon. In like sort the poor man oppressed often, doth as often need the defence of the magistrate ; and therefore hath the magistrate the sword always carried before him, and this sword is always carried before rather than behind the magistrate, that he might rather remember justice than cast the care thereof behind his back.

The last, but not the least thing to be marked of the magistrate, is, that justice is set forth with a pair of balances in the one hand, which admonisheth him to weigh those matters justly which are brought before him ; and within the other hand is a two-edged sword, to the intent that 'justice might return to judgment,' Ps. xciv. 15, that is, that things justly judged might be rightly rewarded on both sides. Whereof king Solomon hath given a good precedent, 1 Kings iii., first, in finding out the true mother of the smothered child, which is a point of judgment ; second, in restoring the living child to his own mother, which was a point of justice. And these parts of a Christian magistrate's duty are so necessarily linked together, that so often as one of them is wanting, the law receiveth a maim at the hand of the magistrate. As when Pilate judged Christ guiltless, but yet put him to death, John xix.; and when Paul's cause was heard and approved, yet he was left in prison, Acts xxiv. Therefore it is good counsel, and worthy to be hearkened unto, which David gave unto all kings and magistrates, that they be 'learned and wise,' Ps. ii. 10; for if the magistrate be not wise, words may carry the matter away. As when Daniel was accused of despising the decree of Nebuchadnezzar the king of Babylon, Jeremiah to be an enemy to the commonwealth of Israel, Jer. xviii.; Elias to be a troubler of the state, 1 Kings xviii. 17; Paul to be a factious and seditious fellow, Acts xxiv. 5; Naboth to have blasphemed God and king Ahab, 1 Kings xxi. 13; and as at the importunate cry of the Jews Christ was put to death, and Barabbas the murderer set at liberty, Luke xxiii. The special wisdom of God matched Moses the magistrate with Aaron the minister, Exod. iv.; thereby giving us to understand, that when the word and the sword go together, there can be none other but good government. As for example, so long as the good priest Jehoiada and the godly king Joash lived together, God was worshipped and his people guided according to his word, 2 Kings xii.; for the man of God counselled virtuously and the king practised carefully, whereto the saying of Solon doth very well agree, who being asked when the commonwealth did best flourish, answered, When the people obey the magistrate, and the magistrate obeyeth the law; for laws are better unmade than unkept. No doubt there want not such as will say with those head-strong people in David's days, ' Let us break their bands in sunder, and cast away their cords from us,' Ps. ii. 3. And our laws have been a long time like to spiders' webs, so that the great buzzing bees break through, and the little feeble flies hang fast in them.

But admit that you reply and say, they are made stronger than in the days of our forefathers; yet are they like to walled cities in the time of war, at the which time, be your walls never so strong, they are beaten down, if they want men and munition; so if your laws wisely made do want patrons to defend them, they will soon be little worth. Therefore it was not the worst warning Jethro gave to Moses, that he should make such magistrates as were 'men of courage,' Exod. xviii. 21. It is good therefore, not only for those men that have the election of magistrates, to make such choice of officers as Jethro enjoineth Moses, and as God himself commanded

Israel, when he said, 'You shall make him king whom the Lord your God shall choose,' Deut. xvii. 15; but also very meet for those magistrates, being so elected, to have a care, that as they are in place above other men, so in good life they go before the people. For this was it that the Israelites desired God to grant unto Joshua, being newly made their governor, namely, a faithful heart to go in and out before them. For, said they, 'even as we obeyed Moses in all things, so will we obey thee; only the Lord thy God be with thee, as he was with Moses,' Joshua i. 17. And it was a necessary prayer; for how foul a fault were it, that the man which is appointed to punish adultery, should be more worthy of correction for the same kind of sin than the party punished? like unto the whore-hunting judges of Samaria, mentioned by the prophet Jeremiah, chap. v., or that he which is appointed to judge according to law, should do anything contrary to law? as angry Ananias commanded that Paul should be smitten contrary to law, Acts xxiii. 2, 3. In this point doth the Lord school the king of Judah by this prophet Jeremiah, who saith, 'Hear the word of the Lord, thou king of Judah, that sittest in the kingly seat of David, thou, and thy servants, and thy people that go in and out at this gate. Thus the Lord commandeth, Keep equity and righteousness, deliver the oppressed from the power of the violent, do not grieve nor oppress the stranger, the fatherless, nor the widow, and shed no innocent blood in this place. And if you keep these things faithfully, then shall there come in at this door of this house, kings to sit upon David's seat, &c. But if you will not be obedient unto these commandments, I swear by my own self (saith the Lord) this house shall be waste,' Jer. xxii. 2, &c. For example, the same prophet speaking there of the wicked government of Shallum, the son of king Josias, who governed Judah, saith, 'Did not thy father eat and drink, and prosper well, so long as he dealt with righteousness? from whence came this, but because he had me before his eyes, saith the Lord?' Now when Jeremiah saith that Josias had God before his eyes, his meaning is all one with David's intent, when he saith, 'God standeth in the parliament of princes, he is a judge among gods;' to give all magistrates a *memento* that God is present in all their assemblies, and judgeth them that judge under him; whereof they had need to be put in mind; for oftentimes Micah proveth too true a prophet in saying, that 'the great man will speak what his heart desires,' and the hearers must allow it well, Micah vii. 3.

Of the which sort of men the very best is but a thistle, which a man can hardly touch unpricked; and the most just like a bramble, whereby the silly sheep, seeking to be shrouded from sharp showers, is often forced to leave his fleece behind. Whose unworthy coming to their places Jotham hath well described in the person of Abimelech, when he said, Judges ix. 8, &c., 'The trees of the wood went to anoint a king over them, and said unto the olive-tree, Reign thou over us. But the olive-tree answered, Shall I leave my fatness, which both God and men praise in me, and go to be promoted over the trees? Then they came to the fig-tree, and said, Come thou and reign over us. The fig-tree answered, Shall I leave my sweetness and good fruit, and go to be promoted over the trees? They said unto the vine, Reign thou over us. But the vine answered, Should I leave my wine, wherewith I cheer God and men, to be promoted over the trees? Then they said unto the bramble, Wilt thou reign over us? Then said the bramble, If it be true indeed that you will submit yourselves to my authority, then put your trust under my shadow; or let fire proceed from the bramble, and consume you.' By this parable we are taught generally, that every man is to be content with that estate wherein God hath placed him; and that for the most part the very best worthy do refuse proffered promotion, and on their part well deserved; whereas, on the contrary, the most unfitly furnished with justice and true judgment, and the least deserving in a commonwealth, are of all others most ambitious. Such a one was Absalom, who stole away the hearts of Israel with this flattering speech, 2 Sam. xv. 4, 'Oh that I were made judge in the land, that every man which hath any plea or matter in law might come to me, that I might do him justice.' But this is the just reward of such as, before convenient time and apt occasion be offered, do ambitiously seek the seat of judgment, even untimely and unnatural death; for Absalom was hanged by the hair of his head, 2 Sam. xviii. 9, and a woman with a piece of millstone dashed out Abimelech's brains, Judges ix. 53. Though Absalom be absent, and Abimelech brained long since, yet it is to be suspected that many men get preferment by their practices, coming in such sheep-skins as are fair words and flattering speeches; but God grant that they prove not like unto those judges whom Zephaniah feared not to liken unto lions and wolves, who finding their prey in the evening, chop up all, not leaving so much as the bones until the morning, Zeph. iii. 3. Solomon saith well, that many would be accounted good doers, 'but where shall we find a faithful man?' Prov. xx. 6. Some men have said well with Absalom, before they came to preferment, but they can now be content to see many men to sue seven years for their right, and yet suffer them to sustain wrong, because necessity hath no law forsooth. Go to, go to, somebody will answer for that one day. A man would think that necessity should have the most law, because she hath least money and fewest friends. 'Are your minds set upon righteousness, O ye congregation? and do you judge the thing that is right, O ye sons of men?' saith the prophet, Ps. lviii. 1; in all his troubles desiring God to stand on his side against his oppressors. He thought it as convenient to crave of God the consideration of his cause, as to ask his aid against his adversaries; and therefore prayeth thus, 'Ponder my words, O Lord, consider my meditations,' &c., Ps. v. 1. So magistrates have not only authority to make and establish good laws, but also to determine betwixt men according to the same; unto whose censure the subject must submit himself, as the apostle proveth to the Romans, when he saith, 'Let every soul submit itself unto the authority of the higher powers; for all power is of God. Wherefore, whosoever resisteth that power, resisteth the ordinance of God, and purchaseth unto himself damnation. For magistrates are not to be feared of them that do well, but of them that do evil. Wilt thou not fear? Do well then, so shalt thou have praise; for he is the minister of God for thy wealth; but if thou doest evil, then fear, for he beareth not the sword for nought, but is the minister of God to take vengeance upon them that do evil,' Rom. xiii. 1; where it is to be remembered, that the civil magistrate, who beareth the sword, is called the minister of God, as well as the spiritual magistrate, that preacheth the word; and that, no doubt, to the intent he might take care as well to maintain true religion, as to minister deserved discipline. For it standeth with all divine and human reason, that if all masters and fathers ought to have a more than ordinary care to instruct and help forward their families in Christian religion, so much as in them lieth; much more ought the magistrate to meditate by all means possible to perform his duty therein, who is a father over all families. I cannot set this forth in any plainer speech than David hath done in this short saying, 'Kiss the Son, lest he be angry, and so you perish in the right way,' Ps. ii. 12. By which speech the prophet teacheth, that God cannot be honoured by any other means than by that which Christ his Son hath taught, who saith himself in the fifth of John, 'He that honoureth the Son, honoureth the Father; he that dishonoureth the Son, dishonoureth the Father.' So that he meaneth in this place, that if you worship not the Son as he hath commanded, then you dishonour him; if you dishonour him, then you anger him; if you anger him, he casteth you off; if he casteth you off, then you err from the right way; and if you err from the right way, then you perish. For the avoiding whereof, all godly magistrates have had a special care to meditate in the law of the Lord; such were Moses, Joshua, David, Solomon, Asa, Jehoshaphat, Hezekiah, &c. Of whose good example God grant all godly magistrates to make good use. Amen.

JACOB'S LADDER; OR, THE WAY TO HEAVEN.

JACOB'S LADDER; OR, THE WAY TO HEAVEN.

So run, that ye may obtain.—1 COR. IX. 24.

BECAUSE I have but one hour to teach you all that you must learn of me, I have chosen a text which is like Jacob's ladder, that shews you the way to heaven. This is all that you would know; and it may please God to open your eyes, that you may know it before ye depart. Hear to practise; hinder not the Spirit, but let it work without resistance; record when you are gone, and you shall see the great power of God, what he is able to do for you by one sentence of this book, if ye digest it well. 'So run, that ye may obtain.' Then we must see first how we should run; secondly, what we shall obtain; thirdly, what will hinder us; that is, we must see the way, the lets, and the end. Four things mark in the way: first, begin betime; secondly, make haste; thirdly, keep the way; fourthly, continue to the end; and thou shalt obtain heaven, whither Christ by these steps is gone before thee. When I have set you in the way, I will point at all the lets, stops, rubs, and blocks which are before you, behind you, beside you; the temptations of prosperity, the temptations of adversity, the temptations of heresy, which stand in the streets, like the fiery sword to stop the way to paradise. Then I will lead you to the mount, as God did Moses, and shew you afar off the blessed land, the country above, that you may see where heaven is, what is the way to it, and what glory and happiness is there. When I have shewed you the way, the lets, and the end, I will commit you to the race, and end as I began; 'So run, that ye may obtain.'

So often as I have read or considered these words which you hear, they seem, methinks, to put us in mind that we are out of the

way, and that there is another way, if we seek it, nearer yet to the
kingdom of heaven than that which we take ; therefore the holy
apostle doth warn every man to ponder his steps, that, running, we
may obtain that which we run for, which is the worthiest prize that
ever was given, and never was given but to him which kept this way
that I will shew you.   The apostle saith that you must run.   It is
not an easy nor a short journey, which a drone, a dreamer, a snail,
or any careless man may perform and take his ease, set forth when
he will, stay at his pleasure, go again at his leisure ; but he must
always run, from the first day he setteth forth till he come to his
journey's end ; for the glorious heaven is far from the dark earth,
and much ado to aspire to the top of mount Sion, but much more
ado to aspire to the top of mount heaven.   The violent take it from
the slothful, and the wicked run to hell ; much more are the pains
which they take to do evil, than the righteous need to take for
heaven.   The apostle putteth the word *so* before *run,* to teach us
to look to our way before we run too far : ' So run,' &c., as if he
should say, More run than come home, as more shoot than hit the
mark.   The heathen philosophers, Plato, Socrates, Aristides, Phocion,
Pericles, Solon, in their way, did run faster than we ; constancy,
temperance, patience, justice, humility, simplicity, integrity, contempt of death, contempt of the world, seem to be buried with them,
and hid in the grave before this iron age was born ; yet, because
they ran without Christ, they did not obtain, but lost their labour,
like a man which, making haste out of his way, takes more pains
than if he kept the way, and yet never comes whither he would.
The blind generations which know not God, in their way, run faster
than we.   Ask the merchants which have seen their life and our
lives, or look into histories, and they will tell you that our religion
is not like their superstition, our knowledge not like their ignorance,
our faith not like their fear, our worship not like their service, our
Christianity not like their idolatry ; yet, because they run to the
creature for the Creator, and follow uncertain dreams before the
word which came from heaven, they run in vain ; for their religion,
devotion, and service, is to them that cannot requite it.   Many of
our adversaries, papists, anabaptists, Donatists, and the grossest
heretics, in their way, run faster than we ; they watch, they pray,
they fast, and distribute more than we ; yet, because they run to
traditions, to angels, to saints, to crosses, to images, to relics, instead
of Christ, and challenge merit of all that they do, and would be
canonised beside, that all posterity might honour them as they do
saints, therefore, as the pharisees had their reward when men praised

them, so have they when one doth worship another. If many run and do not obtain, how easy is it to run in vain! and how happy is he which obtaineth that that all men wish, when so many miss it for nothing but for this, because they run out of the way! You have heard, read, and done much, and more would do, to obtain eternal life with the angels in heaven; for this you pray, and fast, and watch, and obey the laws of God, and come together every Sabbath to hear, to pray, to praise, and serve him which giveth it. How many prayers, how many fasts, how many watches, how many works, how many hours in reading the word, in hearing the word, in receiving the sacrament, in examining your heart, in chastising your flesh, were spent and lost, if you should run in vain! as Esau hunted for a blessing, and went without it. Therefore the Holy Ghost doth say nothing, but it is like a mark in our way, to shew us when we are in, and when we are out; for God would not have us lose our labour, like Laban, which could find in his heart, after Jacob had served him twenty years, to send him away empty; but he would have you to ' seek and find,' to ' ask and receive,' to ' run and obtain;' therefore he saith, ' So run, that ye may obtain.' As there is a heaven, so there is a way to heaven; one way Adam came from paradise, and by another he must return to paradise. The passage is not so stopped but there is a way, though a strait way, and a door, though it be a narrow door, and therefore few do find it; only they which are like Jacob do see a ladder before them, as Jacob did. He had many dreams before, and did not see it; at last ' he dreamed, and, behold, a ladder which reached from earth to heaven, and all the angels descended and ascended by it,' to shew that no man ascendeth to heaven but by that ladder. This ladder is Christ, which saith, ' I am the way,' and therefore he bids us to follow him. If we must follow Christ his steps, let us see how he went to heaven. He begun betime, for at twelve years of age he said, ' I must go about my Father's business,' Luke ii. 49. He made speed; for John saith that 'He spake and did more good things,' in three and thirty years, ' than could be written,' John xxi. 25. He kept the right way; for when he said, ' Who can accuse me of sin?' none could accuse him of any, though they watched him for that purpose. He continued well; for he died like a lamb, and prayed to his Father, and forgave his enemies. Therefore we will call the steps of this ladder, *Maturè, properè, rectè, constanter;* that is, *Begin betime, Make haste, Keep the way,* and *Hold to the end,* and thou shalt go after thy Master.

Touching the first, *Begin betime.* God requiring the first-born for his offering, and the first-fruits for his service, requireth the first labours of his servants, and, as I may say, the maidenhead of every man, because the best season to seek God is to seek him early. And therefore wisdom saith, ' They which seek me early shall find me ;' but to them which defer, she saith, ' Ye shall seek me, but ye shall not find me.' We have long purposed to serve God, and every man thinks that he should be served ; but we cannot accord of the time when to begin. One says, When I am rich ; another says, When I am free ; another saith, When I am settled ; another saith, When I am old, then I shall be fit to fast and pray. Thus, because we are given to set the best last, that we may have a longer time of our sins and pleasures, like the Jews in Haggai i. 2, which said alway, ' The time was not yet come when they should build the temple ;' therefore the Holy Ghost crieth so often, ' This is the acceptable time ; this is the day of salvation ; to-day hear his voice ;' like Rebekah, which taught her son the nearest way to get the blessing. So soon as man was created, a law was given him, to shew that he should live under obedience from the day he is born ; so soon as he is born, he is baptized in the name of God, to shew that when we cannot run to Christ, we should creep unto him, and serve him as we can in youth and age ; so soon as he beginneth to pray, he saith, ' Thy name be hallowed, thy kingdom come, thy will be done,' before he asks his ' daily bread,' to shew that we should seek the will of God before the food that we live by, much more before the sins and pleasures which we perish by. So soon as the Lord distributed the talents, he enjoined his servants to use them, Mat. xxv. 15, Luke xix. 13. Who is so young that has not received some talent or other ? Therefore youth cannot excuse him, because the talent requires to be used of every one that hath it. So soon as God created the man and the woman, he commanded them to 'increase and multiply,' Gen i. 28. Shall we increase and multiply in the flesh, before we increase and multiply in the spirit ? The first thing that God did after he created heaven and earth, ' he did separate light from darkness,' Gen. i. 1, 4 ; shewing us how we should separate our good from evil, before our good become evil. The first lesson that John taught was, ' Repent, for the kingdom of heaven is at hand,' Mat. iii. 2 ; the first lesson that the disciples taught was ' Repent' too, ' for the kingdom of heaven is at hand,' Mat. x. 7 ; and the first lesson that Christ taught was, ' Repent, for the kingdom of heaven is at hand,' Mat. iv. 17, to teach what we should do first. *Repent* was the first lesson to young and old. Therefore David prayed, ' Teach me, O Lord, to number my days,'

Ps. xc. 12; not my years, nor my months, nor my weeks, but my days: shewing that we shall answer for days as well as for years, for to-day as well as for to-morrow, and for our youth as straitly as for our age; even as the little children were devoured with bears for mocking the prophet, 2 Kings ii. 23. This made David to cry, 'Remember not the sins of my youth,' Ps. xxv. 7, which he would not have spoken, if God did not mark the sins of youth as well as age. Therefore the fathers were charged to teach their children the same law which they had themselves, Deut. vi. 7. Therefore Christ rebuked the disciples which forbade the little children to be brought to him, Mat. xix. 14; for, should children honour their father, and not honour God? It was a sweet concert when the children went before Christ to the temple and sung their *Hosanna,* to make their fathers ashamed, which did not know the Messias when he came, when their little children knew him. It is written, when Christ heard a young man answer that he had kept the commandments from his youth, Christ began to love him, Mark x. 20, 21; which shews how Christ loves these timely beginnings, when we make him our nurse, and draw our first milk from his breasts. There is not one confession for old men, and another for young men; in the Creed, the old man saith not, I *did* believe in God, and the young man saith not, I *will* believe in God; but both say, I *do* believe in God. For he which is called I AM, Exod. iii. 14, loveth *I am*, and careth not for *I was*, nor *I will be*. When Christ asked Peter, 'Lovest thou me?' John xxi. 15, he looked that he should answer him, 'Yea, Lord, I love thee'; and not drive off as Felix did Paul, Acts xxiv. 25, 'I will hear thee,' I will love thee, 'when I have time convenient:' nay, when thou hast not convenient time, for if this be the convenient time, after this the convenient time is past. Manna was gathered in the morning, because when the sun arose it did melt away; so virtue must be gathered betime, for if we stay till business and pleasures come upon us, they will melt it faster than we can gather it. Therefore, in Prov. iv. 7, Wisdom is called 'the beginning,' to teach us to seek wisdom in the beginning, as a man taketh the best first. If Elijah would be served before the widow, when she had not enough to serve herself, will God be served after thee? nay, after the flesh, and after the devil? What canst thou owe him to-morrow, which thou art not indebted to-day? Yea, doth not God require morning sacrifice as well as evening sacrifice? It is an old saying, Repentance is never too late; but it is a true saying, Repentance is never too soon; for so soon as ever we sin, we had need to ask forgiveness.

Besides, repentance is a gift, and therefore it must be taken when it is offered; for if Judas conld have repented when he listed, he would never have hanged himself. The time past is gone, and thou canst not call that to repent in ; the time to come is uncertain, and thou canst not assure that to repent in ; the present time is only thine, and thou mayest repent in that, but anon that will be gone too. Therefore when Christ wept over Jerusalem, he said, 'Oh if thou hadst known in this thy day!' calling none *their* day but *this* day. If none can be called thy day but this day, then this is thy day of repentance, or else thou hast none at all. Therefore one resembleth the mercy of God to the pool in Jewry, where the sick and leprous lay ; for at one time of the day 'an angel came and stirred the water, and then he which stepped in first was healed of his disease,' John v. 4 ; he which stepped in first was healed, none but he which stepped in first. So he which taketh time is sure, but he which fore-sloweth time oftener faileth than speedeth; for when golden opportunity is past, no time will fit for it. Yet as when Christ went about to cast out devils, they said that he tormented them before the time, Mat. viii. 29 ; so whensoever thou goest about to dismiss thy sins and pleasures, though thou stay till thou be sick and old, and ready to die, yet they will say still that thou dismissest them before the time. But then is the time, when the devil saith the time is not yet ; for the devil is a liar, and knoweth that what liquor our vessels be seasoned with at the first, they will taste of the same ever after. Therefore linger not with Lot ; for if the angel had not snatched him away, he had perished with Sodom for his delay. They were not wise virgins, but foolish virgins, which sought not for oil before the bridegroom came. Samuel began to serve God in his minority, 1 Sam. ii. 18 ; Timothy read the Scripture in his childhood, 2 Tim. iii. 15 ; John grew in spirit as he ripened in years, Luke i. 80. So whether thou be old or young, thy repentance cannot be too soon, because thy sin is gone before. If thou lackest a spur to make thee run, see how every day runneth away with thy life ; youth cometh upon childhood, age cometh upon youth, death cometh upon age, with such a swift sail, that if our minutes were spent in mortifying ourselves, yet our glass would be run out before we had purged half our corruptions. Thus much of the first step.

The second step in your journey is, to *keep the way.* As God taught the Israelites the way to Canaan, sending a fiery pillar before them, which they did follow wheresoever it went ; so when he ordained a heaven for men, he appointed a way to come unto it, which way he that misseth shall never come to the end. As Herod sought Christ over all Jewry, but none found him but those which followed the star, Mat. ii. ; so there is something still that leadeth men to Christ, which we must follow, or else we cannot come where he is. There be many wrong ways, as there be many errors ; there is but one right way, as there is but one truth. And, therefore, Jacob did not see many, but one ladder, which reached to heaven ; and John Baptist is said, not to 'prepare the *ways* of the Lord,' but 'the *way*,' shewing that there is but one right way in this life; which Solomon understandeth for the mean, and therefore he said, 'Turn not to the right hand nor to the left,' implying that we may err as well of the right hand as of the left. As if he should say, Some are too hot, as others are too cold ; some are too superstitious, as others are too careless ; some are too fearful, as others are too confident ; there is a zeal without knowledge, a love without single-ness, a prayer without faith, and a faith without fruits. Therefore the apostle doth warn us to 'examine whether we be in the faith,' 2 Cor. xiii. 5 ; not whether we have a kind of faith, but whether we be *in the faith*, *i. e.* the true faith. Therefore Paul saith, *Run so.* It is not enough to run, but we must know how we run ; it is not enough to hear, but we must care how we hear ; it is not enough to believe, but we must care how we believe ; it is not enough to pray, but we must care how we pray ; it is not enough to work, but we must care how we work, for we cannot do good unless we do it well, as we may see in this example. Cain offered, and God abhorred ; because he cared not for the manner, God cared not for his offering. Simon Magus believed, Herod listened, Felix feared, Saul obeyed, Jezebel fasted, the Pharisees prayed ; but because they did not believe *so*, hear *so*, fear *so*, obey *so*, fast *so*, and pray *so*, as he which saith, 'Learn of me,' Matt. xi. 29 ; when they say that they have fasted, and prayed, and obeyed Christ, he will answer them as he doth in Matthew, 'I know you not,' Mat. vii. 23. Therefore, if ye ask, like the scribe, how ye shall come to heaven, the right way to heaven is the word, which came from heaven. But here some will say, The word indeed doth contain the right way, but many cannot find that way without a guide. Therefore I have picked out of the word that way which God calleth the right way. The way by which the word doth set thee into heaven is, to do to others as thou wouldst have others do to thee; to exercise good works, and yet believe that Christ's works shall save thee ; to pray without doubting, and yet be content that thy prayer be not granted ; to keep within thy calling, and do nothing by contention ; to bring

thy will unto God's will, and suffer for Christ, because he hath
suffered for thee ; to repent, not only for thine open and gross
faults, but to count every sin great ; to apply all things to the
glory of God, and of every thing to make some use.

Thus the word goeth before us like the fiery pillar, and shews
us when we are in, and when we are out; or else the broad way
would seem the best way, and therefore all which care not for the
word, go, like blind men, to hell for heaven. Look but to the
papists, which have the word in an unknown tongue: some clamber
to heaven by merits, some by angels, some by penance, and some
by pardons; and every man hath a way by himself, and all out of
the way. As Naaman answered Elisha, when he was commanded
to wash himself in Jordan, 'Are not Abanah and Pharpar, rivers
of Damascus, better than Jordan ? may I not wash there and be
healed ?' 2 Kings v. 12; so they say, Are not pardons as good as
works ? are not pilgrimages as good as prayers ? is not sacrifice as
good as obedience? is not reading as good as preaching? may I not
go to heaven this way and that way, as well as by the word ? No ;
as no water but Jordan could cleanse Naaman's leprosy, so no way
but the word can bring to heaven. For which cause the laws of
God are called 'the ways of God,' and the word of God is called
'the word of life;' to shew that there is no way to life but the
word, which is called 'the way and the life.' Therefore, now ye
see the way, I conclude with Isaiah, 'This is the way, walk in it.'
Thus much of your second step to heaven, which is, *Keep the way.*

Now when you are in the way, it's good to make speed; therefore
the next step in your journey is, *Make haste.* For this cause Paul
saith, *Run,* which is the swiftest pace of man ; as though he should
go faster to heaven than to any place else in the world. His meaning
is this, that as a man doth watch, and run, and labour, to be rich
quickly, so he should hear, and pray, and study, and use all means,
to be wise quickly. This the apostle understandeth when he biddeth
us to *add ;* as if he should say, When thou art in the way, and
knowest good from evil, every day kill some vice, and every week
sow some virtue, and make thy two talents five talents, thy five
talents ten talents, and ever be doing; and at last it shall be opened
to thee, because thou hast knocked. Christ saith, 'The kingdom
of heaven is got by violence,' Mat. xi. 12 ; therefore a man must
be earnest and zealous in the religion that he professes, or else it
makes no matter of what religion he is, for, if he be but lukewarm,
God threateneth to spue him out of his mouth, Rev. iii. 15, 16.
Every man hath a kind of religion, and the religion of most is to

be like one another,—as merciful as others, as humble as others, as devout as others ; but God saith, 'Be holy, as I am,' not as others are ; for Christ saith, ' Except your righteousness exceed the righteousness of the pharisees,' although they were holier than others, ' ye shall not enter into heaven ;' that is, except ye be more than statute-protestants, which go to the church, and hear an homily, and receive once a-year, but will not offend any person, nor leave any custom, nor bear any charge, nor suffer any trouble for the glory of God, ye shall come to heaven when the pharisees come out of hell. As love delighteth men, so zeal pleaseth God, for zeal is the love of God. Therefore every sacrifice was offered with fire, to shew with what zeal they should burn which come to offer prayer or praise or thanks unto the Lord ; therefore the Holy Ghost descends in fire, to shew the fervency of them upon whom the Holy Ghost resteth ; therefore the cherubims were pourtrayed with wings before the people, to shew that they should be as earnest and quick about the Lord's business as the cherubims ; therefore God would not take a lame nor halting sacrifice, to shew how he abhorreth slackness in all our duties ; therefore St James says, 'Be swift to hear,' James i. 19. We must be swift to pray, swift to obey, swift to do good ; for he is not cursed only which doeth not the Lord's business, but he which ' doeth it negligently,' Jer. xlviii. 10, i. e. he which doeth anything before it, like him that would bid his friends farewell, and follow Christ after, Luke ix. 61. The hound, which runs but for the hare, runs as fast as possibly he can ; the hawk, which flieth but for the partridge, flieth as fast as possibly she can ; and shall he which runs for heaven creep more slowly than the dial ? Who hath so much faith as the apostles ? yet how oft doth Christ say, 'O ye of little faith'? complaining that their faith was too little. And, therefore, when Peter answered him that he loved him, as though he loved him not enough, Christ asked him again whether he loved him ; and as though he loved him not enough yet, he asked him again, ' Lovest thou me ? For he would have us love him as he loved us when his heart-blood was shed for us ; therefore, when he demanded his love, he measured it by the heart, saying, 'Thou shalt love God with all thy heart, with all thy strength, with all thy mind.' Thrice he repeated all, lest we should keep anything from him. Our Saviour saith not, that his Father is glorified in that we bring forth fruit, but in that we ' bring forth much fruit,' John xv. 8. Is it not better to be vessels of gold than vessels of brass ? Do ye not see how Christ rejected him which said he kept many commandments, because he would not do one commandment ? For one work which he would not do, our Saviour made no reckoning of all that he did. It was good for the apostles that they left all and followed Christ presently ; but this should not be written but to teach us with what speed we should follow Christ, watching the star so soon as it riseth, and the pillar so soon as it removeth. In this strive and go one before another, as Peter and John strove who should come first to the sepulchre. For if Agrippa could be saved when he was almost a Christian, Paul would not have laboured to make him altogether a Christian. Therefore, though purity be counted heresy, yet remember that Christ saith, 'None can see God but the pure in heart,' Mat. v. 8 ; and know that there is no dealing with those mockers, but to answer them as David answered Michal. When she scorned him for his humbleness, he said, 'I will be more humble yet ;' so when they mock thee for thy zeal, spite them with more zeal ; for evil is not overcome but with good. Thus we have passed the third step to heaven.

The fourth step in this happy journey is, *Persevere to the end.* For if you begin betimes, and go aright, and make haste, and continue not to the end, your reward is with them of whom Peter saith, 'Their end is worse than their beginning,' 2 Peter ii. 20. There is nothing in our life which suffers so many eclipses and changes as our devotion ; hot and cold, in and out, off and on, not in one mood so long as the sparrow sits on the ground, but looking, like the chameleon, of the colour of that which we see : if we see good, it puts us in a good thought ; if we see or hear evil, it turns us from good to evil again. Thus man is rolled upon a wheel, that never stands still, but turns continually about, as though he were giddy and treading the maze. He is upon the side of a hill, where it is easy to slide, and hard to get up the flesh. Therefore the apostle, moved with pity, seeing man stand on such a slippery ground, as it were in a ship ready to sink, or a house bending to fall, he cries to them that stand surest, 'Take heed lest you fall ;' *i.e.* when thou hast put on thy 'armour of light,' and art in the spiritual field to fight the Lord's battles against the world, the flesh, and the devil, turn not back like Demas, but remember the comfort of Elisha, that 'there be more with thee than against thee,' and that the tempter can overcome none but them which yield. Other servants change their masters for better masters ; but all that serve God are like the servant which received a print in his ear after the manner of the Jews, in token that he would serve his master for ever, like the vestures which bare their own mark. Therefore the Holy Ghost cries so often, 'Be faithful even unto the death,' 'Be not weary of well-doing,' 'Take heed lest you fall.' For when thou art weary of thy godliness, God doth not count thee good, but weary of goodness; and when thou declinest from righteousness, God doth not count thee righteous, but revolted from righteousness. Therefore Paul saith, 'Pray continually,' as though prayer were nothing without continuance. Jacob did not overcome God so soon as he began to wrestle with him, but when he had wrestled with him all night. And it is said that Christ took pity of them that stayed with him. 'I will not leave thee,' saith Elisha to Elijah; so we should not leave God. Some came into the vineyard in the morning, and some at noon; but none received any reward but they which stayed till night. As God's mercy endureth for ever, so our righteousness should endure for ever. Every thought, and word, and deed of a faithful man is a step towards heaven; in every place he meeteth Christ, everything puts him in mind of God; he seeks him to find him, and when he hath found him, he seeks him still; he is not satisfied, because at every touch there comes some virtue from him. Jacob served seven years for Rachel, and after them he served seven more, and yet he was content to serve six more; and when he had served so many years, 'they seemed unto him as nothing, because he loved her.' He which served so long for Rachel, served all his life for heaven; and if he had lived till this day, he would have served God still, and thought it nothing, because he loved him. To have the ark but a while doeth more hurt to the Philistines than benefit them; so to serve God but a while doth more damage us than help us; for happier is the child which never began, than Judas, whose end was worse than his beginning. What a lamentable thing it is to hear this plaint of him which was once the strongest in the world, Samson hath lost his strength for Delilah, for the love of Delilah, that doth not love him! To shew what a shame it is to end worse than we begin, Christ shews what a reproach it was to him which began to build and could not set up the roof; the passengers pointed with their fingers, and said, This man began a foundation, but he could not cover it; so they will say, This man thought to be holy, but he could not keep promise. 'What shall I say,' saith Joshua, 'when Israel turns the back?' Joshua vii. 8. When Israel turns the back, this astonished him; and this makes the whole temple shake when the pillars tremble. What an offence is it to the church to see Peter to deny Christ, which said even now that he would never forsake him? to see Lot commit incest with his daughters in the mount, which strived so to preserve them chaste in Sodom? to see Solomon worship idols, which erected the temple for the worship of God? to see Noah mocked of his son for drunkenness, for whose righteousness his son escaped? as if the stars should fall from heaven, and light go from the sun. Wisdom is angry with him which leaveth his righteousness to become worse. The vine would not forsake her grapes, the olive would not forsake her fatness, the fig-tree would not leave her sweetness; but the bramble did, Judges ix.; he is not the vine, nor the olive, nor the fig-tree, but he is a bramble made for the fire, which leaveth the joys. Let the dog turn to the vomit, and the swine to the wallow; but thou, like Abraham, hold on thy sacrifice unto the evening, even the evening of thy life, and a full measure shall be measured unto thee. This is a long step, and man is like a horse which loveth short journeys; therefore how can he hold out so far? When one told Socrates, that he would very fain go to Olympus, but he feared that he should not be able to endure the pains; Socrates answered him, I know that thou usest to walk every day between thy meals, which walk continue forward in thy way to Olympus, and within five or six days thou shalt come thither. How easy was this, and yet he saw it not. So is the way to heaven. If men did bend themselves as much to do good as they beat their brains to do evil, they might go to heaven with less trouble than they go to hell. Our idle hours are enough to get wisdom, and knowledge, and faith, till we are like saints among men. If thou look only to the stops, and tell all the thorns which lie in the way, thou shalt go fearfully, wearily, and unwillingly, everything shall turn thee aside, and every snail shall step before thee, and take thy crown from thee; but then lift up thine eyes from the earth, and look to Christ calling, the Spirit assisting, the Father blessing, the angels comforting, the word directing, the crown inviting, and thy fetters shall fall from thee, and thou shalt rise like the sun, and marvel how the thing could seem so hard, and be so easy. When ye do well, remember that ye change not for the worse, and do as ye do then, and ye shall continue to the end.

Now I have encouraged you like soldiers, and taken away your fear, I will bring you to the sight of your enemies, and will set them before your face; not to weaken you, for that were want of charity, but to make you wary, which is true love indeed. To number them surely I cannot, they are so many, and exactly to describe them, it is beyond my skill, they are so subtle; howbeit, to give you a little taste, I may say as Elisha said to his servant, and you shall see it, if you have your eyes open, 'Fear not, for they that be with us are more than they that be with them;' and he that is on our side is stronger than all. But if you will hear what the holy apostle saith touching them, I can tell you; he affirmeth, and that by the very Spirit of God, 'We wrestle not against flesh and blood only, but against principalities, powers, worldly governors, the princes of the darkness of this world, even spiritual wickedness in the high places,' Eph. vi. 12. And St John saith, 'they are the lusts of the flesh, the lusts of the eyes, and the pride of life,' 1 John ii. 16. Let other men think of them what they list; they that hear them thus described, and have felt the force of them in their own souls, could not choose but confess that they have been many in number, mighty in power, subtle in practice, and what not. Who knoweth not this, that the more enemies we have, the more need we have both of force outwardly, and of care inwardly? as again, the more powerful they are, and the more weak we are, the more we should seek for help elsewhere. In outward and bodily foes and forces we confess the truth of this, and do all that we can to shew ourselves wise, circumspect, and courageous; how much more had we need here to express all these things, where the conflict is more hard, though the conquest obtained be more glorious; and where again our foes and their forces be more mighty and many, though their overthrow once performed gives them the fool's foil? But whom shall we look to herein? Other men are as weak as ourselves, if not worse; for all men, 'lay them upon a balance, they are altogether lighter than vanity itself,' Ps. lxii. 9. And if we fear and distrust ourselves, how dare we, or how can we, put confidence in others? specially sith God saith, 'Cursed is every one that maketh flesh and blood his arm,' Jer. xvii. 5. To look up to the holy and elect angels will do us little good; because they go not but being sent, and always wait for a word and warrant from the Lord's own mouth for all their actions; besides that, their own oil and force is little enough for their own supportation. To God, therefore, that is the God of our strength, we must needs come; yea, and to him alone, or else we are utterly overthrown and cast away. And if we cannot say, and do too, as David did, 'Lord, whom have I in heaven but thee? and I have desired none on earth with thee,' we are in a woful taking, and utterly lost. For fear without and fire within, Satan's malice also, men's mischief, and our corruption, will carry and hurry us, as it were a violent tempest or whirlwind. Amongst the heathen they had many odd conceits to chase away bodily and spiritual enemies, as those that have written their histories and actions have plainly set forth: sometimes fire, sometimes water, sometimes blood, and sometimes one thing, and sometimes another; as man's brain is a bountiful shop to forge such devices in. The papists differ not much from them, who think that whippings and scourgings will tame and subdue the corrupt affections of the heart ; and that the casting of a little holy water, as they call it, or the making of a cross in the face, forehead, breast, or any other place, will chase away Satan and all his hellish powers. Of all which actions and ceremonies, either heathenish or popish, were they better than they be (but indeed they are stark naught as they use them), we may say as the apostle saith, ' Bodily exercise profiteth little, but godliness is profitable to all things.' And had Satan's malice and man's presumption stayed here, and gone no farther in gross imaginations concerning this and other matters, it had been the less evil ; but in our light and liberty of the gospel, some suppose that the very saying of *Lord, have mercy upon us*, and that without faith or feeling many times, is all in all ; and the pronouncing of this petition, *Lead us not into temptation*, and that without sense or understanding of it, is sufficient to sunder Satan and our own corruption as far from us as the east is from the west. Upon them their spiritual enemies prevailed by gross ignorance and superstitious conceits ; upon us by careless presumption and presumptuous carelessness ; neither the one of us nor the other understanding rightly, as we should, either our foe's forces, or our own weakness. And that is the cause why they and we, in former times and of late, joined with them and sundered from them, have received very fearful falls and overthrows ; for all is one with Satan, so he catch and snatch men, and have them in possession, he cares not by what means. But wilt thou not escape danger only, but overcome also ? I will shew thee, O man, what thou shalt do. At any hand go out of thyself and other creatures whatsoever ; for if thou stick to them, though never so little, thou dost disadvantage thyself at the least, if not overthrow thyself. The wicked spirits are as strong to effect evil as the elect are to do good ; and so much the more powerful that way, by how much they attempt it with commission from God, and find fit matter in men to work upon. And what then ? Fix the eye of thy faith fast upon God in Christ, and thou shalt never miscarry. For he that cannot lie hath said it, ' I will not fail thee nor forsake thee for ever,' Deut. xxxi. 8, Heb. xiii. 5 ; and in the New Testament Christ hath told us, which is also a word of as sure a promise, ' The gates of hell shall not prevail against this faith,' Mat. xvi. 18. Nay, I will say more ; in the strength and power of this persuasion, thou shalt be made ' more than a conqueror through him that hath loved

thee,' and washed thee in his own heart-blood, Rom. viii. 37. I know
and confess there are many lets and hindrances to the persuasion
and practice of this truth ; but hear and believe only, and I will
shew you yet a more perfect and assured way, by which you shall
be made to walk safe, either in the day of death, or in the time of
temptation, or in any other course or cross that may betide you in
this life. See that you have not only the two side-posts and the
upper door-posts of your houses stricken over with the blood of the
Lamb, but 'your hearts purged' through faith in his blood from
the power of 'dead works,' Heb. ix. 14 ; and then the destroyer,
that overthroweth others, shall pass over thee, and bring thee in
good time to the full fruition of the heavenly Canaan. But thou
wilt say as the slothful person doth in the Proverbs, 'There is a
lion,' yea, many lions, 'in the way.' I answer, Reckon them up and
bring them forth ; they shall all by God's grace be easily removed.
All sorts of afflictions are bitter, I confess it, and so are many things
in meat, drink, and physic ; and yet we refuse them not, but use
them rather, because of the good we know or hope they will effect
in us. And why say we not, as the apostle by the Spirit doth, ' No
chastisement for the present seemeth to be joyous, but grievous ;
howbeit afterward it bringeth forth the quiet fruit of righteousness
unto them which are thereby exercised' ? Heb. xii. 11. Death also
is dreadful ; what then ? but to whom, I pray thee ? Even to the
man that hath his trust in his riches, or hath no hope of a better
life ; but to him that believeth in Christ it is become, through the
power of the death and obedience of Christ, a speedy passage to
eternal life. We endure many dreadful and dangerous things, and
run through fire and water, and all for a corruptible crown ; and
why should we not with patience and prayer pass through this,
which is the very highway to heaven ? Besides, hell is horrible.
Neither will I deny that ; but still I demand, to whom is it so ?
Surely to the devil and his angels, and all manner of wicked ones,
for whom it hath been prepared of old ; but as for the godly and
elect, it cannot come nigh him. For Christ, the very ' way, truth,
and life' itself, hath told us, and therefore we ought to credit it ;
'He that heareth my words, and believeth in him that sent me, hath
everlasting life, and shall not come into condemnation, but hath
passed from death unto life,' John v. 24. Lastly, is not sin a
shrewd and sore enemy to encounter with ? I confess it ; but to
whom ? Tell me, I beseech you ; even to them in whose ' mortal
bodies it reigneth, to fulfil the concupiscences thereof.' To others,
in whom the root of it is dead, it is not so, whether we respect this

life or that which is to come. For here the relics of sin are but as pricks in our sides, to provoke us to better things, and to stir us up to ' hunger and thirst after righteousness ;' and for the life to come, we shall be utterly freed from the same, and have ' all tears wiped from our eyes.' To bring all into a sum, I say, let all objected be as true as anything may be, yet all these, and a thousand more such like, are nothing to him that is in Christ. For the apostle saith, ' There is no condemnation to them that are in Christ Jesus,' Rom. viii. 1 ; and it is he alone that hath destroyed death, and ' became sin for us, that we in him might be made the righteousness of God.' And surely such a one may in some good measure of comfort joyfully say, to the defiance even of death itself, and all other ghostly enemies whatsoever, ' O death, where is thy sting ? O grave, where is thy victory? The sting of death is sin, and the strength of sin is the law. But thanks be unto God, which hath given us victory through our Lord Jesus Christ,' 1 Cor. xv. 55, &c. Yea, he may say, as the saints and martyrs have said in the midst of fiery flames, ' I am persuaded that neither death, nor life, nor angels, nor principalities, nor powers, nor things present, nor things to come, nor height, nor depth, nor any other creature, shall be able to separate me from the love of God which is in Christ Jesus our Lord,' Rom viii. 38, 39. But death is terrible still. I answer, In such a cloud of witnesses and evidence of truth, may I not in some sort and sense say, ' O faithless generation, how long shall I be with you? how long now shall I suffer you ?' Is it fearful to any but to a natural man, and to him that hath his felicity here, and in the things of this life ? Surely it is nothing terrible to him that is made a comfortable partaker of the fruits of the death of Christ, ' who died and rose again, to the end he might destroy death, and him that had the power of death, even the devil himself.' But hell is horrible. True, but yet to them for whom it is prepared ; but thou art in Christ exempted from it. For why did he himself suffer hellish torments both in body and soul ? To leave thee therein, and make it terrible or horrible to thee ? No, but to free thee and all his from the fear of hell, and the feeling of everlasting condemnation. Oh, but what shall I say touching my sin, that is great and grievous, and the peculiar wages of it being death eternal ? That is true in the nature of sin and the justice of God ; but ' with the Lord there is mercy, that he may be feared,' Ps. cxxx. 4. Stand still awhile, and you shall behold the great works of God ; and be not faithless, but faithful, and believe the truth of the word. What is more clear than this, ' Where sin hath abounded, there grace hath abounded much more,' Rom. v. 20. And though it be in a prophet, yet where have we a more plain, plentiful, or evangelical promise than this, 'Though your sins were as crimson, they shall be made white as snow ; though they were red as scarlet, they shall be as wool' ? Isa. i. 18. If we have the hand or writing of an honest man, we think ourselves bound to give credit thereto ; how much more should we believe the most true and unchangeable word of the Eternal ; to which, not for any want in himself, but by reason of the weakness of our faith, he hath been 'willing the more abundantly to shew unto the heirs of promise the stableness of his counsel,' Heb. vi. 17 ; to adjoin and bind himself with an oath, saying, 'As I live, I will not the death of a sinner,' Ezek. xviii. 23, 32 ; yea, 'I will be merciful to their unrighteousness, and I will remember their sins and iniquities no more,' Jer. xxxi. 34, 'that so by two immutable things,' that is, his inviolable oath and assured promise, '(wherein it is impossible that God should lie) we might have strong consolation,' Heb. vi. 18. And as for these objections, or any the like, what are they else but in truth and substance the very evil reports that the spies brought upon the promised land ? and yet there was a very true testimony given by Joshua and Caleb ; yea, the palpable proofs they had by the cluster of grapes and other things which they brought from thence were irrefragate witness. Will you believe them because they are many ? That is flat popery ; and besides, God forbiddeth us to 'cleave to a multitude to do evil,' Exod. xxiii. 2. Will you fear them because they are mighty ? That is to distrust God, who is greater than all, and to make them omnipotent, which is blasphemy. Will you doubt because they double their assaults ? That is no end of temptation, but this rather, to add an edge unto our prayers, that so through them we may hear in our hearts that comfortable speech, 'My grace is sufficient for thee, and my strength shall be perfected through weakness,' 2 Cor. xii. 9. And when we shall have all our senses satisfied in the contrary truth, yea, so far forth as that our eyes may see, our ears may hear, our hands may handle, the good things of God, over and besides the faith we have in him concerning them, it is not gross only, but impious, not to believe. But here in this life are many pleasures and certain delights lawful, as houses, friends, wives, children, goods, honour, and almost infinite such like. That is very true, but with this honey God intermingleth some gall, lest the souls of his servants might run riot to sin. And who is he that can be ignorant of the uncertain estate of all and every one of them ? Our friends fall away as a fruit that is ripe before his time, or as the morning dew ; our houses are overthrown, and are like the ruins of a defaced hold, not one stone of them left upon another; our wives may be lewd in their lips, loose in their lives, and wicked, as was Job's, and wish us to 'curse God and die ;' our children not riotous only and disobedient, but unnatural also, and rising up against us, as Absalom. The goods we possess are not unfitly by Solomon resembled to the eagle, that taketh her to her wings, and flieth aloft into the air. As for our honour, which we make as it were some deity upon earth, it is turned into shame in the twinkling of an eye, or else forgotten as it had never been, and we, that in our own imaginations are lords of all, as the dust or chaff of the earth are carried from all. And what reason is there, then, that these or any such like should hinder us in our race towards heaven ? He that hath an inheritance or land in the world will not be hindered from taking the possession or enjoying of it when it falleth unto him, by the tears of his wife, the entreaty of his children, the heap of his riches, or any such like things ; and why should we suffer these simple conceits to steal away our hearts from the hope and having of heaven ? Besides, who knoweth not that, in respect of the life to come, all these heaped up in the greatest measure that possibly can be in this world, are not so much as a shadow of the good things that shall be revealed ? Hath the Spirit said in vain, 'That which the eye hath not seen, neither the ear heard, neither ever yet entered into man's heart, hath God prepared for them that love him' ? 1 Cor. ii. 9, or shall we think it a lie ? or that God meant to dissemble and dally with us ? Oh, be it far from us to think or speak so. Is that glorious description of that holy and heavenly Jerusalem, mentioned in the Revelation, chap. xxi., but a fiction or forgery ? It were blasphemy for any man's heart to imagine so. We are rather to think that God, by that which is known and can be comprehended, expresseth that which yet is hidden from us, and shall in good measure be comprehended of us also, we 'knowing then even as we are known now,' 1 Cor. xiii. 12. Wherefore let us not fear all or any of our adversaries or pull-backs, for 'true love expelleth fear,' 1 John iv. 18 ; neither let us be faint-hearted in ourselves, but labour rather to 'lift up our hands which hang down, and to strengthen our weak knees,' Heb. xii. 12 ; for 'faithful is he that hath promised, who will also perform it,' Heb. x. 23. 'Be faithful unto death, and I will give thee the crown of life,' Rev. ii. 10. He that so runneth, shall be sure to obtain, and have his portion with the saints in the heavenly inheritance, of a crown that never fadeth nor falleth away.

But he that careth not for this course, must have his portion with hypocrites 'in the lake of fire and brimstone,' that burneth for evermore, and be shut out of the kingdom with 'the fearful, unbelieving, abominable, murderers, whoremongers, sorcerers, idolaters,' and all such like, Rev. xxi. 8. Wherefore, as you love life, and loathe death, run well, I beseech you ; yea, even as our text was at the beginning, so say I at the ending, 'So run, that ye may obtain.' Which I do not only propound unto you by exhortation, but commend and commit, with supplication to God for myself and you, that every one of us, and I myself especially, may in feeling and faith say, 'I am now ready to be offered, and the time of my departing is at hand ; I have fought a good fight, and have finished my course, I have kept the faith. From hence is laid up for me the crown of righteousness, which the Lord, the righteous judge, shall give me at that day; and not to me only, but unto all them that love his appearing,' 2 Tim. iv. 6–8.

THE LAWYER'S QUESTION.

IN THREE SERMONS.

THE LAWYER'S QUESTION.

THE FIRST SERMON.

*And, behold, a certain lawyer stood up, and tempted him, saying,
Master, what shall I do to inherit eternal life?*—LUKE X. 25.

IT is a weighty question, and hath been long discoursed, by what
means a man may come to heaven ; and who is not desirous to be
resolved in it ?   Here the question is propounded by a lawyer, and
answered by the Lawgiver, whose judgment in this case is worth the
hearing. He propounds the question as one desirous to learn,
when indeed he meaneth. nothing less. But as Ahab, when he
asked Micaiah, in the first book of Kings and 22d chapter, if he
should go up to fight against Ramoth in Gilead, meant not to follow the prophet's direction, but only desired to hear his opinion ;
so the lawyer propounds this question, not with a mind to learn of
Christ, but with a mind to tempt Christ, and to try his learning.
As the devil came to tempt Christ in the wilderness, so the lawyer
comes to tempt Christ in the city; and, therefore, whereas the
Evangelist saith, 'Behold, a certain lawyer stood up,' he might have
said, Behold, a certain devil stood up, because for the time he took
upon him the devil's office, to be a tempter. When the devil
tempted Christ, Mat. iv. 10, he bade him 'Avoid, Satan ;' and when
Peter tempted Christ, Mat. xvi. 23, he said unto him, 'Depart,
Satan ;' so when this lawyer tempted Christ, he might have said,
'Avaunt, Satan !' because in his action he was the instrument of
Satan. But though the lawyer was worthy to be repulsed, because
he was so importunate, yet was this question worth the answering,
because it was of such importance.

We see then with what mind the lawyer came to Christ ; now
let us see how he saluteth Christ. Though he came with a bad

mind, yet doth he use good words, that he might deceive with less suspicion ; he salutes him by the name of *Master*, as if he did profess himself to be his disciple. So did Judas salute him, when he meant to betray him, Mat. xxvi. 49 ; and so did the pharisees salute him, when they meant to bring him within the compass of treason, Mat. xxii. 15, 16. And this hath been always the guise of the wicked, to use the smoothest speech when they intend most mischief, and under colour of friendship to practise their treachery. When Absalom meant to be revenged of his brother Amnon for defiling his sister Tamar, he made a great feast, and caused him to be murdered in the midst of the banquet, 2 Sam. xiii. When Joab meant to murder Amasa, he saluted him courteously, saying, 'Art thou in health, my brother?' 2 Sam. xx. 9, and with his right hand took him by the beard to kiss him, and with his left hand sheathed a sword into his belly.

These are such as the psalmist speaks of, Ps. xxviii. 3, which have glozing tongues, and bloody minds; 'which speak friendly to their neighbours, and imagine mischief in their hearts.' As the scorpion hath an amiable face and a poisoned tail, so these men have fair looks and murdering hands. 'Their words are as soft as butter, and as smooth as oil,' Ps. lv. 21; but their deeds are cruel as the deeds of war, and deadly as the dint of swords. The prophet David was sore troubled with such dissemblers, as he complaineth everywhere in his book of Psalms, Ps. xli. 9, that 'even his own familiar friend whom he trusted, and which did eat at his table, had laid great wait for him.' And Ps. lv. 12, 13, 14, that 'it was not an open enemy which had done him dishonour, for then he could have borne it ; nor was it his adversary which had lift up himself against him, for then, peradventure, he would have hid himself from him : but it was even his companion, his guide, and his own familiar friend, which took sweet counsel with him, and walked with him in the house of God as his friend.' At this day the world is full of such feigned friends, which will flatter thee to thy face, and bite thee behind thy back. They will give out hard speeches of some man that is absent in thy hearing, to see if thou wilt speak as hardly of him ; which if thou dost, thy words shall presently be told unto him. Woe unto him, saith the wise man, Ecclus. ii. 12, that hath a double heart, wicked lips, and mischievous hands, and to the sinner that goeth two manner of ways. The Lord hath given but one heart, and one tongue, and one face, to one man ; therefore we should not carry a double heart in our breast, nor two tongues in our head, nor two faces under a hood. It was not lawful for the Israelites to wear any garments made of linen and woollen, Deut. xxii. 11, to signify, that it should not be lawful for Christians to be dissemblers; to carry fire in one hand, and water in the other; to carry honey in their mouth, and gall in their heart; or, as David speaks, Ps. xii. 2, to 'flatter with their lips, and to dissemble with their double heart.'

Of all kind of cattle these are the worst, because they do most hurt where they are least mistrusted. Therefore they are compared in Scripture to the wily fox, for their crafty fetches. And Herod is termed a fox for his dissembling, Luke xiii. 32. For as the fox feigneth himself dead, that he may catch the birds to devour them, so the flatterer feigneth himself to be harmless, and honest, and conscionable, and religious, and holy, that he may 'deceive the hearts of the simple,' Rom. xvi. 18. He is like your shadow, which doth imitate the action and gesture of your body, which stands when you stand, and walks when you walk, and sits when you sit, and riseth when you rise; so the flatterer doth praise when you praise, and finds fault when you find fault, and smiles when you smile, and frowns when you frown, and applauds you in your doings, and soothes you in your sayings, and in all things seeks to please your humour, till he hath sounded the depth of your devices, that he may betray you to your greatest enemies. As the sirens sing most sweetly when they intend your destruction, so flatterers speak most fair when they practise most treachery. Therefore every fair look is not to be liked, every smooth tale is not to be believed, and every glozing tongue is not to be trusted; but as we must 'try the spirits, whether they be of God or no,' 1 John iv. 1, so we must try the words, whether they come from the heart or no; and we must try the deeds, whether they be answerable to the words or no.

Now we are come to the question, which is, 'By what means may a man inherit eternal life?' A weighty question, worthy to be known, not only of lawyers and learned men, but also of all, both men and women, which be persuaded in their hearts, as with their mouth they do confess, that after death their bodies shall rise again. Therefore, though this lawyer were to be blamed, because he came with so bad a mind, yet is he to be commended, because he moved so good a question. Many now-a-days are very curious in idle and unprofitable questions, as, What God did before he made the world? How long Adam stood in the state of innocency? Whether Solomon were saved or no? with many such vain and unnecessary questions. But few there are which will ask, as this lawyer did, what they must do to inherit eternal life. You shall see many very careful and inquisitive how they may get riches, where they may purchase lands and lordships, how they may come to advancement and honour, and by what means they may procure the prince's favour. But we shall see few or none inquisitive concerning the means of their salvation ; you shall seldom hear any ask their pastor what they must do to be saved, or which way they may come to heaven. It is not now as it was in John Baptist's time, when the publicans, the soldiers, and all sorts of people came unto him, with 'Master, what shall we do ?' Luke iii. 10, &c. Nor is it now as it was in the time of Christ, when the people came and asked him, 'What shall we do that we may work the works of God ?' John vi. 28. Nor is it now as it was in Peter's time, when, upon the hearing of Peter's sermon, the people came to Peter and to the other apostles, crying and saying, 'Men and brethren, what shall we do ?' Acts ii. 37. But now every man's mind is on his worldly profit, or pleasure, or preferment. This is the drift of all their devices, the end of all their practices, how they may live here in delight and ease, and leave behind them a rich posterity. As for that heavenly country whereunto they were born, that new Jerusalem wherein they should dwell, it is the farthest end of their thoughts, and the least part of their care, how to inherit it, how to inhabit it.

The question is, How he may inherit eternal life ? wherein he seems to confess that there is an eternal life ; for thereof he makes no doubt ; only the question is, How he may attain to it ? Here therefore it appeareth that this lawyer was not a sadducee, which denied the resurrection of the dead, Mat. xxii. 23 ; nor was he an epicure, which is of this opinion, that after death there is nor joy to be looked for, nor pains to be feared, and therefore is wont to say, *Ede, bibe, lude, &c.*, or, as it is said, 'Let us eat and drink, for to-morrow we shall die,' 1 Cor. xv. 32. But this man was a pharisee, such a one as Paul was before his conversion, one that expounded the law of God to the people, and lived ' after the straitest law of their religion,' Acts xxvi. 5 ; in a word, he was such a one as both for his life and learning was admired and honoured of the Jews. Though this lawyer was learned, yet it was boldly done of him to tempt the Lord. But what is it that learning dare not attempt, if it be not tempered with the fear of God ? Christ Jesus found no greater adversaries than the high priests, the scribes and pharisees, which were all learned men ; and the church of Christ at this day is by none so much afflicted as by those that carry the opinion of singular learning. For look how many heresies are extant in the church, or how many controversies in religion, they have been devised and are maintained by learned men. Let learned men therefore learn to fear the Lord ; let them learn to 'know nothing so much as Christ Jesus and him crucified,' 1 Cor. ii. 2, without which knowledge all knowledge is ignorance, all wisdom is foolishness, all learning is madness, and all religion is error, or hypocrisy, or superstition. 'God hath not chosen many wise men, nor many mighty men, nor many noble men : but God hath chosen the foolish things of the world, to confound the wise ; and God hath chosen the weak things of the world, to confound the things that are mighty ; and vile things of the world, and things which are despised, hath God chosen, yea, and things which are not, to bring to nought the things that are,' 1 Cor. i. 26–28. Our Saviour Christ, in the choice of his apostles, called not one that was learned ; yet hath he not rejected all that are learned, for from heaven he called his apostle Paul, a learned lawyer, Acts xxii. 3, to be the apostle and the preacher of the Gentiles, Rom. xi. 13. And there is no doubt but that in all ages, and even at this day, he calleth some in every place, and endueth them with excellent learning, that they may serve to 'the gathering together of the saints, and to the exercising of the ministry, and to the edifying of the church of God,' Eph. iv. 12. The Lord Jesus so moderate our learning with his holy fear, that we may direct all our studies to the enlarging of his glory and kingdom here on earth, 'that when the chief Shepherd shall appear,' 1 Pet. v. 4, we, that have instructed others and turned many to righteousness, 'may shine as the brightness of the firmament, and as the stars of heaven for ever,' Dan. xii. 3.

Good Master, what shall I do to inherit eternal life? Mark here the discretion of the lawyer in asking this question. As the man was a lawyer, so there is no doubt but that he had read the law and the prophets. If you look into the law, you shall not find, 'Cursed is he that continueth not in all things that are written in the book of the law, to know them.' If you peruse the prophets, you shall not find, 'Cease from doing evil, and learn to speak well.' But the law saith, 'Cursed is he which continueth not in all things that are written in the book of the law, to do them,' Deut. xxvii. 26, Gal. iii. 10 ; and the prophets say, 'Cease from doing evil, and learn to do well,' Isa. i. 16, Ps. xxxiv. 14. And therefore the lawyer saith not, How much must I know ? nor, What shall I believe ? but, 'What shall I do to inherit eternal life?' We have been taught too long, that we are saved by faith, without the works of the law ; which doctrine, though it be most true, and most soundly proved, and flatly concluded, Rom. iii. 28 ; yet being understood amiss, as

Paul's writings sometimes are, 2 Peter iii. 16, it hath been the decay of all good deeds, and brought in epicurism and all ungodliness. It is true indeed that 'eternal life is the gift of God through Jesus Christ,' Rom. vi. 23 ; but yet this gift is bestowed only upon those 'for whom it is prepared,' Mat. xx. 23, which have exercised themselves in the works of mercy, Mat. xxv. 35. In respect of God, our election standeth certain from all eternity ; for 'it hath this seal, the Lord knoweth them that are his,' 2 Tim. ii. 19, and 'I know whom I have chosen,' John xiii. 18. But in respect of ourselves it is uncertain, and therefore we must 'strive to make the same sure' by good works, 2 Peter i. 10. These are the ways to come to heaven, though they be not the cause why we should come to heaven ; therefore we must keep the way, if ever we mean to come to heaven ; for as we are ordained to the end, so are we ordained to the means which bring us to that end. If God have predestinate any to eternal life, he hath also predestinated them to the means whereby they must attain eternal life, that is, 'faith and a good conscience,' 1 Tim. iii. 9. Therefore it is certain, that whosoever is to be saved, shall at one time or other, before they depart out of this life, be called truly to believe, and shall endeavour by all means, as Paul did, 'to keep a good conscience both toward God and toward men,' Acts xxiv. 16. For that which is spoken of Christ in special, Ps. xlv. 7, 'Thou hast loved righteousness, and hated iniquity,' must be verified, and in some measure accomplished in all the members of Christ ; they must love righteousness, and hate iniquity. And this is the difference that the apostle putteth between the children of God and the children of the devil ; that the children of God both love and do righteousness, and the children of the devil love sin, and do it, 1 John iii. 7, 8. Let no man, therefore, think that he is predestinate to salvation, unless he find and feel in himself the effects and fruits of predestination. For 'those whom God hath predestinate, them also in his good time he calleth,' Rom. viii. 30 ; 'not to uncleanness, but unto holiness,' 1 Thes. iv. 7 ; 'and whom he calleth, them also he justifieth,' and endueth with the grace of sanctification, Rom. vi. 2, &c. ; 'and whom he justifieth, them also he glorifieth.' If any be engrafted into Christ by a lively faith, he cannot but bring forth the fruit of good life, John xv. 2, 5 ; and whosoever doth not bring forth such fruit, it is certain that he is not yet engrafted into Jesus Christ. Let us not therefore, I say, flatter nor deceive ourselves, as though we had true faith, when we have not the true fruits of faith ; for as the sun cannot be without light, nor the fire without heat, no more can a saving faith be without good works, which are the fruits and effects thereof. The penitent thief had but a short time of repentance, yet in that short time he wanted not good works to declare his faith, Luke xxiii. 40–42 ; for no sooner was it given him to believe in Christ, but that presently he maketh answer on the behalf of Christ, and cleareth him of all amiss ; he rebuketh his fellow for his incredulity; he confesseth the greatness of their sin, and their just punishment for the same ; he acknowledgeth Christ to be the Lord, and calleth upon him. Therefore, it is not enough for to say, We have faith; for the devils have a kind of faith, James ii. 19. Nor is it enough for us to come to church to call upon the Lord ; for to say, *Lord, Lord,* will not serve the turn, Mat. vii. 21. Nor is it enough for us to preach unto you ; for unto some that have preached in the name of Christ, it shall be said at the last day, ' Depart, I know you not,' Mat. vii. 22, 23. Nor is it enough for you to be ' only hearers of the word;' for then ' you deceive yourselves,' James i. 22. But you that ' say you have faith,' must ' shew it by your deeds,' James ii. 17 ; and you that come to call upon the Lord, must ' depart from iniquity,' 2 Tim. ii. 19 ; and we that preach unto you, must practise that ourselves which we preach unto you, and be an example of holy life for you to follow, 1 Peter v. 3 ; and you that are hearers of the word, must be doers of the word, and then you shall be justified, Rom. ii. 13. What shall I do ? The papists will have other men do good works for them. For some of the holier sort, forsooth, have works of supererogation, that is, more good works than they need themselves, which they can spare and bestow upon those that pay best for them. And we that are protestants, because we will not disable Christ, nor derogate from his merits, will have Christ do all for us, and we will do nothing for ourselves.

But this lawyer was of another mind. He asketh what he shall do to gain eternal life, because he knew that another man could not deserve it for him. ' The soul that sinneth, that same shall die; and the soul that doeth righteousness shall surely live, saith the Lord,' Ezek. xviii. 4, 5. And ' though Moses and Samuel stood before the Lord,' to make intercession for the wicked, it shall not help them, Jer. xv. 1. ' Yea, though Noah, Daniel, and Job were in the land,' when the Lord bringeth his plagues upon it for sin, ' they shall save neither sons nor daughters, but only deliver their own souls by their righteousness,' Ezek. xiv. 20. Therefore it behoveth every man to know what we must do to inherit eternal life ; and not only to know it (for ' he that knoweth his master's will, and

doeth it not, shall be beaten with many stripes,' Luke xii. 47), but
he must do it, and so 'shall he have cause of rejoicing in himself,
and not in another,' Gal. vi. 4. For as another man's sin shall not
be laid to my charge, so another man's righteousness shall not be
reckoned to mine; but 'every man shall bear his own burden,'
Gal. vi. 5.

What shall I do to inherit eternal life? There is a life which
is short and temporal, which Job compareth to a wind, that soon
bloweth over, Job vii. 7; James to a vapour, that soon vanisheth
away, James iv. 14. This lawyer asks not after his temporal life,
for this is common to beasts with men; but here he inquireth concerning that life which is eternal, and shall never have an end. It
is strange to see how every man almost desireth to be eternal, and
yet how few do use the means to be eternal. As the fowls by a
natural inclination delight to fly, the fish to swim, and the beasts
to go, so men are naturally carried with an earnest desire to live
for ever.

And albeit men know themselves to be mortal, yet every man,
according to his several disposition, devises some means to be immortal. Some, like Lycurgus, do publish wholesome laws; some,
Plato-like, pen learned books; and some, like Solomon, build goodly
houses, and 'call the lands after their own names,' thinking by this
means that their names at least shall continue for ever, Ps. xlix. 11.

Thus every man almost, either for some valiant enterprise, like
David's worthies that killed the giants, 2 Sam. xxi., or for some
desperate attempt, like Saul that killed himself, 1 Sam. xxxi., or for
their famous and stately buildings, as the builders of both the
Babels, in the 11th chapter of Genesis, and 4th chapter of Daniel,
ver. 11, will be eternized. But howsoever men by such means may
be remembered after death, yet this is not the way to get eternal
life. For 'this is life eternal, to know the only true God,' John
xvii. 3, and 'to believe in the Son of God,' John iii. 16. But
these knowers must be doers; for 'he that saith I know him, and
keepeth not his commandments, is a liar, and the truth is not in
him,' 1 John ii. 4. And these believers must be good livers; 'for
this is a true saying, and these things I will thou shouldst affirm,
that they that have believed God, should be careful to shew forth
good works,' Titus iii. 8. Therefore to the obtaining of eternal
life two things are necessary. The first is, to believe well; the
second is, to live well. By the first we are justified in the sight of
God, for he respects our faith; by the second we are justified in the
sight of men, for they regard our works. And thus are the apostles

Paul and James reconciled. For when Paul maketh faith the cause of justification, Rom. iii. 28, he meaneth such a faith as 'worketh by love,' Gal. v. 6, whereby we are justified in the sight of God. And when James maketh works the cause of justification, James ii. 24, he meaneth such works as proceed from faith, James ii. 18, whereby we are declared to be righteous before men.

The Scripture describeth this eternal life by divers excellent names, to shew the worthiness and excellency thereof. It is called 'a kingdom,' Luke xii. 32, but yet such a kingdom as 'cannot be shaken,' not like the kingdoms of this world, Heb. xii. 28, for it is 'an heavenly kingdom, Mat. viii. 11. It is called 'paradise,' Luke xxiii. 43, for it is more pleasant than the garden of Eden. And 'Abraham's bosom,' Luke xvi. 22, for it is a place of rest and comfort. It is called 'the house of the Father, wherein there be many mansions,' John xiv. 2; 'The joy of the Lord,' whereinto every faithful servant must enter, Mat. xxv. 21; and all to express and declare unto us the beauty, excellency, and glory of that life which is eternal. And yet as glorious and excellent as it is, such is the love and favour of God unto us, that he hath appointed it to be our inheritance, as here the lawyer termeth it. Inheritance is a kind of tenure, whereby a man in his own right holdeth or possesseth any thing as his own; as when a lawful heir doth inherit his father's lands; even so the kingdom of God belongeth unto us, as our lawful inheritance, because we are the sons of God.

It is a great prerogative to be 'the son of God,' John i. 12. But to be heirs, and heirs with Christ, Rom. viii. 17, of that heavenly inheritance, is a wonderful privilege. How are we bound unto almighty God, that whereas he might have made us stones, or trees, or beasts, or such insensible and unreasonable creatures, it pleased his divine majesty to make us men, the undoubted heirs of eternal happiness! Behold, dear brother, and consider that heaven is thine inheritance, eternal glory is thy patrimony; thou art born to a kingdom, thou hast a title to it, and when thou dost depart this life thou shalt be sure to find it, if before thou depart this life thou do not lose thy right and title by thy sinful life.

Let every one therefore, as he tendereth the salvation of his own soul, forsake his wicked ways, and now begin to walk in the ways of the Lord. If heretofore thou hast profaned the Lord's Sabbath, remember that henceforth thou sanctify it; if thou hast been a blasphemer of the name of God, see that henceforth thou use it with all reverence; if thou hast been malicious, from henceforth be charitable; if thou hast been contentious, now learn to be peaceable; if thou hast been incontinent, now begin to be chaste; if thou hast been a drunkard, from henceforth be sober; and in a word, if thou hast been inclined to any sin, be sorry for it, and forsake it; if thou hast neglected any good work, now begin to do it; that in so doing thou mayest inherit that eternal life which is promised and prepared for them that know the will of God and do it, Luke viii. 21.

The Lord in mercy grant that ye be not forgetful hearers, but doers of the word!

THE LAWGIVER'S ANSWER TO THE LAWYER'S QUESTION.

THE SECOND SERMON.

And he said unto him, What is written in the law? how readest thou? &c.—LUKE X. 26.

Now you have heard the question propounded, you shall hear the question answered: 'And he said unto him, What is written in the law? how readest thou?' as if he should have said, I marvel that thou, being a doctor of the law, which should be able to instruct others in matters of religion, art ignorant of that which it behoveth every man to know, by what means he may inherit eternal life. Wherein hast thou bestowed thy study? wherein hast thou employed thy wit? and how hast thou spent thy time? Thou seemest to be a lawyer: tell me, what doth the law require of thee? Thou seemest to have read the Scriptures; let me see how thou hast profited by thy reading. Thus doth our Saviour send this lawyer to the law to learn his duty, and setteth him to school, that thought himself too good to learn. He came to tempt Christ by asking the question; but now himself must make the answer, unless he will bewray his own ignorance. If he be a lawyer, let him look what the law saith concerning this question; because the law is able to resolve every doubt, 2 Tim. iii. 16, 17. Therefore the prophet Isaiah sendeth us 'to the law and to the testimony,' Isa. viii. 20. And our Saviour Christ biddeth us 'search the Scripture,' John v. 39, and telleth us that the ignorance of them is the cause of all error, Mat. xxii. 29. If then thou wouldest know the will of God, study the Scriptures; there he hath revealed his will unto thee. If

thou desire to please the Lord, look in his word; there he hath
shewed thee what his pleasure is. Finally, if thou wouldst have
thy works to prosper, consider what is written in the law, ask counsel at the mouth of the Lord, examine all thine actions by the
touchstone of the word, and be sure to do nothing for the which
thou hast not the word for thy warrant. If harlots entice thee to lewd-
ness, as Potiphar's wife enticed Joseph, Gen. xxxix., fly from them
as Joseph did from her, and remember what the law saith, 'Thou
shalt not commit adultery.' If sinners, such as have no fear of God
before their eyes, entice thee, 'saying, Come with us, we will lay
wait for blood, and watch to slay the simple man'; consent thou not,
Prov. i. 10, 11, but consider what is written in the law, 'Thou shalt
do no murder.' If they say, 'Cast in thy lot among us, we will
have all one purse; we shall get great riches, and fill our houses
with spoil,' Prov. i. 13, 14; walk not thou in the way with them,
refrain thy foot from their path, and look what the law requires of
thee, 'Thou shalt not steal.' If papists would persuade thee to
change thy religion, because thy fathers were of another religion,
look in the Scriptures, examine thy religion by the word of God;
and then, as Elias said unto the people, 'If the Lord be God, then
follow him; but if Baal be he, then go after him,' 1 Kings xviii. 21;
so answer thou them, If this religion be agreeable to the word, as
in truth it is, then will I be of this religion, though my forefathers
have been of your religion. And to conclude, if thy father that
begat thee, thy mother that bare thee, 'thy wife that lieth in thy
bosom, thy friend that is as thy own self, or thy child which is the
fruit of thy body,' Deut. xiii. 6, shall require thee to do any thing
which the Lord hath forbidden in his law, or shall forbid thee to do
any thing which the Lord hath commanded in his word; then thou
mayest answer them as Job answered his wife, 'Thou speakest like
a foolish woman,' Job ii. 10, or as Christ answered his mother,
'Woman, what have I to do with thee?' John ii. 4; or as he answered his friend Peter, 'Go after me, Satan, for thou savourest not
the things that be of God,' &c., Mat. xvi. 23. Yea, if it come to
this, that thy prince, which hath power over thy life, command
one thing, and the Lord command thee contrary, thou must answer, as Peter and John answered the rulers, Acts iv. 19, 'Whether it
be right in the sight of God, to obey you rather than God, judge you.'
Yea, thou must be content with Shadrach, Meshach, and Abednego,
Dan. iii., to undergo any punishment, even unto the death, rather
than thou wouldst dishonour him, or disobey his word, 'that hath
power to cast both body and soul into hell together, Mat. x. 28.

It followeth, ver. 27, 'And he answered and said, Thou shalt love thy Lord God with all thy heart, and with all thy soul, and with all thy strength, and with all thy thought ; and thy neighbour as thyself.' Before, the lawyer moved the question ; now it is the lawyer's turn to answer; and in his answer he sheweth himself a learned lawyer ; for whereas the law of God consisteth of ten precepts, he reduceth the same unto two. The one is taken (as it seemeth) out of Deut. vi. 5, containing our duty towards God ; the other out of Lev. xix. 13, &c., containing our duty to our neighbour. Here is the abridgment of Moses's law, which as it was delivered in two tables, so it is reduced to two duties ; and both these require but one thing, and that is, *love*, Deut. x. 12. So doth our Saviour Christ divide the law, Mat. xxii. 36, &c., where, being asked, 'Which is the great commandment ?' he answered, as here the lawyer doth, 'Thou shalt love the Lord thy God with all thy heart, with all thy soul, and with all thy mind. This is the first commandment. And the second is like unto this, Thou shalt love thy neighbour as thyself.' Here is nothing but love (my brethren), and yet here is 'the fulfilling of the law,' Rom. xiii. 8. For all the benefits that God had bestowed upon the Israelites, his people, he requireth nothing but love ; and for all favours which he hath done unto us, he asketh no more but love again.

If we were not too unkind, God needs not to crave our love, having so well deserved our love, in loving us before we loved him, 1 John iv. 10, 19. But now he is fain to become a suitor for our love, which he hath dearly bought ; for he sheweth his love to us before he craves our love to him. By his almighty power he created us of nothing, and made us the most excellent of all his creatures. If that be little worth, because it cost him little, for 'he spake the word, and we were made,' Ps. xxxiii. 9, yet this is such a love as cannot be expressed, that when we were fallen from that excellent estate wherein we were created, and become heirs of hell and condemnation, so did he love this sinful world, that he gave his only begotten Son to die for the sins thereof. That he might bring us to heaven, he came down from heaven; that he might deliver us from hell, he came down to hell for us. Not gold nor silver, but his dearest blood, was the price of our redemption, 1 Peter i. 18, 19. What can a man do more than to give his life for his friend ? Rom. v. 7. And what can God do more than to die for sinful men ? And for all this, what doth this loving Lord require of thee, but that thou love the Lord thy God ? Blessed be such a Lord, that requireth nothing of his servants but love. If any prince were so gracious unto his subjects, that he would require no other subsidies, nor tribute, nor custom of them but love, how were the subjects bound to love and honour such a prince? And such an one is our most gracious Lord and King, who, for all the blessings and benefits that we enjoy under his most happy government, craveth no more but love at our hands for recompence. Once he required burnt-offerings; that was a dear kind of service: but now he asketh love; a kind of service which every man may well afford. He asketh not learning, nor strength, nor riches, nor nobility, but he asketh love; a thing that the simplest, the weakest, the poorest, the basest may perform, as well as he that is most learned, most strong, most rich, or most nobly born. If God had required this of thee, that thou shouldst be able to dissolve doubts, like Daniel, and to dispute subtle questions, what should then become of thee that art unlearned? If the Lord should accept of none but such as were strong and valiant, what should then become of women, old men, and children, which are weak and feeble? If God should regard none but the rich and wealthy, what should then become of the poor and needy? To conclude, if God should make choice of none but such as were of noble parentage, what should we do that are the common people? But now he requireth such a thing of us, as the poorest and simplest may perform as well as the wealthiest or wisest man in all the world; for if we cannot love, we can do nothing; especially if we cannot love God, that hath so loved us, we go not so far as the wicked do, for 'sinners also love their lovers,' Luke vi. 32. And therefore blessed be God, that for the performance of so small a work, hath proposed such a great reward; and for the obtaining of such a happy state, hath imposed such an easy task. 'The eye hath not seen, the ear hath not heard, neither can the heart conceive, what God hath prepared for them that love him,' Isa. lxiv. 4, and 1 Cor. ii. 9. And for all these unspeakable joys which God hath prepared, he requires no more of us but love. How is God enamoured of our love? and how unkind shall we be to withhold it from him? He hath an innumerable company of angels, which are inflamed with his love; and not content therewith, he sues to have the love of men. God hath no need of our love, no more than Elisha had need of Naaman's cleansing; but as Elisha bade Naaman wash, that he might become clean, 2 Kings v. 10, so God bids us love, that we might be saved. It is for our good altogether that God requires our love in earth, because he means to set his love on us in heaven. If the man of God had willed Naaman to do some great thing, ought he not to have done it ? So if God had willed us to do some great thing, ought we not to have done it ? How much more when he saith unto us, Love, and you shall live for ever ?

Now, if you would know whether you have this love of God in you, examine your actions, whether they be done with delight and comfort. *In amore nihil amari*, in love there is no mislike. It is like the waters of Jordan wherein Naaman washed; for as his flesh, which before was leprous, became fair and tender after his washing, so all our actions, and labours, and afflictions, which before were tedious and irksome, become joyous, and pleasant, and comfortable, after we are once bathed in the love of God. It is like the salt that Elisha cast into the noisome waters, to make them wholesome, 2 Kings ii. 21, or like the meal that Elisha put into the bitter pottage to make them sweet, as in 2 Kings iv. 41. So the love of God being shed in our hearts by the Holy Ghost, doth make all anguish, and sickness, and poverty, and labours, and watchings, and losses, and injuries, and famishment, and banishment, and persecutions, and imprisonment, yea, and death itself, to be welcome unto us. Such was the love of that chosen vessel, who, for the love that he bare unto God, waded through all these afflictions, 2 Cor. xi. 23, &c., and xii. 10, and could not for all these, and many more, be separated from the love of God, as he protesteth, Rom. viii. 38, 39.

Wherefore, beloved, seeing God, that hath done so much for us, requires no more but love of us, which every one may easily afford, let him be our love, our joy, and whole delight, and then our life will seem delightful. As Jacob served seven years for Rachel, Gen. xxix. 20, and ' they seemed to him but a few days, for the love that he bare unto her;' so when we have once set our love upon God, our pain will be pleasure, our sorrow will be joy, our mourning will be mirth, our service will be freedom, and all our crosses will be counted so many comforts, for his sake whom we love a great deal more than Jacob loved Rachel, because his love to us is like Jonathan's love to David, 'passing the love of women,' 2 Sam. i. 26.

Thus we have heard what it is that the Lord requires of us, namely, love. Now, let us see what manner of love he requireth, ' Thou shalt love the Lord thy God with all thine heart, with all thy soul, with all thy strength, and with all thy thought.' Here the Lord setteth down the measure of that love which he requireth of us; that, first, it must be true and unfeigned, as proceeding from the heart and mind ; secondly, that it must be sound and perfect, ' with all the heart, with all the mind,' &c.

The Lord, which is a Spirit and truth, John iv. 34, will be served in spirit and in truth. He cannot away with hypocrites, which 'draw near unto him with their lips, but their hearts are far from him,' Mat. xv. 8. He cannot abide dissemblers, which 'flatter with their lips, and dissemble with their double heart,' Ps. xii. 2 ; and therefore, though he requireth all the heart, yet he requires not a double heart; to signify, that a single heart is pleasing unto him, and that he detesteth a double heart. As there is a glozing tongue, a wanton eye, an idle ear, a wicked hand, and a wandering foot, so there is a false and dissembling heart, which mars all the rest. As is the eye, such is the sight : 'if the eye be single, the body is full of light ; if the eye be wicked, the body is full of darkness,' Mat. vi. 22, 23. So as is the heart, such are the actions of the body which proceed from the heart. 'A good man, out of the good treasure of the heart, bringeth forth good things : and an evil man, out of the evil treasure of the heart, bringeth forth evil things,' Mat. xii. 35. Therefore, as Christ saith, 'Make clean within, and all will be clean,' Luke xi. 40 ; so I say to you, Look that your heart be sincere and single, and then your tongue, your eye, your ear, your hand, your foot, that is, all your actions, will be holy to the Lord.

The heart of man is a storehouse wherein his treasure lies ; and therefore God, seeking to have the treasure, requires the heart ; for 'where the treasure is, there will the heart be also,' Mat. vi. 21. But he will have it freely, not by constraint ; and therefore he requires the heart, because whatsoever is done with the heart, is done willingly ; and that which is done against the heart, is done, as it were, against the hair : therefore in requiring the heart, God sheweth that he delighteth in voluntary service. Among all the offerings that the Lord in his law required of his people, he liketh none so well as the free-will offerings of their hand. Princes require help of their subjects, because they stand in need of help, not regarding whether they do it willingly, or against their wills ; but God requireth the heart, because he needeth not our help. As God 'gives to all men indifferently, and casteth no man in the teeth,' James i. 5, so he would have us to give that which we give unto him willingly, without grudging. If we give him love, we must give it lovingly ; if we give him our heart, we must do it heartily ; if we give him our alms, we must do it cheerfully. For as he 'loveth a cheerful giver,' 2 Cor. ix. 7, so he loves a cheerful lover ; but he that loves not with the heart, loves not cheerfully ; for 'out of the abundance of the heart the mouth speaketh,' Mat,

xii. 34, the head deviseth, the eye seeth, the ear heareth, the hand worketh, the foot walketh. If the 'heart be inditing of a good matter,' the 'tongue will be as the pen of a ready writer,' Ps. xlv. 1. But if the heart be unwilling, everything will be irksome; like the gift of Ananias, that was loath to part from the price of his land, because Satan had filled his heart with covetousness, Acts v. 3. Such are the gifts of many now-a-days, which either give not so much as their abilities might afford, or if they do, then presently they begin to repent that they gave so much; and as Judas murmured that the oil was not sold, and given to the poor, John xii. 5; so they grieve that their alms was not spared, and put to some other use. Thus though they give sometimes, as Ananias did, for fashion's sake, because they see others give, yet is their gift nothing worth, because it comes not with a willing mind. God more regarded the shepherd's sacrifice of the first fruits of his sheep, Gen. iv. 4, than the husbandman's oblation of the first fruits of his ground; because Abel offered sincerely with all his heart, and Cain offered like an hypocrite, for an outward show. The widow's mite, Luke xxi. 3, was more esteemed than the rich man's much; because she offered of her penury with a willing mind; they of their superfluity, for ostentation. A cup of cold water, or a morsel of bread that is given with cheerfulness, is better than a fat ox with hatred and ill will. When we give to the poor, we lend unto the Lord; and the Lord, to whom we lend, measures the gift by the mind of the giver, and not by the worth of the gift. 'A small thing,' saith David, Ps. xxxvii. 16, "that the righteous hath, is better than riches of the ungodly;' so a small thing that the righteous give is better than great riches of the ungodly, because they give for the love of God, with all their heart; but the ungodly give for other respects, either for the love of the man to whom they give, or, like the pharisees, Mat. vi. 2, for the praise of men before whom they give.

Some will not give at all; wherein they declare that they have no love at all. When a poor man comes to their door, or to their pew, then, as Nabal answered David, when he desired relief for himself and his company, 1 Sam. xxv. 10, 'Who is David? or who is the son of Jesse? There be many servants now-a-days that break every man away from his master. Shall I then take my bread, and my water, and my flesh that I have killed for my shearers, and give it unto men whom I know not whence they are?' so they answer the poor man, Who art thou, and whence comest thou? There are too many such as you are in every place. We have poor enough of our own to help; I must bestow mine alms on them, and have not for you.   Thus do they excuse their niggardice and unmercifulness, by the poor that dwell among them; upon whom God knows they bestow no more than that which the law compels them to bestow, and that for the most part against their will.   Where is the love of God, my brethren? 'If you say you love God, and shew not your love to your brethren, you lie; for if you love not your brother whom you see, you cannot love God, whom you have not seen,' 1 John iv. 20.

As we must love God *with the heart*, that is, sincerely, so we must love him *with all the heart*, that is, with a perfect love.   God is like a jealous husband, loath to have a partner in his love, Exod. xx. 5.   He will not have half the heart, nor a piece of the heart, but all the heart.   When the heart is divided, it dieth; therefore God will not have the heart divided, lest it die, because he desireth a living, and not a dying heart.   He is not like the unkind mother, that would have the child divided, 1 Kings iii. 26, but like the natural mother, who, rather than it should be divided, would forego the child.   So God will have all or none; if he may not have all the heart, and all the soul, and all the strength, and all the thought, he will have none at all.   The devil, or the world, or the flesh, will play small game, as we use to say, before they will sit out.   If they cannot get full possession of our hearts, then they are content to have some part of our love, as it were a little room in our hearts; a wicked thought, or else a consent to sin.   Like Pharaoh, the king of Egypt, who, when he could not keep the Israelites still in bondage, would keep their wives and children back; and when this would not be granted, then he was content to let them go and do sacrifice; but their sheep and their cattle must stay behind; and when this might not be obtained, then he desired them only to bless him before they went, Exod. xii. 32.   But God is of another mind; he that made all the hearts of men, and trieth them, and knoweth them, and reneweth and mollifieth them, and lighteneth them, and ruleth them, and turneth them which way it pleaseth him, will have all the heart, because he hath best right to all. Therefore, as Moses answered Pharaoh, ' There shall not a hoof be left behind us;' so, whensoever the world, the devil, or the flesh are suitors unto us for any part of our heart (as commonly they are, when we have any sacrifice or service to perform unto the Lord our God), then we must answer them as Moses answered Pharaoh, Thou shalt have neither hand nor hoof in this action, Exod. x. 26; or, as Peter answered Simon Magus, when he offered money for the Holy

Ghost, 'Thou hast neither part nor fellowship in this business,' Acts viii. 20, 21. I must not yield one jot to your suggestions; for I must love the Lord my God with all my heart, with all my soul, &c. That God may be our God, he will have the greatest love; because, whatsoever we love best, we make our god. We love our parents, or our wives, or our children, or our friends, or our neighbours, as well as we love ourselves, with a true and unfeigned love; but we must love God better than our parents, or our wives, or our children, or our friends, or our neighbours, or ourselves, with all our hearts, and with all our soul; that is, with a sound and perfect love. As we love a ring or a jewel for his sake that gave it, so we must love all things of this life for his sake that gave them, and him for his own sake above all the rest. This perfect love we can bestow but once, and but one can have it, and whoso hath it must be our God. If we set our heart upon riches, we make riches our god; therefore David saith, Ps. lxii. 10, 'If riches increase, set not your heart upon them.' If our whole delight be in eating and drinking, then we make a god of our belly; and the apostle tells us, Philip. iii. 19, that our end is damnation. If we be given to wantonness and fleshly pleasure, then Venus is our goddess; and Solomon tells us, Prov. vi. 26, that our end will be beggary. But if we have set our love on God, 'the eye hath not seen, the ear hath not heard, neither hath it entered into the heart of man, what God hath prepared for them that love him,' 1 Cor. ii. 9.

Now if you would know how you must love God with all your heart, thus you must do it. When the devil, or the world, or the flesh, shall set anything before thee to love, wherewith thou shalt offend thy God, thou must be content to lose and forego the same, be it never so precious, be it never so lovely. He loveth God above all, which cannot for the love of any thing that is created be brought to sin against his Creator. So Joseph loved God above all, who, though he might have had the love of his lady and mistress without suspicion of man, yet he would not consent, and so lose the love of God, Gen. xxxix. Such was David's love to God, 1 Sam. xxiv., who, when he had gotten Saul (his greatest enemy, that sought his life) into a cave, where he might at once have been revenged on him for all his injuries, was content only to cut off the lap of his garment, and so let him go unhurt, rather than he would sin against the Lord, in laying his hands upon the Lord's anointed. Such also was the love of chaste Susanna, who, when she might have gained the love and favour of the elders without any note of infamy, chose rather to undergo the danger of her life, than to sin in the sight of the Lord.   Therefore thou mayest love the things of this life, thy parents, thy wife, thy children, and the rest ; the Lord gives thee good leave to love them, so long as thou mayest love them without offence to God.   But if once they be unto thee an occasion to sin, thou must leave to love them, and rather choose to sustain any loss, though it be to the cutting off of thy hand, or thy foot, or to the plucking out of thine eye, Mat. v. 29, or to the hazard of thy life, than thou wouldst offend so divine a majesty.

Now thou seest (if thou art not wilfully blind) how far thou art from this perfect love which God requireth of thee.   Thou hast not always preferred God before all thy worldly profit ; thou hast not always preferred God before all thy fleshly pleasure.   When thou hast gotten opportunity to be revenged of thine enemy, thou hast not spared him ; when thou hast gotten opportunity to commit wickedness, thy love to God hath not restrained thee ; where God required all thy heart, thou hast given him no part of thy heart. Sometime all thy heart 'runneth after thy covetousness,' Ezek. xxxiii. 31 ; sometime thy soul is wholly set upon delight and ease ; sometime thy mind is all upon thy corn, Luke xii. 16, &c., or thy cattle, or thy pasture ; and sometime thy thoughts are all upon thy merchandise.   Seldom thou thinkest upon God ; but when thou comest into the church of God, then thy mind is so distracted with divers thoughts, and cares, and affairs of this life, that thou canst not think upon God one hour together.   Therefore what remaineth in this case for thee to do, but confess thine own imperfection, and fly to Christ to supply thy wants, and earnestly to desire the Lord to change thy heart, to take from thee thy old heart, thy vain, thy wandering heart, which hath loved other things more than God, and instead thereof to 'give thee a new heart, and create a right spirit within thee,' Ps. li. 10, wherewith thou mayest love God above all things in this life, that so in the life to come thou mayest find the reward of thy love, such joys and comforts as cannot be expressed.

Thus we have heard what duty we owe unto God himself ; now we shall hear what duty we owe unto our neighbour.   That which we owe unto them both is love, but yet the love which we owe unto them is not alike ; for albeit the second commandment be like unto the first, Mat. xxii. 39, for the necessity thereof, and in respect of the subject or quality which is required, namely, love, yet in respect of the object, which is God, and the measure of our love, which must be perfect, there is great odds between them.   In that they both require but love, they are both alike ; but in that the first requires love to God, the second love to men, the first requireth a greater love than the second : there is the difference. But here a doubt arises. Seeing God requires the love of all the heart, soul, &c., what love remaineth for our neighbour ? If God must have all our love, what love is left for any other ? Whereunto I answer, that the love of our neighbour doth not derogate nor detract from the love of God. As the light of a candle doth not dazzle but rather commend the light of the sun, so our love to our neighbour doth not diminish but rather accomplish our love to God. He that loves the fruit, will love the tree whereon it grows ; and he that loveth the stream, will love the fountain from whence it floweth. Even so he that loveth man, which is a creature, will much more love God that hath created him.

But let us examine the words, ' Thou shalt love thy neighbour as thyself.' Here are four things to be observed : First, what is required, namely, *love ;* secondly, who must love, *thou,* that is, every man ; thirdly, whom we must love, namely, our *neighbour ;* and lastly, how and in what manner we must love him, *as we love ourselves.*

Concerning the first ; as in the former precept, so in this also, the Lord requireth love, wherein he dealeth as a kind father with his children, who is desirous to have them so to resemble him as by their conditions every man may know whose they are. Therefore our loving Father, desirous to have us like himself, requireth us to be kind and loving one to another, as he is kind to the unkind, to the evil, to the just and to the unjust, Mat. v. 45. He will have us perfect as he is perfect, he will have us holy as he is holy, he will have us merciful as he is merciful, he will have us loving as he is love itself. Again, it is the nature of a loving father by all means to procure the welfare of his children ; so our heavenly Father, desirous of our continual happiness, commandeth us love, that so we may lead our lives with delight and pleasure. If he had hated us he would have commanded us to live in hatred, and envy, and malice with our neighbours ; for among all the miseries that are under the sun, there is not a more miserable and irksome life than the life of the envious. Solomon calls it 'a rotting of the bones,' Prov. xiv. 30, and as it were a consumption of the body, because the envious man always repineth, and pineth away at other men's prosperity. As ' all things work to the best to them that love God,' Rom. viii. 28, so all things work to the worst to them that are envious. Therefore one wisheth that the envious man had eyes in every city, that he might be vexed with all men's prosperity. As Christ said, John xiii. 35, ' By this shall all men know that ye are my disciples, if ye have love one towards another,' so the devil saith, By this shall all men know that ye are my disciples, if you have envy, and hatred, and malice one towards another. Therefore, leaving that hateful and loathsome kind of life to the reprobate and damned (who are always malcontent like Cain, Gen. iv. 5, and their countenance cast down; they cannot look on their brother with a cheerful countenance, nor afford him a merry word), God hath prescribed love to those that are his, to shew how desirous he is of their welfare and happiness. But here some churl may say unto me, If this be all, I shall do well enough. If God require no more but love, I should be well content to love, so that I be not bound to give. Alas, this is a silly shift, for it is the nature of godly love to relieve and help him that is beloved. Therefore, whom thou lovest, if thou love him truly, thou canst not see him lack if it be in thy power to supply his want. If thou lovest thy horse, thou wilt give him provender ; if thou lovest thy dog, thou wilt give him thy crumbs ; and if thou love thy brother, thou wilt give him food. Therefore, though nothing be expressed which thou shouldst give unto thy brother, yet in that thou must love him, thou art bound to give him not only thy goods, but even thy life, if need require, to do him good : 'This is my commandment,' saith our Saviour Christ, John xv. 12, 'that ye love one another as I have loved you.' But he so loved us that he gave his life for us, Rom. v. 8 ; therefore 'we also ought to give our lives for our brethren,' 1 John iii. 16. Forasmuch, then, as thy life, which, as Christ speaketh, is more worth than food or raiment, Mat. vi. 25, should not be spared for thy brother's good, from henceforth grudge not to give thy goods to thy needy neighbours, defraud not him of food and raiment to whom thou owest even thy life itself.

But let us come to the second thing, which sheweth who is bound to love : *Thou shalt love.* Under this word *thou*, God comprehends every particular man and woman ; as if he should say, Thou thyself, and not any other : for '*Thou* shalt love thy neighbour.' The poor man is not exempted from this precept, because he may love as well as the rich. If he say, I have no wealth, and therefore I cannot shew my love to my neighbour; though he have no wealth, yet he hath a heart, he hath a mind, he has an affection ; let him have a loving heart, a loving mind, and a loving affection : if he cannot do well, let him wish well unto his neighbour ; if he cannot gratify him with anything that he hath, let him not envy at anything that the rich man hath. For as the rich man shews that he loves his neighbour if he relieves his necessity, so the poor man sheweth that he loves his neighbour if he grieves not at his prosperity. This, therefore, as a general precept, bindeth the poor as well as the rich; it is a common yoke laid upon the neck, and a common burden laid upon the back of every Christian; but yet it is 'an easy yoke, and a light burden,' Mat. xi. 30, because it is love, which maketh all things to seem delightsome. As there are some that would be content to love if they might not give, so there are some would be content to give if they were sure they should not want; therefore, when it comes to giving, they post it over to their heirs, or to their executors, or to their successors, when they are dead; they are never liberal until they die, and then they are liberal of that which is none of theirs. They think to be excused by the liberality of their heirs; but they are bound to be liberal for themselves; therefore they must not lay the burden upon them, because 'every man must bear his own burden,' Gal. vi. 5. If they say, I know not what need I may have before I die, let them remember that 'what they give unto the poor, they lend unto the Lord,' and he is a sure paymaster; he gives great usury. And as David said, 'I never saw the righteous forsaken, nor his seed beg their bread;' so they must needs confess, if they will confess the truth, that they never saw the godly man that was liberal to the poor, by that means to come to misery. By other means many men fall into extreme poverty; *alea, vina, Venus*, dice, wine, and women, have brought many to beggary; but by beneficence and liberality to the poor I never heard that any came to penury. Such a foison[1] hath your alms that, by the blessing of God, which makes men rich, it increases like the widow's meal and oil which she bestowed upon the prophet, 1 Kings xvii. Therefore let no man distrust.

Now we are come to the third thing, which sheweth whom we are bound to love: thou shalt love *thy neighbour*. He saith not, Thou shalt love the rich man, or thy kinsman, or thy friend, or thy companion, but *thy neighbour;* under which word is comprehended every man that is any way capable of thy love; yea, even thy enemy is included in this precept, Mat. v. 44, Rom. xii. 20. As the Jews thought none to be their neighbours but their own nation, so some think none to be their neighbours but their equals. The rich man despises the poor man, and he again envieth the rich man; and every man, as the proverb is, delighteth in those that are like himself. But here this law requireth that whosoever is our neighbour by any means, he is to be loved.

As our Saviour Christ had two kinds of kinsfolk, Mat. xii. 46, 49,

---

[1] That is, abundance or increase. It is a French word.—Ed.

one by the flesh, and another by the spirit ; so we have two kinds of neighbours, one by nature, another by grace. And as Christ preferred his spiritual kindred before his carnal kindred, so we must prefer our spiritual neighbours before our carnal neighbours. Therefore, although by this law we are bound to love all men indifferently, yet, because there are degrees of neighbours, therefore there must be degrees of love. We must love our parents and our kinsfolk more than strangers, because they are bound unto us by a straiter bond of nature ; according to that of the apostle, 1 Tim. v. 8, 'He that hath not a care of his own, specially of them of his household, is worse than an infidel.' So we must love the faithful more than the unfaithful, because they are bound unto us by a straiter bond of faith and religion ; as the same apostle willeth us, Gal. vi. 10, ' While ye have time, do good unto all, specially to them of the household of faith ;' signifying that though we are bound to love all men with a general love, because they are all of the offspring of Adam, yet must we love some with a more special love, because they are the children of God.

Now follows the measure of that love which we owe unto our neighbour, expressed in the last words, *as thyself*. Here is the rule whereby our love must be squared, and a most exquisite example of singular love found in ourselves for us to imitate. He saith not, As he loveth thee, or as he is beloved of others, but *as thyself*.

Who knows not how well he loves himself ? and therefore who can excuse himself and say, I know not how well I should love my neighbour ? But how do we love ourselves ? Feignedly, or coldly, or for an hour ? I trow not ; but truly, and zealously, and every hour. So we must love our neighbour with a true, zealous, and a constant love. We must not pass by, as the priest and the Levite ; but pour our oil into their wounds, with the Samaritan, to help, to relieve them and comfort them. We must love our neighbour though he be envious, as David loved Saul, requiting good for evil ; and as Joseph loved Potiphar, not enticed to sin against him. ' Love is the fulfilling of the law.' It beginneth young, with Moses, to resist the oppressor, and endeth not in old age, but desires to perish for the beloved's preservation ; it calleth infants in the street, with wisdom, to learn ; comforts the imprisoned, with Habakkuk;[1] burieth the dead, with Tobit ; visiteth the sick and possessed, with our Saviour ; ' covereth the multitude of offences,' and shall find this last comfort, 'Come, ye blessed.' To which joy he bring us, that with his love from everlasting death hath bought us !

---

[1] Qu. 'Obadiah'? 1 Kings xviii. 4.—ED.

THE CENSURE OF CHRIST UPON THE LAWYER'S ANSWER.

THE THIRD SERMON.

And he said unto him, Thou hast answered right : this do, and thou shalt live.—LUKE X. 28.

NOW we are come to the answer of Christ unto the lawyer's question. The question was, ' What must be done to inherit eternal life ?' The answer is, Do that which thou hast said, that is, Love God above all, and thy neighbour as thyself; and thou shalt live, thou shalt inherit eternal life. Where first it is to be observed, that though this lawyer came with a mind to tempt Christ, yet because he had truly alleged what was written in the law, Deut. vi. 5, Lev. xix., our Saviour Christ approveth his answer, and commendeth him for it; whereby we are taught to like and allow of those good things that we see in any, though they be our enemies.

Many there are that, if their enemy be endued with many excellent virtues, yet they will not acknowledge it, nor give him his due commendation; but rather seek by all means to disable him, and disgrace him, and dispraise him behind his back. If he be temperate and sober, then they say, as it was said of John Baptist, ' He hath a devil;' if he be sociable and familiar, then they say, as it was said of Christ, ' He is a glutton and a wine-bibber,' Luke vii. 34 ; if he be learned, they say, as Festus said of Paul, Acts xxvi. 24, ' He is mad ;' if he be a good housekeeper, they call him a papist ; if he be religious, they call him a precisian ; yea, if he be a prophet, yet, if he tell the truth, they account him their enemy, Gal. iv. 16, as Ahab termed Elias, 1 Kings xxi. 20. And as the same Ahab cared not to hear Micaiah, because he hated him, 1 Kings xxii. 8, so they despise the doctrine, and mislike the sermon, because they hate the man that preacheth it.

These kind of people are like their father the devil, who both by his name and nature is an 'accuser of the brethren,' Rev. xii. 10. He could not give Job a good word, though he were 'a just man that feared God,' Job i. 1, and no marvel, for he could not speak well of God himself, Gen. iii. But Christ is of another mind; for though this lawyer were his tempter, yet doth he allow his answer. So though a man be thine enemy, yet let him have his due ; if he be learned, report no less of him ; if he be an honest man, defame him not ; if he be humble, say not he is proud ; if he be liberal, say not he is miserable ;[1] if he deal justly, say not he is unconscionable ; and if he hath anything in him that is praiseworthy (as there is no man but hath some good thing in him), acknowledge it, report it, and commend him for it, though he be thine enemy. But here again we see, that though Christ commend this lawyer for his answer, yet doth he not commend him for anything else ; to teach us, that as we must give every man his due, so we must give no man more than his due. The lawyer had answered directly to Christ's demand ; therefore Christ commends his saying ; but the lawyer had not done so well as he had spoken ; therefore Christ doth not commend his doing. So the words of many are commendable, but their works are most detestable. If you come to their sermons, you shall hear them speak marvellous well ; but if you look into their lives, you shall find them far differing from their profession. They are like our bells, which can call the people together to the service of God, but cannot perform any service to God ; so these men can give good counsel to others, but cannot follow it ; they can teach the people to know the will and pleasure of God, but they go not about to do the will of God, that the people might be moved by their example to do the same. And if you seem to mislike their doings, then, as Christ said of the scribes and pharisees, Mat. xxiii. 2, 'they sit in Moses's chair,' &c., so they answer for themselves, Do as we say, and not as we do ; a bad excuse, fit for so bad a cause. As if they should say, We would have you to be godly, but we will not be godly ; we would have you to be saved, but we ourselves will not be saved. How can their doctrine do any good, that live not according to their doctrine ? or how can the people think that the doctrine is true, when they that preach it live not thereafter ? Will not the people reason thus : If his doctrine were good, surely he

---

[1] That is, 'miserly.'—Ed.

would follow it; if his life be good, surely he would teach us to live as he doth; therefore whatsoever he saith, we will not believe him; but as he doeth, so will we do, and we hope to escape as well as he.

Thus with the one hand they build up the church of God, and with the other hand they pull it down; because they do more hurt by their bad example, than they can do good with all their preaching. These are the ungodly, that the Lord by his prophet reproveth, Ps. l. 16, 'Why dost thou preach my laws, and take my words in thy mouth?' So long as Isaiah was a man of polluted lips, the office of preaching was not committed unto him; but when his lips were cleansed, Isa. vi. 7, then was he fit for that office and function. Even so, as long as we delight in sin as much as any, we are not meet to reprove the sins of others; but when we behave ourselves as it becometh the ministers of the gospel, then have we commission to preach the gospel, and to reprove the sins of the people.

Therefore to a good churchman (as you use to call us), two things are necessary : the first is, to teach well; the second is, to live well. For as we are resembled to salt, because we must season the people with sound and wholesome doctrine, Mat. v. 13; so are we resembled to the sun, because we must shine as lights in the world by our holy life, ver. 16. As John Baptist was 'the voice of a crier,' so he was 'a burning lamp;' as the apostles were willed to teach and baptize, so their lights were commanded to 'shine, that men, seeing their good works, might glorify God.'

Thirdly, we here may see that truth is truth, and to be commended, from whomsoever it cometh. For though this lawyer came to tempt Christ, yet, because he told the truth, Christ admitteth his answer, and commendeth him for it. Whereby we have to learn to embrace and receive the truth, by whomsoever it is brought. For as a jewel is to be esteemed, though it be found on a stinking dunghill; so the truth is to be regarded, though it be found in a wicked man.

And last of all, we here may see that to be verified which was spoken of Christ, Isa. xlii. 3, Mat. xii. 20, 'A bruised reed shall he not break,' &c.; that is, he shall not discourage any in the way of godliness. Though this lawyer were Christ's enemy, yet when he answered discreetly and directly out of the word of God, Christ approveth his answer, and exhorteth him to the practice of the same; whereby we have to learn to commend and encourage every man in his well-doing, and by all means to further them in their good beginnings. Praise and honour are spurs to virtue; therefore if a man have done well, commend him, and he will do better. But, alas! with us it is far otherwise; for if a man have done amiss, it shall be often cast in his teeth; but if he have done well, he shall never hear of it.

But let us go forward in the answer of Christ. It followeth, 'Do this.' Having approved his saying, now he exhorteth him unto doing; for it is not enough to say well, or to know much, or to believe aright; but we must do this, that is, we must love God and our neighbour, if we desire to live. Heaven is not gotten with fair words, nor amorous looks, nor gold, nor silver, nor gorgeous array; but with the fruit of a lively faith, or (that I may use the words of the apostle, Gal. v. 6) 'by faith working through love.' God will not come to judge us at the last day, whether we were learned, or wise, or eloquent, or wealthy, or honourable; but whether we have done those deeds of mercy to his needy members. What shall it profit a man in the last hour of his death to have been eloquent and excellent in all kind of learning, that he hath preached many notable and worthy sermons, if he have lived a lewd and wicked life, and carried a corrupt conscience to his grave? In that terrible day, when the books of all men's consciences shall be opened, Rev. xx. 12, and every man's life shall be strictly examined, it shall go better with us if we have served God with a good conscience, than if we have been able to dispute subtle questions; for at that day it shall be said to some that have preached in the name of Christ, 'Depart from me, I know you not,' Mat. vii. 23.

Now, as we shall not be saved for our preaching, no more shall you be saved for your hearing; for God will have you to do as you hear, as well as he will have us to do as we teach. If you look into all the Scriptures, you shall find no promise made to hearers, nor to speakers, nor to readers; but to believers, or to doers. If ye ask God who shall dwell in his holy mountain, he saith, Ps. xv. 2, 'The man that walketh uprightly.' If you ask Christ who shall enter into the kingdom of heaven, he saith, Mat. vii. 21, 'Not they that cry, Lord, Lord; but they that do the will of my Father.' If you ask him how you may come to heaven, he saith, Mat. xix. 17, 'Keep the commandments.' If you ask him who are blessed, he saith, Luke xi. 28, 'Blessed are they that hear the word of God, and do it.' If you ask an angel who is blessed, he saith, Rev. xxii. 7, 'Blessed are they which keep the words of this book.' If you ask David, he saith, Ps. cvi. 3, 'The man is blessed which keepeth judgment, and doeth righteousness.' If you ask Solomon, he saith, Prov. xxix. 18, 'The man is blessed which keepeth the law.' If you ask Isaiah, he saith, Isa. lvi. 2, ' He which doeth this is blessed.' If you ask James, he saith, James i. 25, 'The doer of the word shall be blessed in his deed.' And here, ' Do this, and thou shalt live.' Here is nothing but *doing*, to make us blessed; for as the works that Christ did bare witness that he was Christ, John x. 25, so the works that we do must bear witness that we are Christians.

But here some man may object and say, Is any man able to do this that God requireth? and if he be not, why then doth God command us that which we cannot perform? Herein almighty God deals with us as a father dealeth with his children. If a man have a son of seven years of age, he will furnish him with bow and arrows, and lead him into the fields; set him to shoot at a mark that is twelve score off, promising to give him some goodly thing if he hits the mark; and though the father know the child cannot shoot so far, yet will he have him aim at a mark beyond his reach, thereby to try the strength and forwardness of his child; and though he shoot short, yet the father will encourage him. Even so almighty God hath furnished us with judgment and reason, as it were with certain artillery, whereby we are able to distinguish between good and evil, and sent us into the world, as it were into the open fields, and set his law before us as a mark, as David speaks, promising to give us the kingdom of heaven if we hit the same; and albeit he knoweth that we cannot hit this mark, that is, keep the law which he hath set before us, yet, for the exercise of our faith, and for the testifying of our duty and obedience towards him, he will always have us be aiming at it; and though we come short of that duty and obedience which he requireth at our hands, yet doth he accept and reward our good endeavour; but if we stubbornly refuse to frame ourselves after his will, then may he justly be angry and displeased with us. Therefore, though thou canst not perfectly keep the law of God, yet if thou endeavour thyself to the utmost of thy power to observe the same, the Lord, that ' worketh in us both the will and the work,' will accept the will for the work; and that which is wanting in us, he will supply with his own righteousness.

It followeth, *And thou shalt live.* Here is the promise, even life eternal. Among all earthly things, we count none so dear and precious as our life, insomuch as we can be content to forego anything before our life; our blood and our limbs we lose sometime for the saving of this temporal life, which is no life indeed, but rather a shadow and the image of death. Now if we may make so much of, and suffer so many things for, the life of the body, which is so short and momentary; how far greater things should we suffer for the salvation of our soul, and for the gaining of that glorious and happy life which shall never end! Here Christ speaketh, not of any common life, but of life eternal, which is the inheritance and seat of the blessed.

For seeing Christ must answer the lawyer's question, and his question was, how he might inherit eternal life; when the lawyer had said what was written in the law, Christ answers, *Hoc fac, et vives;* as if he should say, Love God and thy neighbour, and so thou shalt inherit eternal life; this is the assoiling of thy question. Go to then, dear brethren, and consider at how small a rate or price of love eternal life is to be purchased. If we take so great pains and undergo so many difficulties to pursue this mortal life, what pains should we undertake to enjoy that immortal life? If God should bid us go into a hot fiery furnace, and cast ourselves into the burning flames, we ought to do it, that we might reign with Christ. But our gracious loving Lord commandeth us no such thing; but commendeth unto us love, that we may live. Our God is not as the gods of the Gentiles, which will have the parents slay their children, and offer them up in fire for a burnt sacrifice. No; our God ' will not the death of a sinner, but rather that he convert and live,' Ezek. xviii. 23. O how gracious is the Lord unto us, who requireth no more of us but love, and yet requiteth us with no less than life, and that a glorious and eternal life!

Thus have I at length explained the lawyer's question, and the answer of Christ unto the question; wherein I have shewed you one way to come to heaven, which is, to keep the law of God; and this way we find most hard and difficult. Another way there is, by the death of Christ; and this every man thinks most easy to find. But this I assure you, that whosoever doth not endeavour to walk in that old way, that is, to walk in the ways of the Lord, shall never come to heaven by the new and living way, Christ Jesus; because, as John saith, 1 John iii. 3, ' Whosoever hath this hope in him, purgeth himself;' that is, whosoever hopeth to be saved by the death of Christ hath a care to keep himself from sin, and to walk in the commandments of the Lord.

THE SINNER'S CONVERSION.

IN TWO SERMONS.

THE SINNER'S CONVERSION.

THE FIRST SERMON.

Now when Jesus entered and passed through Jericho, behold, there was a man named Zaccheus, which was the chief receiver of the tribute, and was rich. And he sought to see Jesus who he should be; and could not for the press, because he was of a low stature. Wherefore he ran before, and climbed up into a wild fig-tree that he might see him: for he should come that way. And when Jesus came to the place, he looked up, and saw him, and said unto him, Zaccheus, come down at once; for to-day I must abide at thine house.—LUKE XIX. 1–5.

IN the end of the chapter before-going, we may see how Christ healed a man blind in his bodily sight, namely, Bartimeus, whereby he shewed himself to be the physician of the body; here we shall see how he cured one blind in mind, namely, Zaccheus, whereby he sheweth himself to be the physician of the soul, and therefore the saviour of the whole man, Eph. v. 23.

In speaking of Zaccheus and his conversion, we will observe four circumstances: first, the place where he was called, which was Jericho; secondly, the person that was called, Zaccheus the publican; thirdly, by whom and how he was called, by the voice of Christ; and, lastly, the effect and fruit of his calling, his good confession.

First, therefore, for the place where he was converted, it appeareth to be Jericho, a city not far distant from Jerusalem. It was sometimes a notable city, till it was subverted and ruinated by the Lord's champion, Joshua, Josh. vi. It was builded again in the days of Ahab, by Hiel the Bethelite, 1 Kings xvi. 34, and remaineth at this day, with the rest of that holy land, under the Turkish empire. Unto this Jericho the Lord of heaven and earth vouchsafeth to come in the likeness of a servant. And as Joshua compassed Jericho seven times, minding to destroy it, so Christ, the true Joshua, resorted oftentimes to Jericho, minding to save it. But, as in the destruction of Jericho, Joshua spared none but Rahab the harlot, so Jesus, in his journey to Jericho, converted none but Zaccheus the publican. When Joshua had conquered and razed Jericho, he sowed salt in it, to make it barren, and cursed him that should attempt to build it up; yet in this barren soil Christ hath his spiritual harvest, and in this cursed city he hath an holy temple, a blessed building. Samaria, that wicked city, affordeth many that believe in Christ, John iv. 39. And out of Galilee, from whence they thought no good thing might come, John i. 46, Christ called divers of his apostles. And even in Jericho, this cursed city, Christ hath a rich man that is to be saved. In every place Christ hath his chosen. 'There is neither Jew nor Gentile, barbarian nor Scythian, bond nor free, but Christ is in all to all that call upon him,' Rom. x. 12.

Now followeth the description of Zaccheus, which is most plainly and fully set forth unto us. The Holy Ghost, speaking of Zaccheus and his conversion, comes in with an *Ecce, Behold,* as if it were a wonder that Zaccheus should be converted. Zaccheus was a Gentile, a publican, and a rich man, and therefore, behold a miracle; as if, in the conversion of Zaccheus, these three should be converted at once.

Zaccheus was a Gentile: a marvel to see a Gentile become a Jew, that is, to believe in Christ. He was a principal publican: a strange thing to see a chief customer to give over his office. And he was rich also: a rare matter to see a rich man to enter into the kingdom of God, Mat. xix. 23. And, therefore, behold a miracle! as if at this day the Turk, pope, and the king of Spain, were at once persuaded to forsake their idolatry and superstition. Christ going to Jerusalem converteth a Gentile, to signify the calling of the Gentiles; he converteth a publican, to shew that notorious sinners may hope to be saved, if they repent and amend as Zaccheus did; he converteth a rich man, to shew that all rich men are not excluded from the kingdom of heaven.

He was called *Zaccheus* before his conversion, but he was never truly called *Zaccheus* till Christ called him so. His name signified *simple, pure, honest;* but his life was subtle, impure, and most detestable. Thus many are called by honest names whose deeds bewray their dishonest natures, and vices ofttimes are shrowded in the habits of virtue; like Æsop's ass basking in the lion's skin, till his long ears detect his folly; or like the crow that is decked in other plumes, till every bird do pluck his feather.

Zaccheus by his profession was a publican, and therefore much detested of the Jews; for the publicans were Roman officers, appointed to gather and receive public custom or tribute of the Jews, who were at that time in subjection to the Romans. And amongst these officers Zaccheus was the chief, and, as it seemeth, overseer of the rest that were in Jericho, and, therefore, in chief hatred among the Jews, as one that chiefly favoured the Romans' tyranny, and served to abridge their country's liberty, which ought not to be subject to any nation.

Besides, he contemned the ceremonies of the Jews, and regarded not their religion, nor lived after their law; and, therefore, with the rest of the heathen publicans, was excommunicated out of their synagogues, Mat. xviii. 17.

Thus was he hated for his profession, because he was a publican; and for his religion, because he was a heathen. Yet was he beloved for his wealth, for 'rich men have many friends,' Prov. xiv. 20. And though they do never so wickedly, yet have they some to take their parts; if they speak never so proudly, yet are there some to praise their saying, Ecclus. xiii. 23.

Zaccheus was a publican, and therefore rich; for publicans must needs be rich, and usurers will be wealthy. But rich publicans make poor princes, and wealthy usurers make many beggars. In every province there were many publicans, and therefore much poor people in every place; for where there be many caterpillers, the fruit is soon consumed; and where there be many extortioners, beggars must needs abound.

By the law of God there might be no beggars in Israel, Deut. xv; but when so many publicans were suffered to receive tribute of the Jews, contrary to God's law, no marvel though so many sat and begged, contrary to God's law, Luke xviii. 35; John ix. 8; Acts iii. 2. By the law of God there ought to be no beggars among Christians, Ps. xxxvii. 25; but when so many usurers are tolerated in a Christian commonwealth, contrary to the law of Christ, Luke vi. 35, no marvel though we have so many beggars, contrary to the mind of Christ. 'The poor,' saith Christ, 'ye shall have always with you, and when you will you may do them good,' Mark xiv. 7. And we shall be sure to have the poor amongst us always; but we must make such good provision for them, that they be not fain to beg their bread,' Ps. xxxvii. 25.

Thus was Zaccheus rich to himself, for he was a publican; but he was rich towards God also, for he had a desire to see Christ. Almighty God, who was 'rich in mercy,' Eph. ii. 4, hath so inspired his heart with the desire of heavenly riches, that whereas before his whole delight was in seeking of worldly wealth, now his greatest care is to seek for heavenly treasure. He now forgetteth what his profession is, and begins to be of a new profession; and he whose heart was wholly set upon earthly profit, is now, like old Simeon, most desirous to see his Saviour, Luke ii. 27. The tetrarch Herod desired to see Christ, and despised him when he saw him, Luke xxiii. 8, 11; but Zaccheus the publican desired to see Christ, and rejoiced when he saw him, like Abraham, that desired to see the day of Christ, John viii. 56. And, therefore, of the servant of Satan, Zaccheus is now become the child of Abraham, which rejoiced to see the day of Christ. Happy were his eyes that saw so blessed a sight; for many prophets and righteous men have desired to see and to hear those things that Zaccheus both saw and heard, and could not see nor hear the same, Luke x. 24. If Jacob thought himself happy, if that he might see his son Joseph before his death, Gen. xlv. 28; then surely thrice happy Zaccheus, whose hap it was, not only to see, as Jacob did, but to rejoice, as Mary did, in Christ his Saviour.

As Zaccheus was desirous to see Christ on earth, so I would have the rich men of our time desirous to see Christ in heaven; for although with the eyes of our body we cannot see Christ as Zaccheus did, yet with the eyes of our faith we may behold him as Stephen did, Acts vii. 56. But if our faith be so weak-sighted that we cannot see Christ, yet let us have a desire to hear Christ in his word, whereby our faith may be increased; for faith comes by hearing the word of God, Rom. x. 17. And as the queen of the south desired to hear the wisdom of Solomon, so let us be desirous to hear the wisdom of Christ our Saviour.

King Solomon left some books in writing, wherein is seen some part of his wisdom, 1 Kings iv. 32, 33; and Christ our king hath left unto us his most sacred word, as it were a taste of his wisdom, sufficient matter for our salvation. This is that heavenly food, Mat. iv. 4, whereby our souls are fed unto eternal life; let us therefore labour for that heavenly food; and as the Israelites were careful to gather manna to sustain their bodies, Exod. xvi., so let us be as careful to hear the word to feed our souls. The people in the time of Christ, John vi. 24, took great pains to follow Christ both by land and sea; and many now-a-days, I confess, are very forward to follow his faithful ministers; but as they followed Christ so fast to fill their bellies, John vi. 26, so these frequent sermons for fashion, to serve the time.

Zaccheus is desirous to see Christ, a godly care; but yet he could not obtain this purpose, a thing common. For every one that hath any good motion hath always some hindrance to cross the same ; and Zaccheus hath a double impediment to hinder his honest enterprise, the press of the people, and his little stature. Whereof the former, that is, the multitude, is always wont to be an enemy to those that would come to Christ. This hindered the blind man from receiving his sight, Luke xviii. 39 ; for the people 'rebuked him, that he should hold his peace,' till Christ called him, and opened his eyes. This hindered them that brought the man sick of the palsy, Mark ii. 4 ; for 'they could not come at Christ for the press,' till they uncovered the roof of the house, and let down the bed wherein the sick of the palsy lay. This hindered the healing of the deaf and dumb, Mark vii. 33, till Christ 'took him aside out of the multitude,' and cured him. This hindered the raising of the ruler's daughter, Mat. ix. 25, till Christ had thrust out the minstrels and the multitude, and then restored the maid to life. Finally, this hindered Zaccheus here from coming unto Christ, till Christ vouchsafed to call him to himself. Thus always a multitude that is prone to evil doth withdraw and hinder us from approaching unto Christ ; and therefore we must 'not follow a multitude to do evil,' nor decline after many to overthrow the truth, Exod. xxiii. 2.

The second impediment that hindereth Zaccheus from seeing Christ is his little stature. He was so low of stature, that he could not see Christ above the multitude ; but Christ was above the multitude, and therefore could see Zaccheus though he were so low of stature. For 'God looketh not on the countenance, nor on the height of man's stature ; but the Lord beholdeth the heart,' 1 Sam. xvi. 7, and preferreth little David before Eliab his eldest brother ; because he findeth in him a better heart to serve the Lord, ver. 12. And Zaccheus, in his little body, hath a heart and mind prepared to seek and see the Lord. Zaccheus was so low that he could not see Christ ; but many amongst us are so high that they will not see Christ. The common people in the time of Christ were so desirous to follow Christ, that neither lameness, nor blindness, nor sickness, could stay them from coming to him; but the common people in our time are more ready to follow their sport and pastime than to come to the church to hear of Christ. And as for our rich men, who seeth not that they will make great haste to see a commodity, but will scarce come out of doors to hear a sermon ?

They come to Christ as Nicodemus came to Christ, by night, John iii. 2, as if they were ashamed to come to church ; but they run after profit to get riches, as Gehazi ran after Naaman the Syrian to get a bribe, 2 Kings v. 21.

Thus hath Zaccheus two lets that he could not see Christ, the one in the people, the other in himself. And we have many lets to withdraw us from Christ : some are external, and without us, as the enticements of the world ; and some are internal, and within us, as the lusts of our own flesh. The press of the people hindereth Zaccheus from seeing Christ in his humility ; and the multitude of our sins do press us down that we cannot see Christ in glory, Isa. lix. 2. Zaccheus was a man of little stature, and that hindered him from seeing Christ on earth ; and we are men of little faith, and that is the cause we cannot behold Christ in heaven.

Though Zaccheus was a man of little stature, yet it appeareth that he was not a man of little wit ; for when he could not come to the sight of Christ for the multitude, he had the wit to run before, and to climb up into a tree to obtain his purpose. And for the most part it falleth out, that men of low stature are men of high conceit, and the shortest bodies have the sharpest wits ; God so providing, that the defects of their bodies might be supplied with the gifts of their mind. Now Zaccheus, that before was loath to move his foot from the custom-house for losing his profit, begins to run after Christ for fear of a greater loss ; like Elisha, that left his ploughing, and ran after Elias to follow his new vocation, 1 Kings xix. 20. But Zaccheus doth not only run, but also climb up into a tree to see Christ. A strange thing that Zaccheus, a rich man, and a chief customer, should behave himself so childishly in the sight of so great a multitude ; but the desire he had to see Christ made him forget himself, and to commit such things as were not fitting for his state and credit. So they that will follow Christ must make account to do many things contrary to the fashion of the world and their own liking, Rom. xii. 2. If Christ himself were content to leave the glory which he had with his Father to come down to us, shall not we be content to leave the reputation which we have with men to go up to him ?

But, alas ! where is there any almost that preferreth not the fruition of this earthly prison before the possession of that heavenly mansion, and had not rather hazard the hope which they have of eternal glory, than lose the present enjoying of their fading pleasure ?

The ambitious man hunteth after honour, and will not lose an inch of his estimation; the covetous man seeks after profit, and counts, like Judas, John xii. 6, all lost that comes not to his bags; and the voluptuous man bestows his time in pleasure, and thinketh that his chief felicity. Thus every man makes his heaven of that wherein he most delighteth, and is content to take great pains to accomplish his fond desires. But here Zaccheus is of another mind; for being a public officer, he climbs into a tree, which stood not with his gravity; and being a rich man, he runs to see Christ, which was not for his worldly profit, yea, he takes great pains to see Christ, not respecting his ease or pleasure.

Thus must we be affected if we desire to come to Christ, that neither honours, nor preferment, nor profit, nor pleasure, nor kindred, nor friends, be able to hold us back. We must be ready, not only to run, but also to climb (if need require) as Zaccheus did, that is, to take some pain and travail to have a sight of Christ.

The queen of the south undertook a great and tedious journey to hear the wisdom of Solomon, Mat. xii. 42, Luke xi. 31, 1 Kings x. 1, 2; but we are loath to take any pain to hear one that is greater than Solomon.

The people in David's time brought so much treasure, and so many gifts to the building of God's temple, that the priests were fain to bid them cease, 1 Chron. xxix.; but a great part of the people in our time are so sparing of their pain and cost, that they think that time very much misspent which is employed in the service of God; and that money ill bestowed which is given to the maintenance of his ministers.

When Zaccheus could not see Christ for the multitude, he climbs into a tree that groweth in the way where he was to pass, that from a tree he might behold him which was to suffer on a tree for man's salvation; so when we cannot draw near to Christ by reason of our sins that press us down, we will climb up by a lively faith, which is the tree of life, that groweth in the way to eternal life, that so with the eyes of our faith we may behold him that died for our sins upon a tree.

It was a wild fig-tree that Zaccheus climbed; but not like that unfruitful one which our Saviour cursed, Mat. xxi. 19; for this bare most precious fruit, even such as Christ himself vouchsafed to pluck. A happy tree, that bare such precious fruit as Zaccheus was; but thrice happy Zaccheus, that so happily climbed on that happy tree!

This tree grew in the way that Christ was to pass, for else Zaccheus might have climbed to no purpose; so if we desire to find

Christ, we must seek him in the way where he hath promised to shew himself unto us, that is, in his holy temple, where his word is duly preached, and his sacraments reverently administered ; for where two or three be gathered together, he hath promised to be present amongst them, Mat. xviii. 20.

When Christ came to the place, he looked up, and saw Zaccheus.

As Zaccheus ran before Christ, so Christ followed after to see Zaccheus. Satan, for his part, 'went about like a roaring lion, seeking to devour him,' 1 Peter v.'8 ; but Christ, for his part, goeth about like a 'good shepherd,' minding to save him, John x. 11. And although Satan, a 'strong armed man,' had taken some possession in the heart of Zaccheus, yet Christ, a stronger than he, cometh unarmed, and taketh from him his harness wherein he trusted, and rescueth his spoil, Luke xi. 21.

Christ cometh to the place where Zaccheus was, because otherwise it had been impossible for Zaccheus to come to his presence ; for unless the Lord vouchsafe to come unto us, we cannot attain to the presence of God. As no man might have any access to king Ahasuerus, except he stretched out his golden sceptre, Esther iv. 11 ; so no man may come to Christ, unless he be called by the golden sceptre of his sacred word.

Christ looked up, and saw Zaccheus, before Zaccheus could look down to behold him. Thus doth the Lord prevent us with his mercy, whom he might cast off in his justice ; and if he perceive in us a willing mind to come unto him, he is content to come first unto us, and, like that good father, Luke xv. 20, to ' behold us while we are yet a great way off, and to have compassion on us.'

When Job's three friends, that came to visit him in his great calamity, lift up their eyes afar off, they knew not Job, because he was so sore afflicted, Job ii. 12 ; but Christ, who is the mirror of true friendship, cannot so soon forget his friends, howsoever they be disguised. He knoweth his own sheep wheresoever he seeth them, John x. 14 ; whether they be under the fig-tree, as Nathanael was, or upon the fig-tree, as Zaccheus was, he hath respect unto them. And if they have a desire to seek, they shall be sure to find, Mat. vii. 7 ; and if they labour and are heavy laden, he will refresh them, Mat. xi. 28. Christ is now come to the place where Zaccheus is to be called; and as Abraham, Gen. xxii. 13, lift up his eyes, and saw in the bush a ram that was to be sacrificed, so Christ, lifting up his eyes, saw in the tree Zaccheus the sinner that was to be converted. And now begins the conversion of Zaccheus, for now Christ begins to speak unto him.

Zaccheus desired only to see Christ, but now Christ calleth him by name, and offereth his own self unto him. This was more than Zaccheus expected, and yet no more than Christ vouchsafeth, namely, to give more than is desired. The sick of the palsy, that asked health, obtained also forgiveness of sins, Luke v. 20 ; Solomon desired wisdom, ˹and the Lord gave him wisdom, and abundance of wealth beside, 1 Kings iii. 12, 13 ; Jacob asked but meat and clothing, and God made him a great rich man, Gen. xxviii. 20 ; and Zaccheus desired only to have a sight of Christ, and was so happy as to entertain him into his house.

Thus the Lord, that is ' rich in mercy to all that call upon him,' Rom. x. 12, Eph. ii. 4, useth oftentimes to give more than we ask ; and he that is always ' found of them that seek him with their whole heart,' Jer. xxix. 13, is found also sometime of Gentiles that knew not God, Isa. lxv. 1, Rom. x. 20. Let us therefore, that were sometimes sinners of the Gentiles, 'seek the Lord,' as Zaccheus did, ' while he may be found, and call upon him while he is nigh,' Isa. lv. 6. He will be found of them that seek him heartily, and ' is nigh to all them that call upon him faithfully,' Ps. cxlv. 18.

' Zaccheus, come down at once.' Now, Christ begins to call Zaccheus from the tree to be converted, as God called Adam from among the trees of the garden to be cursed, Gen. iii. 8, 9. Before, Zaccheus was too low, and therefore was fain to climb; but now he is too high, and therefore he must come down. And we, for the most part, are either too high or too low, too hot or too cold, too quick or too slothful in the Lord's business. Sometime we flock together to hear a sermon, like the people, Luke v. 1, that 'pressed upon Christ to hear the word;' and anon we run to see some pleasant pastime, like the Athenians, whose ears always itched to hear some news, Acts xvii. 21

Who make more show of conscience and religion than they that shew themselves most irreligious and unconscionable ? Who seemed more confident and valorous in Christ his cause than Peter ? and not long after, who more traitorous and faint-hearted ? Mat. xxvi.

Many can say, with Peter, that they will not stick to die before they will deny Christ ; but when it comes to the trial, they are ready to abjure Christ and his religion, before they will hazard either life or living.

He that will come to Christ, must come at once, without delay ; for delays, specially in the matter of our salvation, are most dangerous, and repentance may not be deferred. We must make no tarrying to turn unto the Lord, nor put off from day to day, lest the wrath of the Lord break forth suddenly, and we be destroyed in our security, and perish in the time of vengeance, Ecclus. v. 7. When the Lord is minded to do us good, he will have us come quickly, like Joseph, Gen. xlv. 9, that in the time of famine would have his father Jacob to come down quickly unto him, to sojourn in Egypt, where there was some plenty of food.

As the children of this world are very nimble to work wickedness, so the children of light should be as nimble to follow goodness. Judas was nimble to betray Christ, John xiii. 27 ; and the bad debtors, Luke xvi. 6, 7, could sit down quickly to mis-reckon their creditor ; so let us come quickly to hear of Christ, that Christ may accept of us quickly ; let us be nimble to make our account before, that we do not, like the foolish builder, Luke xiv. 28, come short of our reckoning.

But why must Zaccheus come down so hastily ? Even to entertain Christ into his house ; 'for to-day,' saith Christ, 'I must abide with thee.' This was joyful news to little Zaccheus. Not long before he wanted means to see Christ, but now he hath an opportunity to entertain him in his house.

There was more humanity in Christ than in Zaccheus ; for if Christ had not bidden himself to dinner, he had not been bidden for Zaccheus. So if Christ do not offer himself unto us in his afflicted members, Mat. xxv. 40, he may go long enough before we will offer him any entertainment. As often as the poor craveth any relief at our hands, let us imagine that Christ asketh something of us. But as Zaccheus must entertain him presently without delay, so let us be ready to help them presently, because they stand in need of present help ; and as he must receive Christ into his house, so we must make account to receive his needy members into our houses. And as the unjust steward procureth himself friends with his master's goods, Luke xvi., so let us make the poor to be our friends by our beneficence and bounty towards them, that so receiving them, when they have need, into our earthly houses, they may receive us, when we stand in greatest need, into everlasting habitations.

They that were invited to the marriage, Mat. xxii. 3, refused to come; but Christ is content to come to Zaccheus's house before he was invited. Wherein also he sheweth his great humility, in coming before he was requested; as they bewrayed their great arrogancy in refusing to come, being solemnly bidden. It was a part of great humility, that he that was most free from sin would vouchsafe to come into a sinner's house ; but it was a sign of greater humility, that he would bewray his great necessity, and seek for succour at a sinner's hand.

Alas, poor, humble Saviour ! who, though thou be the Lord of heaven and earth, as thou art the Son of God, yet, as thou art the Son of man, hast not whereon to lay thy head, Mat. viii. 20.

How justly did thy prophet Jeremiah wonder at thy humble poverty, saying, 'O thou the Hope of Israel, the Saviour thereof in the time of trouble, why art thou as a stranger in the land, or as one that passeth by to tarry for a night?' Jer. xiv. 8. The Son of God vouchsafeth to come, and that unrequested, to a sinful man's house ; a special favour : but he disdaineth not to make his necessity known unto him ; oh strange humility ! Here, therefore, appears the singular humanity and great humility of Christ to sinful men ; he offereth himself to be their guest, if he find them willing to entertain him for their guest. And Zaccheus, no doubt, was willing to entertain him ; for although Christ heard not the voice, yet he heard the affection of Zaccheus inviting him to dinner.

As, therefore, Zaccheus was willing to receive Christ into his house, so let us be ready to receive him into our hearts. For as Christ said to Zaccheus, 'This day I must abide at thy house ;' so he saith to every one of us, This day I must abide in your hearts. Wherefore, as the prophet David saith, 'Open your gates, that the king of glory may come in,' Ps. xxiv. 7, 9 ; so I say unto you, Open your hearts, that the word of God may enter in. This day the word of God may abide in your hearts, for this day the word is preached unto you; and who knows whether he shall live to hear it the next Sabbath ? 'To-day, therefore, if you will hear his voice, harden not your hearts,' as did the Israelites, Ps. xcv. 7, 8, lest if you harden your hearts, his voice be heard no more amongst you.

This day you may gather this heavenly manna, as the Israelites might gather their manna six days together, Exod. xvi. 4, 5 ; but to-morrow, perhaps, and six days after, you may not gather it, as the seventh day manna might not be found.

The Lord grant that you may gather sufficient food for the sustentation of your souls : that as Elias the prophet journeyed in the strength of the meat that the angel brought him, 'even unto Horeb the mount of God,' 1 Kings xix. 8 ; so you, in the strength of this spiritual meat which here I bring you, may be able to pass through the dangerous ways of this troublesome world, unto God's holy mountain, the haven of all happiness ; whither he bring us that hath dearly bought us with his precious blood, even Christ Jesus the righteous, to whom, with the Father and the Holy Ghost, three persons and one God, be given all glory and majesty, world without end.   Amen.

THE SINNER'S CONFESSION.

THE SECOND SERMON.

Then he came down hastily, and received him joyfully. And when all they saw it, they murmured, saying, That he was gone to lodge with a sinful man. And Zaccheus stood forth, and said unto the Lord, Behold, Lord, the half of my goods I give to the poor; and if I have taken from any by forged cavillation, I restore him fourfold. Then Jesus said unto him, This day salvation is come unto this house, forasmuch as he is also become a son of Abraham.—LUKE XIX. 6–9.

YOU heard the last Sabbath how Zaccheus the publican was called to be a Christian, now you shall hear the fruit of his conversion. No sooner had Christ called him from the tree but that ' he came down hastily, and received him joyfully.'

This was the fruit which it had in the heart of Zaccheus, namely, obedience to the voice of Christ, a fruit more precious and acceptable unto God than the most pleasant fruits which Eden yielded, and a sacrifice more sweet and acceptable unto him than all the sacrifices which the law required. This is ' the sacrifice wherewith the Lord is pleased,' Heb. xiii. 16, even when his voice is obeyed, 1 Sam. xv. 22. The voice of the Lord is a glorious voice, and mighty in operation, dividing the flames of fire, and shaking the cedar-trees, Ps. xxix ; so the voice of Christ is a glorious voice ; his voice is mighty in operation, ' dividing the soul and the spirit,' Heb. iv. 12, and shaking Zaccheus from the wild fig-tree whereunto he had climbed.

The same God, to whose command the winds, the sea, the devils, and death itself obey, Mat. viii. 27, here commandeth Zaccheus to come down at once, and he cometh down hastily to receive him into his house, and he receiveth him joyfully. As Zaccheus could not come at Christ till he was called, so 'no man can come to Christ except the Father draw him,' John vi. 44. And as Zaccheus could not choose but come when he was called by the voice of Christ, so when any man is called effectually by the preaching of the gospel, he cannot choose but come to Christ; for where there is an effectual calling, there is grace given also to obey the same, Rom. viii. 30. The Lord is fain sometime to call us often, because we know not the voice of him that calleth us, as he called Samuel three times before he answered, because at that time 'Samuel knew not the Lord,' 1 Sam. iii. 7; but as soon as he understood that it was the Lord that spake unto him, he replied presently, 'Speak on, Lord, for thy servant heareth,' ver. 10. So when the Lord calleth any man effectually by the preaching of his word, all the parts and powers of his body do yield their obedience : the ear listeneth, the tongue confesseth, the heart believeth, the head deviseth, the hand performeth, the foot runneth, the eye directeth, and all concur ' to do thy will, O God,' Ps. xl. 8.

Such and so effectual is the voice of Christ in the hearts of his chosen, that it maketh Saul of a bloody persecutor to become Paul, a painful preacher, Acts ix ; it causeth Peter of a silly fisherman to be a catcher of men, Mat. iv. 19 ; and Zaccheus here, of a vile publican to become a zealous Christian. And such also is the nature of the word preached, wheresoever it pleaseth the Lord to give success and increase thereto, 1 Cor. iii. 7, that it is able to transform the minds of men, to beget faith in the hearts of infidels, and in a word, to save ' such as are ordained to eternal life,' Acts xiii. 48. This is the power of the word of God, even to cause a consenting to the truth thereof; and this is the property of the children of God, to yield all obedience to the word of God. As soon as Christ called Zaccheus, he comes down presently, like the light in the creation, that was made as soon as God said, ' Let there be light.' Here, therefore, of Zaccheus, that obeyed the voice of Christ, let us learn obedience to the voice of Christ; for as Christ biddeth Zaccheus to come down because he was too high, so he saith to every one of us, Come down, because we are too high-minded. But with us the voice of Christ is not so effectual as it was with Zaccheus, for he was content to come down at the first bidding; but we must be often bidden to beware of pride and ambition, and yet we will still be climbing. There are few so high that are content with their calling; but as Haman was always aspiring till he came to the gallows, Esther vii., so many amongst us are always climbing till we catch a fall.

Again, as Christ saith to Zaccheus, 'To-day I must abide at thy house;' so Christ saith to us, To-day my poor afflicted members should receive some succour at your hands. But as the priest and the Levite, Luke x., passed by the wounded man, leaving him half dead; so we (for the most part) pass by our needy brethren, leaving them unrelieved. Thus are we every way disobedient to the voice of Christ. He teacheth us to be humble, as he himself is, Mat. xi. 29, and we wax proud and insolent, as Satan is. He willeth us to be merciful, as our heavenly Father is, Luke vi. 36 ; and we are cruel and unmerciful, as the rich glutton was, Luke xvi. This is the cause why the earth deceiveth, and rendereth not her fruit, Isa. xxiv. ; this is the cause why the sword devoureth abroad, and why the pestilence destroyeth at home, Deut. xxviii., Lev. xxvi. ; and in a word, this is the cause of all the mischiefs and calamities that are threatened, even because we are obstinate and rebellious against the Lord, we are undutiful and disobedient to the voice of Christ, that calleth us so lovingly to come unto him, Mat. xi. 28.

Zaccheus was called but once, and he cometh quickly; but we are called oftentimes, and almost every day, and that by the voice of Christ himself; for 'he that heareth you,' saith Christ, Luke x. 16, 'heareth me ;' and yet we cannot find the way to Christ. The word of God, which is 'the lantern unto our feet, and the light unto our paths,' Ps. cxix. 105, hath been plainly and plentifully preached amongst us these many years, and yet many amongst us have not learned yet to come to Christ. Zaccheus comes quickly when Christ calleth him; let us therefore learn of Zaccheus to come quickly when Christ calleth us. We must be quick in the Lord's business, for God cannot abide loiterers standing all the day idle, Mat. xx.; and as he 'loveth a cheerful giver,' 2 Cor. ix. 7, so he liketh a cheerful follower.

It followeth therefore that Zaccheus received him cheerfully. Still Zaccheus is a receiver. Before he was a receiver of customs, now he is a receiver of Christ. Zaccheus received Christ two ways: first, into his heart, when he desired to see him; and then into his house, when he gave him hospitality. Many received Christ to house, but not into their heart, and therefore received him grudgingly; but Zaccheus received Christ first into his heart, and then into his house, and therefore received him joyfully. Of Zaccheus his joyfulness, we must learn to be joyful when we do anything for the cause of Christ; we must be glad to harbour Christ in his members, as Zaccheus was glad to harbour Christ himself. As before, in coming down from the tree, Zaccheus shewed his obedience; so here, in receiving Christ into his house, he sheweth the great love that he bare unto him. If Zaccheus had not loved Christ, he might have sent him to some common inn; but Zaccheus is content to receive Christ in his own house; yea, he rejoiceth to have gotten so good a guest; like Abraham, that used to sit at the door of his tent, and rejoiced to entertain strangers that went by the way, Gen. xviii. 1. And therefore, though Zaccheus were a Gentile born, yet herein he shews himself the child of Abraham, because he doth the works of Abraham, John viii. 39; so did Abraham, and so must we do, if we will shew ourselves to be the children of Abraham.

When Abraham thought only to have entertained men, he receiveth the angels in the shape and likeness of men, Gen. xviii.; and when Zaccheus thought to entertain the Son of man, he receiveth the Son of God himself. Let us therefore (as the apostle willeth us) Heb. xiii. 2, 'be mindful to entertain strangers, forasmuch as thereby some have received angels into their houses unawares.' And why should we not hope to entertain the like or better guests, if we be given to hospitality, as those godly fathers were? For as the angels came to them in the likeness of men, so Christ himself comes to us in the likeness of a poor man, of a lame man, and of a blind man; and when he cometh he cometh hungry, or thirsty, or naked, or harbourless, or sick, or imprisoned; and happy are they that feed, or clothe, or harbour, or visit him, when he cometh thus afflicted.

When Abraham entertained the angel, he was not only busy himself, but his wife and all his household were careful to make provision for them; so when Zaccheus received Christ into his house, his whole family, no doubt, were no less willing and careful to entertain Christ than their master was. And therefore not only to Zaccheus, but even to his whole house, salvation is promised, because the whole family rejoiced at Christ his coming. Let rich men learn of Zaccheus to entertain Christ in his needy members; and let rich men's servants learn of Zaccheus's family to shew themselves merciful like their merciful masters, that they may receive the reward of mercy and hospitality at the last day, 'Come, ye blessed; for I was harbourless, and ye took me in,' Mat. xxv. 34. Generally, as Zaccheus received Christ, so let every one that is able be glad to distribute to the necessity of the poor saints. If we have much, let us give plentifully; if we have little, let us give gladly of that little; if we be not able to give a penny, yet haply we may afford a morsel of bread; if not that, yet there is none so needy that cannot give a cup of cold water; and even so small a gift shall not lose his just reward, Mat. x. 42. Zaccheus received Christ into his heart; but many amongst us are ready to drive Christ out, and to receive Satan instead of him. Zaccheus received Christ into his house; but there are many rich men amongst us, that, like Dives, Luke xvi., will not afford poor Lazarus the crumbs that fall from their table; but, as the damsel, Acts xii. 14, 'opened not the door for joy when she heard Peter's voice,' so, by contrary, these men for very grief shut their gates, when they perceive a beggar there. Finally, Zaccheus was joyful when he entertained Christ; but many amongst us are sorrowful when they should relieve the poor; like churlish Nabal, 1 Sam. xxv., that reviled David, when he should have relieved him.

So long as Job prospered, he kept a worthy and a worshipful house, he 'suffered not the stranger to lie in the streets, but opened his door to the traveller' that went by the way, Job xxxi. 32. But now many gentlemen of the country are content to suffer the stranger, the fatherless and the widow, not only to lie, but even to starve and die in the streets with hunger and cold, and never receive them to house or harbour, nor afford them any relief or succour. But as 'the voice of Abel's blood did cry from the earth' to God for vengeance against his brother's cruelty, Gen. iv. 10, so the voice of the poor and their piteous cries shall enter into the ears of the Lord; and their guiltless blood (which is poured forth in every place without all compassion) shall pull down hasty and sudden vengeance from heaven upon the heads of those unmerciful cormorants, unless, while this time of mercy lasteth, they shew mercy to their distressed neighbours.

Thus you have heard how Zaccheus behaved himself in entertaining of Christ. Now you shall see the behaviour of the pharisees in disdaining at Christ. 'When all they saw it, they murmured, saying, that he was gone in to lodge with a sinful man.' Before, they hated Zaccheus for his vices, because he was covetous; now they envy him for his virtues, because he was given to hospitality. For the wicked will have always something to find fault with in the children of God, like the sons of Jacob, Gen. xxxvii., that hated their brother Joseph because of his dreams; and like Saul, that unhappy king, that envied David for his happy victories, 1 Sam. xviii. 8. Thus the wicked, when they cannot charge the godly with any grievous crime, they begin to grudge at their well doing. And therefore not only Zaccheus is hated for receiving of Christ, but Christ is hated also for being his guest. When they could not accuse Christ for sin, they accuse him for accompanying with sinners. For they must be still accusing some or other for one thing or other, like their father the devil, that both by name, Rev. xii. 10, and by nature, Job i., is a continual 'accuser of the brethren.' It had been the duty of the pharisees to have received Christ, and made much of him, as Zaccheus did. But they are so far off from entertaining him themselves, that it grieveth them to see Zaccheus give him entertainment. And surely such is the perverse nature of the wicked, that they will neither receive the grace of God when it is offered them, nor willingly suffer any other to embrace the same ; like the wicked Jews, Acts xiii. 50, that would neither believe the doctrine that Paul preached, nor could abide that the Gentiles should be brought to the faith of Christ. The high priests thought themselves too high to have poor humble Christ amongst them ; the scribes and the pharisees in their own conceit were too good, too wise, and too holy to receive him into their company ; and not content to sequester and estrange themselves from Christ, they disdained also that he should be conversant with publicans and sinners, as though he were not worthy to be conversant amongst them.

If it were the office of Christ to convert sinners, why should the pharisees be offended at him, if he were sometimes conversant with sinners to work their conversion ? Mat. ix. 13. If Christ were a physician to cure the sickness of the soul, that is, to save the people from their sins, ver. 12, why should the pharisees murmur at him for keeping of company with Zaccheus, that was sick in soul? For as it is expedient for the physician to visit his patients for their better recovery, so it was convenient Christ should visit sinners for their speedy conversion. But as the physician that resorteth unto sick persons is not straightway infected, so the soul's physician that converseth with sinners is not thereby polluted. And therefore, as Christ performed his office, though the pharisees murmured ; so let the ministers of God learn by this example, to perform their duties, though the wicked be offended. It was the office of Christ, 'to call sinners to repentance,' Luke v. 32. Yea, he came to call pharisee sinners as well as publican sinners, if the pharisees would have confessed themselves to be sinners as the publicans did ; but because they stood so much upon their own righteousness, and despised others, Luke xviii., therefore Christ denounced so many woes against them, Mat. xxiii., and preferreth the penitent publican, that trusted in the Lord's mercy, before the proud pharisee, that trusted in his own merits.

Though Paul was 'a pharisee, and the son of a pharisee,' Acts

xxiii. 6, yet he shameth not to confess himself one of the 'chief sinners' that Christ came to save, 1 Tim. i. 15 ; so if the pharisees that murmured at Zaccheus would have been saved, they should have confessed themselves chief sinners, as Paul did. They should not have accused Christ for keeping company with sinners, but they should have accused themselves for not keeping company with Christ. 'The just man,' saith Solomon, 'is the first accuser of himself,' Prov. xviii. 17 ; but the pharisees are so far from accusing themselves, that they began to accuse Zaccheus and Christ together. Thus the pharisees of our time, that make religion a cloak to cover their corrupt dealing, have this property, to think other men to be heinous sinners, and themselves only to be righteous; insomuch as they will not stick to speak like that proud people, that was wont to say, 'Depart from me, for I am holier than thou ;' and like the presumptuous pharisee, Luke xviii. 11, 'I thank God, I am not as others are, extortioners, usurers, adulterers,' drunkards, or such like. I sanctify the Sabbath, which other men profane ; I frequent sermons, which they neglect ; I reverence the name of God, which they blaspheme ; I pay tithes, which others withhold ; and fast oftentimes, which they do seldom or never. These were the speeches of the pharisees that lived in the time of Christ, whom he so often calleth hypocrites, Mat. xxiii., Luke xi. ; and these are the speeches of the hypocrites of our age, that seem to live 'after the straitest sect of our religion,' Acts xxvi. 5. They 'wash the outside of the cup and of the platter,' Luke xi. 3, Mat. xviii. 25 ; that is, they justify themselves and seem marvellous holy in the sight of men, which can discern by the outward appearance only ; but unto God, that seeth and searcheth the secrets of the hearts and reins, they 'appear like painted tombs, full of dead men's bones and all filthiness,' Mat. xxiii. 27, that is, they have their inward parts full of ravening and all kind of wickedness. Wherefore, as Christ said to his disciples, Mat. v. 20, 'Except your righteousness exceed the righteousness of the scribes and pharisees, you cannot enter into the kingdom of heaven ;' so I say unto you, that except your righteousness exceed the righteousness of these pharisaical hypocrites, ye cannot be saved.

These holy pharisees did use to call the publicans, not usurers, nor extortioners, as they themselves were, but by the general name of *sinners*, as though they themselves were free from sin. Thus the papists at this day do not call the most sincere professors of the gospel, Lutherans, Calvinists, Zwinglians, or protestants, as they were wont to call them; but now they term us *heretics*, a name more odious than any other, whereas in the mean season they themselves are of all others the greatest heretics. So the atheists of our time, when they cannot accuse the godly that are amongst us of usury, or bribery, or extortion, or drunkenness, or any such notorious sin, they call them *hypocrites*, which is the sum of all, whenas in very truth they themselves do best deserve that name. But it makes no matter what they call us, neither are we to be moved at their despiteful speeches; for as the bitter taunts of these murmuring pharisees could not hinder Zaccheus in his conversion, so the slanders of these godless men must not discourage the servants of God from their good profession. The pharisees did Zaccheus great wrong in calling him *sinner*, when he had repented of his sin; and the atheists at this day do greatly wrong the true professors in calling them *hypocrites*, which have truly repented of their former sins, and endeavour by all good means to lead a godly life. Therefore as Zaccheus preferred his soul's health before all their murmuring, so it behoveth us to look to our soul's salvation, notwithstanding all the reproaches and slanders that are devised against us. And as the pharisees might call Zaccheus *sinner*, but could not hinder his conversion, so the malicious worldlings may take away our goods or good names, yea, and our lives also, but cannot deprive us of our salvation.

Wherefore, as our Saviour said to his apostles, Mat. x. 28, 'Fear not them that can kill the body,' and then can do no more; so I say unto you, Fear not the frowns of the wicked, for they are not able to hurt your better part; seek not to gain the favour of the world, for the whole world is not able to save a soul; but fear to offend 'him that is able to destroy body and soul in hell,' and seek to please him that is able to save them both in heaven for ever.

Now followeth another fruit of Zaccheus's conversion, namely, his good confession; for as he 'believed with his heart unto righteousness, so he confessed with the mouth unto salvation,' Rom. x. 10. When Zaccheus was mocked of the pharisees, it seemeth that he should stoop down for shame; but when he was thus reproved and reviled by them, the Scripture saith that he stood up, in sign of gladness. As the apostles 'went away rejoicing that they were counted worthy to suffer rebuke for the name of Christ,' Acts v. 41; so Zaccheus the publican went forth rejoicing that he was reproached for the cause of Christ. Before, Zaccheus was a publican, and therefore stood in sin very dangerously, like the house that is builded upon the sand, ready to be overturned with every tempest;

but now Zaccheus is become a true Christian, and therefore stands in righteousness very safely, like the house that is built upon a rock, free from any danger of falling, Luke vi. 48, 49.

Behold, Lord, the half of my goods, &c. There are two parts of his confession. The first is, his gift to the poor; the second is, the restitution of his unjustly gotten goods. Before, Zaccheus was an oppressor of the poor, now he is a great benefactor to the poor; before, he was an encroacher upon other men's goods, now he is a distributer of his own goods; before, he was a receiver and a taker, now he is a restorer and a giver; neither doth he give sparingly, but he 'giveth liberally, laying up a good foundation against the time to come,' 1 Tim. vi. 18, 19; Mat. xxvi. 7.

Now, Zaccheus found that precious pearl, and for joy thereof he is content, not to sell, but to give all that he hath to enjoy the same, Mat. xiii. 45, 46. When the rich ruler, in the former chapter, was willed to 'sell all that he had, and give it to the poor, he went away very sorrowful, for he was very rich,' Luke xviii. 22, 23; but Zaccheus, perhaps as rich as he, is content of his own accord, and unbidden, to bestow half his goods upon the poor, and that with a cheerful mind. If Zaccheus had given only the third part of his goods, no doubt but Christ would have accepted it, for he accepted the widow's farthing, because it was given with a willing mind, Luke xxi. 3; but if he had 'given all his goods to feed the poor,' as the pharisees gave their alms, to be seen of men, yea, or 'his body to be burned,' as some Romans have done, to get renown, it should have been done to no purpose, because it was done to a wrong end, 1 Cor. xiii. 3.

Now, as Zaccheus was rich in the goods of this life, so was he rich in faith also; neither was it an idle or dead faith that Zaccheus had, but it was a fruitful and lively faith, 'a faith that worketh and laboureth by love,' Gal. v. 6, such as is required at the hands of Christians. St James saith, 'Shew me thy faith by thy works;' and here Zaccheus doth shew his faith by his works. Before, he was exercised in ungodly works, which are the fruits of infidelity; but now he is exercised in the works of mercy, which are the fruits of a lively faith. Zaccheus is very liberal in relieving the poor, but he is liberal of that which is his own, so there are many now-a-days that are very liberal, but it is of that which is none of theirs; for as Nadab and Abihu offered strange fire unto the Lord, Lev. x. 1, so these men offer strange goods unto the Lord. There are some amongst us that think to make amends for their unjust dealing, giving part of that to some good uses which they have gotten

by bad means; if they have gotten a pound by usury and oppression, they are content perhaps to give a penny to relieve the poor.
But as it was not lawful for the Israelites to bring the price of the
hire of an harlot into the house of the Lord, Deut. xxiii. 18, so it
is not lawful for us to apply the gain of our ill-gotten goods to the
service of God.

The half of my goods I give, &c.   Zaccheus saith not, *I have
given,* as an upbraider of God; or, *I will give,* as a delayer that
means to give away his goods after his death, when he can keep
them no longer; but he saith, *I give,* to signify that his will is his
deed, and that he meaneth not to take any days of payment for the
matter; for as before he ran apace to see Christ, and came down
hastily to entertain Christ in his own person, so doth he here give
quickly to relieve Christ in his needy members.   This is Zaccheus's
last will and testament that he maketh before his death, and seeth
the same proved and performed before his eyes.   If, therefore, we
desire to do any good to any of our poor brethren, let us learn of
Zaccheus to do it quickly while we are alive, for time will prevent us,
and death will prevent us.   I know there be many that would be
willing to give some part of their goods to the poor before their
death, as Zaccheus did, but that they know not what need themselves may have thereof before they die; and therefore, for the
most part, they will hardly forsake or leave their goods, till their
goods forsake and leave them.   But herein they shew themselves
to doubt of God's providence, and as it were to distrust his payment, who hath promised to 'repay whatsoever is given unto the
poor,' as it were lent unto himself, Prov. xix. 17; and that not
secretly, though they did their alms never so secretly, but the Lord
'will reward them openly,' as our Saviour speaketh, Mat. vi. 4.   The
wise preacher, Eccles. xi. 1, willeth us to 'cast our bread upon the
waters,' that is, to be liberal to the poor, whose watery eyes bewray
their great necessity, or, as others expound it, to hazard and adventure some of our goods upon our needy brethren, as merchants do
adventure their goods upon the seas; for although they may seem
to be in great peril and danger of perishing in the waters, yet commonly it falleth out that, by the blessing of God, they return with
greater profit.   So, albeit the relief that is bestowed upon our distressed neighbours may seem to be lost, yet, as the wise man saith,
after a time we shall find it again.   And as the precious oil descended from Aaron's beard to the skirts of his clothing, Ps. cxxxiii. 2,
so certainly the oil of mercy and charity, which we pour into the
wounds of our distressed brethren, Luke x. 34, shall descend into

our own souls. And as the widow's oil was increased in the cruse, because she relieved the Lord's prophet, 1 Kings xvii., so shall this precious oil, bestowed upon the poor, be returned upon our heads in great measure. Thus is Zaccheus liberal, as you see, for he giveth away half his goods. But he gives it not to the rich, that might give to him again; but he gives it to the poor, that cannot requite him, to teach us upon whom we should bestow our alms. As God, that is rich in mercy, giveth all things unto us that cannot requite him, so the rich men of this world, if they have any spark of mercy in them, should give unto the poor that cannot requite them. But amongst us, in every place almost, it is far otherwise; for if anything be to be given, not they that are poorest and stand in greatest need, but they that can make best friends are best preferred. Thus Dives is still enriched, and Lazarus is still rejected, Luke xvi. If we send to a great man, we send an ox for a present; but if we send to a poor man, we send a crust for an alms. Therefore, as Christ said to the Jews, that 'the Ninevites should rise in judgment against them, because they repented at Jonas's preaching,' Mat. xii. 41; so it may be said unto us, that Zaccheus shall rise in judgment against us, and condemn us, for he shewed great mercy upon the poor, but we are void of all compassion.

Thus you have heard the first part of Zaccheus's confession, wherein you see his liberality to the poor. Now you shall hear the second part of his confession, wherein he promiseth restitution of his unjustly gotten goods. Before, Zaccheus gave to the poor the half of that which was his own; now, he restoreth that which is none of his to the right owners. And because he had detained their goods so long, to their great loss and hindrance, therefore he doth not only restore the principal, which he had taken from them, but he alloweth them their costs and damages that they had sustained. As Joram, king of Israel, caused to be restored to the Shunammite her house and land, and all the fruits and profits of the same, which were wrongfully kept from her seven years together, 2 Kings viii. 6; so Zaccheus the customer restoreth to those that he had oppressed, their goods which he had gotten from them by fraudulent dealing with all the fruits and profits that might come thereof during the time of his unjust possession. So liberal was Zaccheus to the poor, that he gave them half his goods; and so little got Zaccheus by his usury and oppression, that for every penny he restoreth four. If the usurers and extortioners of our time would restore fourfold for that they have wrongfully gotten, I fear they would have but a small half to give to the poor, and but a little left to help them-

selves.   There was no law to compel Zaccheus to make such restitution, except he will confess himself to be a thief because he was
an usurer, and then the law of God requireth such restitution.   And
surely Zaccheus seemeth after a sort to confess his theft, because
he promiseth fourfold restitution.   If a man had stolen a sheep,
the law of God requireth that he should restore four sheep for one,
Exod. xxii. 1, 2 Sam. xii. 6 ; and the ancient Romans had this law,
that usurers should forfeit four times so much as they took for
usury.   If the same law were now to use against our thievish
usurers, as it was sometime among them, we should not have such
complaining of the poor, both in prisons and streets.   But if these
great thieves (I mean our biting usurers), that rob and spoil without ceasing when they have no need, might find no more favour
than those petty thieves which rob and steal sometime when they
are driven unto it by extreme necessity ; then, surely, the commonwealth would soon be disburdened of that pestilent brood of caterpillers wherewith it is pestered.   I wish them betimes to look to
their own estate, and with Zaccheus to forsake their damnable trade.
If they have lived hitherto by the gain of usury, let them now
lament their sin, and call to God for mercy and forgiveness ; let
them make restitution of that they have wrongfully taken, and
grieve that they have so long detained that which is none of theirs.
For as no sin is pardoned without repentance to God, so usury is
not pardoned without repentance to God ; and as the sin of theft
is not removed before restitution be made to men (if the party be
able), so the sin of usury, which is a secret theft, is not remitted
before restitution be made to those that are oppressed and spoiled
by this secret theft.

Thus you have seen how Zaccheus, that was once a hoarder of his
goods, as our rich men are, is now a liberal disposer of his goods, as
I wish they were.   He that lately was a camel laden with riches,
and therefore unapt to go through a needle's eye, Mat. xix. 24, hath
now, like the camel, cast off his rich lading, and therefore may
enter in at the narrow gate, Mat. vii. 14.   Some rich men would
rather have lost their lives than foregone their goods, and for half
that loss would have proved very pensive ; but this was the joy-
fullest news that ever came to Zaccheus's house, sweeter to him than
all his gold and silver : that whereas before he was in the state of
damnation, now salvation is promised to him and his house ; and
whereas before he was the servant of Satan, now he is become the child
of Abraham.   Now Zaccheus's house is become God's house, and Zaccheus himself is the son of Abraham, and therefore no cause why

Christ should not resort to Zaccheus's house. As Christ said to the penitent thief, Luke xxiii. 43, 'This day thou shalt be with me in paradise;' so he saith here to the penitent publican, 'This day salvation is come unto thy house,' and this day thou art become 'the child of Abraham.' Christ loves not to be long in any man's debt; for as he saith to Zaccheus, 'To-day I must abide at thy house,' so he saith to the same Zaccheus, To-day and henceforth for ever thou and thy house must abide with me in heaven. Here is a happy change: instead of a little worldly treasure, subject to loss by thieves, and to spoil by rust and moth, to have all store of heavenly treasure, which neither thieves can steal, nor canker can corrupt, Mat. vi. 19, 20; instead of an earthly house, subject to fire and falling, to have a house given of God, 'not made with hands, but eternal in heaven,' 2 Cor. v. 1. Who would not rather choose, with Zaccheus, to give half of his goods to the poor, that he may be an heir of salvation, and the son of Abraham, to rest in his Father's bosom, than, with Dives, to keep all from the poor, and be tormented in those eternal flames? Luke xvi. That rich glutton that denied the crumbs from his table, challenged Abraham for his father; but he was refused, because he had not the faith nor works of Abraham. But Zaccheus, though by nature he were not the child of Abraham, yet by grace he is become the child of Abraham, because he walked in the steps of that faithful father, John viii. 39. Abraham believed before he was circumcised, Rom. iv. 12; so Zaccheus believed before he was circumcised. As Abraham left his country, and all that he had, when God called him, Gen. xii. 4, Acts vii. 3, 4; so Zaccheus left his office, and the most part of his riches, when he was called by the Son of God. And as Abraham desired to see the day of Christ, and saw it, and rejoiced, John viii. 56; so Zaccheus desired to see Christ, and he saw him, and rejoiced. Now is Zaccheus, a Gentile, become the child of Abraham; and not only he, but his whole house also is become the house of Abraham; for when Zaccheus is converted, his whole house is converted. As the master is, such are the servants; if he be godly and religious, they prove godly and religious; if he be an atheist, they prove atheists likewise. Therefore keep no company with the wicked, for it is most pernicious; but associate thyself with those that fear the Lord, that thou also mayest learn to fear the Lord; who for his mercy grant that we may with Zaccheus be desirous to see Christ, joyful to receive Christ, liberal to receive the members of Christ, and ready to make amends when we have wronged any of our brethren; that so, with Zaccheus, we may be heirs of salvation, and the true sons of Abraham, to reign with Christ in heaven for ever, by the means and merits of Him that died and rose again for us. To whom with the Father and the Holy Ghost be all glory. Amen.

THE SWEET SONG OF OLD FATHER SIMEON.

IN TWO SERMONS.

THE SWEET SONG OF OLD FATHER SIMEON.

THE FIRST SERMON.

Lord, now lettest thou thy servant depart in peace, according to thy word. For mine eyes have seen thy salvation, which thou hast prepared before the face of all people; a light to be revealed to the Gentiles, and the glory of thy people Israel.—LUKE II. 29–32.

THIS is the sweet song of old father Simeon, wherein is set forth the joyful and peaceable death of the righteous, after that they have embraced Christ Jesus with heart and mind unfeignedly, as he did, seeing their death is to be the beginning of a better and more joyful and pleasant life than the former.

But before we proceed farther in it, let us hear a little of that which went before. The evangelist saith, ver. 25, &c., 'And, behold, there was a man in Jerusalem, whose name was Simeon; this man was just, and feared God, and waited for the consolation of Israel, and the Holy Ghost was upon him. And a revelation,' &c.

Simeon feared God. Religion may well be called fear, for there is no religion where fear is wanting; for 'the fear of the Lord is the beginning of wisdom,' Prov. i. 7. And this privilege hath God given to those that fear him, that they need to fear nothing else.

And waited for the consolation of Israel. Simeon also waited for the consolation of Israel, until he had embraced in his arms him whom he so long longed to see and feel. How many waiters be there in the world! yet few wait as Simeon did; but some wait for honour, some for riches, some for pleasures, some for ease, some for rewards, some for money, some for a dear year, and some for a golden day, as they call it; but Simeon waited, and expected with many a long look, until he had seen and embraced Christ Jesus, the light of the Gentiles, the glory of Israel, the salvation of all that with a faithful and zealous affection and love do wait for his coming, to the comfort of the afflicted, and to the terrifying of the wicked and ungodly, which have not already waited, neither embraced him, as Simeon did.

And waited for the consolation of Israel. Faith in all afflictions doth lift up her head, waiting in assured hope beyond all hope; and seeing the clouds scattered over her head, yet she is ever comfortable to herself, saying, Anon it will be calm; and although all the friends in the world do fail, yet it never faileth nor fainteth, but ever keepeth promise in that which by the verity of the Spirit of God it assureth, until her joy be fulfilled. 'All are not Israelites that are born of Israel,' Rom. ix. 6. Simeon was an Israelite indeed, for he waited for the Messias from God with patience and expectation; so the Spirit of God dwelleth always with them which always say, 'Thy will be done.'

And a revelation was given him. If we wait as he did, the Spirit will assure us, as it did him, that we shall see God before we die; and they that long in faith to see the joys of heaven, the Spirit assureth and promiseth faithfully unto them that they shall see them.

And he came by the motion of the Spirit into the temple. Simeon came into the temple at this time by the providence of God. The worldlings will call it chance, but the evangelist would not chop that in, because it is manifest that all things come to pass by the providence of God, without which there is nothing done, Mat. x. 29. By this providence Rebekah came forth to wait on her father's cattle, when Abraham's servant prayed, and looked for her coming, that he might take her for Isaac to marry withal, Gen. xxiv. 14, &c. By this providence Saul was anointed king by Samuel, when he had no such thought in his heart, but went about seeking for his father's asses that were lost, 1 Sam. ix. 20, and x. 1.

And he came by the motion of the Spirit. The devil led Christ unto the top of an high mountain, that he might shew him the glory of the world, which deceiveth unstable minds; so would he do you, if you would be led by such a guide. But I would not have you to mark the vain motions of such a spirit, which leads to nothing but to vanity and pride; for after he hath led you to the top, and allured you by carnal pleasures as much as he can, if you then fall down to worship mammon, and embrace the world, the same spirit will afterward lead you, nay, rather cast you down from the top of all unto hell. Therefore, I beseech you, and heartily entreat you, that you would be the servants of God, and servants of the Spirit of God, to be led by it, to obey it, and to do nothing contrary to his will that you can refrain, but all those good things which you would were done by you, and go thither whither you would come; for all would come to heaven, but all will not not go to heaven. If you will all hear, I will teach you all; yea, I will undertake this, hear and mark my words, and you shall be led by the power of the Spirit to our Lord Jesus Christ. And I pray to the Lord that I may never preach to the condemnation of any among you all; yea, I wish that every one of you were more zealous and more godly than myself. But to whom shall I compare you? even to the vagabond Jews, of whom Luke mentioneth in the Acts, chap. xix. 13–16, that they 'took upon them to adjure evil spirits by the name of Jesus, whom Paul preached. To whom the evil spirits answered, saying, Jesus we know, and Paul we know; but who are ye? And those which had the evil spirits ran upon them and overcame them, so that they fled out of that house naked and wounded.' And thus the devil prevailed against them at that time, because they sought to work with another's instrument, and prevail with another's weapon. If they would have said, 'In the name of Jesus, whom we preach,' they might have prevailed; but they thought it sufficient that Paul preached him, though they never professed him. And so we lean upon another's staff, and think to be saved, because God saveth others. We shall be dealt withal as were those vagabond Jews; for he will answer, Such I know, and such I know, but who are ye? Therefore it behoveth us all to pray unto the Lord, that he would furnish us with weapons to encounter against all the evil motions of the spirit of Satan, that we may overcome, and not be overcome and put to flight, like those vagabond Jews; but that we may have oil always in our lamps burning, and be always armed with watchfulness against our enemy, lest Satan steal upon us unawares in the dark, and lead us to fulfil his lusts, and spoil us, and strip us, and leave us stark naked.

And he came by the motion of the Spirit into the temple, &c. If we would think that his Spirit doth lead us into the temple, we would mark very diligently the motions thereof when we are there, whether it speaketh to us in our own souls by the mouth of the minister of God, who is the minister, not of the letter, but of the Spirit and grace of God.

And when the parents brought in the child Jesus to do for him according to the customs of the law, then he took him in his arms.

Happy Simeon embracing Christ; but not happy that he embraced him with his hands; but therefore happy, because he embraced him in heart. 'Happy are the eyes and blessed which see the things that ye see, and the ears that hear the things that ye hear,' saith Christ, Mat. xiii. 16; but cursed are we that hearing and seeing do not repent; for we cannot be blessed by hearing and seeing only, unless we hear and see with profit, so that we in heart embrace Christ. But we will object that we are Israelites, and are circumcised, and have received the sacrament of Christ's blood, that we might be his people, and he our God. But this will not excuse us, nor make us seem any thing better in the sight of God, but rather worse, if we have not ceased to embrace the world, to embrace vanities, and have not unfeignedly embraced the word of God, and also the Lord Jesus Christ. For it is said, that Christ 'came amongst his own, and his own received him not,' John i. 11; but therefore accursed are so many of them as reject their own salvation, which being freely offered unto them, they will not stretch forth their hands to receive it; that is, will not attend with their ears to hear it, or at least will not enlarge their hearts to embrace it.

And praised. If Samuel had heard the first time that God called him, then God needed not to call him the second or third. If Peter had marked the crowing of the cock at the first time, as he did at the third, Luke xxii., the cock needed not to crow thrice. Now therefore, when you hear the same sound again which you have heard before, remember now that the cock croweth the second time; for you know what discommodity doth come by negligence, and what commodity by attention. For if you attend and follow, justice shall be swallowed up of mercy.

Simeon praised God. Simeon was thankful. Here is the example, but where be they that follow it? If nine lepers be cleansed, yet but one returneth to give thanks; then one is all. Unthankfulness is the first guest that sitteth at the table; for some will not stick to say, that they never said grace since they were children; but if they had said, they never had grace since they were children, I would rather believe them. Do you not say, 'Give us this day our daily bread?' If you do, for shame say so no more, beg no more at God's hands, until you be more thankful for that you have received. For, behold, the heaven frowns upon you for your sins, and the earth denieth her fruit, and is become barren, because of your unthankfulness, Lev. xxvi. 19, 20.

And praised God, and said, &c. Here Simeon prayed and

praised God, yet but in few words; for God delights not in much babbling. He prayed not like the Ethnicks, the pharisees, or the priests of Baal; but Simeon prayed with the heart, like Moses, and was heard.

And said. He joyfully praising God spake, yea, sweetly as it were sung it. Though you sing all David's psalms over, and have not David's spirit, it profiteth nothing; and though David was heard when he sung them, yet you cannot be heard. Therefore let us pray so that our prayers may be heard. But we cannot with the heart, and so that we may be heard, pray, if we turn away our ears from the word; for so doing, whatsoever prayers we make, they are abominable, Prov. xxviii. 9. Therefore let us hear so, that hearing we may profit by it. Let us not hear still so unprofitably as we were wont to do; if we do, it shall be required at our hands. Do you think you shall never be called to account of that which I have preached unto you? And therefore as soon as ye are gone out of this place, all is shut up, and all is forgot, God is exempted from your minds. Our Saviour Christ saith, 'The word I speak unto you shall judge you at the last day,' John xii. 48. Mary is commended for that she heard our Saviour very diligently, laying up his words in her heart, Luke x. 39, 42; and Jacob was wiser than all his children, in that he remembered the dream of Joseph until he saw it fulfilled. Those that love the Lord with an unfeigned love do gladly hear his voice, and become obedient. 'My sheep hear my voice,' saith Christ, John x. 27; and they that love the ark as David did, will dance about the ark as David did, and that with joy and gladness, 2 Sam. vi. 14. Isaac was a good man, his name signifieth *laughter*, Gen. xxi. 6; whereby was shewed what joy and laughter there should be about Christ Jesus; for he was the figure, the truth was Christ himself. The virgin sung when she knew that she should bear him, Luke i. 46; the angels sung joyfully when he was born, Luke ii. 13, 14; and Simeon sung when he was brought into the temple.

If Simeon had not longed, and so waited for the consolation, should he now have had this joy and exultation? He could not have felt it; for as our desire is, so is our joy. And surely, therefore, we receive not sound comfort, or feel small joy, by the preaching of the gospel, because we with longing wait not for it; we have no lively desire of it; we hunger and thirst not after it.

Lord, now lettest thou thy servant depart. Simeon, waiting for the consolation of Israel, longing to see the Saviour, was like the hart panting for the water-brooks, till he had beheld his best beloved ; but as soon as he had taken him in his arms whom his soul desired to see, he so thirsted for death, that he thenceforth thought of, sought after, besought God for, nothing, but to leave this life, and hence to depart ; for he forthwith, singing, prayed, 'Now lettest thou thy servant depart.' But do you, say some, commend him herein ? did he well ? May not any man desire death ? May not the fastened ship in a strange land desire to be loosed, to hasten to his longed-for port at home ? May not a man imprisoned amongst bitter enemies desire to be set at liberty, to return to his own country, in freedom to live amongst his sweet friends ? Are we not strangers here, and by unpeaceable, most deadly enemies, our own flesh, the world, and the devil, held prisoners in the chains of sin and manifold infirmities ? and is not our home heaven, and the saints and angels our most dear friends ? No marvel, then, that Simeon here desireth to be loosed, or let depart. And Paul professeth he desireth to be dissolved, Philip. i. 23, or unloosed, as ships in a strange land fastened, as strangers amongst cruel enemies imprisoned. They were unnatural if they did not ; it were unreasonable to require they should not ; for we not only may think it lawful, but must also acknowledge it even a necessary duty, to desire death. For is there till then in us any perfect, yea, any pure obedience of God ? Doth not sin, as long as this life lasteth, dwell in our members ? Is there any passage to the perfect life but by the first death ? The fish which is taken in the net out of the sea struggleth to get in again ; and Adam, thrust out of paradise, would fain have been within again : how much more should we be desirous to be settled in the new paradise, in assurance never to be put from thence ? Therefore also it is not only our duty to desire death, but also as soon as any clearly seeth Christ, presently he desireth to die. For though his state be never so pleasant, though his life be most delightful, though he excel in riches, and pleasures, and honours, and knowledge, and glory, and far exceed all that ever were ; yet at the sight of Christ he even rejoiceth to forego all ; the love of the world falling away like the mantle of Elias, when he was rapt into heaven ; and so crieth with the apostle, 'I desire to be dissolved,' that he may be with Christ. For Christ is light, and as soon as they see him, they see also themselves, and the world's false happiness ; his glory, and their shame and filthiness, which maketh them wish for death, that they may cease to sin against God, and perfectly please him, and enjoy true happiness with him ; for all sin is blood in their eyes, and all worldly pleasures vanities.

But why then, say you, have Heman the Ezrahite, Ps. lxxxviii. 15, &c.; and Hezekiah that godly king, Isa. xxxviii. 10, &c.; and that man after God's own heart, the sweet singer of Israel, David, Ps. vi. 4, and xxx. 8, 9, so prayed, and taught others to pray, against death? Why? Because they all were, and would have others to be, in the fervent love of God, both to die and to live desirous; to live, that they might amongst men uphold and further the true worship of God, so to save their brethren's souls, and advance the glory of God the more; to die, that they might, perfectly obeying God, fully please him, and freed from all evil, enjoying all good, with him most blessedly live. For not only the apostle Paul, but all these, and whosoever is grounded in the faith of Christ, but especially all that have strong hope to advance the honour of God, are in a strait, as the apostle speaketh, Philip. i. 23, and crushed on both sides, even with two contrary desires; to be with Christ, which is best of all for themselves; and to continue amongst men, which is most needful for them, So that this remaineth still a manifest and most necessary duty, and of all that have truly, as Simeon, believed in Christ, performed; namely, thenceforth still to be desirous of death, though they also withal desire life, life for others, death for themselves.

Yet all that desire death perform not a duty; for the wicked often desire to die, but not duly; for though they wish sometimes for it, and be willing also to abide it, yet do they not in heart desire it, because they think it is not a thing in the ordinance of God good, and that for them, but utterly hate it, holding it an extreme evil. For they acknowledge, as the truth is, it will deprive them of all their delights which here they desire; and they cannot but at least fear it will take from them all pleasure, and bring them to easeless, and yet endless, pain, and torments intolerable, and yet unspeakable. For the sentence of the unchangeable God is already given: 'The fearful, and unbelieving, and the abominable, and murderers, and whoremongers, and sorcerers, and idolaters, and liars, shall have their part in the lake which burneth with fire and brimstone: which is the second death,' Rev. xxi. 8. And the just judge shall say to all workers of iniquity, 'Go, ye accursed, into hell fire, prepared for the devil and his angels,' Mat. xxv. 41; hell fire, 'where the worm never dieth, and the fire never goeth out,' Mark ix. 41, 44, 48. Whereupon this the prophet avoucheth, 'There is no peace to the wicked, saith my God,' Isa. lvii. 21. For in their strong hope they feel a stinging fear, their greatest confidence is not without trembling of conscience. Therefore, fearing the event of death to be for them, as indeed it is, most horrible, they utterly abhor it, they detest it extremely. How then, say some, should they seek death so eagerly? How should they murder themselves so willingly? They do it not altogether willingly, but wittingly; not freely, but forced with fear of some supposed greater evil. The troubles of this world, the anguish of body, the horror of mind, they are most impatient of, they cannot, they will not endure them; and thereupon they sometimes prefer death before life, less willing to live in vexation, than dying to try whether they shall feel what they fear, even deserved damnation. For they are never willing to die, but unwilling to live often; and so work themselves endless woe, in hope of supposed happiness; abhorring life, not truly desiring death. For how die they when they most voluntarily bereave themselves of life? Not in love of God, longing to please him, performing all service to him; but either in pain of body, or else anguish of mind; either raging that they cannot satisfy their lusts, or have lost outward things immoderately loved; fearing, if they die, deserved torments; if they live, they shall either continue in felt horror, or lose hoped-for honour; either impatient of God's rod, fretting against him that they so heavily feel his fury, and cannot fiercely fulfil their malicious minds, or freely feed on the rest of their fleshly lusts, or impotent in their desire of some false fondly-conceived good; hoping, with dreadful doubting, by death to better their state; that choose rather to prove the truth of God's threats, and of the terrors of their trembling minds, than in life to remain any longer; rather abhorring life, than any way truly desiring death. Therefore, in that Simeon duly desired death, that which we heard of Simeon in the beginning is proved true, to wit, that he was 'just, and feared God.'

For none but the truly righteous, none but they that by faith are assured they are before God righteous, can rightly desire death. For who would desire a change but for the better? But all that are ignorant of God, all the unfaithful, what knowledge soever they have, cannot be in better ease dead than they are now in living, though most miserably pained; nay, they cannot be without just fear, when they forego this life, to feel for ever the second death. But the faithful, having their consciences quiet, and also joyful in Christ, free from the fear of that death they have deserved, and assured by death to pass to that life which God to all the faithful hath promised, earnestly wish to die, in all fervent love of God, and zeal of his glory, that so they may cease from offending their good God, and never cease magnifying his mercy; shewing thereby that they are weary of the service and bondage of Satan and sin, and assured after death to enjoy the true life, most fully glorifying God, and most perfectly pleasing him for ever; and therefore also they desire death, not shortening their life, but waiting his leisure and calling, thereby glorifying God, as in their lives they have done and sought to do.

For man was not born at his own will, and therefore may not die at his own pleasure. Therefore they beg it of God, referring themselves ever to his good will, when, where, and how by death they shall glorify him, still desiring it, but never wilfully procuring it.

If any object that Samson plucked the house on his own head as well as on the Philistines, we must understand that Samson was a figure of Christ, and therefore as it were offering himself to God a sacrifice, first prayed, and then glorified God at his death more than in all his life, in killing so many of God's enemies. And because they wait the Lord's leisure, they not only wilfully murder not themselves, but are careful also lest foolishly, unwittingly they hasten their end. For all they are guilty of their own blood, that either by foolhardy, rash, or unwise behaving, or with surfeits, drunkenness, or any intemperate using of themselves, shorten their life. Yea, though they tender their lives never so dear, yet are they guilty, because they willingly use the means that brings death.

Simeon had seen much in his many days; but when he saw Christ, he was unwilling to live any longer to see more. His desire is accomplished, his long longing at length is satisfied, his fervent expectation with free joy now fulfilled. It is enough, saith Simeon, that I have seen my Saviour; as Jacob said, 'It is enough that my son Joseph liveth,' Gen. xlv. 28. How much more then should we be satisfied with this, and in all thankfulness rest in it, that we have seen Christ, not, as Simeon, in weakness and baseness, but victorious, most glorious, over sin, death, and hell triumphing, and are more assured than Jacob was, that he, not as Joseph under Pharaoh in Egypt, liveth, but in heaven with his Father in highest majesty, reigneth Lord over all, having all power both in heaven and earth, Mat. xxviii. 18; and, moreover, where he is, thither shall we come, John xvii. 24, and be like him, 1 John iii. 2; and with him as fellow-heirs reign in the kingdom of our Father for ever, Rom. viii. 17.

Simeon knew Christ as soon as he saw him, and embraced him as soon as he knew him, and enjoyed him as soon as he embraced him. So some know the word of God as soon as they hear it, and believe it as soon as they know it, and feel the comfort of it as soon as they believe it; but others hear it as though they heard it not, like deaf adders, that stop their ears at the voice of the charmer. So Pharaoh would not hear the voice of Moses, Exod. v., &c., nor Baal's priests the voice of Elias, 1 Kings xviii. And others, though they know it, yet will not believe it; as if God were untrue. So all malicious wretches that prefer the pleasures of sin before the glory of God. And others, though they believe it, yet can they not, either presently or when they will, feel the comfort of it, much less the joy which is offered by it, namely, the heart-oppressed, the desolate afflicted soul.

The seed is not cast all on a heap, but is cast abroad; therefore where be the fruits of the Spirit that you have brought forth? For the Spirit of God is not like a dead potion in the stomach, which worketh not; neither can we have this Spirit in us and feel it not. For if thou hast it, it will lead thee, as it did longing Simeon (as we have hitherto seen), to the temple; and when thou art there, it will lead thee to Christ; and when thou hast received and embraced him, it will possess thee with joy, and so with thankfulness, and godly care to keep him, and to entertain him, and to be obedient unto him; nay, also with a longing to be loosed hence, and evermore perfectly to please him. Therefore, beloved, 'judge yourselves, that ye be not judged of the Lord.'

Thy servant. The godly would not leave this privilege for all the riches in the world; for that they are the servants of God, fellows to princes and angels; for we serve him whom David, Solomon, Hezekiah, Josiah served; yea, to whom a thousand thousand, Dan. vii. 10, even innumerable angels minister, Heb. xii. 22, even him who is most blessed for ever. Every serving man bears the cognizance of his master upon his sleeve. What then will the Lord say when he cometh and findeth us marked with the badge of Satan? Surely he will say, Give unto Satan that which is Satan's. But all the houses of Israel are sprinkled with the blood of the Lamb, Exod. xii. 22, 23, and all mourners in Jerusalem are marked, Ezek. ix. 4, and all the chosen are sealed with the seal of the living God, Rev. vii. 3, &c.

Well was it said, 'The poor receive the gospel.' The young men are more forward in the truth and more zealous than the aged, the son than his father, the servant than his master. Once the younger brother stole away the blessing from the elder, therefore the elder hated him even for his zeal. And when was Jacob hated more than he is now? When was he so hated and persecuted as he is now by Esau? Yet, in the old time, men were more zealous in their age than ever we hear of them to be in their youth ; yea, they were zealous in the Lord's business.

Age hindered not Noah from building of the ark when God commanded him, Gen. v. 32 and chap. vi. ; age hindered not Simeon from rejoicing and mirth when he beheld and embraced the Lord Jesus Christ. Then old Simeon embraced Christ, and he enjoyed him with hearty joy in zeal ; but now where is old Simeon ? There be but few of them to be seen coming to the temple to receive Christ ; but now young men receive him, young Simeons, young Daniels, Dan. i. 8 ; young Samuels, 1 Sam. iii. ; young Timothies, 1 Tim. iv. 12, 2 Tim. iii. 15 ; and young Onesimuses, Philem. 10 ; and the young infants begin to speak again, Mat. xxi. 15.

The young have him, they are zealous ; and I hope they will keep him, though old men neglect him. Satan, thou hast too much for nothing already.

In peace, &c. Christ brings peace with him, not the peace of the world, but that 'peace which passeth all understanding.' 'My peace I leave with you,' John xiv. 27. My peace remain with you, saith he. Our peace is laid up in Christ, and all the peace we have, we have by him, else it is not true peace. Simeon was just, and feared God in his life, and therefore he departed in peace. So mark the end of the just, Ps. xxxvii. 37, and follow their steps, and you shall then depart in peace, like the Lamb upon the cross.

Fain would Balaam die the death of the righteous, Num. xxiii. 10, but Balaam must then live the life of the righteous ; therefore, all men look to this. Happy are they that depart in peace; who, when death saith *fear*, and the serpent saith *despair*, they say by the Spirit to the flesh *crouch*, and bid the serpent fly, while death openeth the prison doors.

If the papists would have men to depart in peace, they would never say that those which depart go to purgatory, for so, by their own saying, the worst part is behind ; for they affirm that the pain thereof is far grievouser than any that in this life may be sustained. But again, some say this purgatory is in the earth, near to hell, and so it is too far from heaven to be saved. Some do say they are punished there by fire, and some say by water, and some say by fire and water. Some, lastly, do say that the good angels torment, and others say that the evil spirits do it. In this variety of most uncomfortable opinions, how is it possible hence to depart in peace ? But we must understand it is a painted sepulchre, made for the pampering of the living, not for the punishing or purifying of them that be dead. For the locusts of Rome do live altogether upon such trentals, and by such traditions; and this is the profitablest dream that ever any of them dreamed. But it is manifest by the word of God, that 'where the tree falleth, there it lieth,' and shall lie for ever, Eccles. xi. 3. Dives and Lazarus are dead, and where they are thither shall we all go, Luke xvi. 22. Satan hath many sleights to deceive us, of which this is one of the greatest, to bring us from the word of God to dreams and traditions, and things invented by the brains of mortal men, which have not the Spirit of God in them.

According to thy word. All the seed falleth not into good ground : and therefore though I have shewed you it is ungodly, as being not according to the word, some think it but a small matter to say for the dead, *Lord, have mercy upon them ;* at least they think it a venial sin, if it be a sin. But let us take heed how we make trifles of sins ; for there is no dallying with God, who is jealous as 'a consuming fire,' Heb. xii. 29, when his people make such small account of his words. Others demand whether it be not better to say, *God be with them,* than *The devil be with them,* both which are naught, and to be eschewed. And herein they ask this question like a thief, who, having robbed a man by the highway, and being taken with it, and demanded why he did such a villany, saith, Is it not better to rob him than to kill him ? as though he must needs do one of them. Then what a shameless answer is this, for it is manifest that of two evils none is to be chosen.

Some will say, It is a testimony of our good will. To such we must reply, saying, So it is a testimony of your ignorance. And then, after a little conference, they will grant that indeed it doth not profit them. Then we must reply, and say, God hath made all things to profit us, and hath commanded that nothing be used unprofitably, no, not so much as a vain word speaking, saying, that 'for every idle word we must give account at the day of judgment,' Mat xii. 36. Then they reply again, saying, If it do them no good, it doth them no harm. But we must answer, It were good to beware lest it do thyself harm.

Another sort will reply and say, I pray God I never do worse. But to such we must answer, I pray God you may do better ; and you should first know whether you do not harm, before you do it. For indeed it must proceed of harm, being spoken in doubting, without faith, Rom. xiv. 23. For if you believed that they were laid up in peace whom you pray for, what need you pray for them at all ? But it shews an unbelieving heart, and we know that 'whatsoever is not of faith is sin;' and the Lord will say of them, 'Who hath required these things at your hands?' you have wrought vanities. Now therefore you will not leave it, because you used it; then will you say also, We will not leave our lying, nor swearing, nor our cursing, because we have used it. It will grieve me if I hear you use these speeches hereafter, having no reason nor proof of Scripture to maintain it by, or to be your warrant in it; therefore I charge you in the name of God that you use them not; but rather, when you hear this or any other sin condemned, lay hands upon it, and see that you put it to death without delay, according to the law of God.

According to thy word. When Satan hath thus possessed us with this opinion, that in the service of God we may neglect the word of God, then profits and pleasures guide us in our profession; but they that do profess religion and godliness can never have any comfort by it all their life. For their own hearts accuse them for hypocrites, because they wait not for the consolation of God according to his word; and whatsoever is not done according to that word cannot be acceptable: and this word they care not for, neither have it in estimation. When Adam seeth his nakedness, the subtle serpent can deceive no longer; but before he seeth his nakedness, he is ever deceived, and led away with the multitude into innumerable errors. Some say they shall be saved by good works, and some by the pope's pardon, others say by purgatory; and these will have a mass sung for them as long as the world standeth, and all for one silly soul, thinking to be saved by it. And yet see their blindness; for they seem to think that their torment shall not cease as long as the world standeth, else why should they find and hire men to say mass for them so long? But these are the fat morsels of Baal's priests, and for this cause is the popish creed made very favourable to the clergy. Well say they that ignorance is the mother of devotion; for when the covetousness of the priests and the ignorance of the people joined together, then they invented purgatory, masses, prayer for the dead, and then all their trinkets. For if they had not held our fathers in ignorance, keeping them from the word, they would never have been papists. But when they cast a mist before the eyes of men, then the blind fell into the ditch, which doth contain so many gross corruptions.

For mine eyes have seen thy salvation. Because the Holy Ghost by inspiration had declared unto him that he should not die till he had seen Jesus Christ, therefore the same Spirit led him to the temple, and shewed that which it promised; and having seen the same, he desired and wished to die, and be released from his earthly prison, that he might live with God. As idle and evil wishes are vain, because they are not according to faith, nor grounded upon the word of God, so, though we ask as cunningly as Jacob, Gen. xxvii. 18, &c., and as earnestly as the sons of Zebedee, Mark x. 35, 37; yet, if we ask not in faith, according to knowledge, we cannot obtain. But we should ask so that we may receive, that we may not return empty, James i. 6, 7. Therefore the ground whereon Simeon settled himself to wish for death was, that he had received a promise of God that he should be delivered from this miserable life when he had once seen the light of the Gentiles, the Christ; and now he had seen his Saviour, and embraced the true Messiah, which was promised by the Father, figured in the law, and spoken of by the prophets, foretold by the fathers, and pointed at by John Baptist. For thus he reasoneth : Now that I see thy salvation according to thy word, and therefore the condition is now performed, let thy promise also be fulfilled, 'Now let thy servant depart,' &c. 'For mine eyes,' &c.

Mine eyes have seen, &c. Then we see that Christ was no spirit, neither was his body a fantastical body; for if he were a spirit, Simeon could not see him; and if his body were a fantastical body, then could not he have embraced him. Therefore we see that the words of the Scripture are true, which saith that Christ was perfect man in all things, sin only excepted. For he sometime wept, as at the death of Lazarus, John xi. 35, and likewise over Jerusalem, Luke xix. 41. Sometime he thirsted, as at the well where the woman of Samaria disputed with him, John iv. 7. And also sometime ate, as at Martha's house, Luke x. 38 ; as also among publicans and sinners, Luke v. 29. And in everything he shewed himself to be perfect man.

Have seen, &c. O Lord, saith he, I desire now to be dissolved and free from the bondage of sin, which so long hath inhabited in my mortal body ; for now he is come by whom thou hast promised to free us and set us at liberty ; he is come by whom thou hast promised to break the serpent's head ; and he is come that will heal our infirmities, and give strength against sin and Satan, by faith and peace towards God, through love. And now, saith he, I have embraced him, and thankfully do receive him. I believe and am persuaded that this is the same Messiah whom the Father promised, and the prophets foretold, all Israel longed for and expected, who is the light of the Gentiles, the glory of Israel, and the God of the whole world. So they which love the truth of God, and wait with desire to be fulfilled with the knowledge thereof, such shall not die until they have their hearts' desire with contemplation thereof. For as Peter was sent to Cornelius, Acts x., and Philip to the eunuch, Acts viii., so the Lord will stir up such of his servants as may be fit instruments to minister the same unto us. Judas, indeed, died before the time, and lived not to see Christ crucified; but the disciples which loved Jesus did see him die like an undefiled innocent lamb, and that to their exceeding joy and comfort, when they understood how that he suffered death for love of them, and for their redemption. Now if Christ cannot hide him from such as hunger after him through love, then what shall we say of our fathers, which lived in the time of ignorance, that longed to see his light, although they had a mist cast before their eyes? Surely such died not till they saw Christ, and embraced him in their hearts. And this is our judgment concerning them that died in the time of popery. And likewise as concerning the rest, which thought to be saved by purgatory and masses after that they were dead, we say that they which sleep without oil in their lamps, they die ere they are aware of, and ere they wish for it; like the Philistines, which sent for Samson to laugh and mock at him, and to sport themselves, upon whom the house fell and destroyed them all, Judges xvi.; or like the Egyptians, which thought that the waters had made passage for them as well as for the Israelites, Exod. xiv.; both which died in and for their security, because they were not watchful, nor prepared against the Lord called them.

Have seen thy salvation. Seeing now he is come for whom Simeon longed, what are the troubles that are past, and the sorrows that are come to an end? So when we have our desires accomplished, feeling the sound comforts of the gospel, what should we, how may we think, either on the length of time wherein we waited for them, or the tediousness, or also grievousness, of the troubles whereby we have obtained them?

Have seen thy salvation. As Moses died on the mount, where he saw the land of Canaan, Deut. xxxiv., so the godly die in the sight of God, and in the contemplation of his glory; like Stephen, who, at the very instant of his death, saw the heavens open, and Christ Jesus sitting at the right hand of his Father, Acts vii. 56; and like Simeon here, which desireth to be loosed, and no doubt shortly died, viewing joyfully, and so thankfully beholding, the Lord of life.

Beloved, you are not ignorant that the great day of the Lord is near at hand; and therefore they that have not yet seen Christ,

M

they that have not yet embraced him, but still sleep without oil in
their lamps, shall suddenly be overtaken without the wedding garment, and shall be cast into eternal torment for ever.

Have seen thy, &c. There be many sights of Christ; all go not
up to the mount, as Peter, James and John, Mat. xvii. 1; all see
not his face, with Moses, Exod. xxxiii.; all sleep not in his lap, with
John, John xiii. 23, xxi. 20; all are not taken up into heaven, like
Paul, 2 Cor. xii. 2; all embrace him not in their arms, with Simeon.
But as pleaseth God, so he sheweth himself unto us; and all that
love him, both see him and embrace him.

To some he shews himself as in a glass, to some generally, to
some particularly; some he calleth early, and some he calleth late;
and there is no hour in the day wherein he calleth not some to go
labour in his vineyard, Mat. xx. To some he sheweth himself by
angels, and to other some by visions. Abraham saw three angels,
Gen. xviii. 2, Lot saw but two, Gen. xix. 1, Manoah's wife saw but
one, Judges xiii. 3; and yet one was enough. It is said that Abraham saw Christ's days, John viii. 56; but we see him clearer than
Abraham, and clearer than John, if we believe in him as we should.
Some see Christ, and not his salvation; and some see his salvation,
and do not embrace it. We see Christ when we hear his word, and
we embrace his salvation when we believe it; they see him that
hear him, they embrace him that follow him. But how can they
believe the word of God which hear it not? how can they embrace
Christ which know him not? and all through ignorance, having not
the means to see him, because their leaders are either blind guides,
sleepy watchmen, or hireling shepherds. And surely it is a woful
case, when shepherds go to task, and let their own sheep alone
summer and winter. They shear them, but neither summer nor
winter do they feed them. How should those people under their
charge see Christ and his salvation, when they are so debarred of
wholesome food, and many thousands of their souls even starved to
death, because they have not the food that nourisheth the soul unto
salvation! And how many be there that are as old as Simeon, and
yet have not embraced Christ Jesus! Yea, they know him not
though they see him, neither do they wait for his coming, because
they have no desire to embrace him; and therefore they defer that,
and put it off from their youth to their middle age, from their
middle age to their old age, from their old age to death; and so
they can have no leisure in all their life to embrace him. But to
such as do seek him, and wait for him with unfeigned diligence, we
say as the angel said unto the woman at the sepulchre, 'Fear not,

you seek the Lord Jesus,' Mark xvi. 6. How is this world set to deceive us? We can find leisure to do evil at any time, but we can find no leisure all our life long to do good, that we may at length enjoy the true salvation.

I have somewhat to say to you of this parish. A dainty was prepared for you, and you let the strangers take it from you; you were required to a fast, and you did feast yourselves; you were required to come and pray unto the Lord, and to humble yourselves in his sight, that he may turn away his wrath from you; and you let the temple stand open and empty for your parts, and your shops were all open, and you were about your merchandise, forsaking God, and seeking to win the unjust mammon, and the vanities of the world.

Thy salvation. He came not by angels, or by men, or by any other means, but only from the alone and eternal God. He calleth him 'thy salvation;' for his name was not given him by Joseph, nor by Mary, but by the angel of God, Luke i. 31, signifying that he was come from heaven. The Father saw him when he was born, the Spirit came upon him when he was baptized, the angels ministered unto him in the wilderness, his enemies subscribed unto him upon the cross, the virgin travailed, the star walked, the wise men came out of far countries to worship him. Then is not this Jehovah the mighty God, whose birth is glorious, whose life is famous, whose death is meritorious? None can take upon him the authority of God, but he on whose shoulders the Lord layeth it, being sent of God, and from God. Then we see that our Saviour is the true Saviour sent from God; for all creatures bear witness unto him, yea, the very devils with all the evil spirits do obey his voice, Mark i. 24–26, at whose name all knees shall bow, Philip. ii. 10. He came not to bring health, wealth, pleasures, or profits; for if he had, then multitudes of worldlings would have followed him; but he came to bring salvation, righteousness, peace, truth, and life; therefore few care for him. He came to save sinners; not all sinners, 'nor every one that saith, Lord, Lord,' Mat. vii. 22; but he came to save penitent sinners, which turn unto God by their repentance. Therefore he prayeth, in John, for those only that were given unto him, John xvii. 9. So soon as the seed is sown, the stones refuse it, or the sun parcheth it, or the thorns choke it; and what comfort hath the lily among thorns? Therefore wisdom taketh her unto her wings, and whispereth, saying, You shall seek me before I come; 'you shall seek me, but shall not find me,' Prov. i. 28; because ye have refused me when I offered myself to you.

Christ is their salvation that believe in him, and make much of him, and thankfully receive him. The godly he delivereth from sin, but the wicked he leaveth bound in the chains of their iniquity, to be tormented of him which had tempted them thereunto, whose will they always endeavoured to fulfil, and not the Lord's ; and he sheweth them a hand upon the wall, writing their condemnation, Dan. v., and another catching them by the hairy scalp, which maketh all their joints to tremble, and their hearts to despair ; and he saith unto them, 'What doest thou here without the wedding-garment?' Mat. xxii. 12. How darest thou come to steal the children's bread? The spirit of Saul worketh in him, in his bed, and everywhere, and he calleth for the harp of David to comfort his heart, which cannot be comforted, 1 Sam. xvi. And this spirit saith to Judas, Thou hast betrayed the Lord, and crucified him, therefore go and hang thyself, Mat. xxvii. 4, 5 ; for even at the preaching of salvation, the horror of damnation, the mark of Cain, Gen. iv. 15, sticketh within thee whosoever believest not in God's salvation. But the godly heart goeth home, having embraced this salvation, chewing the cud, and rejoicing like the apostles, which 'rejoiced in that they were counted worthy to suffer for his name's sake,' Acts v. 41. And they say, Oh what a good banquet we have had this day ! what delicious dainties hath God feasted us with ! And so the bee goeth loaden to the hive, and goeth longer in the strength thereof than Elias did.

Thy salvation. The only Saviour is here called *salvation* itself ; for if he were called a bare Saviour only, then you might likely understand by him some other saviour; but here he is called salvation itself, to shew that there is no other. For there be more saviours, but no more salvations; as there be many ways to death, and yet but one death. The brazen serpent was a figure of Christ, Num. xxi., John iii. 14, 15, that they which are stung by sin, by fire, and by the serpent which beguiled Eve, may make speed, because there is no remedy but to come to Christ.

The papists have found out many salvations ; they have found out a salvation by saints, a salvation by angels, a salvation by masses, a salvation by merits, a salvation by idols ; as though Christ had least to do in his own office, for they have other salvations to fly unto. They will have it, but they will buy it ; and what will they give for it ? Why, they will fast so many days, go so far on pilgrimage, hire a priest to say so many masses, build so many abbeys, and give so many sums of money to the monks and friars. Therefore the Scripture goeth against them, and dishonours their shamelessness, who, like Nimrod, that, heaping stone upon stone, would have built up to heaven, Gen. xi., heap sin upon sin; and every hour some one heresy or superstition groweth up from this filthy root.

For what papist dare say that Simeon thought on any of these, or put confidence in any other Saviour, but only in him whom he embraced in his arms? for salvation is by the promise of God, Gal. iii. 18, and all promises are in Christ, 2 Cor. i. 20. And though Jacob wanted bread, Joseph wanted not money; therefore he gave them back again their money, and likewise he gave them that corn that they would have bought with it, Gen. xlii. 1, 2. I would wish them therefore to say, as Joseph's brethren did, that they have their corn for nothing, and their money too; let them, I say, be content and rejoice to say, that they have mercy for nothing, and their works too, for God cannot be won by men's works, because they profit not him, but themselves.

There is no water can wash Naaman but Jordan, 2 Kings v.; no water can wash the leprosy of sin but the blood of the Lamb. By this the Israelites were saved when the destroyer passed by, Exod. xii. By this the Lord knoweth us to be his people. And by this the devil knoweth us to be none of his. As it is proper unto God to be called goodness, so is it proper unto Jesus Christ to be called salvation. He is also called ' the way, the truth, and the life,' John xiv. 6; for that life which we have is but a spark and shadow of life, but he is the true and eternal life.

Then seeing Christ is both our righteousness, salvation, and also the way, the truth, and the life, to lead us thereunto; it is as possible for us without Christ to be justified or glorified, as it is to be wise without wisdom, righteous without righteousness, or saved without salvation. Therefore let us not be ashamed to take our water from the fountain, seeing Christ is the fountain of all wisdom, of all righteousness, of all truth, of all knowledge, of all salvation, and briefly of all goodness; for there is no other ark to save us from the flood, no other ladder to ascend with into heaven, no other Joseph to feed us in the famine, no other Moses to lead us through the wilderness.

But as the river Siloa runneth through all the land of Judea, and watereth the whole city of God; so Christ doth shew himself all in all, and all-sufficient in mercy to save and bless all his church with spiritual gifts. If Christ be salvation, what shall make us despair? Shall Satan? No, for he hath overcome Satan. Shall death? No, for he hath overcome death. Shall hell? No, for he hath overcome hell. Shall the law? No, for he hath fulfilled the law. Shall wrath? No, for he hath trodden the wine-press of his Father's wrath, Isa. lxiii. 3. Therefore it was a sweet saying of one at his death, When mine iniquity is greater than thy mercy, O God, then will I fear and despair.

Salvation is born; therefore we were all in the state of condemnation before. Light is come; therefore we sat all in darkness before. Glory is come; therefore we were all loaden with shame before. Life is come; to shew that we were all dead in sin before. Life is come, and light, and salvation; life to the dead, light to the blind, and salvation to the damned. For Christ is called *salvation*, to shew that without him we are all damned, fire-brands of hell, heirs of condemnation, and forsaken of God. To him that is sick, it is easy to be thankful when he is whole; but when he is whole, it is harder to be thankful than to be sick. I would fain be disproved, that Nineveh might be saved, though Jonah would not.

Thy salvation. This word salvation is a sweet word, yea, the sweetest word in all the Scripture; and yet many despise this worthy jewel, because they know not what it is worth; like the daws, which would rather have a barley-corn than a pearl or a jewel, because they know not the value thereof.

'O Lord, what is man, that thou art so mindful of him?' Ps. viii. 4. O man, what is God, that thou art so unmindful of him? If a friend had given us anything, we would have thanked him heartily for it; but to him that hath given us all things, we will not give so much as thanks. Now, therefore, let the rock gush out water again, and let our stony hearts pour forth streams of tears in unfeigned repentance. We have all called upon you, but none regardeth us; as though God were as Baal, and as though Dives felt no pain, nor Lazarus joy, but all were forgotten. Many times Christ cometh into the temple, and there is scarce a Simeon to embrace him. The babe is here, but where is Simeon?

If God had not loved us better than we loved ourselves, we should have perished long ere this; and yet we embrace not Christ, as Simeon, who hath saved us from temporal and spiritual punishment. We are invited to a banquet; he who calleth us to it is God. What is the banquet? Salvation. Who are the guests? The angels and the saints. What is the fare? Joy, peace, righteousness. This is the fare, and we invite you every one; yet who will come at our bidding? Some for want of faith, some for want of love, some for want of knowledge, have despised his holy banquet; yet unto this art thou called still, O soul unworthy to be beloved.

THE SWEET SONG OF OLD FATHER SIMEON.

THE SECOND SERMON.

Thy salvation which thou hast prepared before the face of all the people ; a light to be revealed to the Gentiles, and the glory of thy people Israel.—LUKE II. 30–32.

Thy salvation. This word *salvation* is a sweet word, and holds me to it like an adamant ; for when I thought to proceed, this word said unto me, Stay here, teach this, and teach all ; learn this, and learn all ; for it is the pith of all the mercies of God towards his children. Christ is called *salvation,* because no man shall despair, and because it is impossible to be saved without him, for salvation is only in him. Christ can do anything but this ; he cannot save him that will not repent. He is called 'the salvation of God,' because he came not from men, nor from angels, nor by chance, but from God himself; and therefore his name was not given him after the manner of men, which was that every father should name his own child; but so did not Joseph, for the angel had given direction for his name.

The virgin, the oracles, the babes, the shepherds, the star, the wise men, the voice of the crier, the devils, the lepers, the sick, the dead, the earthquake, the sun, the moon, and all the creatures, do bear witness unto the Son of God, which is our salvation. He is called the salvation of God, because he is salvation according to God's own mind. He came not to bring ease and liberty, but he came to bring the spiritual sword and condemnation to all obstinate sinners, yet salvation to the penitent.

I shewed you how many despised this jewel, because they know not what it is worth; how few Simeons there be in the temple, how few Nathanaels, how few men that fear God. These plants grow not on every ground.

Who would be unthankful, if he knew what the Lord gives, and what he forgives? He gives the Son for the bastard, the Lord for the servant, the righteous for sinners, the innocent for the wicked, and the almighty Lord for the sinful sons of men. Do you not marvel how you can offend this Lord willingly, which hath done so much for you? Here I reprove unthankfulness, security and negligence, striving as it were to crucify Christ again, as the wicked Jews did, who never prospered since they said, 'His blood be upon us and upon our seed,' Mat. xxvii. 25. They were not like Simeon, who, as soon as he saw him, embraced him and rejoiced over him. There is no show of grace in them which shew no liking of godliness in themselves or in others; for this is the first part of our conversion, to love them that love God, and so we are drawn to the Son. No man will build an ark until the flood come, Gen. vi.; no man will seek for corn until the famine come, Gen. xlii.; and scarce will Lot be gone out of Sodom before the time of execution of God's wrath do come upon them, Gen. xix.

We preach unto you, and call upon you, we have even wearied ourselves among you, we have reproved you for sin, and we must still reprove you until you amend; now, therefore, if there be any grace in you, if you have any knowledge, any fear of God in you, if you have any goodness in you, if you have any leisure to be saved, turn back now from doing evil, come out of hell, and pluck your limbs out of the clutches of the serpent. For verily we have not done so well in this city as the Ninevites did, for all the preaching and teaching we have had. For who hath determined in his heart to amend his life? who hath left his pride? who hath restored that which he hath taken by extortion, usury, and wrong? Surely they that have done thus are monsters; I cannot see them, they walk invisibly and cannot be found. The heavens trembled at the death of Christ; the sun did hide his face, the earth quaked, the veil of the temple rent in sunder, the dead bodies rose out of the graves, Mat. xxvii. 45, 51, 52, 53; and all this was to shew that the Prince of the world suffered violence, and that the Lord of life suffered death for the ransom of us, and of all whosoever throughout the world do believe the gospel, and live in obedience thereof; and withal, that he suffering for sinful and wretched man, was a conqueror over hell and all evil, and hath overcome death. The scribes were against him, the pharisees were against him, the rulers band themselves against him, the atheists against him, and all the spiteful and envious Jews against him; whose birth was base, whose life was contemptible, and whose death was ignominious; but God was with him, and in him, by whose power he overcame them all, and so became the salvation of God.

David being to encounter with Goliath, Saul took and put on him his own harness; but he could not wear it, it was too heavy for his little body; therefore he took nothing but a staff, and a few stones in a scrip; and so David slew the pride of the Philistines, and the fear of Israel, 1 Sam. xvii. 38–40. And even thus the Lord set his Son to fight with the prince of this world, not with swords and targets, bows and bills, but with the word and Spirit of God, with the which he hath overcome, and through him we also have the victory.

Which thou hast prepared before the face of all people, &c. He speaks this to the end that the eyes of all mankind may be fixed upon him, as the eyes of all Israel were fixed upon the brazen serpent in the wilderness, Num. xxi.; and when they be stinged with the sting of that fiery serpent which deceived our forefathers, they may fly unto him for help, lest they perish in their sin, and their blood be on their own heads.

Which thou hast prepared. He was prepared long ago, as it doth most plainly appear; for the virgin which bare him, the place of his birth, the poor state wherein he was, his miracles, his apostles, his torments, his cross, his death, his resurrection and ascension into heaven, all these were foreshewed and foretold long before they came to pass. Therefore some said, Who is this that is so often spoken of by the prophets? Who is this that can do many miracles that the scribes and pharisees cannot do? that can raise the dead, that can cease the winds, that can calm the waters, at whose suffering the earth quaked, the sun hid his face, darkness came over all, and who, being dead, rose again by his own power, and ascended into heaven in the sight of a great multitude? How can it be then but it must be known 'before the face of all people,' which was so manifest by dreams, by visions, by oracles, by power, by authority, and everything? For there was nothing which had not a tongue to speak for God. Everything was prepared for him before he came to be revealed. He came not in the beginning nor in the ending. He came not in the ending, that we which come after him might long for his second coming. He came not in the beginning, because that such a Prince as he should have many banners and triumphs before him. He came not in the beginning, because the eyes of faith should not be dazzled in him, and lest they which should live in the latter times should forget him and his coming, which was so long before; even as you forget that which I have said as soon as you are gone hence. He came not in the beginning, because if he had come before man had sinned, man would have acknowledged no need of a physician; but he came when man had sinned, and had felt the smart of sin. For when they were cast out of paradise, they ran unto Christ, as the Israelites did to the serpent. He came not in the beginning, but in the perfect age of the world, to shew that he brought with him perfection, perfect joy, perfect peace, perfect wisdom, perfect righteousness, perfect justice, perfect truth; signifying thereby, that notwithstanding he came in the perfect age thereof, yet he found all things imperfect. The Jews thought that he should come like some great prince, with pomp and glory, which was a carnal conceit, and herein they were marvellously deceived; his father was but a poor carpenter, and his mother but a simple woman, and he a silly babe wrapt in clouts. Then ought not we to reverence our Lord, and to praise his name, for that he became so humble for us most vile wretches, that are worthy of nothing? Yet we see how cruelly they dealt with this blessed one, which came to save them. Ignorance sat in the chair, deceit gave the sentence, and cruelty executed him with the most painful and shameful death of the cross. Oh that your eyes do not dazzle, and your ears tingle, and your hearts marvel, at this dealing of yours to our loving Saviour, which came to save them that would, and specially in that now you see that he abased himself for our sakes, even to the uttermost! Oh wonderful thing to think of! If you would mark, I would make you in love with him before I have done with you. I say unto all those that come hither to be edified, Take your fill of pleasure, enter into paradise, lift up your eyes, stretch forth your hands, and eat your fill of the tree of life, and the Lord will go home with you; embrace him, and kiss him, entertain him well, and he will dwell with you for ever. But you that come hither for fashion's sake, either to see or to be seen, to find fault with somewhat, or to make an hypocritical show of godliness, where there is none, I tell you, that comfort shall shake hands with you at the door: mark it, and you shall see my words are true. Shew me what is it that is better than salvation. I would have none of you to be damned, if I might prevent it; not so much as a piece of you to be given unto Satan; therefore I would I knew that stone that would kill Goliath, for I would strike it with my might into his temples. If you will you may be saved, and the Lord will one day put those words into my mouth that will touch your hearts. Therefore now arise, kiss and embrace the sweet babe Jesus, and then afterwards frame yourselves to obey him ; for then the Lord will knock at your hearts, and if you will let him in, he will teach you all things. The Lord came not in the beginning, nor in the ending, but he came in the middle age of the world, to shew, that if it will not learn now, it will never learn to come unto God by repentance and amendment, that they may learn to 'kiss the Son, lest he be angry, and so they perish in his wrath,' like Sodom, Ps. ii. 12. He came in the middle age of the world, to shew that he was indifferent for the world, to give light and life unto all that return unto him. For 'God respecteth no persons ; but every man, of what nation or country soever he be, that feareth God and worketh righteousness, is accepted of him,' Acts x. 34, 35, and he will fulfil their joys through Christ ; yet not when we will, but, according to his own good pleasure, and when he thinketh good. Therefore stay, Elias, anon the ravens will bring thee meat, and thou shalt have enough, 1 Kings xvii ; anon Moses will deliver Israel, Exod. xiv. 13. So salvation is already prepared of God, and hath been long since, with fulness of knowledge and all excellent gifts ; and he will give them to us when he seeth good. But we are like whining children, that will not stay until their milk be cold, but would have it though they be scalded with it ; so we would have the knowledge of God and liberty before we know how to use it ; we would know the high mysteries and deep counsels of God before we know ourselves ; we would have the liberty of the gospel, when we know no way how to use it but in security. But the Lord will wisely give unto us as it were our bellies full, when he seeth it good, and when he seeth us ready for it, who knoweth our hearts better than we ourselves.

A light to be revealed to the Gentiles, and the glory of thy people Israel. You have heard Simeon shewing the cause why the Son was sent from the Father, why he became man, which reigned before in paradise. What moved God to leave his joy and his bliss, and suffer more than all the world could suffer together ? A great cause it is that would make a king leave his kingdon and fall to beggary. A great and wonderful cause it was that made Jehovah to come down from heaven to suffer misery upon the earth. Two causes Simeon sheweth why this Messiah came from heaven : the first, that he might enlighten the Gentiles, which sat in darkness ; and the second, that he might be the glory of Israel, which gloried in their sacrifices and in their ceremonies, and so had no glory before he came, but were like the moon when the sun doth shine upon it, or like Rachel, which despised Leah, and became barren, Gen. xxix. 31 ; and they despised the Gentiles' light, like that son which was angry because his lost brother came home again, Luke xv. 28 ; or like those labourers which checked the lord of the vineyard, because he gave unto the other labourers as much as he gave unto them, Mat. xx. 11.   But the Gentiles are like Leah, who being despised became fruitful, Gen. xxix. 31.   Simeon did rejoice in Christ, not only for that he was 'the glory of Israel,' but also for that he was 'the light of the Gentiles.'   Shall the head be sorrowful because the hand is well ?   Nay, rather the hand should be glad because the head is well, and the head because the hand is well.   The father should be glad because his son is stronger than himself; the mother should be glad because her daughter is wiser than herself ; the brother should be glad because his brother is richer than himself ; the mistress should rejoice because her maid is a better housewife than herself.   But we envy our brethren and neighbours, because they are better than we, and because God hath blessed them with temporal or spiritual things above us.   If we see they have learning, then we envy them for their learning ; if he have more gifts, we envy him for his gifts ; if he have more knowledge, we envy him for his knowledge ; if he have more zeal, we envy him for his zeal ; if he have more riches, we envy him for his riches.   And how can we rejoice, when everybody's good is our evil, and everybody's joy is our sorrow ?   But fix your eyes upon Christ alone, and he will fulfil your joy, if you look not back to Sodom, like Lot's wife, Gen. xix. 26.   If you love joy and gladness, Christ is joy and gladness ; if you love comfort, why, Christ is the comfort of all that bear his cross ; if you love life, Christ is eternal life ; if you love peace, Christ is peace ; if you love riches, Christ is full of heavenly riches, and full of liberality, to bestow them upon all such as love God.   So Christ is all in all unto the godly, and they have more joy in Christ always, and in all things, than the richest and most glorious and sumptuous prince in the world, than Solomon himself had in worldly riches, honours, pleasures, joy, ease, or felicity.   For the wicked, which put their trust in riches, and make them gods of gold and money, of ease and pleasures, though they do all that they can to fulfil their lusts, and take never so much pleasure, and be never so merry, yet they can have no true joy, nor peace of conscience ; for all the peace, the mirth and sport they have is but deceit, all false and undurable, like the grass, green in the morning, and withered ere night.   But when the Lord doth knock at their hearts, and strike them with a feeling of their horrible transgressions, as no doubt he will, then they are all in a maze, and they can have no joy, no peace, no rest; but they may say, In laughter my soul is sorrowful, in ease my soul hath trouble, in mirth moan, in riches poverty, in glory shame, in life my soul is even dead, in plenty my soul wanteth all things wherein it should rejoice; it is destitute of all comfort, and possessed with all slavish fears; like Cain, who, being lord of all the earth, yet had no joy in it when God had once forsaken him, Gen. iv. Likewise Saul, when God had forsaken him, he had no joy of his kingdom, nor of all his riches, 1 Sam. xvi.; and then who had more joy, Saul the king, or David the subject? So then we see, that perfect joy can be had in nothing but in God and in Jesus Christ. Wherefore, as by the stream you may be led to the fountain; even so let the joy and peace of this life serve to lead us to God, who is perfect joy and peace; and there let us rest, like the wise men, which were guided by the star to come to the true Son[1] of grace, Jesus Christ, when he was born. And if we rest not in him when we have found him, there is no rest for us; we shall be like the restless dove, which fluttered about, and found no rest anyway till she returned to the ark. But we seem as though we sought him and found him, whenas we do but play the hypocrites. Solomon saith, that the ways of the whore are prosperity and welfare; for she ever putteth on a vizard, that she might not be known to be so vile as she is. Under the colour of goodness evil is always lurking.

Therefore also is Christ called the light, because we should leave our foolishness, seeing light is come, and that we should forsake all our lights, which are but darkness, and cleave unto his light, which is the true light indeed.

A light to be revealed to the Gentiles, &c. He came to lighten the Gentiles, and they received him with thankfulness, of whom there was no hope of goodness left. Who would suppose that the barren woman should become fruitful, or the prodigal son return home again? It is like as if an owl should be converted to see light, or as if the stream would return into the fountain, or as if an old man should become young again.

A light to be revealed to the Gentiles. To be revealed, not yet *revealed.* The Jews must first reject him before the Gentiles receive him; and when the Jews did oppress him, condemn him, and crucify him, then were his arms spread into the whole world. When the guests would not come, then he sendeth into the high-

---

[1] Qu. 'Sun'?—ED.

ways to compel others that would not come willingly into it, Luke xiv. 21, &c. Comfort is on foot, and that which will come shall come, &c. The queen of Sheba came from the uttermost parts of the earth to hear Solomon's wisdom, Mat. xii. 42 ; and the wise men came from the east to see Jesus Christ. But we may say, The Lord was here in the temple, and I was in my shop selling and buying, lying, deceiving, and swearing. Well, when he comes back again, I will be better acquainted with him ; and so we esteem not of his presence in any reverent sort. The Shunammite said, ' Let us build a chamber for the man of God,' 2 Kings iv. 10 ; then we should build an house. Zaccheus climbed up into a tree to see our Saviour, and the Lord, seeing his diligence, called him, ' Zaccheus, come down, for I will dine at thy house this day ;' and that was a joyful day with Zaccheus, for then 'salvation came into his house,' and upon all his family, Luke xix. He gave the Lord a feast, and the Lord made him a far better feast, a feast of peace, a feast of joy, a feast of heavenly things ; and so for his zeal and endeavour to see Christ bodily, he shewed himself unto him spiritually, even to his heart's desire.

To be revealed. Have an eye to the future tense ; that which is not, shall be. As for example, Solomon *was* wise, but he *is* foolish ; Samson *was* strong, but he *is* weak ; Judas *was* a preacher, but he *is* a traitor ; Paul *was* a persecutor, but he *is* a preacher ; Peter *was* a denier of Christ, but now he *is* a bold professor of Christ ; Moses *was* learned in the wisdom of the Egyptians, but now he *is* learned in the wisdom of God, by which the wisdom of the Egyptians is made but mere foolishness in the sight of God. Others, as heathen philosophers, Plato, Aristotle, Cato, Crates, and such like, were counted very wise men in the sight of the world ; yea, they wrote so many books full of wisdom, and also adorned with notable sentences and witty sayings, that one would think all wisdom were buried with them, so famous were they, and so full of earthly understanding, teaching manners, counsels, and policies. Yet, for my part, I have neither seen nor heard of any such being wise in worldly things, and without the wisdom of God, but that they have committed some notorious foolishness in the sight of all men. Like Ahithophel, of whom we read that he was so wise a counsellor that 'his counsel was like as if one had asked counsel at the oracle of God,' 2 Sam. xvi. 23, and yet see the end of him, he hanged himself, and all for the want of the knowledge of God, 2 Sam. xvii. 23. It had been better, therefore, for him to have had more wisdom and less wit. Crates, Aristotle, Plato, and others of the wise philosophers, have either poisoned, burned, or drowned themselves. And so we see that the end of the worldly wisdom is mere foolishness, 1 Cor. i. 19, 20, and the foolish have more peace than the wise; for their wisdom without the fear of God doth them no more good than the ark did to the Philistines, which did nothing but torment them, because they knew not how to use it, and therefore unreverently abused it, 1 Sam. v. For if your wisdom consist in eloquence of words, in profundity of wit, to gain craftily and spend warily, to invent laws, to expound riddles, and interpret dreams, to tell fortunes, and prophesy of matters by learning, all your wisdom is but vexation of the spirit; for all these, without the fear of God, do us no more good than their wit did these philosophers, which notwithstanding sat in darkness. And I am afraid, though Christ brought light unto the Gentiles, yet it may be said that the Gentiles sit in darkness still, saving a few Levites scattered upon the mountains, for whose sake Sodom is spared. And because those had not the knowledge of God, therefore they worshipped Mars and Cupid, sun and moon, beasts and serpents, 2 Kings xvii. 30. So the Philistines worshipped Dagon, Judges xvi. 23; the Ephesians worshipped Diana, Acts xix. 27; the Assyrians Nisroch, 2 Kings xix. 37; the Israelites worshipped a calf, Exod. xxxii.; Ahaziah worshipped Beelzebub, 2 Kings i. 2; the Moabites worshipped Chemosh, 1 Kings xi. 33; the Samaritans did worship unto Baal, 1 Kings, xvi. 32; so the truth to such seemeth falsehood, and error seemeth truth. As for example, that the world should be made of nothing, that the Word became flesh, that God and man was joined together in one person, that one man may be righteous in the righteousness of another, which is Christ, and that the dead shall rise again; these seemed foolishness unto the Gentiles, neither could they believe them. No more can some Gentiles amongst us at this day, which are but natural men; therefore they do not believe them; for 'when they professed themselves to be wise, they became fools,' saith the Holy Ghost, Rom. i. 22. So then we see now what Christ hath done for us; he hath bound that serpent which hath sown all the tares, so that the devil is fain, for want of better lodging, to enter into swine.

Heretofore, where one followed God, a thousand followed Baal; but now kings and princes lift up their heads, desiring Christ to reign with them, and in them. Heretofore we made ourselves like the wounded man, we were spoiled, we were stripped naked, and we were bathed in our blood, being full of wounds; but now Christ hath furnished us, he hath washed us, he hath clothed us, and we are now become true Israelites; us, which were the vile and wild olives, he hath grafted upon the true olive, and planted us in a fruitful soil. And what cause can we shew for this, but only mercy? For heretofore we were called foolish; but the Lord hath made us wise, according to the wisdom of God, in these days by his Spirit. But if we deserve to be called 'the foolish nation' again, then we are most unhappy and most cursed. So now we have heard that the Lord doth reveal his counsel unto his prophets, and how the glory of Israel is now revealed to be the light of the Gentiles. And you have the cause why; because the Jews rejected their own salvation. You have heard that the cause was only his mercy and his love, because mercy cannot contain itself within Jerusalem.

A light to be revealed to the Gentiles, and the glory of thy people Israel. You have heard why Christ is called light, why he is called the light of the Gentiles, why the Lord did change a curse into a blessing, and why the Gentiles did change darkness for light, and a thousand gods for one true God. Then the Gentiles received more grace than they desired; for the Lord came uncalled unto their houses, and made a feast unto them in their own houses. The light of the Gentiles is our light, your light and my light; Christ is our grace, your grace and my grace; and Christ is our salvation, your salvation and my salvation. He came unto the Jews, and for the Jews; and yet his coming unto the Gentiles was better than to the Jews. He came into the world when the world did abound in all wickedness, and saved us when we most deserved wrath. Wonder at this, you that wonder at nothing, that the Lord would come to bring salvation, to redeem our lost souls, even, as it were, against our wills; so that now we would not be as we were for a thousand worlds.

The blessedness of the Jews was and is wonderful, who heard of their rejection, and of our conversion, and yet understood it not, neither sought to prevent God's wrath in rejecting of them. Therefore the rock which should have saved them, shivered them in pieces. Wherein was shewed their wonderful blockishness, having it so often foretold by their prophets, figured in their law, shadowed in their sacrifices, and read in their churches from Sabbath to Sabbath. Everything that cometh to pass in churches, in commonweals, in cities, in countries, in kingdoms, and in provinces, these are all foretold in the Scriptures; and yet none do understand it, saving a few chosen ones whom God loveth. For, the coming of antichrist, the overthrow of kingdoms, the darkness of popery, the light of the gospel, the conversion of the Gentiles, and the rejecting of the Jews, all these are set down in the Scriptures, and yet we cannot understand it, though we hear it day by day, because we do not give our minds to understanding.

Such hearers shall stand in amaze before the righteous and terrible throne of God. The dead shall rise, the trump shall blow, and all the world shall be in an uproar, and they shall stand quaking, when their hearing without profiting shall be laid to their charge; and they shall say, Oh, we have known no such thing. But surely if the Jews could come out of hell, they would admonish us to take better heed how to hear; for we hear as though we did not hear at all, our minds are otherwise occupied. Now when we see anything come to pass as it is foretold in the Scripture, then we must say as Christ said, This prophecy is fulfilled; for all things that are written are come to *Scriptum est, et factum est;* that is, as sure as it is written, so surely doth it come to pass. It prophesieth nothing but that which truly is fulfilled in due time; and the more often it speaks of a thing, the more certain, the more excellent, and the more to be believed it is. Like a jewel that is beset with pearl, so is our calling adorned with Scriptures; for so doth God tender our calling, which is often in his mouth, and we so often in his remembrance, that he speaketh of us in every book throughout the whole Scriptures; like a kind spouse, whose love is in a strange country, and he delighteth himself with thoughts and meditations of her. So he did long until the Gentiles were come to him again; like the prodigal child, whose father did long till he had embraced him, Luke xv. When shall my prodigal son come home again, saith he? I will put my best garment on his back, and my gold ring on his finger, and his fare shall be the daintiest morsel. And thus God longeth for our salvation, and he knocketh at our doors. Is faith here? Is love here? Is one called the fear of God in this place?

And as love maketh lovers sometime to speak plainly and familiarly one to another, sometime by dark speeches and riddles, sometime by letters, sometime by dumb shows and signs, and sometime to hide themselves one from another; so our God speaketh sometime plainly to his church, sometime darkly and mystically; sometime he turneth his face from his church and dear spouse, as though he would not speak unto her for love, as it appeareth in the book of the Canticles.

Of the casting off of the Jews, and calling in of the Gentiles, the first type or figure was Cain and Abel, Gen. iv. Cain was the eldest son of Adam, and Abel the younger; yet God loved Abel, and accepted his sacrifice; but God rejected Cain for his wickedness, and he became a reprobate. Even so doth God: he rejected the Jews, which were the eldest son, the true olive, and the natural seed, and God's dear children, if they had continued in obedience; and he taketh us, being but the youngest son, the wild olive, the seed of the wicked, and maketh us children by adoption unto him, only of his mercy, without any other cause.

The second example was Shem and Japhet, both which were Noah's sons, Gen. ix. Shem was the second son, and Japhet the first, and of this Japhet came the Gentiles; of him said Noah, 'God persuade Japhet, that he may dwell in the tents of Shem,' ver. 27; that is, that they may be united together, as we see it is come to pass. 'Other sheep I have,' saith Christ, 'which are not of this fold: them also will I bring, and they shall hear my voice; and there shall be one sheepfold, and one shepherd,' John x. 16.

The third type or figure was Ishmael and Isaac, both the sons of Abraham, Gen. xxi. Ishmael was the eldest, Isaac the younger; yet Isaac was chosen of God, and enjoyed the promise; and Ishmael, his elder brother, a mocker of Isaac, was put away, the Lord was not with him.

The fourth type or figure was Jacob and Esau, both the sons of Isaac, Gen. xxv. Esau was the elder brother, and Jacob the younger; yet God loved Jacob, and hated Esau, because Esau contemned his birthright, and sold it to Jacob for a mess of pottage; and therefore Jacob stole the blessing from him. So God blessed Jacob, but cursed Esau; whereby he shewed, that the Lord did for the contempt of the Jews take away their birthright and their blessing, and hath given it unto us.

The fifth type or figure was Leah and Rachel, the two daughters of Laban, Gen. xxix. Leah was the elder, but blear or squint-eyed; Rachel the younger, beautiful and fair, ver. 17; therefore Rachel was beloved of Jacob, and Leah despised, ver. 18; yet Leah was first married, ver. 23; and also made fruitful, ver. 31; but Rachel also was after married, ver. 28; and more beloved, ver. 30; and having envied her sister's fruitfulness, chap. xxx. 1, and repented, God remembered her, and made her fruitful. So Christ first married the Jews, and made them glorious; but when they despised their glory, he married with the Gentiles, and they envying their happiness, of barren in all goodness, became fruitful in true holiness.

The sixth figure was Manasseh and Ephraim, the two sons of Joseph, Gen. xlviii. Manasseh was the eldest, and Ephraim was the youngest. Both of them Joseph having brought to Jacob his father, that he might bless them, he took Manasseh, and put him towards Jacob's right hand, that he might bless him first and more plentifully; and he took Ephraim, and put him towards Jacob's left hand; but Jacob stretched out his right hand, and laid it upon Ephraim's head, which was the younger, and his left hand upon Manasseh, directing his hands so of purpose, for Manasseh was the elder of them. Thus the Lord blessed us, when there was no hope left for us.

The seventh figure was Rahab, a harlot in Jericho, who was a Gentile, yet her heart was touched so that she received and entertained the spies that Joshua sent, and in time of danger hid them, that they should take no harm, Joshua ii.; signifying thereby, that the Gentiles should receive and embrace the Israelites and messengers of the gospel, and keep them as safely, and defend them as diligently, as Rahab did the spies of Israel.

The eighth figure was Ruth a Moabite, Ruth iv. Of her Christ Jesus vouchsafed to come as concerning the flesh; to shew, that he came not only of the Jews, and for the Jews, but also of and for the Gentiles, which were the lost sheep, unhoped for, being strangers from the covenant.

The ninth figure was Samson, who, being a Jew, would needs marry with a Gentile, Judges xiv.; signifying, that Christ Jesus would also marry with the Gentiles, as he did with the Jews.

The tenth figure was Solomon, who married Pharaoh's daughter, which was an Egyptian and Gentile, 1 Kings iii,; signifying thereby, that Christ would take him a spouse among the Gentiles to marry with himself, as David in the Psalms declareth, Ps. xlv.

The eleventh figure was Naaman the Syrian, whose leprosy is turned upon Gehazi, the leprosy of an heathen and ignorant man turned upon an Israelite, and one that had the knowledge of God, being the servant of a prophet, 2 Kings v.; signifying, that our leprosy of sin and ignorance should be turned from us upon the Jews, who had the knowledge of the law of God, but esteemed it not, but were unthankful for it. Many like examples there are in the New Testament. For like as the cherubims, though severed in sunder, yet looked one towards another, and both upon the mercy-seat; so the Old Testament and the New look one towards another, and yet point at one and the same thing.

The first type or figure in the New Testament was the wise men, which were the first fruits of the Gentiles, and came from the east, being guided by a star, Mat. ii.; signifying, that by the guiding of the word and Spirit of God, the Gentiles should come from all the places of the world to embrace Christ Jesus with joy.

The second type or figure was Christ his going into Egypt, Mat. ii.; signifying thereby, that he should go from the Jews to the Gentiles, because the Jews refused him through unbelief, abundance of wickedness, and want of reformation. So we see that nothing can drive away Christ but sin.

The third type was Christ's whipping the Jews out of the temple, Mat. xxi. 12; shewing thereby, that the Jews should be whipped or cast out of the spiritual temple, and the Gentiles should occupy it. This, beloved, belongeth unto us, to whom the Lord so wonderfully hath made his light to shine.

The fourth figure is the parable of the vineyard, that was taken from them that possessed it, and given to them that should bring forth the fruits thereof, and yield better increase unto the Lord of the vineyard, Mat. xxi. 33, &c.

The fifth figure was the parable of the two sons, that were bidden to go and work in their father's vineyard; of whom the first said, he would, and did not; the second said, he would not, and did repent, and went to labour in the vineyard, Mat. xxi. 28, &c. The first signified the Jews, which made many vows, with such a show of godliness, which was but hypocrisy, whom the Lord rejected and cast off, and said, that the publicans and sinners should stand in judgment to condemn the greatest of them.

The sixth figure was the feast that the Lord made unto the disobedient guests, whom the Lord invited to his banquet, which was only ordained for them, and who promised to come unto it, and yet refused and would not come, but alleged slight excuses, taken from their love of earthly and transitory things above God; therefore the Lord sent into the highways, to call and compel the Gentiles to come, which came, though some left their wedding garments behind them, Mat. xxii. 2, &c.

The seventh type or figure was the vision of Peter in Joppa, when he was on the top of the house, when he saw the vessel come down that had in it all manner of four-footed beasts of the earth, and wild beasts, and fowls of the air, and creeping things; where also the voice said unto him, 'Arise, Peter, kill and eat,' Acts x.; wherein the Lord shewed unto him that he should count no man unclean, although the Gentiles then were counted unclean, as were the unclean beasts set down in the law of God; therefore when Peter was sent to Cornelius's house, he said, 'Of a truth I perceive that God hath no respect of persons: but in every nation he that feareth God, and worketh righteousness, is accepted of him,' ver. 34.

Many other examples there are of our calling; as the strayed sheep, the lost groat, the prodigal son, Luke xv., and Christ's eating with publicans and sinners, Luke v. ; which when we read we should cast our finger, and say, Of whom is this spoken ? of the Gentiles ? then is it of me, for I am a Gentile. But am I converted? If I be not, then have I not fulfilled this prophecy ? Therefore let us strive to do well, and to mortify and subdue sin which dwelleth in our mortal bodies ; for none but the valiant can enter into the kingdom of heaven.

Now, all these prophecies are fulfilled, the blind see, the lame go, the dumb speak, the deaf hear, the maimed work, the dead are quickened, the lepers are cleansed, and the poor receive the gospel,' Mat. xi. 5, Luke vii. 22. Therefore who will despair, and say, Light is not revealed unto me, whenas he seeth it to be revealed unto whole nations ? And so solemn is our calling, as that in so many places of the Scripture it is foretold ; whereby we see how dearly the Lord tendereth our salvation, like as a kind spouse, which was longed for while she was in a strange country ; for Christ longed for the Gentiles, till they came home again unto him. Therefore let us now consider what he giveth us, namely, righteousness and salvation ; first righteousness, then salvation ; first repentance, and then forgiveness of sins, the sun of the gospel, lest we should see heaven in hell, and light in darkness, and joy in anguishes. Let us not contemn our light, or grow careless of it ; let us not build with one hand, and overthrow with the other by profaneness ; like those men which, while they surfeited at their gluttonous tables, called upon God for health. Christ is not received with the left hand. If the father, offering a gift, do see the son stretch forth his left hand, he will withdraw his gift from him. I say, let us not contemn our light, as the Jews contemned their glory.

For what is light to him that will shut his eyes against it ? What is this light ? It is such a glorious light, and such an excellent revelation, that great and mighty kings have earnestly desired to see, and princes have laid down their crowns to reveal it, Mat. xiii. Let us embrace this light, let us take and put on the wedding-garment, and go to the banquet unto which a thousand messengers have invited us, and allege no excuses ; say not, ' I have married a wife,' ' I have bought oxen,' ' I go to see a farm,' &c., ' and therefore I cannot come,' neither will I come, Luke xiv. 18, &c. Well, do so, if that ye will needs ; but remember that thou wast invited, and therefore the blessing shall be given to another ; and Esau shall weep for the blessing, but shall not have it, Heb. xii. 17.

But give me a reason, I pray thee, why thou wilt be called the servant of God, which dost not serve him; or the child of God, which dost not love him; or the disciple of Christ, which dost not learn of him; yet his rain falleth upon all, just and unjust, and he giveth thee all things for nothing. The sun doth give his light for nothing, the dew doth give his moisture for nothing, the rivers do give their waters for nothing, and the earth doth give her fruit for nothing.

What shall we do then when the sun shineth? We must not do as we do in the dark, for then men ought to betake them to their labour, Rom. xiii. 12, Eph. v. 8, 11. Learn of the savage beasts, who as soon as the day springs betake them to their travel, and every bird welcometh it with many a sweet song. Christ is light, and this light is come; therefore he that seeth now is blind. Are not they then blind which yet see not that prayer for the dead is vain, needless, and bootless? But thick darkness needs a mighty light to chase it away. So that he which beginneth to root out some error or superstition, at the first shall have much ado; for custom and natural corruption are the first causers of heresy, and shall cry against him in the maintenance thereof; and withstanders of reformation shall say, 'Great is Diana of Ephesus;' and so for a long time they seem to wash the Ethiopian, or blackmoor; the more they wash him, the more they gall him, and yet he is an Ethiopian still; but in the end the ark standeth, and Dagon falleth down, 1 Sam. v., and truth triumpheth over falsehood, having got the victory, and light chaseth away darkness with the brightness thereof. Why then doth this darkness continue amongst us still? To him that asketh, What scripture have you against it? it is sufficient to answer, What scripture have you for it? For if the word command it not, God rejecteth it, and will say, 'Who hath required these things at your hands?' But what is this? 'For every idle word you must give account,' as our Saviour Jesus Christ saith, Mat. xii. 36. And 'whatsoever is not of faith is sin,' Rom. xiv. 23. They ask, What, shall we not say, *God be with them?* Why should you? Why, say they, must we say nothing? What if thou do not? What sayest thou when thou mentionest the death of thy first fathers, Adam, Seth, Enos, Enoch, Noah? Dost thou less love these, not praying for them, than thou dost them for whom thou sayest, *God be with them, &c.?*

But thou hast speeches enough to use, if thou wilt needs say somewhat, and leave such superstitious and offensive sentences. If he be a good man, thou mayest say, The Lord be thanked for his deliverance, and the like ; but if he be not, then thou mayest say, God grant we may do better than he hath done, and that by his fall we may learn to rise from sin, or some such thing. Whatsoever he be, thou mayest say as David said of his child, giving a reason why he would not pray for him any longer being dead, 'Can I call him back again? I shall go to him, but he shall not return to me,' 2 Sam. xii. 23 ; or any other words, so they be wise, and therefore not against the word. What then is to be done? As Jacob said to his wives and children, Give me your idols, that I may bury them, Gen. xxxv.; so say I unto you, Give me your superstitions, that I may bury them, that they may remain with you or in you no longer, to the dishonour of God, offending of your weak brethren, or to my grief. For I am jealous over you ; and because you are mine, and I am yours, oh that my voice were as the whirlwind, to beat down, root out, and blow away all your superstitions, that they may no longer reign amongst you! Or rather, oh that Christ, which is our light, were come into us all, and shined so bright, that we were ashamed of all our darkness ; of all, not of mind only, but of will also, and of works, that we no longer would walk in darkness ; for few have the will to walk according to the word either in darkness or light. We can see to sin in the dark as well as in the light ; and do rather, because the light discovereth both the harlot and the thief, so they are afraid of the light. But assured be we, where light is not, Christ is not, for Christ is light, John i. 9. And let none be afraid to seek this light, which is so good, so excellent, and so profitable for us ; for it doth not only descry itself, but all other things round about it. Therefore if thou have this light, thy faith, thy fear, thy love will shew itself, and good things cannot now hide themselves, for he that is light doth delight to please God in the light. It is no marvel though a man stumble in the dark ; but he which stumbleth in the light is not very strong, because he seeth his way before him. Once we stumbled at every straw, when we walked in darkness ; for then wrath had a fall, pride had a fall, lust had a fall, drunkenness had a fall, penury had a fall, ignorance had a fall ; or, if you will, pride rose, and we fell ; lust rose, and we fell, &c.

Were Egypt as light as Goshen, we should have idolaters as joyful as true worshippers ; but there is palpable darkness, tedious, fearful, and of long continuance in Egypt, clear light only in Goshen ; therefore fly Egypt. But if thou live in Egypt, that is, walk in darkness, or commit wickedness, though thou sin in the dark, the light will bewray thee, and thy conscience will accuse thee and condemn thee for it. Therefore, now give over darkness, and arm thee with light, for our light shineth as the light ; therefore, now we should be Israel, for Israel is revolted. But many scrolls may be written of our sins ; and thus the Gentiles are as Gentiles still. He that believeth not the word is an infidel ; he that believeth not God is an atheist ; he that worshippeth anything more than God is an idolater ; every man's conscience shall condemn himself. Yet men will leave godliness for riches, but they will not leave riches for godliness. What madness ! Yea, the Jews never served God at any time with such devotion as many do now their gold and their riches. Oh, intolerable wickedness ! For many there are that could be content never to die, but to live here with their riches and pleasure. And is not the godly more despited for his godliness than the wicked for his wickedness? Are not the members of Christ more hated and worse entertained by us than the limbs of Satan ? So dearly every one loves sin, and draws sin upon sin, till there be a chain of many links, and monsters therein drawn most loathsome. And though we of ourselves run swiftly to hell, yet the most drive us, to make us hie faster ; they come unto us and say, Your fathers loved us well, and said unto us, If you will be fair, you shall be wise ; if you will be drunk, you shall be rich, &c. Yea, every one pointeth and sheweth us the way that leadeth to destruction, but how few are the number of them that do shew us the way of virtue and godliness !

And thus we are even as forward as those Jews that strive who shall come into hell first. Who did ever thank God that he was not born an hundred years ago, when ignorance spread over all, and all Egypt was smitten with darkness ? Or that the Lord hath not left him to himself to become an atheist or an epicure, which lives without God in the world ? We have all God's gifts offered us, but we have refused them. Christ brought light, but we had rather he had brought darkness ; for we loved darkness more than light. The angels, the heavens, the word, the Spirit, are light, and we that see it are darkness ; for we cannot abide light, but are like an owl that flieth out of a bare field from the light of the day : such a death is day unto us. Faith is flown away, truth is become a pilgrim, and every string is out of tune. He that should weep and be sorrowful, laughs ; and truth is brought to the ground, yea, poor truth is persecuted to death ; but sinners are stubble, and their sentence is, *Burn them.*

How fine would be the way of virtue, if you would pare away the rubs that are in it ; if you would take away all occasions of sin, and give it gall to eat ; and when you have done so, set a crown of thorns upon the head thereof; and when you have thus crowned it, make it carry the cross ; and when it hath carried the cross, condemn it ; and when you have condemned it, put it to death ; and when you have put it to death, bury it ; and when you have buried it, roll a great stone upon the head of it, and set watchmen to keep it, even fasting and prayer, that it may never rise again to reign any more. The which the Lord for his mercy's sake grant. Amen.

THE CALLING OF JONAH.

IN FOUR SERMONS.

THE CALLING OF JONAH.

THE FIRST SERMON.

*The word of the Lord came to Jonah the son of Amittai, saying,
Arise, and go to Nineveh, that great city, and cry against it,
for their wickedness is come up before me.*—JONAH I. 1, 2.

YOU have heard the sweet song of old father Simeon, like the
pleasant song of a sweet bird before her death, setting forth the joy
of the righteous that embrace Christ Jesus. Before Christ Jesus
vouchsafed to come to us, we would not come unto him, but in all
our doings we wrought our condemnation, and through the innumerable heaps of our iniquities, laboured to drive him, without all hope
of mercy, from us. So we continued, like flies which flutter about
the candle, till they have consumed themselves. When we had
done as much as in us lay to drive him away from us, then he
saved us, and recompensed good for evil unto us. So that if God
had loved us no more than we loved ourselves, we might have
perished in our sins, and our blood should have been upon our own
heads. If Christ be the light of the Gentiles, let us embrace him,
and every one walk as becometh the children of light. But many
do shut their eyes against it, lest they should see ; and not only many
smother their own light, but the sun saith unto the moon, Shine
not, and the moon saith unto the stars, Be not bright ; and many
have smothered their light so long, that the damp hath put out the
candle. And thus they labour to bring the darkness of Egypt upon
Goshen, so that their eyes have forgotten to see, and so many go
out of the way, because they would not look upon the candle ; and
the devil giveth to every one that which he wisheth, so it may be
for his hurt. But who can but pity that, with the same manna

which cometh from heaven, and feedeth many to life everlasting, so many are poisoned, and find it is nothing but the savour of eternal death.

The Jews had no cause to envy our light, for he gave them glory; he was poor, and yet he gave them riches; he was counted base, and yet he made them honourable; he was contemned, and yet he made them beloved; they were full of darkness, and he brought them light; but they contemned his light, and so procured their own condemnation. And therefore now it is come to pass, that they are become vagabonds upon the earth, and most contemned of all other nations, and in every people have a dwelling. Ever since they prophesied evil unto themselves, saying, 'His blood be upon us and our children,' goodness hath put on the face of bashfulness amongst them.

If thou embrace Christ, as Simeon did, then Christ is thy glory; but if thy glory consist in beauty, which fadeth; in gay clothing, which weareth; in wealth, which wasteth; or in gold, that rusteth; then Christ is not thy glory.

We have gone long with an old man, and now we have lost him; but we are loath to part with him, he is such a good companion; nevertheless we hope to find him again in Jonah. We have gone but slowly with him, as with an old man that is not very swift of foot; but now we must run with Jonah as with a post, lest Nineveh be destroyed.

The prophecy of Jonah. I need not to shew the authority of prophets; but, concerning their sorts and differences, there are three sorts of prophets. The first were such as called upon the name of the Lord in prayer for the people, and received an answer from the Lord in the people's behalf, of which sort was Samuel; and these were called seers, 1 Sam. ix. 9. A second sort of prophets were such as God raised to expound the law, and declare the will of God unto the people, when the priest and such as should do so were slack in their callings; of which sort was Isaiah, Jeremiah, Ezekiel, Daniel, Hosea, Joel, Amos, Obadiah, and the rest of the holy prophets. A third sort were such as have been since Christ, working such like effects; of which sort was the prophet Agabus, of whom mention is made in Acts xi. 28.

Now in the second sort of these was Jonah, whom God sent to declare his will to the people; unto whom also the Lord did reveal the subversions of kingdoms, the overthrow of tribes, the captivity of nations, the calamities that were to come unto the sons of men for iniquity and rebellion against God.

As all wise men were not born at once, nor lived together, so these holy prophets have not been at once, but were raised up by the Lord God, some here, some there, according to his pleasure, and as he saw the people stand in need of them, by reason of the corruption of the times.

And, furthermore, the Lord hath not at any time revealed unto one of these all things that might be revealed, but as much as was sufficient for them, every one in their time and place. Neither hath any of them told as much of the will of God as might be declared, nor fully expounded his laws; but the patriarchs left some to the prophets, and the prophets left some to the apostles; but they have left none for us, but they have all set open the whole will of God unto us; and every prophet now bringeth only gold, myrrh, and frankincense, like the wise men that came to see our Lord.

There are three things that moved me to take this story in hand above all others. First, because you know the story, and therefore can the better conceive of the matter as I go forward with it. Secondly, because it is brief, and doth contain a great deal in a little. Thirdly, because it is most agreeable for the time and state of this sinful age wherein we live, and therefore most convenient for us. It is manifest that Jonah lived in a very troublesome time, namely, in the time of Jeroboam the son of Joash, king of Israel, a wicked king, though not he that is called the Jeroboam that made Israel to sin. For of this second Jeroboam, in whose time he prophesied, it is written, 2 Kings xiv. 24, 'He departed not from any of the sins of Jeroboam, that made Israel to sin;' which commendeth the holiness of Jonah, in that he, in the midst of their corruption, wherewith all the people were overflown, was uncorrupted and unspotted, and called to be a prophet amongst the people of God. For he had prophesied in Israel before he was sent to Nineveh, as the word also doth argue, 2 Kings xiv. 25. Which layeth open and magnifieth the great love of God, in that he sent a prophet to admonish this ungodly people, whenas he should have sent a thunderbolt to terrify them, or rather utterly to destroy them; so that there mercy stepped before judgment.

His name was *Jonah*, which signifieth a *dove*, which admonisheth us that, as we labour to be as wise as serpents, so we should also desire that we might be as simple as doves. His father's name was *Amittai*, which signifieth *truth*. I would that truth were every preacher's father.

There are two special things contained in this history. The first, the great mercy of God shewed unto three sorts of men: the Ninevites, Jonah, and the mariners. In respect of the Ninevites, that he sent a prophet to Nineveh, a city of the Gentiles, which were strangers from the covenant, from the promise, and 'strangers from the commonwealth of Israel,' and converted them by his preaching, and so spared them now.

In regard of Jonah, that being, for his disobedience in flying to Tarshish when he was sent to Nineveh, thrown into the sea, he prepared a great whale to swallow him, and in his belly, even in the bottom of the sea, where there was no hope of life for him, preserved him, and after three days delivered him thence safe ; and then cast him not off, but continued him in his calling, and wrought powerfully by him, both in the ship, converting the idolatrous mariners, and in Nineveh, humbling the king and the whole city. And, lastly, when he had most unworthily doubly murmured and justified himself against God, he contented himself with a gentle and mild reproof of him.

In consideration of the mariners, that, having been idolaters all their lives, and now in danger, giving the honour of God to their own fancies, God yet converteth them, so that they called upon him and sacrificed and made vows unto the true God, and, by his mighty power having the wind and seas calmed, were then and for ever saved.

The second thing is Jonah's fall and rising again. His fall, first sinning, both flying from God and murmuring, and therein justifying of himself ; secondly, sustaining his punishment, manifold and long fears, casting into the sea, and continuing in the whale's belly three days, and afterward his reproof and conviction. His rising : first, repenting in the ship, in the belly of the whale, and being cast out of it ; then also faithfully discharging his duty, crying against Nineveh courageously.

We have seen Jonah afar off ; if we would, we might see him nearer. 'He that receives a prophet in the name of a prophet, shall receive a prophet's reward.' Therefore let us prepare our ears to hear and receive the word of God preached by the ministers, and let us think that Jonah is come again to our houses to preach ; and whether it be forty days, or forty weeks, or forty years, they that live like Sodom shall be punished like Sodom. But as our Saviour saith to his disciples, 'Pray that your flight be not in winter, nor on the Sabbath,' Mat. xxiv. 20 ; so say I unto you, Pray that the Lord's coming be not on the week days, for if he come then, how shall he find you ? Therefore I pray you learn at least now and give good ear, that you may hear sufficient for all the week.

The word of the Lord came to Jonah, the son of Amittai, saying, Arise, and go to Nineveh, &c.

Herein I observe that Jonah went not before he was sent; for going to preach unto Gentiles, it was needful that he should have a special calling and commission from the Lord himself; for it was unmeet to 'cast the children's bread unto the dogs,' unless he had a special commandment from God so to do.

None ought to take upon them the function of preaching in the church, unless they have their warrant or authority from God, as Aaron had, Heb. v. 4. And although they have not their authority in that form and manner as Jonah had his, namely, as it were, by word of mouth even from God himself, 'Arise, and go to Nineveh,' yet they must have their warrant from him, else their calling is unlawful.

But now here is another authority crept into the church, that makes so many idols, which have eyes and see not, tongues and speak not, ears and hear not; and that is this, when one stalleth up another into Moses's chair, not having Moses's rod, nor Moses's spirit. But this gall will not hold spurring. Farther, I observe that, as the word of the Lord came to Jonah, so the word of the pope came to his priests, Jesuits, and seminaries, but so and in such sort many times, that they are drawn to Tyburn, while masses are said for them at Rome.

The word of the Lord came to Jonah, &c. That which came unto him was not always with him; but so it was, that when the word of the Lord came unto any of the prophets, then they were well furnished with ability to teach, to preach, to reprove, or to command, whomsoever the Lord would have so handled. As by example, Nathan the prophet bid David the king that he should build a temple, 2 Sam. vii. 3, and 1 Chron. xvii. 2. And a little after he came and bid him that he should not build it. Where we see, that when he bid him build it, then the Spirit of the Lord came not unto him, to bid him so to do. And therefore the Spirit of God came unto him the very same night, and bid him that he should go to David, and bid him that he should not build it. For this is evident, that as God himself is constant, so his Spirit and his word are constant, and therefore never saith and unsaith one thing.

Again, the prophet Elisha said, 2 Kings iv. 27, that the Shunammite's heart was grieved, but the Lord had hid it from him, and had not as then declared the same unto him; which doth note unto us, that the same word whereby the Lord hath and doth reveal marvellous things unto the prophets was not now upon him, neither is always upon any prophet; but according to the will of God it comes unto them, to reveal unto them what he would have them to do, and when it pleaseth him.

Also Daniel said, that the Lord did not reveal the king's dream unto him for any wisdom that he had more than any living, but only for the king's sake, and for the poor people of God's sake, Dan. ii. 30. And so you must think of us that are the ministers of the gospel, that the Lord doth not reveal his will unto us for any wisdom or worthiness that is in us more than other men, but for your sakes, and that we might reveal it to you. Therefore hear us even for this cause, because the Lord hath revealed unto us these things for your sakes and good.

From the calling we come to the charge.

Arise, and go to Nineveh, that great, &c. God cometh and findeth us all asleep, then he bids us arise; for they are not fit to convert others which are not yet converted themselves; according to that saying of Christ to Peter, 'When thou art converted, strengthen thy brethren,' Luke xxii. 32, teaching them by your experience.

Now-a-days men take upon them to reprove others for committing such things as themselves have practised, and do practise without amendment, notwithstanding their diligence in teaching others their duty; they can teach all the doctrine of Christ saving three syllables, that is, *Follow me.* Therefore these are like some tailors, which are busy in decking and trimming up others, but go both bare and beggarly themselves. Yet they will not let us pluck out the beam that is in their eyes, until we have plucked out the mote which is in our own eyes.

Go to Nineveh. Nineveh was the greatest and ancientest city in the land of Assyria, and the name of it signified *beautiful;* which name was rather given it, for the greatness and beauty thereof, than the name of Ashur, which was the builder and first founder thereof, as we read in the book of Genesis, Gen. x. 11. It had a fair name, but foul deeds, like this city.

Go to Nineveh, &c. God would not suffer any people to be untaught; therefore he hath written his name in great letters, easy to be read of all. 'The heavens declare the glory of God; and the firmament sheweth the works of his hands. They have no speech nor language, without them is their voice heard. Their line is gone forth through all the earth, and their words into the ends of the world,' Ps. xix. 1, 3, 4. 'In them is manifest for all what may be known of God, for his eternal power and Godhead are seen by the creation of the world,' Rom. i. 19, 20. But especially he teacheth some by his word also. Therefore he sent unto the old world Noah, Lot to Sodom, Moses to Israel, and here Jonah to Nineveh. But when Paul with Silas and Timothy 'had gone throughout Phrygia, and the region of Galatia, they were forbidden of the Holy Ghost to preach the word in Asia; then came they to Mysia, and sought to go into Bithynia: but the Spirit suffered them not,' Acts xvi. 6, 7.

Go to Nineveh. The Jews would not hear the word of God by Jonah, and therefore the Lord sent him to Nineveh. They that grieve the Spirit quench the Spirit. Then goes the prophet from Samaria to Nineveh. The word was in Samaria, it went thence to Nineveh. The gospel was at Ephesus, Rev. ii., it is come into England, it is gone out of the city; but it may depart from England again. 'If any think that he standeth, let him take heed lest he fall,' 1 Cor. x. 12.

But the prophet goes from Samaria to Nineveh. That was, first, to shake off the dust of his feet, to witness against them their obstinacy and hardness of heart; and secondly, to let them see that the wicked Gentiles were more righteous than they, in that they repented at the voice of one prophet, yea, and that with one sermon; whereas themselves refused and resisted all the holy and worthy prophets that God sent unto them; and thirdly, it may be, to signify, that the Jews, for their contempt and negligence, should be rejected, and the Gentiles should be received into the favour of God, that they might be an holy and sanctified people unto the Lord in their stead.

That great city. Nineveh had fifteen hundred towers in it, as some do write, and an hundred and twenty thousand little children, as it is noted in the end of this story, Jonah iv. 1; therefore it may well be called a great city; but the greater it was, the more ungodly it was. For as one man taketh sickness of another, so one man is infected by the wicked words and evil example of another, and so taught to sin the more, till the measure of sin be full.

And cry against it, &c. First, God biddeth him arise, and shake off all impediments, and then go and call them to battle; and now he bids him cry out against them, and so terrify them. Every prophet is a crier, as appeareth where the Lord biddeth Isaiah to 'lift up his voice like a trumpet,' Isa. lviii. 1. Every prophet must both be plain and bold; and this many times maketh the poor servants of God to speak their minds as plain and bold as if they sat in judgment. John was 'a voice;' a voice would not serve, he was 'the voice of a crier;' and yet he could not 'make all the crooked straight, nor the rough plain,' Luke iii. 4.

And because all the preachers of the gospel should cry, that is, preach zealously; in the second of the Acts it is written, the Holy Ghost came down in fire and tongues. But this fire is quenched, and the tongues are tied up, so that they that should cry are stark dumb. But though they cannot speak, they can see if a great benefice fall, though it be an hundred miles off; and Pharaoh had more care of his sheep than we have of our souls.

If preachers were not dumb, and their hearers deaf, they needed not to cry one to another; but such is the dumbness of preachers, and the deafness of all sorts of hearers, that there is great slowness of followers, so that there is but little good done, and but a few fruits gathered.

If ye were not deaf, we need not cry; but because ye be dull of hearing, therefore we cry with mouth, with heart, with hand, with foot, and with all the powers of our bodies, unto you; and yet how little do you regard it? But are not ye commanded to hear, as well as we to cry? Yea, the cock croweth when men are asleep; yea, the cock croweth, and yet Peter still denieth his master, Mat. xxvi.

Before you cry unto the Lord, hear what the word crieth unto you, and let not your works cry for vengeance while your tongues cry for mercy.

When men hear the preacher speak against pride, hypocrisy, covetousness, or against any other sin, then they look one upon another, as though it belonged not unto them; but 'who can say his heart is clean?'

And cry against it. Our sins buffet God on every side, as the Jews buffeted Christ, first on the right side, then on the left side, and never leave, till they have provoked him to cry against us. When God cries, then we should weep, considering wherefore he cries; for there is nothing that can provoke the Lord to cry but sin, and that he ever crieth against. Do what you will, and say what you will, and the Lord will not be offended with you, unless you sin; but if you commit sin, he is just, and therefore will not leave, till he hath by crying slain either you, or sin that reigns in you. For as an angry man ever pursueth that which he hateth, until he hath destroyed it, so the Lord crosseth and followeth us with his judgments, until he hath slain that which most deadly he hateth, sin.

And cry against it, &c. Reproof is the necessariest office, yet it is least regarded, yea, most abhorred. For now we think, if one reprove us, he hateth us. But the Lord saith, Lev. xix., 'Thou shalt not hate thy brother in thy heart: thou shalt reprove him, and suffer him not to sin;' noting thereby, that if we flatter any in their sin, or see them sin, and not reprove them for it, it is a manifest sign that we do it of hatred, how great love and good will soever we pretend toward them ; seeing the matter tends to the hurt of their souls, and the offence of God.

Yea, if a preacher reprove sin, he is thought to do it of hatred, or of some particular grudge, and to be too busy, too bitter, too sharp, too rough ; and therefore they say he should preach God's love and mercy, for he is a preacher of the gospel ; he tells us of, and threatens us with, the law, and so throws us down too low, some to despair. As though we preached the law only or chiefly, and not the gospel also continually, to them that loathe and strive against their sins, though they sin grievously. Others, as though they were galled, will say, Let him keep his text ; or they will say, He is beside his book : as though no text in Scripture reproved sin. And so of all doctrines, the doctrine of reproof and reprehension of sin is most contemned, and least esteemed. But let a preacher preach dark mysteries, or profane speeches, or unprofitable fables, or frivolous questions, or curious inventions, or odd conceits, or brain-sick dreams, and any of these will be more welcome unto them than reprehension, which is most profitable and necessariest of all. Balaam's ass never spake but once, and then he reproved, Numb. xxii. 28. Then, if Balaam's ass reproved Balaam, how much more ought Balaam to reprove asses, or such as will be no otherwise than beasts in their behaviour ! But persuade yourselves, beloved, which is most true, though we speak as if we were angry with you, and threaten as if we would hurt you, and cry against you as if we hated you, yet we love you in the dearest blood we have ; and therefore, though with persecution we preach the law, to lead you to the gospel, we preach judgment that you may find mercy, we preach hell to bring you to heaven ; whatsoever and howsoever we preach, we do all to fill your hearts with joy in believing, and, having made you fruitful in all good works, present you without spot, nay, glorious also, as a virgin most beautiful, to the Lord of all grace and glory, Christ Jesus.

Hitherto we have heard of Jonah called and charged to cry ; but what should he cry ? Indeed, it is not expressed in this place. But what then ? Why, then, the papists may say that he was charged to cry against them for neglecting their traditions. Assuredly they may with as great truth, and as much probability, as they do gather out of divers places of the New Testament,[1] that they ought to be observed. But Jonah hath not left it doubtful what he was to cry; for in the third chapter, ver. 2, the charge is repeated, and thus expressed, 'Go, and proclaim against it the proclamation which I speak unto thee.' He was then to cry what God had commanded him. Oh that none would cry but what God hath commanded!

But what did God command him to cry? Even that which he afterward cried, 'Yet forty days, and Nineveh shall be overturned.' Overturned? Yea, ancient Nineveh, fair Nineveh, proud Nineveh, must be destroyed. No man sits so high but destruction sits above him, and will fall on all that persist in their defection. Justice would have come against them before it cried against them; but God the most gracious would have them cried against, that they might cry out woe and alas for their sins, so preventing deserved and threatened vengeance; for they, hearing the cry of God, cried out themselves, and that in great humbling to God; so God heard their cries, and took pity on them.

Isaiah was commanded to cry, and he cried, 'All flesh is grass, yea, all the glory thereof like the flower of the field: the grass withereth, the flower fadeth, when the Spirit of Jehovah bloweth on it: surely the people is grass,' Isa. xl. 6, 7. John was commanded in the spirit of Elijah to cry, and he cried, 'Prepare the way of Jehovah, make even in the desert a path for our God,' Mat. iii. 3. And Jonah was commanded to cry, and he cried, 'Yet forty days, and Nineveh shall be overthrown,' Jonah i. 2 and iii. 2. And all the preachers of the gospel are commanded to 'cry,' and that aloud, not to spare: to lift up their voices like a trumpet, to shew God's people their defections, and the house of Jacob their sins,' Isa. lviii. 1. And then, also, if they thereby be truly humbled, to proclaim unto them, 'their iniquity is pardoned, they have received at the hand of Jehovah double for all their sins,' Isa. xl. 2. 'It is required of the disposers of God's secrets, that they be found faithful,' 1 Cor. iv. 1, 2. And woe be to them that love the pleasures of sin more than the glory of God.

For their wickedness is come up before me. For, &c. We have heard the charge itself given; heavy news, that a most beautiful city, a most rich city, a most populous city, and a most ancient city, must be overturned, and that within forty days. What is

[1] John xvi. 12; xxi 25; Acts i. 3; 1 Tim. vi. 20; 2 Tim. i. 13, and ii. 2.

the cause? 'Their wickedness is come up before me.' As if he had said, Nineveh hath followed her lusts and forgotten the law, to satisfy her desires; she hath notoriously despised her sovereign, defied all well-meaning, all good dealing; and this is known to the just judge, and at his bar she is arraigned, and her accusers stand crying at the bar of justice. Therefore she may no longer be forborne, execution of justice must needs be done. Let her, therefore, prepare for death, and that she may, 'cry against her, Yet forty days, and Nineveh shall be overturned; for their wickedness is come up before me.'

When God sends criers unto a people, it is a most manifest sign that their wickedness is come up before him, which doth cause him thus to exclaim, thus to cry out against them. And then, if they will not repent, whilst God's cries continue crying amongst them, the Lord of hosts will rise up in arms against them.

Their wickedness. Will you see the Ninevites in a scroll, that withal you, the daughters of Nineveh, may see that wealth and wickedness were got together, prosperity and security kissed each other? Nineveh, saith Nahum, was like 'a pool of waters,' most populous and 'full of all store,' Nahum ii. 3; which to increase, it was wholly full of lying, deceit, and fraud, full of robbery, oppression, and all violence, a bloody city, whereby it increased in wealth, and flourished in honour and glory; and therefore, as Zephaniah hath it, was 'a rejoicing, a rioting city, sat securely,' and proudly contemned others, saying, 'I am, and none is beside me,' Zeph. ii. 15. Moreover, it was 'the mistress of witchcrafts,' a most idolatrous city; yea, 'sold people through her whoredoms, and nations through her witchcrafts,' Nahum iii. 4, and made others idolatrous like herself, as 2 Kings xvi. 10.

Their wickedness is come up before me. Sin mounts up on high, like the tempter, which led Christ unto the top of the pinnacle, to behold all the pleasures of the world at once; and then, because we have fallen down before the god of this world, and tempted the God of heaven, whether he be just or no, therefore wrath speaks out of the fire, Now thou hast taken thy pleasure, thou must also take thy punishment.

A most heavy and grievous thing it is, if you knew what you are doing here, and what your sins are doing at the bar of God's just judgment. For even now, before you came hither, you were serving the devil in sin; but now it is too late to speak of it. And where are they now? Flesh and blood could not stay them, nature could not stay them, pleasures could not stay them, riches could not stay them, nor they could not stay themselves, but they are ascended up before the face of the eternal God, to stand at his bar, and cry for vengeance to fall upon us, for committing such heinous sins against the majesty of God.

An arrow is swift, the sun is swifter, but sin is swiftest of all; for in a moment it is committed on earth, it comes before God in heaven, and is condemned to hell. For though Nimrod could not climb to heaven, his sins flew up to heaven; and though we stay below, our sins ascend high, like the tower of Nimrod; but they fling us down to confusion, and we become Babel. For when we sin, we are as the shell-fish, which the eagle taketh, and flieth into the air with, and then letteth it fall upon the rocks, and so dasheth it in pieces, and then devours it. For the wrath of God taketh us up on high, and throweth us down low upon the rocks of shame, and contempt, and terror of conscience; and so, having crushed us, and bruised our very bones, consumes us with double death, the grave devouring us, hell swallowing us.

Is come before me. To them which ask how our sins ascend and fly up before God, I answer, God here speaks unto us after the manner of men, who cannot see a thing afore it be brought unto them, even where they are, and before them. So that hereby is signified, God had seen their wickedness.

We fast as before him, we pray as before him, we give alms as before him, and we do every good thing as before him; because we do it freely, and as it were not caring who looks upon us. But we sin as behind him; because we hide and cloak our sins, and commit them in secret, loath that men should spy them; our conscience in such actions accusing us, and instantly telling us, we are about that which we cannot justify. And we suppose that we sin behind him, because we sin here below; saying with ourselves in the consideration of our blinded hearts, as Eliphaz accused Job to have said, 'Is not God in the height of heaven? and see the highness of the stars, how high are they! Therefore how should God know it? should he be able to see through the dark? The thick clouds are a covering to him, that he may not see; and he walketh up and down the round circle of the heavens,' Job xxii. 12–14. But then chiefly we imagine that God beholds us not, when men cannot see us; as if God could not know when men cannot spy. But let us not deceive ourselves, for 'God seeth not as man seeth.' Man can see but only outward things committed in action; but God seeth, and knoweth, and searcheth the secrets of the heart, yea, the secretest thoughts and imaginations of it. Again, man can but see one thing at once; he cannot turn his right eye one way and left eye another; he cannot see before him and behind him with one look; but God seeth all things at all times. Though we sin as closely as we can for fear of hatred or shame of the world, or for any other respect, yet God saith, Your sin is come up before me. For though we cover it, and hide it, and colour it, yea, and, as it were, bury it as much as lieth in us, yet all is open unto him; therefore he saith, Your sin is come up before me.

For when we speak evil, he is all ears to hear us; and when we do evil, he is all eyes to behold it. Therefore, O foolish man, do not think that God seeth not that which man seeth not; for when he looks up, he sees all below also; and when he looks down, he sees all above also. If he should not, much wickedness should lie in darkness unregarded, and men should not be terrified from sin, but rather by the example of others allured to sin freely, secretly. For Ananias might have gained by his craft, if God had not seen his heart, which men saw not; but God saw his distrustful and dissembling and corrupt heart; therefore he lost his goods, and his life too, Acts v.

If God had not seen that which men see not, Gehazi might have gained a bribe for his labour, when he ran after Naaman the Syrian, and told him a lie for his profit, 2 Kings v. But God seeing his fetches, which men saw not, turned his bribe to a leprosy, and so made him a leper for his labour. A fearful example for such as take bribes; yet many care not what bribes they take, so men see it not.

The man that said, 'Be merry, my soul, and take thy pleasure for many years,' might have done it, had not God seen him. But he espied him falling to godless security, and threatened him that night to bereave him of his soul, Luke xii. 19. Forget it not, ye that abound in wealth, whose cup runneth over. If God had not seen Achan take up the piece of gold, Joshua vii., he had kept it to himself for his labour, and no man should have known where he had it. But God seeing it, though closely done, rewarded him with shame in the sight of all Israel. O Lord, what is man, that thou so watchest him? Achan would never have stolen, if he had known that God did see him; Gehazi durst never have taken a bribe, if he had thought that God beheld his doings. Wilt thou steal, the owner looking on thee? Wilt thou speak treason in the king's hearing? Neither should we lie, nor swear, nor steal, nor hurt, nor be profane at any time, if we considered that the Lord seeth us, and remembered that he watcheth us. If we would do this, sin might go a-begging for want of service. Therefore if you would mark but this part of my sermon, that God seeth all, you would refrain from those things secretly that are to the offence of God, which you for fear or shame will not do before men ; and you would say, even when your hand is at it, I will not do it, because the Lord seeth me. But as when we sin, though in secret, he is all eyes to see us ; and he sees it requisite to make some example, to teach all, that when men cannot nor will not dicover us, he will shew that he saw us, then he is all hand to punish and plague us, and in the end to root us out from all our pleasures ; so when we repent, he is all mercy and love ; and when we amend our lives, and leave all our wicked ways, to walk before him ever after in holiness, then he is all truth and righteousness, to forgive us all our former wicked life, and to wash us from all our uncleanness. Now, therefore, repent thee of all the evil that thou hast done, lament truly, run and hie thee as fast as ever thou canst to the throne of grace ; prove whether thy repentance will not as boldly stand before God and as powerfully cry for pardon, as thy sins speedily came up before God, and vehemently cried for punishment. No doubt the angel that cried, ' Fallen is, fallen is Babylon the great,' Rev. xviii. 2, though he ' cried vehemently with a loud voice,' cried not so audibly as thou shalt hear the Spirit of truth crying and assuring thee, Thy sins are forgiven thee, The God of glory loveth thee, Sin shall no longer reign in thee, Rom. vi. 14 ; no evil shall hurt thee; no good thing shall be wanting to thee, Ps. xci. 10, and xxxiv. 10, and lxxxiv 11 ; all things shall work together to the best for thee, Rom. viii. 28. Wilt thou any more ? He shall ever dwell with thee, ' in whose presence is the fulness of joy, and at his right hand pleasures for evermore,' Ps. xvi. 11. Repent therefore, but repent truly, loathe all sin, grieve that thou hast committed any, fly every sin, yea, whatsoever occasions of it, and ' all appearance of evil,' 1 Thes. v. 22; but ' love the truth' also, 2 Thes. ii. 10, and ' follow all holiness, and, as much as in you is, have peace with all men,' Heb. xii. 14 ; and the God of peace will increase your peace in Christ Jesus.

All which, even this point that we speak of, viz., whatsoever we do God seeth us, most sufficiently assureth us of. For this so often repeated speech, Rev. ii. 2, 9, 13, 19, and iii. 1, 8, 15, ' I know thy works,' is spoken as to rouse the dead Sardians, iii. 1, and to heat the lukewarm Laodiceans, iii. 15, so to commend the faith, hope, love, patience, &c., of the other churches, and so to establish and set them forward therein, knowing he is just, and ' a liberal rewarder of them that seek him,' Heb. xi. 6.

Their wickedness is come up before me. Sin once committed casts no doubts of coming presently before God; but the thoughts of the heart of the carnal man, thinking of the way to heaven, are the faint spies that went to the land of Canaan, which say, that journey is farther than you are able to go all your life, the way is like a thicket, and the door like a needle's eye; therefore it is impossible for you to come thither. But when you send faith, hope, and love, those messengers of peace and truth, they will bring you word, saying, Your ruffs must be ruffled, and your farthingales crushed, pride must be put off and other sins; and none shall be kept out of heaven, but such as love the world better than heaven, or such as will take their sins with them; for they be unbeseeming the fashion of that country. So that ere we come thither we must leave them, like the shadow when we go in at the door, and we must shake hands with them, and bid them farewell.

THE REBELLION OF JONAH.

THE SECOND SERMON.

But Jonah rose up to fly to Tarshish from the presence of the Lord, and went down to Joppa; and found a ship going to Tarshish : so he paid the fare thereof, that he might go with them to Tarshish from the presence of the Lord.—JONAH I. 3.

THE charge given to Jonah hath hitherto been spoken of; now it followeth to be shewed how it was by Jonah discharged. First, Jonah rebelliously neglected it; then, being chastised, and so repenting, he faithfully discharged it. First, therefore, let us consider his rebellion; afterward we shall see his correction.

But Jonah rose up to fly to Tarshish from the presence of the Lord. We cannot stand to speak of Tarshish, nor what it is to fly from God, but this shall be our meditation, Jonah the prophet was commanded to go to Nineveh, and there to cry out against sin, to preach against pride and all kind of ungodliness, thereby to reclaim them, and stir them up, in laying open their sin, and the punishment that hanged over them, that they might speedily repent, and so turn away from them the wrath of God thereby deserved. How beautiful should have been the feet of him that should have brought so powerful a message as should have wrought such an happy effect! How blessed should Nineveh have been, when the Lord had vouchsafed them so great mercy! But still one fly or other mars the whole box of ointment, Eccles. x. 1. As soon as he was commanded to go thither, Satan stood in the gap, and enticed him to go to Tarshish; for he thought that if he could let Jonah from going to Nineveh, then, first of all, he should put a singular prophet out of God's favour, and bring upon him some judgment, not only inward, as torment of conscience, decay of gifts, or the like, but visible also, whereby the people to whom he had preached might think he was some false prophet, as they are ever ready to condemn for hated of God whom they see grievously afflicted; and so, secondly, the people should be hardened in their sins, and obstinately condemn ever after, him, his like, and their preaching too ; and, thirdly, the goodliest, the most populous, and the wealthiest city in Assyria should be destroyed ; the good with the wicked, the young with the old, one with another, all should unrepentant die in their sins, and so the very angels in heaven should mourn. So that he thought he should, by stopping Jonah, every way gain well by his labour.

Therefore he comes to Jonah, he flatters him, he tempts him ; thus he begins with him. It is good that men look before they leap ; haste makes waste ; words are not always to be taken as they properly signify, one thing is often spoken and another meant ; but thinkest thou God meaneth thou shouldst go to Nineveh ? Why, doth he regard idolaters, and his professed enemies, so that, to have them admonished of their ruin, he will bring shame upon his own people ? For the very going of a prophet from Israel to preach to Nineveh, must needs proclaim that there is more hope of most sinful Gentiles than of natural Israelites. And how couldst thou seem so to think of thine own nation, thine own brethren, thine own blood, the chosen of God ? Or if thou do, shalt thou not thereby procure their utter hatred for ever, and make them to detest both thy person and thy preaching, whatsoever thou hast heretofore, or hereafter shalt teach them ?

What ! for thy faithful prophesying here among God's people, will God, thinkest thou, recompense thee, thee whom he hath made reverend, and to be honoured of kings and princes of Israel ; recompense, I say, thee with shame and contempt among heathens, yea, with a cruel death, or with a more miserable life ? For what other success may be hoped for at the Ninevites' hands of such a message by thee ? For thou knowest they have all Jews in contempt ; therefore when thou shalt come among them, and tell them not these few words only, and in this form which God hath spoken them in (for if thou so do, who will not count thee rather a madman than God's prophet ?), but at large, that there is one all-seeing, most just, almighty, and ever-living God, and no more ; and so all their gods are no gods, but idols ; and that they above all others have given his glory to stocks and stones, worshipping them for gods, alluring and enforcing others likewise to dishonour him ; that they have abused his blessings most unthankfully, most ungodly, to all excess, and are most proud contemners of their betters, and most notorious drunkards, gluttons, fornicators, adulterers, thieves, oppressors, witches, murderers, and the like; and therefore have so provoked him that is most merciful and patient, that he will without all pity destroy man, woman, young and old, high and low, amongst them, yea, their very city also, and all that is therein, whereby they have been so wicked, and that within forty days. When, I say, thou, being a Jew, shalt tell them this, thus in despite revile (for so they will take it), thus utterly condemn them and their gods, will not the best of them mock and despise thee? will not the rest gnash their teeth at thee, be ready to tear thee in pieces, put thee to exquisite torments, condemn thee to some horrible death, or continue thee in intolerable pains, in a most bitter life? No question. Think not therefore that thy good God, thy most kind and tender Father, will recompense thy faithfulness with sending thee so far, to sustain such misery; it were impiety to think he willed it; it is blasphemy, terrible blasphemy, to think he commands it. For it is to condemn him of unkindness, for thou hast shewed fervent love; of untruth, for he hath promised it should go well with the just; of injustice, for godliness should have the reward due only to wickedness. Yea, he should seem contrary to himself, to charge thee cruelly to murder thyself, which hath commanded all to kill none, if he should will thee to provoke that bloody city so. But the very thing itself also argueth, God meant nothing less than to commit thee to such danger, or that thou shouldst do to the proud Ninevites such a message. For to what end shouldst thou so cry against that city? To make them fly, and so to free them from destruction. How shouldst thou then not be found a false prophet, and God a liar? What then? To bring to repentance, and then to spare them? How should not God so again be found untrue, and thou his lying messenger? What then? To convert them, and so to destroy them? What justice were that, and how contrary to his promise to Solomon? 2 Sam. vii. 14, 15. Therefore it is manifest, God meant not thou shouldst go and cry so against Nineveh; but signified that thou wert as good, for any good may be done here, to exclaim so like a frantic man against Nineveh, as to preach in Samaria any longer now. Men here are so hardened, that they contemn all; part are so cloyed, that they loathe all; the best part little esteem all that is preached; of none is the word accounted precious, of none reverently heard. And therefore, thou shouldst for a time, to make the word precious, and to sharpen men's affections towards it, give over preaching here, and, where thou wilt, re-

fresh thyself a while. Now, here thou mayest not be idle ; at
Tarshish thou mayest be quiet ; thou mayest at Tarshish, that
famous city, among the strangers of many countries, hear many
strange things, much delight thee in the variety of their manners,
in the abundance of all things with great pleasure live. No time
so fit as this to see the world. At Joppa thou canst not want
shipping thither. Seem not to make small account of this kindness of God, defraud not thyself of the granted good.

Thus Satan is ever crossing, tempting. enticing us, when we are
or should be addressing ourselves to do the will of our God. So
was Moses, Exod. iii. 11, and chap. iv. ; Jeremiah, Jer. i. 6 ;
Ezekiel, Ezek. iii. 14 ; Nehemiah, Neh. ii. 19, and iv. ii. 8 ; Christ
himself tempted, Mat. iv. 1 ; being about most notable works.
What said our Saviour to Peter ? 'Satan hath desired to sift and
winnow you as wheat,' Luke xxii. 31. Who are these whose peril
Satan so earnestly desireth ? Even Peter's, and James's, and
John's. No marvel, for Christ himself, though acknowledged the
Son of God, was most fiercely assaulted of the tempter forty days,
and then indeed was left, but it was only for a season, Luke iv. 13.
Therefore never dream of a truce with Satan, whosoever thou be,
whatsoever thou art about to do. For the enemy, the envious foe,
the tempter, the false accuser, 'goeth about continually seeking
whom he may devour,' 1 Peter v. 8. Now his manner of tempting
is, first, and most usually, with flattering, but yet very often with
most terrible threatening. For whatsoever we do or feel cometh
from one of these three spirits, the spirit of Satan, the Spirit of
God, or our spirit. Now our own spirit of itself is always occupied
about worldly things, seeking delights in pleasures, not disquiet by
threats. The Spirit of God is gentle, loving, and meek ; not forcing,
not threatening. Therefore Christ saith, 'If any will follow me,
let him deny himself, and take up his cross daily,' &c., Luke ix. 23.
And mark his spirit. He saith not, *You shall* follow me, and *You
shall* deny yourselves, and take up your cross ; but, If any will
follow me, let him deny himself, and take up his cross. *Let him.*
The same is to be seen in the Canticles, where he saith, 'Open
unto me, my sister, my love, my dove, my undefiled ; for my head
is full of dew, and my locks with the drops of the night,' Cant. v. 2.
For when she opened not unto him, making most unmeet excuses,
though he had most lovingly prayed, and lively urged her to open,
and she most unkindly, most unworthily, had denied ; yet he went
his way mildly, without any threats. But the spirit of Satan takes
another course ; for, when by lying and deceit he cannot allure to

sin, he threatens most fearfully with grief, or loss of goods, solitari-
ness, and want of pleasure ; and sometime by his ministers, imps
of his own likeness, he threatens death and deadly torments, whatsoever they may inflict upon any.

Christ saith, ' If you will follow me.' If you will ; but he saith,
I will make you follow me, and do as I bid you ; else you shall have
fire and faggot, scalding lead and burning pitch ; if you will not
follow me, you shall, whether you will or no. We will make you
do as we command, saith his eldest son antichrist, usurping
authority over nations, and inflicting torments on the saints. His
order of tempting is, first, to make us doubt of the word of God,
whether such or such doctrine be true, such and such an action be
commanded, such and such a promise, such and such a threatening,
be certain. Then, secondly, he falls to flat denying of it. This
doctrine, these promises, these threatenings, are false ; this thing
is not commanded, this action is not commended. And then comes
he in with his contradiction, contrary assertions, and countermands.
For there is no commandment of God, but the devil commands the
contrary, and he is ever gainsaying that which God saith. For our
God saith unto Adam, If you eat of the forbidden fruit, you shall
surely die, Gen. iii. 3, 17 ; the devil came and he told them, first,
It is not certain you shall die; then, ' You shall not die;' then,
thirdly, ' You shall be as gods, knowing good from evil,' Gen. iii.
4, 5. God saith, ' Submit yourselves one to another in brotherly
love, 1 Peter v. 5 ; the devil saith, first, You need not to abase
yourselves so much ; secondly, You should not yield to others ;
then, thirdly, Advance yourselves, and contemn others. God saith,
' Love thy neighbour as thyself,' Mat. xxii. 39 ; the devil saith,
first, Love little, and outwardly ; then, Love none but thyself;
then, inwardly, hate thine enemies, envy thy betters, disdain thine
equals, despise thine inferiors. God saith, ' Labour for that food
that perisheth not,' John vi. 27 ; the devil saith, first, Care not
much for it ; then, secondly, Contemn it ; then, thirdly, Stir not
an inch for it. God saith, Forsake the world, Rom. xii. 2 ; the
devil saith, first, Neglect not the world ; then, Love the world;
then, thirdly, Give over yourselves unto the world ; above all,
Follow the world, with all the lusts thereof.

Now the means whereby the devil tempts are arguments fetched,
some from the wit and reason of man, or from the customs of the
world ; some from the holy Scriptures, either corrupted, or wrong
applied ; now in consideration of the persons, then in regard of the
thing itself, &c. In respect of the persons to whom he should

preach, and himself, Jonah is here tempted, and so thus reasoneth with himself : I have long preached unto the Jews, which are the chosen people of God ; and seeing they will not hear me, it is in vain to preach unto these Gentiles, which never heard of God or godliness, and therefore will esteem my words the less.

Thus Jonah is loath to lose his labour, and puts in a doubt where he needs not, because he considered not the great power of God in men's hearts. The Ninevites are heathen people, and therefore, saith Jonah, why should I venture myself amongst them ? For seeing my own countrymen kick against my words, and cannot abide to hear the word which cometh from the Lord to reprove sin ; then how much more shall I be despised by these, and persecuted to death ? Thus flesh and blood stand staggering when it should do any good, misdoubting troubles, jealous of his own case ; but when it goeth about to do any mischief, it never considereth the danger, it weigheth not the following woe. Yet doing good, it is uncertain whether all will not according to, or even above our hope, succeed ; it is more likely we should be kept safe ; but doing evil, mischief most certainly is procured, not danger only, but loss of the best things commonly, peace of conscience or spiritual graces, of some blessings alway, or at least not receipt of those things which much would rejoice us. For sure this was a sore temptation, to bid a man, being in reasonable good estate touching his body and life, that he should go and preach unto a savage heathen people, that never heard of preaching, and that this doctrine, that there is but one only true God, Deut. vi. 4, to them who will serve a thousand, and cannot abide the contrary to be spoken.

If a preacher were commanded to go and preach at Rome's gates against antichrist's jurisdiction, and the idolatry that is so inordinately used in that synagogue of uncleanness ; seeing that is a matter for which they torment and kill all that preach it sincerely, I fear it would hardly come to pass at all, that this preacher would go from a reasonable quiet estate touching his body, to venture his life among such cruel tyrants ; I fear he would rather content himself with his present case, than commit himself to so likely misery.

If I go to preach unto these infidels, saying. ' Yet forty days, and Nineveh shall be destroyed,' then, saith Jonah, it may be they will repent, and God will have mercy upon them, so I shall be counted a false prophet for my labour. And thus we regard our credit, more than the glory of God in the obedience of his will ; and rather than we would receive any reproach by our doings, in the sight of the world, we rather choose to enter into no great action touching the glory of God, and the good of the church.

In respect of the Israelites and himself he is thus tempted : If I leave mine own people, and preach unto the Gentiles, saith Jonah, I shall bring shame upon Israel before all people ; because a prophet is gone from them for their obstinacy, choosing rather to preach unto uncircumcised Gentiles than unto them, as if there were more hope of the Gentiles than of them.   So Jonah more feareth the children's disgraces than the Father's dishonour, and their despite than his displeasure.   Satan is too well acquainted with man's nature, and so more certainly knows than we wisely consider, that all Adam's sons are from labour easily brought to loiter ; more willingly from fear and pain to security and pleasure ; therefore seldom or never doth he in tempting omit this enticement, It will be for thy ease, for thy delight, for thy security.   Therefore he saith to Jonah, not only, The way to Nineveh is long and dangerous, thy person and message odious ; therefore thy travel must needs be tedious, thy troubles grievous, &c., but also, Thy passage to Tarshish is easy, thy security there sure, thy pleasures many, thy delight great.   Yea, with this he assaulted Christ himself, saying, when he had 'shewed him all the kingdoms of the world, and the glory of them,' 'All these will I give thee,' &c.   And doth he not so also evermore persuade us, this good, this gain, this glory, this pleasure, or this preferment shalt thou get, if thou thus and thus deal.   If you will leave the society, the exercises, the profession, and the company of the children of God, and serve me, and worship me ; preferring your covetousness, your pride, your lust, before the service of God ; not being scrupulous to swear for your gain sometime, nor to lie for your pleasure, nor to cozen for riches ; then you shall not only be free from the reproaches wherewith professors are overwhelmed, and the contempt wherein they are had, and the many heavy sighs that they are forced to fetch ; but you shall also grow rich soon, and so be well thought of, and had in estimation, and by your wealth live in ease, with all pleasure, procuring everything at your heart's desire.

Thus Jonah, which way soever he look, is tempted on every side ; tempted to sin, but not constrained ; urged, but not compelled; for the devil hath power to entice to sin mightily, but not to enforce violently.   Lo, then, comforts against this cross.   Our enemy's power is in our Father's hands, and our Saviour prayeth for us, being most glorious in heaven, as he on earth in humility prayed for his apostles, that our faith fail us not, Luke xxii. 32.   Behold, then, also encouragements to fight against his assaults ; yet see a greater. God hath given us this privilege, this promise have we, 'Resist the devil, and he shall flee from you,' James iv. 7. God hath given no promise to the devil, that if he persuade he shall prevail ; if he urge, we shall yield. What a shame is it to us that Satan is bolder in tempting than we are in resisting. Is he not ? Oh that we could truly say, We are as wise, as watchful, as thought-ful to withstand Satan's assaults, as he is wily, vigilant, and more than diligent to assault !

But what doeth Jonah, thus, as we have heard, by Satan assaulted? Resists he as manfully as the devil hath set on him cunningly ? Alas ! no ; Jonah is no sooner dissuaded to go to Nineveh, than he is persuaded it were great folly ; he is as soon resolved, as he is enticed, to go to Tarshish, thinking it a chief point of wisdom to seek his own ease, his own pleasure, his own sweet delight. Once, it is said, 'God spake, and it was done,' Gen. i. Surely the devil also but speaks, and it is done ; for he is such an orator as no man can deny him. For who can gainsay him that counselleth as a special friend, yea, as a most holy angel ? For he would seem to be not only careful both to keep us from danger and the fear thereof, and to procure us all good, but also jealous of God's honour, fearful lest men should despise the word, and so their own salva-tion. Therefore he made not only Gehazi to take a bribe, 2 Kings v. 22, 23, Demas to embrace the world, 2 Tim. iv. 10, Judas to betray his Master, Mat. xxvi. 48, 49, and Cain to kill his brother, Gen. iv. 8 ; but Rebekah also to persuade Jacob, and Jacob to be bold by lying to seek for the blessing, Gen. xxvii. 6, &c. ; yea, the father of the faithful to commit folly with Hagar, Gen. xvi. ; as here Jonah not to go to Nineveh, lest, forsooth, God should not be true of his word ; as if what to man seemeth unlikely, that were with God impossible ; and he could not be righteous, unless we shew ourselves impious.

We have seen some causes why Satan assaulting us, straight over-comes us ; would any see more ? We have been taught his power, malice, watchfulness, and wiliness ; we have most fit and sufficient armour ministered unto us, Eph. vi. 11, &c. ; we have a promise that, resisting him, we shall make him fly from us, James iv. 7. Therefore, surely we forget our enemy, or neglect the promise, or take not to us the whole armour of God, specially we like not that armour-bearer humility : 'Submit yourselves to God,' and then 'resist the devil.' But moreover, we to our own certain peril and pain, so corrupt are we, join with our enemy, more ready to do his will than God's word. Hereof, no doubt, foolish Balaam asked again and again, till God seeing him bent contrary to that he had been commanded, left him unto himself; and so Balaam went on in sin so long, till the very ass whereon he rode was constrained to reprove him, Num. xxii. But would you, howsoever Satan tempts, not to be turned by him out of the right way; howsoever he fights, not to be foiled by him? Would you have him soon to forsake you, speedily to fly from you; that is, would you resist him? for when we begin valiantly to fight, then forthwith he flies. Consider how shameful a thing it is, being every way encouraged to fight, to shew ourselves most dastardly cowards; how dishonourable to our captain, Christ, to yield the victory to his deadly enemy; how dangerous for ourselves, knowing he is a most cruel tyrant, and most inexorable, that most glorieth, and specially takes pleasure in putting us to the most bitter pain that possibly he can, and therefore having overcome us, will for ever continue us in most intolerable torments. Yea, sayest thou, these things considered would make us courageously to encounter with Satan, and so soon to conquer him; but he comes often as a friend, as an angel of light, how shall I then descry him, that I may defy him, and make him to fly?

How? Here, indeed, is the hardness, for he is a notable hypocrite, the father of hypocrisy; but thou must follow the counsel of Christ, Rev. iii. 18; thou must 'anoint thine eyes with the eyesalve, that thou mayest see;' thou must be 'fulfilled with the knowledge of God's will in all wisdom and spiritual understanding,' Col. i. 9; and moreover, 'watch and be sober,' 1 Peter v. 8. And lastly, consider, first, how thy spirit is affected; for our own spirit, by nature evermore hard, if it be moved by the Spirit of God, is sad, and soft, and slow; but if it be moved by the spirit of Satan, is proud, boisterous, and stout. Then, whether that which thou art indeed moved to be good or evil. If good, that is, agreeable to God's word, then acknowledge it comes from God; for all good motions are the work of the Spirit of God, howsoever they seem to proceed of ourselves. But if it be evil, that is, not agreeable with the word of God, then it is always either a lust of our corrupt nature, or a suggestion of Satan. Wherefore it is a sure way to say when we are tempted to evil, This motion is of the devil, for even our corruption came of his suggestion. For the spirit of man is always tossed between these two contrary spirits, the Spirit of God procuring our salvation, and the spirit of Satan seeking our condemnation. So that if any will get the victory of Satan, he may not be without the spiritual 'sword, which is the word of God,' Eph. vi. 17 ; yea, he must have 'the word of God dwell in him plenteously,' Col. iii, 17, and cry still, ' Open mine eyes, O Lord,' Ps. cxix. 18 ; ' Give me understanding,' ver. 34 ; and, ' Incline mine heart unto thy testimonies,' ver. 36, and beware that he submit himself duly, and diligently watch.

Thus, Jonah tempted, hath consented to neglect his charge ; and doth he forthwith repent ? No; he prepares himself to his pur-posed journey. ' But Jonah arose to fly unto Tarshish.' As Jonah was no sooner tempted to go to Tarshish but he yielded, so, as soon as he had yielded, forthwith he [began] to go. So Jonah made himself a runaway, and shewed himself a disobedient servant to his God. And in the meanwhile Nineveh set on the score, and had no ho with them in working wickedness, but still filling the cup of all abominations, ran down to hell with as much force and speed as they could. So Nineveh is still Nineveh, but Jonah is not like Jonah ; for the prophet is flying, and sin is crying, and so all falls to confusion.

But Jonah arose up to fly unto Tarshish, &c.   Jonah flieth unto Tarshish before he would go to Nineveh ; and every one is like that son which said he would not before he went ; and so sin is born first, as Esau was born before Jacob, Gen. xxv. 25, 26.   Therefore, if evil may compare with goodness in particular actions, evil may say in all mankind corrupt, he is the ancienter. But as soon as thou perceivest any evil cogitation or motion in thyself, be thou wroth with it, nip it in the head, put it to death ; and then the un-clean spirit, that hath long been strong, and with delight dwelt in thee, will soon be weary of thy house, and say as the evil spirit said, Here is no dwelling for us, let us go into yonder herd of swine, Mat. viii. 31.

But Jonah arose up to fly unto Tarshish, &c.   Jonah was sent to Nineveh, but he went towards Tarshish. And so it is always with us, we are ever doing that we should not do ; for either we do nothing, or that which we are not commanded, or else otherwise than we are commanded. Sometime most rebelliously we do that which we know the Lord straitly forbiddeth ; and as Jonah took Tarshish for Nineveh, so we take the devil for an angel, darkness for light, &c.

But Jonah rose up, &c. They that should preach at Nineveh are flying to Tarshish ; and though he be like a drone, yet doth he, even the non-resident, keep his benefice fasting, feasting himself ; but wilt thou keep it still ? go and preach at Nineveh, as ye have been doubly commanded, or for shame leave your privilege and benefice. But they stand staggering, ashamed to keep it, and loath to leave it. For the sweet morsels of Baal's priests are pleasant unto them, that they cannot find in their hearts to leave them, as long as they are able to keep them. But no marvel that Jonah fled to Tarshish, when he should go to Nineveh. For this is a stumbling vocation amongst men, yea, rejected by the children of this world, which alway kick against it; so that if you would ask for a painful vocation, this is it; if for a thankless vocation, that is it; if for a contemptible vocation, this is it; for reproving, we are reproved; blessing, we are cursed; preaching peace, we make war; proclaiming liberty, we are imprisoned; do what we can, we are persecuted; and for our work worthy of love, we receive of the most hatred; of few, yea, very few, not any more than a cold affection. Hereof it hath come to pass, that Moses and Jeremiah, being called, excused themselves, Exod. iii. 11, and iv. 10, 13, Jer. i. 6; Ezekiel, having received his charge, 'went in bitterness and indignation of his spirit,' and seven days neglected his charge, Ezek. iii. 14, 15, as Jonah here doth his; Moses, Elijah, and Jeremiah at length complained, Exod. v. 22, Jer. xx. 7, 1 Kings xix. 10, 14. And, which to the best men is the greatest grief, it is as easy almost to wash a blackmoor white, as to convert a sinner; because Satan is ever crossing men doing God's will, but specially hindering the course of right preaching. For the Lord was not so earnest to stop the way of Balaam lest he should commit wickedness, as the devil is earnest to stop the way of every Jonah lest he fulfil righteousness, that is, cry against Nineveh, longing and duly, that is, wisely and earnestly, labouring to convert Nineveh.

But Jonah rose up to fly unto Tarshish from the presence of the Lord. The righteous fall, and now no less than a prophet, yea, such a prophet as was the figure of Christ. But who would have thought that such a prophet should fly from the Lord, yea, and that when he should do him most service; who counted that no wickedness now that he ever thought and taught was rebellion, while he was among the wicked? A fearful example; therefore let him that thinks he standeth take heed lest he fall, for the way is slippery wherein we are to walk. When thou rememberest the fall of the prophet, then, first, consider that thou art much weaker than a prophet, and therefore the easier to be encountered and overthrown, and the likelier to have a most grievous fall, except the Lord do mightily uphold thee, seeing such a one cannot stand in the sight of his so mortal enemy, but by him receiveth so grievous a fall. Secondly, if thou see Jonah fly, Moses murmur, David fall to adultery, Solomon to idolatry, and Peter to forswear his master, then mayest thou learn not to trust to thy own strength, for it is weakness; nor to thine own wisdom, for it is sinful;[1] but seek help and crave strength at the hand of almighty God, who 'giveth to every one that asketh indifferently, and hitteth no man in the teeth,' James i. 5; which 'doth not bruise the broken reed, nor quench the smoking flax,' Mat. xii. 20, but doth rather increase our zeal than diminish it. Thirdly, judge wisely of the fall of Jonah, not rashly condemning him for his fault; for although David joined murder with adultery, yet he repented, and is the dear child of God.

And he found a ship going to Tarshish. Jonah was no sooner come to Joppa, but he goes to the haven, or meets with mariners, and presently understands of a ship, not going to Nineveh, but to Tarshish. As soon as he set forward to fly from God, Satan straightways prepared a ship; so that temptation and occasion of sin do always go together. Shall Judas lack money, or Jonah stay for a ship? No; Satan saith by the mouth of his ministers, Here, Judas, take the money, and betray thy master; and, Jonah, here is a ship for thee, go, haste thee away, and fly from the presence of the Lord. For the devil is always a very serviceable and pleasant devil to such as fly from God; he can find occasion at all times, and means and instruments fit for that purpose. If thou wilt fly from God, the devil will lend thee both spurs and a horse, yea, a post-horse, that will carry you swiftly and lustily away unto all vanity and ungodly lusts. Therefore, if any will ask what the devil's occupation is; it is, to tempt, to entice by all means, to provoke to sin; and then to provide us of the means to practise our purpose, to commit, and, as James speaketh, to bring forth sin.

And he paid the fare thereof. This money was cast into the sea, it did him as little good as if he had utterly lost it; it had been good for him if he had lost it, for it did him much harm. There are many that will spend and waste they care not how much upon cards and dice, and unlawful games; this money also is cast into the sea, for it doeth them much more harm than they know of, it doeth them no good; it were good for them they had not a penny to lose. And so men care not what they pay for vanities and braveries, the most part of which is unprofitable, and rather hurtful than necessary for them, but only for the vain use of the present time, and for some vain respect; this also is cast into the sea, and

---

[1] Qu. 'folly'?—ED.

better should they be if they had it not to lavish, and to their own and many others' hurt so to garnish themselves. Men care not what they pay for their vanity, so it doth please their mind for the present, without consideration of the end and use thereof; but they will give little or nothing to do good withal; so that Lazarus can get nothing, Luke xvi. 21, and David can get no meat, 1 Sam. xxv. 11. 'Shall I take my bread and my wine, and the flesh which I have provided for my shearers, and give them unto one whom I know not?' saith churlish Nabal. We can be content to give anything, or do anything, to win the world; but we will give nothing, nor do nothing, thereby to win the kingdom of God.

We have heard Jonah confessing that he received a charge to go to Nineveh, but he arose and fled toward Tarshish, and went down to Joppa, and found a ship going to Tarshish, and paid the fare thereof, and went down into it; hereafter we shall hear, that being entered the ship, he went to sleep, and slept soundly, and being wakened, he confessed not his sin, but suffered the mariners to devise, to find out for whose cause they were so troubled, and at length also the lots to be cast, never confessing it, until he was enforced to it. What needed he to rehearse all this? Had it not been enough to have said, that he left his business undone, he was a sinner? No; for God would have men to know the stubbornness and disobedience of Jonah, in that this thing was not done upon the sudden, but upon deliberation, and in no short time, but in some continuance, while he went from Samaria to Joppa, and thence was departed, and had some while sailed, in which space he had leisure enough to have repented, but did not. Jonah confessed his sin, that he should not once have listened to Satan's assaults, or reasons of the flesh; and when he had listened, he should not have liked them; and when he had liked them, he should not have consented to obey them; and when he had consented, he should not have put them in practice, he should not have fled toward Joppa; and when he was come to Joppa, he should not have gone to the haven; and when he came to the haven, he should not have paid the fare; and when he had paid the fare, he should not have entered the ship; and when he was entered the ship, he should not have hoised up the sails, and sailed, and gone to sleep. But this he did, teaching that sin runs on wheels, as it were, down a hill in all post-haste, and never stays till it arrive even in hell. For Jonah thought, because he came safe to Joppa, therefore he might go to the haven; and because he came well to the haven, therefore he might pay the fare; and because he paid the fare in peace, therefore he might take shipping; and because he entered the ship in safety, therefore he might hoise up the sails to go; and because he hoised up the sails without danger, therefore he might go securely to sleep, and safely sail to Tarshish.

So sins follow one another like links of a chain, till the tempest of destruction break it in sunder. So saith the forlorn sinner, I have sworn, and God did not punish me, therefore I will steal; I have stolen, and God did not punish me, therefore I will kill; I have killed, and God did not punish me, then why may I not do what I list? I may do this as well as I have done other things heretofore. But if Jonah had considered with himself that God is the Lord, who is all-seeing and almighty, from whom nothing can be concealed, he would never have taken his journey to Joppa; or when he came to Joppa, he would not have paid the fare; or when he had paid the fare, he would not have entered the ship; or when he was gone into the ship, he would not have hoist the sails, but rather would have leaped out of that ship that would carry him from his God, carry him from his duty; for he forgets himself, thinking the creatures can hide him from the Creator, which is an absurd thing to think, seeing nothing can be hid from him, Heb. iv. 13. Neither would any, I say, add drunkenness to thirst, or heap sin upon sin, or suffer any evil thought to take place in him, if they considered that the just Jehovah beheld them in all their very thoughts. All those that pity Jonah, let them pity themselves; for if we consider our own estate, we have as many and as foul sins in us as there were in Jonah, yea, in Nineveh. Jonah confessed his sin that we might confess. He confessed it freely, he confessed it fully, that he knew his Master's will, but not only did it not, but also took another course quite contrary to that which he commanded; and that not in purpose only, but in deed also; not for an hour, but a long time; not in struggling with his weakness, but in a profound ungodly carelessness, or in striving to overmaster his conscience accusing him for his wickedness. And wherefore hath he written it, but to admonish us narrowly to look to ourselves, and manfully to fight, that we may stand where he fell; and when we have fallen, as freely and fully to confess it to God always, and to man also when wisdom commands.

THE PUNISHMENT OF JONAH.

THE THIRD SERMON.

*But the Lord sent a great wind into the sea, and there was a
mighty tempest in the sea, so that the ship was like to be broken.
Then the mariners were afraid, and cried every man unto his
god, and cast the wares that were in the ship into the sea, to
lighten it of them : but Jonah was gone down into the sides of
the ship, and laid down, and was asleep. So the shipmaster
came to him, and said unto him, What meanest thou, O sleeper ?
arise, and call upon thy God, if so be that God will think upon
us, that we perish not.—JONAH I. 4–6.*

THE sin is past, but the punishment is to come ; for after disobedience followeth wrath, the heavy companion of wickedness. For
although she love not sin, yet she will be always where wickedness
is ; yea, also full of strength, like a lion which will not be tamed.

He that made the winds commands them, and they obey his
voice ; the winds and the waters obey him, but man will not obey
him. He saith not that a wind arose, but saith, ' The Lord sent a
great wind.' Therefore we see the cause of this tempest, and so of
Jonah's punishment. The just Judge of the whole world may not
suffer sin unpunished, therefore he says, ' The Lord sent out a
mighty wind.' Then it was not by chance, nor yet by witchcraft ;
for the mariners (notwithstanding they were infidels) were not so
gross as to ascribe it to any such cause ; but rather thought it to be
sent from some revenging power, being provoked to indignation by
some particular person among them, that committed some heinous
fact ; else why did they cast lots to know him, and find him out
that had sinned, and whose sins did procure this tempest to be
sent ? Though this wind had almost drowned Jonah, yet he said,

The Lord sent it; so the Lord sendeth wind to bring ships to land in safety, Ps. cvii. 25–31, and the same Lord sendeth wind to drown and break and sink other ships. Therefore Job said, when he was bereft of all his substance at once, and left as poor as might be, that 'the Lord had taken' them from him, who had first 'given' all to him, Job i. 21; adding also thanksgiving, even for the persecuting hand of God which did so molest him. If some had so much loss by tempest as Job, and such dangers as Jonah, they would surely say with Job, 'Blessed be the name of the Lord' for it; but more (it is to be feared) would say with Job's wife, 'Curse God, and die,' Job ii. 9.

And there was a tempest in the sea. First, God spake gently to him: 'Arise, Jonah, go to Nineveh;' then he would not go; but seeing words would not serve, the Lord would take another way, and try whether that could make him obedient to his voice. So the Lord caused a mighty tempest to arise in the sea, like the messengers that were sent to compel folks to come to the banquet, that seeing the commandment could not, the tempest might bear rule. For unless it be an imperious cross, we will not yield; so headstrong is sin.

Therefore it is said that as God sent out a great wind, so that there was a mighty tempest; that sin might have the foil, and God the victory.

He that sails to Tarshish, or whither he is forbidden to go, would have as good a wind as he that sails to Nineveh, or whither he is commanded to go. But he that doeth one thing for another shall receive one thing for another; as Ahab did, who hoped, according to the saying of four hundred false prophets, to go up and prosper; but he went up and perished. As surely as Jonah thought to arrive at Tarshish, so surely the Spaniards thought to arrive in England; but as Jonah's company wondered at this tempest, so at these Spaniards' destruction their fellows at home wondered, yea, were astonished, how their invincible power could be destroyed. But God is strong enough for them that kick against him, and disdaineth to be crossed of dust and ashes.

And there was a great tempest in the sea. The ship went on roundly for a time, the prophet sleeping, the mariners sporting, their sails flaunting, the waters calming, the winds guiding; so merrily sin goes on before the tempest comes. The wind blows not yet; therefore go on yet a little, and yet a little more; but suddenly the tempest rushes upon them before they are aware of it, and tumbles them up and down, and suddenly all is like to be undone.

He came to the haven, and paid the fare, and entered the ship, and hoist up sails, and went on forward, and all to fly from God ; but now it appears he fled not from him, but to him.   Therefore David saith, ' If I take the morning wings and fly aloft, lo, thou art there. If I go into the nethermost depth, thy hand will find me out ; therefore whither shall I fly from thee ?' Ps. cxxxix. 9, 10.   So that when we think that we fly from God, in running out of one place into another, we do but run from one hand to the other ; for there is no place where God's hand is not ; and whithersoever a rebellious sinner doth run, the hand of God will meet with him to cross him, and hinder his hoped for good success, although he securely prophesieth never so much good unto himself in his journey.   What ! had he offended the winds or the waters, that they bear him such enmity ?   The winds and the waters and all God's creatures are to take God's part against Jonah, or any rebellious sinner.   For though God in the beginning gave power to man over all creatures to rule them ; yet when man sins, God giveth power and strength to his creatures to rule and bridle man.   Therefore he that even now was lord over the waters, now the waters are lord over him.

But if Jonah had thought that God would have thus brought things to pass, he durst not have been so bold in this enterprise. Therefore we may see that sin hath no eyes while it is doing. Tush, saith the fool, it is fair weather yet, while he goeth to the stocks, Prov. vii. 22.

So that the ship was like to be broken.   We have heard of the cause and greatness of this tempest, the effects follow, whereby the greatness of it is the better expressed; first, in the ship, then in the mariners.

The ship was like to be broken.   The ship was fair and goodly, so strong that it might have encountered with instruments of war, and so sure made that it might have endured great tempest, and made many voyages.   Yet now with one tempest, and at one voyage, it was so deformed, so weakened, in such a taking, that it was like to be shivered in pieces ; and all because Jonah was in it. Such strife is always betwixt God's wrath, and man's disobedience. When God's word will not turn us, God's winds and other instruments of his wrath must threaten to overturn us.

Then the mariners were afraid, and cried every man to his god, and cast the wares out that were in the ship, to lighten it thereof.   The effects of this tempest in the mariners were two : first, they were afraid ; then used means to appease the tempest, and save themselves.

Then the mariners were afraid. Mariners living in the sea almost as fishes, having the waters as their necessariest element, are commonly men void of fear, venturous, and contemners of danger. Yet now, seeing the tempest so vehement on a sudden, that their goodly and tall ship was tossed almost to a cock-boat, and cracked so that it was like to be torn all to pieces, and thereby were fully persuaded it was no common nor ordinary storm, but a revenging tempest, for some extraordinary cause sent out upon them by some great power provoked ; now they are afraid, they tremble for fear, like women that shrink at every stir in the wherry, and like little children when they are frighted, lest their ship break or leak, and so sink, and they lose their goods, their ship, their lives and all.

Now, these nought-fearing fellows, these high-stomached men, which desire danger, are brought down by danger, fear and quake like a young soldier, which starteth at the sound of a gun.

And cried every man unto his god, and cast forth their wares into the sea, &c. The means which the mariners use to save themselves are divers : first, they cry to their gods : then, when that appeased not the tempest, they cast out their wares.

They prayed. This is then a manifest sign that the heathen acknowledged there is a divine power seeing and governing the whole world ; for they would not have prayed at all, but that they were convinced there was a God who beheld the affairs of men, and could in extremest danger deliver whom he would. Nature convinced them, the works of God made them to acknowledge it. For in man, though the lamps be wasted since Adam consulted with the devil to be a god, yet there is some little light left, which dwelleth in darkness, like a spark hid in the ashes, whereby the stately and most glorious frame of the world, with all the wonderful variety of the singular effects of all the excellent creatures therein, considered, man cannot but acknowledge there is a God. Yea, his mighty power the blinded Gentiles saw so expressly in all the creatures, that they imagined it to be impossible for one God to work them all ; therefore they thought that there were divers gods, as there were divers seasons, divers nations, divers trades, divers languages, divers and sundry kinds of all things ; and so divers nations worshipped divers gods. When the wicked see that all their inventions will not bring their enterprise to pass according to their mind, but they are in extremity, and like to be cast away for want of succour, then they fly unto God, being driven by compulsion, as a bear unto a stake, and they crouch and kneel, and make great shows outwardly of humiliation and piety, all in hope of help from God, and as it were thinking to deceive him by their hypocrisy.

Every one unto his god. This sheweth that they were of divers nations; for among the Gentiles every nation had a several god to worship. Chemosh was the god of the Moabites, 1 Kings xi. 7, 33; Beelzebub the god of the Ekronites, 2 Kings i. 2; Dagon the god of the Philistines, 1 Sam. v.; and the Ephesians worshipped Diana, Acts xix. 35. In our necessity we fly every one unto his god : that is, in the time of necessity every one doth fly for help and ease unto that which most feedeth his own humour, or best pleaseth him, that wherein he reposeth most confidence, persuading themselves of sufficient relief from that; some run to their coffers, thinking that there it is that is able to procure ease from any troubles; other some turn to their delights and wanton sports, supposing that there is no trouble so great but they will cause them to forget it; some to their glorious attire and costly jewels, imagining they will now as well rejoice their hearts, remedying their grief, as at other times they have delighted others' eyes, pleasing their sight; some to their dainty meats, and some to their soft beds, and easy standing, hoping by those to feel relief. In sickness we cry, Come, physic, help me; in heaviness we call, Come, music, cheer me; in war we sound, Come, soldiers, succour me; in quarrels we say, Come, law, defend me; evermore leaving the Creator, which is all goodness and powerful in himself, running to the creatures, which have no goodness nor power, save that they receive of him; neither by their goodness can they do us good, but by his blessing.

And cried every man unto his god. They did well in that they prayed, but they prayed not well; for they prayed every man unto his god; that is, unto feigned gods, gods in name, but not in nature; and gods they were that could not help so much as themselves.

Every man unto his god. Every of these mariners did now in their extremity call upon his god, every one upon that god which he thought most highly of, and whom he had in his prosperity reposed most confidence in. Now while none could help but one, they cried to many; and by this means, while they sought to lay the tempest, they stirred it more; for their prayers being idolatrous, were so wicked, that the Lord had utterly destroyed them, if his mercy had not been wonderful over all his works, Ps. cxlv. 9. They prayed much like the papists, which in extremity cry out, some to one saint, some to another, some to saints of this place, others to saints of that place, thinking, as these mariners did, if one will not help, another will.

They cried, &c.   They prayed, and their prayers did beat the sky, though they could not lay the tempest.   They were not, as many of us be when we pray unto God, without a sense of their danger, or without great desire to obtain their requests.   What an hypocrisy is this that is common among us, to have vehement speeches, and loud cries, and long prayers, without lively affection within !

They cried.   Here is a distinction of crying to be observed.   The righteous cry, and as well when they are in prosperity as when they be in calamity, though many nothing so fervently ; but the ungodly then only when the hand of God is upon them, and then also like bears without their prey, always much doubting, sometimes despairing of help, although they cry for it.   And therefore blessed is he that hath the Lord for his God ; and let them know that cry without faith, without confidence in God, they do but cry in vain.   'Let not the wavering-minded man think to receive any good of the Lord,' James i. 6, 7.

And cast the wares that were in the ship into the sea.   Here is the second means which they used to help themselves.   Now, the mariners are content to cast their wares into the sea, in hope of some furtherance to save their lives thereby ; for though many will venture their lives for riches, yet they rather part with all their riches than with their lives.   But they cast them out to appease the tempest, or lighten their ship ; but it was sin that procured danger, and being cast away would have saved all, which being retained, the tempest abating not, the ship is not the safer, though it be the lighter.   'If I regard wickedness in my heart,' saith David, 'the Lord will not hear me,' Ps. lxvi. 18.   And Paul saith, 'Though I cast my life into the fire, if I have no charity,' if I retain malice in my heart, 'it profiteth me nothing,' 1 Cor. xiii. 3. If I cast not away sin, I cast away all.   Some will give to the poor, and yet use extortion and usury to get money by ; but God saith to such, that if they regard wickedness in their hearts, it profiteth nothing ; though they part with all that they have, and bestow it upon never so good actions, they do but as the mariners did, cast all away, their desire nothing satisfied.   For though they think themselves beneficial to the poor thereby, and hope for reward therefor, yet God will but accept of them as hypocrites ; he will none of their oblations, he abhorreth their very prayers, Prov. xv. 8, until they have humbled themselves, and reformed their own hearts before him from such uncleanness.

They cast out the wares into the sea.   They would fain have laid the tempest, that thus readily lose their wares, and cast out

their very tackling into the sea; but the sea will not be satisfied;
the waters must wash the sinner, or there is no safety; nay, the danger
is greater, the sea continually more and more troublesome, vexing
them. But Jonah was no sooner cast into the sea, but all was quiet,
the winds are calm, and 'the sea ceaseth from her raging,' Jonah i.
13, 15. Oh that justice were executed, and he that troubleth the
ship were in the sea! He that troubleth, not he that against all
reason is thought to trouble; then should all be safe, yea, peradventure Jonah too.

And they cast the wares that were in the ship into the sea.
Observe here that oftentimes many are punished for one man's sin,
as all the host of Israel were punished for the sin of Achan, Joshua
vii. 5, 12; and here all the mariners and owners of ship or wares
for Jonah's sin, &c., to the end that men may learn thereby to admonish one another when they see they do amiss, with love, and
not to say, with Cain, 'Am I the keeper of my brother?' For he
that is not careful to keep his brother from sin, is not careful to
keep himself either from sin or from sorrow. Therefore, let us take
heed that a wicked one be not found amongst us unadmonished. I
would there were not many worse than Jonah among us. Will
you know what I think of you? I think you are worse than infidels, Turks, or pagans, that in this wonderful year of wonderful
mercies[1] are not thankful, believe not in God, trust not in him,
glorify not his name; but like Pharaoh's sorcerers, who, seeing the
great works of God which Moses wrought passing their skill, confessed, saying, 'Surely this is the finger of God,' Exod. viii. 19; for
you confess, it is the great work of God, as you must needs, but
where are the fruits it hath brought forth in you? The captain
saith, I have done nothing; the soldier saith, I stirred not; but the
Lord sent out a mighty tempest upon them, and after that they
escaped our hands, the Lord stretched out his mighty arm against
them, and Pharaoh is drowned in the sea; so that he never attained
the land of promise which he gaped for, and made full account to
possess. Farther, herein we may note that extremity is God's opportunity; for when the wind had almost overturned all, and the
waters had almost drowned all, and destruction had almost devoured all, then, and not afore, was God's opportunity to set forth
his glory.

First, they used prayer unto the divine powers for assistance;
then they used such ordinary means as they knew best in such a

* This Sermon must have been preached in 1588, the year of the Spanish Ar-
mada.—ED.

time, by casting out their wares, to lighten the ship of them. Which order is necessary to be used of all Christians in their necessity : first, to seek for aid and assistance at the hands of God ; and then to use all such good means to help themselves as God shall enable them to, trusting that of his goodness he will bless their endeavours, or else may they go over all the earth to seek help, and have none; for there is no other way. God indeed is the last refuge, but he is also the first refuge which is to be sought unto ; for he will have us to acknowledge that 'man liveth not by bread only,' and, 'a horse is but a vain thing to save a man,' and, 'except the Lord keep the city, the watchman waketh but in vain ;' no means can help without his blessing. But then he will not have us careless and negligent to use lawful means ; for he never or very seldom worketh without means, when the means may be used by us. Danger then, we have seen, made them to fear, but fear astonished them not, but gathered their wits together ; for they used means with wisdom to save themselves. But when the Lord sendeth calamity upon many of the ungodly, they have so guilty a conscience, that whilst they feel the great hand of God, they are even distraught of their wits, and made as it were senseless, that they know not what they do ; yea, when troubles come, it makes them like a headless bee, which buzzeth about she knows not whither; or like the swallow which, by compulsion of the wind, flieth backward and forward till it fall into the sea ; or like Cain, whose head was fraught with fears, so that he knew not whither to go, doubting to be slain of every one whom he saw. But whatsoever befalleth the child of God, he hath ever matter of consolation, and some moderation of mind to bear it withal, expecting a joyful issue of all. Therefore blessed is he that hath the Lord for his God.

But Jonah was gone down into the sides of the ship, and laid down, and was fast asleep. They prayed unto their gods, and their gods were now deaf, while they were thus tossed ; and Jonah is gone to sleep, when he should have been better occupied. We come hither to hear the word, and here we fall asleep, but it were far better we were away ; for we sleep when we should hear, and so sleeping sin, and sleep in sin, Therefore let them now give ear that are asleep, for we are come to Jonah's sleeping, not that we should sleep with him, but by his sleeping to be warned of our security ; and we shall see him waked, that we may learn to wake with him. Jonah's fast sleeping is noted, to declare the occasion of

the shipmaster's speech to Jonah, but chiefly to note the dead
security of Jonah in his sin; forasmuch as though the mariners
cried for fear, and cast out their goods, nay, the very senseless ship
seemed to feel the anger of God, and to cry to Jonah by rolling
and cracking; yet Jonah was not once moved thereat, but lay still
fast asleep. So by Jonah his sleeping we see the nature of all the
sons of Adam: when they listen to the serpent, they are like
changelings, they are cast into a dead sleep; for when they forget
God and his word, and bid conscience adieu, they sleep in sin, and
that to death, like one sick of the lethargy.

Jonah signifieth *a dove.* Jonah therefore was now indeed
Jonah; I mean, like the dove which Noah sent forth of the ark.
For as the dove, being gone out of the ark, could find no rest for
the sole of her foot, till she returned into the ark again; so when
Jonah arose up from the presence of the Lord, he could find no rest
for his mind, neither by sea nor land, until he returned again unto
the Lord. For the cause of Jonah's going down to sleep was, it
seemeth, to ease his mind, for it was disquieted, he felt it grievously troubled, the conscience of his sin tormented it. Therefore,
now, oh that Jonah could sleep till the tempest were past: But
it will not be, for the tempest is sent purposely to wake him.

And he was fast asleep. See how little Jonah is ashamed of his
sin; all the world smarted for it, and yet he sleeps. As if we should
say, neither the winds blowing, nor the waters roaring, nor the ship
reeling, nor the wares casting, nor the mariners crying, with all the
stir, could move him, waken him from his sleep or raise him from
his sin. Now, Jonah might say, I was asleep, and all might have
perished for me, if one God had not helped more than all the
rest; for Jonah slept, but God waked, and called to the winds and
the waters, saying, Toss him, but you shall not drown him; fear
him, but you shall not kill him; whip him, and when you have
whipped him, send him to me, that I may send him to Nineveh.
Jonah was fast asleep, when the winds over him were blowing, the
waters under him tossing, the ship about him reeling, the
mariners by him crying, the wares overboard casting; in all the
stir Jonah felt nothing, but slept, as if there were no stirring.
Yet we go far beyond Jonah in security. For the Lord causeth the
tempest to blow down houses beside us, the heavens to thunder
over us, the earth to quake under us, the water to overflow the
land about us, the fire to consume all that we have before us, the
air with cold ready to kill us, and all things in an uproar round
about against us, thereby always crossing us one way or another,

and all to put us in mind of our duty, the neglect whereof is the cause of all these troubles which the Lord doth send us; but we sleep more deadly than Jonah in our negligence, void of feeling because we consider not what we have done, we look not back on our sin; yet every cross should cause us to examine ourselves thoroughly, and leave no sin unviewed, that we might lively feel our wickedness, and so duly repent it, and soon find release of our miseries. Therefore if we sleep still, and will not be wakened, God will deal more roughly with us than he did with Jonah; for the Lord caused a whale to swallow him, and afterward to cast him up again; but we shall be swallowed of that serpent which never restoreth again.

He should have been their teacher, if he had not been asleep; he should have taught them to pray aright, if he had had any good feeling in him. But all this while we read not that Jonah once condemned his thoughts, nor so much as once said to himself, Jonah, take heed what thou doest; thou knowest how God may handle thee upon the waters: though thou fly, he can overtake thee; though thou hide thyself, he will find thee out; though thou give thyself to sleep, he shall give thee no rest, and awake thee to thy greater woe. How should we be strong, if a prophet, and such a prophet as was the figure of Christ, could not withstand this one temptation, but suffer himself to be led away so far that, when he should run, he lay still, and when he should cry, he held his peace, and when he should zealously bestir himself, he is fast asleep?

In Jonah his sleeping we observe two things: the first is, that when we think ourselves most at rest, then we are in greatest danger. When shipwreck is most likely, then Jonah is asleep; when Herod is vaunting, then he is stricken, Acts xii. 21–23; when Nebuchadnezzar is in his greatest pride, then he is turned out, Dan. iv. 29, &c.; when Belshazzar is banqueting, the hand writ his condemnation, Dan. v. 4, 5; when the rich man saith unto his soul, Thou hast enough, then his soul is taken from him, Luke xii. 19, 20; when the Philistines are sporting, then the roof is falling, Judges xvi. 25, 30. So destruction overtaketh sinners when they least think of it, like a leopard which is taken while he sleepeth, or a bird when she singeth; therefore suspect thy pleasure like a bait.

The second note is, the nature of sin, which is here expressed (while it is a-doing) to be, not bitter, but sweet; not painful, but pleasant; like a harlot which sheweth nothing but her bravery and beauty. Adam swallowed the forbidden fruit with pleasure, Gen. iii.; Gehazi lied for gold with gladness, 2 Kings v.; Noah drank his wine with mirth, Gen. ix. 21 ; David committed whoredom with delight, 2 Sam. xi. 4 : so sinners go on merrily till wrath overtakes them at unawares ; like the fool, I will sleep a little longer, and fold my hands together a little, yet a little, and a little longer, till poverty comes as an armed man, and God's just judgment as the whirlwind, suddenly and unresistibly, Prov. xxiv. 33, 34. Then, though thou hast gotten gold with Gehazi, or honours with Haman, or Naboth's vineyard with Ahab, or all the delights of the world ; if thou have not an assurance of thine own salvation, if sin be still pleasant, if it be not bitter in thy belly, though it be sweet in thy mouth, deceive not thyself, believe God, thy hope is but doubting, thy strongest confidence but a vain trust.

Then the shipmaster came unto him, and said, What meanest thou, O sleeper ? arise, and call upon thy God.   Here Jonah is taken napping : sin hath brought him asleep, and now the shipmaster wakens him. The mariners may do him more good than the tempest. Whom sin should waken, peril cannot waken ; the winds are not loud enough, nor the waters rough enough, therefore the shipmaster must waken him, else all shall be endangered. If the winds will not waken him, let the waves waken him ; if the waves will not waken him, let the mariners waken him ; if he will not be wakened, let him perish in his sleep, and die in his sin.

Now mark who is asleep, and who wakens him. Jonah is asleep, and the mariners waken him : an Israelite, an infidel. What a thing is this, that he which is the son of Abraham, who is wiser than a thousand mariners, is now wakened and told his duty by a mariner ! This is a shame for Jonah, that he which had taught princes should now be told his duty by mariners. He that long had and should still wake others, needs oftentimes to be wakened by others ; and he that should reprove sinners, is often reproved of sinners. And thus the Lord sometimes shameth his servants, and doth vex them with a foolish nation ; as he reproved Abraham by Abimelech, Gen. xx. 9, and Balaam by an ass, Num. xxii. 28.

Now, we might ask Jonah, saying, Why didst thou write that thou fledst from God, or that when thou hadst most need to pray, thou didst sleep ? If thou hadst not thus laid open thine own shame, thou mightest have been reckoned as one of the best prophets ; therefore why didst thou so ? Jonah did it to this end, that in him we may see the reward of disobedience ; for, as Paul saith, 'whatsoever is written, is written for our instruction ;' and Jonah would never have written it, had it not been for our sakes. If he have done thus much for us, which way shall we requite him ?

That which he would have us to do for him is this, to be warned by him to suppress all evil motions, not suffering them to take effect, as he did.

What meanest thou, O sleeper ? arise. As if they should say, O wretchless, altogether careless, quite senseless man ! art thou dead, that thou wakest not ? or benumbed, that thou feelest not ? or deaf, that thou hearest nothing ? or carest thou not whether thou live or die ? Have not the winds nor waters raging, nor our loud cries so long thundering, wakened thee ? Canst thou sleep in all this stir ? Do not our troubles, nor labours, nor losses, nor the common danger, move thee ? What meanest thou ? Why dost thou not come and labour with us in this dangerous time ? Is this a time to sleep in, when we are all in peril of our lives ? Shall we cry, and thou hold thy peace ? shall we labour, and thou rest ? shall we cast away all our goods, and thou lie sleeping, caring for nothing ? This is no time to sleep ; it is a time to pray unto thy God for his assistance, and to use the means that may save our lives : up, arise, help what thou canst. Jonah, hearing this, did not snap like some currish dogs, and bite him that wakened him ; neither did he (as in public danger most are wont) sit still, devising with himself to shift for himself, neglecting others ; but he ariseth, he thanked him that waked him.

Many of you come to hear the word, and here you fall asleep when you have most need to be waking ; but I am glad I have now gotten a text to waken you, for now I cannot read my text but I must say, ' What meanest thou, O sleeper ? arise.' But I pray you, have I not wakened you, and yet you sleep again ? If you mark not what is said unto you, you are asleep, though your eyes be open. But if you were as wise as Jonah, you would not sleep here in the sight of all the people, but would rather get you to sleep in some corner ; for Jonah went under the hatches to sleep, and would not sleep in the sight of the mariners. If you were as wise as Jonah, you would thank him that wakened you, as no doubt Jonah did. Solomon saith, that ' he which reproveth, shall have more favour of a wise man than he which flattereth,' Prov. xxviii. 23. The Lord Jesus saith, ' Woe be unto that servant, that when his master cometh he shall find sleeping,' Luke xii. 45, 46. ' Canst thou not watch one hour ? ' saith he to Peter, Mark xiv. 37. Can you not wake while I speak to you ? You would all be found in the church when the Lord cometh, but you would not be found sleeping in the church. You are watched, though I see you not below ; and none of you can steal a nap, and not be espied ; but when your eyes be most shut, and see least, then most eyes be upon you; and I can as well stand in the pulpit unseen, as you can sit and sleep there and not be espied. I marvel how you can sleep, having so many eyes looking on you, so many clamours in your ears, and God himself speaking unto you. Shall I continue jogging till you be wakened? How long shall I preach afore I can convert the usurer, the extortioner, the drunkard, or the blasphemer, seeing I speak thus long, and cannot convert you from your sleeping? What would you do if I read some homilies unto you; whereas you cannot wake while I preach unto you, and speak against you? If you should see a traitor sleep on the hurdle, or if you should see men sleep with meat in their mouths, would you not marvel? Yet even so do you; while I denounce the great judgments of God against you, and while I am feeding some of you, you fall asleep, and so I preach in vain. There is a country whereof it is said, that it is night with them when it is day with us. I think that country be here; for how many are here which have lost their eyes and their ears since they came thither? If all of you were as many of you be, I mean asleep, the strangers which came hither to hear would think that you were all dead, and that I preached your funeral sermon; therefore for shame leave your sleeping. What meanest thou, O sleeper? arise, sleep no more, and I will waken you no more.

Arise, and call upon thy God, if so be he will think upon us, &c. This is another means which they use, Jonah being wakened, to appease the tempest; now that they see they cannot themselves allay the winds, nor assuage the waters, they desire, they exhort Jonah, to try what he can do by calling upon his God. 'Arise, call upon thy God,' &c.

After that the shipmaster had wakened Jonah, he bids him call upon his God; as if he had said, 'Watch and pray.' He speaks like a saint, yet he is an infidel; he said not, Call upon *gods;* but, Call upon thy *God.* The shipmaster would not call upon his God; but saith he, Call upon thy God, and it may be he will help us. If he had said, Call upon our God, when he said, Call upon thy God; and if he had said, He will help us, when he said, If so be he will help us: then he had shewed some spark of faith. Because he wanted help and comfort, he bids him arise; and because he was fearful, he bids him pray. 'It may be,' saith he, 'he will think upon us, that we perish not.' As if he had said, Jonah, we know that thou hast a God as well as we, and therefore we say, Call upon thy God, for now every god is to be tried; therefore if ever thou didst pray in thy life, fall to it now. Thus Satan leads men a blind way with zeal, in hope of some relief, being in trouble. They called upon them for help which were neither willing to assist them, nor able to hear them; and when they perceived by woful experience that there was no kind of succour to be had that way, they fly to God; and then Satan laboureth to undermine the confidence and expectation of help, and to place instead thereof doubtfulness and infidelity. Thus Satan will be sure to lose nothing by this bargain any way. Jonah, say they, call upon thy God; for if he cannot help us, we are all undone and lost; for we have called upon our gods, we have laboured hard to amend our state, we have cast away our goods to lighten the ship, but all in vain, for we are no whit the better; like the woman which had spent all her substance about physic, yet all could not help her till Christ came, Luke viii. 43. So the papists, while they are well, they pray unto every saint and angel for succour against the troublesome times; but in extremity, or at the point of death, none of them can help, so that then they are fain to fly unto God, or be destitute; as like idolaters as one fly is like another. They are like the heathen, which worship Juno, Venus, Neptune, Pallas, Jupiter, and the rest; some hold on the one, and some on the other. Some say, If Jupiter be with me, I care not for all the petty gods, because I hold him chief; so another saith, If St Gabriel be with me, I care not for the rest. And some raise great disputations whether this saint or that saint, this angel or that angel, be better; whether our lady of Bologna or our lady of Rome be surest; whether St James of Calais or St James of Compostella be strongest; and so, like beggars which run from door to door, they run from one saint to another. If one god will not help, another will, think these; as though the gods were contrary one to another, and where the one bids, the other forbids. So some thought that Venus was a friend to the Trojans, and Pallas was not their friend; as fools think of witches, one strikes, another heals.

Call upon thy God. They bid him call upon his God, before they knew him; but the faithful will not worship a false god, though they may be helped by him. By the example of these mariners, if they thought that their god was the true God (and why else did they worship him?) we may learn the substance of every temptation that doth undermine us, namely, that it will bid us do this evil, that good may come of it; mark, whensoever thou art motioned to evil, if it do not promise thee some goodness to come of it. But the servants of God ought not to do that which is evil, though they were sure to gain all things that can be wished by so doing; for they have learned their lesson, and how to answer Satan at such

times, Why temptest thou me, Satan? for it is written, Thou must
not do evil that good may come of it, Rom. iii. 8. And this is the
armour called *Scriptum est*, wherewith the Lord overcame the devil
in the wilderness.

Here also we may see the difference between the faithful and infidels; for, 'Call upon thy God,' saith the shipmaster and the rest.
The mariners bid Jonah pray unto his God in their behalf; but
Jonah saith not to the mariners, Pray to your gods in my behalf.
And this is also manifest, that a papist will say unto a protestant,
and one that lives well, Pray for me; but a protestant, if he be anything zealous, will not say unto a papist, Pray thou for me; knowing
that when a papist doth pray, he doth it to idols, saints, or angels,
or at least without faith, and therefore their prayers are abominable
in the sight of God; and therefore they will not bid them do it,
because they will not do evil to the intent that good may come of
it. Whereby it is manifest that our religion is the true religion,
our adversaries themselves being judges. And so Pharaoh said to
Moses, 'Pray for me,' Exod. viii. 8, &c.; but Moses said not to Pharaoh, Pray for me. Saul said to Samuel, 'Pray thou for me,'
1 Sam. xv. 25, but Samuel said not to Saul, Pray thou for me.
Therefore the mariners had need of Jonah to pray for them; but
Jonah had no need of ignorant idolaters to pray for him. And why
should not all pray to Jonah's God, and Pharaoh pray to Moses's
God, seeing God hath said, 'Call upon me in trouble, and I will
hear thee'? Call upon thy God (say they) when they cried and
saw no help; they distrusted their gods, they thought they would
not help; indeed they could not; therefore they ran to another
whom they knew not, hoping to be helped by him, because they
thought some god there was that could do it. So the papists run
from one god to another, from St Dominic to St Francis; and why
should they run from St Dominic to St Francis, but that they
mistrusted St Dominic? They think he will not hear them, and
so they go forward. But in the end 'the unknown God' is thought
to be the best. Yet the Lord taught not Peter one prayer, and
John another, but taught them all one prayer unto one only God, and
to wait still upon him, praying still with assurance that he will be
a help   due time.

If peradventure he will think upon us, that we perish not. This
if, *perhaps*, and *peradventure*, cost Adam paradise. God said to
Adam, 'If thou dost eat of this tree, thou shalt surely die.' Then
Eve reported these words thus, 'Lest peradventure we die.' The
serpent seeing her in such a mind, so careless and forgetful of the

commandment, he came and quite changed the matter, and said, 'You shall not die.' Thus sin creeps upon us, while doubtfulness remaineth in us. So God saith, You shall be saved; the trembling flesh saith, Peradventure I shall, &c., then cometh Satan, and he saith, Thou shalt die. So that if you will ask what is the faith of sinners, or if you would have it defined; it is this, Peradventure yea, peradventure no. If you will ask me whereupon this faith is grounded; it is upon *ifs* and *ands :* this is the faith of the ungodly, to say, If so be God will help us; for they cannot assure themselves of any help. But we may not doubt of our God, and say, *It may be,* or, *If peradventure ;* for we may freely pray to our God with confidence, and may say, Our God, and the God of Jonah, will surely help us, and hath helped us. But yet let us know that we have sinned like infidels, and do deserve to be punished like the Egyptians.

If so be he will, &c. Thus it cometh in like a little leaven, which soureth the whole lump of dough; and like the moth, which eateth the whole wedding garment; and this same little thief hath stolen away all the papists' faith. Therefore with them wickedness lieth sick in bed, and calleth to every one that cometh by, Call upon God, and pray for me, if so be he will look upon me and help me; and so their hope, when the tempest cometh, is either an easeless horror, or a comfortless doubting.

If so be he will think upon us. Our God thought upon us in the time of trouble; he thought upon us, and laid the tempest, when our enemies called upon their gods, saints and angels. But what do we mean, beloved, when mercy is come, to send for judgment? For though we be saved with Israel, we deserve to be plagued with Pharaoh, because we are not thankful for this, namely, that the Lord hath thought upon us in our distress; for he travaileth with mercy, and laboureth till he be delivered; he goeth laden like a bee, but wants a hive. There are two hands, a hand to give, and a hand to receive; God's hand to give, and man's hand to receive. The hand of God is a bountiful and a merciful hand, a hand loaden with liberality, full of gracious gifts; therefore let us stretch forth the good hand to receive it, thankfully to embrace it, cheerfully to entertain it, and carefully to keep it; let us receive it by the hand of faith, the hand of love, and the hand of prayer; for whoso cometh with this hand shall be filled, and whoso cometh without it shall go empty away, because they have despised the ways of God; for when I instructed them they would not hear, and what I taught them they would not learn, saith the Lord, Prov. i. 24, 25. Jonah, wakened thus, and thus exhorted to call upon his God, soon no doubt perceived his danger, and partly with the horror of his sin, partly for fear of the deserved, and thus threatened, drowning and other punishments, without question was grievously vexed. For he could not but see that the very dumb creatures were bent against him for his disobedience; the wind blows, as though it would overturn all; the waters roar, as though they would drown all; the ship tumbles, as though she were weary of all; and albeit the mariners had cried, and cast out the wares, as though they would lose all; yet the tempest rageth still, their danger is greater than ever.

Wherefore now one might have said to Satan, Satan, thou persuadedst him to fly from his defence for his safety, and madest him believe that he should come safe to Tarshish, and there live at liberty and ease, enjoying all temporal benefits at his pleasure; but now thou hast brought him into the prison of the ship, and it is tossed thus by this tempest likely to destroy him, thou leavest him in the greatest danger, and rejoicest that Jonah quaketh at the tempest, and hath his heart aching for fear of the danger thus threatened, due to rebellion; yea, seekest also to drown him, and that also in hell, howsoever thou pretendest a desire to preserve him from troubles, and procure him many pleasures, with much security. O most wretched and deceitful liar! he that trusteth his enemy, and he that believeth thee, shall ever be deceived. And now might Jonah say, Beware by me, for thus hath the tempter deceived me; he hath allured me with flattering fantasies, and persuaded me that it was but an easy thing to fly from the presence of the Lord, that seeth always all things, and from whom no man, no, nor secret lurking in any man's heart, can be hid, but all are always in his presence. He made me believe that light could be brought out of darkness, that good may come of evil; for he assured me, that if I would set forth towards Tarshish, I should not only shun the presence of the Lord, but should live at ease like one unknown, both for my vocation, and also for my behaviour in the execution thereof; and so I might creep into a familiarity with these people, and enjoy the benefit of their society. Otherwise, if I went to Nineveh, as the Lord commanded, they would hate and persecute me, yea, and so I should end my life in misery; both because they being Gentiles, and I a Jew, they cannot abide me, for the one holdeth the other in contempt; and also because of my message, namely, a prophecy of destruction, grounded upon a reproof of their vile and sinful pleasures. Which message Satan persuaded me would be so heinously taken, that no death nor torment that they could devise for me would be thought sufficient, and so I should be sure never to escape their hands alive, if I went; as though the eternal and most glorious God, which sent me thither, were not able to defend me from all evil when I came thither, as well as he did Daniel in the den of lions, and Christ in the wilderness among the savage beasts. And when Satan had thus persuaded me, I believed him, and so took my journey to fly from the presence of the Lord, if I could have performed my intention. But the Lord hath beheld the stubbornness and disobedience of my heart, and therefore followeth me with great displeasure: he hath sent out this tempest upon the sea, whereby we are like to be overwhelmed; and so near as we are to the water, so near we are to death by all likelihood.

THE PUNISHMENT OF JONAH.

THE FOURTH SERMON.

Afterwards they said every one to his fellow, Come, and let us cast lots, that we may know for whose cause this evil is come upon us. So they cast lots, and the lot fell upon Jonah.—
JONAH I. 7.

Now followeth another mean which the mariners use to appease the tempest. 'They cast lots.' But first they consult and consent to cast lots. The tempest was so strong, that they concluded with themselves it was the revenging power of some angry god, for the sin of some notorious wretch that was among them.

Seeing, therefore, neither they nor Jonah praying had appeased the tempest, but it was rather increased, and no man confessed he was the sinner, they take counsel, and agree to find him out by lots. Wherein let us observe, first, never a one of them is of David's spirit, who, when he saw the people plagued, said, Lord, it is I. Every man excuseth himself; for every man would extenuate his own sin and diminish it, and every one thinketh his sin salved when he hath excused himself. Let Adam be his own judge, and he will say, The woman tempted him to sin; and let the woman be her own judge, and she will say, Yonder serpent persuaded her to it. Let every one be his own judge, and there will be such posting off of sin, that never a one will be found guilty. There is none that will be so impudent as to say he hath no sin at all; yet few that will freely confess they have grievously sinned. Therefore these here say, every man within himself, though he be a sinner, yet he is no great sinner. None are accounted sinners, unless they be openly detected of some notable and heinous crime. If they be dicers, swearers, drunkards, brawlers, pickers, flatterers, profaners of the Sabbath, sleepers at church and such like, they be not thought sinners ; these actions are counted no sins, but rather recreations. For the multitude count none sinners, unless they be thieves, traitors, open and gross idolaters, and taken with such like capital crimes ; no, nor these neither, were it not fear of the law : as none among the Jews but the publicans were counted sinners ; all the rest were good fellows, and just men.

The papists say, some thoughts, affections, words and outward actions not agreeing with the law of God, are easily washed away with a little holy water, &c. They are not deadly, they deserve not the wrath of God, they are but venial. Did you ever read of these venial sinners in the Scripture ? But think you they have nothing but Scripture ? Yes, they have decrees, they have decretals, the ceremonies whereof observed, these venial sins are soon pardoned, and they have a pope that can forgive any sins. Thus they lessen sins, thus they abate the price of sins, and they can buy out sins with money, or redeem them with masses, and by a little short penance purchase a large and long pardon.

And as the mariners every man thought he was no great sinner ; so Jonah thought with himself, Though I be a great sinner, yet am I not so grievous a sinner as these idolatrous heathens. Or if he thoroughly condemned himself, yet, unwilling to be known such a rebel, he thought, it may be, and it is most likely, they are many, I but one, peradventure therefore the lot will not fall upon me. Like a thief, which, notwithstanding in his own heart he acknowledge himself guilty of that wherewithal he is charged, yet will not confess, until the matter be thoroughly sifted, and clearly proved to his own face, in such sort that he cannot for shame (though with shame he confess) deny it. Therefore if God had not sifted out this sinner the better, Jonah would not have been known the man, and the mariners would still have contended who was the lesser sinner ; therefore they consult to cast lots.

Let us cast lots. They did not use to cast lots, this was no custom among the mariners; but the tempest was so wonderful, that it made them seriously to think of God, and willing to use the means prescribed by God for the ending of doubtful matters, acknowledging that he ordereth all, and the lot is the sentence of God ; by the falling of the lot he revealeth the truth, Prov. xviii. 18, xvi. 33.

These, like worldlings, never confess God but when he cometh
in a tempest; they will not see his mercy, until his justice appear;
they will not acknowledge God's government, before he bring on
them some judgment; like Pharaoh's sorcerers, who confessed
not God's majesty while they lived at ease; but when the Lord
plagued them, they cried out, 'This is the finger of God,' Exod.
viii. 19.

*Let us cast lots, that we may know for whose cause this evil is
come upon us.* Why? What are they the better when they know
him? What would they do with him on whom the lot should fall?
Surely they supposing, or rather clearly seeing, this tempest to be
sent from some wrathful power, and that for some one man's sin
among them, they determined, having found him, to sacrifice him
unto the god that was so offended by him. God turneth evil unto
good, but the devil turneth good into evil. The Gentiles had a
a custom in the time of the common plague, to sacrifice one for the
rest. This custom they took by imitation of the Jews in offering
beasts, and of Abraham in offering his son; the devil, that father
of lies and schoolmaster of all mischief, teaching them. So the
devil took advantage to do evil by the service of God, in moving
the Gentiles to work abomination by offering men, imitating the
Jews' commanded sacrifices. But if they had rightly known the
true God, they would have taken their sins by the throat, and have
sacrificed them.

Come, let us cast lots. The mariners were not so wise to prevent
the tempest before it came, as they are diligent to allay the tempest
when it may not be laid. We, once overtaken with God's just
judgments, are very careful always to use all means to be rid of
them. But who keepeth a watch of his own ways, and diligently
laboureth to keep himself free from that which necessarily draweth
on itself God's judgment? Who purgeth himself of his sins, lest he
be sick? Who letteth or fetcheth out his corrupt blood of pride,
lust, covetousness, lest he be sore? Who keeps a good diet, and
maketh his choice of holy exercises, godly companions, religious
conferences, &c.? But know we, he is not safe that is sound,
neither he sound that is intemperate.

So they cast lots. Whether it be lawful to cast lots, it is not
evident by this example, because they were Gentiles, and therefore
no precedent for us; but so far may we use them as the word doth
lead us, and no farther.

There are two goats brought to Aaron, that he might cast lots
to see which goat should be killed, and which should not, Lev.

xvi. 8, &c. These goats signify Christ; for, as he died, he lived again; and as he was buried, he rose again. Again, the land of Canaan is parted by lots, to see what part each tribe should inhabit, Josh. xiv. 2. Again, that thief Achan is found out by lots, first by his tribe, then by his family, and, lastly, by his particular person. Josh. vii. Again, it is said that Saul was chosen king by lots, 1 Sam. x. 17, &c.; and, lest any should have said that it was his good luck, his good lot or chance, to be king, therefore the Lord appointed that he should be anointed before he was chosen by lots, ver. 1. Again, Matthias is chosen by lots to the apostleship instead of Judas, Acts i. 26. So that it is lawful in some cases to cast lots, so that they do attribute nothing unto them, and acknowledge that 'the lot is cast into the lap, but the disposition thereof is from the Lord,' Prov. xvi. 33. For they must not say that it is their chance, fortune, or good luck, for so they make an idol of it, and rob God of the honour due unto him. For it was not Saul's fortune to be king, but God's mercy; it was not Achan's chance to be caught, but God's judgment. Lots may be used to prevent strife, when all other means have been used; and sometimes before all other means, when in wisdom it is thought the best means. Brethren often, and godly men, at first divided their inheritance by lots, as the children of Israel divided the land of Canaan. Therefore in the church of Geneva there is an order, that in the time of plague there should be an house set apart for the sick to lodge in; and, lest they should be uncomforted, they choose out a minister by lots to do it.

So they cast lots. Now we are come to put up ourselves to the court of lawyers, to see if they will do anything for God, for conscience, or for love; viz., that they would end men's suits quickly, and let the poor clients have equity. Some say that lawyers be good until they be counsellors; like lions, which will be gentle until their talons grow. Be not offended, but amend, for malice speaks not.

I am persuaded that, if the lots were cast to see who troubles the ship, it would fall upon the lawyers. Be not offended, but amend, for malice speaks not. A poor client cometh forth accusing one, and going home accuseth a hundred; for so few seek to further him, and so many seek to hinder him, that all his gain is but labour and loss.

For a small matter many will come to law, to strive for that which, with reason, might easily be attained without such contention; and others seek to enrich themselves with contending for a small matter with their neighbours, yet in the end lose that they sought, and that they had beside; and so they contend and strive about a thing commonly, till the lawyer hath gained more by them than the thing which is in controversy is worth. These are like the mouse and the frog, which strove so long about marsh ground, that at length the kite came and took them both from it. Others will come up to law about a small matter, and therein so entangle themselves, that they cannot rid their hands of it until it have almost undone them; like a silly sheep that is hunting a fly, which runneth from bush to bush, and every bush catcheth a lock of him, so that the poor sheep is threadbare ere he hath done, and hath not a fleece left him to cover himself withal. So he runs from court to court to sue, to complain, to plead, till he have spent his cloak and his coat; were it not better to have cast lots for the coat at first? For the law is like a butler's box;[1] play still on, till all come to the candlestick. Therefore it is lawful, to end any controversy in a hard matter, to use this means.

Now whether it be lawful to cast dice; if lots may not be used (as Solomon's words, Prov. xviii. 18, 'The lot causeth contention to cease,' compared with Heb. vi. 16, prove) but in hard matters and weighty causes, when the thing is doubtful, and all good means are tried before to avoid strife, that question is decided which none but voluptuous men make question of, namely, whether dice-play be a meet exercise for a Christian soul. Solomon saith, 'The lot causeth contentions to cease;' therefore lots are to end strife; but these lots make strife. For before thou takest the dice, thou knowest thine own, and no man striveth to take it from thee; but when thou castest the dice, thou dost (as it were) ask whether thine own be thine own, and makest a strife of no strife. Art thou not worthy to lose the gifts of God, which venturest to lose them when thou needest not? Dost thou not deserve to forego thine own, which art so greedy of another's, that thou wouldst have his living for nothing but for turning of a die? Esau did not sell his birth-right so lightly, but he had somewhat for it which refreshed his hunger; but God hath given thee a living, and thou spendest it for nothing. The mariners did cast lots to find out the sinner; they did not cast dice to see who should win, as dicers do; for to whom the lot falls, he taketh all, which deserves to lose all as well as the other, and hath no right unto it by any law. For God hath not allowed one man to take another's goods for the tripping of a

---

[1] For an explanation of this allusion, see Vol. I. p. 99.—ED.

die ; but either they must be merited, or they must be given, or they must be bought, or else it is unlawful, ungodly, unconscionable, to take them. Besides the brawls, the cozenages, the oaths annexed to this game, which would not agree with it, unless it had been a meet companion for them. Thou takest another man's goods for nothing, whereas God hath appointed thee to get thy living with the sweat of thy brows; for thou takest away that which others sweat for; and whereas thou shouldst live by working, thou seekest to live by playing, like as the ape, which lives by toying. Doth any dicer think he doeth well ? Tell me, what thinkest thou? for every sinner doth condemn in his prayer to God that which he excuseth before men. If they which are gamesters repent it, how can they which are gamesters defend it ? Thou shouldst do nothing but that thou wouldst have God find thee doing, if he should come to judgment. Wouldst thou have him take thee at dice ? I am sure thou wouldst not have God see thee so vainly occupied. Neither canst thou think that Christ, or his prophets, or apostles, or evangelists, were dicers; for no such lots are named in the holy Scripture ; and yet the Lord's day is most profaned with this exercise, cards and dice, as though they kept all their vanities to celebrate holidays. What hast thou to allege for dice, now evidence is given up against them? Hast thou any patron to speak for them, but thy vain pleasure and filthy covetousness, which are condemned already, and therefore have no voice by law ? Take away these, and take away dice. The patron condemns the clients, when one vice condemns another. If the exercise were lawful, such patrons as pleasure and covetousness would not speak for it. Take thy pleasure therefore in that which is good, and the angels will rejoice with thee. If this were good, God would prosper them better that use it; but neither winners nor losers are gainers. I know not how, but there is not so much won as lost, as though the devil did part stakes with them, and draw away with a black hand when no man seeth ; for the winner saith, he hath not won half so much as the loser hath lost. One would think that one of them should flow, when so many ebb ; there is never an ebb without a flowing, never one loseth but another winneth, but at dice. What a cursed thing is this, that turns no man to good, which robs others, and beggars themselves ! The school of deceit, the shop of oaths, and the field of vanities. Thou dost not only hazard thy money in this game, but venturest thy salvation, and casteth dice with the devil, who shall have thy soul. For everything that cometh well to man, he giveth thanks; but for that which cometh by dice, he is ashamed to give thanks; which sheweth, that in conscience that gain is evil gotten, and that he sought it without God. Can this be good, when worst men use it most? If it were good, the evil would like worse of it than the good; but the more a man savoureth of any goodness, the more he begins to abhor it, and his conscience doth accuse him for it, as for sin. They which doubt whether God doth allow it, need but look how he doth prosper them that use it; but they trust not in God, the terms of their occupation descry, for they call all their casts *chances*, as though they relied not upon God, but upon chance. Therefore if dice make strife without cause; if they take away others' good for nothing; if we may not live by playing, but by labour; if they which have been dicers repent it among their sins; if the holy men never used this recreation, but the worst most delight in it; if thou .wouldst not have God see thee when thou playest at dice, nor take thee at it when he comes to judgment; if nothing but pleasure and covetousness speak for them; if they do not prosper which take pleasure in it; if they trust not upon God, but rely upon chance; if thou dost not only venture thy money, but hazard thy soul: then the best cast of dice is, to cast them quite away.

And the lot fell upon Jonah. The lot fell upon Jonah, not because he was the greatest sinner of them all (for so is the opinion of the common people, to censure them worst whom they see most afflicted, Luke xiii. 2, &c. If any one be seen to bear his cross, then many will say, This is a wicked man, and so think well of themselves, supposing that God is not bent against them to punish them as well), but because Jonah should feel the hand of the Lord both punishing and preserving him, and be reformed. For God correcteth all as he did his Son, to learn them obedience, Heb, v. 8. But 'if judgment begin with the house of God, what shall become of the ungodly?' 1 Peter iv. 17, 18.

And the lot fell upon Jonah. Now, when the sinner that troubled the ship is taken, Jonah can hide himself no longer. Now he might also fear to be sacrificed by the mariners presently. For the mariners, partly for the pain they had endured, partly for the loss they had sustained, partly for the danger wherein they remained, were no doubt as the she-wolves robbed of their whelps, out of measure furious, and fully bent to sacrifice him on whom the lot fell, to appease the wrathful God. But God stayed and restrained the rage of the mariners, and made them afterward willingly to abide the tempest a while, and put themselves to more pain to save him, endeavouring by rowing to recover land. For having heard of the true God, and, though they lost their goods, having found who is all good, shall we, say they, destroy him that hath saved us? Shall we give him up to death unnecessarily, that hath brought us to life, and assured us to reign with God in all glory everlasting? Surely the thankless are graceless; especially they that love not, and shew not forth the labour of love for, their gracious guide to God. But therefore we may see that 'the hearts of men are in the hands of God, and he turneth them which way he list,' Prov. xxi. 1; he fashioneth their hearts every one, Ps. xxxiii. 15; yea, even king's hearts as rivers of water doth he turn, to water and make fruitful his vine, to pity and to persecute, to honour and to shame, to love and hate his people, Ps. cvi. 41, &c., Isa. v. 2, &c., Ezra i. 4, Isa. iii. 24, Neh. ii., to deliver their power to the beast, Rev. xvii. 13, and again to eat the whore's flesh, and to burn her with fire, Rev. xvii. 16. Therefore let us never fear to perform our duties whatsoever, to whomsoever; for he formeth the hearts of all, who hath promised to ' honour them that honour him, but to make them contemptible that do despise him,' 1 Sam. ii. 30. Neither let us 'put confidence in man, nor in princes,' Ps. cxlvi. 3; for their hearts are rivers of waters of themselves, fleeting easily, as they be led following. But especially let us not forget chiefly to make prayers, supplications, intercessions, and to give thanks, for all those on the godliness or profaneness of whose hearts the flourishing or defacing of the gospel of Christ Jesus and the chosen of God doth most depend, 1 Tim. ii. 1.

And the lot fell upon Jonah. Now Jonah could not deny he was that sinner, unless he would accuse God of unrighteous judgment; for ' the lot is cast into the lap, but the whole disposition thereof is of the Lord.' Now therefore he must needs confess it. The winds thundering, the waves tumbling, the ship cracking, the mariners quaking, upon their gods crying, their wares forth casting, Jonah's prayers requesting, to cast lots consulting, Jonah kept himself close; he would not be thought that sinner. The wind said, I will overturn thee; the water said, I will drown thee; the ship said, I cannot hold thee; the mariners said, We cannot help thee; his prayers said, We cannot profit thee; his conscience within bleeding, and God at the door of his heart knocking, and the lots now ready for casting, said threateningly, For thee the tempest is come, thou fugitive, and we will discover thee.

Yet Jonah conceals his sin; so much did he abhor the shame of men, of strange men, a few men, frail men, or the fear of the fury of the flesh. Therefore, after the winds had roared, the waves raged, the ship reeled, the mariners cried, and the lot, his conscience, and God himself threatened him ; the lot also condemned him, and the fear of being sacrificed by sinners to Satan terrified him, so that he forthwith repented thoroughly, he declared it openly, and confessed his sin freely. Such a stir hath God before he can come by his own ; he must cross us, set himself and all his creatures against us, strain our bodies, or leave our souls, and constrain us to it, before we will return from our wicked ways, and thoroughly humble ourselves to yield him due obedience. Oh the goodness of the great God ! Oh long-sufferance and bountifulness unspeakable, which not only leadeth, but also in the chains of love draweth, us to true repentance !

It was God's great goodness to Jonah, that the mariners sacrificed him not ; greater, that he truly repented ; that God continued him in his calling, whose flying from God deserved flying to Satan, and blessed his, not so much solemn preaching, as sudden confession, and short denunciation of vengeance ; yea, made it so powerful, that it converted idolatrous heathens, most hardened idolaters ; first mariners, then Ninevites.

For what a blessing felt Jonah, God vouchsafing him of this honour, to offer them a lively, holy, and acceptable sacrifice to God, by whom he presently before greatly feared to have been offered dead, unholy, and so a delightful, sacrifice to Satan ! This fear banished, and that joy possessing him, what a mercy of the Almighty did Jonah think it ! But before he converted the Ninevites, he was more to be humbled, fuller to be strengthened, better every way to be prepared. Therefore God would have the sea to wash him, the whale to fast him, and yet miraculously safe to preserve him, that, being purified, he might pray fervently ; and being delivered, find power, comfort, and courage abundantly. Therefore when by lot being taken, and by his own confession found the man that procured the tempest, the mariners, in love and compassion of him, had essayed by rowing to get to land, but could not, the sea raging more and more, and Jonah himself professed he knew the tempest was sent for his cause, and would be laid, he being cast into the sea ; Jonah at length was cast out of the ship into the swelling surge of the tempestuous sea. What hope of life then left ? is there any ? To swallow up all, soon after he is swallowed whole of a whale. Here let us mark, that after the tempest had terrified Jonah, the mariners reproved him ; when they had reproved him, his conscience pricked him ; when his conscience had pricked him, the consulting to cast lots grieved him; after grief for consulting, their concluding to cast lots vexed him; vexed at the conclusion, the lot condemns him; the lot having condemned him, in what an agony think we was Jonah; partly, that he should be held that notorious wretch that had brought this woe; partly, lest they in their raging grief, for their great trouble of body, loss of goods, and danger of life, should forthwith kill him for a sacrifice, to appease the unknown angry God? But after this agony the terror of drowning followed, and after that the horror of that huge fish: first, lest it tear him in pieces; then, lest it melt him; afterward, lest it poison him; lastly, three days and three nights the comfortless horror of darkness and noisome stink in the fish's belly tormented him.

First then see, the winds could not further him, the waters could not bear him, the ship could not hold him, the mariners could not help him; and, being cast out, lest all for him be cast away, the whale would not spare him, the stench would ill feed him, the darkness would less glad him, and light might not visit him. Now, see then what Jonah got by his journey: notwithstanding all the promises of which Satan assured him, and all the furtherances which the serpent procured him, he lost his labour, lost his money, lost his joy, lost his credit, lost his quiet, and saw no hope but to lose his life too, finding plentifully and bitterly feeling dreadful fears. He trusted to the winds, the winds could not save him; he trusted to the ship, the ship could not keep him; he trusted to the mariners, the mariners could not help him; he trusted to the lot, the lot would not spare him; he trusted to the waters, the waters could not bear him; neither would the whale forbear him, neither did anything make show of likelihood to save him. Therefore we may see in Jonah what it profiteth a man to fly from God, forsaking his calling, and so practising the evil motions of Satan, instead of the known will of God. Assuredly, if we follow his flatteries, as Jonah did, we shall have, as he had, accusing consciences, fearful hearts, and the wrath of God upon our heads. For he hath nothing to give us, although he promise and make us believe he hath kingdoms. Yet, indeed, he hath horror of mind for all that obey him, and hell for the reward of his, which will make all their hearts ache which receive it.

See, secondly, in this punishment of Jonah, the justice of God. The bee, when she hath once stung, doth lose her sting, so that she can sting no more; so doth not God's justice punishing sin; for it retaineth power, it hath store of stings to vex still. When one

judgment is executed, he ever hath others enough ready, either of
the same kind in another degree more sharp, or of another sort.
For all the creatures, with their several powers, are God's darts to
strike us when he commands. Therefore, if we be sick, sickness is
not dead with us ; if we be poor, poverty endeth not ; if we be in
danger, danger is not therefore put down for ever after ; and if we
be vexed, vexation hath not therefore lost his sting. His dart, his
weapons also, are as sharp now as they were at the first, and sharper
too, because we are sinfuller. For according to the sickness is the
medicine ; and wounds more dangerous require more dolorous
plasters.

And if thou be disobedient, then he will lead thee through them
all, until he hath humbled thee, and made thee to glorify him with
obedience, or utterly destroyed thee, Lev. xxvi. 16, &c.

Thirdly, let us not forget, neither lightly think of this, that God
knoweth how to punish for sin, yea, most severely to correct his
children, though repenting. If our prophet Jonah here may not
keep thee some good while in a due meditation of it, let that man
after God's own heart, the sweet prophet of Israel, come to thy
mind, and in him see whether God cockereth his entirest friends, or
doth not something sharply, if not bitterly, handle them, if they
settle themselves in their dregs, or securely serve the Lord, 2 Sam.
xviii., xii., and many other places.

Lastly, yet consider God is rich in mercy, and full of compassion ;
loath to punish, unless too far provoked ; content to shake his rod
over us, to make us fear only, and keep us free from feeling his
strokes, if that may have his due work in us, that is, recall, reform,
and confirm us. For as the winds could not overthrow Jonah, nor
the waters drown him, so neither could the whale consume, poison,
or annoy him, or aught but fear him, though it had swallowed him ;
for Jonah remembering God, God shewed he forgot not Jonah.
Therefore when and where Jonah thought verily and speedily to
have perished, then and there God caused him to be three days and
as many nights most safely preserved. Oh power omnipotent ! oh
goodness all-sufficient, in all things, at all times ! God then as well
knoweth to deliver his out of all distress in due time, as to reserve
the wicked to the day of judgment to be punished. And in what
danger shall we despair ? in what extremities ought not we to hope
in our most mighty Saviour, remembering Jonah in the whale's
belly, Jonah ii. 10 ; Jeremiah in the mire of the deep dungeon,
Jer. xxxviii. 13 ; Daniel among the fierce lions, Dan. vi. 23 ; his
three companions in the hot burning furnace, Dan. iii. 26 ; nay,

600,000 men of war, and three times as many more, men and women, young and old, in the wilderness, lacking now drink, then meat, Exod. xvii. 6, and xvi. 13 ; and all these delivered out of all danger, these last miraculously satisfied with drink out of the rock, and with meat abundantly from heaven ?

Secondly, though Jonah be cast into the troublous sea, and swallowed of a huge whale, yet he must preach at Nineveh ; though Moses fly out of Egypt, yet he must be the leader of God's people thence, Exod. ii. 15, and iii. 10 ; Joseph is in prison, but he must be the lord of Egypt, and preserve the church alive, Gen. xxxix. 20, xli. 40, and xlv. 11. Who would have thought that Saul should become Paul ? Acts ix., 1 Cor. xv. 10 ; or forswearing Peter a faithful preacher ? Mark xiv. 71, Acts iv. Suspend, then, thy judgment, and wonder at God's works, whether of mercy or justice ; and think not the worse of a man though he were cast out of the sea, as Jonah, Jonah ii. 10 ; or basely brought up, as Amos, Amos i. 1 ; for the deliverer of Israel was brought out of the flags, Exod. ii. 3, and the converter of Nineveh out of a whale, Jonah ii. 10, and the salvation of the whole world out of a stall, Luke ii. 16.

And the lot fell upon Jonah. The lot fell upon Jonah, that he might be cast out of the ship ; that as the ship was almost broken, but not altogether ; so Jonah might be almost drowned, but not altogether ; almost consumed, almost poisoned in the belly of the whale, but not altogether ; that being in the double deep duly humbled, and as gold in a furnace, fined and fitted for God's works, he might thence in a miraculous manner come forth, like Lazarus in his winding-sheet, that he might glorify God once again, and courageously cry against Nineveh.

And the lot fell upon Jonah. The lot fallen upon Jonah, the justice of God (both manifesting the truth incorruptly, and chastising his disobedient servant severely), did appear, but with all singular mercy shined ; and the mariners' minds were mollified, in that they sacrificed him not to Satan ; but much more was God's mercy, that he by that means truly repented. Insomuch that the old idolatrous mariners presently by him were converted ; and he, cast into the sea, was not drowned, swallowed of the whale, and three days continuing therein perished not, but miraculously was preserved, and most preciously cast on land safe ; and, lastly, crying against Nineveh, that sinful city, had his preaching so mightily prevailing, that he wonderfully humbled them all. This mercy was marvellous, this goodness of God to Jonah most glorious ; for the Ninevites hearing 'Yet forty days, and Nineveh shall be overthrown,' first, as the mariners had before done, believed the word of God, though they never heard it before. If we heard of the word of God preached, as the mariners and Ninevites did, with trembling hearts in the sense of God's majesty, it would not be but we should feel the power of it lively, and filled with all joy in believing speedily ; but ineffectual and fruitless is preaching, because there is nothing almost but unreverent and senseless hearing. And why should God teach the heedless to learn ? why should he give pearls to dung-hill cocks, nay, to very swine ? But they believed the word as soon as they heard it, though they never heard it before. What doth that argue ? Surely it sheweth, that the foolish and simple are more diligent and ready, both to hear and receive the word of God, than those that are wise in their own conceit, or also in the view of the world. What saith Christ ? 'The poor receive the gospel,' Mat. xi. 5. What saith Paul ? 'Not many rich, not many wise,' 1 Cor. i. 26. For though we have knowledge, if our knowledge be like the pharisees', Mat. xxiii. 13, &c., that is, in show of sincerity only, in counterfeit holiness, and hollow-hearted friendship through hypocrisy, it had been better for us that we had been ignorant, for it will but leave us the more inexcusable; it will be found insufficient to save us, but sufficient the more fearfully to condemn us, because we 'know our Master's will, and do it not,' Luke xii. 47, 48. Therefore, as Peter said to Simon Magus, 'Thy money perish with thee,' Acts viii. 20 ; so will the Lord say unto such, Thy knowledge perish with thee, seeing it is fruitless.

But when Nineveh had believed God, what did they secondly ? They speedily, they notably repented ; they proclaimed a fast, they put on sackcloth, they humbled themselves before the Lord, they earnestly besought him to turn away his wrath from this woful city. Jonah preached at Nineveh, crying against it, Jonah iii. 4 ; it seemeth to have humbled them, and that without a miracle, without which scant any doctrine is of credit among the Gentiles ; for not only within forty, but within four days, much within forty days, he converted Nineveh, ruffling Nineveh, old and idolatrous Nineveh ; long before forty days be ended, the seed is sown, grown, increased mightily, and full ripe, in a soil in reason most barren. Sow therefore, ye seedsmen, where ye are set. If ye sow cheerfully, ye shall reap plenteously in due time ; faint not. Say not, I have a stony, or a starved, or a thorny ground: Nineveh repents in sackcloth.

In which willing submission of theirs, and speedy lively repentance at the words of the prophet, after he had been three days and three nights in the whale's belly, the calling of the Gentiles by Christ, after he had been three days and three nights in the bowels of the earth, might well be signified ; for they no less willingly than the Ninevites submitted themselves to the gospel preached ; no less speedily, and peradventure more truly, repented. For though they now thus wonderfully humbled themselves, not the fearful multitude only, but the richest and greatest, the noble and king also, and so all escaped now, Jonah ii. 5, 6 ; yet soon after they returned to their vomit, and never ceased to add sin to sin, till they were by open wars miserably weakened, and at length, fulfilling the prophecy of Nahum, utterly consumed, Nahum iii. Therefore, first, for the comfort of the godly, since Ahab humbled himself before the Lord ; Ahab, I say, that had done exceeding abominably in following idols, and sold himself to work wickedness in the sight of the Lord; submitted himself under the hand of God, fasting in sackcloth, though he did all in hypocrisy, and had not the evil threatened brought upon him in his days, 1 Kings xxi. 25, 26, 27, 29 ; seeing Rehoboam and the princes of Israel who had 'for-saken the Lord,' 2 Chron xii. 1, and the whole tribe of Judah, 'which wrought wickedness in the sight of the Lord, and provoked him more with their sins than all that their fathers had done,' 1 Kings xiv. 22, humbling themselves before the Lord, and confessing him just, had not the wrath of the Lord poured on them by Shishak, king of Egypt, were not destroyed, but shortly delivered, 2 Chron. xii. 6, 7, 12 ; yea, also, things prospered in Judah, though the Lord had threatened to 'leave them in the hands of Shishak,' albeit they truly repented not, verse 5 ; lastly, forasmuch as Nineveh, that 'bloody city, full of lies and robbery, the beautiful harlot, with multitude of fornications, that mistress of witchcrafts, which sold the people through her whoredoms, and the nations through her witchcraft,' Nah. iii. 1, 4, humbling themselves with fasting, and putting on sackcloth, the Lord repented of the evil he had threat-ened them, and did it not,' Jonah iii. 5–8, 10 ; how assured may we be, that whatsoever judgment the Lord threateneth us, and howso-ever he threaten it, it shall not light on us, when we unfeignedly humble ourselves in true fasting, turning from our evil ways, and from the heart vowing to serve God in all holiness ? For this is the clear promise of the faithful God. 'If I shut the heaven that there be no rain, or if I command the grasshopper to devour the land, or if I send pestilence among my people ; if my people, among whom my name is called upon, do humble themselves, and pray, and seek my presence, and turn from their wicked ways ; then will

I hear in heaven, and be merciful to their sins, and heal their land,' 2 Chron. vii. 13, 14. Again, as generally most plainly saith just Jehovah, 'I will speak suddenly against a nation, or against a kingdom, saying, I will pluck it up, and root it out, and destroy it. But if this nation against which I have pronounced this turn from their wickedness, I will repent of the plague that I thought to bring upon them,' Jer. xviii. 7, 8. Let us then, O beloved of the Lord, whosoever love the Lord Jesus, be careful to fulfil the condition; and then be confident, not doubting of the performance of the promise, by so much the more, by how much the fewer we be, and by how much the longer and clearer the Lord hath threatened most terrible judgments.

Now for the terror of the ungodly, as many of them as repent only when God's hand is upon them, and then humble themselves outwardly only, and that but only when the fierceness of his wrath appeareth, or else after they have escaped the feared judgment fall to their wonted wickedness again; let them be sure, the strong and just God, that consumed Nineveh slidden back, will overtake them also in wrath, and for ever turn them over to ceaseless woe. For the greatness, the beauty, the strength and riches of Nineveh could not withstand the hand of God, or keep it from destruction, but rather furthered and hastened it. For with the more excellent ornaments that it was adorned by the Lord, the more heinous and grievous in his sight was the abuse of them. Therefore the hugeness or the strength of this or any other city cannot save it from the judgment of God, being sinful in his sight.

Great Sodom is destroyed, great Jericho is destroyed, great Nineveh is destroyed, great Jerusalem is destroyed; and great Rome, the room of all unclean spirits, stayeth for her destruction, like a whore that stayeth for her punishment till she be delivered; and these were and shall be punished for unthankfulness and contempt of the word of God. Yet Nineveh, Jericho, Sodom, nor Rome, have had half the preaching that we have had; yet we are unthankful too; then what have we to look for? But when Sodom was burned, Zoar stood safe; when Jerusalem was destroyed, Bethlehem stood still. So the Lord doth always provide for his people, though he make never so great a slaughter and destruction among his enemies. For the Lord, because of his covenant, doth always provide for his chosen, although they be but a remnant, like the gleaning after harvest, or like a cluster of grapes on the top of the vine after the vintage, and though there be never so great calamity or trouble; as we see in the book of Genesis, when there was a great time of dearth and scarcity to come upon the land where Jacob was, the Lord had sent Joseph to provide for his father Jacob, lest he should want bread, he or any of his sons and folks, and so ordered the matter that Joseph was treasurer over all the corn in Egypt. And so among the Turks and Spaniards, and infidels, the Lord will find means to do them good which unfeignedly love him; and in the dungeon, in prison, and in bonds, yea, and in death, the godly shall find God.

THE BENEFIT OF CONTENTATION.

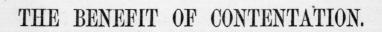

THE BENEFIT OF CONTENTATION.

Godliness is great gain, if a man be content with that he hath.—
1 Tim. VI. 6.

BECAUSE when we preach, we know not whether we shall preach
again, my care is, to choose fit and proper texts, to speak that
which I would speak, and that which is necessary for you to hear.
Therefore, thinking with myself what doctrine were fittest for you,
I sought for a text which speaks against covetousness, which I may
call the Londoners' sin. Although God hath given you more than
others, which should turn covetousness into thankfulness, yet as
the ivy groweth with the oak, so covetousness hath grown with
riches; every man wisheth the philosopher's stone; and who is within these walls that thinks he hath enough, though there be so many
that have too much? As the Israelites murmured as much when
they had manna, as when they were without it, Exod. xvi. 2, Num.
xi. 4; so they which have riches covet as much as they which are
without them; that conferring your minds and your wealth together, I may truly say, this city is rich, if it were not covetous.
This is the devil which bewitcheth you, to think that you have not
enough, when you have more than you need. If you cannot choose
but covet riches, I will shew you riches which you may covet: 'Godliness is great riches.' In which words, as Jacob craved of his
wives and his servants to give him their idols, that he might bury
them, Gen. xxxv. 4; so Paul craveth your covetousness, that he
might bury it; and that ye might be no losers, he offereth you
the vantage; instead of gain, he proposeth great gain. 'Godliness
is great gain;' as if he should say, will you covet little gain before
great? You have found little joy in money, you shall find great
joy in the Holy Ghost; you have found little peace in the world,

you shall find great peace in conscience. Thus seeing the world strive for the world, like beggars thrusting at a dole, lawyer against lawyer, brother against brother, neighbour against neighbour, for the golden apple, that poor Naboth cannot hold his own, because so many Ahabs are sick for his vineyard, 1 Kings xxi. 4; when he had found the disease, like a skilful physician, he goeth about to pick out the greedy worm which maketh men so hungry, and setteth such a glass before them that will make a shilling seem as great as a pound, a cottage seem as fair as a palace, and a plough seem as goodly as a diadem; that he which hath but twenty pounds, shall be as merry as he which hath an hundred; and he which hath an hundred, shall be as jocund as he which hath a thousand; and he which hath a thousand, shall be as well contented as he which hath a million; even as Daniel did thrive with water and pulse, as well as the rest did with their wine and junkets, Dan. i. 12. This is the virtue and operation of these words; if you hear them with the same spirit that Paul wrote them, they will so work upon your hearts, that you shall go away every man contented with that which he hath, like Zaccheus, which before he had seen Christ, knew nothing but to scrape, but as soon as he had heard Christ, all his mind was set upon giving, Luke xix. 8; this was not the first day that Zaccheus seemed rich to others, but this was the first day that Zaccheus seemed rich unto himself, when riches seemed dung, and godliness seemed riches. Christ doth not will others to give all their goods away to the poor, as he bade the young man, to see what he would do, Mat. xix. 21; but he which forbade him to keep his riches, forbiddeth us to love riches, and makes our riches seem poverty. When ye contemn riches, ye shall seem rich, because no man hath enough, but he which is contented; but if ye covet, and groan, and thirst, as Jacob gave Reuben a blessing, but said, 'Thou shalt not be excellent,' Gen. xlix. 4; so God may give you riches, but he saith, You shall not be satisfied. For ye will be covetous until ye be religious. He that will have contentation, must leave his covetousness in pawn for it. This is the spirit which we should cast out; if we will leave but this one sin behind, you shall depart out of this church like Naaman out of Jordan, 2 Kings v. 14, as if you had been washed, and all your sins swept away, like the scales from Paul's eyes, Acts ix. 18. For what hath brought usury, and simony, and bribery, and cruelty, and subtilty, and envy, and strife, and deceit into this city, and made every house an inn, and every shop a market of oaths, and lies, and fraud, but the superfluous love of money? Name covetousness, and thou hast named the mother of all these mischiefs, other sins are but hirelings unto this sin, usury, and bribery, and simony, and extortion, and deceit, and lies, and oaths, are factors to covetousness, and serve for porters to fetch and bring her living in. As the receiver makes a thief, so covetousness makes an usurer, and extortioner, and deceiver, because she receiveth the booty which they steal. Even as Rachel cried unto her husband, 'Give me children, or else I die,' Gen. xxx. 1; so covetousness crieth unto usury, and bribery, and simony, and cruelty, and deceit, and lies, Give me riches, or else I die. How they may save a little, and how they may get much, and how they may prolong life, is every man's dream from sun to sun, so long as they have a knee to bow unto Baal, Rom. xi.; so many vices bud out of this one, that it is called, 'The root of all evil,' 1 Tim. vi. 10, as if we would say, the spawn of all sin. Take away covetousness, and he will sell his wares as cheap as he; he will bring up his children as virtuously as he; he will refuse bribes as earnestly as he; he will succour the poor as heartily as he; he will come to the church as lightly as he. If ye could feel the pulse of every heart, what makes Gehazi take the bribe which Elisha refused? 2 Kings v. 11; what makes Demetrius to speak for images which Paul condemned? Acts xix. 4; what makes Nabal deny David that which Abigail gave him? 1 Sam. xxv.; what makes Judas grudge the oil which Mary tendered? Nothing but covetousness. When thou shouldst give, she saith it is too much; when thou shouldst receive, she saith it is too little; when thou shouldst remit, she saith it is too great; when thou shouldst repent, she saith it is too soon; when thou shouldst hear, she saith it is too far; like Pharaoh, which found one business or other to occupy the Jews, when they should serve God, Exod. v. 6.

Thus every labour hath an end, but covetousness hath none; like a suitor in law, which thinks to have an end this term, and that term, and the lawyer which should procure his peace, prolongeth his strife, because he hath an action to his purse, as his adversary hath to his land; so he which is set on coveting, doth drink brine, which makes him thirst more, and sees no haven till he arrive at death; when he hath lied, he is ready to lie again; when he hath sworn, he is ready to swear again; when he hath deceived, he is ready to deceive again; when the day is past, he would it were to begin again; when the term is ended, he wisheth it were to come again; and though his house be full, and his shop full, and his coffers full, and his purse full, yet his heart is not full, but lank and empty, like the disease which we call the wolf, that is always eating, and yet keeps the body lean. The ant doth eat the food which he findeth; the lion doth refresh himself with the prey that he taketh, but the covetous man lieth by his money, as a sick man sits by his meat, and hath no power to taste it, but to look upon it; like the prince to whom Elisha said, that he should ' see the corn with his eyes, but none should come within his mouth,' 2 Kings vii. 22. Thus the covetous man makes a fool of himself. He coveteth to covet; he gathereth to gather; he laboureth to labour; he careth to care; as though his office were to fill a coffer full of angels, and then to die like an ass, which carrieth treasure on his back all day, and at night they are taken from him, which did him no good but load him. How happy were some, if they knew not gold from lead? 'If thou be wise,' saith Solomon, ' thou shalt be wise for thyself,' Prov. ix. 12. But he which is covetous, is covetous against himself. For what a plague is this, unless one would kill himself, for a man to spend all his life in carking, and pining, and scraping, as though he should do nothing but gather in this world, to spend in the next, unless he be sure that he should come again when he is dead, to eat those scraps which he hath gotten with all his stir? Therefore covetousness may well be called *misery*, and the covetous *miserable*, for they are miserable indeed.

Of them which seem to be wise, there be no such fools in the world, as they which love money better than themselves; but this is the judgment of God, that they which deceive others deceive themselves, and live like Cain, which was a vagabond upon his own land, Gen. iv. 14, so they are beggars in the midst of their wealth; for though they have understanding to know riches, and a mind to seek them, and wit to find them, and policy to keep them, and life to possess them, yet they have such a false sight and blear eye, that when their riches lie before them they have poverty, and he which hath not half so much, seems richer than they. Will you know how this comes to pass? To shew that the covetous men belong to hell, they are all like hell while they live. Hell is never filled, and they are never satisfied, but as the horse-leech crieth, Give, give, Prov. xxx. 15, so their hearts cry, Bring, bring; and though the tempter should say to him, as he said to Christ, ' All these will I give thee,' Mat. iv. 9, Luke iv. 6, yet all will not content them, no more than heaven contented him. But as the glutton in hell desired a drop of water, Luke xvi. 24, and yet a river would not satisfy him; for if a drop had been granted him, he would have desired a drop more, and a drop to that; so they will lie, and swear, and deceive for a drop of riches. The devil needs not offer them all, as he did to Christ, for they will serve him for less; but if he could give them all, all would not content them, more than the world contented Alexander. For it is against the name and nature of covetousness to be content, as it is against the name and nature of contentation to be covetous. Therefore one saith, that no man's heart is like the covetous man's heart, for his heart is without a bottom.

A prentice is bound but for nine years, and then he is free; but if the covetous might live longer than Methuselah, Gen. v. 15, yet they would never be freemen, but prentices to the world, while they have a foot out of the grave.

It is a wonder to see; as the devil compasseth about, seeking whom he may devour, 1 Peter v. 8, so men compass about, seeking what they may devour; such love is between men and money, that they which profess good will unto it with their hearts, will not take so much pains for their life, as they take for gain, Prov. i. 13. Therefore no marvel, if they have no leisure to sanctify themselves, which have no leisure to refresh themselves. Christ knew what he spake, when he said, 'No man can serve two masters,' Mat. vi. 24, meaning God and the world, because each would have all. As the angel and the devil strove for the body of Moses, Jude 7; not who should have a part, but who should have the whole; so they strive still for our souls, who shall have all. Therefore the apostle saith, 'The love of this world is enmity to God,' 1 John ii. 15; signifying such emulation between these two, that God cannot abide the world should have a part, and the world cannot abide that God should have a part. Therefore the love of the world must needs be enmity to God, and therefore the lovers of the world must needs be enemies to God, and so no covetous man is God's servant, but God's enemy. For this cause covetousness is called idolatry, Eph. v. 5, which is the most contrary sin to God, because as treason sets up another king in the king's place, so idolatry sets up another god in God's place.

This word doth signify that the covetous make so much of money that they even worship it in their hearts, and would do as much for it as the idolaters do for their idols. Paul, seeing such sins committed, and such pains taken for gain, thought with himself, if they could be persuaded that godliness is gain, it is like that they would take as much pains for godliness as they did take for gain. Therefore he taketh upon him to prove this strange paradox, that godliness is gain, against all them in the verse before, which hold that gain is godliness. These two opinions are very contrary, and here are many against one. A man would think that Paul should be very eloquent and sharp-witted, and that he had need to use some logic, for he hath chosen a hard text: What, Paul, will you prove that godliness is gain? You shall have more opponents against you than Micaiah had when he forbade Ahab to fight, 1 Kings xxii. 17. If you had taken the former verse, which saith that 'Gain is godliness,' then you should have had matter and examples enough; the merchant, and mercer, and lawyer, and landlord, and patron, and all would come in and speak for gain, as the Ephesians cried for Diana, Acts xix. 28. But if you will be cross to all, and preach 'Godliness is gain' to them which count gain godliness, men will think of you as Festus did, that you speak you know not what, Acts xxvi. 24. These lessons are for Paul himself. As Christ saith, 'All do not receive this word,' Mat. xix. 11; so all do not count this gain, but loss; we count him rich that hath his barns full, like the churl, Luke xii. 18; his coffers full, like the glutton, Luke xvi. 19; his table full, like Belshazzar, Dan. v. 1; his stable full, like Solomon, 1 Kings iv. 26; his grounds full, like Job, Job i. 3; his purse full, like Crœsus. You speak against your Master, for Christ sent word unto John, that the poor receive the gospel, Luke vii. 22, as though the godly were of the poorer sort; and David calleth the wicked rich: 'They prosper and flourish,' saith he; their seed blasteth not, their cow casteth not, Ps. lxxiii. 3, 12; as if he should say, It is not as you take it, Paul, that godliness doth make men rich; for this I have observed in my time, that the wicked be the wealthiest; and good Lazarus is the poor man, and wicked Dives is the rich man, Luke xvi. 19, 20. Again, we read that the officers were asked, Which of the pharisees or of the rulers did follow Christ? John vii. 48; yet these were counted rich men, though they had no godliness; and if you should examine yourself, it seems you were no rich man for all your godliness, when you did work with your hands for your living, 1 Thes. ii. 9; therefore, if godliness be such gain, how happeneth it that your share is no better? So they which are like Nicodemus, when Christ saith that they must be born again, think that they can have no other meaning, but that they must return into their mothers' womb, John iii. 4; and when he calls himself bread, that he must needs mean such bread as they dine with, John vi. As the Jews, hearing the prophets speak so often of Christ's kingdom, and call him a king, looked for a temporal king that should bring them peace, and joy, and glory, and make them like kings themselves, Mat. xx. 20 ; so the carnal ears, when they hear of a kingdom, and treasures, and riches, straight their minds run upon earthly, and worldly, and transitory things, such as they love, to whom Paul answereth, as Christ answered his disciples, 'I have another meat which you know not of, John iv. 3, so there are other riches which you know not of ; I said not that godliness is earthly, or worldly, or transitory gain, but 'great gain.'

He will not only prove godliness to be *gain*, but *great gain; as* if he should say, more gainful than your wares, and rents, and fines, and interests, as though he would make the lawyer, and merchant, and mercer, and draper, and patron, and landlord, and all the men of riches believe, that godliness will make them rich sooner than covetousness. I fear this saying may be renewed, 'If a man tell you, ye will not believe,' &c., Hab. i. 5. As the Lord looked down upon the earth, to see if any did regard him, and said, 'There is not one,' Ps. xiv. 2, liii. 2 ; so this sentence may go from court to city, from city to country, and say, there is scarce one in a town that will subscribe unto it. 'Many,' said David, 'ask who will shew us any good ?' Ps. iv. 6, meaning riches, and honour, and pleasure, which are not good. But when he came to godliness itself, he leaves out *many*, and prayeth in his own person, 'Lord, lift thou up the light of thy countenance upon us ;' as if none would join with him. 'Yet wisdom is justified by her own children,' Mat. xi. 19, and the godly count godliness gain ; to make us love godliness, he calleth it by the name of that we love most, that is, gain. As the father calleth his son which he would love more than the rest, by his own name, to put him in mind of such a love as he beareth to himself. Here we may see that God doth not command men to be godly, only because it makes for his glory, but because godliness is profitable to us. For godliness is not called gain, in respect of God, but in respect of us ; it is gain to us, but it is duty to him. So it is called a health in respect of us, Prov. iii. 8, because it is the health of our souls ; so it is not called a kingdom in respect of God, but in respect of us, because we are entitled to the kingdom by this difference from the reprobates. Put all the good things in the world together, and the goodness of all is found in godliness, and therefore godliness is called by the names of those things that men count best, to shew that the godly are as well, as merry, as content with their love towards God, and God's love towards them, as others are with health, and wealth, and pleasures. Therefore it is said of the godly, 'The fear of the Lord is his treasure,' Isa. xxxiii. 6. Therefore saith Jeremiah, 'The Lord is my portion,' Lam. iii. 24, as though he desired nothing else ; and therefore it is said of Moses, that he ' esteemed the rebuke of Christ greater riches than all the treasures of Egypt,' Heb. xi. 26. If crosses be riches, as Moses thought, what riches are in godliness ? But is this all the harvest ? shall godliness be all the godly man's riches ? Nay, saith Paul, godliness ' hath the promise of this life, and of the life to come,' 1 Tim. iv. 8, that is, the godly shall do well in heaven and here too. And therefore Christ saith, ' First seek the kingdom of God, and all the rest shall be cast upon you,' Mat. vi. 33, even as the sheaves fell before Ruth, Ruth ii. 16; so riches shall fall in your way, as they did to Abraham, and Lot, and Jacob, and Job, and Joseph ; riches were cast to them they knew not how ; but as if God had said, *Be rich,* and they were rich straight. For all good things were created for the good, and therefore they are called good. Because the good God created them for good men to good purpose, therefore as Jacob got the blessing, so he got the inheritance also, Gen. xxvii. 8 ; to shew that as the faithful have the inward blessing, so they have the outward blessings too, when they are good for them. For, said David, 'They which seek the Lord shall want nothing that is good,' Ps. xxxiv. 10. Now God knoweth better than we what is good for us, as the nurse knoweth better than the child when the milk is ready for it. Therefore Christ saith, ' Your heavenly Father knoweth what you have need of,' Mat. vi. 32. He saith not, that we know what we have need of, but that our Father knoweth. As if he should say, when you have need of health, your Father will send you health ; when you have need of riches, your Father will send you riches; when you have need of liberty, your Father will send you liberty ; for he saith not only, that our Father knoweth what we have need of, but that he will give us the things which we need. Therefore, as children take no care for their apparel, what clothes they shall wear, nor for their victuals, what meat they shall eat, but leave this care for their father, so saith Christ, ' Take you no care, for my Father careth for you,' Mat. vi. 31 ; Ps. xxxiv. 10, xxv. 5.

He was not content to call godliness *gain,* but he calleth it *great gain;* as if he would say, *gain,* and more than *gain;* riches, and better than riches ; a kingdom, and greater than a kingdom. As when the prophets would distinguish between the idol-gods and the living God, they call him the great God; so the gain of godliness is called great gain. The riches of the world are called earthly, transitory, snares, thorns, dung, as though they were not worthy to be counted riches; and therefore, to draw the earnest love of men from them, the Holy Ghost brings them in with these names of disdain, to disgrace them with their loves; but when he comes to godliness, which is the riches of the soul, he calleth it great riches, heavenly riches, unsearchable riches, everlasting riches, with all the names of honour, and all the names of pleasure, and all the names of happiness. As a woman trims and decks herself with an hundred ornaments, only to make her amiable, so the Holy Ghost setteth out godliness with names of honour, and names of pleasure, and names of happiness, as it were in her jewels, with letters of commendation to make her be beloved. Lest any riches should compare with godliness, he gives it a name above others, and calleth it great riches, as if he would make a distinction between riches and riches, between the gain of covetousness and the gain of godliness, the peace of the world and the peace of conscience, the joy of riches and the joy of the Holy Ghost. The worldly men have a kind of peace, and joy, and riches. But I cannot call it *great*, because they have not enough, they are not contented as the godly are; therefore only godliness hath this honour, to be called *great riches*. The gain of covetousness is nothing but wealth; but the gain of godliness is wealth, and peace, and joy, and love of God, and the remission of sins, and everlasting life. Therefore only godliness hath this honour, to be called great gain. Riches makes bate, but godliness makes peace; riches breeds covetousness, but godliness brings contentation; riches makes men unwilling to die, but godliness makes men ready to die; riches often hurt the owner, but godliness profiteth the owner and others. Therefore, only godliness hath this honour, to be called great riches. Such gain, such joy, such peace is in godliness, and yet no man covets it; and this is the quality of virtue, it seemeth nothing unto a man until he hath it, as Solomon saith of the buyer, while he is in buying, he dispraiseth the things which he buyeth, and saith, 'It is naught,' it is not worth the price which ye ask, Prov. xx. 14; but when he hath bought it, so soon as he is gone, he boasteth of his pennyworths, and saith, it is better than his money. So godliness, before a man hath it, he saith it is not worth his labour, and thinks every hour too much that he spendeth about it; but when he hath found it, he would not lose it again for all the world; because he is now come to that which followeth, to 'be contented with that he hath.' Here Paul sheweth with what a man should be contented, not with one thousand pounds, nor one hundred pounds, nor twenty pounds, but with that he hath; and there is great reason why he should so, because no man knoweth what is fit for him so well as his carver. And therefore every one should esteem so reverently of God, that he think nothing better for him, for the time present, than that which God measureth forth unto him. For when Christ had no money, he was content; and when he wanted money to pay tribute, he sent for no more than he needed, Mat. xvii. 27; he might have commanded twenty pounds as well as twenty pence. But to shew that we should desire no more than will serve our turn, he would have no more than served his turn. Now, because contentation is of such a nature that it can please itself with poverty as well as riches, therefore it is called the great gain, as though it had all which it wanted. And this contentment, saith Paul, we owe to godliness, because it is not possible for a wicked man to be contented; for as he is not satisfied with sin, so is he satisfied with nothing. Riches come, and yet the man is not pleased; liberty comes, and yet the man is not pleased; pleasure comes, and yet the man is not pleased; until God come, and then he saith, 'My cup is full,' Ps. xxiii. 5; 'Shew us thy Father,' saith Philip, 'and it sufficeth,' John xiv. 7. Nay, shew us thy truth, and it sufficeth. 'Now, my soul,' saith the churl, 'take thy rest.' Nay, 'Now, my soul, take thy rest, for thou hast laid up for many years,' Luke xii. 19. The godly man hath found that which all the world doth seek, that is, *Enough*. Every word may be defined, and every thing may be measured, but *enough* cannot be measured or defined, it changeth every year; when we had nothing, we thought it enough, if we might obtain less than we have; when we came to more, we thought of another *enough;* now we have more, we dream of another *enough;* so enough is always to come, though too much be there already. For as oil kindleth the fire which it seems to quench, so riches come as though they would make a man contented, and make him more covetous. Therefore, seeing contentation was never found in riches, the apostle teacheth to seek it in godliness, saying, 'Godliness is riches,' as though it did not only make a man contented, but make a man contented with itself. He speaks as though he had found a new kind of riches, which the world never thought of; that are of such a nature, that they will satisfy a man like the water that Christ spake of, ' He that drinks of this water shall thirst no more,' John iv. 13. So they that taste of these riches shall covet no more; but as the Holy Ghost filled all the house, Acts ii. 2, so the grace, and peace, and joy of the Holy Ghost filleth all the heart; that as Joseph had no need of astronomy, because he had the spirit of prophecy, Gen. xliv. 15, so he which hath contentation hath little need of riches; he thinks not of the philosopher's stone, nor the gold of Ophir, 1 Kings ix. 28, nor the mines of India, but he hath his *quietus est*, without suit of law ; for he retaineth a peacemaker within, which would make all lawyers preachers, if men were so wise to take counsel of it.

When the law is ended, if the man be not content, he is in trouble still ; when his disease is cured, if he be not content, he is sick still ; when his want is supplied, if he be not content, he is in want still ; when bondage is turned into liberty, if he be not content, he is in bondage still ; but though he be in law, and sickness, and poverty, and bondage, yet, if he be content, he is free, and rich, and merry, and quiet, even as Adam was warm though he had no clothes, Gen. ii. 25.

Such a commander is contentation, that wheresoever she setteth foot, an hundred blessings wait upon her ; in every disease she is a physician, in every strife she is a lawyer, in every doubt she is a preacher, in every grief she is a comforter, like a sweet perfume, which taketh away the evil scent, and leaveth a pleasant scent for it. As the unicorn's horn dipped in the fountain makes the waters which were corrupt and noisome clear and wholesome upon the sudden, so, whatsoever estate godliness comes unto, it saith like the apostles, 'Peace be to this house,' Luke x. 5, peace be to this heart, peace be to this man.

I may liken it to the five loaves and two fishes, wherewith Christ fed five thousand persons, and yet there were twelve baskets full of that which was left, which could not fill one basket when it was whole. Thus their little feast was made a great feast ; so the godly, though they have but little for themselves, yet they have something for others, like the widow's mite, Matt. xii. 41 ; that they may say as the disciples said to Christ, they want nothing, though they have nothing, Luke xxii. 35. Contentation wanteth nothing, and a good heart is worth all. For if she want bread, she can say as Christ said, ' I have another bread,' John iv. 32 ; if she want riches, she can say, I have other riches ; if she want strength, she can say, I have other strength ; if she want friends, she can say, I have other friends. Thus the godly find all within that they seek without. Therefore, if you see a man contented with that he hath, it is a great sign that godliness is entered into him, for the heart of man was made a temple for God, and nothing can fill it but God alone. Therefore Paul saith after his conversion, that which he could never say before his conversion, 'I have learned to be content,' Philip. iv. 12. First he learned godliness, then godliness taught him contentation. Now (saith Paul), 'I have learned to be content;' as though this were a lesson for every Christian to learn, to be content. For thus he must think, that as God said to Moses, when he could not obtain leave to go to Canaan, 'Let this suffice thee to see Canaan,' Deut. iii. 26; so whatsoever he giveth, he gives this charge with it, 'Let this suffice thee.' As Jeremiah saith, 'This is my sorrow, and I will bear it,' Jer. x. 19; so thou must say, This is my portion, and I will take it. This is the sign whether godliness be in a man, if he have joy of that which he hath for things which God giveth to the righteous. Paul saith, that he 'giveth them to enjoy,' 1 Tim. vi. 17, that is, if he have much, he can say, with Paul, 'I have learned to abound;' if he have little, he can say with Paul, 'I have learned to want,' Philip. iv. 12; that is, if he have much, as Abraham, and Lot, and Jacob, and Job, and Joseph, yet it cannot corrupt his mind, but as the net was full of fishes, and yet not rent, because they cast it in at Christ's command, John xxi. 11, so, though the godly man be full of riches, yet his heart is not rent, his mind is not troubled, his countenance is not changed, because he remembers that these things were given him to do good, as Esther thought of her honour, Esther iv. 14; for if we have little, it is like the little oil which served the widow, as little as it was, 2 Kings iv. 7. 'A little to the righteous,' saith David, 'it is better than great riches to the ungodly,' Ps. xxxvii. 16; for when a man hath found the heavenly riches, he careth not for earthly riches, no more than he that walks in the sun thinks whether the moon shine or no, because he hath no need of her light. Therefore we conclude with Christ, 'Blessed are they which thirst after righteousness, for they shall be satisfied,' Mat. v. 6; not they that thirst after riches, nor they that thirst after honour, nor they that thirst after pleasure, shall be satisfied, but thirst more, as the ambitious, voluptuous, and covetous do; but 'they that thirst after righteousness shall be satisfied,' albeit they have no riches, nor honour, nor pleasure. If ye ask, like the virgin, 'How can this be?' I answer, Even as Adam was warm without clothes, Gen. ii. 25, so God doth satisfy many men without riches. Though he was naked, yet he did not see his nakedness, so long as he was innocent; but when he began to rebel, then began he to want clothes; so though a man be poor, yet he sees not his poverty, so long as he is contented; but when he begins to covet, then he begins to want riches, and from that day the curse (in the first of Haggai, ver. 6), takes hold on him ; ' Ye eat, but yet have not enough ; ye drink but ye are not satisfied ; ye clothe yourselves, but you are not warm.' Indeed, the covetous man seems to draw the world to him with cords ; his coffers are of loadstones, his hands like nets, his fingers like lime-twigs ; there it comes, and there it comes ; one would think this man should be happy one day.

When the churl's barns were full, he bade his soul take rest, thinking to gain rest by covetousness, that he might say, Riches gain rest, as well as godliness ; but see what happened : that night when he began to take his rest, riches, and rest, and soul, and all, were taken from him, Luke xii. 16. Did he not gain fair ? Would he have taken such pains if he had thought of such rest ? Covetousness may gain riches, but it cannot gain rest ; ye may think like this churl, to rest when your barns, and shops, and coffers are full ; but ye shall find it true which Isaiah saith, ' There is no rest to the ungodly,' Isa. xlviii. 22 ; therefore the wise man, to prevent all hope of rest, or honour, or profit by sin, speaks as though he had tried, ' A man cannot be established by iniquity,' Prov. xii. 3. Therefore he cannot be quieted, nor satisfied by the gain of deceit, or bribes, or lies, or usury, which is iniquity. Therefore blessed is the man whom godliness doth make rich ; ' for when the blessing of the Lord maketh rich,' saith Solomon, ' he doth add no sorrow to it ;' but, saith he, ' the revenue of the wicked is trouble,' as though his money were care. Wherefore let patron, and landlord, and lawyer, and all, say now, that Paul hath chosen the better riches, ' which thief, nor moth, nor canker can corrupt ;' these are the riches at last, that we must dwell with, when all the rest which we have lied for, and sworn for, and fretted for, and cozened for, and broken our sleep for, and lost many sermons for, forsake us, like servants which change their masters ; then godliness shall seem as great gain to us as it did to Paul ; and he which loved the world most, would give all that he hath for a dram of faith, that he might be sure to go to heaven, when he is dead, though he went towards hell so long as he lived.

Here then is an answer to them which ask, ' What profit is it to serve God ?' Mal. iii. 14. How happy was Barzillai, that would not be exalted ? 2 Sam. xix. 33. What quiet had the Shunammite, which cared not for preferment ? 2 Kings. iv. 13. When did the disciples seem so rich, as when they were willing to leave all ? Luke v. 11. This shall be your gain, when you are usurers of godliness. Is not the word gone forth yet, which hath killed covetousness, that I may end my sermon ? Either you go away contented, or you go away condemned of your own conscience ; before, you were vexed with covetousness, but now the word shall vex you too ; for you shall never covet, nor lie, nor deceive hereafter, but a serjeant shall arrest you upon it, and some sentence which you have heard, shall gnaw you at the heart with a memorandum of hell, that ye shall wish, Oh that I could adandon this sin, or else that I had never heard that warning which makes it a corrosive unto me before I can leave it. If they which are greedy still, could see what peace and rest, and joy go home with them that are contented, though they may say with Peter, ‘Gold and silver have I none,’ Acts iii. 16, every man would be a suitor to godliness, that he might have the dowry of contentation.

If any here be covetous still, let him always think why David prayeth, ‘Turn my heart to thy law, and not to covetousness,’ Ps. cxix. ; he might have named pride, or anger, or lust, but that no sin did so keep his thoughts from the law, as covetousness when it came upon him ; he saith, ‘Turn my heart unto thy law, and not to covetousness,’ as though a man could not be covetous, and have any leisure to think upon any good. But as John baptized with water, Luke iii., so I can but teach you with words.

Now you have heard what contentation is, you must pray to another to give it unto you. It is said of this city, that many citizens of London have good wills, but bad deeds ; that is, you do no good until you die. First, ye are ungodly, that you may be rich ; and then you part from some of your riches, to excuse for some of your ungodliness. It may be that some here have set down in their wills, When I die, I bequeath an hundred pounds to a college, and a hundred pounds to an hospital, and an hundred gowns unto poor men. I do marvel that you give no more when you are at that point ; for Judas, when he died, returned all again, Mat. xxvii. 1 ; so ye die, and think when ye are gone, that God will take this for a quittance. Be not deceived, for God doth not look upon that which ye do for fear, but upon that which ye do for love, 2 Cor. ix. 7 ; if ye can find in your heart to do good while you are in health, as Zaccheus did, Luke xix. 8, then God hath respect to your offering ; but before God hearkens how ye give your riches, first, he examines how ye came by them ; for a man may be hanged for stealing the money which he gives to the poor, because, if he should count godliness gain, much more should he care to gain by godly means.

Thus you see the fruits of godliness, and the fruits of covetousness, to stay Balaam’s posting for a bribe, Num. xxii. 17, and the sons of Zebedee suing for preferment, lest, seeking for asses, they lose a better kingdom than Saul found, 1 Sam. x. 1. If you be covetous, ye shall never have enough, although you have too much ; but when ye pray, 'Thy kingdom come,' Luke xi. 2 ye shall wish, My kingdom come. If ye be godly, ye shall have enough, though ye seem to have nothing, like to the Smyrnians, of whom God saith, 'I know thy poverty, but thou art rich,' Rev. ii. 9. Therefore what counsel shall I give you, but as Christ counselled his disciples, Be not friends to riches, but 'make you friends of riches ;' and know this, that if ye cannot say as Paul saith, 'I have learned to be content,' Philip. iv. 12, godliness is not yet come to your house ; for the companion of godliness is contentation ; which, when she comes, will bring you all things. Therefore as Christ saith, 'If the Son make you free, you shall be free indeed,' John vii. 36 ; so I say, if godliness make ye rich, ye shall be rich indeed. The Lord Jesus make ye doers of that ye have heard. Amen.

THE AFFINITY OF THE FAITHFUL.

THE AFFINITY OF THE FAITHFUL.

Then came to him his mother and brethren, and could not come near him for the press. And it was told him by certain which said, Thy mother and brethren stand without and would see thee. But he answered and said unto them, My mother and brethren are those which hear the word of God, and do it.— LUKE VIII. 19-21.

HERE is Christ preaching, a great press hearing, his mother and his friends interrupting, and Christ again withstanding the interruption, with a comfortable doctrine of his mercies towards them which hear the word of God and do it. When Christ was about a work, and many were gathered together to hear him, the devil thought with himself, as the priests and Sadducees did in the fourth of the Acts : If I let him alone thus, all the world will follow him, and I shall be like Rachel, without children; therefore, devising the likeliest policy to frustrate and disgrace but one of his sermons, thereby to make the people unwilling to hear him again, as he set Eve upon Adam, Gen. iii. 6, and made Job's wife his instrument, Job ii. 9, when he could not fit it himself; so he sendeth Christ's mother, and putteth in the minds of his kinsmen, to come unto him at that instant, when he was in this holy exercise, and call upon him while he was preaching, to come away, and go with them. Christ seeing the serpent's dealing, how he made his mother the tempter, that all the auditory might go away empty, and say where they came, We heard the man which is called Jesus, and he began to preach unto us, with such words, as though he would carry us to heaven; but in the midst of his sermon came his mother and brethren to him, that it might be known what a kinsman they had;

and so soon as he heard that they were come, suddenly he brake off his sermon, and slipped away from us, to go and make merry with them.   Christ, I say, seeing this train laid by Satan, to disgrace him (as he doth all his ministers), did not leave off speaking, as they thought he would ; but as if God had appointed all this to credit and renown him, that which was noised here to interrupt his doctrine, he taketh for an occasion to teach another doctrine, that there is a nearer conjunction between Christ and the faithful, than between the mother and the son, which are one flesh.   Therefore when they say, 'Thy mother and brethren are come to speak with thee,' he pointeth to his hearers and saith, 'These are my mother and brethren, which hear the word of God, and do it;' as if he should say, I have a mother indeed which brought me forth, but in respect of them which hear the word of God, and do it, she is like a stepmother, and these are like a natural mother.

With this wise answer he quieted the auditors, and made them hear him better than they did before.   For now they thought with themselves, What man is this, which loveth us more than his mother ?   His mother called him, and yet he would not go from us ; his brethren stay for him, and he maketh as if he did not know them, but saith, 'Who is my mother ?   Who are my brethren ?'

Thus Christ stood up, as it were, in an indignation against Satan, and said, Satan, this sermon was not begun for thee, neither shall it end for thee ; this work was not done for my mother, neither shall it be left for my mother.   Thus he caught the devil with his own bait, and made his people more loving and attentive towards him, by that which Satan thought to disgrace him.   He was so armed with the Spirit, that, let the devil tempt him, or the woman tempt him, or princes tempt him, all is as one.

Here are two doubts : the first is the difference between the evangelists ; for Matthew saith, that one brought this message, Mark and Luke attribute it to more, Mat. xii. 47 ; Mark iii. 31 ; Luke viii. 20.   Both may stand, for the word which his mother gave of calling him forth, was received of the rest, and so passed amongst many, till it came to Christ, so that one may be said to bring this message, because one noised it first, and many may be said to bring this message, because many noised it after.

The second doubt is, because Christ had no brethren, how they said, 'Thy brethren would speak with thee.'   You must understand that they which are here called Christ's brethren, were his cousins by the mother's side ; that is, her sister's children, for there were three Marys, and these three were sisters, Mary the virgin, Mary the mother of James, and Mary the daughter of Cleophas, whose sons these were; their names were James, Joseph, Judas, and Simon; and they are called the Lord's brethren, because they were kin unto him. Therefore note, that in holy Scripture there be four sorts of brethren: brethren by nature, so Esau and Jacob are called brethren, Gen. xxvii. 30, because they had one father and one mother; brethren by nation, so all the Jews are called brethren, Deut. xv. 1, because they were of one country; brethren by consanguinity, so all are called brethren which are of one family, and so Abraham called Lot his brother, Gen. xiii. 8, and Sarah his sister, Gen. xii. 13, because they were of one line; brethren by profession, so all Christians are called brethren, Mat. xxiii., because they are of one religion. These are brethren of the third order, that is, of consanguinity, because they were of one family.

Now, when his mother and his brethren were come to see him, it is said, that they could not come near him for the press. Here were auditors enough. Christ so flowed now with his disciples, that his mother could have no room to hear him; but after a while it was low water again. When the shepherd was strucken, the sheep were scattered, Mat. xxvi. 31; when he preached in the streets, and the temples, and the fields, then many flocked after him; but when he preached upon the cross, then they left him which said they would never forsake him; then there was a great press to see him die, as there was here to hear him preach. And many of these which seemed like brethren and sisters, were his betrayers, and accusers, and persecutors, Mat. xxvii.; so inconstant are we in our zeal, more than in anything else. Thus much of their coming and calling to Christ. Now, to the doctrine which lieth in it.

Here be two speakers: one saith, 'Thy mother and thy brethren are come to speak unto thee;' the other saith, 'Those are my mother and brethren which hear the word of God and do it.' The scope of the evangelist is this: first, that Christ would not hinder his doctrine for mother, or brethren, or any kinsman; then, to shew that there is a nearer conjunction between Christ and the faithful, than the mother and the son. The first is written for our comfort; touching the first, he which teacheth us to honour our father and mother, Exod. xx., doth not teach here to contemn father and mother, because he speaks of another mother, for it is said, that 'he was obedient to his parents.' This he sheweth, when, being found in the temple amongst the doctors, he left all, to go with his mother, because she sought him; so he honoured her, that he left all for her, Luke ii. 46. This he shewed again at his death;

being upon the cross, he was not unmindful of her, for pointing unto John, he said, ' Mother, behold thy son ;' and pointing unto her, he said, ' Behold thy mother,' John xix. 26 ; so he commended her to his beloved disciple before he died. Therefore, this is not a doctrine of disobedience, but a rule how to obey.   As he taught his disciples to give unto Cæsar that which is Cæsar's, and to God that which is God's, Mark xxii. 21, Luke xx. 25 ; so he teacheth us here, to give unto parents that which is parents', and to the Lord that which is the Lord's.   When God said, ' Honour thy father and thy mother,' Exod. xx., he did not give a commandment against himself ; and therefore he saith, *Honour me*, before he saith, *Honour them*.   The first commandment is, *Honour God ;* the fifth commandment is, *Honour thy parents*, lest you should honour your parents before God.   When Solomon bid his mother ask him anything, 1 Kings ii. 20, he signified that the mother should be obeyed in many things ; but when he denied his mother that one thing which she asked, he sheweth, that the mother should not be obeyed in all things.   When Christ said, ' You have but one Father and master,' Mat. xxiii. 9, he speaks of faith and religion, shewing that when it concerneth our faith and religion, we should respect but one father, and one master, which is the giver of our faith, and the master of our religion.

When Paul said, ' Children, obey your parents in the Lord,' Eph. vi. 1, he means not that we should obey them against the Lord. As when he saith, ' Obey princes for conscience' sake,' Rom. xiii. 5, he meaneth not that we should obey them against conscience. Therefore, when it cometh to this, that the earthly father commandeth one thing, and the heavenly Father commandeth another thing ; then, as Peter answered the rulers, so mayest thou answer thy parents, ' Whether is it meet to obey God or you ?' Acts iv. 19. Then these are the hands which thou must cut off, then these are the eyes which thou must pull out, or else they should be as much unto thee as thy hand or thine eye.

In Mat. xix., a man must forsake his father and his mother to dwell with his wife.   In Luke xvi., he must forsake father, and mother, and wife, to dwell with Christ ; for, ' he which forsaketh father or mother for me, shall receive more,' saith our Saviour, Luke xiv. 26.   Nay, ' he which doth not hate father, or mother, or wife for me, cannot be my disciple.'   Shewing that our love towards God should be so great, that in respect of it, our love towards men should be but hatred.   Thus he which obeyed his parents more than we, yet would have some rule, some sentence, some example in Scripture, of not obeying them too, because it is such a hard point, to know how far they are to be obeyed, which are set in authority over us.

As none but God speaks always right, so none but God must always be obeyed. We are not called only the 'sons of men,' but we are called 'the sons of God,' Gen. vi. 2. Therefore, as Christ answered his mother, when she would have him turn water into wine, 'Woman, what have I to do with thee?' John ii., so we should answer father and mother, and brethren and sisters, and rulers and masters, and wife too, when they will us to do that which is not meet, 'What have I to do with you?' For to leave doing good, and do evil, were not to turn water into wine, but to turn wine into water. Peter was not Satan, but when he tempted Christ like Satan, Christ answered him as he answered Satan, 'Come behind me, Satan,' Mat. xvi. 23; shewing that we should give no more attention unto father or mother, or master, or wife, when they tempt us to evil, than we would give unto Satan, if he should tempt us himself.

Three things children receive of their parents, life, maintenance, and instruction. For these three they owe other three; for life, they owe love; for maintenance, they owe obedience; for instruction, they owe reverence. For life, they must be loved as fathers; for maintenance, they must be obeyed as masters; for instruction, they must be reverenced as tutors. But as there is a King of kings, which must be obeyed above kings, so there is a Father of fathers, which must be obeyed above fathers; therefore sometimes you must answer like the son, when he was bid to go into his father's vineyard, 'I will go;' and sometimes you must answer as Christ answered, 'I must go about my Father's business.'

When two milch kine did carry the ark of the Lord to Bethshemesh, their calves were shut up at home, 1 Sam. vi. 10, because the kine should not stay, when they heard their calves cry after them; so when thou goest about the Lord's business, thou shalt hear a cry of thy father, and thy mother, and thy brethren, and thy sisters, and thy kindred, to stay thee, but then thou must think of another Father, as Christ thought of another mother; and so, as those kine went on till the Lord brought them where the ark should rest, so thou shalt go on till the Lord bring thee where thou shalt have rest. It is better to fly from our friends, as Abraham did, Gen. xi. 3, and xii. 11, than to stay with some friends, as Samson did with Delilah, Judges xvi. 14, &c.

I may say, Beware of kinsmen, as well as our Saviour said, 'Beware of men, for this respect of cousinage made Eli his sons priests, 1 Sam. ii.; and this respect of cousinage hath made many like priests in England. This respect of cousinage hath made Samuel's sons Judges, 1 Sam. viii. 1; and this respect of cousinage hath made many like judges in England. This respect of cousinage brought Tobias into the Levites' chamber, Neh. xiii. 4, 5; and this respect of cousinage hath brought many gentlemen into preachers' livings, which will not out again. As Christ preferred his spiritual kinsmen, so we prefer our earthly kinsmen. Many privileges, many offices, and many benefices, have stooped to this voice, Thy mother calleth thee, or, Thy kinsmen would have thee. As this voice came to Christ while he was labouring, so many such voices come to us while we are labouring. One saith, Pleasure would speak with you; another saith, Profit would speak with you; another saith, Ease would speak with you; another saith, A deanery would speak with you; another saith, A bishopric would speak with you; another saith, The court would speak with you.

When a man is in a good way, and studies the Scriptures to be a teacher of the church, a voice cometh to his ear, as this came to Christ's, and saith, Thy friends would have thee study the law, for by divinity thou shalt attain to no preferment, and thine own flock will vex thee, or the bishop will stop thy mouth. The mind sometime turneth Jonah his sails from Nineveh to Tarshish, and makes him bury his talents.

If he be a divine already, and preach his conscience, a voice cometh unto him again, as this did to Christ, and saith, Thy friends would have thee to be quiet; or, There be spies which do note what thou sayest; or, There be fellows that lie in wait for thy living; so sometimes, with a little entreaty, he beginneth to draw up his hand, and lay his finger upon his mouth, and preach peace, when he is sent with war. Thus we are cumbered like our Master, before our sermons, and in our sermons, and after our sermons; even of them sometime, which should encourage us; and therefore, as Christ saith, ' Beware of men,' Mat. x. 17, so say I, Beware of kinsmen.

So soon as the children be born, their parents bring them to the temple, and baptize them, and offer them to God; but so soon as they be able to serve him, they tempt them away from him to law, or physic, or merchandise, or husbandry, and had rather they should be of any tribe, than of the tribe of Levi, which serveth in the temple, Num. iii. 6–8. He which will be hindered shall have blocks enough; but we must learn to leap over all, as Christ leaped over this. If we should 'leave father, and mother, and wife, and children, for Christ,' much less should we care for labour, or loss, or shame, or trouble, or displeasure, for we should adventure these for our friends. Thus much of his natural kindred; now of his spiritual kindred.

Here is a genealogy of Christ, which Matthew and Luke never spake of. As Christ saith, 'I have another bread which you know not;' so he saith, I have other kinsmen which you know not.

St John, writing to a lady which brought up her children in the fear of God, calleth her 'the elect lady,' 2 John 1, shewing that the chiefest honour of ladies, and lords, and princes, is to be elect of God. St Luke, speaking of certain Bereans, which received the word of God with love, calls them 'more noble men than the rest,' Acts xvii. 11, shewing, that God counteth none noble but such as are of a noble spirit. As John calleth none elect but the virtuous; and Luke calleth none noble but the religious; so Christ calleth none his kinsmen but the righteous; and of those only he saith, 'These are my mother and my brethren, which hear the word of God and do it.'

As Abraham's children are not counted after the flesh, but after the spirit, Rom. ix. 8, so Christ's kindred are not counted after the flesh but after the spirit; for the flesh was not made after the image of God but the spirit, Gen. i.; therefore God is not called the Father of bodies, but the Father of spirits, Heb. xii. 9. Now God, which is a Spirit, preferreth them that are kin to him in the spirit. Therefore Esau was not blessed because he was of Isaac's flesh; but Jacob was blessed, because he was of Isaac's spirit, Gal. iv. 28, 29. As we love in the flesh, so Christ loveth in the spirit; therefore he calleth none his kinsmen, but them 'which hear the word of God, and do it.'

It seemeth that Paul thought of this saying whenas he said, 'Till Christ be formed in you,' Gal. iv. If Christ be formed in us, as Paul saith, then we are Christ's mother; every one which will have Christ his Saviour, must be Christ's mother. The virgin asked the angel, 'How she could bear Christ, seeing she had not known a man,' Luke i. 34. So you may ask how you can bear Christ, seeing he is born already.

As there is a second coming of Christ, so there is a second birth of Christ. When we are born again, then Christ is born again; the virgin was his mother by the flesh, and the faithful are his mother by his Spirit; the Holy Ghost conceived him in her, the Holy Ghost doth conceive him in them; he was in her womb, and he is in their hearts; she did bear him, and they do bear him; she did nurse him, and they do nurse him. This is the second birth of Christ. As the soul of man may be called 'The temple of the Holy Ghost,' which is the third person, 2 Cor. vi. 16; so it may be called, the womb of the Son, which is the second person.

Before these words, it is said that Christ asked, 'Who are my brethren?' as if he should say, You think that I am affected to my kinsmen, as you are. But I tell you that I count them my kinsmen 'which hear the word of God and do it.' To shew that Christ loveth us with an everlasting love, he sheweth that he doth not love us for any temporal things, but for that which endureth for ever.

If Christ loved us as Isaac loved Esau, for venison, Gen. xxv. 28, then we might miss the blessing as Esau did. But as John saith, He 'loveth in the truth,' so Christ loveth in the truth. To love in the truth is the true love. Every love but this, at one time or other, hath turned into hatred; but the true love overcometh hatred, as the truth overcometh falsehood.

Now for this love. Christ calls them by all the names of love; his father, and his brethren, and his sisters. In Rom. vi. they are called his servants; if that be not enough, in John xv. they are called his friends; if that be not enough, in Luke xxiv. they are called his brethren; if that be not enough, in Mark i. they are called his children; if that be not enough, here they are called his mother; if that be not enough, in Canticles the 5th they are called his spouse, to shew that he loveth them with all love; the mother's love, the brother's love, the sister's love, the master's love, and the friend's love.

If all these loves could be put together, yet Christ's love exceedeth them all; and the mother, and the brother, and the sister, and the child, and the kinsman, and the friend, and the servant, would not do and suffer so much among them all, as Christ hath done and suffered for us alone. Such a love we kindle in Christ, when we hear his word, and do it, that we are as dear unto him as all his kindred together.

Now as we are his mother, so should we carry him in our hearts, as his mother did in her arms. As we are his brethren, so we should prefer him, as Joseph did Benjamin, Gen. xliii. 34. As we are his spouse, so we should embrace him, as Isaac did Rebekah; if thou be a kinsman, do like a kinsman.

Now we come to the marks of these kinsmen, which I may call the arms of his house. As Christ saith, 'By this all men shall know my disciples, if they love one another;' so he saith, By this shall all men know my kinsmen, if they 'hear the word of God, and do it.'

As there is a kindred by the father's side, and as a kindred by the mother's side, so there is a kindred of hearers, and a kindred of doers. In Matthew it is said, 'He which heareth the will of my Father, and doth it;' here it is said, 'He which heareth the word of God, and doth it;' both are one, for his word is his will, and therefore it is called his will, Ps. cxix.

As he spake there of doing, so he speaks here of a certain rule, which he calls, the word of God, whereby all men's works must be squared; for if I do all the works that I can to satisfy another's will or mine own will, it availeth me nothing with God; because I do it not for God. Therefore he which always before followed his own will, when he was stricken down, and began to repent himself, he presently cried out, 'Lord, what wilt thou have me do?' Acts ix.; as if he should say, I will do no more as men would have me, or as the devil would have me, or according as the flesh would have me, but as thou wouldst have me. So David prayed, 'Teach me, O Lord, to do thy will,' not my will; for we need not to be taught to do our own will, no more than a cuckoo to sing *cuckoo*, her own name. Every man can go to hell without a guide.

Here is the rule now; if you live by it, then you are kin to Christ. As other kindreds go by birth and marriage, so this kindred goeth by faith and obedience. Hearers are but half kin, as it were in a far degree; but they which hear and do, are called his mother, which is the nearest kindred of all. Therefore if you have the deed, then are you kin indeed; there is no promise made to hearers, nor to speakers, nor to readers; but all promises are made to believers or to doers.

If you ask God who shall dwell in the holy mountain; he saith, 'The man which walketh uprightly,' Ps. xv. 2; here are none but doers. If you ask Christ who shall enter into the kingdom of heaven, he saith, 'Not they which cry, Lord, Lord,' Mat. vii. 22, (though they cry twice Lord), 'but they that do the will of my Father;' here are none but doers. If you ask him again, how you may come to heaven, he saith, 'Keep the commandments;' here are none but doers. If you ask him again, who are blessed, he saith, 'Blessed are they that hear the word of God, and do it,' Luke xviii.; here are none but doers. If you ask an angel who are blessed, he saith, 'Blessed are they which keep the word of this book,' Rev. xxii. 7; here are none but doers. If you ask David who are blessed, he saith, 'The man is blessed which keepeth righteousness,' Ps. cvi. 3; here are none but doers.   If you ask Solomon who are blessed, he saith, ' The man is blessed which keepeth the law;' here are none but doers.   If you ask Isaiah, who are blessed, he saith, ' He which doth this is blessed,' Isa. lvi. 2; here are none but doers.   If you ask James who are blessed, he saith, ' The doer of the word is blessed in his deed,' James i. 25 ; here are none but doers.   The blessing and doing run together, Mat. vii. 21 ; Rom. ii. 13.

Lest any man should look to be blessed without obedience, Christ calleth love the greatest commandment ; but Solomon calleth obedience the end of all, as though without obedience all were to no end.

When Micah had got a Levite into his house, ' Now,' saith he, ' I know the Lord will be good unto me, seeing I have a Levite in my house,' Judges xvii. 13 ; so many think, when they have gotten a preacher into their parish, Now the Lord will be good unto us, now Christ will love us, now we are good sons, seeing we maintain a preacher amongst us.   But Micah was not blessed for a Levite, nor you for a preacher ; but as you would have us to do as we teach, so God would have you to do as you hear, for you shall be no more saved for hearing, than we are for speaking.

When God created the tree, he commanded it to bring forth fruit, Gen. i. ; so when he createth faith, he commandeth it to bring forth works, and therefore it is called a ' lively faith.'   When our Saviour would prove himself to John, to be the true Messiah indeed, he said to his disciples, ' Tell John what things you have heard and seen,' Mat. xi. 4, Luke vii. 22, not only heard, but seen ; so if we will prove ourselves to be Christ's kinsmen indeed, we must work that which may be seen, as well as heard.   John was not only called, ' The voice of a crier,' Mat. iii. 3, but ' a burning lamp,' which might be seen ; so all which are crying voices, must be burning lamps.

James doth not say, Let me hear thy faith, but ' let me see thy faith,' James ii. 18.   As the angels put on the shape of men, that Abraham might see them, Gen. xviii. 2 ; so faith must put on works, that the world may see it.   ' The works which I do,' saith Christ, ' bear witness of me;' so the works which we do, should bear witness of us.   Therefore Christ linketh faith and repentance together, ' Repent and believe the gospel,' Mark i. 15.   Therefore I conclude, ' That which Christ hath joined, let no man separate,' Mark x. 9.

Thus have I shewed you Christ preaching, a great press hear-

ing, his friends and kinsmen interrupting, and Christ again withstanding the interruption; by this you may see what a spite the
devil hath to hinder one sermon; therefore no marvel though he
cause so many to be put to silence; no marvel though he stand so
against a learned ministry; no marvel though he raise up such
slanders upon preachers; no marvel though he write so many books
against the Christian government in the church; no marvel though
he make so many non-residents; no marvel though he ordain so
many dumb priests; for these make him the god of this world; the
devil is afraid that one sermon will convert us, and we are not
moved with twenty; so the devil thinketh better of us than we are.

Again, by this you may learn how to withstand temptations;
whether it be thy father which tempteth, or thy mother which
tempteth, or thy brother which tempteth, or thy sister which
tempteth, or thy kinsman which tempteth, or ruler which tempteth,
or master which tempteth, or wife which tempteth. As Christ would
not know his mother against his Father, so thou shouldst not know
any father, or mother, or brother, or sister, or friend, or kinsman,
or master, or child, or wife, against God.

If the mother's suit may be refused sometime, a nobleman's letter
may be refused too; he that can turn his hindrance to a furtherance,
as our Saviour did here, maketh use of everything. Again, by this
you may learn how to choose your friends. As Christ counted none
his kinsmen, but such as 'hear the word of God, and do it;' so we
should make none our familiars, but such as Christ counteth his
kinsmen. Again, you may see the difference between Christ and
the world; Christ calleth the godly his kinsmen, be they never so
poor, and we scorn to call the poor our kinsmen, be they never so
honest; so proud is the servant above his Master. Again, by this
you see how Christ is to be loved; for when he calleth us his
mother, he shews us the way to love him as a mother; for indeed
he is the mother of his mother, and his brethren too. Again, by
this, all vaunting and boasting of kindred is cut off. Glory not in
that thou hast a gentleman to thy father, glory not that thou hast
a knight to thy brother, but glory that thou hast a Lord to thy
brother. He which calleth Abraham his father, fried in hell, because God was not his Father. If Mary might not be proud of such
a Son as Christ, much less may you brag of any friend, or son that
you have.

Again, by this you may know whether you be kin to Christ; as
those priests were shut out of the temple which could not count
their genealogy from Aaron, so they shall be shut out of heaven

that cannot reckon their pedigree from Christ. Here are the arms now whereby you may shew of what house you came. If you hear the word of God and do it, then Christ saith unto you as he said unto them, 'These are my mother, and my brethren, and my sisters.' You women are his sisters, and you men are his brethren. If you be Christ's brethren, then are you God's sons; and if you be God's sons, then are you his heirs; for all God's sons are called heirs, Rom. viii. 17.

Lastly, by this you may know the devil's kinsmen, and therefore Christ saith, ' You are of your father the devil,' John viii. 44; shewing that the devil and the wicked are as near kin as Christ and the faithful.

Now, as David saith, ' Seemeth it a light thing unto you to be the son of a king, seeing I am a poor man, and of small reputation?' 1 Sam. xviii. 23; so may I say, Seemeth it a light thing to you, to be the sons of the King of kings, seeing you are poor men, and of small reputation? It is counted a great honour to Abraham, Isaac, and Jacob, that God was not ashamed to be called their God, Heb. xi. 16. What an honour then is this, that God is not ashamed to be called our Father, nay, our brother?

If the Israelites had such care to match with the servants of God, what a blessing is this to marry with the Son of God? Therefore, if any affect rich kinsmen, or great marriages, here is a greater than Solomon, marry thou him. This kinsman of ours is now gone up into heaven, that we may have a friend in court.

Joseph desired the butler to remember him when he stood before Pharaoh, and he forgot him, though he had pleasured him, Gen. xl. 23. But a thief desired Christ to remember him when he came into his kingdom, and he received him into paradise the same day, though he had always offended, Luke xxiii. 42; to shew, that though we have been as bad as thieves, yet we may have hope in Christ. Therefore, now we may conclude. You have heard the word; if you go away and do it, then you are the mother, brethren, and sisters of the heavenly King, to whom, with the Father and the Holy Spirit, be all praise, majesty, and dominion, now and evermore. Amen.

THE LOST SHEEP IS FOUND.

THE DECLARATION OF HENRY SMITH, TO THE LORD JUDGES HOW HE FOUND, AND HOW HE LEFT, ROBERT DICKONS.

When I came first to Mansfield with your honours' precept, I found this Robert Dickons in these and like opinions, which he presumed he would hold unto death.

He said that he had seen three visions by an angel, which shewed him strange things, promised him rare gifts, and power to come.

He said that the angel called him Elias, whereupon he affirmed that the prophecy of Malachi remains to be fulfilled in him.

He said that the angel told him, that he should be a leper two years, and a bondman eight years.

He avouched, that his father should be cast over into ignorance, and that all he had should perish.

He avouched, that there should be neither battle nor dearth in his country for eight years, which is the time of his service.

He pretended that after two years, his time should come to preach, and that no man should be able to confound him.

But before I left him, as the word of God doth always exercise his natural power, he pronounced before us all, Now I am converted by Scripture; whereupon he requested me to set down his recantation, which he uttered in these words:

The Confession of Robert Dickons upon the first day's Examination.

I did believe my visions to be true before I heard the Scriptures prove the contrary, and now I esteem them but a delusion of Satan. Therefore I desire to be set to learning for my own salvation, and for the edifying of my brethren. Witness, Will. Dabridgecourt, Esq., Henry Smith, Edward Immims, Will. Whaly, Hugh Peace his master, and a number more.   ROBERT DICKONS.

This, I trust, he spake unfeignedly; and for so much as his desire to learn is commendable, and his gifts not common to men of his degree, as your wisdom shall better see if you talk with him alone; I leave this motion to your honour's good consideration, which can best judge how to quench, or how to kindle such sparks.

The lost sheep is found. HENRY SMITH.

The Examination.

Robert Dickons's confession upon my second examination, wherein he declareth, that he had no visions at all, but that he coined them, and to what end.

The matter of the first vision.

I did see, upon Valentine's day was eight years, green leaves, which was strange, in winter, for which cause I brought them home, and the leaves of the same oak in summer became red; it chanced at the same time to thunder and lighten; after that I was visited, as pleased God, for two years.

The matter of the second vision.

Four years after I dreamed much like to the matter of the first vision, and the same night it chanced to lighten (yet of this I take God to be my judge). I found a leaf printed in my chamber next morning, with those six sentences, saving only the first line; which leaf, unless it was lost out of my fellow's books, I know not how it came.

The matter of the third vision.

This time twelvemonth, I saw light in the shop alone, whereat I was astonished, and imagining with myself what it should mean, it came into my head to tell my fellows, which came in and found me afraid, that I had seen an angel in a flame of fire, which called me Elias, and bade me write all that I had seen and heard; hereupon I, remembering my former sights and dreams, thought to make me strange unto men, and so turned all that which I had seen, as if God had shewed me visions. Here is all the matter and sum of my supposed visions. To this confession I take God for my judge, as I shall be saved in the latter day; but to the other I never swore, though I was never so often examined.

ROBERT DICKONS.

Upon this he yielded up his books into my hands, which I have and keep; and now he hath nothing to shew for that false title.

HENRY SMITH.

THE LOST SHEEP IS FOUND.

Prove the spirits whether they are of God or no.—1 JOHN IV. 1.

NEITHER too bold, nor too credulous, as John sent to Christ, 'Art thou he that cometh, or look we for another?' Luke vii. So send I unto him which calleth himself *Elias*, Art thou he which was prophesied, or is he come already? But will Elias answer as well for himself, as Christ proved his authority to St John? 'Go your way, and bring word again to John what things ye have seen and heard, how that the blind see again, the lame go, the lepers are cleansed, the deaf hear, the dead rise, the poor receive the gospel.' These tokens the Lord used for an answer, because he would not that men should endanger their salvation, to believe every man that calleth himself Christ, or Elias, or a prophet, unless he bring the testimony of the Holy Ghost in fulness of power, Mat. xxiv.; therefore he requireth himself, 'If I do not the works that no man doth, believe me not,' John x.; therefore he saith again, 'the works that I do bear witness of me, that the Father hath sent me,' John v.; therefore it is written, 'All that heard him were astonished at his understanding and answers,' Luke ii.; therefore the servants came back, and could not bring him, but told the pharisees how their hearts were stricken, 'No man ever spake as this man speaks,' John vii.; therefore it is written of Stephen, 'they could not resist his wisdom and the spirit by which he spake,' Acts vi.; therefore the disciples would not receive Paul before Barnabas gave witness of him, Acts ix.; therefore all the prophets prophesied of Christ's coming, that when he came we should know him, and receive our salvation, Acts iii. 24; therefore Christ hath foretold us all the tokens of his second coming, and all the signs which shall go before his day of judgment, Mark xiii. 33 ; and as he had left nothing out, he saith in a full conclusion, 'Take heed, let no man deceive you, I have shewed you all things before.' But what hath Elias done? Or what hath Elias spoken? Or who cannot dispute with Elias? Or who giveth witness of Elias? Or who hath prophesied of Elias? Or who hath received Elias? Or who hath said, 'Of a truth this is a prophet'? John vii. 40. Oh how necessary had it been, that Christ, amongst all other tokens of his coming, should especially have noted us that Elias, that great prophet, that crier, that trumpet, that destroyer, that Noah, that Lot, that soldier of the Lord, that son of righteousness, that man which no man shall accuse of sin, if there had been any such to come! sure we would have respected more that sign, than all the rest. But so it is that Christ hath forewarned us of many false prophets, Mark xiii. 6, but of any one singular prophet of God, he hath not in all his tokens once remembered. Alas! Elias, where wast thou that the Lord did so forget thee? Hath the Lord revealed all tokens unto us, and yet wilt thou be a token above number? He that cometh in without his wedding-garment shall be thrust out, and shame shall come upon him which is without shame, Mat. xxii.

Is it enough for our belief, to say, that an angel called thee Elias? Satan is transformed into an angel of light ; 'search the Scripture, saith Christ, 'those be they which testify of me,' John v. 39. Will it excuse Adam to say, The woman deceived me? Be not deceived, saith Christ, 'If an angel from heaven teach you any other doctrine than this, believe him not,' Gal. i. 8 ; 'He whom God hath sent, speaketh the words of God,' John iii. 'If ye continue in my word, then are you my very disciples,' John viii. ; he which hath the gift of prophecy, let him have it according to the faith. You say, we are true in religion; if thou wert Elias, thou wouldst let us so continue. Why are we in the true religion? Because we truly believe the Scriptures; but the Scriptures so plainly, so often, so vehemently point unto us, that Elias is come already, that now we cannot believe him that calleth himself Elias, unless we falsify the word of God. You, therefore, which say we stand in the true faith, and yet would inveigle us from the faith which we do hold, to believe contrary to his infallible word, have a secret meaning to call us to one heresy after another, which he may easily do, whosoever can prove the Son of man a liar, and go under the name of Elias. It is hard for thee to kick against the prick, Acts ix. 5. Read, see, and behold, how the Spirit consents against thee ; 'I say unto you that Elias is come already, and they knew him not, but have done to him whatsoever they listed,' Mat. xvii.

'All the prophets and the law itself prophesied unto John; and if ye will believe it, this is Elias which was for to come; he that hath ear to hear, let him hear,' Mat. xi. 'Elias, verily when he cometh, first restoreth all things; but I say unto you, Elias is come, and they have done unto him what they would, as it is written of him.' John shall 'go before him in the spirit and power of Elias, to turn the hearts of the fathers to their children.' What say you to all these which bear witness against you? Do all the evangelists speak in parables? Was not Elias come, because they knew him not? If the scribes and pharisees had taken John for Elias, then would you have said the cause is plain, for all men believe that Elias is come. But now the scribes knew him not; though Christ say, he is come, yet you will not know him. What is this but to confess the scribes, and deny Christ? You, therefore, which speak not the words of God, are not sent of God; you which continue not in his saying, are not his disciple; you which prophesy not according to the faith, have not the right gift of prophecy. This is the sentence of truth, under which, if Elias fall, all the false prophets cannot raise him up again.

Now shew thy testimony, Elias; thou art of age, answer for thyself, John ix. 23. How many Eliases will you make? Or of what Elias did Christ speak? His disciples understood him of John, Mat. xvii.; for unto him the Jews had done what they would; or what Elias was to be fulfilled? not he that was prophesied? or what Elias did the scribes think should first come, before the Son of man should rise from the dead? or to what prophecy did they lean, why they should look for Elias? Did they not stand upon the prophecy of Malachi? Mal. iv. 5. Yea, no question, for they had no other to trust unto; but Christ made answer to his disciples, that Elias which the scribes looked for, was come already; therefore the Elias of Malachi was come already, for they knew no other but of Malachi; and the apostles asked him in their meaning, to give answer unto the scribes, Mat. xvii. 10. If Christ say, Elias is come already, doth he not mean that Elias, which was prophesied and expected, is come already, that the Scripture might be found true? No truth can say that he meant other; then if Elias which was prophesied be come already, how canst thou be he which was prophesied?[1] The apostles said, the scribes looked for Elias; Christ said Elias is come

---

[1] You have as much reason for Elias, as the Jews that thought Christ called for Elias when he said, *Eli, Eli, lama sabachthani.*

already; is not this as much as if he had said, Let them look for
him no more, for he that is come shall not come again; if we were
now to look for another, he that comes not in at the door, is not
the right shepherd, John x.; and you are as worthy to be welcome,
as he which comes before he be bidden; but if you had done wisely,
you would have come before Christ, ere he had broached these
things to the people; then if you had made this tale, and framed
your matters cunningly, perhaps some credulous person would have
said, This may be Elias. If Christ had not come when Christ came,
then St Patrick had been Christ.[1] Can you not be content to think
as the apostles did? Sure it is, they knew not that any Elias should
arise in those days, but accounted the prophecy of Malachi fulfilled,
when they heard Christ give sentence thereof, and they all in one
spirit understood him of John, Mat. xvii. 13. Furthermore, all the
prophets prophesied to John, Mat. xi. 13; but after John we read of
no prophet, but the ministers of the Lord. So that if you will interpret a prophet as they were in the old law, by this sentence, you
cannot be a prophet; but if you say that place of Matthew is not so
to be understood, then you must needs construe it thus, that all the
prophets prophesied to John, that is, that all which any of the prophets said to Elias they prophesied in meaning to John, and so
Malachi's prophecy is fulfilled in John. Thus Matthew construeth
himself in the next verse, saying, This John, to whom the prophets
prophesied, was the Elias which is to come.

You grant that John had the spirit, the power, and office of
Elias, and that he did fulfil his duty; stand there, for in this point
Luke's words do agree with the words of Malachi. Now, demand
I of you whether names be anything with God, and when the
Spirit prophesied a prophet, whether he prophesied the name, or
the office and the power? Christ had faith,[2] they which do the
works of Abraham are children of Abraham, and none but they,
John viii. So, when Malachi prophesied that Elias should come,
he meant not that Elias, which was taken up in a fiery chariot,
should descend again, but that one should come in the spirit and
power of Elias, as Luke interpreteth the prophet, saying, 'He shall
go before him in the spirit and power of Elias.' The prophecy is
fulfilled when the thing prophesied is come to pass, and that is
done which was spoken. He is not a prophet that bears the name
of a prophet, but he that hath the spirit and power, and doth the
office of a prophet. But if your name be Elias, why were you not
so called from your birth? If you be Elias at all, you are Elias

---

[1] An Irish devotion.   [2] Qu. 'Christ had said'?—ED.

as well at one time as another. Elizabeth could not choose but call her son John, Luke i. Mary was warned before she was delivered to call her fruit Jesus. Your angel speaks to none but to yourself. Makes God prophets in such secret? The Holy Ghost lighteth upon Christ in the likeness of a dove, that John might see and bear witness, Luke iii.; Paul was stricken down to the ground in the sight of all his companions, Acts ix.; a voice came from heaven that the people heard, and Jesus answered, 'This voice was not because of me, but for your sakes,' John xi.; but of this angel I may say, he which intendeth evil hateth light. But John said, I am not Elias, John i.; he said well, for Elias was taken up into heaven, and nothing was prophesied to come again, but one in the spirit and power of Elias, as I have proved before, and this was John; but he would not call himself Elias, nor say he came in the spirit and power of Elias, though God had given him both his spirit and power. This was John's modesty, to humble himself, as Christ advanced him; so he said, I am not a prophet, and yet he was a prophet, and more than a prophet. 'Thou, child,' saith his father, 'shalt be called a prophet of the Highest,' Luke i.; so little John respected the name of Elias, or of a prophet. But are the prophets of the Old Testament, or the prophets of the New Testament, to be fulfilled in our days? I thought the prophets had determined about Christ, and that Christ had prophesied of us. Thus St Paul taught the Hebrews before Elias came, Heb. xi.; hold fast, Elias, for if this be true, thy kingdom is but short. But I come nearer unto you; do you believe, as St John, as a prophet, or an apostle? Then you can shew me your faith by your works. 'These tokens,' saith Christ, 'shall follow them that believe. They shall cast out devils in my name, they shall speak with tongues, they shall drive away serpents; if they drink poison, it shall not hurt them; and they shall heal the sick, by laying on their hands,' Mark xvi. If you cannot do all these, or none of these, then I may believe as well as Elias; shall he that is full of the Holy Ghost, Luke i. 15, be unable to yield one token of faith? Hold fast, Elias. But whether you be a true prophet or a false, yet you shall have power to cast out devils; for the false prophets, shall come unto me, saith Christ, and shall say, We have cast out devils in thy name, Mat. vii. 22. But if thou be but a pettifogger, and have no cunning, but set a face on things, then take heed how you adjure these spirits, lest they turn upon you again, and say, 'Jesus I know, and Elias I know, but who art thou?' Truly, Elias, make account of this, that whomsoever thou servest, the same shall pay

to thee thy wages. Yet a little nearer to you, you ask your brother,
as I read in a piece of a letter, under your name, If I be a false
prophet, what false doctrine have I taught ?   Indeed, if you were
the prophet of God, the Holy Ghost should speak within you, and
the Spirit of truth should lead you into all truth, as it is written,
John xvi.   And if you had the spirit of John, as John had of Elias,
then you shall be full of the Holy Ghost from your mother's womb.
The prophet of God cannot speak, but that which God puts into his
mouth, 1 Kings xxii. 14 ; but you err, and that against God, and
against his word, and yet you ask, What false doctrine have I taught ?
First, you call yourself Elias, to which now I say no more, but set
you the ensample of Christ, which you should follow. ' If I bear
witness of myself, my witness is not true,' John v.   You presume,
further, that Christ descended into hell both in soul and body,
which is so absurd, that never either protestant or heretic avouched;
the creed saith plainly his body was buried, and if in this article
we do not believe truly, how say you that we are in the true religion, which are not yet come to the knowledge of our salvation ?
You avouch stiffly that the patriarchs before Christ remained in
hell, where was no darkness but light ; I stand not to refell absur-
dities, I rather look for your proof, than you to expect my con-
futation. Some have said in Abraham's bosom, some in *limbo
patrum*, some in heaven, and some in hell ; but shew me Scripture,
or one doctor or true professor since the world began, which ever
said as Elias saith.   Did the angel tell you this ?   Ask him, when
you talk with him again, where this delicate hell is, and to what
purpose it serveth since Christ fetched his patriarchs forth of it.
You say that Christ knew all things saving the day of the resurrection ; which will not stand with his humanity, for so he knew not
all things ; nor with his deity, for so he knew the day of resurrection, and all things else.   In this point you overshoot yourself, for
want of learning to distinguish of the two natures in Christ,
whereby I perceive there is nothing in you, but that which is of
practice, and you know no more than you have learned at school.
You pervert the words of Mat. xvii.; he saith, ' Elias shall first
come and restore all things ;' you say, Elias shall come and destroy
all things ; and so, upon a false foundation, you ground a busy
argument to no purpose.   Shall this be your proceedings to falsify
the truth, to prove a lie ?   What doctrine is this that shall destroy
all things?   Antichrist is called the son of perdition, because he
destroyeth others, and shall be destroyed himself, 2 Thes. ii. 3. My
power, saith Paul, is to edification, not to destruction, 2 Cor. xiii. 10 ;

construe my words wisely, for if the sheep hear his voice, they will think that the wolf comes rather than the true shepherd. Did John thy office, and did he not destroy? Had John thy power, and could he not destroy? In this word all thy doctrine is manifest; if Matthew say *destroy*, then Elias's doctrine shall stand for truth; but if Matthew say *restore*, then Elias shall be content to go for a false prophet, because thou hast changed the truth into a lie. You prophesy that your father shall be cast over into ignorance, and all that he hath shall perish. Now, Elias expounds how he meaneth to destroy, and first he beginneth with his father: O miserable child, for whom his father is accursed! Was John Baptist's father cast over into ignorance? was Mary accursed? did their cattle perish? No; 'Thou shalt have joy and gladness,' saith Gabriel to Zacharias; 'Elizabeth was filled with the Holy Ghost,' saith Luke; 'Blessed art thou among women,' saith the angel. Is it true, Elias? This will go hard on thy side. You would bear men in hand, that never plague, nor dearth, nor earthquake, nor waters shall touch your country, so long as you continue amongst them. This is more than ever was granted Christ; what shall we think? 'They promise liberty,' saith Peter, 'and they themselves are bondservants.' Ah, Lord God!' saith Jeremiah, 'behold, the prophets say to them, Ye shall not see the sword, neither shall famine come upon you; but I will give you assured peace in this place,' Jer. xiv. 13. Then the Lord said unto him, They prophesy lies in my name. I have not sent them, I speak not to them, but they prophesy unto you a false vision, a divination, a vanity, a deceitfulness of their own heart, and they themselves shall perish by the plagues from which they exempt their country, without my commandment. You avouch that religion is most sincerely professed, and thoroughly purged from ceremonies in England: now I would that Elias were not a false prophet. But here I descry, that Elias the prophet knoweth not what is done beyond seas. No, Elias, Geneva is yet to learn of England. I would all the wisdom of Elias could move England to learn of her sister Geneva; then should we have more religion and less ceremonies.

You pretend that Calvin was a good man, and yet in your article of Christ's descent, you make him a plain reprobate, for he never believed as Elias doth. You term your three apparitions, visions; and yet you do say they were true; wherein you will beguile yourself, because you go further than your knowledge; you know not what a vision meaneth; but read, and you shall find that visions are false. Though Elias make a mingle-mangle of truths and seemings together, as though you could dream and be awake; either all must be a vision, or part of a vision; all truth, or no truth. You say, your soul was taken from your body; indeed, St Paul durst not say so, lest any man should think of him above that which he did see him to be, and that he heard of him, 2 Cor. xii. 11; but Elias had need speak for himself, for no man will speak for him. But Christ saith, ' the word which I speak is not mine, but the Father's which sent me,' John xiv. Mark the strong reasons of our new prophet, he proves not as we do, by *scriptum est,* but doth speak as one that hath some authority, *ipse dixit;* for how would you have him prove else that he walked upon the clouds, and that the roof opened to let forth his soul? I fear this time is not yet come to prove this by *scriptum est.* But what saith Paul? 'Say I these things of myself? saith not the law the same also?' This gear will not hold, Elias; you did not look well at the knitting, how these things would agree.

Paul refraineth to glory of himself, because men should not account him above that which they saw in him, 2 Cor. xii. 6. Elias boasteth himself of secret visions, because he would that men should account of him above that which they see him to be. Christ would not be known before his time, Mat. xvi. 12; Elias will be a prophet before he can prophesy. ' Be ye followers of me,' saith Paul, ' and look on them that walk so, as ye have us for an example,' Philip. iii. 17. Therefore fashion thyself to Paul, and we will look on thee, for ' he that commendeth himself is not allowed, but he whom the Lord commendeth.' Is this man likely to have revelations, which cannot reveal any more unto us than we know? God did bear witness unto the doctrine of the apostles, with signs and wonders, divers miracles and gifts of the Holy Ghost. Is Elias also among the apostles? Well, he is the least of the apostles, we will not look for wonders, we will crave but truth.

The prophet which speaketh a word which I have not spoken, shall die; and if thou think in thy heart, How shall we know the word which the Lord hath not spoken? mark if the thing be not, nor come to pass, then the Lord hath not spoken, but presumption, Deut. xviii. 20.

Is it come to pass that the word of Matthew, *restore,* is turned to *destroy?* Is it come to pass, that England is before Geneva in sincere profession? We see, alas, it is not so; therefore we know the Lord hath not spoken to this man, but he speaketh of himself; therefore thou shalt not be afraid of him, saith God. You were sick as nature inclined, and you say that the angel prophesied you should be a leper; you were bound prentice as others be, and you say the angel prophesied you should be a bond-man; your country hath done well, as many more, and you say the angel prophesied it should fare well for your sake. This is to prophesy of the weather, when the time is past. Who cannot have enough of such angels, if men would believe them? Yet Hanno wrought with more credit than this: he taught birds to sing, *Hanno is a god;* and when they had learned their lesson, he lets them fly in the air, and wheresoever they came, they cried *Hanno is a god.* This had some miracle in it, but Elias will face us out with a card of ten.

This is but a young devil. You affirm, that at the desire of the proud, Elias is beheaded; this is prophetical indeed, it passeth my understanding. The Spirit of truth speaketh plainly to edify in truth, and giveth understanding to the simple, Ps. cxix., but the spirit of Satan leadeth men's minds to construe his saying as they list, that under ambiguous words he might sow erroneous opinions, and contention amongst men. These are the wells without water, or those which be deep that men can draw no water out of them. This sentence cannot be verified, unless you make John, Elias; and and so we receive your *submittimus;* see how Satan shall be taken in his own snares. You demand confidently, If I be a false prophet, what evil have ever I done? or where is the person that can accuse me of sin? Christ might very well say so, which had power and reigned over sin; but Elias is a man subject to infirmities, as we are; so saith James, James v. 5. But was there any prophet or apostle whom man could not accuse of sin? O Solomon, thou wast not the wisest man, if a child be wiser than thou! O David, thou wast not a man after God's own heart, if thy heart were not as pure, and thy life as holy as a simple prentice's; if no man rebuke thee of sin, thou hast no faithful friend; if no man could accuse thee before, now I accuse thee of sin; thou hast made thyself wiser than the wisest, and thou hast said, I am purer than he which is a man after God's own heart. Woe be to that holiness which leadeth in hypocrisy unto damnation. Indeed, I hear well of your conversation towards all men, and I am heartily sorry that such a good name should impart credit unto a false doctrine. I lament that the wisdom of the flesh should be readier to godly works than the wisdom of the spirit. It may pity a good heart that a body so well mortified from sin, should not have a spirit fitted unto it. But what do you think of these false prophets? Shall they not make a show of godliness? Shall they not set forth a kind of good works (as the papists do to merit heaven); yea, no doubt, else Christ would never have said, 'They shall be able (if it were possible) to seduce the elect,' Mat. xxiv. 24. 'Satan himself is transformed into an angel of light, therefore it is no great thing if his ministers be transformed into the ministers of righteousness,' 2 Cor. xi. 14. The damsel cried after Paul and Barnabas, 'These men are the servants of the most high God, which shew unto us the way of salvation,' Acts xvi., and yet she had a foul spirit; Judas kissed, and yet he betrayed; Pilate washed his hands, and yet he was guilty; Satan alleged Scripture, and yet he was but a devil; 'some preach Christ of envy and strife, and some of good will,' saith Paul, Philip. i. 15. If the false prophets rise not in these days, when shall they come? If they confess not many truths, how shall their lies be credited? If they make not a show of good works, how shall they be held for prophets? Whatsoever thou art, Elias, the false prophets shall come daily, they shall come in sheep's clothing, and they shall call themselves great men; and they shall speak strange words, they shall work wonderful things, and they shall seem holy amongst men, and shall deceive many, but the end shall try them. Judas received thirty pieces, but after he cast them down. Thou mayest win glory among some, but when desperation shall see from whence his torments came, then they shall cry, Woe unto that prophet, Woe unto that prophet. Cast down those thirty pieces, if thou be not a child of perdition, as Judas was; cast down thy false name, cast down all which thou hopest to gain by that cursed spirit; dost thou not know that he is a liar? What dost thou look for at his hand? 'Build again the things that thou hast destroyed,' Gal. ii. 18, then Saul shall be called Paul; if it be such a glory to be called a false prophet, why dost thou call thyself a true prophet, and detract from thy praise? If thou hast not thy reward here, where wilt thou call for it? Is the dragon become so familiar? is hell-fire become so tolerable, that any man should look for ease with the devil, and make his pastime to lead a number after him into hell? Truly, Elias, thou canst not seduce the elect, for their names are written in the book of life, and the Lord hath promised, 'no man shall pluck them out of my hands,' John x. Alas, wilt thou lose thyself, to lose those that are the children of perdition already? This is a strong delusion; yet a little nearer to thee, and if thou canst suffer me, even to thy heart, thou art Elias, and thou must preach, wilt thou teach a new doctrine? Accursed be that man, Gal. i. Wilt thou teach the truth? Thou sayest we know that already; but yet thou wilt labour with us, and preach together. It is spoken like a friend, why then canst thou not join thyself with the disciples?

Why doth not the Spirit put into their hearts to receive thee ? If God had sent thee to us, no doubt he would have sent us to thee, that as many as be elected might believe ; for so did the Jews when Peter came; and so did the Gentiles where Paul preached, Acts xiv. ; and as the angel warned Peter to come, so he warned Cornelius to send, Acts x. 'Surely the Lord will do nothing, but he revealeth his secrets to his servants and prophets,' Amos iii. 7. Amongst the people, some said he is Elias, some John Baptist, some a prophet, Mat. xvi. ; but the disciples had him strait before he told them, 'Thou art the Son of the living God.' For 'the spirits of the prophets are subject to the prophets,' 1 Cor. xiv. ; so saith Paul, which had the Spirit of God. 'My sheep know my voice,' saith Christ, 'but a stranger they will not follow,' John x. What prophet is he that the Spirit brooketh not, and the elect do not believe ? It is I, saith Elias, and none else ; God grant that never false prophet find no more credit.

But you pretend your time is not yet come, &c. Nay, Elias, your time is past, Mat. xvii. 12 ; you were filled with the Holy Ghost from your mother's womb, Luke i., and do ye not believe, or is not your time yet come, wherein men shall believe you ? Why then do you speak for credit before your time ? or why do you bid us believe you ? I am weary of these tales, and have been too long in reproving that spirit, which I trust no brother will believe. Mark, therefore, you shall hear, in a word, all which I have spoken ; you which bear witness of yourself; which have done nothing wonderful ; which speak like other men ; which cannot answer in disputation ; of whom no disciple beareth witness ; of whom no prophet hath prophesied ; whom no brother hath received ; which are not in the number of all the tokens ; which come without your wedding-garment ; which prophesy not according to the faith ; which lead us from our belief ; which make the Son of man a liar ; which construe the simplicity of the apostle, in parables and figures ; which confess the scribes and deny Christ ; which presume Christ did not respect the prophecy ; which come before you be bidden ; which come in at the wrong door ; which come to prophesy when the prophets are gone ; which think not as the apostles did ; which understand not Christ as his disciples ; which make the Spirit prophesy names ; which were not called Elias from your birth; whose angel speaks to none but yourself; which claim your calling from the prophecy of the Old Testament fulfilled before Christ ; which have not the tokens which follow them that believe; which come to destroy ; whose father is accursed ; which privilege your country above all the promises that were granted to Christ; which teach false doctrine; which pervert the text of the Scripture; which prophesy of things when they are past; which speak darkly to divers senses; which cast yourselves[1] in your own sayings; which proclaim, Who can accuse me of sin? which glory of yourself above that which all men see in you; which will be wiser than the wisest, and more righteous than he which is a chosen man after God's own heart; which rise in these suspicious days; which make a show of holiness; which confess truths to infer lies; which cannot join yourself to the disciples; what are you, a true prophet or a false? If these be the marks of a true prophet, how shall we try spirits of Satan? Our religion taketh these for the marks of a false prophet. Elias saith, we believe the truth; therefore he which takes Elias with all these marks for a true prophet, by Elias's own sentence, is in a wrong belief. 'Let us therefore keep the profession of our hope without wavering, for he is faithful that promised,' Heb. x. 23. 'Be not suddenly moved from your mind, nor troubled, neither by spirit, neither by word, neither by letter, as it were from us,' 2 Thess. ii. 2. 'If a dreamer or prophet rise amongst you, and give you a sign or wonder, and the same sign come to pass, and he notwithstanding say, Let us go another way, ye shall not hearken unto his words; for the Lord proveth you, to know whether you will love him with all your heart,' Deut. xiii. 1. The prophet at whom Jeroboam stretched out his hand, was charged by word from heaven, neither to eat nor to drink, nor turn again the same way he came; but when he was gone, a man of Bethel overtook him, and said, 'I am a prophet also as thou art; and an angel spake unto me, Bring him again to thy house, and let him eat and drink with thee. But he lied unto him. Yet he went with him, and did eat; but as they sat at the table, the Lord spake to the man of Bethel, Because thou hast not done as the Lord commanded thee, but turned again and eaten, thou shalt not come home to be buried with thy fathers. And as he was gone, a lion met him by the way, and slew him,' 1 Kings xiii. God spake once to Balaam, but Balaam besought God to speak unto him again, and so the foolish prophet was rebuked of his ass, because he tempted God to alter his commandment. How long look we after deceitful signs? How long halt we between two opinions? 1 Kings xviii. If the apostles speak the truth, believe them; if Elias speak the truth, hear him; a prentice in Mansfield calleth himself Elias; but Thomas will not believe. How shall Thomas be made to believe? 'Put to thy hand, Thomas,

---

[1] Qu. 'yourself'?—ED.

and feel my wound.' So shew me thy testimony, Elias, let me feel your heart, let me see your works, let me hear your faith, your wisdom, your knowledge, and what you can foretell to come. If you will not come to this reckoning, then I say no more, but warn all men to beware. If I had not known the truth, I would have thought this man had spoken truth.

God is my witness, I have suffered the Spirit to speak unto thee, because I seek thy conversion; but if thou wilt not return, while mercy is ready, I bring thee sorrowful tidings, when Satan shall not help thee, the rack must prove this doctrine. Wilt thou heap God, and the devil, and man upon thee all at once? O wretched creature, and miserable prophet! Who is able to sustain? 'My son,' saith Solomon, 'if thy heart be wise, my heart shall rejoice, and I will be glad over thee,' Prov. xxiii. 15. So I, which have gone thus far to bring thee unto Christ, if thy portion be amongst the righteous, and thou hast an hour yet wherein thou shalt be called, if thou canst go with me, and it may please the divine providence to call thee at my voice, I will sing praises, I will give thanks, I will say unto my soul in all her troubles, Rejoice, my soul, remember since thou prayedst for Elias, and the Lord heard thee out of his holy sanctuary, and thy conversion shall not be hid from Israel; pity thyself before the day of payment, and always remember the sentence of Gamaliel, which never lighted false, 'If thou be not of God, thou shalt come to nought, and thy end shall be worse than thy beginning,' Acts v. 38.

'The word that I have spoken, the same shall judge you in the last day,' John xii. 48.

QUESTIONS GATHERED OUT OF HIS OWN[1] CONFESSION, BY HENRY SMITH, WHICH ARE YET UNANSWERED.

Whether you are sure you shall live these three years, because you say, after three years you must preach?

Whether may a man expect visions from God, because you say, for these three years you are to look for more visions?

Whether shall you be able at any time to interpret the truth of the Scripture in all places without error, better than all the doctors?

One of your sentences saith, you shall live chaste in wedlock. When must you take a wife? and why should you not rather continue single?

Whether there hath been neither pestilence, nor dearth, nor war, nor earthquake in your country these five years, nor shall be any time of your continuance there, because the angel so promised? Is this more than ever was granted to Christ?

What Bible or translation mean you, when you say, this Bible is truly translated?

Whether it be necessary to salvation to believe all the articles of the creed?

Whether any man, since the apostles, did stand so right in the whole doctrine of the Scripture, that he did hold and believe the true interpretation of all the words and sayings through all the prophets and apostles in all the Bible?

Whether predestination, election, &c., are to be preached unto laymen? What free will had Adam? and what free will remaineth unto us?

What scriptures are canonical, and which are not canonical?

Whether a man may marry his child with a papist, or other heretic, hoping to convert him?

Whether ministers should have livings or stipends?

Whether, in some cases, a minister may not be non-resident?

[1] That is, the confession of Robert Dickons.—ED.

Whether heretics, living to themselves without corrupting others, are to be punished with death ?

Whether Satan knoweth the inward thoughts, further than by the outward habit of the body ; and whether he can read and say, *Verbum caro factum est ?*

Whether Christ was, or is, or shall be known and preached unto all nations of the world ?

Where is hell ? and what shall be the manner of punishment there to the reprobate ?

What think you of the antipodes, and those monstrous people which live in Asia, and of monsters in general ?

What think you of that saying of Christ, ' This day shalt thou be with me in paradise' ? what kind of place is this, and where, and to what purpose now it serveth ? and whether it was a material apple that Adam did eat ?

How esteem you of astronomy, physiognomy, palmistry, casting of a figure, of music in the church, &c. ?

What think you of our common prayer-book and litany ?

What esteem you of fairies, hobgoblins, &c. ? whether their money be true, and how they have it ?

Whether should one meaning to be a preacher first study the arts, or else study nothing but divinity, as you have done ?

Whether the font, surplice, caps, tippets, bells, holidays, fasting-days, and such like ceremonies, are better observed, or omitted ?

Whether they which are called protestants, or those whom we call puritans, be of the purest religion, and most reformed to the primitive church ?

What is meant by the prison, in Peter, whither Christ descended in spirit ?

Whether our joys in heaven shall be to all equal, and the torments in hell to every one alike ? and whether we shall see and know one another ?

Where was the soul of Lazarus while his body was in the grave ?

Whether Elisha, cursing the little children, did not sin ?

At what age and stature shall all rise in the resurrection ? and whether the wounds and scars shall remain in our bodies glorified.

What think ye of the scribes in the third of Mark, that said, Christ had an unclean spirit, and casted out devils by Beelzebub, did they sin against the Holy Ghost ?

Whether images be in no respect tolerable, and whether a man remembering Christ by seeing the cross, doth sin ?

Which is the greatest sin that reigneth this day in England ?

How is the soul created in man, and when it cometh, and how, or in what part it is placed in the body?

In what estate shall the sun, and moon, the heavens, and elements be after the last day, when there shall be no creature upon earth?

What think you of plays, and representing divine matters, as in pageants?

Whether all things amongst the faithful Christians ought to be common? Acts iv. 32.

What do you think concerning the bishoping of children?

What city is described of John in the seventh of his Revelation?

Whether did the apostles know sufficiently their salvation before Christ died and rose again?

Answer to every point, or yield.

Henry Smith of Husband's Boreswell, at the commandment of the Right Worshipful his Uncle, Master Brian Cave, High Sheriff of Leicestershire.

THE TRUMPET OF THE SOUL SOUNDING TO JUDGMENT.

THE TRUMPET OF THE SOUL SOUNDING
TO JUDGMENT.

---

*Rejoice, O young man, in thy youth, and let thy heart be merry in thy young days, follow the ways of thine own heart, and the lusts of thine eyes : but remember, for all these things thou must come to judgment.—*ECCLES. XI. 9.

WHEN I should have preached under the cross, I mused what text to take in hand, to please all, and to keep myself out of danger ; and musing, I could not find any text in the Scripture that did not reprove sin, unless it were in the Apocrypha, which is not of the Scripture. This text bids them that be voluptuous, be voluptuous still; let them that be vainglorious, be vainglorious still; let them that be covetous, be covetous still ; let them that be drunkards, be drunkards still ; let them that be swearers, be swearers still ; let them that be wantons, be wantons still ; let them that be careless prelates, be careless still ; let them that be usurers, be usurers still; but, saith Solomon, 'Remember thy end, that thou shalt be called to judgment at the last for all together.' This is the counsel of Solomon, the wisest then living, What a counsel is this for a wise man, such a one as was Solomon !

In the beginning of his book he saith, 'All is vanity,' and in the end he saith, 'Fear God, and keep his commandments ;' in the twelfth chapter he saith, 'Remember thy Maker in the days of thy youth;' but here he saith, 'Rejoice, O young man, in thy youth.' Here he speaketh like an epicure, which saith, Eat, drink, and be merry; here he counsels, and here he mocks ; yet after the manner of scorners, although they deserved it in shewing their foolishness; as in the first of the Proverbs, 'He laughed at the wicked in derision ;' as in the second Psalm, God seeing us follow our own ways. For when he bids us pray, we play ; and when he bids us run, we stand still; and when he bids us fast, we feast, and send for vanities to make us sport ; then he laughs at our destruction. Therefore, when Solomon giveth a sharp reproof, and maketh you ashamed in one word, he scoffingly bids you do it again, like a schoolmaster which beateth his scholar for playing the truant, he biddeth him play the truant again. Oh, this is the bitterest reproof of all. But lest any libertine should misconstrue Solomon, and say, that he bids us be merry and make much of ourselves, therefore he shutteth up with a watch-word, and setteth a bridle before his lips, and reproveth it, as he speaketh it, before he goeth any further, and saith, ' But remember that for all these things thou must come to judgment.' But if we will understand his meaning, when he saith, Rejoice, O young man, he meaneth, Repent, O young man, in thy youth ; and when he saith, Let thy heart cheer thee, Let thy sins grieve thee ; for he meaneth otherwise than he speaketh : he speaketh like Micaiah in the first book of Kings, the twenty-second chapter, ' Go up and prosper ;' or like as Ezekiel, ' Go up and serve other gods ;' or as St John speaketh in the Revelation, ' Let them that be wicked, be wicked still.' But if there were no judgment-day, that were a merry world ; therefore saith Solomon, when thou art in thy pleasures, flaunting in the fields, and in thy brave ruffs and amongst thy lovers, with thy smiling looks, thy wanton talk, and merry jests, with thy pleasant games, and lofty looks, ' Remember, for all these things thou shalt come to judgment.'

Whilst the thief stealeth, the hemp groweth, and the hook is covered within the bait. We sit down to eat, and rise up to play, and from play to sleep, and a hundred years is counted little enough to sin in ; but how many sins thou hast set on the score, so many kinds of punishment shall be provided for thee ; how many years of pleasure thou hast taken, so many years of pain ; how many drams of delight, so many pounds of dolor. When iniquity hath played her part, vengeance leaps upon the stage: the comedy is short, but the tragedy is longer; the black guard shall attend upon you, you shall eat at the table of sorrow, and the crown of death shall be upon your heads, many glistering faces looking on you. And this is the fear of sinners ; when the devil hath enticed them to sin, he persuadeth like the old prophet in the book of Kings, who, when he had enticed the young prophet contrary to the commandment of God, to turn home with him and to eat and drink, he cursed him for his labour, because he disobeyed the commandment of the Lord, and so as a lion devoured him by the way. The foolish virgins think that their oil will never be spent; so Dinah straggled abroad, whilst she was deflowered. What a thing is this, to say, *Rejoice,* and then *repent;* what a blank to say, *Take thy pleasure,* and then *thou shalt come to judgment.* It is as if he should say, Steal and be hanged, steal and[1] thou darest; strangle sin in the cradle, for all the wisdom in the world will not help thee else; but thou shalt be in admiration like dreamers, which dream strange things, and know not how they come. He saith, 'Remember judgment.' If thou remember always, then thou shalt have little list to sin; if thou remember this, then thou shalt have little list to fall down to the devil, though he would give thee all the world, and the glory thereof. Solomon saith, the weed groweth from a weed to a cockle, from a cockle to a bramble, from a bramble to a brier, from a brier to a thorn; lying breeds perjury, perjury breeds haughtiness of heart, haughtiness of heart breeds contempt, contempt breeds obstinacy, and brings forth much evil. And this is the whole progress of sin; he groweth from a liar to a thief, from a thief to a murderer, and never leaveth until he hath searched all the room in hell, and yet he is never satisfied; the more he sinneth, the more he searcheth to sin; when he hath deceived, nay, he hath not deceived thee; as soon as he hath that he desireth, he hath not that he desireth; when he hath left fighting, he goeth to fighting again; yet a little, and a little more, and so we fly from one sin to another. While I preach, you hear iniquity engender within you, and will break forth as soon as you are gone. So Christ wept, Jerusalem laughed; Adam brake one, and we brake ten; like children which laugh and cry, so as if we kept a shop of vices, now this sin, and then that, from one sin to another.

'Oh remember thy end,' saith Solomon, and 'that thou must come to judgment.'

What shall become of them that have tried them most? Be condemned most. 'Rejoice O young man in thy youth.'

But if thou mark Solomon, he harps upon one string, he doubles it again and again, to shew us things of his own experience, because we are so forgetful thereof in ourselves, like the dreamer that forgetteth his dream, and the swearer his swearing. So we beg of every unclean spirit, until we have bombasted ourselves up to the throat, filling every corner of our hearts with all uncleanness, and then we are like the dog that cometh out of the sink, and maketh

---

[1] That is, 'if.'—ED.

every one as foul as himself; therefore saith Solomon, If any one will learn the way to hell, let him take his pleasure.

Methinks I see the dialogue between the flesh and the spirit : the worst speaketh first, and the flesh saith, ' Soul, take thine ease, eat, drink,' and go brave, lie soft ; what else should you do, but take your pleasure ? thou knowest what a pleasant fellow I have been unto thee, thou knowest what delight thou hast had by my means. But the soul cometh in, burdened with that which hath been spoken before, and saith, I pray thee remember judgment, thou must give account for all these things, for unless you repent, you shall surely perish.

No, saith the flesh, talk not of such grave matters, but tell me of fine matters, of soft beds and pleasant things, and talk to me of brave pastimes, apes, bears, and puppets, for I tell thee, the forbidden fruit is sweetest of all fruits, for I do not like of your telling me of judgment; but take thou thy jewels, thy instrument, and all the strings of vanity will strike at once, for the flesh loves to be brave, and tread upon corks, it cannot tell what fashion to be of, and yet to be of the new fashion.

Rejoice, O young man, in thy youth. Oh this goes brave, for while wickedness hath cast his rubs, and vengeance casts his spurs, and his foot ; and thus she reels, and now she tumbles, and then she falls ; therefore this progress is ended.

Pleasure is but a spur, riches but a thorn, glory but a blast, beauty but a flower ; sin is but an hypocrite, honey in thy mouth and poison in thy stomach ; therefore let us come again and ask Solomon in good sooth, whether he meaneth in good earnest, when he spake these words : Oh, saith Solomon, it is the best life in the world to go brave, lie soft, and live merrily, if there were no judgment. But this judgment mars all, it is like a damp that puts out all the light, and like a box that marreth all the ointment; for if this be true, we have spun a fair thread, that we must answer for all, that are not able to answer for one ; why Solomon maketh us fools, and giveth us gauds to play withal ; what then, shall we not rejoice at all ? Yes, there is a godly mirth, and if we could hit on it, which is called, ' Be merry and wise.' Sarah laughed, and was reproved; Abraham laughed, and was not reproved. And thus much for the first part.

But remember, for all these things thou shalt come to judgment.

This verse is as it were a dialogue betwixt the flesh and the spirit, as the two counsellors ; the worst is first, and the flesh speaketh proudly, but the spirit cometh in burdened with that which hath been spoken, The flesh goeth laughing and singing to hell; but the spirit casteth rubs in his way, and puts him in mind of judgment, that for all these things now ends *rejoice,* and here comes in *but;* if this *but* were not, we might rejoice still; if young men must for all the sports of youth, what then shall old men do, being as they are now? Surely, if Solomon lived to see our old men live now, as here he saith of young men; so high as sin rageth, yet vengeance sits above it, as high as high Babel.

Methinks I see a sword hang in the air by a twine thread, and all the sons of men labour to burst it in sunder. There is a place in hell where the covetous judge sitteth, the greedy lawyer, the griping landlord, the careless bishop, the lusty youth, the wanton dames, the thief, the robbers of the commonwealth; they are punished in this life, because they ever sinned as long as they could, while mercy was offered unto them; therefore, because they would not be washed, they shall be drowned. Now put together *rejoice* and *remember,* thou hast learned to be merry, now learn to be wise. Now, therefore, turn over a new leaf, and take a new lesson, for now Solomon mocked not as he did before; therefore, a check to thy ruffs, a check to thy cuffs, a check to thy robes, a check to thy gold, a check to your riches, a check to your beauty, a check to your muck, a check to your graves. Woe from above, woe from below, woe unto all the strings of vanity; dost thou not now marvel, that thou hast not a feeling of sin? For now thou seest Solomon saith true, thine own heart can tell that it is wicked, but it cannot amend; therefore it is high time to amend. As Nathan cometh to David after Beelzebub, so cometh accusing conscience after sin. Methinks that every one should have a feeling of sin; though this day be like yesterday, and to-morrow like to-day, yet one day will come for all, and then woe, woe, woe, and nothing but darkness. And though God came not to Adam until the evening, yet he came; although the fire came not upon Sodom until evening, yet it came; and so comes the judge: though he be not yet come, though he have leaden feet, he hath iron hands. The arrow stayeth, and is not yet fallen; so is his wrath; the pit is digged, the fire kindled, and all things are made ready and prepared against that day, only the final sentence is to come, which will not long tarry.

You may not think to be like to the thief that stealeth and is not seen; nothing can be hid from him, and the judge followeth thee at the heels; and therefore, whatsoever thou art, look about thee, and do nothing but that thou wouldest do openly, for all

things are opened unto him. Sarah may not think to laugh, and
not be seen; Gehazi may not think to lie, and not be known; they
that will not come to the banquet, must stand at the door.

What ! Do you think that God doth not remember our sins,
which we do not regard ; for while we sin, the score runs on, and
the judge setteth down all in the table of remembrance, and his
scroll reacheth up to heaven.

Item, for lending to usury; item, for racking of rents ; item, for
deceiving thy brethren ; item, for falsehood in wares; item, for
starching thy ruffs ; item, for curling thy hair ; item, for painting
thy face ; item, for selling of benefices ; item, for starving of souls;
item, for playing at cards ; item, for sleeping in the church ; item,
for profaning the Sabbath day ; with a number more hath God to
call to account, for every one must answer for himself : the forni-
cator for taking of filthy pleasure ; O son, remember thou hast
taken thy pleasure, take thy punishment ; the careless prelate, for
murdering so many thousand souls ; the landlord, for getting
money from his poor tenants by racking of his rents. See the rest,
all they shall come like a very sheep, when the trumpet shall
sound, and the heaven and earth shall come to judgment against
them ; when the heavens shall vanish like a scroll, and the earth
shall consume like fire, and all the creatures standing against
them ; the rocks shall cleave asunder, and the mountains shake,
and the foundation of the earth shall tremble ; and they shall say
to the mountains, Cover us, fall upon us, and hide us from the presence of his anger and wrath, whom we have not cared for to offend.
But they shall not be covered and hid ; but then they shall go the
black way, to the snakes and serpents, to be tormented of devils
for ever. Oh pain unspeakable ; and yet the more I express it,
the more horrible it is ; when you think of torment passing all
torments, and yet a torment passing all that, yet this torment is
greater than them, and passing them all.

Imagine you see a sinner going to hell, and his summoner gape
at him, his acquaintance look at him, the angels shout at him, and
the saints laugh at him, and the devils rail at him, and many look
him in the face, and they that said they would live and die with
him, forsake him, and leave him to pay all the scores. Then Judas
would restore his bribes, Esau would cast up his pottage, Achan
would cast down his gold; and Gehazi would refuse his gifts, Nebuchadnezzar would be humbler, Balaam would be faithful, and the
prodigal would be tame.

Methinks I see Achan running about, Where shall I hide my

gold that I have stolen, that it might not be seen, nor stand to appear for a witness against me?

And Judas running to the high priests, saying, Hold, take again your money, I will none of it, I have betrayed the innocent blood.

And Esau, crying for the blessing when it is too late, having sold his birthright for a mess of pottage.

Woe, woe, woe, that ever we were born! Oh, where is that Dives that would believe this, before he felt the fire in hell, or that would believe the poorest Lazarus in the world to be better than himself, before the dreadful day come when they cannot help it, if they would never so fain, when repentance is too late? Herod shall then wish that he were John Baptist, Pharaoh would wish that he were Moses, and Saul would wish that he had been David; Nebuchadnezzar, that he had been Daniel; Haman, to have been Mordecai; Esau would wish to be Jacob, and Balaam would wish he might die the death of the righteous; then he would say, I will give more than Hezekiah, cry more than Esau, fast more than Moses, pray more than Daniel, weep more than Mary Magdalene, suffer more stripes than Paul, abide more imprisonment than Micaiah, abide more cruelty than any mortal man would do, that it might be; *Ite, Go, ye cursed*, might be, *Come, ye blessed*. Yea, I would give all the goods in the world, that I might escape this dreadful day of wrath and judgment, and that I might not stand among the *Go*. Oh that I might live a beggar all my life and a a leper; oh that I might endure all plagues and sores, from the top of the head to the sole of the foot, sustain all sickness and griefs, that I might escape this judgment!

The guilty conscience cannot abide this day. The silly sheep, when she is taken, will not bleat, but you may carry her and do what you will with her, and she will be subject; but the swine, if she be once taken, she will roar and cry, and think she is never taken, but to be slain. So, of all things, the guilty conscience cannot abide to hear of this day, for they know that when they hear of it, they hear of their own condemnation. I think if there were a general collection made through the whole world, that there might be no judgment-day, then God would be so rich, that the world would go a-begging, and be as a waste wilderness. Then the covetous judge would bring forth his bribes; then the crafty lawyer would fetch out his bags; the usurer would give his gain, and the idle servant would dig up his talent again, and make a double thereof. But all the money in the world will not serve for our sins; but the judge must answer for his bribes, he that hath money must answer how he came by it, and just condemnation must come upon every soul of them; then shall the sinner be ever dying, and never dead, like the salamander, that is ever in the fire, and never consumed.

But if you come there, you may say as the Queen of Sheba said of King Solomon, I believed the report that I heard of thee in mine own country, but the one half of thy wisdom was not told me. If you come there, to see what is done, you may say, Now I believe the report that was told me in my own country concerning this place, but the one half, as now I feel, I have not heard of; now choose you whether you will rejoice, or remember; whether you will stand amongst you[1] blessed, or amongst you[1] cursed; whether you will enter while the gate is open, or knock in vain when the gate is shut; whether you will seek the Lord whilst he may be found, or be found of him when you would not be sought, being run into the bushes with Adam to hide yourselves; whether you will take your heaven now here, or[2] your hell then there; or through tribulation, to enter into the kingdom of God, and thus to take your hell now here, or[2] your heaven then there in the life to come, with the blessed saints and angels, so that hereafter you may lead a new life, putting on Jesus Christ and his righteousness.

[1] Qu. 'yon'?—ED.   [2] Qu. 'and'?—ED.

THE SINFUL MAN'S SEARCH.

THE SINFUL MAN'S SEARCH.

*If thou wilt early seek unto God, and pray unto the Almighty;
if thou be pure and upright; then surely he will awake unto
thee, and make the habitation of thy righteousness prosperous.
And though thy beginning be but small, yet thy latter end shall
greatly increase.*—JOB VIII. 5–7.

IN a sick and evil affected body, dearly beloved, we usually see pre-
paratives ministered, that the maladies may be made more fit and
pliable to receive wholesome medicines. The like, yea, and greater
regard ought we to have of our souls, which not being crazy only,
or lightly affected with sin, but sick even unto death, had need to
be prepared with threats and exhortations, comforts and consolations,
one way or other, that they may be made fit, not to receive the
preparative, but the perfection of happy salvation. And for this
cause have I made choice of this part of Scripture, as of a light to
shine unto us in darkness, a direction to our steps, and a lantern to
our paths, while we wander through the boisterous waves of this
wicked world. The text is plain, and object to every man's capacity,
naturally budding unto blossoms : the first containing our duty
which we are to perform towards God ; the second, God's promises,
if we perform this duty.

Our duty towards God is implied in these three conditions ; first,
If thou wilt early seek unto God ; secondly, *If thou wilt pray
unto the Almighty ;* thirdly, *If thou be pure and upright ;* so
that the whole consisteth on these three points. First, what it is
that God requireth, namely, a diligent and speedy search, in these
words, *If thou wilt seek early.* Secondly, how thy search is to be

made ; in prayer, in these words, *If thou wilt pray to the Almighty.* Thirdly, what effect these things ought to work in us ; a purity and sincerity of life, in these words, *If thou be pure and upright.*

As our duty towards God consisteth in three points, so God's blessing towards us is also threefold, answerable to the same. First, for seeking, he promiseth, *He will awake unto thee.* Secondly, for praying unto him, *He will make the habitation of thy righteousness prosperous.* Thirdly, for being pure and upright, *He will make thy latter end increase exceedingly ;* yea, though the beginning be but small.

First, therefore, considering the search, it is a work both in desire and labour to be joined to God. In the Psalms, this standeth for the burden of the song, 'They called upon the Lord in the time of their trouble, and he delivered them,' Ps. cvii. It is but, 'Ask and have, seek and find, knock and it shall be opened unto you,' Mat. vi. Saving that here these things are to be regarded, to wit, *how,* by *whom,* and *when* we must seek the Lord.

How. First, *faithfully ;* for if ye have but 'as much faith as a grain of mustard seed, and say unto this mountain, Remove, it shall remove, and nothing shall be impossible unto you,' Mat. xvii. 20.

Then next, *humbly,* for it is the humble petition that pierceth the skies, and that shewed the publican to depart home to his house more justified than the boasting pharisee ; and they alone that be humbled and meek, find rest for their souls.

And last of all, *continually ;* for we must not 'faint in well-doing,' Gal. vi., because the reward is not promised to him that doth, but to him that continueth to do, 1 Thes. vi.

But we may long seek and never find, except we seek the Father by the Son ; for 'no man knoweth the Father but the Son, and he to whom the Son shall disclose him.' He is 'the way, the truth, and the life, and no man cometh to the Father but by him.' 'There is one God, and one mediator betwixt God and man, the man Christ Jesus,' 1 Tim. ii. So that 'if we sin, we have an advocate, Jesus Christ the just, and he is the propitiation for our sins ;' only let us seek the Lord while he may be found.

And to this end, the word *seeking* is used in this place, that we may learn, that as the heavens and the planets, and the whole frame of nature, were ordained to finish their course by motions and operation ; so man, as he was ordained to a most blessed and happy end, should attain thereunto, not by sloth and idleness, but by an earnest seeking of the same.

The kingdom of heaven is like a treasure, which cannot be found without seeking and digging, Mat. xiii. 44. It is like the precious pearl, for which the wise merchant was content not only to seek, but to sell all that he had to buy it. God hath placed us here in this world as husbandmen, to plough upon the fallow of our hearts; as labourers to work in the vineyard, as travellers to seek a country, as soldiers to fight the battle of the Lord, against the flesh, the world, and the devil.

And for this purpose hath he proposed unto us an untilled land, a vineyard, a triple enemy to fight against; that we might remember, that we must till the ground, if we will reap the fruit, that we must prune the vine, if we will drink of the grape; that we must fight, if we will overcome. 'He that tilleth the land,' saith the wise man, 'shall be satisfied with bread, but he that followeth idleness shall be filled with poverty,' Prov. xxviii. Idleness is a moth or canker of the mind, and the fruits thereof are wicked cogitations, evil affections, and worse actions; corrupt trees without fruit, twice dead, and plucked up by the roots, engendering in the mind a loathing of God and godliness.

Eschew therefore idleness, I beseech you, and by the want ye find in others, learn instruction for yourselves. Be not forgetful how busy your enemy is, if he find you idle; first, he putteth you in mind of some vanity; then offereth opportunity to practise; then he craveth consent, and if you grant him that, he triumpheth by adding practice; he leaveth no means unattempted, whereby he may subvert and bring you to perdition. To one, as to Eve, he promiseth the knowledge of good and evil, Gen. iii. Another he seduceth with lying speeches, as he did Pharaoh the king, whom he deceived by false prophets, Exod vii. 22. To the Jews he pretended the temple of the Lord, 1 Kings xiii. To the heathen he sheweth universalities and antiquities, 1 Cor. ii. And to other particulars, he leaveth nothing unattempted, whereby he may entangle the soul of the simple, and wrap them in the snare of death. Fly idleness therefore, and seek virtue, and the way thereof; seek learning as for a jewel, make diligent search and inquisition after her; seek early and seek late; in the morning sow thy seed, and in the evening let not thy hand rest; seek him in the day of trouble, and he will deliver thee, and thou shalt glorify him.

Seek him, there is the commandment; *he will deliver thee*, there is the promise; and *thou shalt glorify him*, there is the condition. To disobey the commandment is rebellion; to distrust his promise is infidelity; to refuse the condition is vile ingratitude. Wherefore let us seek, and seek earnestly, with a fervent spirit and humbleness of heart, and let us persuade ourselves that there is no finding without seeking, no opening without knocking.

The second circumstance to be considered in this point, is to *whom* we must seek for these things. Our direction is made unto God, for 'every good and perfect gift is from above, descending from the Father of lights,' James i. 17. And as for many causes we are to seek God, and to God alone, so especially for these four.

First, because we have nothing of ourselves, nor of any other creature ; but whatsoever we have, we have it of God ; for 'what hast thou that thou hast not received ?' 1 Cor. ii. 'In him we live, we move, and have our being.' Art thou wise in thine own conceit ? Oh remember that the wisdom of the world is foolishness with God, Rom. i. Oh consider that the natural man understandeth not the things of God ; these things are hid from the wise and prudent, and are revealed to babes and sucklings. Alas, what were man if he were once left to himself? A map of misery, and a sink of calamity. Alas, how were he able to resist the fiery darts of the adversary, who continually goeth about like a roaring lion, seeking whom he may devour ? Here ye may note, first, his malice, for he daily accuseth us before the chief judge of the king's bench ; when he cannot prevail in this court, but seeth his bills of accusation repelled, then he removeth the matter to the court of our own conscience, where, on the one side, he layeth the books of the law, and statutes made against sin ; on the other side, the bills of accusation brought in against us out of the book of the law, alleging these strict places against us, 'The soul that sinneth shall die the death ;' 'Cursed is he that abideth not in every point of the law, to do it.' On the other side, he bringeth in our consciences to witness against us, and then inferreth this hard conclusion, *Therefore there is no hope in salvation.*

Then if he see that we appeal from justice to mercy, and say, At what time soever a sinner repenteth, the judge putteth all his wickedness out of his remembrance ; he dealeth with us as crafty worldlings deal in matter of law, who, when they see their matters pass against them in higher courts, bring down their case into the country to be decided by their neighbours ; who, either for their simplicity cannot, or for their favour dare not, judge of the truth of the matter.

1. So our adversary, though God himself do discharge us, though our conscience doth testify our innocency, yet he accuseth us in the third court, before men, where he is bold to pour out his whole venom and poison of his malice against us, and so forge what lies

and slanders, and libels he list, because he knoweth they shall be received as true.

Thus he accused Christ Jesus, our blessed Lord and Saviour, before Pontius Pilate, and caused divers false and untrue witnesses to come in against him. But if he were malicious only to wish our destruction, and not mighty to wreak his malice, we should have little cause to fear; but he is mighty, therefore he is termed a lion, the power of darkness, a great dragon, which drew to the earth the third part of the stars of heaven; that is, with earthly temptation to have overthrown them, which seemed to shine in the church of God as lamps and stars. Oh then how easy is our overthrow if the Lord did not hold us up; which shine not as stars in heaven, but creep like worms on earth.

3. Yet if he were but malicious and mighty, it were better with us; but he is fierce, and therefore called a roaring lion, who, laying wait for the blood of the godly, stirreth up bloodthirsty persecutors to make themselves drunk with the blood of saints; as most grievously he did from the time of John Baptist to the reign of Maxentius, the space of 294 years, slaying some by the sword, burning others with fire, hanging some on the gallows, drowning some in rivers, stabbing some with forks of iron, pressing others unto death with stones, devouring many thousands of the tender lambs of Christ's flock.

4. To this malice, might, and rage, is added his subtle policy, which he useth in circumvening the faithful. He doth not pitch his tents in any one place, but walketh about from place to place to spy out his best advantage, Job i.; in the night he soweth tares, and in the day he hindereth the growth thereof.

5. He proceedeth after further, and addeth to his policy industry, he considereth our natures and dispositions, and to what sins we do most incline; and thereunto he applieth himself. Sometimes by flattery, sometimes by fear, sometimes by feeding our humours, he subtilly enticeth us; sometimes by violence he goeth about to enforce us, sometimes by changing himself into an angel of light, he endeavoureth to betray our souls into his hands, and in whatsoever estate he findeth us, he thereby taketh occasion to lay siege to our souls.

Thus you see noted in a word the force of our adversary; examine now yourselves whether you have anything in yourselves, and you shall find nothing but weakness and corruption. It is God that giveth strength to the mighty, wisdom to the prudent, and knowledge to the understanding; he teacheth David's hand to fight, and his fingers to battle, he giveth strength to his arms to break a bow, even a bow of steel, Ps. cxliv.; wherefore let neither the wise man glory in his wisdom, nor the strong man in his strength; but let him that glorieth glory in the Lord.

Secondly, We are to seek unto God alone, because none is so present as he; for God, because he is Almighty, and with his power filleth both heaven and earth, is present always with them that fear him, and ready to succour them in distress. 'The Lord is near to all that call upon him in truth;' he heareth our groanings and sighs, and knoweth what things are necessary for us before we ask.

The third reason why we must seek unto God is, none is so able to help as he. But of this I shall have particular occasion to speak when I come to this point, *And pray unto the Almighty*.

The fourth reason why we must seek Christ alone is, because there is none so willing to help as he. It is a great courage to us to make suit, when we are persuaded of the willingness of him to whom we make suit; and I pray ye, who was ever more careful for our salvation, and more watchful over us than the Lord? Who ever put his trust in him, and was confounded? In this respect he is called a Father, because as the father tendereth his son, so the Lord doth all those that put their trust in him. Can there be any more willing to help us than Christ, whose whole head was sick, and whose heart was heavy for our sakes? yea, in whose body, from the sole of the foot to the crown of the head, was nothing but wounds, and swellings, and sores? But, alas, this was nothing to that he suffered for our sakes. He was compassed about with fear and horrors, till his sweat was drops of blood, and his bones bruised in the flesh; he was whipped, and scourged, and chastised with sorrows, till he cried out in the bitterness of his soul, 'O Lord, if it be possible, let this cup pass from me.' The heavy hand of God was so grievous upon him, that he bruised his very bones, and rent his reins asunder; he could find no health in his flesh, but was wounded, yea, wounded to the death, even the most bitter death upon the cross. His tender fingers were nailed to the cross; his face was wrinkled with weeping and wailing; his sides imbrued and gored with his own blood, spurting and gushing fresh from his ribs; the shadow of death was upon his eyes.

Oh what a grief could be like this, or what condemnation could be so heavy, sith there was no wickedness in his hands! sith he was the brightness of his Father's glory, and the Sun of righteousness that shined in the world, as to see his days at an end, to see such throbbing sighs and careful thoughts without cause of his, so deeply engraven in the tables of his breast! But was this all? No, my brethren; sith his excellency was such above all creatures that the world was not worthy to give him breath, it was a greater grief unto him, to see himself made a worm, and not a man, a shame of men, and contempt of the people; to see his life shut up in shame and reproaches, how could it but shake his bones out of joint, and make his heart melt in the midst of his bowels! Who was ever so full of woe, and brought so low into the dust of death? Upon whom did the malice of Satan ever get so great a conquest?

This, though it were exceeding, yet it was not all; no, it was but a taste of grief in comparison of the rest; behold therefore, if your weary eyes will suffer you to behold, the depth of all miseries yet behind; the sin that he hated, he must take upon his own body, and bear the wrath of his Father poured out against it. This is the fulness of all pains that compassed him round about, which no tongue is able to utter, or heart conceive; the anger of the Father burned in him, even to the bottom of hell, and deep sink of confusion; it wrapped him in the chains of eternal death; it crucified him, and threw him down into the bottomless pit of calamity, and made his soul by weeping and wailing to melt into these bitter tears trickling from his eyes: 'O God, my God, why hast thou forsaken me?'

Oh that my head were a well of water, and a fountain of tears, that I might weep day and night at the rememberance thereof; but lest I linger too long about one flower, while I have many to gather, I will conclude this one point in a word.

Sith Christ hath suffered these, and an infinite number more such like torments for our sakes, it is blasphemous once to dream or imagine any to be more willing to help us than he; nay, he is more ready to hear our prayers, than we to offer them unto him, insomuch as he complaineth by the prophet Isaiah, 'I have been found of them which sought me not; all the day long have I stretched out my hand unto a rebellious people, which walked in a way that was not good, even after their own imaginations,' Isa. lxv. And unto Jerusalem he saith, 'O Jerusalem, Jerusalem, how often would I have gathered thee together, as a hen gathereth the chickens, but ye would not,' Mat. xxiii.

Wherefore, to end this point: seek for knowledge as for a treasure, and for wisdom, as for the wedge of gold of Ophir. No mention shall be made in comparison of it, of coral, gabish, or that precious onyx, for 'wisdom is more precious than pearls.' But above all things, seek it where it may be found; and where is the place of understanding? Surely man knoweth not the path thereof. The deep saith, It is not in me; the sea saith, It is not in me; death and destruction say, We have heard the fame thereof with our ears; all creatures say, It is not with us: but God understandeth the way thereof; and unto man he saith, The fear of the Lord is the beginning of wisdom, and to depart from evil is understanding, Job. xxviii., Prov. ix.

The third circumstance is, *when* we must seek unto God; and holy David answereth, 'Early, even in a time when he may be found,' Ps. xxxii. Let us redeem the day which we have fore-slowed so many days, wherein we have so long hardened our hearts; let us take up this day, and make it the day of our repentance; let us make it a day of newness of life, as it is the first day of the new year; let even this moment be the last of a sinful life, and the first day to godliness; and as the wise man saith, 'Make no long tarrying to turn unto the Lord, and put not off from day to day; for suddenly shall the Lord's wrath break, and in thy security thou shalt be destroyed, and shalt perish in the time of vengeance,' Ecclus. v.

Art thou a magistrate, placed in high room and authority, and seated in the throne of dignity? Then use not this thy might to wrong and oppression, grind not the face of the poor, swell not with pride, despising his low estate. Sell not thy righteousness for silver, preferring the merchants of Babylon before the citizens of Jerusalem, Amos viii.

Art thou a private labouring man? Do thy duty truly, be subject, and live in dread to displease the good magistrate, 1 Peter iii.

Art thou old, and hast consumed the flower of thy youth in wantonness? Break off thy course, and frame thy life to sobriety; give the water no passage, no, not a little; for if it have never so little issue, it will overflow thee; and if thou do slack the reins never so little, thy sins will carry thee, like a wild horse, through brambles and bushes, and will leave no soundness in thy flesh; work this reformation in thyself betimes, even to-day, even this first day of the new year: 'If you will hear my voice, harden not your hearts.'

Art thou young, and dost begin to flourish like the young palm tree? Oh consider, that the only way to retain the blossoms of thy beauty, and to keep thy flower from withering, and thy life from fading away, it is to seek early unto God, and to apply thy mind to understanding, to prevent the morning watches, and to give thy body to be moistened of the morning dew. For beside the good hours, that are well employed in some good study and holy exercise, early rising bringeth health to thy body, and increaseth the number of thy days.

Seek therefore, and seek early, consecrate yourselves Nazarites unto the Lord, touch no unclean thing, give no provocation to the flesh. Strive with the cock in watchfulness, and rise with the chirping of the birds, Eccles. xii.; sacrifice your body a sweet smelling sacrifice unto the Lord. This sacrifice is like a sacrifice of fine flour ; it is like the fat taken from the peace-offering ; yea, it is better than any sacrifice, it is like the flower of roses in the spring of the year, and as the lilies in the springs of water, and as the branches of frankincense in the time of summer : And as a vessel of massy gold beset with rich precious stones, as a fair olive that is fruitful, and as the tree that groweth up to the clouds, Ecclus. xxxii., xlvii., l.

Having spoken of the search, it followeth that I speak of the manner how it is to be made. In prayer, by these words, *If thou pray unto the Almighty.*

I shewed you before the force of our adversary ; receive now a shield against his force, even the shield of prayer. He is not to be resisted by ringing of an hallowed bell, nor by sprinkling of holy water, nor by the relics of saints, nor by our own works and merits ; for these are weapons of his own making ; but by an earnest seeking to God, which search and seeking must be made by prayer, against which his poisoned venom taketh no effect.

It is his malice that accuseth ; prayer pleadeth thy case before God, and repelleth all his accusations ; for all the prophets do witness, that whatsoever we ask in prayer, if we believe, we shall receive it. Is it his rage and fury that should terrify us ? No; that prayer that strengthened Samson to rent a young lion, as one should have rent a kid, having nothing in his hand, shall smite and shut up the mouth of the lion. As for his policy in walking up and down, seeking to devour us, it cannot prevail. For 'the prayer of the faithful shall save them ; and the Lord shall raise them up, and if they have committed sin, it shall be forgiven them,' James v. 15 ; and after this conflict ended, they shall triumph for ever with Jesus Christ our Saviour. But in any case see you unite to your prayer knowledge, that you be not seduced to offer your petitions to strange gods, as saints, stocks, or stones. Then consent that we ask only in the name of Christ Jesus, not for any desert of our own ; for whosoever believeth in Christ shall have remission of sins, he shall not perish, but have life everlasting ; he 'shall not come into judgment, but shall pass from death to life.' Lastly, a confidence, which is a certain persuasion of God's mercy towards us. This is that prayer, of which the Lamb testifieth, that ' whatsoever we ask by prayer, it shall be given us by God the Father.' A thing, dearly beloved, so precious, that nothing is more accepted in heaven, nothing more grateful to God ; a service commanded of God himself, taught by Christ our Saviour, and frequented by the angels ; a thing of more force with God than any oration of the eloquent.

Hast thou not heard how the sun stood still in the firmament, and was not suffered to run his course ? Joshua and Hezekiah prayed, and the sun stood still, Joshua vi., 2 Kings xx. Hast thou not heard of the stopping of the lions' mouths ? Daniel prayed, and this prayer stopped the lions' greedy and devouring throats, Dan. vi. Hast thou not heard of the dividing of the Red Sea ? The Israelites prayed, and the waters of Jordan were dried up ; yea, the Israelites prayed, and the waters stood about them like to a wall, Exod. xiv. Hast thou not heard how the fiery furnace lost his heat ? The three children prayed, and the fire lost his heat, Dan. iii. Hast thou not heard how the heavens were opened and shut ? Elias prayed, and the heavens were shut up three years. Elias prayed, and the clouds poured down rain from heaven, 1 Kings xviii.

Oh sure fortress, more forcible than any engine, and stronger than the gates of hell ; and to conclude the sum and substance of all in few words, the only thing whereby mortal men have the clouds, and the stars, and the angels, and all the powers of heaven at commandment. For as Deborah sung in her song, ' They fought from heaven, even the stars in their courses fought against Sisera.' For all creatures have been subject to the prayers of the faithful to revenge the Lord's quarrel, to 'help the Lord, to help the Lord against the mighty.' Prayer hath ever been the cognisance, and the victory, and the triumph of the faithful, for as the soul giveth life to the body, so prayer giveth life to the soul.

Oh that I could engrave the love of it in your hearts, as with a diamond, and so instil your minds, that my words might be pricks to your consciences, and thereby give you occasion to pray often. It is a wonderful matter to be able to persuade men ; but if prayer be able to persuade the living God, oh how great is the force thereof, it goeth through the clouds, and ceaseth not till it come near, and will not depart until the Most High have respect thereunto. Oh that you would therefore pray often, and learn of

Christ (the most absolute pattern of our life) to pray continually. He prayed in his baptism, in the wilderness, in preaching, in working of miracles, in his passion on the mount, in the garden, in his last supper, in commending his spirit to God at all times and in all places, that he might leave unto us an example of the same. It followeth, *And pray to the Almighty.* To those three former reasons which I brought, why we must seek and pray to God alone, I added this as a fourth; because there is none so able to help us as the Lord. 'He that trusteth in the Lord shall be as mount Sion.' 'If God be on our side, who can be against us?' 'It is God that justifieth, who condemneth' 'The Lord destroyeth the counsel of the heathen, he maketh their devices to be of none effect.' Christ is the angel of great counsel, wisdom, and understanding, and there is no device against the Lord. The world notwithstanding, is come to that frame, that every man has got him a strange kind of belief. Some believe not the law, but the prophets; some be persuaded in the supremacy, but not in the sacrament; some in free-will, but not in merit; some in invocation on saints, but not in purgatory; some in pilgrimages and pardons, but not in images; some like the doctrine well enough, but not the preachers; the most believe little, yet many believe somewhat, few believe all; therefore to deal plainly, because plain dealing is best, you must not believe by the half; I mean you must not repose some trust in God, and some in saints, but all in the Lord. 'The gods of the Gentiles they have mouths and speak not, eyes and see not, ears and hear not,' Ps. cxv. 5. Then what can be looked for at their hands? But the Lord is strong and mighty, a merciful God, and therefore through the Scriptures he is called a rock, a fortress, a strong tower, a shield, a horn of salvation, a refuge, the Lord of hosts, with other such like appellations, that we might be assured that our help and deliverance cometh from the Lord.

Puttest thou any trust in man, whose breath is in his nostrils? Cursed is he that maketh man his strength, and flesh his arm. Surely Pharaoh, and all princes, are 'a broken staff, on which, if a man lean, it will strike into his hand and pierce it,' and lay him grovelling in the dust. 'It is better, therefore, to trust in the Lord, than to put any confidence in princes.' Thinkest thou, that angels, or saints, or images can help thee? Oh foolish and impious piety, to attribute more unto the angels than they dare arrogate unto themselves. The angel in the Revelation forbiddeth John to worship him, Rev. xix. As for the image, we read that to turn the glory of the incorruptible God into the similitude of a corruptible creature, is idolatry, Rom. i. Well may I then affirm with Moses, 'Cursed be the image and the image-maker,' Deut. xxvii. The conclusion therefore of this point is this, that we seek the Lord and his strength evermore, that we pray unto God in humility and sincerity, and in full assurance of faith continually, who without end is to be sought, because without end he is to be beloved.

The third thing contained in our duty is, what effect this seeking and praying ought to work in us, comprehended in these words, *If thou be pure and upright.* If the clouds be full, they will pour forth rain upon the earth, and impossible it is, that a man that seeketh after God, and prayeth unto the Almighty, should not bring forth the fruit of a good life ; for if the tree be good, the fruits cannot be bad, and if the head of the water be pure, it will send forth pure waters into the cisterns. Wherefore as good motions are stirred up by prayer, so must they be fostered by practice of life, according to that of the apostle, 'Quench not the Spirit, nor grieve the Holy One of God, by whom ye are sealed to the day of redemption,' 1 Thes. v.

He quencheth, dearly beloved, the Spirit, which being once lightened with the sparkles of faith, and felt God's motions in his heart, doth neglect to increase the one to a flame, and the other to good works in his life, but with the dog turneth to his vomits, and with the sow that was washed, to her wallowing again in the mire. Therefore, beloved, love and seek the Lord, pray to the Almighty, be pure and upright in conversation, fly from sin as from a serpent, for if thou come near, it will bite thee. The teeth thereof are as the teeth of a lion, to slay the souls of men, and all iniquity is as a two-edged sword, the wounds that it gives cannot be healed. I dare not stand as I would upon these points, fearing tediousness; wherefore let this suffice for the former general part, concerning the duty we owe unto God.

Now God's promises for the performance hereof, yield unto us most plentiful matter of doctrine and consolation. First, of his justice, that as he will suffer no sin unpunished, so he will suffer no good work unrewarded, but giveth to every several action his several hire, and just recompence of reward. Shall 'the hour come, in which all that are in their graves shall hear a voice, and come forth, they that have done well, to the resurrection of life ; they that have done evil, to the resurrection of condemnation'? Shall the Lord 'search Jerusalem with lanterns'? Shall all foul corners be swept, and all plaits and wrinkles be unfolded? Shall the grave, death, and hell give up all that is in them? And shall all dead, both small and great, stand before God, when the books are opened ? and shall every man have praise of God according unto his deserving ? Shall we then discern between the vessels of honour and of wrath, between sheep and goats, the just and unjust ? Finally, shall there be an infallible, general, and incorrupt judgment, wherein the book of all our offences shall be laid wide open ? Now God be merciful unto us ; be favourable, O Lord, be favourable. But to proceed ; it is thy nature, O Lord, to gather up the wheat, and burn the tares, to cut down all fruitless trees, and cast them into the fire, yea, into a fiery furnace, that never shall be quenched, into an utter darkness, where is weeping, wailing, and gnashing of teeth; then be favourable, O Lord, be favourable.

Doth not the Lord spare David, a king and a prophet, for murder ? Doth he not spare the Shechemites for adultery ? Nor Absalom for treason ? Nor Saul for tyranny ? Nor Eli for negligence ? Nor Ahab, Jeroboam, nor Jezebel for cruelty ? Nor Herod, Nebuchadnezzar, and Lucifer for pride ? Nor Pharaoh for incredulity ? Then be favourable, O Lord, be favourable unto us, in whom almost every one of these sins do dwell and remain. Did the Lord for corruption overflow the world with water ? Did he burn Sodom for her villany ? Did he cast Adam and Eve out of paradise for eating of the forbidden fruit ? Did he stone a poor wretch to death for gathering chips on the Sabbath day ? Then be favourable, O Lord, be favourable unto us. But doth not the Lord spare the cedar-tree for his height, nor the oak for his strength, nor the poplar for his smoothness, nor the laurel for his greenness ? No, verily, from the cedar that is in Lebanon, even to the hyssop that groweth out of the wall ; yea, 'every one that bringeth not forth good fruit is hewn down and cast into the fire ;' it is a righteous thing with God, to render vengeance to those that disobey him, and to destroy such as have forsaken the law, by everlasting perdition.

Behold, the Lord shall come in the great and latter day of judgment, when none shall escape his judgment-seat, with clouds shall he come, and every eye shall see him ; even they which pierced him through, shall also wail before him, being summoned all to appear most fearfully before his imperial throne of majesty ; then be favourable, O Lord, be favourable. Alas, with what eyes shall we miserable sinners behold him, so glorious, sitting in his royal kingdom, with all his mighty and holy angels, and whole number of saints, sounding with the voice of the archangel, and trumpet of God, causing the heavens to pass away with a noise, and the elements to melt like wax, and the earth to burn with the works thereof ?

Yea, with what eyes shall we behold him, when we see the sun darkened, the moon eclipsed, and the stars fall down from heaven? But, alas, when he taketh the furbished blade into his hand, when he is ready to throw the fiery thunderbolts of his wrath, when he summoneth before him the worm that never dieth, the fire that never shall be quenched, to revenge upon the wicked, into what a plight are they then driven? Then leave they off, be favourable, O Lord, be favourable, and say to the hills, O ye mountains, come and cover us; O ye waters, come and overwhelm us; woe, woe, woe, how great is this darkness! The godly on the other side are bathed in such streams of bliss, and advanced to such happiness, as neither tongue can utter, nor heart conceive.

The second thing we have to note in his promises, is his mercy, which exceedeth all his works. For God, though he hath given a curse of the law against sinners, yet seeing Christ for the penitent hath borne the curse, whereby his justice is not impaired, he is content to accept our weakness as our strength, to recompense our imperfection with reward of greatest perfection; and that which we can perform but in small part, he is content to accept as whole, not for any desert of ours, but in satisfaction of his Son, who paid with the seal of his own blood, the ransom for our sins, he hath cancelled the handwriting that was against us. Wherefore we are to pray unto God, that whensoever our sins shall come in question before him, that he would look upon Christ Jesus, the true looking-glass, in whom he shall find us most pure and innocent, and to shine most clearly in the righteousness which he hath given us by faith; so that we appear not in our own righteousness, but in the righteousness of the Lamb, who having taken away the sins of the world, and having made us as white as snow, though we were as red as crimson, saith, he will be merciful to our iniquities, and will remember our sins no more. Of him do all the prophets bear witness, that 'through his name all that believe shall receive remission of their sins.' Again, 'Drink ye all of this, for this is my blood which is shed for the remission of sins.' Christ gave himself for our sins, that he might deliver us from the curse of the law, even according to the will of the Father. Christ 'bare our sins in his own body on the tree, that we being delivered from sin, might live in righteousness, by whose stripes we are healed, for we were as sheep going astray, but are now returned to the shepherd and bishop of our souls.' It is no more but believe and be saved; believe and receive remission; believe, and lay off thine own righteousness, and invest thyself with the righteousness of the unspotted Lamb.

David was young, and after was old, yet in all his days he never saw the righteous forsaken. Sometimes he scourgeth his children, but like a loving father, he layeth no more upon them than they are able to bear ; for he afflicteth them for his own justice, because they are sinners ; for his wisdom, to exercise their faith ; for his mercy, to cause them to repent ; but this is the end of all, he helpeth them in their distresses, he revengeth himself upon his enemies, and giveth to his people rest and quietness. Oh that we would therefore praise the Lord, and forget not all other his singular benefits. O that we would confess, that his mercy endureth for ever.

The third thing to note in his promises, is his bountiful kindness, in requiring so small a thing, with so great and liberal blessings ; and bindeth himself by obligation, as it were, that as sure as we perform the one, so he will not fail to accomplish the other.

The fourth is, his patience and longsuffering, which is not slackness, as some men account slackness ; but is patience, because willingly he would have no man to perish, but gladly would have all men come to repentance. He is content to stay our leisure, till we seek and pray unto him, and never smiteth till there be no hope of redress.

The fifth is, his love, in that he is content to stir us up to holy exercises and purity of life, and to allure us with fair promises of aid, and prosperous increase of all his blessings in this world. The particular examination of these blessings would require a larger discourse than, fearing tediousness, I dare presume to trouble you withal ; wherefore, a word of each, and so I end.

Touching the first, where it is said, *God will awake up unto thee*, it is a greater benefit than the words import ; for it signifieth not only that he will hear thee, but that he will also do what thou desirest, and satisfy thy request. As long as the sinner sleepeth, the Lord is said to be asleep ; but as soon as the sinner awaketh from sin, 'God will arise,' saith David, 'and his enemies shall be scattered ; and they that hate him shall fly before him : as the smoke vanisheth before the wind, and as the wax melteth before the fire, even so shall the wicked perish at the presence of God,' Ps. lxviii. Wherefore, as St Paul exhorted the Ephesians, so I exhort you, 'Awake, thou that sleepest, stand up from the dead, and Christ shall give thee light,' Eph. v. 14 ; awake unto God, and God will awake unto thee, and Christ, even the Son of God, the bright morning Star, shall give thee the light of life.

In the second, he promiseth abundance of worldly blessings in recompence of prayer; for it is said, *He will make the habitation of thy righteousness prosperous,* that is, the Lord will make peace within thy walls, and prosperity within thy palaces; he will command his blessings to be with thee in thy store-house, and in all thou settest thy hand unto; he will open unto thee his good treasure, even the heavens, to give rain on thy land in due season. 'Thou shalt lay up gold as the dust, and the gold of Ophir as the flint of the river; thou shalt wash thy paths with butter, and thy rocks shall pour out rivers of oil; thou shalt call salvation thy wall, and praise shall be in thy gates. Lo, thus shall the man be blessed that feareth God.'

Lastly, for being pure and upright, he will make thy latter end greatly increase, and, that thou mayest the less mistrust his promises, he will do it though thy beginning be but small.

Here, brethren, ye see what a sea of matter is offered me, whereunto, if I would commit myself, I might discourse unto you what strange events, by God's providence, have happened in the world, what great kings and potentates have been plucked down from their thrones, and what contemptible persons in the eyes of the world have been advanced to their rooms: how Mordecai, a stranger, was exalted into Haman's place, Esther viii.; how Joseph and Daniel, the one a bondman in Egypt, the other a captive in Babylon, were made princes in those kingdoms, Gen. xli., Dan. vi. But because I will not overmuch transgress the bounds of modesty, or hold you longer than in this place I have been accustomed, only remember what the prophet saith, 'He raiseth the needy out of the dust, and lifteth the poor out of the mire, that he might set him with the princes, even with princes of the world,' Ps. cxiii. 5.

Remember the example of David, whom the Lord chose and took from the ewes great with young, that he might feed his people in Jacob, and his inheritance in Israel, Ps. lxxviii. Remember the example of Job, how the Lord turned the captivity of Job, as the rivers of the south; how he blessed the last days of Job more than the first; how he gave him sheep, and camels, and oxen, and she-asses in more abundance than he had before; how he increased him with sons and daughters, even to the fourth generation, so that he died being old and full of days, Job xlii. Remember even our own estate, for whom the Lord hath done great things already; as created us, and redeemed us, and sanctified us, and not long since delivered us from the gaping jaws of those that sought to suck our blood. Upon some he hath bestowed humility, whereby their minds are adorned with virtue; honour upon others, whereby their persons are invested with majesty; upon others comeliness, whereby the other two are graced; upon others orchards, which they planted not, at least into which they gave no increase; upon others, increase of virtuous children, whereby their posterity is preserved; upon others, the free passage of his word, which a long time had been obscured by ignorance, the mother of devotion, as the shavelings call it, but under[1] a stepdame of destruction, as we perceive it; and though he bestow but some one or two of his blessings upon us, yet how much are we bound for these blessings to sing praise, and honour, and glory, unto him that sitteth upon the throne, and unto the Lamb for ever. But upon whom he hath bestowed all these blessings, oh how strictly by good cause are they bound to magnify the Lord, and to rejoice in God their Saviour. Examine then your own consciences, I beseech you, whether God hath bestowed all these blessings upon you, or no; and if he have, oh what great cause have you to come before his face with praise, to sing loud unto him with psalms, to worship and to fall down before him, to give unto the Lord the glory of his name, to bring an offering of thanksgiving, and to enter into his courts with praise. And yet who knoweth whether the Lord hath greater blessings for you in store? Ye may be sure he will pull down the mighty from their seat, and exalt the humble and meek. Surely the Lord doth use virtue as a means to bring us to honour, and whosoever you shall see endued with the virtues of this text, I mean with seeking unto God with prayer and purity of life, ye may be sure there is a blessing reserved for him of the Lord, yea, such a blessing, as though his beginning be but small, yet his latter end shall greatly increase.

God increase the love of these things in our hearts, and make us worthy of Christ's blessings, which he hath plentifully in store for us; that after he hath heaped temporal blessings upon us, he will give us the blessing of all blessings, even the life of the world to come.

[1] Qu. 'rather'?—ED.

MARY'S CHOICE.

MARY'S CHOICE.

Now it came to pass, as they went, that he entered into a certain town: and a certain woman, named Martha, received him into her house. Now she had a sister called Mary, which also sat at Jesus' feet, and heard his preaching. But Martha was cumbered about much serving, and came to him, and said, Master, dost thou not care that my sister hath left me to serve alone? bid her therefore that she help me. And Jesus answered and said unto her, Martha, Martha, thou carest and art troubled about many things. But one thing is needful; Mary hath chosen the good part, which shall not be taken away from her.—LUKE X. 38–42.

As Christ had shewed himself loving unto Lazarus and his sisters, in raising him from the death of the body, and then from the death of the soul, John xi.; so do they here shew their thankful minds to Christ again, the one by receiving him into her house, and the other by entertaining him into her heart. As he was God, he was received of Mary; as he was man, he was received of Martha. They both desired to entertain our Saviour, as Jacob and Esau desired to please their aged father, Gen. xxvii.; but Mary made choice of the better part, and was preferred before her sister, as Jacob sped soonest of most dainty venison, and prevented his brother of the blessing. And although the care of Martha in entertaining of Christ be not to be misliked, yet Mary's diligence in hearing his doctrine, is of purpose preferred, to teach us, that it is much better with Mary to study in the word, and first to seek the kingdom of God, than with Martha to labour in the world, and to neglect that heavenly kingdom. And yet notwithstanding, such is the corruption of this rusty age, that our greatest care is to provide for this present life, as the rich man, Luke xii., enlarged his barns, wherein to put his store for many years; but we never or very late remember to provide for the life to come, like that other rich man, Luke xvi., that never thought of heaven, till he was tormented in the flames of hell.

In the eleventh of John, Christ is said to love the whole family, and here he is said to come unto them; for whom he loveth, he cannot choose but visit, like the friends of Job, that came to comfort him in his great adversity, Job ii.; yea, and the greater love he beareth unto any, the oftener he will resort unto them, yea, he will come and dwell with them, John xiv. 23; like Jacob, that came down into Egypt, to his beloved son Joseph, and dwelt in Goshen, Gen. xlv. But Christ is yet more kind than Jacob was, for he came not till he was sent for with horses and chariots, but Christ came of his own accord to this beloved family.

Thus doth he always prevent us with his blessings: before he was desired, he came into the world; he called his apostles before they came to him; and before he was requested, he came unto this noble house. Oh happy house, that entertained such a guest! but thrice happy inhabitants, to whom such a guest would vouchsafe to come! When he came to the swinish Gadarenes, they desired him to depart out of their coasts, preferring their swine above their Saviour, Luke viii.; but this godly family received him into their houses, preferring their God before their gold, and the health of souls before their worldly wealth. They received him into their house, who had not a house wherein to put his head, Mat. viii. 19, wherein their hospitality is commended, and shall certainly be rewarded at the dreadful day; for with this and such like works of mercy, the Lord shall answer the sentence of judgment, which is to be denounced against the wicked, that never exercised those works of mercy.

Let us learn by their example to be harbourers, and given to hospitality, which is so often commended unto us in the Scripture, and shall be so richly rewarded at the last day. Those godly fathers, Abraham and Lot, entertained angels in the habit of strangers, Gen. xviii. and xix.; so we may duly entertain Christ Jesus in the habit of a poor man, of a blind man, or of a lame man; and whatsoever is done to any of these that are his members, he accounteth and accepteth as done unto himself.

Now, as the virtue of hospitality is commendable in all sorts of men, so is it more especially commended to the ministers, who are expressly commanded by the apostle amongst other things, to be given to hospitality, 1 Tim. iii. 2. Unto the Levites in time of the law, the Lord appointed cities of refuge, Num. xxxv., to signify that the minister's house should be the poor man's harbour, and his store their treasure; but the true ministers of our days have no cities of refuge for others, for they have none for themselves; they have not wherewith to relieve the wants of others, for they have not to relieve their own.

When Martha had thus entertained Christ, as he was man, into her house, Mary began to entertain him, as he was God, into her heart; she sat at his feet to hear his preaching; for no sooner was Christ come into the house, but that he took occasion to teach and to instruct the family; and instead of bodily food, which they bestowed upon him, to give unto them the food of the soul. Thus doth he always shew himself a thankful guest, into what house soever he entereth; he leaveth better things behind him than he findeth. He loves not to be in Zaccheus's debt for his dinner, for instead thereof he bringeth salvation to his house, Luke xix.; neither doth he leave his supper unpaid for here, for instead thereof he bestoweth upon them an heavenly sermon. This should be the exercise of faithful ministers, when they are invited to great feasts, that as they are called the salt of the earth, Mat. v. 13, which serveth to season the meats, to make them savoury, and preserve them from putrefaction, so they should season the table-talk with some godly conference, to minister grace unto the hearers, Eph. iv. 29.

These sisters were godly women, and both earnest favourers of Jesus Christ, and yet in the manner of their devotion there is such difference, that the worldly affection of the one may in some sort be misliked, in respect of the godly exercise and practice of the other. Martha is sore encumbered with much serving, where a little service had been sufficient; but Mary is attentive to hear the word of God, which never can be heard sufficiently.

Mary sitteth to hear the word, as Christ used to sit when he preached the word, Mat. v., Luke iv., John viii., to shew that the word is to be preached and heard with a quiet mind. In a still night every voice is heard, and when the body is quiet, the mind most commonly is quiet also. But Martha is troubled with other affairs, and therefore unfit to hear the word, as the ground that is surcharged with stones, or overgrown with weeds and thorns, is unfit to receive the seed, or yield any fruit to him that tilleth it. As often therefore as we come to hear the word of God, we must not come with distracted minds, we must not trouble ourselves with the cares of this life, which, as our Saviour said, are thorns to choke the word, and to make it unfruitful. For Moses was unfit to talk with God, till he had put off his shoes, Exod. iii., and the blind man unfit to come to Christ, till he had thrown away his cloak, Mat. x.; so we must think ourselves unfit to hear the word, and unapt for every heavenly exercise, till we have put off our shoes, that is, our worldly cogitations and affections, and till we have cast away our cloak, that is, all lets and impediments which might hinder us from profiting in our profession.

When our minds are quiet, we are fit to deal with heavenly matters ; therefore the doctors conferred sitting in the temple, and God delighteth to deal with us when we are most private ; he appeareth to Abraham sitting in the door of his tent, Gen. xviii. The Holy Ghost came down upon the apostles, and filled all the house where they were sitting, Acts ii. The eunuch, sitting in his chariot, was called and converted by Philip's preaching, Acts viii.

Mary sat at Jesus' feet, yet sat she not sleeping, as many sit at the preacher's feet, but she sat at Christ his feet, and heard his word ; as Paul was brought up at the feet of Gamaliel, and was perfectly instructed in the law of the fathers, Acts xxii.

Her humility is commended, in that she sat at Jesus' feet, to shew that the word is to be heard with all humility ; her diligence and earnestness appeareth in that she would not depart to help her sister, to signify that the hearing of the word must be preferred before all worldly businesses.

Her diligence and humility serveth to condemn our negligence and contempt of Christ and his word ; we do not sit at Christ his feet ; nay, we rather set Christ at our feet, when we are so negligent in hearing his word.

We are as slow to come to the church as the raven was to come to the ark, Gen. viii.; and as loath to spend any time in the service of God as Pharaoh was loath to let the Israelites go to serve the Lord, Exod. viii. 32. If a commodity were to be seen, whereout some profit might arise, how careful would we be to procure it ! what pains would we take to get it ! Absalom was not more desirous of a kingdom, 2 Sam. xv., than the rich men of our time are desirous of golden gain. But if it be a matter of cost or trouble, if they cannot hear the word preached without some hindrance to their worldly business, and some extraordinary charge to their purse, then, like the Gadarenes, Luke viii., they are content to take their leave of Christ and his word, and had rather lose that heavenly pearl, Mat. xiii. 47, than they would part from their worldly pelf.

Thus in Christ we have the patience of a good pastor, and in Mary the pattern of a good hearer. Let ministers learn by his example to take all occasions to preach the word, to be instant in season and out of season, 2 Tim. iv. 2 ; and let Christians learn by her example, first, to seek the kingdom of God and his righteousness, and then to provide for the things of this life, Mat. vi.

While Mary was careful for the food of the soul, Martha was curious to provide food for the body ; her greatest care was to entertain Christ, and to make him good cheer, to testify her thankful mind unto him that had done so great things for them : he had raised her brother Lazarus from death to life ; therefore he was worthy to be well entertained.

If Elias deserved to be well dealt withal at the hand of his hostess, whose son he had restored to life, 1 Kings xvii. ; or Elisha deserved such entertainment for her son's reviving, 2 Kings iv., then surely our Saviour Christ is worthy to be welcome hither, where he had raised Lazarus out of his grave, wherein he had lain by the space of four days before, John xi.

It was well done therefore of Martha to shew her thankful mind unto Christ, but it was not well done *at that time* to shew herself thankful *in that manner;* it was then time to hear the word, for at that time Christ preached the word ; it was no time for her to spend that time in other affairs, and to neglect the greatest affairs, the means of her own salvation.

It was not unlawful for Martha to labour on, more than it was unlawful for Peter to sleep, Mat. xxv.; but when Christ was preaching, it was no time for her to be so busy in serving, no more than it was time for Peter to sleep when Christ willed him so earnestly to watch and pray, When Christ preached out of Simon's ship to the people that stood upon the shore, Luke v., it was no time for Peter to play the fisherman. But when Christ had left speaking, and commanded him to launch into the deep, then it was time for Peter to let down the net.

There is a time wherein we ought to labour in our vocation, and a time wherein we ought to hear the word ; and as we may not utterly neglect our lawful callings to follow sermons, so must not we bestow the Sabbath, which is consecrated to the service of God, in following the works of our vocation. All things have their appointed time, saith the wise man, Eccles. iii., and everything is seemly in his convenient season; but when things are done pre-posterously and out of order, there followeth confusion.

Although Martha did not hear Christ, yet did she labour for Christ; many in our days will neither labour for Christ, nor hear of Christ; but as the Israelites were weary of their journey in the wilderness, and loathed that heavenly manna, Num. xxi., so these men are weary of every godly exercise, and are soon cloyed with the word of God.

The five foolish virgins wasted their oil to no purpose, and, while they went to buy, were excluded the marriage, Mat. xxv.; and these foolish men spend this time of grace vainly and wantonly, as though after this life there were no time of justice and vengeance to be feared. The day serveth for their pride and profit, the night is spent in sport and pleasure, and no time is left to hear the word. When we are praying, they are playing, Gen. vi.; when we are preaching, they are eating and drinking, like the old world, that ate and drank, married wives, and gave in marriage, while Noah was preparing the ark for the saving of his household, Heb. xi. And as Baal's priests wounded themselves to serve their idols, 1 Kings xviii., so these men take dangerous courses, and strangely trouble themselves to serve the devil.

Now Martha findeth herself aggrieved, and begins to envy her sister's exercise, as Joseph's brethren envied him for his dreams, Gen. xxxvii.; and the sons of Jesse, that disdained their brother David for his forwardness in the combat with Goliath, 1 Sam. xvii.

These two sisters, that in other things agreed so well together, in this do differ so much that Christ must have the hearing of the matter, and decide the controversy; Martha playeth the plaintiff, and accuseth her sister. Mary, the defendant, answereth by her advocate; and Christ himself, that took upon him the office of an advocate, is become the judge, and giveth sentence on Mary's side. Martha complaineth of her sister's slothfulness, and seemeth, after a sort, to blame our Saviour for winking at it, requiring him to see the matter redressed speedily. But Christ reproveth Martha's curiosity, and then excuseth, yea, and commendeth, Mary's care.

In Martha it appeareth how willing we are to please ourselves in our own conceits, and how ready to conceive amiss of others' doings; yea, sometimes to prefer our own defects before the perfections of other men. If David chasten his soul with fasting, it shall be turned to his reproof, Ps. lxix. If he put on sackcloth to testify his contrition, they jest at him, and the drunkards make songs of him. If John Baptist be temperate in his apparel and diet, they will say he hath a devil, Luke vii. 33. If Paul answer discreetly for himself, he shall be charged to be mad with overmuch learning, Acts xxvi. ; yea, if our Saviour Christ himself frequent the company of sinners, to reclaim them from sin, they will not stick to call him a friend and companion of publicans and sinners, Luke vii. 34. Amongst us, if there be any that be more forward in religion than the rest, and more diligent to hear the word, as Mary was, there shall not want some or other to censure them at their pleasure, yea, to find fault, and condemn them for so doing ; yet are not the godly to be discouraged herewith, or to desist from their godly exercises ; for as the Lord answered for Mary, when she held her peace, so the Lord will defend their cause, and take their part against their adversaries. The Lord cannot abide to hear his servants ill spoken of, but is always ready to maintain their right, and to answer for them. He will not suffer Laban to speak an ill word to his servant Jacob, Gen. xxxi. 24 ; and if Aaron and Miriam murmur against Moses, the Lord will punish it with leprosy, Num. xii. What a comfortable thing is this to the godly, that the King of kings will take their parts, and will not suffer them to sustain any wrong ! He is a most sure and trusty friend, that will not abide his friends to be back-bited or ill-spoken of, but either he will answer in their defence, or he will find some means to stop their mouths, and restrain the slanderous tongues of their enemies, as sometime he stopped Balaam's passage, when he went to curse God's people, Num. xxii., and caused the dumb beast to speak and reprove the madness of the prophet, rather than he would have his people to be cursed, 2 Peter i. 5.

The repetition of Martha's name argueth the vehemency and earnestness of this admonition. The Lord is fain to be very earnest and importunate with us, before he can reclaim us. So when God spake unto Abraham, he called him twice by name ; Christ called Peter thrice by name, John xxi., to cause him to make his threefold confession, to make amends for his threefold denial. And when the Lord spake unto Samuel, he called him four several times by name before he answered, for such is the great mercy of God, that he is content to admonish us often of our duty ; and such is the dulness and perverseness of our crooked nature, that we cannot be gained by the first admonition ; but the Lord must call us often and earnestly, before we will hearken unto him.

There are two things in the speech of Christ to be observed : the first is, his modest reprehension of Martha's immoderate care ; the other is, his friendly defence of Mary's choice. Though Martha was very careful to entertain Christ in the best manner, yet if he perceive anything in her worthy reprehension, he will not stick to tell her of it ; he will not soothe her in her saying, nor smoothe her in her own conceit, for all the trouble and cost that she bestows upon him.   If we be often invited to some man's table, and kindly entertained, it would be unkindly taken if we should find fault with any disorder ; but forasmuch as all Christ his actions are the instructions of Christians, therefore every Christian, but especially preachers, whom it more specially concerneth, must learn by this example how to behave themselves, when they are invited to great feasts, namely, speak their conscience freely when they see a fault.   The best requital that we can make for our good cheer, is to give good counsel and wholesome admonitions to them that invite us.   When Christ dined with the pharisee, Luke xi., and was misliked for not washing before dinner, he took occasion to reprove their hypocrisy, their outward show of holiness, which was the sin of the pharisees ; and at another time he noteth them for pressing to the chief places at banquets, and sheweth what modesty is to be observed in sitting down to meat, and what guests should be bidden to our table, Luke xiv.   So should preachers behave themselves towards those that invite them to great feasts, when they see perhaps some fault or disorder, either in the master of the house, or in some other of the guests, to say unto them thus, or otherwise as the case requireth, I will warn you of one thing that will do you good, that you would leave your usury and extortion, your covetousness and oppression, that you would leave your swearing and blaspheming the name of of God, that you would forbear to profane the Lord's Sabbath, that you would leave your pride and excess in your diet and apparel, that you would forbear to speak ill of any behind their backs, or to bear any malice or hatred to any of your neighbours.

These are the faults which are easy to be espied almost in every place, and these are the faults which the faithful minister of Christ Jesus should not leave unreproved, wheresoever he cometh.   But as Elias told Ahab of his idolatry, though he were his king, 1 Kings xviii., and John Baptist told Herod of his adultery, though he did many things for him, and heard him gladly, Mark vi. 23; so should the preacher reprove the people for their notorious offences, notwithstanding some favours and courtesies received from them.   If Christ had cause to find fault with Martha for her too much diligence in his entertainment, it seems he was not curious in his diet, but would have been content with simple cates ; he was no delicate or dainty guest ; he did not affect or delight in sumptuous banquets, or costly fare; he rather required a religious heart, a constant faith, a willing mind to hear the word, with an earnest care to live thereafter. These are the things wherein the Lord delighteth; these are the junkets which he desireth, and which he preferreth before all earthly cheer.

Thus is Martha reprehended for her curiosity; now let us see how Mary is excused, and commended for her godly care. One thing is necessary, saith Christ; and what is that one thing? Even to hear the word preached, which is the power of God to salvation, to every one that believeth. A man may better want all things than that one needful thing; and yet we desire all other things, and neglect that one thing, which is so needful.

This one thing hath Mary chosen, and therefore hath chosen the better part. Martha's part is good, because it provideth for this present life; but Mary's part is better, because it leadeth to eternal life. It is good to be occupied about our calling, to get our living; but it is better to be occupied in hearing the word, which is able to save our souls. As the head and the foot are both needful in the body, so Mary and Martha are both needful in a commonwealth; man hath two vocations, the one earthly by his labour, the other heavenly by his prayer. There is the active life, which consisteth in practising the affairs of this life, wherein man sheweth himself to be like himself; and there is the contemplative life, which consisteth in the meditation of divine and heavenly things, wherein man sheweth himself to be like the angels; for they which labour in their temporal vocations, do live like men; but they which labour in spiritual matters, live like angels. When they hear the word, God speaketh unto them; when they pray, they speak unto God; so that there is a continual conference between God and them, because they are continually exercised in hearing and praying.

Christ loved Martha for her hospitality, as Isaac loved Esau for his venison. So did he love Mary for diligence in hearing his word, as Rebekah loved Jacob for hearkening to her voice. A nurse which hath her breast full of milk, doth love the child that sucks it from her; and Christ which hath his breast full of heavenly milk, is glad when he hath children to suck the same; let us therefore, as the apostle willeth us, 1 Pet. ii. 12, 'laying aside all maliciousness, and all guile, and dissimulation, and envy, and all evil speaking, as new born babes, desire the sincere milk of the word, that we may grow thereby,' to be perfect men in Christ Jesus. Let us breathe after the fountain of the living water, which springeth up into eternal life; and as the fainty hart desireth the water-brook to quench his thirst, Ps. xlii. 1. And forasmuch as many things are so trouble-some, and one thing is so needful, let us seek that one needful thing, the end of all things, even to fear God and keep his commandments, Eccles. xii. 13, which we learn by hearing the word of God, whereby faith, without the which it is impossible to please God, Heb. i. 6, is begotten and nourished in the hearts of men, Rom. x. 17.

This is that good part which Mary hath chosen, by so much better than her sister's choice, because it concerneth a better life, and hath the fruition of this present life, 1 Tim. iv. 8. Mary hath a double portion, she heard the word and ate of the meat which her sister dressed; for godliness hath the promise of this life, and of the life to come. As for all other things, whether they be honours, pro-motions, pleasures, and what not, they serve only for the mainte-nance of this present life, which is so short and subject to mutability; but the word of God is the food of the soul, the bread of life, that immortal seed which bringeth forth fruit unto eternal life, 1 Peter i. 13. Let the word of God therefore be precious unto us, because it is so permanent; for heaven and earth must pass, but the word of God endureth for ever, Luke xxi. 33, 1 Pet. i. 25. If we make choice of anything beside, it must be taken from us, or we shall be taken from it; but if we make choice of this one thing, it shall never be taken from us, neither in this world, nor in the world to come. The Lord grant that we be not only hearers, but doers of the word, James i. 22; that it may be truly said of us, as Christ said of his disciples that heard his preaching, 'Behold my brother, my sister and mother,' Mat. xii. 50; or as he answered the woman that com-mended his carnal kindred, 'Blessed are they that hear the word of God, and keep the same,' Luke xi.

GOD'S ARROW AGAINST ATHEISM AND IRRELIGION.

THE EPISTLE DEDICATORY.[1]

To the Right Worshipful, Virtuous and Godly Lady Katherine Hayward, Wife to Sir Rowland Hayward, the grave Father and Ancient Alderman of the famous City of London, John Danter, wisheth health, with increase of authority.

The gardener (right virtuous and godly lady) walking in the prime of summer, in a fragrant and odoriferous garden, where grows all sorts of sweet flowers, commonly gathereth the pleasant rose to gratify his master: so I (right worshipful) having come to my hand many excellent works to be published abroad the world, have from amongst them all chosen this book, entitled, *God's Arrow against Atheists*, as the purest rose for your ladyship to delight in: hoping upon this favour, that you will be the sweet patroness of this my poor good will, and to shadow it under the wings of your clemency from the bitter storms of all heretical schismatics. In so doing, my mind will be fully satisfied, that long hath waited the time, to shew my bounden duty to the grave fathers and ancient governors of this famous city of London, but especially to the right worshipful Sir Rowland Hayward, your reverend husband, who thrice hath been lieutenant under Her Majesty, and borne the chiefest office in the city, to the preservation of London's charter; and you, sweet lady, his renowned wife, whose virtuous mind hath ever yet been willing to prefer scholars

---

[1] This dedication has been kindly brought under our notice by the Rev. J. Knight Jennings, of Wellington House, Weston-super-Mare. It was prefixed to the first edition of the 'Arrow,' printed at London, 1593; but not, so far as we have been able to learn, reproduced in any subsequent edition. It is evident that it was unknown to Fuller, else he would not have fallen into the mistake of supposing that Smith lived till about 1600, since it speaks of his death as having occurred before the date of its issue in 1593. The copy from which we take it was lately presented by Mr Jennings to the British Museum.—ED.

to the setting forth of God's truth, and to beautify the true endeavours of us citizens. I therefore, still expecting your wonted and favorable liking, that you will spend away some part of winter's weary nights and summer's pleasant evenings in perusing over this worthy book, made by that famous learned man Master Henry Smith, before he departed this life, wherein is discoursed, the vain heresies of sundry religions now used in England, to the great hurt of this flourishing commonwealth: In so doing I have my desire, wishing you the increase of all dignity in this world, and in the world to come everlasting happiness. Amen.

　　Yours in all humble and dutiful service to his poor power,

　　　　　　　　　　　　　　　　　JOHN DANTER, Printer.

GOD'S ARROW AGAINST ATHEISM AND IRRELIGION.

CHAPTER I.

That there is a God, and that he ought to be worshipped.

ATHEISM and irreligion was ever odious even among the heathen themselves, insomuch as that Protagoras, for that he doubted whether there were any God or no, was by the Athenians banished out of their country. Diagoras was such a notorious infidel, that he held there was no God; him, and all such like atheists, the very heathens have abhorred and detested, as being more like rude beasts than reasonable men. For Cicero, the heathen philosopher, doth condemn them all; and further saith,[1] 'There was never any nation so savage, or people so barbarous, but always confessed that there was a God; whereunto they were led even by the light of nature, and natural instinct. For the very same is confirmed by the common use of all heathens, in lifting up their eyes and hands to heaven, in any sudden distress that cometh upon them.[2] Yea, by experience of all ages it hath been proved that atheists themselves, that is, such as in their health and prosperity, for more liberty of sinning, would strive against the being of a God, when they came to die or fall into great misery, they of all others would shew themselves most fearful of this God, as Seneca himself declareth;[3] insomuch as Zeno the philosopher was wont to say, that it seemed to him a more substantial proof of this matter, to hear an atheist at his dying day preach God, when he asked God and all the world forgiveness, than to hear all the philosophers in the world to dispute the point. For that at this instant of death and misery, it is like that such do speak in

[1] Cicero, de natura Deor.   [2] Tertul. in Apolog.   [3] Seneca, lib. i. de Ira.

earnest and sobriety of spirit, who before in their wantonness impugned God. It is remembered of Caius Caligula, that wicked and incestuous emperor, that he was a notable scorner and contemner of God, and made no reckoning of any other to be God but himself;[1] yet this abominable and wicked atheist, as God let him not unpunished, for by his just judgment he was slain by some of his own officers; so whilst he lived, he was wont, as the historiographers report of him, at the terrible thundering and lightning, not only to cover his head, but also to get himself under his bed, and there to hide himself for fear. Whence, I pray you, came this fear upon him; but that his own conscience did tell him, howsoever in words perchance he would not affirm so much, that there was a God in heaven, able to quail and cast down his pride and all the emperors of the world, if he listed; whose thunderbolts were so terrible as that justly by his own example he shewed, he was to be feared of all the world? And hereof it is that some say, that God is called *Deus*, of the Greek word, *Theos*, which signifieth *fear*, because the fear of him is planted and ingrafted in the very natures and conscience of all reasonable creatures, yea, even in the conscience of the greatest contemners and rankest atheists of the world, who say what they list, and do what they list, yet shall they never be able to root out this impression, namely, that there is a God, whose fear is engraven in the hearts of all men.

And whence, I pray you, cometh shame in men after an offence committed? Or why should men, by natural instinct, put a difference between virtue and vice, good and evil, if there were not a God, who, because he loved the one, and hated the other, hath written that difference in every man's heart? Therefore conclude, that every man's knowledge, conscience, and feeling, is instead of a thousand witnesses to convince him, whosoever he be, that there is a God which is to be feared, which hateth iniquity and wicked ways, and which in time of trouble and deep distress is to be sought unto for refuge and relief, as the acts of the very heathen themselves do plainly demonstrate.

2. Moreover, as God is to be felt sensibly in every man's conscience, so is he to be seen visibly, if I may so speak, in the creation of the world, and of all things therein contained; for that this world had a beginning, all the excellent philosophers that ever were, have agreed, except Aristotle for a time, who held a fancy, that this world had no beginning, but was from all eternity;[2] but at last in his old age, he confessed and held the contrary, in his book

---

[1] Sueton. in Cal. i. 51, Dion. in Caligula.   [2] Vide Plutarch. *de placit. philos.*

De Mundo,[1] which he wrote to king Alexander (which book Justin Martyr esteemed greatly,[2] and called it the epitome of all Aristotle's true philosophy). This then being so, that the world had a beginning, it must needs follow, that it had an efficient cause or maker thereof. I demand, then, who it was that made it ? If you say it made itself, it is absurd ; for how could it make itself before itself was made, and when it had no being at all ? If you say that something within the world made the world, that is, that some one part of the world made the whole, that is more absurd ; for it is as much as if a man should say that the finger (and this before it was a finger or part of the body) did make the whole body. Wherefore it may be convinced by force of this argument (which is plainly demonstrative), that a greater and more excellent thing than is the whole world put together, yea, that something which was before heaven and earth were made, was and must needs be the maker and framer of this world ; and this can be nothing else but God, the creator of all things, who was before all his creatures, and is termed in the sacred writings, ' Alpha and Omega, the first and the last,' for that he only was without beginning himself, and shall be and remain without ending. For he is eternal, being the *primus motor*, and the only Almighty Creator of all things. So true it is which Paul the apostle doth testify, when he saith, that ' the invisible things of God (that is, his eternal power and divine essence), are seen perfectly in the creation of the world, being perceived by his works which he hath made,' Rom. i. 20. If, therefore, men would but cast up their eyes to heaven, and from thence look down again upon the earth, and so behold the excellent beauty and building of this world, they cannot be so sottish or dull conceited, but they must know there was and is a God, which was the maker of them ; and be moved in some sort to glorify so incomparable and excellent a Creator. Yea, the poets and others have affirmed of God, that he is *Pater hominum*, the Father of men, to shew that men have their original and creation from him ; so that if we should draw our eyes from the beholding of the great world, and consider but man (who for his beauty and excellency is called in Greek *Microcosmos*, the little world), still we shall be enforced to acknowledge God the author of us, the Father and Creator of us. So true is that which Paul the apostle noteth out of the poet Aratus, which saith that *ejus progenies sumus*, we are the issue or offspring of

---

[1] Aristot. lib. viii. de Mundo, et vide Plot. lib. de Mundo.
[2] Justin in Apol.

God, Acts xvii. 29. And as true it is, which he further saith in that place, that 'in him we live, move, and have our being.' And therefore we owe all dutiful obedience and subjection unto him, which duty and nature commands us to perform in regard of our creation. For the son honoureth his father by natural duty, and all men are naturally carried to be grateful to their founders, to whom they are specially bound, and whom they ought not to forget, neither will, except they be extreme unthankful and dissolute.

3. Not only the creation of the world, and of all things therein contained, doth proclaim that there is a God, who is to be honoured for his infinite extended authority and almighty power (for he made all things of nothing ; only he spake the word, and they were created), but his daily blessings and benefits sent down upon the earth do shew also there is a God, which is provident, and hath care of men, and therefore of men to be praised, thanked, and glorified for ever). For true it is which St Paul saith in this behalf, that 'God left not himself without witness, when he bestowed benefits from heaven, giving unto us rain, and seasonable weather, and filling our hearts with meat and gladness,' Acts xiv. 17. By means of these and all other his blessings, men might, and still may daily be induced not only to believe that there is a God from whom they receive all these, but also to acknowledge and attribute all praise and thankfulness unto him, as to their first principal and special benefactor. For the ox doth know his owner, and the ass his master, feeder, and maintainer. And therefore how can it be but reasonable men should much more know God, not only their first founder and creator, but their daily feeder, preserver, keeper, and upholder ? For so oft as they think upon these things, and see and have them, they cannot choose but be put in mind of God the sender and author of them all, and be moved with a grateful mind towards him : and hereof is it that he is called *Deus, à dando, of giving.* And in English we call *God, quasi good,* because he is only and perfectly good of himself alone, Mat. xix. 17, and the giver of all goodness, and of all good gifts and blessings unto others, James i. 17, Rom. ix. 16 ; from whom, as from the fountain, all benefits whatsoever do come, descend, flow, and be derived unto them.

4. I might here shew how God is also known to the world by his judgments upon wicked and unrighteous people, whom divers times he maketh visible examples of his severity and justice, if men did well consider them, for hereby also hath God manifested himself,

as Paul the apostle teacheth. These premises, I trust, may suffice, if there were no more to be said, for by them we may easily see and prove that there is a God, which created the world, and all things therein, which preserveth and upholdeth the same with his mighty puissance, supporteth the earth, and all the creatures thereof with his providence and helping hand. Yea, besides the heavens and the earth, which are the work of his hands, every man's own conscience doth plentifully teach, as I said before, that there is a God which is to be feared. For howsoever many a man, that hath spent his life in a wicked way, and most damnable course, could wish in his heart there were no God, because he seeth God no otherwise than in his vengeance ; yea, howsoever many a wicked person doth soothe himself in his wickedness, and flatteringly say unto himself, like the fool in the Psalms, 'There is no God,' Ps. xiv. 1 ; yet at other times his own conscience will so provoke him, and enforce this matter, that there is a God, that with horror and dread of him it will make him quake, fear, and tremble ; for the fear of him is so deeply printed in the natures of all men, as that it is impossible to shake it off. And which is more, a kind of devotion to worship him, being the Creator and Preserver of men, and of all things else, and the provident Father of all, is planted, and inseparably fixed in the hearts of all men, though all men of all nations know not how to worship him aright, and in such sort as he requireth. This is manifest by the examples of all nations and people in the world, who all have some one kind of religion or other, though all find not the right religion. All be devoted to the worship of God, howsoever all do not find out the true God, nor his right manner of worship, but worship him according to the devices of their own brain. Considering, then, that there is no nation under the sun so barbarous, nor ever was, but aimed at the worship of God, and either worshipped him, or something else in his place, it appeareth to be a most vain and foolish conceit which atheists sometimes utter, namely, that religion is nothing else but a matter of policy, or a politic device of human invention ; for it is evident that religious affection to worship God is naturally seated, and ever was, in the hearts of all men ; and the conscience of every man, even of the greatest scorner and contemner of God, which sometimes trembleth before his judgment-seat, doth abundantly testify that a religious devotion of fear towards God is bred and born with every man ; and therefore it cannot be any policy of human invention, inasmuch as if there were no laws of men, yet this religious affection to worship God, and the fear of him, would and doth remain written by the finger of God in the hearts and consciences of all men living, how rude, savage, or barbarous soever they be. What law of men, I pray, was there to make Caligula the emperor, when he heard the terrible thundering in the air, and saw the flashing flames of lightning about him, to run under his bed, and to hide himself for fear of this terrible and great God ? or what maketh the rankest atheist in the world, in the like case, and at the like tempest, to do the like ? Or what made the heathens in any dangerous or sudden distress to lift up their eyes or hands to heaven, mightily to fear and to be astonished ? None can say it is the law of men, for no law of men doth enforce this attempt. But it is a natural instinct of the fear of God, whom he hath offended, and whose vengeance he dreadeth, and from whom he thinketh succour may come, seated in all men's hearts even from their nativity, which doth make him to fear, and cause him to seek to God for refuge. Let this, therefore, remain firm and most undoubted, that the fear of the great God, and a religious disposition to worship the same God, is not enforced by the laws of men, but naturally sown in the hearts of all men, though all find not out, nor observe the right religion. Let us therefore now seek and search out which is the true religion, which is acceptable to God ; and which is without wavering and doubting, to be observed of men. For all nations and people have a kind of religion, as I said before, but all have not the true and right religion.

CHAPTER II.

Wherein, and in the next chapter, is shewed that the Christian religion is the only true religion in the world, and wherewith only God is pleased.

IN ancient times, all the world was divided and distinguished into Jews and Gentiles; and this distinction doth, and may still, remain among us. If, therefore, I can prove the truth of this our Christian religion against both Jews and Gentiles, I shall then prove it against all the world. In this chapter I will first prove it against the Jews, and in the next against the Gentiles. Concerning the Jews, they will easily grant our religion to be the true religion, if we can prove Jesus Christ, whom we believe to be that Messiah which was foretold by the prophets, being the true and undoubted prophets of God. And this, we are sure, may easily be proved; and therefore, in vain do the Jews look for any other Messiah than he that is already come, namely, Jesus Christ our Mediator, Saviour, and Redeemer, in whom God his Father is well pleased, and for whose sake, if we believe in him, he will not be offended with us, but be reconciled to us, and save us. Whatsoever was foretold to belong unto their Messiah is fully performed, and perfectly accomplished in our Jesus Christ, and in no other ; and therefore, our Jesus was and is the true Messiah, and no other. Let us herein consider the marks of the Messiah, whereby he might be known ; and so shall we see that our Saviour Jesus Christ is the only true Messiah, and none but he.

1. One mark for us to know the Messiah by is, that when he came he should not be known or acknowledged to be the Messiah, but should be rejected and refused of the Jewish nation, to the end he might be put to death amongst them, according to the fore-appointment and determinate counsel of God, Ps. xviii. 22, Isa. vi., Deut. xxviii., Isa. lv., liii., Dan. ix. ; for had they received him for the Messiah, they would never have used him so shamefully as they did, neither should he then have been slain amongst them, as was foretold he should. This, then, being one mark of the Messiah, that he should be refused for the Messiah of the Jewish nation, and of the chiefest rulers amongst them, is a great confirmation of our faith, inasmuch as it is found fully performed in our Saviour Jesus Christ, whom they scorned, rejected, condemned, and put to death. And therefore, if the Jewish nation had received our Jesus for the Messiah, it had been an undoubted argument that he had not been the right Messiah ; so, on the other side, because they did refuse him, it is a very strong persuasion to us that he was and is the very true Messiah indeed. In vain, therefore, it is, if any do look for such a Messiah as should be wholly received of the Jewish nation ; for none such was promised ; yea, it was foretold, contrari-wise, that he should be refused of them, as our Jesus was, that so he might be made an offering for sin, according to the preordina-tion of God.

2. It was foretold of the Messiah, that he should be born of a virgin, Isa. vii. 14 ; that the place of his birth should be Bethlehem, Micah v. 1 ; that at his birth all the infants round about Bethlehem should be slain for his sake, Jer. xxxi. 15 ; that the kings of the earth should come and adore him, and offer gold and other gifts unto him, Ps. lxxii. 15 ; that he should be presented in the temple of Jerusalem, for the greater glory of the second temple, Mal. iii. 1 ; that he should fly into Egypt, and be recalled thence again, Hosea

xi. 2 ; that a star should appear at his birth, to notify his coming into the world, Num. xxiv. ; that John Baptist, who came in the spirit and power of Elias, and therefore was called Elias, Luke i. 17, Mat. xi. 10, 14, should be the messenger to go before him, and to prepare the way, and to cry in the desert, Malachi iii. 1, Mark i. 2. Isa. xliii. ; after this, that he should begin his own preaching with all humility, quietness, and clemency of spirit, Isa. xlii. 2 ; that he should be poor, abject, and of no reputation in this world, Isa. liii. Dan. ix., Zech. ix., Jer. xiv. ; that he should do strange miracles, and heal all diseases, Isa. lxi. 1 ; that he should die and be slain for the sins of his people, Dan. ix., Isa. liii.; that he should be betrayed by one that put his hand in the dish with him, and was his own disciple, Ps. xli. 9, and lv. 13, 14 ; that he should be sold for thirty pieces of silver, Zech. xi. 12 : that with those thirty pieces, there should be bought afterwards a field of potsherds, Jer. xxx.; that he should ride into Jerusalem upon an ass before his passion, Zech. ix. 9 ; that the Jews should beat and buffet his face, and defile the same with spitting upon it, Isa. l. 6; that they should whip his body before they put him to death, Isa. liii. 2, Ps. xxxvii. 18 ; that they should put him to death among thieves and malefactors, Isa. liii. 12; that they should give him vinegar to drink, divide his apparel, and cast lots for his upper garment, Ps. lxviii. 22, and xxii. 11 ; that the manner of his death should be crucifixion, that is, nailing of his hands and his feet upon the cross, Ps. xxii. 16, Zech. xii.; that his side should be pierced, and that they should look upon him when they had so pierced him, Zech. xii. ; that he should rise again from death the third day, Ps. xvi. 10, Hosea vi. 3 ; that he should ascend into heaven, and sit at the right hand of his Father, in glory and royalty, and like a conquering potentate over-ruling all, Ps. cx. 1, 2.   All these things, and whatsoever else belonging to the Messiah, are found perfectly fulfilled in Jesus Christ, and in no other ; and therefore he alone and no other is the true Messiah.

3. Hitherto have I spoken of such circumstances and accidents as did belong unto the Messiah, concerning his incarnation, birth, life, death, burial, resurrection, and ascension into heaven, and there sitting at the right hand of his Father ; and also of his rejection by Jews, and the Jewish nation ; which things, albeit they be very wonderful, and sufficient to establish any man's belief in Christ Jesus our Lord, in whom only they are found faithfully fulfilled, yet if we shall consider withal the time of the Messiah his appearing, and when he should come into the world, our faith will be so much the more confirmed towards him.

Daniel, the prophet of God, who lived in the time of the first monarchy, foretold that there should be three monarchies more, and the last of these four monarchies greatest of all, Dan. ii. 39, 44; and that in the days of this fourth and last monarchy, which was the Roman monarchy or empire, the eternal King or Messiah should come, and build up God's kingdom throughout all the world. And this happened accordingly, for Jesus came and was born in the fourth monarchy, which was the Roman, namely, in the days of Augustus the Roman emperor. But yet let us go more strictly to the matter.

The temple of Jerusalem, as all men know, was builded twice— first by king Solomon, which lasted about 440 years, and then was destroyed by Nebuchadnezzar, king of Babylon; wherefore about seventy years after it was builded again by Zerubbabel, who reduced the Jews from their captivity. But this second temple, for pomp and riches of the material building, was nothing like unto the first, which the old men in the book of Esdras (1 Esd. iii.) do testify by their weeping when they saw this second and remembered the first, and which Haggai the prophet doth expressly testify, Hag. ii. 4. And yet saith God by his prophet Haggai, in the same place, ver. 5–10, that after a while, 'the desired of all nations shall come, and then should that second house or temple be filled with glory, and that greater should be the glory of this last house than of the first.' Which prophecy was fulfilled by the coming of our Saviour Jesus Christ into this second temple, which being personally done, was of far greater dignity, and more glory thereunto, than any dignity whatsoever was found in the first temple builded by Solomon. It is therefore manifest that 'the desired of all nations,' that is, the Messiah, should come whilst the second temple stood. And so doth Daniel also shew, that the second temple, after the building thereof, should not be destroyed until the Messiah were first come and slain, Dan. ix. 26. And Malachi the prophet doth also most plainly testify that he should come during the second temple, Mal. iii. 1. And so, indeed, he did; for Christ Jesus came into the world during that second temple, and did himself likewise foretell the destruction thereof ere that generation passed, which came to pass accordingly, for it was destroyed, about forty-six years after the ascension of our Saviour into heaven, by Titus, son to Vespasian the Roman emperor. Most vainly, therefore, do the Jews, or any other, expect for a Messiah to come after the destruction of that second temple.

Let us yet, moreover, consider the prophecy of old Jacob concerning the particular time of the Messiah his appearing : 'Come hither, my children,' saith he, 'that I may tell you the things that are to happen in the latter days,' &c. 'The sceptre shall not depart from Judah until Shiloh come, which is the expectation of the Gentiles,' Gen. xlix. By *Shiloh* is meant the Messiah, as both Jews and Christians expound it. This prophecy, so long foretold, was performed at the birth of Jesus Christ, in the days of Herod king of Jewry ; for from the time that the sceptre was given to king David, who was the first king of the tribe of Judah, it did not depart from that tribe, but remained always in it, until the days of king Herod, in whose time, and not until whose time, all government was taken away, and clean departed from the tribe of Judah, and committed to a stranger ; and therefore in the time of Herod was the Messiah to be born, and neither before nor after his time. That the sceptre or government was not clean taken away, or departed from the house of Judah, after it was once settled in it in the person of king David, even till the days of Herod the king, is evident ; for from David, who was the first king of that tribe, unto Zedekiah, that died in the captivity of Babylon, the Scripture sheweth how all the kings descended of the house of Judah ; and during the time of their captivity in Babylon, which was seventy years, the Jews were always permitted to choose unto themselves a governor of the house of Judah,[1] whom they called Reschgaluta. And after their delivery from Babylon, Zerubbabel was their governor of the same tribe, and so others after him until you come to the Maccabees, who were both governors and priests,[2] for that they were of the mother's side of the tribe of Judah, and by the father's side of the tribe of Levi, as Rabbi Kimhi[3] affirmeth; and so from these men down to Hircanus, king of Jewry, who was the last king which was lineally descended of the house of David, and of the tribe of Judah.

For after Hircanus came the aforenamed Herod, a mere stranger, whose father, as Josephus,[4] who well knew, reporteth, was called Antipater, and came out of Idumea. He came into acquaintance and favour with the Romans, partly by his said father's means (who was, as Josephus saith, a well moneyed man, industrious, and factious), and partly by his own diligence and ambition, being of himself both witty, beautiful, and of most excellent and rare qualities, by which commendations he came at length to marry the

---

[1] Sambed. cap. Dinei Manmouth.   Rab. Moses Egypt in præfat.   Maimonim.
[2] Esd. lib. 1 cap. i. 23 ; Mac. lib. 1, cap. ii. 3.   [3] Rab. Kimhi, com. in Agg.
[4] Joseph. lib. i. 1, 3, and 14 Ant.

daughter of Hircanus aforesaid, king of Jewry, and by this marriage obtained of his father-in-law to be chief governor and ruler
of the province and land of Galilee under him. But Hircanus
afterwards, in a battle against the Parthians, fell into their hands,
and was taken and carried prisoner into Parthia.

Herod then took his journey to Rome, and there he obtained to
be created king of Jewry, without any title or interest in the
world, for that not only his father-in-law, Hircanus, was then
living in Parthia, but that also his younger brother Aristobulus,
and three of his sons, viz., Antigonus, Alexander, Aristobulus, with
divers others of the blood royal in Jewry, were alive also.

Herod, then, having procured by this means to be king of Jewry,
procured first to have in his hands the king Hircanus,[1] and so put
him to death. He brought also to the same end his younger brother Aristobulus, and his three sons likewise. He put to death,
also, his own wife Mariamne, which was king Hircanus's daughter,
as also Alexandra her mother, and soon after two of his own sons,
which he had by the same Mariamne, for that they were of the
blood royal of Judah ; and a little after that again he put to death
his third son, named Antipater. He caused also to be slain forty
of the chiefest noblemen of the same tribe of Judah ; and as Philo
the Jew, who lived at the same time with him, writeth,[2] he put to
death all the Sanhedrim, that is, the twenty-seven[3] senators or
elders of the tribe of Judah that ruled the people. He killed the
chief of the sect of the Pharisees ; he burned the genealogies of all
the kings and princes of the house of Judah ; and caused one
Nicolaus Damascenus, an historiographer, that was his servant, to
draw out a pedigree for him and his line, as though he had descended from the ancient kings of Judah. He translated the
priesthood, and sold it to strangers ; and finally, he so razed, dispersed, and mangled the house of Judah in such sort as no one
jot of government or principality remained therein. Now, then,
in the days of this king Herod, and not till then, was the sceptre,
that is, the government, departed from Judah ; and therefore then,
and not till then, was the Messiah to appear, according to that
prophecy of Jacob. And so it came to pass accordingly ; for Christ
Jesus, the true and undoubted Messiah, was then born, viz., in the
time of Herod king of Jewry. In vain, therefore, do the Jews, or
any other, look for any other Messiah to come after the days of
that Herod, in whose time, and not before, was the sceptre and all
principality and government departed utterly from the house of

---

[1] Joseph. lib. xv. Antiq.   [2] Phil. lib. de tem.   [3] Qu. 'seventy-two'?—ED.

Judah ; and therefore in his time, and neither before nor after, was the Messiah to appear and come, according to Jacob's prophecy.

Daniel the prophet yet goeth nearer to work, and foresheweth even the very day and time of the day when the Messiah should be slain for the sins of the people ; for in the first year of Darius, son of Ahasuerus, king of the Medes, about the time of the evening oblation, he prayed to his God for the people and their deliverance, inasmuch as then he perceived that the seventy years of their captivity, foretold by Jeremiah, were now come to an end.

So Daniel thus praying, about that time of the evening oblation, God sent his angel Gabriel to signify and shew unto him, that at the very beginning of his supplications the commandment came forth for the return of the people from their captivity, and to build again Jerusalem ; and sheweth likewise, that as the people had now been in the captivity of Babylon seventy years, and then were delivered from that their earthly bondage, so it should come to pass, that within seventy weeks of years the Messiah should come, who should finish wickedness, seal up sins, blot out iniquity, and bring in everlasting righteousness, and be a deliverer not only from the outward, but from the spiritual Babylon and hellish Egypt.

The words of the angel be these following : ' At the very beginning of thy supplications the commandment came forth, and I am come to shew thee ; for thou art greatly beloved : therefore understand the matter, and consider the vision. Seventy weeks are determined over thy people, and over the holy city, to finish wickedness, and to seal up sins, and to blot out iniquity, and to bring in everlasting righteousness, to seal up the vision and prophecy, and to anoint the Holy of holies [or the most Holy]. Know therefore and understand, that from the giving forth of the commandment to bring again the people, and to build Jerusalem, unto Messiah the Prince, there shall be seven weeks and three score and two weeks, &c. After these three score and two weeks shall Messiah be slain, but not for himself, &c. He shall confirm the covenant with many for one week, and in the midst of the week he shall cause the sacrifice and the oblation to cease.' For the better understanding of which words, it must be remembered that this word *hebdomada*, signifying a week or seven, is sometimes taken for a week of days, that is, seven days, and then it is called *hebdomada dierum*, a week of days ; as in this prophecy of Daniel he saith of himself that he did mourn three weeks of days, Dan. x. 2. But at other times it signifieth the space of seven years, and that is called *hebdomada annorum*, a week of years ;

as in Levit. xxv. 8, where it is said, 'Thou shalt number unto thee seven weeks of years,' that is, seven times seven years, which make forty and nine years.

Now, it is most certain that these seventy weeks are to be understood of weeks of years, and not of days; for that, even by the Jews' own confession, as also by the books of Esdras, it is manifest, that the temple and Jerusalem were many years in building before they were finished. These seventy weeks of years, therefore, are seven times seventy years, which makes in a sum total four hundred and ninety years, within which time the Messiah should be slain; for from the going forth of the commandment to bring the people back again, and to build Jerusalem, which command-ment went forth at the beginning of his supplications, which were the first year of Darius, as the text sheweth, unto the time that Messiah the Prince was anointed to preach the kingdom of God, which was after his baptism, when he began to be about thirty years of age, there must be seven weeks and three score and two weeks, that is, sixty and nine weeks, which make four hundred, four score, and three years; which number of years being rightly accounted from that time of Darius, wherein the commandment went forth, are fully accomplished in the fifteenth year of Tiberius Cæsar, at which time Christ Jesus was baptized and anointed, by the Spirit of God descending down upon him in the form of a dove, a voice also being heard from heaven, saying, 'This is my beloved Son, in whom I am well pleased.'

Yet is there one week more to make up the number of seventy, in the midst of which week the Messiah should be slain, which came to pass accordingly; for in the midst of that week, that is, about three years and a half after Christ's baptism, Christ Jesus, the true Messiah, was put to death, and died for our sins, which was in the eighteenth year of Tiberius Cæsar. In vain, therefore, do the Jews or any other look for another Messiah to come after the days of that Tiberius Cæsar, the Roman emperor.

4. The Scriptures, Ps. lxxxviii., 2 Kings vii., 1 Chron. xxii., do shew that the Messiah should come of the seed of David, according to the words of God, 'I have sworn unto David my servant, I will prepare thy seed for ever; and will build up thy seat to all genera-tions,' which cannot be applied to king Solomon his son, as the latter Jews apply it; for these words, that his kingdom shall stand for ever and for all eternity, cannot be verified in Solomon, whose earthly kingdom was rent and torn in pieces straight after his death by Jeroboam, and not long after, as it were, extinguished; neither

can they be understood of any terrestrial king ; but they must needs be understood of an eternal king, which should come of David's seed. The promise then made to David for Christ to come of his seed is again repeated after his death by many prophets, and confirmed by God: as in Jeremiah, where God useth these words, ' Behold the days come on, that I will raise up unto David a just seed ; and he shall reign a king, and shall be wise, and shall do judgment and justice upon earth. And in his days shall Judah be saved, and Israel shall dwell confidently ; and this is the name that men shall call him, Our Just God,' Jer. xxiii. 6, &c., xxxiii. 16. All this was spoken of David above four hundred years after David was dead, which proveth manifestly that the promises and speeches were not made unto king David, for Solomon his son, nor for any other temporal king of David's line, but for Christ, who was particularly called ' the Son of David;' for that David was the first king of the tribe of Judah, and not only was Christ's progenitor in the flesh, but also did bear his type and figure in many other things. For which cause likewise in Ezekiel (who lived about the same time that Jeremiah did), the Messiah is called by the name of David himself, Ezek. xxxiv. 3, &c. ; for thus saith God at that time to Ezekiel, ' I will save my flock, neither shall they any longer be left to the spcil ; I will set over them a shepherd, and he shall feed them, even David my servant, he shall feed them ; and he shall be their shepherd, and I will be their God, and my servant David shall be their prince.' In which words, not only we that are Christians but the latter Jews also themselves do confess in the Talmud, that their Messiah is called David, for that he was to descend of his seed.

Now then, let us see whether Jesus Christ our Lord did come of the seed of David, as was foretold the Messiah should. It is plain that he did, for never any man doubted or denied but that Jesus was directly one of the tribe of Judah, and descended lineally, by his mother, of the only house of David (as was foretold he should), which is confirmed most clearly by the two genealogies and pedigrees set down by Saint Matthew and Saint Luke, Mat. i., Luke iii.; of the blessed virgin, whose descent from David ; and Joseph, that was of the same tribe and kindred with her ; for according to the laws of the Jews, they used to marry in their own tribe. And therefore the evangelists, shewing the line of Joseph, do thereby also declare the lineage and stock of Mary (the mother of Jesus), as being a thing then sufficiently known unto all, though they spake no more.

Secondly, It is confirmed by their repairing unto Bethlehem

(when commandment was given by Augustus Cæsar, that every one should repair to the head city of their tribe and family, to be taxed or assessed for their tribute, Luke i. 1–5,), for by their going thither it is shewed, that they were both of the lineage of David, inasmuch as Bethlehem was the proper city only of them that were of the house and lineage of David, for that king David was born therein.

Thirdly, it may appear by this, for that the Jews, who sought out all exception they could against him, yet never excepted this, nor alleged against him, that he was not of the house of Judah, nor of the house of David, which they would never have omitted if they might have done it with any colour; for such a speech, if it could truly have been spoken, would easily have convinced our Jesus not to be the true Messiah. But it appeareth they never doubted of this. Yea, I add further, that it remaineth registered in the Jews' Talmud itself[1] that Jesus of Nazareth crucified was of the blood royal from Zerubbabel of the house of David. Wherewith agreeth that saying of Paul the apostle, Rom. i. 3, 4, where he testifieth thus, 'Jesus Christ was born of the seed of David according to the flesh,' though he were also 'the Son of God in power, according to the spirit of sanctification.'

5. That the mother of Jesus was a virgin is plentifully testified by the evangelists, and that so the Messiah's mother should be, the Scriptures of the Jews do sufficiently shew. For in Isa. vii. 14, it is told as a strange thing to king Ahaz, and so it is indeed, that a virgin should conceive and bring forth a son, and they should call his name *Immanuel*, that is, *God with us*. Which could not be strange, if the Hebrew word in that place did signify only a young woman, as some later rabbins do affirm, for that is no strange or new thing, but common and ordinary, for young women to conceive and bear children. Wherefore the Septuagint do rightly translate the word *parthenos*, which properly and fully signifieth a virgin, and so did also the elder Jews understand it, as Rabbi Simeon well noteth.[2] And Rabbi Moses Hadarsan,[3] of singular credit among the Jews, upon these words of the psalm, 'Truth shall bud forth of the earth,' saith that it is not said, 'Truth shall be engendered of the earth,' but 'Truth shall bud forth,' to signify thereby that the Messiah, who is meant by the word *truth*, shall not be begotten as other men in carnal copulation; he also citeth Rabbi Berechius to be of the same opinion; and, finally, Rabbi Hacadosch proveth

---

[1] Tal. tract. Sab. cap. Higmar.
[2] Rab. Sim. Ben. Johai. in chap. ii. Gen.   [3] Rab. Moses Hadars. in Ps. xiv.

by art cabalistical out of many places of Scripture,[1] not only that the mother of the Messiah shall be a virgin, but also that her name shall be *Mary.* Likeas also the same Rabbi Hacadosch proveth by the same art out of many texts of Scripture,[2] that the Messiah's name at his coming shall be *Jesus.* And that the mother of the Messiah should be a virgin, may further appear in the prophecy of Jeremiah, where God saith, 'I will work a new thing upon earth, a woman shall environ or enclose a man,' Jer. xxxi. 22, which were no new thing, but usual and wonted, except he understood of a virgin that should bear a child.

6. Now because Christ Jesus by the wonderful works and surpassing miracles which he did, being such as no man could do (if he had been but a bare man) as also by his heavenly doctrine, words, and deeds, did declare himself to be the Son of God, sent from the bosom of his Father, let us also, as we have found the Messiah to be man, so search whether he ought not to be God also. The sacred scriptures of the Jews give answer, that he ought to be God also, and so to be both God and man. Which thing is signified by the prophet Isaiah, when he saith, 'They shall call his name Immanuel, which is by interpretation, God with us,' Isa. vii. 14. Again, the same Isaiah testifieth that they shall call his name 'Wonderful, Counsellor, the mighty God, the everlasting Father, the Prince of peace,' Isa. ix. 6. Again, by Isaiah he is called 'the issue of the Lord,' and also 'the fruit of the earth,' Isa. iv. 2, to signify him to be both the Son of God and the Son of man. And Jeremiah the prophet doth testify of him, that he shall be called 'the righteous God,' or 'God our righteousness,' Jer. xxiii. 6, and xxxii. 26. And God himself saith of him, 'Thou art my Son; this day have I begotten thee,' Ps. ii. 7. And David proveth him plainly to be the Son of God; for though he knew he should come of his seed as touching the flesh, yet doth he also call him his Lord, saying thus, 'The Lord said unto my Lord, Sit thou at my right hand till I make thine enemies thy footstool,' Ps. cx. 1. Sith David calleth him his Lord, it is manifest that he maketh him not only to be man, but God also, even the Son of God, the second person in the Trinity. This matter is testified almost everywhere in the scriptures of the Jews, and therefore I need no further to amplify.

7. Yet, because the Jews do look for the Messiah to be a terrestrial king which should reign in Jewry, and subdue all their enemies with his terrestrial power and force, wherein how grossly they err,

---

[1] Rab. Mos. Had. in Gen. xxiii.; Rab. Hacad. ad qu. iii. in Isa. cap. ix.
[2] Rab. Hacad. in Isa. ix. 11.

as the premises do partly shew, so is it not impertinent here to speak somewhat to convince their so gross an opinion. For, first, the time is past long ago wherein the Messiah should come, and yet no such terrestrial king as they dream of hath been reigning in Jewry ; and therefore very experience and knowledge of the times might teach them to abandon so foolish a conceit. Daniel calls him 'the eternal King,' Dan. ii. 44. Micah saith, 'He shall reign for ever,' Micah iv. 5, which cannot be supposed of an earthly kingdom. Again, 'Ask of me,' saith God to his Son, the Messiah, 'and I will give unto thee the heathen for thine inheritance, and the uttermost part of the world for thy possession,' Ps. ii. Which words do shew that the Messiah should be an universal king, to rule not only over the Jews, but over the Gentiles also, even over all the world. Again, it is said that 'he shall endure with the sun, and before the moon from generation to generation ; he shall reign from sea to sea unto the end of the world. All kings shall adore him, and all nations shall serve him ; all tribes of the earth shall be blessed in him, and all nations shall magnify him,' Ps. lxxii. And it was told Abraham that in his seed, that is, in the Messiah which should come of his seed, all nations of the earth should be blessed, Gen. xviii.; how, then, should he overthrow any nation for the Jews' sake, as they dream, when all nations were to receive their blessing from him ? In the prophecy of Isaiah, chap. xlix. 6, the commission of God his Father unto him is thus set down. 'It is too little that thou be unto me a servant to raise up the tribes of Jacob, and to convert unto me the preserved of Israel ; Behold I have appointed thee also to be a light unto the Gentiles, that thou be my salvation unto the uttermost parts of the earth.' Everywhere almost it is testified, that the Gentiles should have every way as much interest in the Messiah as the Jews, and should be as beneficial unto them. The Messiah therefore, though he be termed a king, and is so indeed, yet is to be supposed a spiritual and eternal king, as the prophets declare him ; for it is too childish and fond to imagine him to be an earthly king, which should reign only in Judea, and be a great and mighty terrestrial conqueror. Doth not Zechariah, as touching his estate in this world, shew that he should come poorly, riding upon an ass ? Zech. ix. Doth not Isaiah say, that in this world he should be a man despised, abject, and of no reputation ? Isa. liii. Doth not Daniel expressly say, that he should come to be slain, that with his sacrifice he might take away sin, and cease all other sacrifices ? Dan. ix. Doth not Zechariah say, that they should look upon him after they had pierced or crucified him ? Zech. xii. And doth not the prophet Isaiah say of him, that he gave his soul an offering for sin, and that he should be led as a sheep to the slaughter, and as a lamb dumb before his shearer, so opened he not his mouth? Isa. liii.   Where then is his pomp, when he was to be poor ?   Where was his earthly honour, when he was to be abject and of no reputation ?   Where was his worldly conquest, when he was himself to be slain ?   Where should his fleshly resistance be, when he was not so much as to offer it, yea, when his enemies were to lead him to death as the sheep to the slaughter, and as a lamb dumb before his shearer, not opening his mouth to save himself?   Yea, how should the Jews think, if they would thoroughly consider, that the Messiah should be such a one as they dream of, when they were the men that should pursue him to death, and whom they should look upon when they had pierced him ?

These things which have been spoken, though in very brief and plain sort, are, I trust, sufficient to convince the Jews, that our Lord and Saviour Jesus Christ is that seed of the woman which should break the serpent's head, which deceived Adam and Eve our first parents ; and he in whom all the nations of the earth should be blessed, and is in all points the very true, certain, and undoubted Messiah, which was fore-promised and foretold by their prophets; for all things which were foretold of the Messiah, do fitly, fully, and only agree to him, and to no other. And therefore I conclude against them, that the Christian religion, which we profess, and which we hold derived to us from that Christ the true Messiah, the author thereof, is the only true religion which is acceptable to God.

CHAPTER III.

Wherein is shewed that the Christian religion is the only true religion, against the gentiles and all infidels of the world.

THAT there is a God, the heathen have evermore confessed ; that there is but one God, as the Christian religion holdeth, all the learned sort of the heathen philosophers have acknowledged ; for howsoever they dissembled at some times, and applied themselves outwardly to the error of the vulgar sort in naming of *gods*, yet surely they never spake of more than of one *God*.   Which thing may appear by Plato in an epistle which he writeth unto Dionysius, king of Sicily,[1] wherein he giveth him a sign when he spake in

[1] Plato, Epist. 13 ad Dionys.

jest and when in earnest: *Hinc disces tu scribam ego serio necne ; cum serio, ordior epistolam ab uno deo ; cum secus à pluribus.* Hereby, saith he, you shall know whether I write in earnest or not ; for when I write in earnest, I begin my letter with one god, and when I write not in earnest, I do begin my letter in the name of many gods. And three of the most learned that ever professed the Platonic sect, Plotinus, Porphyrius, and Proclus,[1] do all testify and prove in divers parts of their works, being themselves but heathens, that both themselves and their master Plato never believed indeed but one God. Aristotle, that ensued Plato, and began the sect of the Peripatetics, though he were a man so much given to the search of nature, as that sometime he seemed to forget God, the author of nature, yet in his old age, when he wrote the *Book of the World*,[2] he resolveth the matter more clearly, acknowledging also one God ; and saith, moreover, in the same place, that the multitude of gods was invented to express the power of this one God by the multitude of his ministers. Whereby doth appear, that belike the foolisher sort of heathens did imagine of God as of earthly princes ; for they saw that every earthly prince had a great many men ministers, otherwise called servants and attendants upon him, thereby to declare and shew his power, his magnificence, and high honour ; and therefore they thought likewise, that the great and high God could not be sufficiently conceived of except it were supposed that he had a great number of inferior gods, waiting and attending upon him, in like sort to shew his greatness and magnificence. This opininion of their master concerning one god, Theophrastus and Aphrodiseus,[3] two principal Peripatetics, do confirm at large.

Zeno, the chief and father of all the Stoics, was wont to say, as Aristotle himself reporteth, that *either one god or no god*. Which opinion of one God is averred everywhere by Plutarch and Seneca, two most excellent writers, and great admirers of the Stoic severity ; and before them by Epictetus, a man of singular account in that sect, whose words were esteemed oracles : *Dicendum ante omnia, unum esse Deum, omnia regere, omnibus providere.* Before all things, saith he, we must affirm that there is one God, and that this God governeth all, and hath providence over all.

[1] Plotin., Enneæ i. lib. viii. 1, 2, et En. vi. lib. iv. cap. 12, 3, 4 ; Porph., lib. ii. de Abst., et lib. de occa. cap. ii. ; Procl. in Theolog. Platon., et lib. de Anima, et dæm. i. 31, 42, 55. [2] Arist. lib. de Mundo.
[3] Theoph. in Metaph. Alex. Aphro., lib. de provid.

As for the Academics, although their usage was to doubt and dispute everything, as Cicero seemeth to do in his discourse concerning the gods,[1] yet at last he concludeth in this point with the Stoics, who believed one God. And as for Socrates, who was the father and founder of the Academic sect, and who was judged by the oracle of Apollo to be the wisest man in all Greece, the world doth know that he was put to death for jesting at the multitude of gods among the gentiles.

All these four sects of philosophers, then, who in their time bare the credit of learning, made, as we see, profession of one God, when they came to speak as they thought. And yet if we will ascend up higher, to the days before these sects began, that is, to Pythagoras and Architas Tarentinus,[2] and before them again to Mercurius Trismegistus, that was the first parent of philosophy to the Egyptians, we shall find them so plain and resolute herein, as none can be more. It is true that the heathen did honour such men as were famous either for their valiant acts, their singular invention in matters, their good turns to others, or their own rare gifts and qualities above others, with the title of gods, but yet they believed not that those men were gods; yea, they knew them to be no other than mortal men, which thing Trismegistus sheweth[3] when he saith, *Deos non naturæ ratione, sed honoris causa nominamus.* We name them gods not in respect of their natures, but for honour's sake; that is, we call them gods not for that we think them to be so, but because, under that title, we would honour some famous acts or rare parts and qualities which were in them. Cicero likewise testifieth the same in these words, The life of man, saith he, and common custom have now received to lift up to heavenly fame and good will such men as for their good turns are accounted excellent; and hereof it cometh that Hercules, Castor and Pollux, Æsculapius and Liber, which were but men, are now reckoned for gods. Perseus, likewise, Zeno's scholar, testifieth the same. And therefore did the Grecians truly think, who, as Herodotus reporteth, thought that their gods, whom they so called, were no other at first than mortal men, and so is the common opinion of all. And when men and women that were famous, excellent, and surpassing others, died, because the memory of them should not die with them, but remain as precedents to follow, or as persons to be admired at, those that were living could not be

---

[1] Cicer., lib. de natura Deor. Apuleius Aleg. et Lacri. in vita Socrat.
[2] *Vide* apud Plutarch de placit. Philos. Trismeg. in pæman, et in Asclep.
[3] Trism. in pæman, cap. ii. 3, 4, 5, &c., in Asclep., cap. xxvi, &c.

content to honour them with the title of gods and goddesses, but also would needs have their pictures or images drawn, and set up somewhere for posterity to behold. Hereof it came that they after a while began, as man's natural corrupt inclination is too prone that way, to give honour and to do reverence unto them ; and not so contented, they proceeded further, and builded altars and temples unto them, and at length consecrated priests and appointed certain rites, ceremonies, and sacrifices to be done there. The devil hereupon taking occasion and fit opportunity, purposing always to seduce the world, and to hold them in error so far forth as he might, entered at last into those altars which were dedicated to those men, and under the names of those men made way to have himself worshipped instead of the true God ; for true it is, which the sacred psalm witnesseth, that the gentiles 'sacrificed their sons and daughters unto devils,' Ps. cv. ; and which Paul saith, that 'whatsoever the gentiles offer, they offer to devils, and not to God,' 1 Cor. x. 20 ; for the devils, being entered into those altars, received their sacrifices offered to them, being glad they had them in such a predicament; and because their delusion should be the stronger under the names of those men, they would yield forth answers to such as came to demand any questions of them, and those their answers were written by their priests, and called oracles ; and with such sleights those devillish spirits bewitched the world, and deceived them. Of which their oracles, more shall be spoken hereafter ; but here first I make this argument against them.

They which, howsoever ignorantly, worship devils, are far from the true religion ; this is plain.

But the Gentiles worshipped devils, *ergo*, &c.

That the Gentiles worshipped devils, not God, may appear, first, by this reason, for that those their gods allowed, yea, required, not beasts, but men to be sacrificed unto them, delighting themselves in such infinite murders and manslaughters as were most cruel and unnatural, signifying themselves to be thereby appeased, wherein God is most displeased. For, as Polydor[1] Virgil hath collected, the people of Rhodes sacrificed a man to Saturn ; in the island Salamis, a man was sacrificed to Agraula. To Diomedes, in the temple of Pallas, a man was offered, who, being thrice led about the altar by young men, was at last by the priest run through with a spear, and put into the fire and burnt. Among the people of Cyprus, Teucrus sacrificed human sacrifice unto Jupiter, and left the same to posterity to follow. To Diana likewise human sacri-

[1] Polyd. de Inv. lib. v. cap. viii.

fices were offered. The like was done to Hesus and Teutates. Amongst the Egyptians, three men a day which were sought out (if they were clean) were sacrificed to Juno. Amongst the Lacedæmonians, they were wont to sacrifice a man to Mars. The Phœnicians, in the calamitous times of war and pestilence, were wont to sacrifice unto Saturn their dearest friends. The people called Curetæ sacrificed children unto Saturn. At Laodicea, a virgin was sacrificed to Pallas. And amongst the Arabians, every year a child was sacrificed and buried under the altar. Also the Thracians, Scythians, the Carthaginians, and almost all the Grecians, especially when they were to go to war, sacrificed a man. All barbarous nations have done the like, yea, the Frenchmen and Germans; yea, the Romans themselves did the like sacrifice, as namely, to Saturn in Italy, a man was sacrificed at the altar; and not only so, but he was also to be cast down from a bridge into the river Tiber. Dionysius [of] Halicarnassus writeth,[1] that Jupiter and Apollo were marvellously angry, for that the tenth part of men were not sacrificed unto them, and therefore sought they revenge upon Italy. Diodorus reporteth that the Carthaginians, when they were overcome of Agathocles, king of the Sicilians, thought their gods to be angry with them, and therefore, to appease them, sacrificed unto them two hundred of the noblemen's sons at a time. Oh monstrous cruelty! Who, then, can possibly be persuaded otherwise, but that these gods of the Gentiles, which they thus worshipped and sacrificed unto, were mere devils, considering that such monstrous, unkind, and unnatural slaughters of men, which must needs offend God the more, were the appeasements of their anger and wrath?

Again, these gods of the gentiles were not only well pleased with the sacrifices of the blood of men, but also well liked and allowed of fornication, adulteries, and all uncleanness; for at Alexandria, the image of Saturn was most devoutly worshipped, whose priest, Tynannus by name, brought certain matrons of the city, which he had selected out, unto that image or idol, as being sent for by their god, and there, when the lights were put out, had to do with them in the name of that their god.[2] Also, among the Nasamones, it was the custom that the bride, the first night after her marriage, should lie with all the guests, in honour of the goddess Venus. I therefore conclude, that those gods of the gentiles, which delighted in the slaughter of men, and likewise in their filthiness and uncleanness, must needs be devils; for the kind and

---

[1] Dionys. Halic. 1 Antiq.   [2] Polyd. de Inv. lib. v. cap. viii.

righteous God can abide none of these things, as any man's own reason, sense, and understanding may teach them.

2. Another argument to prove that the gods of the Gentiles were devils is this, because the oracles which they gave forth in matters merely contingent, were either false, or else so ambiguous and uncertain, as that they were deceitful, and therefore could not come from God, but from the devil. This falsehood and deceitfulness of their oracles, Porphyry himself, the great patron of paganism, testifieth in a special book of the answers of the gods,[1] wherein he professeth that he hath gathered truly, without addition or detraction, the oracles that were most famous before his time, with the false and uncertain event thereof, in consideration of which event, he setteth down his own judgment of their power in prediction after this manner : The gods do foretell some natural things to come, for that they observe the order of their natural causes; but in things which are contingent, or do depend upon man's will, they have but conjectures ; only in that by their subtilty and celerity they prevent us ; but yet they oftentimes lie, and deceive us in both kinds ; for that as natural things are variable, so man's will is much more mutable. Thus far Porphyry of the prophecies of his gods; whereunto agreeth another heathen among the Grecians, named Oenomaus,[1] who for that he had been much delighted with oracles, and more deceived, wrote also a special book in the end of their falsehoods and lies; and yet sheweth, that in many things wherein they were deceived, it was not easy to convince them of open falsehood, for that, cunningly, they would involve their answers, of purpose, with such obscurities, equivocations, amphibologies, and doubtfulness, as that always they would leave themselves a corner wherein to save their credits. As for example, when Crœsus, that famous and rich king of Lydia, consulted with the oracle of Apollo, whether he should make war against the Persians, and thereby obtain their empire, the oracle gave answer thus, If Crœsus, without fear, shall pass over Halys, which was a river that lay between him and Persia, he shall bring to confusion, a great and rich kingdom. Upon which words, Crœsus passed over his army, in hope to get Persia ; but he lost Lydia, his own kingdom, and was deceived by that uncertain oracle.

Like answer gave the oracle of Apollo to Pyrrhus king of Epirus, demanding whether he should prosper in the war against the Romans ; for it was delivered in these words : *Aio te Æacida Roma-*

---

[1] Porph. lib. de resp. et oracul.
[2] Oenomaus de falsitate oraculorum, et de artificibus malefic.

nos vincere posse, I say that the son of Æacus the Romans may overcome. Upon which oracle Pyrrhus, the son of Æacus, thinking to be the conqueror, was himself vanquished by the Romans.

A number more such oracles there were, wherewith the world was deceived, that trusted them; but I need not recite them; for (as it appeareth) the oracles and answers which their wicked spirits gave forth in matters future and merely contingent, were such as might be taken and construed two ways; and therefore their worshippers (if they had been wise to have noted their cunning and deceitful answers, containing no certainty at all), they had been as good never to come at them to inquire of any matter future; for they had such ambiguous answers as whereby they might remain as doubtful, and as unresolved as they were at first, and so depart home as wise as they came, or rather more fools than when they went. But what might be the reason why these devils, or devilish spirits, gave no certain answers to their worshippers in these matters future, whereof they were demanded?

The reason is manifest; for no doubt they would if they could, that so their credit might have been the more. But it was a thing not in their power, but only reserved unto God, to know and foretell certainly the things that are to come; for herein God provoketh all the gods of the Gentiles to make trial and experience of their power, in these words, ' Declare unto us,' saith he, 'what shall ensue hereafter, and thereby we shall know that ye are gods indeed,' Isa. xli. 23. Which sheweth, that the certain foretelling of things future doth manifest a divine power, whereof these devilish spirits are not partakers; for had these wicked spirits such a power in them, as certainly to know and foretell such things as were to come, out of all doubt they would then have given such certain, plain, and undoubted oracles and answers in this behalf as would have purchased them everlasting credit in all the world. But now the falsehood and uncertainty and deceitfulness of them, have got them justly perpetual discredit in all the world, and manifested them to be no better than lying spirits, whose worshippers were miserably deluded by them, as even the heathen themselves have testified.

Having thus briefly, yet I trust sufficiently, disproved the religion of the gentiles, as being a cruel, wicked, false, lying, and deceitful religion, having in it no certainty at all whereupon men might rest or assure themselves; it remaineth now that I shew and prove against them the truth of the Christian religion, which we profess. Where the first argument, to shew the powerful and undoubted truth thereof, shall be this, namely, the confession of the gods of the Gentiles, that is, of devils and hellish spirits themselves, who have given testimony thereof, even to their own worshippers, especially when the time of Christ his appearing in the world (who should be the light of the Gentiles) drew near and approached. For the manifestation whereof, two oracles of Apollo may suffice ; the one whereof was to a priest of his own, that demanded him of true religion, and of God, to whom he answered thus in Greek :[1] O thou unhappy priest, why dost thou ask me of God, that is the Father of all things, and of this most renowned King's dear and only Son, and of the Spirit that containeth all ? &c. Alas, that Spirit will enforce me shortly to leave this habitation and place of oracles. The other oracle was to Augustus Cæsar, even about the very time that Christ was ready to appear in the flesh ; for the said emperor now drawing to age, would needs go to Delphos, and there learn of Apollo who should reign after him, and what should become of things when he was dead. Apollo for a great while would make no answer, notwithstanding Augustus had been very liberal in making the great sacrifice called hecatomb ; but in the end, when the emperor began to iterate his sacrifice, and to be instant for an answer, Apollo (as it were enforced to speak) uttered these strange words unto him,[2] An Hebrew child, that ruleth over the blessed gods, commandeth me to leave this habitation, and out of hand to get me to hell ; but yet do thou depart in silence from our altars. Thus it appeareth that this Hebrew child (which is our Christ Jesus) hath power over the gods of the Gentiles, to command them unto hell, from whence they came, to enjoin them silence, and to remove them from their habitations ; and therefore the religion of this powerful Jesus (whereof he is the author) must needs, even by the acknowledgment of the devils themselves (whom he doth command), be the true religion.

3. Another argument of the divinity and truth thereof is this, namely, that it hath removed by the puissant force thereof, all the gods of the Gentiles, in despite of them, ceased their oracles, and driven them clean out of the earth, so that now they are nowhere to be found. And so it was foretold by the prophets, that Christ, when he came, *attenuabit omnes deos terræ*, shall wear out all the gods of the earth, Zeph. ii. The truth whereof, all the world doth now see clearly to be certain and undoubted by the event.

The oracles and answers of these gods, even in Cicero's time, as

---

[1] Suidas in Thulis et Porphyr. et Plut de Oraculis.
[2] Suidas in vita Augusti. Niceph. lib. i. hist. cap. xvii.

Cicero himself witnesseth,[1] who lived somewhat before the coming of Christ, began to cease ; and at last by little and little they ceased altogether, and were utterly extinct. It is reported that in Egypt, when Christ was there with Joseph and his mother Mary, all the idols of that foolish and superstitious nation fell down of their own accord. Afterwards, in the time of the emperor Adrian, all sacrifices unto those gods ceased, as also the oracles of Apollo, and all other oracles became dumb.[2] Wherefore Juvenal saith, *Cessant oracula Delphis*, that is, The oracles cease at Delphos. And another poet saith,

> " Excessere omnes adytis, arisque relictis,
>   Dii, quibus imperium hoc steterat," &c.—*Lucan.*

that is, all the gods whereby this empire stood, have departed from their temples, and left their altars and place of their habitation. Plutarch affirmeth the like,[3] and is much busied to search out the cause and reason of the ceasing of their oracles, who, being a heathen, was much troubled herewith, guessing at the matter, and vainly devising fond conceits in his brain, not able indeed to pierce into the very cause thereof. But Porphyry, even that great patron of paganism, and enemy of Christian religion, can teach him, or any other, the true cause thereof, shewing them that since the coming of Jesus, their gods are dumb, and can do them no good, but all are gone and departed from them. His words be these,[4] *Nunc vero mirantur (inquit) si tam multos annos civitas peste vexetur, cum et Æsculapius et alii dii longe absint ab ea; postea enim quam Jesus colitur, nihil utilitatis a diis consequi possumus.* Now, saith he, they marvel why this city is so many years vexed with pestilence, whenas, indeed, Æsculapius and other gods be far gone and departed from it ; for since the time that Jesus is worshipped, all our gods have been unprofitable to us. Considering then that Jesus, the author of the Christian religion, hath silenced and utterly destroyed the gods of the Gentiles, as histories and the visible event shew, his religion must needs be the only true religion.

4. What should I say more ? Even the Gentiles themselves, the most ancient, and the best, have testified of Jesus Christ, and of the truth of his religion ; for inasmuch as Christ was appointed before the creation of the world, to work the redemption both of the Jew and Gentile, and to make them both one people in the service of his Father, here-hence it is that he was foretold, and not alto-

---

[1] Cicero, lib. de divin. ii.
[2] Polyd. lib. v. cap. viii.
[3] Plutarch, de defectu oraculorum
[4] Porphyr. advers. rel. Christ.

gether unknown or unheard of to both these nations, and therefore divers forewarnings and significations of him were left, as well among the Gentiles as the Jews, to stir them up to expect his coming. For, first, by the consent of writers it is agreed, that in those ancient times there were three famous men that lived together,[1] namely, Abraham, who descending from Heber, was the father or beginner of the Hebrews, who were afterward called the Jews, and with him Job, and Zoroaster, that were not of that lineage of Heber, but, as we call them for distinction's sake, heathens or gentiles. Job, we know, testifieth of Christ, calling him the Redeemer, Job xix. 25-27, and was most assured to see him one day with his own eyes, and none other for him, although worms should destroy that body of his, as he himself testifieth. Zoroaster living thus in Abraham's time also, might, by account of Scriptures, see or speak with Noah, for Abraham was born threescore years before Noah deceased; and hereof it is, that in the writings of Zoroaster, which are yet extant, or recorded by other authors in his name,[2] there be found many plain speeches of the Son of God, whom he calleth *Secundam mentem*, the second mind; but much more is to be seen in the writings of Hermes Trismegistus, who received his learning from this Zoroaster, by whom appeareth, that these first heathen philosophers had manifest understanding of this second person in Trinity, whom Hermes calleth, The first begotten Son of God, his only Son, his dear, eternal, immutable, and incorruptible Son, whose sacred name is ineffable; so are his words, and after him again amongst the Grecians, were Orpheus, Hesiodus, and others, that uttered the like speeches of the Son of God, as also did the Platonists, whose words and sentences were too long to repeat.

Moreover, the Gentiles must remember, that they had also some prophets among them, for Balaam was a prophet among the Gentiles, Num. xxiv., and a Gentile, and he is such a one as testified of Christ, and of the star that should appear at his birth; by means of whose prophecy, it should seem, the wise men in the east seeing that star, were assured that Christ was born, and therefore came a long journey to Judea to see him, as one Gospel sheweth. The same star is mentioned by divers heathen writers, as by Pliny, under the name of a comet,[3] for so they term all extraordinary stars, which appeared in the latter days of Augustus Cæsar, and was different from all others that ever appeared. And Pliny saith of it, *Is cometa*

---

[1] Euseb. in Chro.
[2] Clem. Alex. lib. i. Strom. et Orig. lib. vi. cont. Celsum et Procl. lib. ii. et iii. Parm. Plato. Herm. in Pæman, cap. i.   [3] Plin. lib. ii. cap. xxv.

unus toto orbe colitur, that only comet is worshipped throughout all the world. Calcidius, a Platonic, doth say,[1] that the Chaldean astronomers did gather by contemplation of this star, that some god descended from heaven to the benefit of mankind.

The Gentiles also had certain women called *Sybillæ,* which were prophetesses, who, being endued with a certain spirit of prophecy, uttered most wonderful particularities of Christ to come ; one of them beginning her Greek metre in these very words, *Know thy God, which is the Son of God.* Another of them maketh a whole discourse in Greek verse, called *acrostici,* expressly affirming therein that Christ Jesus, by name, should be the Saviour, and that he was the Son of God ; and expressly saying that he should be incarnate of a virgin, that he should suffer death for our sins, and that he should be crucified ; that he should rise again and be exalted into the glorious heavens, and from thence, at the time appointed, and at the day of the resurrection of all flesh, come again to the last judgment.[2] Of these sybils there were ten in number ; and, talking of his first coming into the world, they also say that *rutilans eum sidus monstrabit,* a blazing star shall declare him. These sybils speak so plainly of Christ Jesus as the prophets among the Jews did, yea, more plainly, and as plainly as may be, and in a manner as fully as our gospel speaketh ; and therefore, if the Gentiles will believe their own prophets, they must likewise believe the Christian religion, whereof Jesus Christ is the author, of whom they abundantly testify. Now, lest it might be thought by some suspicious heads that Christians have devised and invented these things, as also that it may yet more fully appear that Christ, before his coming, was notified over the world by means of those verses of the sybils, it must be remembered that Marcus Varro, a learned Roman, who lived almost a hundred years before Christ, maketh mention at large of the sybils,[3] who in number, he saith, were ten ; and of their writing, countries, and ages, as also of the writers and authors that before his time had left memory of them ; and both he and Fenestella, another heathen, do affirm[4] that the writings of the sybils were gathered by the Romans from all parts of the world where they might be heard of, and laid up with great diligence and reverence in the capitol. Sybilla Erythræa, who made the former acrostic verses, testifieth of herself, as Constantine the emperor

---

[1] Calcid. apud Marsit. Picin. tract. de Stella Mag. Lact. contra Gent.
[2] Sybil Samia apud Betul.
[3] Var. lib. de reb. divin. ad Cæsarem Pont. Max.
[4] Fenest. cap. de xv. viris.

doth record,[1] that she lived about six hundred years after the flood of Noah ; and her countryman, Apollodorus Erythræus, and Varro, do report that she lived before the war of Troy, and prophesied to the Grecians that went to that war that Troy should be destroyed, as it came to pass, which was more than a thousand years before Christ was born. Cicero also, that died more than forty years before Christ was born, translated into Latin the former acrostic verses, as Constantine saith, which translation was to be seen in his works when Constantine wrote that his oration. See Cicero of these acrostic verses of Sybilla, lib. ii. *de Divinatione.*[2] And finally, Suetonius, an heathen, recordeth[3] that Augustus Cæsar, before our Saviour Christ was born, had such special regard of the sayings of the sybils, that he laid them up in more straiter order than before under the altar of Apollo, in the hill Palatine, where no man might have the sight of them but by special license. And so much for the credit of the sybils, who gave full testimony of our Saviour Jesus Christ, by name ; and therefore, if the Gentiles will believe them, who were their own prophets, and highly reverenced of all the world, they must also believe our gospel, and the Christian religion to be the only true religion.

Lastly, the Gentiles might have the understanding of Christ the Messiah by the Hebrew Scriptures, which were in the Greek language divers ages before Christ was born. For Ptolemy, king of Egypt, which had the famous library, was studiously inquisitive to search out the original of all nations and religions, and he found that the people of the Jews was the most ancient, and that they only had the most certain and undoubted history of the creation of the world ; and therefore he sent unto them to send to him from Jerusalem seventy men, by whose help the sacred Bible might be translated out of Hebrew into their tongue, which was done accordingly. As also the Gentiles might have knowledge of this Messiah, either by access into the Jewish country, or by the access of the Jews into their country, as, namely, by their long bondage in Egypt, as also their long captivity in Babylon, &c. But I conclude this matter thus : Sith the prophets of both Jews and Gentiles, that is to say, the prophets of all the world, have given full, plain, and evident testimony of Jesus Christ, the Son of God, that therefore his religion is the only true religion, and all other to be rejected and detested.

5. That religion which is most ancient is the true religion, for

---

[1] See the oration of Const. in Euseb. lib. iv. cap. xxxiii. de vit Const.
[2] Cic. lib. ii. de divinat.   [3] Sueton. Trans. cap. iii. de vita.

truth was first, insomuch as error is nothing else but the corruption of truth, or wandering from truth ; but the religion whereof Christ is the author is the most ancient, inasmuch as Christ, the author thereof, is the most Ancient of days, being the Son of God, as also because he is testified of by the Hebrew records, which are the most ancient writings in the world ; *ergo*, the Christian religion is that which must needs be the only true religion in the world. For it is a true saying of Tertullian,[1] *Verum quod primum, quod posterius adulterium est :* that is true whatsoever is first, and that is adulterate which is not the first. That the Hebrew records do testify and foreshew Christ to come, is declared before in the second chapter, and none can deny it. For he was promised to Adam, the first man that ever God made, under the name of ' the seed of the woman,' that should ' break the serpent's head ;' he was foretold to Abraham, that he should come of ' his seed, in whom all the nations of the earth should be blessed.'

Jacob foretold of him, calling him *Shiloh,* and that he should be the expectation of the Gentiles. God telleth Moses of him, and foresheweth to him that he should be ' the prophet whose voice all should hear and obey,' &c. Considering, then, that he is come, and that he is the very same that was foretold by the writings of Moses, and by the Hebrew records, which are the most ancient records in the world, I conclude that his religion, whereof he is the author, is the only true religion.

The antiquity of the Hebrew history to be long before all other, is acknowledged by the heathen themselves, and therefore I need not to prove it ; only this I say, that Eupolemus and Eusebius[2] also do say, that letters, which are the beginning of words that should be written, were first found out by Moses, and by him delivered to the Jews, and that the Jews taught them to the Phœnicians, and that lastly the Grecians received them of the Phœnicians, and therefore the Hebrews must needs be they amongst whom the first and most ancient records of the world were to be found, as Ptolemy also, king of Egypt, did find and affirm, and therefore made much of the Hebrew Scriptures. Now, then, forasmuch as the Hebrew writings and histories be the most ancient, they must also needs be supposed true, inasmuch as in themselves they all agree in a sweet harmony, and no other records are able to disprove them. Yea, if men will be so incredulous as to doubt of Moses's history, because it is so ancient, why may they not, with as good reason also, doubt of any other history which is ancient, and long before

---

[1] Tertul. contra Prax.   [2] Euseb. lib. x. de præpar. Evang.

their times ? But because some are of so little belief, although the history do sufficiently give credit to itself, yet for better settling of their minds in this behalf, I will briefly shew that even the heathen historiographers and writers do confirm the same, that so the credit and reverence due unto Moses may be reserved, and wicked tongues that bark against him may be stopped. The very heathen and profane writers themselves, that spake of Moses, spake of him most reverently ; insomuch that Trebellius Pollio,[1] speaking of Moses, *solum Dei familiarem vocet,* doth call him the only man with whom God was familiar. Cornelius Tacitus, although he speaketh what he can against the religion of the Jews,[2] yet cannot discredit Moses's history, but is enforced to confess, according to the history written by Moses, that after there were botches and swelling sores sent into the land of Egypt, which were noisome both to men and beasts, the king of Egypt then took order, that the people of the Hebrews should go out of his land, and depart whither they should be directed. Procopius also mentioneth Joshua the son of Nun, Moses's successor, and saith, that the people of Phœnicia, for fear of Joshua and the Israelites, left their own country, and departed into Africa ; he mentioneth, likewise, the Jebusites, Gergesites, and the other people mentioned in the sacred Bible. Orpheus, one of the most ancient writers next to Moses, and an heathen, doth mention the two tables of stone wherein the law of God was written, and wisheth, moreover, all such as be studious of virtue to learn out of his verses divine knowledge, whereby, saith he, they shall understand and know the Author of the world, which is one God, which created all things, cherisheth all things, nourisheth all things ; who is not seen with mortal eyes, but is perceived only by the mind ; which doth no hurt to mortal men, insomuch as he is the causer and procurer of all good things. Furthermore, he addeth, that no natural man hath seen God at any time, except only a certain most godly old man that came of the Chaldeans, viz., Moses. At last he concluded with this saying, that he had learned these things out of the monuments which God in times past had delivered in two tables of stone. Linus also saith, that God created all things, and in the seventh day had finished all things. Homer, also, and Hesiodus, testify the same—the one saying that the seventh day did perfect and finish all things ; the other, *septimam lucem fuisse sanctam et præfulgidam,* that the seventh day was most holy and bright. How the earth was without form before it was fashioned

---

[1] Treb. Pol. in Claud.   [2] Tacit. Annual. lib. xxi.

by God, Ovid testifieth, calling it a *chaos*, which is *rudis indigestaque moles*, a rude and unfashioned heap ; which Homer and Hesiodus also testify, calling it *hyle*, a certain unshapen and rude matter, which God afterwards brought into good form and fashion. These have testified, we see, of the creation of the world, which is the great marvel of marvels, affirming in manner the very words of Moses which he writeth in Genesis, shewing that the world had a beginning, and that God created heaven and earth, and all therein, in seven days, and that the seventh day was holy unto the Lord. And this truth of Moses's history concerning the creation of the world, all the chief and best learned philosophers[1] amongst the heathens did also firmly believe. The flood that drowned the world, which we call the flood of Noah, not only Ovid testifieth in his Metamorphosis, but also divers ancient heathen writers, namely, Berosus Chaldæus, Jeronimus Ægyptus, Nicholaus Damascenus, Abydenus, and others, according as both Josephus and Eusebius[2] do prove.

Concerning the tower of Babylon, and confusion of tongues there, which Moses recordeth, Gen xi., testimony is given by Abydenus, that lived about king Alexander's time, and by Sybilla, and by the words of Hestieus,[3] concerning the land of Shinar, where it was builded ; and these Gentiles do shew by reason, that if there had not been some such miracle in the division of tongues, no doubt but that all tongues being derived from one, as all men are of one father, would still have retained the same language, which we see was seen long not to be in the world. The difference of languages in the world, is a proof of that confusion of tongues.

Of the long life of the first patriarchs, not only the forenamed Berosus Chaldæus, Jeronimus Ægyptus, Nicholaus Damascenus, Abydenus, but also Mænetheus, that gathered the history of the Egyptians, Molus Hestiæus, that wrote the Acts of the Phœnicians, Hesiodus, Hecatæus, Abderica Helanicus, Æusilaus, and Ephorus, do testify, that these first inhabitants of the world did live so long; and they allege the reason thereof to be for the multiplication of people, and for the bringing of all sciences to perfection, especially astronomy and astrology, which, as they write, could not be brought to any sufficient perfection by any one man that had lived less than six hundred years, in which space the great year, as they call it, returneth about.

[1] Vide Plut. de placit. Philos.
[2] Jos. lib. de ant. Jud.   Euseb. l. ix. de præp. Evang.
[3] Euseb. lib. ix. de præp. cap. iv.

Of Abraham and his affairs, I have alleged from heathen writers before, as Berosus, Hecatæus, and Nicholaus Damascenus; but of all others, Polyhistor[1] allegeth Eupolemus most at large of Abraham's being in Egypt, of his fight and victory in the behalf of Lot, of his entertainment by king Melchisedec, of his wife and sister Sarah, and of other his doings, especially of the sacrifice of his son Isaac. To whom agreeth Melo, in his books written against the Jews; and Artabanus, of the strange lake wherein Sodom and Gomorrah were turned, by their destruction, called *Mare Mortuum*, the Dead Sea, where nothing can live; both Galen, Pausanus, Solinus, Tacitus, and Strabo,[2] do testify and shew the particular wonders thereof.

From Abraham down to Moses writeth very particularly the said Alexander Polyhistor, albeit he mingleth sometimes certain fables; whereby it appeareth that he took not his story wholly out of the Bible. And he allegeth one Leodemus, who, as he saith, lived with Moses, and wrote the self-same things as Moses did; and with these also do concur Theodorus, a most ancient poet, Artabanus and Philon, gentiles; and therefore it is manifest that Moses's history, as also all the rest of the sacred and canonical Scriptures, is no fable or feigned matter, as the devil would make us believe, but a true, certain, and most undoubted history in all points. All which matters be sufficiently and substantially shewed also even by the heathen writings, which are too tedious to be here rehearsed.

But the great wonders and miracles which Moses did, being acknowledged to be done, not by his own power, but by the power of God, do sufficiently do credit unto him, of whom and of whose acts do bear witness, not only the forenamed, especially Artabanus in his book of the Jews, but many others also, especially Eupolemus, out of whom Polyhistor reciteth very long narrations of the wonderful and strange things done by Moses in Egypt. Yea, the miracles done by him, the greatest enemies that ever he had in the world, that is, Appion in his fourth book against the Jews, and Porphyry in his fourth book against the Christians, do confess.[3] And Porphyry adjoineth more for proof thereof, namely, that he found the same things confirmed by the story of one Sanctonathon a gentile, who lived, as he saith, at the same time with Moses; but all those miracles, say those two his great enemies, were done by art magic, and not by the power of God. But first, where could Moses, a simple shepherd, learn so much magic? Or why could

---

[1] Alex. Polyhist., lib. de Judaica Historia.
[2] Galen de simpl., Paus. in Eliæ., Solin. in Polyh., Tacit. in lib. ult.
[3] Appion lib. iv., contra Judeos. Porph. lib. iv., adversus Christian.

not then the great magicians of Egypt either do the like, or at leastwise deliver themselves from those plagues that were in Egypt, especially since their study was in art magic from their infancy? yea, why did they cry out, 'The finger of God is here,' Exod. viii. 18, when they could not do as he did? Or let them answer, why Pharaoh, king of Egypt, did speak to Moses and Aaron, saying, 'Pray ye unto the Lord, that he may take away the frogs from me, and from my people,' Exod. viii. 9–11, &c. His great magicians belike could not do it; yea, he signifieth in that speech that none can do it but God; yea, and that neither Moses nor Aaron could do it any otherwise than by praying unto God; and indeed Moses and Aaron did by prayer unto God effect it, at the very same time that the king did appoint it to be done, that he and all the world might know, that there was not any like unto the God of Israel.

Where did you ever hear of such works done by art magic as Moses did? when he divided the great and mighty Red Sea, that the people of Israel might go through the dry land? when the waters came together again upon Pharaoh and all his host, and drowned them, and all their glory, in the sea? Exod. xiv.; when he called so many quails upon the sudden into the camp, as sufficed to feed six hundred thousand men, besides women and children? Exod. xvi.; when he made a very rock, by smiting it, to yield forth abundance of water, sufficient for the whole company of Israel? Exod. xvii.; when he caused the ground to open and swallow down alive, three of the greatest of his army, Korah, Dathan, and Abiram, together with their tabernacles, bags, and baggages? Num. xvi.

Besides, what wondrous works or miracles soever Moses did, he always acknowledged to come from God, rejecting utterly all glory from himself, and attributing and yielding all the glory unto God. Again, in his writings he doth not excuse nor conceal his own sin, nor the sin of his people, no, not the sin of Aaron his own brother, nor of Miriam his sister, nor of Levi his grandfather, nor of any other of his lineage or kindred. Neither did he once seek or go about, although he were in place of power and authority to do it, to bring in any of his own sons into the rule and government after his decease, although he had many, but left the only rule and government unto a stranger, named Joshua, as God commanded.

All which things do shew, and many more too tedious to rehearse, that Moses, both in his writings, in his words, and in his works, was no man of ambition, or of worldly spirit; but a meek, humble, dutiful, obedient, and faithful servant of God in all matters.

The history of Moses, therefore, being the most ancient, and the same being most undoubted and certain true, insomuch as he and his history do plentifully testify of Christ which was to come, and should be heard in all that he should say and teach; it remaineth that his religion which he hath taught unto the world, is the only true religion, and all other religion, not grounded on the like antiquity and truth, to be abandoned.

6. None can discredit Moses, nor the Psalms, nor any of the prophets amongst the Jews, but they must withal discredit Christ; for Christ saith thus of himself, that 'All must be fulfilled which were written of him in Moses, the prophets, and the Psalms,' Luke xxiv. 44. Again, he sendeth such as would know of him whether he were the true Messiah, to the Scriptures of the Jews, saying thus, 'Search the Scriptures, for they are they that testify of me,' John v. 35. So that Christ, Moses, the Psalms, and the prophets, in a word, the whole canonical Scriptures of the Jews, do go arm in arm, and be linked together, like inseparable friends that will not be sundered; and therefore the one is always a proof for the other; as likewise a disproof of the truth of the one is a disproof of the other; and therefore is it, that though the incredulous Jews be so false in friendship, as that they will not, through unbelief, take part with the Christians, yet the Christians be more firm, and will hold with the Scriptures of the Jews to the death. Now if there were no more to prove the divinity of Christ but the great and wonderful miracles which he did (some whereof were such as never any did before, nor could do, but God only), it were sufficient to prove him to be the Son of God, and that he came from the bosom of his Father. The great and many miracles that he did (being famous not only in Judea, but in all the Roman empire, and so over all the world) are and were such as none of the heathen dare, do, or can deny, but all acknowledge. And therefore I conclude, that the Christian religion, proceeding from so divine a power, and from one whose works and wonders are above all the world, is the most undoubted true religion.

7. Christ did never any hurt on earth, but he did marvellous much good; he healed all manner of diseases; he caused the dumb to speak, the halt to go, the blind to see, and the deaf to hear; he stilled the raging of the winds and seas, gave sight to him that was born blind, raised the dead to life again, cast out devils, knew men's thoughts, and did such works as no man could do, except God were with him, yea, except himself were God. Moreover, his life was such as none was able to accuse him of any sin, so pure and unre-

provable was he. Again, the doctrine he taught was far from a worldly spirit, being most heavenly, most innocent, and most divine; for never any man spake as he spake, nor with such authority. Again, he always pronounced that he sought not his own glory, which deceivers are wont to do, but the glory of his Father; and as he spake, so it was indeed. The whole course of his life and death, resurrection and ascension, doth shew the same; for when the Jews would have made him an earthly king, he would none of it, but conveyed himself away, John vi. 15, teaching his ministers to do the like, Luke xxii. 25, 26. For he proclaimed that his kingdom was not of this world, John xviii. 36, but that he came to do the will of his Father. Over and above all this, he was the greatest prophet that ever was, and foretold divers things, as namely, that he should be crucified of the Jews, and the third day rise again; that Jerusalem and the temple should be destroyed ere that generation passed; that after his ascension, the Holy Ghost should come upon his disciples assembled at Jerusalem; and divers others; all which the world doth know came to pass accordingly. And nothing which he hath spoken, but it shall be performed; for there was never any fraud within his lips, or falsehood within his tongue. And therefore I conclude, that the religion of him, who was most holy in his life, most harmless towards others, most bountiful towards all, most wonderful in his works, most true in his prophecies, most heavenly in his doctrine, not savouring of any carnal delight or worldly affection, nor by any way or means seeking his own glory, but the glory of God, and to do the will of his Father, is and must needs be the only true religion.

8. Another argument I frame thus: That religion which proceedeth undoubtedly from God is the true religion; but the Christian religion proceedeth undoubtedly from God, *ergo*, &c. That it proceedeth undoubtedly from God, I prove thus: either it must proceed from God, or from the devil, or from men; but it is too holy to proceed either from men or devils; for it overthroweth the works and kingdom of the one, and forbiddeth the revenging spirit of the other; commanding men to love their enemies, to do good to them that hate them and persecute them; and it condemneth their wanton eye, and the adulterous thoughts of their hearts, and their covetous humour, admitting no uncleanness or impurity, and forbidding all iniquity and wickedness, be it never so secret or close. Sith, therefore, it is so opposite and contrary to men's affections, wherewith naturally they be carried, and that it commandeth to be holy, even as God is holy, it is manifest that it can neither be

of man's devising, nor of the devil's invention ; it remaineth there-fore that it must needs be of God, and consequently the only true religion.

9. Another argument is this: That religion which respecteth only the glory of God, is, and must needs be, the only true religion. But such is the Christian religion, for it alloweth not any man to glory in himself, but sheweth that whosoever glorieth, should glory in the Lord, 1 Cor. i. 30, 31, Rom. iv. 2. Therefore the Christian religion is the only true religion.

10. Lastly, the spreading and prevailing of the gospel of Christ over the universal world, whenas all the world, both Jews and gentiles, were set and opposed against it, doth demonstrate plenti-fully and effectually, that the Christian religion proceedeth from God, and that God is the author thereof ; for if it had not had a God to protect and patronage it, and to make it pass currently through the world, it must needs have been utterly suppressed and choked, even in the springing and first rising thereof. For after the ascen-sion of Christ Jesus into heaven, what were his few apostles, in the judgment of reasonable men, able to do, for the spreading and pre-vailing thereof, against the force and power of all the world, which was then ready bent with all both fury and fraud, violence and vengeance, and with all their devices which they could invent to suppress it? Or what eloquence had his few apostles to persuade the world, or any therein, to the receiving and embracing of that Christian religion which they were appointed to preach? They, as all men know, were reputed and known to be unlearned men, but only that they were taught and instructed by the Spirit of God, which, according to the promise of Christ their Master, at the time appointed, descended down upon them, being assembled at Jeru-salem; by which Spirit they were enabled to speak all languages, and emboldened to preach his gospel and religion in such sort, and with such puissant and divine wisdom, as none should be able to resist that Spirit they spake by, howsoever their persons might be hindered, molested, vexed and persecuted. This, even this is a wonder of wonders, and an infallible demonstration of the divine virtue of the Christian religion, that it having so few to publish it, and such as they were, and being encountered by all the princes and potentates of the world, it should notwithstanding so strangely prevail, as within a short time to be universally spread over the face of the whole earth. Who can now say but that it was pro-tected and prevailed by the power of God? For the power of all the world was against it; and if the Christian religion had been no

better protected by God than by men, alas, it had perished long ago; yea, it had never lived until this day, but had been choked even at the first uprising, and as it were in the cradle or infancy thereof. Let all wits therefore throw down themselves, and let all tongues freely confess the divine virtue of the Christian religion, which could not be stopped nor suppressed; but was so mighty, as that the power of all the world, and all the devils in hell joining with them, was not able to stay the course and passage thereof, but that it did prevail, and that within short space, over all the earth. And therefore the Christian religion, without all doubt, is the only true religion, which came down from heaven, being brought by Jesus Christ the true Messiah, from the bosom of God the Father. Of which, having so many and so infallible arguments to prove to every man's sense the truth thereof, none can doubt, except he will also doubt whether the eye doth see, the ear doth hear, and the heart doth understand; the evidence thereof is so clear and manifest, as that it is able, if not to convert, yet to convince all gainsayers whosoever, and to make us, that already profess, firmly to hold the same; knowing for certain that the Christian religion is the only true religion in the world, and that salvation is nowhere else to be sought. For run over all the religions of the world, and where shall you find any so pure, so divine, so powerful, so miraculous? It hath all the signs, tokens, arguments and proofs that may be, for the splendent truth thereof, and to demonstrate that undoubtedly it came from God.

CHAPTER IV.

Wherein is briefly shewed the religion of Mahomet to be a false and wicked religion.

IF I shall speak something of the Mahometish religion, I think the truth of the Christian religion will appear so much the more; for when black and white are laid together, the white carrieth the greater estimation and glory with it. And beside, Mahomet himself testifieth of Christ to be a great prophet of God, and a great worker of miracles;[1] and that the same Jesus Christ was born of the virgin Mary, that he lived without sin among men, that he was a prophet, and more than a prophet, and that he ascended into the heavens. And therefore he reproveth the Jews, for that they would

[1] Mat. Paris Hist. Ang. in Hen. iii.

not believe him to be born of a virgin. But, on the other side, because he would not have Christ to bear credit above him, he disliked that he should be called or reputed the Son of God. But beside, the testimony of all the former prophets of the world, both Jews and Gentiles, as is afore shewed, do all teach that he should be the Son of God. Suidas doth moreover confute this false prophet, who reporteth in his History that the pharisees at Jerusalem called a council to find out the father of Jesus ; they enjoined certain women to search his mother ; the women affirmed they found her a virgin ; then was it recorded in the famous register book of the temple, *Jesus the Son of God, and of Mary the virgin.* This proveth, not only that the mother of Jesus was a virgin (which Mahomet truly held), but also that Jesus was the Son of God, which Mahomet alloweth not. And indeed Mahomet's religion is a patched religion, mixed partly with Judaism, partly with Gentilism, partly with Papism, partly with Christianism, being subtilely contrived for the erecting of the same, and to bring followers after him, whereof shall be spoken more hereafter.

The beginning of Mahomet's usurping, and of his sect, was thus many hundred years after Christ, namely, in the year of our Lord 597; and in the reign of Mauritius the emperor, whenas Gregorius Magnus was bishop of Rome, this Mahomet was born (being of the line of Ishmael, the son of Abraham, by Hagar the bondwoman, having unto his father one Abdara, and unto his mother one Emma, being very obscure and base parents) in Mecca, a city of Arabia. His parents deceased, and left him a very young orphan, who in short time, by misadventure, was taken captive.[1] This being once known unto his kindred, one Ademonaples, saith Volateran,[2] an Ishmaelite, bearing him good will for his favour and forwardness of wit, paid his ransom, and made him servant and factor in all his merchandise.

Not long after, his master died without issue, and his servant Mahomet matched with his mistress, a widow of fifty years of age, called Eadigam, and, saith Paulus Diaconus, his own kinswoman ;[3] so that, his master being of credit and substance, and his mistress (afterwards his wife) of no less account, and so shortly after departing this life, he succeeded them both in credit and all their substance, and by this means grew to a great power and estimation. Diaconus further saith that this Mahomet, for the space of ten

[1] Matthæus Pal. Masleus Chron. lib. xiii. ; Dreenchsleer, Chron. de Saracen. et Turc. Orig.
[2] Volat. Georg. lib. xii.　　　　　[3] Paul. Diac. rec. Rom. lib. xviii.

years, gave himself secretly by persuasion to bewitch the people ; and other ten years after, with rogues and vagabonds that repaired unto him with force of arms, with sword, and shedding of blood, he spent in subduing of countries ; and lastly, nine years he openly and manifestly enjoyed as a deceiver, a false prophet, and a king, over those whom he had already infected throughout Arabia.

Sabellicus writeth[1] that Mahomet's father was an heathen, and his mother an Ishmaelite, whereby it came to pass that, while his mother taught somewhat of the religion of the Hebrews, and his father, on the other side, the religion of the Gentiles, Mahomet, like a dutiful child, but not like a discreet son, obeyed both, and that was some cause of the mixed and patched religion. He had the falling sickness, which took him so extremely that he grovelled along the ground, and foamed piteously at his mouth. His wife, being of great honour and substance, bewailed her hard hap in matching with a beggarly rascal, and a diseased creature ; but he, with his wily companions, having taught a dove to feed at his ear, wherein he had put grains of corn, persuaded his wife to be content, and that he was another manner of man than she took him to be, namely, that he was a prophet, that the Spirit of God fell upon him, and that the angel Gabriel, in the form of a dove, came to his ear and revealed to him secrets from God, whose presence he was not able to abide ; and therefore was it that he so prostrated himself, and lay in a trance. His wife being herewith satisfied, she began to chat the same amongst her gossips, saying, Say nothing, my husband is a prophet. The women, after their manner (whereof some of them can keep no counsel), blazed abroad that Mahomet was a prophet, and so from women it came to men.

This being once noised, they flocked unto him from all parts of Arabia.[2] He being thoroughly instructed in Satan's school, and well seen in magic, observed the present opportunity. The Romans and Persians then warring together, Mahomet, with his Arabians, went and first took part with the Romans, but afterwards served them a sly touch, and forsook them, and thereby weakened that side. In a while after, he espied the Persians go to wreck ; and, having despised the Romans, he setteth less by the Persians,[3] and then setteth forth himself with might and main, with his captains and lieutenants, called Amirel, to subdue nations, and to destroy the Christians, to the end that he might establish that false religion, devised by himself and his wicked confederates. He prevailed

---

[1] Sabel. Ænead. viii. lib. viii.
[2] Aventine. Annal. lib. iii.
[3] Zonaras Annal. tom. iii.

wonderfully, and in short time after his decease, in the time of
Ebubezer and Haumer, that successively reigned after him in
Arabia, there were got and subdued to the Arabians the region of
Gaza, the city of Bostra in Arabia, Damascus, Phœnicia, Egypt,
Palestina, the city Jerusalem, all Syria, Antioch, Edessa, Mesopo-
tamia, all Persia, yea, and in a manner all Asia. But I may not forget the end of Mahomet, who in an evening sitting up late in his
palace, and having taken his fill of wine, wherein one of his companions had poured some poison, felt his wonted sickness approaching, and made haste forth, saying he must needs depart to confer
with the angel Gabriel, and go aside lest his glorious presence
should be an occasion of their deaths. Forth he went, and remembering that a soft place was best for his falling-sickness, down he
fell upon a dunghill, grovelling along with great pain, foaming at
the mouth, and gnashing his teeth; the swine came about the dunghill, fell upon him, wounded him sore, and had eaten him up had
not his wife and others of his house heard the noise of the hogs,
and rescued the false prophet. Antoninus reporteth[1] that he was
not without sundry diseases, which intemperate diet brought to
him, namely, the pleurisy and a kind of lethargy; for oftentimes
his senses seemed to be taken from him. He continued drooping
the space of fourteen days; at length he departed this life. His
belly had such a swelling, that it seemed ready to burst, and his
little finger bowed backwards. In the time of his sickness he commanded them that were about him that, when breath departed his
body, they should not straightway bury him, for he said that within
three days he would ascend into heaven; but hereby appeared that
he was a false prophet, for they kept him above the ground the
third and fourth day, yea, as *Flores Historiarum* testifieth, the
space of thirty days, in great hope he would rise and ascend according to promise; but they saw nothing, saving that they felt an intolerable stench, so that in great disdain, saith Antonius, *eum
longe à domibus projecerunt*, they cast him far from houses. But
his companions, such as consulted with him, and concealed his
falsehood and treachery, remembering themselves, and judging that
the disdain of Mahomet would be their discredit, and his fall their
foil and shame, they fetched him again; they chest him in an iron
coffin, saith Sabellicus and Nauclerus;[2] they bring him unto the
famous temple of Mecca, in which city he was born, with great so-

---

[1] Ant. Chron. part ii. tit. xiii. cap. v.
[2] Sabel. Ænead. viii. lib. vi.; Anton. Chron. part ii. cap. v.; Wolfang. Drenster.
Chron. Naucl. Gen. xxii.; Sabel. Ænead. viii. lib. vi.

lemnity, as if he had never been seated upon the dunghill with swine; they convey to the roof of the temple mighty loadstones; they lift up the iron coffin, where the loadstones, according to their nature, draw to them the iron and hold it up, and there hangs Mahomet on high.

Those that embrace the religion of Mahomet are called *Saracens*, for it was the pride of Mahomet to have them so called, to advance his own doctrine and profession, because he knew himself lineally descended of Ishmael, the son of Hagar the bondwoman; therefore, to avoid this reproach, he bare the world in hand that he came of *Sarah* the free woman, the wife of Abraham, and called himself and his followers *Saracens*. Sabellicus writeth, that the Grecians of spite are wont to call the Saracens *Agarenes*, for that they came not of Sarah, but of Hagar.

This Mahomet, while he lived, used the company of Christians, Jews, and Infidels; *et ut popularior esset ejus lex, ex omnium gentium sectis aliquid assumpsit*, and to the end his law might be the more favoured, he borrowed something of every sect.[1] Satan furnished him with three instruments, as helps to bring his mischievous intent about. The first was a Jew, a great astronomer and a magician, who opened to him at large the Jewish follies; the second, one John of Antioch; the third, one Sergius, a monk, both abominable heretics. Every one played his part. To flatter the Christians, he was content to be baptized of Sergius; and of these heretics he learned with the Sabellians to deny the Trinity; with the Manichees, to establish two beginnings;[2] with Eunomius, to deny the equal power of the Father and the Son; with Macedonius, to call the Holy Ghost a creature; and with the Nicolaites, to allow many wives and wanton lust. Sergius, the monk, also persuaded Mahomet in his Alcoran (so is the book of the law termed) to commend the humility of Christian monks and priests;[3] he made him also deliver the Saracens a monk's cowl, which they use to this day; also *instar monachorum multas genuflexiones*, many duckings and crouchings, like the monks. Matthias à Michovia addeth,[4] that they use shaving, and this, no doubt, was the monk's doctrine. They commend the blessed virgin Mary, confess God to be the governor of all things, and that Jesus Christ was the apostle of God, begotten by the angel Gabriel on Mary the virgin, who never knew man, and that he was greater and worthier than man.

[1] Sabel. Ænead. viii. lib. vi.; Fascicul. Temp.
[2] Sabel. Ænead. viii. lib. vi.   [3] Ant. Chro. par. ii. tit. xv. cap. ii.
[4] Matthias à Michov. de Sarmat. Asian. lib. i. l. vii.; Laonic. de Turc. lib. iii.

They allow the miracles that Christ did, and the gospel, so far forth as it agreeth with the Alcoran, and Moses, and the Old Testament, correcting therein, so presumptuous is the spirit, certain errors.[1] He called himself a prophet, and that he was sent of God to supply the imperfections of all laws. He forbade his followers all pictures and images in their temples ; he forbade the eating of swine's flesh ; he commanded purifyings and washings, *ad similitudinem Judæorum*, after the manner of the Jews. The Christians have Sunday for their Sabbath, the Jews Saturday, and Mahomet Friday, to dissent from the Hebrews and Christians, or, as Antonius writeth, in the honour of Venus, the goddess of Arabia, thereby the rather to win that country people. And thus it pleased him to devise a religion mixed of all these, to the end he might have of all religions some to build up his kingdom. And indeed Mahomet took the advantage of the time, for that time was a time of dissension among princes, and a division amongst those which called themselves Christians. Heraclius the emperor, and Chosroes king of Persia, were at deadly enmity, one warring against another. The Scythian nation were of neither side, but at last against both, raising a power of themselves, having Mahomet their ringleader. The church was troubled with divers sects and heresies, as with Nestorians, Jacobites, Monothelites, &c. And then was there contention amongst the bishops, who should have the proud title of universal bishop. God was highly displeased with this wickedness, and suffered nations to rise as a rod or scourge to whip his people ; for where the hedge is broken, there it is easy for the beasts of the field to enter and spoil. Now the vanity and falsehood of this religion may be proved thus :—

First, By the newness of it ; for it is but of late years begun, and there was never any prophecy that did allow of such a prophet, or of the doctrine of such a one ; and therefore he cometh in his own name, and so, consequently, not to be received.

Secondly, He did no miracle at his coming, and therefore no reason that any should believe in him. He spake unto the Saracens of himself, *non sum miraculis, aut indiciis ad vos missus :* I am not sent unto you with miracles and signs.[2] There was no divine power shewed in all his practice.

Thirdly, It is manifest that Mahomet was a false prophet, because he said, that within three days after his death he should ascend into heaven,[3] which was notoriously false, as before appeareth.

---

[1] Sabel. Ænead. viii. lib. vi.   [2] Matth. Paris Hist. Ang. in Hen. iii.
[3] Flor. hist.

Fourthly, The religion of Mahomet is fleshly, consisting in natural delights and corporal pleasures, which shew that man, and not the divine Spirit of God, is the author thereof; for it is permitted the Saracens by that his law to have four wives (though these be of nigh kin), yea, five, marrying them virgins; and to take besides as many of them which they have bought and taken captives, as their ability will serve to maintain.[1]　The paradise likewise promised to his followers is this, namely, they shall have garments of silk, with all sorts of colours; bracelets of gold and amber; parlours and banqueting-houses upon floods and rivers; vessels of gold and silver, angels serving them, bringing in gold, milk, silver, wine; lodgings furnished, cushions, pillows, and down-beds; most beautiful women to accompany them, maidens and virgins with twinkling eyes; gardens and orchards, with arbours, fountains, springs, and all manner of pleasant fruit; rivers of milk, honey, and spiced wine; all manner of sweet odours, perfumes, and fragrant scents; and, to be short, whatsoever the flesh shall desire to eat. Thus fleshly people have a fleshly religion, and a fleshly paradise to inhabit. But like prophet, like people, and like religion; for Mahomet himself was such a fleshly fellow, as that though modest ears are loath to hear, yet because the filthiness of this prophet may not be concealed, I must utter it. He committed buggery with an ass; Bonfinius writeth it.[2]　Again, he committed adultery with another man's wife, that upon displeasure was from her husband; and when he perceived the murmur of the people, he feigned that he had received a paper from heaven, wherein it was permitted him so to do, to the end he might beget prophets and worthy men.[3]　Again, Mahomet (as Cælius reporteth[4]), had forty wives; and further, he gloried of himself, that it was given him from above to exceed ten men (saith Cleonard[5]), fifty men (saith Antoninus[6]), in carnal lust and venery. Avicenna, one of Mahomet's own sect, is himself brought in disliking of this religion, for this reason,[7] because Mahomet (saith he) hath given us a law, which sheweth the perfection of felicity to consist in those things which concern the body; whereas the wise and sages of old had a greater desire to express the felicity of the soul than of the body. As for the bodily felicity, though it were granted them, yet they regarded not, neither esteemed it, in comparison of the felicity which the soul requireth. His paradise and doctrine is

---

[1] Jacob de Vor. legend. 157; Laonic. de reb. Turc. lib. iii.; Ant. Chron.
[2] Bonfin. lib. viii. Decad.
[3] Bernard. in Rosar. part. i. Serm. xiv.; Ant. Chro. par. iii. tit. xv. cap. ii.
[4] Cœlius Nichol.
[5] Cleon i. Epist.
[6] Antonin. Chron. part ii. cap. v.
[7] Avicenna Metaphys.

such, as there seemeth small difference between epicurism, atheism, and Mahometanism.

Fifth, Mahomet's law is a tyrannical law; for he made it death to dispute of it; and if any man speak against it (saith he), *Proditore occidatur*,[1] let him be traitorously put to death. And again, *Sine audientia occidatur;* let him be put to death without coming to his answer. *Qua sanctione* (saith Sabellicus[2]) *palam fecit nihil sinceri in ea lege esse, &c.* By which decree he manifested, that there is nothing sincere in that law, &c. Moreover, he wrote in the Arabian tongue, and taught his followers, that his religion, *A gladio cœpit, per gladium tenetur, et in gladio terminatur*,[3] began by the sword, is holden by the sword, and is finished or ended in the sword; which sheweth that the sword and arm of flesh is all the author and protector that his religion hath. Again, Mahomet made this law amongst them, saying, He that slayeth his enemy, or is slain of his enemy, let him enter and possess paradise. He spake like a man with a carnal spirit; teaching revenge to the uttermost, and promising paradise to such;[4] but no proof of a divine Spirit appeareth in him.

Sixth, As Mahomet's religion is defended by force of sword and fraud, insomuch as he made it death to call it into question; so likewise did it begin, as by the force of sword, so likewise by notable fraud, and was established through wiles, deceit, subtilty, and lies. For, first, he having the falling-sickness, persuaded his wife and others that it was the power of God, and the presence of the angel Gabriel, that caused him to fall down. Sergius the heretical monk was at hand, and bare false witness to the same (saith Zonaras[5]). He told them that the same dove which he taught to feed at his ear, was sometimes an angel, and sometimes the Holy Ghost. He had three companions all of a confederacy, to devise and face out lies with him. When he perceived that men gave ear to him, he feigned that the angel Gabriel had carried him to Jerusalem, and thence to have lifted him up to heaven, and there to have learned his law.

He made the Saracens believe, that before God made the world, there was written in the throne of God, *There is no God, but the God of Mahomet.*[6] When he had framed his Alcoran, and bound it up fair, he caused secretly a wild ass to be taken, and the book to be bound about his neck; and as he preached unto the people, upon

---

[1] Anton. Chron. part ii. tit. xiii. cap. iv.
[2] Sabel. Ænead. viii. lib. vi.
[3] Matth. Paris. hist. Aug. in Hen. iii.
[4] Paul. Diac. rer. Rom. lib. xviii.
[5] Zonaras, Annal. tom. iii.
[6] Ant. Chro. part viii. tit. xiii. cap. v.

a sudden he stood amazed, as if some great secresy was revealed to him from above, and brake out, and told the people, Behold, God hath sent you a law from heaven ; go to such a desert, there you shall find an ass, and a book tied about his neck. The people ran in great haste, they found it so as he had said ; they take the ass, they bring the book, they honour the prophet.[1] Touching divorced and separated wives, he told the Saracens he had received a paper from heaven. He used soothsaying and divination, the which at Fessa, a city of Mauritania, unto this day is called *Zarragia*. He persuaded his followers, that at the end of the world he should be transformed into the form of a mighty ram, full of locks and long fleeces of wool ; and that all that held of his law, should be as fleas shrouding themselves in his fleeces, and that he would jump into heaven, and so convey them all thither. These, and such like were his flights, to beguile a foolish, rude, and barbarous country people ; the foolery, pride, and vanity of whose religion, I trust every one doth sufficiently perceive.

Seventhly, Mahomet's religion is no true religion, but a mere device of his own, and of three others his false conspirators ; for he hath patched together his Alcoran of the doctrine of heathens, Indians, and Arabians ; of superstitious Jews, of Rechabites, of false Christians and heretics, as Nestorians, Sabellians, Manichees, Arrians, Cerinthians, Macedonians, Eunomians, and Nicolaites, of illusions and inventions of their own ; and lastly, for further credit, he borrowed some out of the Old and New Testament. But God will not thus be served ; for he delivered his mind of old unto Israel, and he is not changed, but continueth the same God still. ' Ye shall not,' saith God, ' do every man what seemeth him good in his own eyes. Whatsoever I command you, take heed you do it ; thou shalt put nothing thereto, nor take aught therefrom,' Deut. xii. Satan being conjured to deliver the truth of the Alcoran of Mahomet, said that therein were comprised twelve thousand lies,[2] and the rest was truth ; by all likelihood very little. And therefore I conclude, that there is no evidence to prove Mahomet a true prophet ; many prove him to be a false prophet, and blasphemous, and presumptuous ; and his religion to be a wicked, carnal, absurd, and false religion, proceeding from a proud spirit, and human, subtle, and corrupt invention, and even from the devil, the crafty father of lies, a murderer and man-killer from the beginning. And so much hereof may suffice.

[1] Avirus lib. ii. cap. xii. ; Joh. Leo. lib. iii. cap. xxiii. ; Aphric. Bern. in Rosan. part. i. serm. 10.　　　[2] Fascicul. temp.

CHAPTER V.

Wherein is shewed that the Church of Rome is not the true church of God, nor observeth the true religion.

I AM now entering into that great controversy between the protestants and the papists, whether of them should be the true church, and true worshippers of God in Christ; for they both acknowledge God, and Christ his Son; and all the sacred and canonical books of the Scriptures, they confess to come from God, and from his divine Spirit, as indeed they could come from no other. But whiles they both confess this book, it is good reason that they should both stand to the arbitrament and judgment of these books, for the trial of the true church, which, if they do, as indeed they must, this controversy is at an end, and not worthy to be made a question, or to be doubted of; for by the sacred and canonical writings it shall by and by be manifest that the church of Rome cannot be the true church possibly. But first let us hear what it saith for itself, and what good grounds it hath for the fortification thereof. For if it be not builded upon a good foundation, and upon such grounds as will hold, the whole building is like to lie in the dust, and to come to ruin.

1. They hold very stiffly, but not so strongly, that the church of God militant here upon earth is visible to the outward eye, and may be pointed out by the finger at all times, in such sort as that one may know whither to resort, as to the congregation of God's people, there to join himself unto them, and to praise and pray unto God with them, and to do those things that he requireth at their hands. But all this cannot profit them, nor hurt us; for as in the primitive churches, persecuted by those tyrannical and heathen emperors, there was a church of God, though not seen of them, who had their meetings and assemblies amongst themselves, though secretly, because of their enemies; so likewise in the days of Queen Mary, as also in all other times of the persecution of our church by the Romish bishops and their partakers, our church no doubt was, and might be; and they likewise had their meetings and assemblies, though both they and the place of their resort were unknown to those their persecutors.

In the time of Diocletian the emperor, especially, Christians were so wasted as to the judgment of men none were remaining, their books were burned, the churches destroyed, and themselves put to death. In the end, when this great havoc was made, and cruelty had wasted and destroyed all that could be found, where was then the visible church? It must needs be then enforced to hide itself, and so it was, and the glory thereof so eclipsed, that for a while it shined nowhere. And therefore the church is not always visible and seen to the outward eye, nor splendent in the faces and sight of men, and yet a true church notwithstanding, as then it was; for it is the sun, though it be sometimes overwhelmed with a cloud; and it is fire still, though it be sometimes raked up in embers; and so the true church is and may be, although not seen or known to the world; yea, though it seem overwhelmed with tyrannical malice, and hide itself as though it were clean extinct.

2. Let them tell me where the church was visible, when, being assembled at Jerusalem, there arose a great persecution against it, insomuch as they were all dispersed and scattered, as the text sheweth, Acts viii. 1. Or let them tell me, where or how the church was visible when Christ was smitten, and all the rest were scattered and hid, and concealed themselves. The face of the visible church was then not in Christ and his apostles, but in the Jews, among the scribes and pharisees, Mark xiv. 27; and therefore, if visibility be such a mark of the true church, then these who crucified Christ were the true church, and not Jesus Christ and his apostles; which who dare affirm? Yea, who will not deny? Yea, when the shepherd was smitten, and the sheep scattered, and yet a true church, who can deny but that a true church may be, though it be not apparently visible, and seen to the world? What shall I say more? Doth not St John in his Revelation testify expressly, that the church of Christ, signified there by a woman, *fugit in solitudinem*, fled into a desert, or wilderness, where she had a place prepared for her of God, and where she could not for a certain season be found of her persecutors? Rev. xii. 6, 7. Let them further shew me how the church was visible in the time of Elias the prophet, when he complained that he himself was left alone. 'O Lord,' said he, 'they have forsaken thy covenant, they have destroyed thine altar, and slain thy prophets with the sword, and I am left alone,' 1 Kings xix. 11, &c. Elias did not think himself to be *solus propheta relictus*, as Campian answered in the Tower; I say he spake not of himself only in that respect; but in this respect, that he took himself to be the only true worshipper that was left in Israel; which is manifest by the answer which God gave him, namely, that besides him he had seven thousand true worshippers yet remaining, which had not bowed their knee to Baal. I demand

of the papists, when Elias knew no other true worshipper of God but himself, how the church was visible? for whither he should go to find a true worshipper, he knew not. Again, it is written in 2 Kings xvi., that under the reign of Ahaz, there was taken a pattern of the altar of the idolaters of Damascus, and that Urias the high priest removed the altar of the Lord; whereby it appeareth, that the priesthood was corrupted, the altar removed, and consequently the sacrifices ceased, &c. What visibility of the true church could there be in those days, either of Ahaz, Manasseh, and other kings, being idolaters, when the temple itself, where only by the law of God the Jews were to offer the sacrifices, was polluted and defiled with heathenish idolatry? What church or congregation could any man, in this case, have resorted unto, to have performed a true and acceptable sacrifice unto God in those times, when the temple of Jerusalem, which was the place to worship at, would admit no true worshippers, but only idolaters? It is therefore manifest that a true church may be, though they know not a congregation of God to resort to; yea, though it be close and not seen or known one to the other, nor yet to the world. And consequently visibility, which the papists make a mark of the church, is no perpetual mark thereof. Yea, if such visibility should be a mark of the true church, then were the idolatrous people in the time of Elias, in the time of Ahaz, Manasseh, and many other kings of Israel that were idolaters, the true church, who indeed were the false church; and then were Elias and all others the true worshippers of God, who had in those times no places left to sacrifice in, the false church, which is absurd. Chrysostom saith,[1] that in the time of 'the abomination of desolation,' spoken of by Christ Jesus in Mat. xxiv., that is, in the time of wicked heresy, which is the army of antichrist, as he expounds it, *nulla probatio potest esse Christianitatis, neque effugium potest esse Christianorum aliud volentium cognoscere fidei veritatem, nisi scripturæ divinæ,* no proof can be made of Christianity, neither can there be any other refuge for Christians, which are desirous to know the true faith, but only the divine Scriptures. And therefore I conclude, which is apparent, that the true church sometime is in such a state, as that visibleness cannot discern or prove it, but only the divine Scriptures must demonstrate and declare it; and consequently it is demonstratively manifest, that it is no true position of the papists, that the church of God is always and evermore visible, seen, and splendent, to the outward eye and view of the world. Wherefore the papists do us great injury, and bewray

---

[1] Chrys. in Mat. xxiv.

their own ignorance, when they would have us to shew our church in all times and ages; which notwithstanding perhaps may be done, for our church was always, though it were not seen or known to them, but lay hid and kept itself close from their fury and tyranny, as the first and primitive churches did from their bloody persecutors. Our church was then persecuted in those times when it could not be seen, and many then, like constant martyrs, endured the tyranny of that Romish religion; so that some were banished, others fled into other nations, some endured martyrdom at home, others hid themselves, but the whole church generally was vexed and oppressed. And therefore when our church was thus persecuted, it is a good argument, I think, to say, we had our church then and always, though a persecuted church, though a church chased and pursued, though a church scattered, though a church not seen or visible to them, yea, though in itself it were enlightened from God many ages together, namely, till the tyranny of antichrist were over-past.

Secondly, Another erroneous position whereby they are miserably deceived is this: They hold the church cannot err, and therefore suppose, because the church of Rome was once the church of God, therefore it is so now and evermore. As though there might not be an apostasy in the church, which St Paul affirmeth there should, 2 Thes. ii. 3, 4. Or as though a particular church, for the church of Rome is but a particular church, could not err. Yea, as though general councils, which represent the whole church, could not err; for so they affirm: but how truly, let the world judge. And if it may be shewed that general councils have erred or may err, then they yield their cause in this behalf. I wish they would for their own sakes; for false Jesuits and seminaries do but deceive themselves and others to their own confusion in this world, and, except they repent, in the world to come.

That general councils may err, is manifest by Augustine, who plainly teacheth that only the Scriptures cannot err; all other writers may err, provincial councils may err. Lastly, he saith,[1] *Concilia quæ fiunt ex universo orbe Christiano, priora posterioribus sæpe emendari, cum aliquo experimento rerum aperitur quod clausum erat, et cognoscitur quod latebat:* that general councils, which are gathered of all the Christian world, are often corrected, the former by the latter, when by any trial of things that is opened which was shut, and that is known which was hidden. A general council may be corrected, saith Augustine,

[1] August. tom. vi. lib. ii. contra Donatist.

ergo, it may err ; and therefore Augustine speaketh plainly to Maximinian the bishop of the Arians;[1] Neither ought I to allege the council of Nice, nor thou the council of Ariminum, to take advantage thereby; for neither am I bound nor held by the authority of this, nor thou of that : set matter with matter, cause with cause, or reason with reason ; try the matter by the authority of the Scriptures, not proper witnesses to any of us, but indifferent witnesses to us both.

In the time of Constantine, that Christian emperor, was the first and last council of Nice,[2] wherein, according to our creed, was decreed that Christ was God as well as man. In the time of Constantius, Constantine's son, favouring the error of the Arians, it was decreed in the council of Ariminum that Christ was not God, but man. This council of Ariminum did err, and that grossly, in a matter of faith ; *ergo*, it is palpable that a general council may err even in matters of faith.

Again, general councils have been contrary one to the other, and that in matters of faith, as the council of Constantinople condemned the setting up of images in the church, and the council of Nice afterward allowed images. One of them, being contrary, must needs be erroneous ; *ergo*, a general council may err.

The general council confesseth itself that it may err; for the whole council prayeth in the end of a general council in a set form of prayer that is appointed to be said after every council,[3] namely, that God would *ignorantiæ ipsorum parcere et errori indulgere*, spare their ignorance and pardon their error ; *ergo*, a general council may err.

The pope of Rome, whom the papists hold for head of their church, may err, *ergo*, their whole church may err. Augustine proveth it errs[4] : *Beatæ memoriæ Innocentius papa sine baptismo Christi, et sine participatione corporis et sanguinis Christi, vitam non habere parvulos docet*, Behold, pope Innocentius of blessed memory doth teach that young children cannot be saved except they receive the baptism of Christ, and also the communion of the body and blood of Christ.

But this is taxed for an error, *ergo*, the pope of Rome may err, and consequently the whole church under him, except perchance members have a privilege above the head. But what shall I need

[1] Aug. con. Maximin. lib. iii. cap. iii.   [3] Concil. tom. i. de ord. celeb. concil.
[2] Theodor. lib. ii. cap. xviii.   [4] Lib. ii. ad Bonif. contra Epist. Pelag. cap. iv.

to stand hereupon? Their own canon law, as it is evident in the decrees,[1] doth say expressly that if the pope be found negligent of his own and his brethren's salvation, yea, though he lead innumerable people by heaps to the devil of hell, no mortal man may presume to reprove him, because he himself being to judge all, is to be judged of none, *nisi deprehendatur a fide devius*, except he be found erring from the faith; whereby it appeareth that they thought he might err in matters of faith, or else that exception was put in vain. But the pope is no other than a man, as also the members of his church be, and *humanum est errare*, all men are subject to error. Let every man take heed how he trusteth the pope, or any man mortal; for it is written, Jer. xvii., *Maledictus homo qui in homine confidit*, 'Cursed is the man that putteth his trust in man.' And why? Because, as the prophet David saith, Ps. cxvi., all men are liars in their words, and sinners in their works. But when the doctrine of that man of Rome and of his church is in divers things clean contrary to the express word of God, who can deny but it is an apparent erring church?

As when it established ignorance to be the mother of devotion, which Christ calleth the mother of error, saying, 'Ye err, not knowing the Scriptures,' Mat. xxii., 29; who can choose but think that it hath no good meaning in it, but purposed only to build up the pride of the pope, of his cardinals, bishops, priests, monks, and other their ecclesiastical men? Christ biddeth the people to 'search the Scriptures,' John v. 39; this antichrist forbiddeth them, saying it is perilous, it causeth schisms, sects, and heresies, as though they were wiser than Christ. Again, the apostle Paul commandeth that 'the word of God should dwell plentifully' in the people, whereby they might teach themselves, Col. iii. 19. But the pope of Rome and his church alloweth not plentiful knowledge of the word in them; yea, ignorance is the knowledge that he would desire them to have. Who would not justly suspect such a church and such a religion, yea, condemn it, when to maintain and continue their church in errors, they would have none of the people to search any Scriptures, whereby they might be discovered? Thus the silly papists, whom I pity, are led like blind men they know not whither, and with their *implicita fides*, which is to believe for their part they know not what, are lamentably seduced. It is good themselves should see and know what they believe, and that their faith and belief be right, lest at last they be, through overmuch trust of their teachers, extremely deceived. The people

---

[1] Part. i. dist. xl. cap. *Si Papa*.

of Berea were highly commended, and it is noted to their praise that they searched the Scriptures, to see whether those things were true or no which Paul himself teached, Acts xvii. ; for whosoever he be, yea, though he were an angel from heaven, if he teach matters contrary to the doctrine of the holy and canonical Scriptures, we are to hold him accursed, yea, and accursed again, as the apostle of Christ Jesus, St Paul, commandeth, Gal. i. 8, 9.

Again, the church of Rome when it taught and holdeth that the Scriptures were to be read unto the people, or congregation, in an unknown tongue, what were the people the wiser? St Paul would have all things done to edifying in the church. For saith St Paul, *Is qui supplet locum indocti, quomodo dicturus est Amen ad tuam gratiarum actionem, quando quidem quid dicas nescit?* 'How shall he that supplieth the place of an unlearned man say Amen to thy thanksgiving, when he understandeth not what thou sayest?' 1 Cor. xiv. ; and in that whole chapter he utterly disliketh service in an unknown tongue ; and therefore, if the church of Rome will not confess their error herein, she is past all shame, and hath the impudent and shameless face of an harlot.

They have all devised and defended a place of purgatory, wherein all that depart this life be put, and there punished, being a punishing fire, until they help to fetch them out with their masses, and other their inventions and devices, which they will not do, nor think they have reason to do, except they have good current coin for the same.

And therefore it may be well and justly called *purgatory-pick-purse;* and it is manifestly apparent hereby, that wealth and great riches of the clergy, was the only mark they aimed at. For it hath no warrant in the canonical books of the Scriptures ; yea, the canonical books of Scriptures shew the contrary, and so do the ancient fathers. Christ in the Gospel, Luke xvi., sheweth only but two places, namely, heaven and hell ; saying, that the rich man's soul, which was unmerciful to Lazarus, went after his death to hell, and there was tormented ; and that Lazarus's soul, he being dead, was carried into Abraham's bosom, a place of joy and comfort. To the thief which was executed at the passion and suffering of Christ, and believed in him, Christ answered, *Hodie eris mecum in paradiso,* 'This day shalt thou be with me in paradise,' Luke xxiii. 43; which sheweth that the souls of the faithful never come in purgatory fire to be boiled and punished, for all their sin is forgiven, and consequently, the punishment incident to the same is forgiven also, and their souls pass from death to life, and into paradise, a place of comfort, delectableness, and all sweetness, namely, heaven, where Christ is. 'Verily, verily, I say unto you,' saith Christ, 'he that heareth my word, and believes in him that sent me, hath eternal life, and cometh not into condemnation, but passeth from death to life,' John v. 25. What is become then of this purgatory? St Paul saith, 'I covet to be dissolved, and to be with Christ,' Philip. i. 23; shewing thereby, that presently after his dissolution, he was to be with Christ in glory. 'For we know,' saith he, 'that when this earthly tabernacle of ours is dissolved, we have a building not made with hands, but eternal in the heavens,' 2 Cor. v. 1. St John in his Revelation saith, 'Blessed are the dead which die in the Lord from henceforth: they rest from their labours, and their works follow them,' Rev. xiv. 13. If from the time of their death they have blessedness and rest, as he sheweth, then are they not in any purgatory-fire to be scorched and molested. St Peter telleth the saints and children of God, and assureth them of it, that 'the end of their faith is the salvation of their souls,' 1 Peter i. 9. If salvation of their souls begin at the end of their faith, which lasteth unto the end of their life, and no longer, for then they have the fruition and possession of that which they believe and hope for, then it is manifest there is no purgatory. Ambrose saith,[1] *Qui hic non receperit remissionem peccatorum, illic non erit is in cœlo; quia remissio peccatorum vita œterna est*, He that here in this life receiveth not remission of sins, shall never come into the kingdom of heaven; for life eternal is remission of sins. Cyprian saith,[2] *Quando istinc excessum fuerit, nullus jam locus penitentiœ, nullus satisfactionis effectus; hic vita aut amittitur aut tenetur; hic saluti œternœ cultu Dei et fructu providetur.* And again, by and by, he saith, *Tu sub ipso licet exitu et vitœ temporalis occasu pro delictis Deum roges, qui verus et unus est; venia datur confitenti, et credenti indulgentia salutaris, et ad immortalitatem sub ipsa morte transitur;* that is, when men are once departed hence, there is then no more place of repentance, no effect of satisfaction; here life is either lost or kept; here provision is made for eternal salvation by the worship of God, and fruits; and therefore, saith he, do thou call upon God, though it be at thy last gasp and departure of this thy temporal life, but call upon that God which is one and true; pardon is given thee if thou confess thy sins, and saving forgiveness if thou believe; and from death presently thou shalt pass to immortality. Jerome saith,[3] that the time of sowing

---

[1] Ambr. lib. ii. de bono mortis.   [3] Hier. in Gal. c. vi.
[2] Cyprian. contra Demet. tract. i.

their seed for Christians is this present life, and that as soon as this life is ended, they reap everlasting life. Augustine saith, *Primum fides catholicorum divina authoritate regnum esse credit cœlorum; secundum gehennam ubi omnis apostata, vel a Christi fide alienus, supplicia experitur; tertium penitus ignoramus, nec esse in scripturis sanctis reperimus.* The first place, saith he, the faith of catholics doth, by divine authority, believe to be the kingdom of heaven; the second, hell; a third place we are utterly ignorant of, neither can we find any such in the holy Scriptures. And the same Augustine writeth in another place,[1] that they which believe a purgatory-fire are much deceived, and that through an human conceit. How then can the papists be the true catholics, which believe not the faith of the catholics, which Augustine doth affirm?

They also hold, that a man, since the fall of Adam, hath free will of himself, and of his own power to come unto God, and to do things acceptable and well-pleasing in his sight. Whereas God saith after that time, that 'the imaginations of men's hearts are only evil every day,' Gen. vi. If they be *only evil,* then have they of themselves no affection to goodness acceptable to him. And Christ saith, 'No man can come unto me, except my Father draw him,' John vi. 44. If he must be drawn before he can come, he hath no proclivity or willingness of himself to come. And therefore it is that the prophet saith, 'Convert thou me, and I shall be converted,' Jer. xvii., shewing, that he hath no power in himself to be converted. And St Paul sheweth, that till God give grace, 'there is none that doth good, no, not one,' Rom. iii. 10, &c. For all the philosophical virtues and good deeds which men do before they have faith, which is the gift of God, are sin, and not acceptable to God, John vi. 29. For the apostle witnesseth, that 'without faith it is impossible to please God,' Heb. xi. 6; and that 'whatsoever is not of faith is sin,' Rom. xiv. 23. Christ himself again saith, that 'except men be engrafted into him, they can bring forth no fruit,' John xv. 1, 2, &c. Paul often teacheth that we must be new men, and 'cast off the old man,' Eph. iv. 22. And again, he bids us to be 'renewed in the spirits of our minds,' ver. 23. And moreover he saith, that 'the natural man perceiveth not the things that are of God, neither can he, for they are spiritually discerned,' 1 Cor. ii. 14. And again, that 'it is God that worketh the will and the deed,' Philip. ii. 13. And he plainly confesseth of himself and of all others, that 'we are not able of ourselves so much as to think

[1] Aug. Enchir. ad Laurent. c. 67.

a good thought,' and that 'all our sufficiency is of God,' 2 Cor. iii. 5.
Which premises do shew, that our understanding is blind, and our
will perverse in any divine matter, or acceptable service unto God,
till God do enlighten the one, and draw and move the other unto
himself. Thus hath God ordered matters, to the end himself might
have all the glory ascribed to him, as good reason he should. For
what is man since his fall in Adam, but an abject and runaway
from God, of himself seeking by-paths and crooked out-ways,
leading from God, and from his worship, except he be assisted from
above ? which is signified by Adam's hiding himself from the
presence of God after his fall. And therefore Augustine saith well
and truly,[1] *Hominem libero arbitrio male usum, et se et illud
perdidisse,* that man, having ill-used his free will that he had, hath
now both lost himself and that. And again, *Liberum arbitrium
captivatum, ne quid possit ad justitiam,* that free will is taken
captive, that it can do nothing towards righteousness. And again,
Hominis non libera sed a Deo liberata voluntas obsequitur, not
the free will, but the freed will of man, which is set free by God,
doth obey and yield obeisance. And again, *Liberum non fore,
quod Dei gratia non liberavit,* that the will is bound, and not free,
till God deliver it and set it at liberty. Cyprian, which Saint
Augustine so often citeth, saith, *De nullo gloriandum, &c.,* man
must glory of nothing, because nothing is ours ; therefore every man,
annihilating his own power, must learn wholly to depend upon God.
And Chrysostom saith,[2] that *omnis homo non modo naturaliter
peccator, sed totus peccatum est,* every man is not only sinful
naturally, but is altogether sin. And therefore Saint Paul sheweth,
that till a man be regenerate or born anew, and until he be renewed
in the spirit of his mind, he hath in him nothing else but *con-
cupiscentias erroris,* lusts and affections after error, Eph. iv. 23,
24, saying likewise, that ' by nature we are the sons of wrath,' Eph.
ii. 3. Which also Christ himself testifieth to Nicodemus, saying,
that ' that which is born of the flesh is flesh, and that which is born
of the spirit is spirit,' and that 'except a man be born anew by that
spirit, he can never so much as see the kingdom of God,' John iii.
3, &c. And therefore St Paul telleth, 2 Cor. xv. 17, that there must
be a new creature, whosoever will be in Christ Jesus, and a renew-
ing and metamorphosis of the mind (he useth the very word) before
men can find out the good and acceptable will of God, and what

---

[1] Aug. ad Arst. Epist. xliv. et Enchir. ad Lau. cap. xxx. et lib. iii. cap. vii. et ad
Bonif. cap. viii. et iii. et alib. passim.
[2] Lib. de præstest. sanct. item ad Bonif. lib. iv. in Gen. Hom. i.

pleaseth him, Rom. xii. 2. I therefore conclude, that the papists are far wide, and know not the misery and thraldom of men, whereinto they are fallen by that great sin and disobedience of Adam, whilst they stand to defend free will in natural men. Indeed, it appeareth to be free and too free unto evil, but it is so bound and fast tied from desire of any divine duties, that God must first draw it out of that servitude wherein it is, and set it at liberty, and move it to come, before it will shew any readiness that way. I trust therefore they see, that their church not only may err, but erreth most grossly in many points.

They hold that, in the sacrament of the Lord's supper, it is lawful to debar the people of the cup, and so they use; which is contrary to the institution of Christ, *Bibite ex hoc omnes*, ' drink ye all of this,' Mat. xxvi. 27. And as well, and by as good authority, may they take the bread from the people likewise. And it is contrary to the express doctrine of St Paul, 1 Cor. xi. 23, 28, who, as himself testifieth, delivered the institution of Christ, for he saith, ' Let a man examine himself,' *et sic edat, et bibat,* 'and so let him eat of this bread, and drink of this cup.' So that he must drink, as well as he must eat. And that the people should be partakers, and receive in both kinds, was observed many hundred years in the church after Christ; insomuch as pope Gelasius decreed, that all they should be excommunicate which would receive but in one kind. But Rome that now is, is not Rome that then was; but with her council of Constance,[1] is not ashamed to go against all antiquity and all divinity.

But they hold, which is a marvellous gross error also, transubstantiation in the sacrament, namely, that after the words of consecration, the bread and wine are changed into the very substance of the body and blood of Christ. And this they would seem to ground upon these words, *Hoc est corpus meum*, ' this is my body,' Mat. xxvi. 26, which they will have to be expounded literally. But why, then, do they not expound the other words of Christ literally also concerning the cup? For the text saith, in the 27th and 28th verses, that ' he took the cup,' &c., and said, 'This is my blood.' I am sure they will not say that the cup was the blood of Christ, as the words be, but they will grant a figure in those words, namely, *continens pro contento*, that by the cup is meant the wine in it. If, then, they will admit a figure in this, why may there not be a figure in the other, namely, *signatum pro signo*, that these words, ' this is my body,' should be understood thus,

[1] C. Comperimus de consecra. dist. 2.

the bread is a sign of my body, which was broken for you? If we look into the old sacraments of the Jews, namely, circumcision and the paschal Lamb, we shall find the phrase of speech observed. For circumcision was called 'the Lord's covenant,' when indeed it was not the covenant, as all men do know, but a sign and seal of the covenant; for the covenant was this to Abraham, *Ego Deus tuus, et seminis tui, &c.*, 'I will be thy God, and the God of thy seed,' &c., Gen. xvi. Rom. iv. 21. So likewise the paschal Lamb is called *the passover*, when indeed it was but a sign of the passover, or passing over or through the Red Sea, which was a mighty and most wonderful deliverance, Pharaoh and all his host being drowned in the sea, when they passed through as on dry land. Insomuch, therefore, as it is usual in sacraments so to speak, it is not against reason, but standeth with very good reason to think that Chris Jesus, in instituting this sacrament, which to the Christians is the same that the paschal Lamb was to the Jews, did likewise call the bread his body, in such sort as the paschal Lamb was the passover, that is to say, figuratively; that as the paschal Lamb was called the passover, and yet was but a sign and remembrance of their passover, so the bread was called his body, and yet it was but a sign and remembrance of his body.

And that this is the right exposition, may appear by the words of Christ, where he saith, 'Do this in remembrance of Christ,' Luke xxii. 19. Tertullian likewise doth so expound them; for he saith,[1] Christ said, *Hoc est corpus meum, id est, figura corporis mei :* this is my body, that is, a figure of my body. Augustine likewise saith,[2] *Christi miranda patientia adhibuit Judam ad convivium, in quo corporis et sanguinis sui figuram discipulis tradidit :* the admirable patience of Christ admitted Judas to the banquet, wherein he delivered to his diciples a figure of his body and blood. And again he saith, *Non dubitavit Dominus dicere, Hoc est corpus meum, cum daret signum corporis sui :* the Lord doubted not to say, This is my body, when he gave but the sign of his body. And this exposition must needs be true ;[3] for St Paul saith plainly and expressly, 1 Cor. xi. 26, 28, that the communicant doth eat bread, *ergo*, it remaineth bread after the words of consecration ; for if it were transubstantiate into the body of Christ, then were there no bread to eat, but the body of Christ is the thing that should be eaten. But none do eat the very body of Christ ; for if every communicant did eat the very body of Christ naturally, carnally, and

---

[1] Tertul. cont. Marcion. lib. iv.
[2] Aug. in Ps. viii.
[3] August. in tom. vi. cont. Adamant.

really, as they grossly suppose, Christ should have a number of bodies, which is palpably absurd and monstrous ; and beside, then every communicant should be saved, yea, even Judas himself, which is known to be the child of perdition; for Christ saith, ' He that eateth my flesh, and drinketh my blood, hath eternal life,' John vi. 54. Indeed, the elect and godly do eat Christ, and drink Christ, but how ? not carnally, but spiritually, and by a true faith, apprehending Christ, and applying Christ with all his benefits, as firmly into their souls as the bread and wine is applied to their bodies. Besides, if Christ gave his body to be eaten really by his disciples, at the time of the institution of this sacrament, what was it that did hang on the cross on the morrow ? Moreover, St Peter saith, Acts iii. 21, that as touching the body of Christ, the heavens must contain him unto the end of the world. If his body be in heaven, and that he hath a true body, as all men know he hath, how can it be that he should be both in heaven and in earth, as touching his body, at one time ? For though he have a glorified body, yet he retaineth the nature and property of a true body still, which can be but in one place at once. And so saith Augustine,[1] saying, *Corpus Domini in quo resurrexit, uno tantum loco esse potest,* the body of the Lord wherein he rose again, can be but in one place only. But the papists, to help themselves, are driven to this, to say that there is a miracle in the sacrament, and that Christ is there miraculously. Whereunto I answer, that if the bread be turned into the very body of Christ by a miracle, then should it appear visibly so ; for the nature of every miracle is to be visible to the outward eye and senses, as when Christ turned water into wine, it was visibly wine ; when Moses's rod was turned into a serpent, it was visibly a serpent ; and so, if the bread be turned into the very body of Christ, it is visibly his body, if you will hold a miracle to be wrought therein. But Augustine answereth,[2] there is no miracle in the sacrament, saying thus, *Honorem tanquam religiosa possunt habere, stuporem tanquam mira non possunt,* the sacraments may have honour as things religious, but they are not to be admired at as miracles. Theodoret, also, is most express against transubstantiation, for thus he saith,[3] *Neque enim signa mystica post sanctificationem recedunt a natura sua : manent enim in priore substantia, figura et forma, et videri et tangi possunt sicut prius ;* that is, the mystical signs after consecration do not depart from their nature, for they abide

---

[1] Aug. in Joh. tract. iii.
[2] Aug. Tom. iii. de Trinit. l. iii. c. x.
[3] Theod. dialog. ii.

still in their former substance, figure, and form, and may be both seen and felt as before.

Gelasius, a pope himself, doth say most plainly that there is no transubstantiation in the sacrament. His words be these,[1] *Non desinit substantia vel natura panis et vini; et certe imago, et similitudo corporis et sanguinis Christi in actione mysteriorum corporis Christi celebratur:* the substance or nature of bread and wine doth not cease, and verily there is the image and similitude of the body and blood of Christ, celebrated in the action of the mysteries of the body of Christ. And therefore I conclude, that the church of Rome which now is, is not the same which it was in former times, but it is become degenerate, and revolted from that former purity which once was in it; and, consequently, it is expressly manifest that that church both may and doth err.

The church of Rome doth further hold, that their pope hath authority to depose kings and princes. But by what title? It is clear that in his either so doing, or attempting to do, he is both a notable traitor unto God, whose authority he doth claim and arrogate, and unto princes, to whom he should be subject. For the raising and pulling down of princes God hath reserved to himself alone in his power. For it is he, not the pope, that 'deposeth the mighty from their seats, and exalteth them that are of low degree,' Luke i. It is he, not the pope, that 'putteth down kings, and giveth kingdoms to whomsoever he will.' And it is he that testifieth of himself, saying, *Per me reges regnant, et principes dominantur:* 'By me kings reign, and princes bear dominion,' Dan. ii. 20, and chap. iv. 14 and 22. Seeing, therefore, it is God that hath this high authority proper to himself, which way can the pope claim it, without injury and treason unto God? Will he claim it by reason of his keys, and in his apostolical right? That he cannot do; for he must remember that the keys given were 'the keys of the kingdom of heaven,' Mat. xvi. 19. And therefore by authority of the keys he cannot meddle with terrestrial kingdoms, to open an entrance for any into them, or to shut out or exclude any that be in them. And beside, St Paul the apostle doth say expressly, both of himself and of the rest of the apostles, that how great authority soever they have for the overthrowing of strongholds, that is, of rebellious thoughts, and proud conceits, and stiff-necked opinions seated in men's hearts against God, as himself expoundeth in the same place, that all their power and means to convert men is only by the sword of the Spirit, which is

[1] Gelas. contra Eutich.

the word of God, and by the power of the keys committed to them. In all which their authority, given unto them from Christ, he confesseth plainly, 2 Cor. x. 4, that the weapons of their warfare are not carnal, but mighty through God, that is, spiritual. Which words do demonstrate, that by their ecclesiastical ministry, they have clearly no civil authority committed to them.

And, moreover, it is manifest, by the practice of the apostles, and all their precepts, commanding all Christians to obey their rulers, their kings, and princes, yea, though they were persecutors, that the apostles never had any such authority committed to then , Rom. xiii. 1–4; 1 Pet. ii. 13; Tit. iii. 1. And therefore it is undoubtedly true, that the pope of Rome cannot claim it by any such authority. Again, the bishop of Rome can claim no more authority by the power of the keys, or of binding and loosing, than any other bishop elsewhere may do ; for the keys, that is to say, the power of opening and shutting, and of binding and loosing, John xx. 22, 23, were given to all the rest of the apostles as well as to Peter. And, consequently, for any minister of the gospel thereby to claim authority above another is absurd ; for they be all indifferently joined in one commission, and therefore have all equal authority ; and therefore the bishop of Rome, by virtue of the keys, hath no more authority than any other bishop hath, that is to say, none at all, to depose princes. Their duty is rather to practise obedience themselves to them, and to teach the same obedience to others, as the apostles of Christ did. Yea, Christ himself said, 'his kingdom was not of this world,' John xviii. 36 ; himself likewise refused to be made a king, John vi. 15 ; himself paid tribute unto Cæsar, and commanded others to give the same, and all other duties of subjection and obedience unto Cæsar, Mat. xxii. 21. If he were subject to Cæsar, it is a shame for the bishop of Rome to exalt himself above Cæsar.

But perchance the bishop of Rome will challenge this his sovereign authority over princes by donation from Constantine, or some other Christian emperor. Indeed, such fables sometimes he is not ashamed to utter. But let it be the strongest way for him, if you will, that some Christian emperor was so foolish as to give him his empire, which is neither likely nor credible, yet say I, it was neither lawful nor tolerable for him to take it, if he will be a minister of the gospel, or successor of the apostles. For Christ hath expressly forbidden his apostles, and in them all the ministers of the gospel, all such dominion, and civil jurisdiction, saying thus unto them, ' The kings of nations reign over them, and they that be great amongst them bear rule or dominion ; but it shall not be so with you,' Mat. xx. 25, 26 ; Mark x. 42, 43 ; Luke xxii. 25, 26.

Which words be most prohibitory, and shew that they may not reign like kings of nations, nor bear rule as great men in those nations do ; but they must serve in the church, be diligent to discharge that great charge in the church which their master Christ Jesus hath laid upon them. And therefore every way the pope of Rome hath no title, but is hereby an usurper, and an intruder, and a notorious and odious traitor, both to God and princes. And besides, all the ancient churches have affirmed and acknowledged the supreme authority of princes above and over all, both priests and people. And therefore, saith Tertullian,[1] *Colimus imperatorem ut hominem a Deo secundum, et solo Deo minorem,* we honour the emperor as the next man to God, and inferior to God only. And again he saith[2] that princes are *a Deo secundi, post eum primi, ante omnes, et super omnes,* the second to God, the first next after God, and before and over all men.

Optatus in like sort saith,[3] *Super imperatorem non est nisi solus Deus, qui fecit imperatorem,* there is none above the emperor but God only, which made the emperor. And Chrysostom saith,[4] *Parem ullum super terram non habet,* he hath no equal on earth. And Gregory, bishop of Rome, himself affirmeth[5] that the power is given to princes from heaven, not only over soldiers, but priests. And therefore I conclude that the church of Rome which now is, is not the church which once it was, but is wonderfully fallen into corruption, and grown into pride, both against God and his anointed prince ; and consequently not only may err, but doth err, and that most detestably and abominably in the highest degree.

The bishop of Rome doth further hold that he hath authority from God to forgive sins ; and thereupon he sendeth forth his charters of pardon, his bulls and indulgences, to such as he meaneth to assoil. The scribes in the Gospel could say, ' None can forgive sins but God,' Mark ii. 7, Job xiv. 4, Isa. xliv. 25. If, therefore, the pope of Rome will take upon him to forgive sins, in that sort he doth, he must prove himself to be God, otherwise his actions will not be warranted. How often in the Scriptures is it said of God that he forgiveth iniquity and transgressions, ascribing that authority only to God, and to no other ?

I need not recite any particular places ; the whole book of God

---

[1] Tertul. ad Scap.
[2] Tertul. in Apologet.
[3] Optatus cont. Parmen. lib. xiii.
[4] Chrysost. ad populum Antioch. homil. ii.
[5] Gregor. Epist. lib. iii. cap. c. et cap. ciii.

is plentiful herein. I do not deny but ministers of the gospel have power to bind and loose sinners, as Christ himself sheweth, Mat. xvi.; but how, and whom ? They can neither justify the unrighteous, whom God abhorreth, nor yet condemn the godly and faithful, whom God dearly loveth. Inasmuch, therefore, as they cannot pardon such as God condemneth, nor yet condemn such whom God acquitteth, Rom. viii. 33, 34, it is manifest that all their power of binding and loosing sinners is limited and bounded within the compass of God's word, which they may not pass ; for if they do, they go beyond their warrant, and so all that they do will be of no force. The incredulous and obstinately wicked persons they may, by warrant of God's word, pronounce condemnation against, except they do repent ; and to the assuredly faithful, repentant, and godly persons, whose continual care is to please God, and walk in his ways, they may pronounce the sentence of undoubted and certain salvation, because the word of God doth affirm as much ; and this is all the binding and loosing of sinners which they have. For in all their pronunciations of pardons and forgiveness of sins, they must be sure they speak not in their own names, nor their own wills and pleasures; but they must do it in the name of God, being first assured that it is his word, will, and pleasure which they utter. But the bishop of Rome observeth not the rule of God's word to square and measure his pardon by, but pardoneth whom he list and as he list, as if he were a god himself, having absolute power in himself, without respect of God's word or will, to do what he list. Insomuch as traitors and rebels against God and their lawful princes, he will not only pardon without exception, but he will abet them in their damnable courses, till at last, when it is too late for them to repent, they will, if they take not good heed in time, feel the smart of it in hell torments together for ever. What the religion of Rome is may appear by this, that any man for money may get a pardon for his sins ; and then what sin need rich men fear to commit, when a pope's pardon will salve all ? Or how can it be otherwise than a religion of licentiousness, when for money a man may have a license or dispensation against any sin whatsoever? These things be such open blots to the Romish religion as that worthily every good and godly mind hath it in detestation, and doth justly condemn it. Yet further will I prove that the church of Rome cannot be the true church possibly.

1. The church of Rome doth hold that the divine and sacred Scriptures do not contain all things necessary to salvation ; but their unwritten traditions must, forsooth, all be received with equal

and like authority, for so hath their council of Trent determined.[1] And Pope Leo the Fourth feareth not to pronounce with a loud voice, that he that receiveth not without difference the popish canons, as well as the four Gospels, believeth not aright, nor holdeth the catholic faith effectually. The decretal epistles also, they number with the canonical Scriptures. And pope Agatho saith that all the sanctions and decrees of their Romish see are to be taken as established by the divine voice. Which blasphemies who can abide? For hereby they make both the Scriptures imperfect, and, not so content, do further add unto those Scriptures.

Wherein they commit two notable sins: first, accusing the sacred and canonical Scriptures, that they contain not all matters necessary to salvation, which is directly contrary to the testimony of St John, who saith, that 'these things are written that ye may believe, and that in believing you may have life eternal;' and clean contrary to the testimony of St Paul, who saith, that 'the Scriptures given by divine inspiration are profitable to reprove, to teach, to correct, to instruct, and perfect the man of God,' 2 Tim. iii. 15. *Ergo*, the Scriptures, or word of God written, is a true, sound, and perfect whole doctrine, containing in itself fully all things needful for our salvation. Yea, St Paul saith expressly to Timothy, that 'the Scriptures are able to make him wise unto salvation,' 2 Tim. iii. 15. And therefore the church of Rome, being clean contradictory, doth marvellously err; and therefore also we need none of their unwritten traditions.

And again, how should we be assured that those traditions which they call apostolical, be apostolical, considering them not written by the apostles? Augustine speaking hereof,[2] saith thus, *Si quæ reticuit Jesus Christus, quis nostrum dicet hoc vel illud esse? Et si quis hoc dicat, quomodo probabit?* That is, If Jesus Christ have kept anything close, which of us shall say it is this or that? And if any say, it is this, how will he prove it? For all the errors of the church of Rome shroud themselves under the harbour of traditions. And Chrysostom saith flatly,[3] Whatsoever is requisite for our salvation, is contained in the Scriptures. And again he saith, All things be clear and manifest in the Scriptures, and whatsoever things be needful be manifest there. And Jerome, in the prologue of the Bible to Pauline, after he had recited the books of the New Testament and the Old, saith thus, I pray thee, dear brother, among

---

[1] Concil. Trident. i. decret. iv. sess. Distinct. xx. c. *in libellis*; Dist. xv. c. *in Canon;* Dist xv. cap. *Sic omnes.*   [2] August. in Epist. ad Januar.
[3] Chrysost. in Mat. xxiv. hom. iv., Chrysost. in 2 Thessa. ii.

these live, muse upon these, know nothing else, seek for none other thing. And again, upon the books of the Old and New Testament : These writings be holy, these books be sound, there is none other to be compared to these ; whatsoever is beside these, may in no wise be received amongst these holy things. And again he saith,[1] All other things which they seek out or invent at their pleasure, without the authority and testimony of the Scriptures, as though they were the traditions of the apostles, the word of God cutteth off. Let us therefore stand fast to the written word of God ; and as for their traditions, which they cannot prove, but obtrude unto us without testimony of Scriptures, let us contemn them. For as Athanasius saith,[2] the holy Scriptures inspired from God are sufficient to all instruction of the truth. And as for the other point of the papists in equalling and adding their traditions, their decretal epistles and canons, to the pure and divine word of God, it is blasphemy intolerable, and who can endure it ? For doth not God say thus, ' Ye shall put nothing to the word which I command you, neither take aught therefrom,' Deut. iv. And again he saith, ' Whatsoever I command you, that take heed ye do only to the Lord ; put nothing thereto, nor take aught therefrom,' Deut. xii. And doth not St John in his Revelation say, that ' if any man add to this book, God shall add unto him the plagues which are written in this book, and shall take away his part out of the book of life ?' Rev. xxii. I conclude, therefore, that the church of Rome, which doth not content herself with the sacred and holy Scripture, which the chaste spouse of Christ evermore doth, is not the true church of God ; for there she sheweth herself to bear the mark of a strumpet. But when she proceedeth and addeth her own traditions, decretal epistles and canons, to the word written, and maketh them to be of as good and equal authority as the canonical and sacred Scriptures themselves, what greater pride could have been shewed, or what higher blasphemy ? But these are the right notes of an adulteress, to equal herself with her husband. Yea, what should I say more ? They hold, that the authority of the church is above the Scriptures, which sheweth fully the notable pride and spiritual whoredom of their church.

2. The church of Rome is idolatrous, and therefore it is not the true church. They fall down before idols and images, as the heathen did, and therefore commit idolatry as the heathen did ; I speak of the manner of their worship ; for the heathen, howsoever they worshipped not the true God, yet they thought they worship-

---

[1] Jerome upon Hag. ii.　　　　[2] Athanas. contra Gentiles.

ped the true God, and their meaning was to worship the true God in the image or idol, as the papists likewise do mean; for they say they be not such fools as to think, or believe, that an image or idol, made of wood or stone, could be God; neither were the heathen so foolish as to think, or believe, that their idols or images were God, for they knew they were made of wood or stone, or such like; but, as they took it, they worshipped God in the image, as the papists say they do; and therefore the case for the manner of worship is all one. Again, if the papists do not worship the idol or image, why do they bow down unto it? God commandeth, saying, 'Thou shalt not make to thyself any graven image,' Exod. xx.; so that the very making of images to represent God withal, who is a spirit, eternal and invisible, is idolatry. Again, he saith, 'Thou shalt not bow down to them nor worship them,' &c. So that to bow down unto them, though they be supposed to represent God, is idolatry; for God must be worshipped in such sort as himself hath prescribed, and not otherwise. And that it is flat idolatry to worship God in any image, is expressed and manifest by the children of Israel, when they made the golden calf to be a representation of God; for the text sheweth that it was idolatry, for which many of them were plagued and punished, Exod. xxxii.; and yet their meaning was to worship the true God in the calf; for they were not so simple as to think or believe that that dead idol or image was God, and therefore the idolatry of the church of Rome is as gross and wicked as theirs was. Neither can the papists help themselves in their wonted distinction of δουλεία, and λατρεία, affirming that they give to images but *duliam,* that is, *service;* and to God *latriam,* that is, *worship;* shewing thereby, that both they worship God and serve images. But, 'how agreeth the temple of God with images?' saith Paul, 2 Cor. vi. 15, 16; or what warrant have they to serve images beside God? when Christ himself saith, 'It is written, Thou shalt worship the Lord thy God, and him only shalt thou serve,' Mat. iv. 10, Deut. ix. 13, and x. 20.

And Paul the apostle doth likewise persuade expressly, that men should 'turn from idols or images to serve the living God' (where the word *dulia* is used), whereby the apostle doth shew, that there is such an opposition between images and the service of God, that he that serveth the one cannot serve the other. God himself disliketh idols and images utterly, saying by the prophet, that they are so far from being laymen's books, as the papists term them, that they are no better than teachers of lies, Hab. i. And St John himself commandeth all Christians to keep themselves from idols,

1 John v. 21 ; besides, it is idolatry to pray unto any but God; for Christ biddeth when men pray, not to call upon the virgin Mary, nor any other saint departed this life, but upon God only. 'When ye pray,' saith he, 'say thus, Our Father which art in heaven,' &c., Mat. vi. Again, St Paul saith, 'How shall they call upon him in whom they have not believed?' Rom. x. 14, declaring thereby, that faith and prayer go together. We can call upon none, but we must consequently also believe on him ; but we are to believe on none but God, therefore we may pray to none but God ; and therefore the church of Rome, calling upon saints departed, committeth gross idolatry ; for the Scripture sheweth, that God only is to be prayed unto. Besides, they teach in their idolatrous mass, or sacrament of the altar, as they term it, after a certain mumbling of words by the priest, there is no bread nor wine remaining, but the very body and blood of Christ; and that piece of bread which is shewed, for bread it still appeareth to be, for all their magical mumbling, they command to be adored and worshipped. To adore or worship any creature, such as bread is, is idolatry; the papistical church doth the same ; *ergo*, it is idolatrous. I have proved it before, that it remaineth bread after the consecration; and that Christ cannot possibly be there, as touching the bodily substance, because in that respect he is 'ascended up into heaven, and there sitteth at the right hand of God his Father, until he come to judge the quick and the dead.' And if they will not believe divine testimonies therein, yet the authority of Cicero, a heathen man, might somewhat move them, for in one place he saith,[1] *Quem tam amentem esse putas, qui illum quo vescatur, Deum credat esse?* that is, Whom do you think so mad, as to believe that which he eateth to be God? Insomuch, therefore, as the church of Rome doth worship bread as if it were God, it is manifest they be gross idolaters ; and consequently their church cannot be the true church of God on earth.

3. The papists do not deny Christ in words, but if we examine them by particulars, we shall find that in deed they do. As for example, we know that the right faith believeth Christ Jesus to be both God and man, which the church of Rome in words will also affirm; but urge them in this point of the sacrament, and then they bewray themselves, that they believe not Christ to have a true body ; for when they are pressed with this, that the body of Christ cannot be both in heaven and in earth at one and the selfsame time, because it is against the nature of a true body so to be, then

---

[1] Cicero, lib. de natura.

they become *ubiquitaries*, and say, that because the Godhead of Christ is everywhere, therefore his humanity is everywhere. But this is no good consequent, for the Godhead and humanity are of several natures. And if his body and flesh were everywhere, as his Godhead is, how is that true which the angel spake, saying, *Surrexit, non est hic,* 'He is risen, he is not here,' Mat xxviii. 6 ; for these words shew that his body and flesh is not everywhere. Again, if he were everywhere in respect of his humanity, how is it true that he ascended into heaven ? For that word *ascension* doth shew that his bodily presence did remove from one place to another ; and then was it not in that place from whence it did remove.

Lastly, It is the property of a divine nature to be everywhere, and therefore whilst they defend this ubiquity of the flesh of Christ, it is as much as if they should say, that the flesh of Christ is turned into God, which is a gross heresy. And thus it appeareth, that the papists do, with the Eutichians, deny that Christ hath a true body, when they hold that, contrary to the nature of a true body, it may be in divers places at once, yea, everywhere ; and therefore denying Christ to have a true body, they are not the true church. And so much for their error concerning the person of Christ.

4. Now for the office of Christ, for his person and his office be two chief things which we are all to regard. The papists will yield with us, that it consisteth in these three points ; namely, that he is both a prophet, a priest, and a king. This I say in words they will acknowledge, but in deeds and verity they do not ; for in respect that Christ is our prophet, which should and did reveal his Father's will unto the world, we ought to be content with his voice, and search no further than he hath revealed in the Scriptures. But the papists are not so contented, but they hold that their unwritten traditions and popish canons must also be received upon like peril of damnation, as before I shewed. Concerning the priesthood of Christ, it consisteth in two things ; namely, the offering up of himself once for a full, perfect, and sufficient sacrifice ; and his intercession with his Father, which yet remaineth also, and shall do to the world's end. Both these the papists annihilate, as I will prove.

First, concerning the sacrifice and oblation of Christ, there is no doubt but being once done upon the cross it was a most full, perfect, and satisfactory sacrifice to deliver both *à culpa et pœna* from the guiltiness, and the punishment incident to that guiltiness ; for otherwise how should Christ be *Jesus*, that is, a Saviour, if he did not deliver us from the punishment as well as from the sin ? But the papists hold that Christ hath obtained by his passion remission for our sins going before baptism ; but for sins committed after baptism, that his passion hath taken away only the guiltiness, that the punishment remaineth notwithstanding ; which is to be paid in purgatory, as they say, and to be redeemed by our own satisfactions ; and so they make the punishment due to sin, which is indeed eternal in hell, to be but temporary in purgatory, upon satisfactions as they have devised. But what can a man give for the ransom of his soul ? And it appeareth before, even by the report of Augustine, that the catholic faith believeth no purgatory, such as they have invented ; for as St John saith, ' The blood of Christ is that which purgeth us from all sin,' 1 John i. 7 ; and that his most precious blood is the only purgatory we hold, and doth deliver his people from the punishment due to sins as well as from sins ; for our punishment was laid upon him, and with his stripes we are healed, as the prophet Isaiah speaketh, Is. liii. Again, the papists do say they offer up Christ in their mass, which mass, they say, is propitiatory both for the living and the dead. First, for the dead it cannot be propitiatory, nor do good unto ; for as the tree falleth, so it lieth, and as a man is found to die, so he goeth either to heaven or to hell. A third place, which the papists call *purgatory*, there is not ; and if any be in heaven, their masses can do them no good ; for they enjoy all good already. And if any man be in hell, we know that *ex inferno nulla redemptio,* from hell there is no redemption, Luke xvi. ; and therefore for the dead it cannot be propitiatory, nor anything else available ; and for the living it cannot be propitiatory. Yea, it is blasphemous and derogatory to the passion of Christ once for all ; for inasmuch as he is a priest for ever, after the order of Melchisedec, he is to die but once, which he did upon the cross ; whose oblation being perfect, as the author to the Hebrews speaketh, needed not any other help, as of mass or whatsoever else, to make it perfect ; yea, it is wicked, gross, blasphemous, and damnable to suppose any imperfection in the sacrifice and oblation of Jesus Christ ; for God twice cried with a loud voice from heaven, saying, ' This is my beloved Son, in whom I am well pleased,' Mat. iii. 17, xvii. 8.

5. As touching the other part of his priesthood, namely, his intercession with his Father, whereby he maketh request unto God for us, although the papists ascribe that chiefly unto Christ, yet what do they else but clean rob him of it, when they associate others with him ? And, namely, the virgin Mary, they call her the queen of heaven, the gate of paradise, their life and sweetness, the treasure of grace, the refuge of sinners, and the mediatrix of men.

I pray what do they now leave to Christ? Yea, when they say thus to her, *O felix puerpera, nostra pians scelera, jure matris impera redemptori,* that is, O happy mother, satisfying for our sins, by thy motherly authority, command the Redeemer, what greater blasphemy to Christ could they have uttered? It is clear that St Paul saith, 'There is but one God, and one mediator between God and man, the man Christ Jesus,' 1 Tim. ii. 5. But the papists be not content with him, but will have many mediators. St Paul saith, moreover, that 'by him we have boldness and access unto God,' Eph. iii. 12; and therefore what foolish fear is it of papists to appoint to themselves other mediators? Sith therefore the church of Rome doth not repute the one oblation of Jesus Christ and his intercession to be perfect, but accuseth them of imperfection, as appeareth by their doctrine, it cannot possibly be the true church. Christ himself biddeth to ask in no other name than his, and promiseth that whatsoever shall be asked in his name it shall be done, John xiv. 13, 14. Chrysostom, speaking of the woman of Canaan, who, though she were a sinner, was bold to come unto Christ, saith thus:[1] *En prudentiam hujus mulieris; non precatur Jacobum, non supplicat Johanni, non adit ad Petrum, nec apostolorum cœtum respicit, aut ullum eorum requirit; sed pro his omnibus pœnitentiam sibi comitem adjungit, et ad ipsum fontem progreditur:* Behold the wisdom of this woman; she doth not pray James, she doth not beseech John, she goeth not to Peter, she looketh not to the company of the · apostles, neither doth request of any of them, but for all this she taketh repentance for her companion, and goeth to the very fountain itself. And again he saith,[2] that to have access unto God, *nihil opus est atriensi servo vel intercessore, sed dic, Miserere mei Deus: is enim te audit quocunque sis loco, et undecunque invocetur,* we have no need of any courtly attendant or intercessor, but say, Have mercy upon me, O God; for he heareth thee in what place soever thou art, and from what place soever thou callest upon him. Ambrose likewise answereth the carnal reason of the papists:[3] *Solent,* saith he, *misera uti excusatione, dicentes per istos posse iri ad Deum, sicut per comites itur ad reges. Ideo ad regem per tribunos, et comites, itur, quia homo utique est rex; ad Deun autem, quem utique nihil latet, suffragatore non est opus, sed mente devota. Ubicunque enim talis locutus fuerit, respondebit illi.* That is, They are wont to use a pitiful excuse, saying, By these saints they may have access unto God, as by earls

---

[1] Chrysost. hom. xii. de Cananæa.   [2] Eadem hom.   [3] Amb. in Rom.

there is access to kings; therefore is it that by officers and earls access is made to the king, because the king himself is a man; but to come to God, from whom nothing is hid, there is no need of a spokesman, but of a devout mind; for wheresoever such a one speaketh to him, he will answer him. The church of Rome, therefore, which accounteth not of the sufficiency and perfection of that one oblation of Christ, nor of his continual intercession, cannot possibly be the true church.

6. The papists in words will not deny but Christ is a king, which hath all power in heaven and in earth. But indeed it appeareth they do exile and banish him out of his kingdom, or at least leave him but a small portion, or rather none at all; for in respect that he is a spiritual king, and the king of his church, he is also (as Saint James speaketh) the only lawgiver thereunto, and therefore by his laws only the church is to be governed, which they cannot abide; for they add their popish canons, constitutions, and customs, whereby they will have the church governed; yea, they will have these take place, though they utterly displace the word of God for the maintenance of them. Secondly, Christ only is to reign in the consciences of men, and yet the pope claimeth power to bind men's consciences by his laws, statutes, and decrees. Thirdly, he claimeth most traitorously to be the head of the whole universal church, which title by way of prerogative is given and attributed only to Jesus Christ, to whom it only appertaineth. But before I proceed any further herein, I demand of the pope and papists, when, and by what right, he their proud pope taketh upon him this title to be head of the church, or universal bishop over all the Christian world (by virtue of which title he taketh upon him to rule as he list, and to do what he list). First, to claim it as successor to Peter, is impossible; for that Peter the apostle never had any such title, preeminence, or authority over the rest of the apostles.

It is true, that Christ said to Peter (after he had confessed Christ to be that Christ, the Son of the living God), 'Thou art Peter, and upon this rock will I build my church,' Mat. xvi. 18. These words hitherto give no superiority to Peter above the rest, only they shew that the church is builded *non super Petrum, sed super Petram*; not upon the person of Peter, but upon the rock; and upon what rock? namely, upon that Christ Jesus, whom Peter confesseth to be the Son of the living God. For that confession of Peter concerning Jesus to be that Christ the Son of the living God, is the rock whereupon the church is builded; for as St Paul expoundeth and affirmeth, 'Other foundation can no man lay, but that which is laid

already, namely, Jesus Christ,' 1 Cor. x. 4.' And in another place
he saith expressly, 'that that rock was Christ.' And Christ himself affirmeth likewise, that 'he that heareth his words, and doth
them, is likened to one that buildeth his house upon a rock,' Mat.
vii. 24 ; shewing thereby, that he, and his words and doctrine, be
'the rock against which the gates of hell shall never prevail.'
Agreeable hereunto speaketh St Paul again, when he saith, that the
church is 'builded upon the foundation of the prophets and apostles,
Christ Jesus himself being the head stone in the corner,' Eph. ii. 20.
Where then shall we find that Peter was made prince of the
apostles, to rule over all the rest, as the pope now doth ? The papists answer, that in the next words, when Christ gave unto Peter
by special name the keys of binding and loosing, Mat. xvi. 19, he
thereby made Peter the prince and universal bishop of the whole
church. But hereunto I say, that Christ therein gave no authority
more to Peter than to the rest ; that at this time the keys were not
given to him, nor to the rest, only there was a promise that they
should be given, John xx. 22, 23 ; for the words be not in the present tense, *do tibi, I give unto thee ;* but in the future tense, *dabo
tibi, I will give unto thee :* which promise of Christ was afterward
truly performed, and when it was performed, the keys, that is, the
power of binding and loosing sinners, was given not only to Peter,
but to Peter and all the rest put together, as St John in his Gospel
clearly declareth and avoucheth. Now, because Peter was the man
that gave answer for himself and the rest, therefore our Saviour
Christ spake personally unto Peter ; and so both Cyprian and
Augustine do expound and declare it. Otherwise, neither in the
promise of the keys, nor yet in the receipt of the same, did Peter
receive any more authority or superiority than the rest of the apostles
did. I grant he was called *primus,* because he was of the first
that was called to the apostleship ; or because he was the first of
all the apostles that confessed Christ to be the Messiah and Son of
the living God ; or because he was readiest always to speak and
answer. But all this doth not prove that he had authority over
all the rest, or a larger commission than the rest. Yea, the words
of their commissions do shew the contrary, namely, that they had
all equal authority ; for it was thus made unto them all indifferently, and without putting a difference, namely, 'Go ye and teach
all nations, baptizing them in the name of the Father, and of the
Son, and of the Holy Ghost ; teaching them to observe all things
whatsoever I have commanded,' Mat. xxviii. 19, 20. Run over all
that remaineth written, and you shall find that Peter was one of

the twelve, equal with the rest, and their fellow, but not their lord. Where was Peter's superiority, when Paul reproved him to his face? Gal. ii. 11, when, being accused, he pleaded no privilege, but for the clearing of himself, and satisfaction of others, he answereth to that accusation? Where was Peter's authority over the rest, when the rest sent him and John unto Samaria? Acts xi. 3, 4, and Acts viii. 14. In that he went at their sending, he plainly sheweth that he had no principality over them. Where was his preeminence or authority, when, in a council held at Jerusalem, where the apostles were, yet not Peter but James ruled the action, and according to his sentence was the decree made? Acts xv. 13, &c. Yea, I say moreover, that when there was contention amongst the apostles, who should be chief amongst them, Christ told them plainly, that kings of nations might bear rule over their people, and that great men under those kings might likewise exercise authority over other, but so might not they do one over another, Luke xxii. 25, 26, &c.; but the greatest among them should be as the least, and as a servant; yea, should be the least, and should be a servant, as is declared in Mat. xx. 25, 26, and in Mark x. 42, 43.

If the greatest must be as the least, what authority hath he above the least? For then hath the least as great authority as the greatest, that is, they have all equal authority. I marvel, therefore, what the pope and papists mean contrary to the tenor of the commission of Christ, contrary to the practice of Peter himself, and contrary to this decree made by Christ of their equality, to say notwithstanding that Peter was prince of the apostles, and had authority over them all; whenas, indeed, it is manifest by all the Scriptures and course of his life, he neither claimed nor had any authority over the rest, more than the rest had over him, and consequently the pope of Rome can never claim that as successor to Peter which was never in Peter, his supposed predecessor.

The papists perceiving that the Scriptures make nothing for, but against, them, because they would have the matter coloured with some antiquity, or show of antiquity at least, have devised some counterfeit and forged authors, as Anacletus and Anicetus, and such like, to speak something for them. But the falsehood of all those is discovered by other writers, if they be well marked. In Cyprian's time, it was deemed a matter odious for any to take upon him to be bishop of bishops, as appeareth by that voice which he crieth in the council of Carthage. It was likewise decreed in the African council that none should be called priest of priests, or arch-priest, or any such like. The council of Nice did decree that the bishop of Rome should keep himself within the compass of his province, and not exceed his bounds ; as likewise the bishops of Antioch, Jerusalem, and Constantinople were to do the like. Other councils did affirm as much, which, because they are sufficiently known, I need not to recite. But they all shew that, at those times, the bishop of Rome had no greater jurisdiction than within his own province, and that he could not meddle within the provinces of other bishops. And Jerome of his time saith[1] that the bishop of Eugubium, or any other the least see, is equal to the bishop of Rome. The title of universal bishop was much desired of John, bishop of Constantinople, and much contention there was about it, but it was never obtained of the bishop of Rome until the time of Boniface the Third, who procured that title of Phocas, the wicked emperor of Rome ; after which the bishops of Rome never ceased still to augment their dignity, and increase the pride of the Romish see. And even at the very first time, when John, bishop of Constantinople, sought to get that title of universal bishop to his see, Gregory, then bishop of Rome, did himself stand against it mightily, and affirmeth that he could be no less than antichrist whosoever did take unto him that title. First, therefore, it is manifest that until the time of Gregory, bishop of Rome, an universal bishop was not heard of in the church ; and Boniface the Third was the first bishop of Rome that got this title, which was about six hundred years after Christ. And besides, how will the bishop of Rome that now is avoid himself to be antichrist, sith by the express determination of Gregory, bishop of Rome,[2] his predecessor, he is condemned for antichrist, inasmuch as he hath this title, and is not ashamed thereof ? For what is this else but to come in the place of Christ, and consequently to be antichrist, usurping the prerogative title of Christ Jesus ? But the pope saith that though he claim thus to be the head of the church, yet he doth not name himself to be otherwise than a ministerial head, and to be Christ's vicar on earth. But why will he be so arrogant as to challenge this title without lawful conveyance made unto him from Christ, which he cannot shew ? For who dare take upon him to be a lieutenant to an earthly prince without letters patent first had from the prince ? Again, the church of Christ on earth being as a chaste spouse of her husband and head Christ Jesus, neither can nor ought to acknowledge any other for her head than that her husband to whom

---

[1] Hieron. ad. Evagrium.
[2] Vide Greg. lib. iv. epist. 32, 34, 36, 38, 39 ; et lib. vi. epist. 20, 28, 29.

she had plighted her troth. Lastly, there can be no successor but when the predecessor is gone and absent; but Christ is always present with his church, according to his own words, 'Behold, I am with you to the end of the world,' Mat. xxviii. 20. And therefore he can have neither successors nor vicar to represent his person, or to guide his church; for his Spirit, since his bodily ascension, is the guide and governor of the church in his room, John xiv., xv., and xvi.; for no man mortal is appointed thereunto. I conclude therefore that, for all these causes, the church of Rome cannot possibly be the true church.

7. The church of Rome doth not ascribe justification to faith in Christ Jesus only, but saith, that men's works be meritorious, and to them partly is justification to be ascribed; and so they make men's imperfect works to be causes of salvation, which is a gross error, even in the foundation or fundamental point. St Paul saith, 'that all are justified freely by his grace,' Rom. iii. 24. If they be justified gratis, freely, as he affirmeth, then are they justified without any desert of theirs. And St Paul setteth down this axiom in the conclusion, 'We hold that a man is justified by faith without the works of the law,' Rom. iii. 28. And the apostle in very many places, whereof mention shall be made hereafter, doth expressly exclude works from being any causes of our justification, for indeed they are the effects thereof. And therefore it appeareth to be a true position, that faith only doth justify, inasmuch as justification is, in the sight of God, imputed to our faith, not to our works. For 'Abraham believed God, and that was imputed to him for righteousness,' as Paul speaketh, Rom. iv. 8. And he sheweth that Abraham was not justified by works before God; for if Abraham were justified by works, then should he have wherein to glory, but not before God; and because he had not wherein to glory before God, therefore he was not justified in the sight of God. I grant that St James in his second chapter doth say, that Abraham was justified by his works when he offered up his son Isaac at God's commandment; and likewise that he saith, that a man is justified by works, and not by faith only. But before whom is he justified by works? Not before God, but before men; that is to say, his works do declare unto men that faith whereby he is justified before God. And that this is the meaning of St James may appear by that his saying, where he saith, Shew unto me thy faith by thy works; thou sayest thou hast faith, that is not enough; thy words do not prove it, thy works will; therefore, saith he, shew me thy faith by thy works. This word, *shew me*, doth manifest

what manner of justification he speaketh of, namely, that he speaketh of a justification before men. For it is God that respecteth the faith of a man, whereby only he is justified in his sight; and it is men which respect the works, whereby, indeed, they testify unto the world their faith to be good before God. For, as St James saith truly, faith without works is but a dead faith, and not good, nor sound, nor available. But faith and works must go together. And indeed, where a true faith is, there good works will shew themselves as the fruits thereof. And thus Paul and James are to be reconciled ; which things Thomas Aquinas, a schoolman of the papists, doth himself plainly testify, saying that Christ Jesus doth justify *effective*, effectually ; faith doth justify *apprehensive*, by taking hold of Christ ; and good works do justify *declarative*, that is, do declare unto men their justification before God. And so it is clear, that howsoever a true faith cannot be without works, as fire cannot be without light and heat, yet our justification before God is to be imputed to our faith, not to our works, as warmth is to be imputed to the heat of the fire, not to the light of the fire. For so saith St Paul expressly, that 'God imputeth righteousness without works,' Rom. iv. 6 ; and again, that 'it is by grace, not of works,' Rom. xi. 6 ; and again, 'not of works,' Rom. ix. 11. Again, St Paul telleth the saints at Ephesus, that God hath ordained men to walk in good works; yet he saith that they may not trust to be saved by them ; for he affirmeth, and assureth them, that they are saved by grace, and not by their works, Eph. ii. 8–10. Again, he speaketh in the person of himself, and of all the children of God, and saith, that we are saved, not by works, but by his predestination and grace, 2 Tim. i. 9. And again, God is our Saviour, ' not for any works which we have done, but according to his own mercy he hath saved us,' Tit. iii. 5. And divers other like places be. Wherefore St Hilary[1] hath these very words, which we hold, *sola fides justificat*, faith only doth justify. And Ambrose, among other sentences, hath this, *non justificari hominem apud Deum nisi per fidem*, that a man is not justified before God but by faith ; which is as much as faith only doth justify before God. St Basil doth say, that this is perfect and sound rejoicing in God, when a man doth not boast of his own righteousness, but knoweth that he wanteth in himself true righteousness, and that he is justified by faith only. And Gregory Nazianzen saith, that to believe only is righteousness. And therefore it is evident, both by the express testimony of the Scriptures

---

[1] Hilar. in Mat. cap. viii. ; Ambr. in Rom. iii.

and of the fathers, that we hold the truth in this behalf, and that the church of Rome is in a marvellous error. It is true which is written, that every man shall be rewarded according to his works ; because the faith of men is esteemed and estimated by their works, as the tree is known by the fruit. But there is no text of Scripture to shew that any man is saved *propter merita,* for his works or merits ; but many texts of Scripture to the contrary, as before appeareth. For when we have done all that we can, yet we must say, as Christ commandeth, We are unprofitable servants, Luke xvii. 10. And therefore the papists, which teach works meritorious, yea, works of supererogation available to salvation, as well for others as for themselves, hold not the right faith, and consequently are not the true church.

But if I should shew all the corruptions of the Romish church, I should be infinite, neither am I able to number them. I will therefore conclude all this discourse only with this argument following. The pope of Rome, being the head of that church, is that famous antichrist that was foretold by Paul the apostle, and that is prefigured in the Revelation of St John. *Ergo,* it is impossible that the church of Rome should be the true church ; for the church of antichrist, though it boast never so much, cannot be the true church, though it would fain be so accounted ; as many an harlot desireth to be reputed an honest woman.

1. One mark of that antichrist Paul sheweth to be this, 2 Thes. ii. 8, that he should exalt himself above every one that is called god ; he doth not say above God, but above every one that is called god, John xx. 34. Now, those whom the Scripture calleth gods, we know to be such as be the judges and magistrates of the earth, Ps. lxxxii. 6; who, for that they be in the place of God and his lieutenants, are vouchsafed in Scripture this high and honourable title of gods. That the pope of Rome is such a one as doth exalt himself above any such god of the earth, namely, above all princes and magistrates, is a thing so well known, as I need not to prove it ; himself, by his wicked practices, and his Jesuits, seminaries, and priests, do in their books manifest the same unto the world.

2. Another mark of antichrist St Paul setteth down to be this, namely, 2 Thes. ii. 4, that he should sit in the temple of God, shewing himself to be God. And I pray, what doth the pope else but sit in the temple of God as God ? Who, claiming the apostolic see, he taketh upon him to be the head of the church, and to rule as he list ; to erect princes, and to depose them from their thrones ; that he cannot err ; that he can forgive sins, matters that belong

particularly to God, and to no other; what doth he else but by these demonstrations shew himself to be God, insomuch as he arrogateth to himself most proudly the authority of God himself? which things the sixth book of the Decretals, the Clementines, and the Extravagants, do abundantly testify. For these men were not content with that which Angelicus wrote in his poetry, the beginning whereof is *Papa stupor mundi,* the pope is the wonder of the world; *Nec Deus es nec homo, sed neuter, et inter utrumque,* thou art not God, neither art thou man, but neuter, mixed of both! But these popes were bold to take unto themselves the very name of God, and to accept it, given of others; according as pope Sixtus the Fourth, when he should first enter into Rome in his dignity papal, had made for him a pageant of triumph, cunningly fixed upon that gate of the city he should enter in at, having written upon it this blasphemous verse, dedicated unto him:

> Oraculo vocis mundi moderaris habenas,
> Et merito in terris crederis esse Deus.

> By oracle of thine own voice the world thou governest all,
> And worthily a god on earth men think, and do thee call.

Yea, shall I say more? The pope, if any man in the world, doth take upon him much more than Luciferian pride; howsoever, to deceive the world with words, he calleth himself *servus servorum Dei,* a servant of the servants of God; that he exalteth himself above God himself, and his worship; for he taketh upon him to be above the Scriptures, and to dispense with them at his pleasure, and to allow matters contrary unto them, which God himself, whose will is immutable, and revealed therein, will not do; for he and his word will not be contrary. Again, hereby it is manifest, that he exalteth himself above God, inasmuch as there is less danger and punishment for any that breaketh any of God's laws, than for one that breaketh any the least constitution of the pope. Moreover, he claimeth authority in three places, heaven, earth, and purgatory, and that is the reason he weareth a triple crown; so that by this account and claim, he hath more and larger extended authority than God himself; for such a third place as purgatory is, he knoweth not of. And what do these things but manifest him, to exalt himself even above God, and all that is worshipped?

3. Antichrist is described to be such a one as should come in lying signs, and false miracles, and wonders, 2 Thess. ii. 9, whereby, if it were possible, he would deceive the very elect. And

that this is verified in the pope and popish church, as all men know that have been acquainted with their knavery, deceits, and frauds, so let their *Aurea Legenda*, and Book of Trophies, testify to the whole world.

4. St Paul, 2 Thess. ii. 8, sheweth by his name, that he that he speaketh of should be ὁ ἄνομος, that is, a lawless person, or one subject to no law; which is also manifestly verified in the pope, for no laws will hold him, neither divine nor human, for he claimeth to be above them all, and to change and alter what he list, and when he list, and to whom he list, which the gloss upon the Decretals do testify, saying thus of the pope, *Legi non subjacet ulli;* that is, He is not subject to any law. What is this else but to be ὁ ἄνομος, a lawless person, even the very same whom St Paul speaketh of?

5. St John in his Revelation doth pourtray antichrist and his seat by the name of the great whore, with whom have committed fornication the kings of the earth, and the inhabitants of the earth have been drunken with the wine of her fornication. This woman is that great city which had dominion over the kings of the earth at the time of this Revelation, as St John expressly affirmeth, Rev. xvii. 18. It is well known that there was then no other city which reigned over the kings of the earth but only Rome, and therefore Rome only is, and must needs be, the seat of antichrist, for no other can be, by this evident and plain description of St John; for Rome was the only city of the world that reigned over the kings of the earth, the head whereof was then the emperor, but now the pope; for the condition of the first beast (namely, of the Roman empire civil) is altered and changed into an ecclesiastical and Roman empire.

6. St John in his Revelation, xiii. 11, saw a beast rising out of the earth which had two horns, like the lamb, but he spake like the dragon; and then all that is spoken of this beast doth fitly and only agree to that man of Rome, the pope, who though in show he were the lamb,—for what is more mild or humble, than to call himself the servant of the servants of God?—yet, indeed, he playeth the part of the dragon, or devil, having learned this cunning of Satan, who, though he be never so bad a spirit, yet will transform himself into an angel of light to deceive souls, 2 Cor. xi. 14, as the apostle sheweth. But here is wisdom, saith John in that Revelation, 'Let him that hath any wit count the number of the beast, for it is the number of a man, and his number is 666.' Now, because the number of this wicked beast

containeth six hundred sixty and six, Irenæus thinketh that this antichristian beast should be Λατεῖνος, that is, a man of Italy, for the number of the beast is set down in great letters, and this Greek word, *Lateinos,* doth make up the just number of six hundred sixty six, which is the number of the beast's name. If any do think that, though this Revelation were written in Greek, as being the more known and common language, yet that it was uttered to St John in Hebrew, because the Hebrew tongue is the holy tongue, and that St John himself was an Hebrew or Jew by nation, and that likewise divers Hebrew words are found in the Revelation; whose opinion is not unlikely, but very probable, then let him seek out an Hebrew word, which containeth that just number, and herein he need not search far, or to study much upon the matter; for the Hebrew word *Romiith,* that is, *Romanus,* a man of Rome in English, doth in those Hebrew letters contain the just number of six hundred sixty-six, which is the number of the name of that antichristian beast. And so by the number of the name to be accounted either by Greek letters or by Hebrew letters, it is perfectly agreeing to that man of Rome, the pope. All the marks agreeing to antichrist, whatsoever they be, are found fully and only accomplished in the pope; and, therefore, there is no doubt but he is that notable antichrist, of whom Paul and St John in his Revelation do testify, and consequently, the church of Rome being not the true church of Christ, but contrariwise, the visible church of antichrist, is justly forsaken, and for ever to be forsaken, of all Christians, as they tender their salvation in Jesus Christ, to whom only they have bethrothed themselves, and to whom they must remain constant for evermore, which God grant us all to do. Amen.

CHAPTER VI.

Against schism and schismatical synagogues.

MANY there be who, out of a godly and zealous mind, do in good sort seek reformation, and for that church government, which Christ himself hath instituted in his church, whom I neither dare nor do reprove. Others there be, that seek reformation amiss, with venomous and slanderous tongues, railing and reviling against those which understand it; which things do neither grace themselves, nor yet the cause which they would prefer; other some there be, who, to make the cause of reformation odious, do say, that it abolisheth her majesty's supreme government, and authority in causes ecclesiastical. I would wish all men to speak the truth, and to seek the preferment of God's truth, in a dutiful, peaceable, and charitable sort. Let the cause be made no worse than it is. For my part, I desire no more than every Christian ought, namely, that the truth of God should carry the pre-eminence, whatsoever it be.

And I would to God that, all malice and contention set apart, all of all parts would grow more charitably affected, both in their words and in their writings, one towards another; for so would this controversy sooner come to an end, and the more speedily be decided. Others there be, who for that in so long time they cannot see their desired discipline and church government to be established, run from our church, and make a schism and separation from us, erecting discipline by their own authority, condemning our church to be no church, that they may make their detestable schism the more allowable. These are the Brownists and Barrowists, who will not stay the chief magistrate's pleasure for the establishing thereof, nor yet allow unto us any church in England, but themselves. But they, for against them I deal, and you, must understand, that a church may be, yea, a true church may be and is, though it have neither elders, nor deacons, nor discipline in it; for we read in Acts ii. 41, 42, 43, 47, of an assembly of people at Jerusalem, that received the word of God and believed, and which are expressly called a church, and who can or dare deny them to be the true church of God, sith the Holy Ghost doth so testify of them? and yet at that time no deacons were chosen, nor consistories of elders erected. For they were not erected till afterward. And therefore a true church of God may be, though as yet it have not these, for this desired discipline is not an essential part of the church; for it doth resemble the wall of a city, or an hedge or ditch about a vineyard; and it is a city, though the wall be wanting, and it is a vineyard, though the hedge or ditch be wanting; though so much the less fortified, I grant. Inasmuch therefore as we have the preaching of God's holy word, and the right administration of the sacraments, which be the essential marks of the true church, none ought to forsake our church for any other defect, corruption, or imperfection. For there may be corruptions both in doctrine and discipline some, and yet the church where they be, the true church of God. Admit, if they will, that ministers in the church of England be not rightly created and brought into the church, will they therefore count they be no ministers? By as good an argument they may say, that he that is brought and born into the world, not according to the right course or order of nature, but otherwise, as by ripping of his mother's belly, is no man, for the one cometh unorderly into the world, as the other doth into the church. I am sure the corrupt ordination of a minister doth not prove him to be no minister; neither doth any other corruption in our church take away the life and being of a church; for if a man be diseased and full of corruptions, will any man therefore say he is no man? They say we do not only want the right discipline, but we have also put a wrong discipline in the place thereof. But what of this? The error then, I confess, is great, but yet not such as doth make a nullity of our church, so long as it holdeth Christ Jesus the life and soul of the church, and is ready to reform her error whensoever by good proof it shall be manifested unto her. In the mean time, their argument is nothing worth; for if a man lose a leg or arm, yet none will deny him to be a man for all this blemish or defect; yea, though he put a wooden leg instead of his leg which he wanteth, yet he remaineth a man still, because his principal parts remain; so though we want that discipline, yet we have the principal parts of the church, namely, the right preaching of the word of God and administration of the sacraments, and therefore a true church of God undoubtedly. And if we have a true church, though not a perfect church, let the Brownists and Barrowists consider from whence they are fallen; for if the church of Christ be the body of Christ, as St Paul affirmeth, what do they else but by their schism and separation rent themselves from the body of Christ? And then let them remember whose members they be until they be reunited. Let them no longer for shame charge our church with idolatry, except they were better able to prove it, which neither they nor all the world shall do. To say, as they say, that a set form of prayer is used in the church and exhibited unto God, the prayer being framed according to the rule of God's word, is idolatry, is detestable; for by as good reason they may condemn all prayer made to God by the preacher or pastor of the congregation, which they will not do; and besides, all the reformed churches in Christendom have a set form of public prayers for public meetings and congregations.

They say that we observe saints' days, and dedicate churches unto them; but they should shew that we do these things in honour of the saints, else have they no reason to charge our church with idolatry, as wickedly they do; for the statute itself doth express, that our church doth call them holidays, not for the saints' sake, but for the holy exercises used upon them in the public assemblies.

Again, true it is, that divers churches amongst us are called by the names of those saints they are dedicated unto ; but to say, therefore we do dedicate churches unto them, it is very ridiculous. For when we call St Peter's church, or St Paul's church, it is but to distinguish them from other churches by their names. In Athens there was a place which bare the name of Mars, and St Luke, in Acts xvii., calleth it *Mars Street*. Will any man therefore be so foolish, or so fond, as to say therefore he committeth idolatry, or that therefore he dedicated that place to that heathen god of battle ? None, I think, will be so wicked or absurd.

Moreover, it is true, that we observe fasting days ; but therein we observe no Romish fasts, nor place therein the worship of God, nor the remission of our sins, nor the merit of eternal life, as the papists do. But the politic laws of this land, which appoint that men shall not eat flesh upon certain days, do it in respect of the commonwealth, as to maintain navigation so much the better, and for spare of the breed of young cattle ; appointing moreover a penalty for such as shall take the days to be observed as meritorious Romish fasts.

I therefore wish them to cease their slander against this church, and to cease their damnable schism, and to be reconciled to that church of ours, from whence they have foolishly departed; for how imperfect a church soever it be,—whose imperfections God cure in his good time,—yet shall they never be able to shew otherwise, but that the Church of England is the true church of God, from which it is utterly unlawful to make a separation. God forgive us all, and reconcile us unto him. Amen.

PRAYERS, &c.

PRAYERS, &c.

A GODLY PRAYER TO BE SAID AT ALL TIMES.

BECAUSE I have sinned, O Lord, and done wickedly in thy sight, and provoked thee to anger by my abominable wickedness, making my body, which thou hast ordained as a vessel for thine honour, an instrument of most detestable filthiness; O Lord, be merciful unto me, and pardon me this great wickedness. Look not upon me, good Father, with the eyes of justice, neither do thou draw against me the sword of judgment, for then how shall I that am but dust stand in thy presence, when thy wrathful indignation cometh forth as a whirlwind, and thy heavy displeasure as a mighty tempest, seeing the earth trembleth, the depths are discovered, and the very heavens are shaken, when thou art angry? Exercise not therefore thy fury against me, that am but chaff before the wind, and as stubble against a flaming fire; though I have sinned grievously in thy sight, preferring my wicked desire before thy holy commandments; esteeming the pleasure of a moment before eternal and everlasting joys. Nay, which is worse, making more account of vileness and vanity, and extreme folly and madness, than of the glory and majesty of the most excellent, wonderful, and blessed God, nothing dreading his displeasure, whose wrath maketh the devils to quake, and burneth unquenchable unto the bottomless pit of hell; whose might is so great, that by the breath of his nostrils, he can in the twinkling of an eye destroy a thousand worlds; yet am I bold, prostrating myself before the throne of thy majesty, heartily to beseech, and humbly to entreat thee, thou wilt not deal with me according to my merits, for I have deserved that thou shouldst rain down fire and brimstone from out of heaven upon me to devour me, or to open the earth under me, to swallow me up quick into hell; but thou art gracious and full of compassion, and rich in mercies, there-fore do men put their trust under the shadow of thy wings. I have none in heaven to fly unto but thee, nor in earth, of whom I may receive any comfort, but at thy favourable hands, which are stretched out day and night, to receive all that by earnest repentance turn to thee, being ready to ease all those that are laden with the burden of their sin, and to refresh their distressed consciences. In the multitude of thy mercies I approach unto thee, O Lord, desiring thee to look down from the height of thy sanctuary, upon me poor and wretched sinner, and to wipe away mine offences, and to blot out my misdeeds ; especially this my ungracious, unclean, and un-godly act, that it may not come up in remembrance with thee, nor be imputed to me for ever for thy Son's sake, O Lord, in whom thou art well pleased, in whom thou wast fully satisfied upon the cross for my sins. Grant me free pardon and remission of that I have so foolishly, by my exceeding frailty, committed against thee in this shameful deed. But, O thou my unclean and unthankful soul, my ungodly and rebellious heart, what did I, sinful wretch and execrable caitiff, so blindly and desperately attempt ? How art thou become quite senseless that thou wast so ready to anger thy most loving God, and to provoke thy most mighty Judge, that thou mightest satisfy thy filthy flesh, suborned both by thine and God's most malicious adversary, to grieve and vex the Spirit of the Lord, and so damn thyself for ever. Hath not God, of his singular favour, made the heavens of old, and placed the sun and moon in them, two glorious lights, with innumerable stars, a wonderful workmanship for thy use and benefit ? Hath he not lifted up the clouds by his strong arm, and heaped treasures of rain, hail, and snow, to do thee service ? Hath he not in the midst of the world laid the foundations of the earth, that thou mightest have a stable habitation, and mightest from thence behold every way thou lookest, the walls of his beautiful palace ? Hath he not gathered the waters into one place, and made the dry land appear, and drawn forth by his power a pure substance of air between heaven and earth, that fishes might multiply in the seas, fowls in great abundance fly in the open face of the firmament, tender plants, herbs, flowers, trees in all variety grow and fructify upon the ground ; yea, creeping things, cattle and beasts, increase in infinite number, in pastures, fields, gardens, orchards, and groves, and all these to do thee pleasure ? Hath he not further given thee springs and rivers, gold and silver, pearls and jewels, even plenty of streams, stones, and metal, to further thee with whatsoever for profit thou needest, or for pleasure desirest ? Hath he not made thee lord and ruler over all his creatures, even over all the huge elephants, the whale, the strong lion, and unicorn, and horse of war? over the savage tigers, bears, and wolves? over the mighty eagle, griffin, vulture, ostrich, and hawk ? Art thou not clad and defended, fed and enriched, cheered and renowned by these his creatures, and that all the parts of the body, and senses of the mind, might be partakers of his goodness, and with his sweetness refreshed, comforted, and delighted in great measure ? Yea, above all this, hath he not breathed into thy body an immortal soul, that thou mightest remain with him in glory for ever? Did he not at the first frame thee like unto himself, that he might therefore love thee as his son ? Did he not cast into thy spirit the beams of his wisdom, that thou through thy understanding mightest behold him and his glory, and stir up sparks of goodness in thy heart, that thou mightest by thy affection embrace him and his bounty, and be made perfectly blessed by his infinite happiness, who, when Adam thy ungrateful father, by distrusting him that hath faithfully promised, was thoroughly able to fulfil his will, and resolutely determined exceedingly to advance him, having given him this whole world in testimony thereof, by discontenting his mind with the excellent estate he was placed in of unspeakable love, unless he might be as good as God himself, proudly desiring to make dust the fellow of him who was from everlasting, infinitely full of wisdom, power, grace, and majesty, and had done all this at the persuasion of the most traitorous rebel of his right gracious King, and spiteful enemy of his most bountiful Master, even then when this most villainous conspiring with God's notorious adversary had deserved immortal hatred against him, and all that pertained unto him ; yea, they are yet unborn, but contained in him, whose whole mass, by this impious disobedience, became by just judgment a temple of cursed estate for ever and ever ; thou also thyself bringing forth fruit of contempt of his law, which is most holy, merciful, and mighty ; yet even then, I say, of unspeakable pity and compassion intended, nay, promised, nay, laboured to deliver him and thee from that dreadful vengeance which ye have purchased by your wicked and ungracious demerits, and to reconcile you, base abjects and vile castaways, and yet stubborn and spiteful haters of the great God Jehovah, who, when there was no means to be found in heaven, nor seas, nor in the earth, nor under the earth, but that he should damn his only begotten Son, the very brightness of his glory, who never offended him, but was an eternal delight unto his soul, and rejoicing unto his Spirit, that thou mightest be saved, a gross lump of slime and clay, still vexing him by thy wickedness; yet delivered his Son into the full power of Satan, to put him to a most shameful death, by the hands of most detestable persons, and did cast him far away out of his favour, and threw him down into the bottomless pit of his unsupportable wrath and indignation, that thou mightest be placed between his own arms in the kingdom of heaven, in all royalty and glory, as his dear and entirely beloved son. Why therefore wast thou, O my unholy and unthankful nature, so ready and prone, so violent and headstrong to commit things highly displeasant in his sight, who in a manner, and as far as was possible, slew himself for thy safety, when he had no creature so disobedient as thee? O thou my inward soul, and spirit of my mind, awake and stand up to defend thyself, for thou art besieged with mighty enemies, the prince of darkness, the rulers of the air, the spiritual craftiness and policies of hell! Why arisest thou not, thou sluggard? Thy foes in great number are prepared with many ambushments, having a huge army all maliciously bent with venomous darts to pierce through thy heart; they are entered thy holds at all five gates of thy outward sense, yea, they have broken down thy inward door, and have left thee but one window towards heaven to escape by, even by thy prayers, whereto the Spirit of God waiteth thy speedy coming. Make haste, O thou heavy with sleep, or thou art taken by thy cruel enemies, whose hands are of iron, and their teeth of steel, to grind thy very bones to powder. Hearken no longer to that stinking harlot, thy wicked appetite, which, lying in thy bosom, desireth nothing but thy utter destruction; she persuadeth thee that thou art in no present danger, that she may rejoice at thy miserable end. It may be thou art led to the slaughter, that though thou go on a little way in thy pleasant path, thou mayest return back when thou wilt, and thy little wandering will not greatly be regarded. O thou unwise and sottish heart, when wilt thou understand? Hath the Son of God endured such pain for the smallest of thy sins, and makest thou so light account of so grievous crimes? Doth the law thunder curses, and plagues, and everlasting torments, against thy least inordinate motions, and didst thou not dread to perform so shameless a practice? Knowest thou not that the eyes of God and his angels behold thee doing that thou wouldest be ashamed to do in the presence of ungodly men or unclean beasts? or dost thou consider how thou didst grieve the Spirit of God, who hath vouchsafed of his infinite mercy to dwell in thy body to this end, chiefly that he might mortify thy carnal lusts? Why didst thou then defile this temple which he hath sanctified to be a house for himself to dwell in ? Take heed thou drive not out so worthy a guest by such swinish and fleshly behaviour, who, if he once depart, then shalt thou be a hold for devils and legions of damned spirits, that they may stuff thee full of all manner of iniquity, and then at length become pitch and brimstone to maintain the fire of God's scorching wrath in thy sinews, spirit, and inward bowels, drinking out in full measure the dregs of the wine of his rage and fury ; and canst thou be blind and reckless, that for the vain pleasure of sin for a little while thou wilt constrain God to torment thee everlastingly, who, it may be, even at this instant, if thou wilt still try his patience and longsufferance, will suddenly take thy spirit from thee, or come in judgment to recompense to all sinners, by his final sentence in the burning of the whole world, the stipend of horror, shame, confusion, and utter reprobation. And weigh with thyself that to approach to God is the chiefest joy of his chosen, to behold his glorious countenance in the face of his Son, whereas thy sins do separate thee from him, and make thee afraid to speak to him by prayers, which is thy chiefest and greatest solace in this mortal life ; how much more will thy ungodliness make thee wish delay of the last judgment, the speedy and present coming whereof is a chief prop of our faith ; and withal remember how the devil, that roaring lion, laboureth by his impure act to make thee most filthy and loathsome in the sight of God, and rejoiceth to see thy gracious Father, merciful Saviour, and comfortable Sanctifier so abused and withstood, and angered by thee, whom he hath wonderfully made, carefully preserved, and dearly redeemed, and tenderly loved, that if it may be, thou shouldest by utter apostasy dishonour him in the face of the world who hath advanced thee in the presence of all his angels ; and though thou be so sure in faith that thou canst not utterly fall, the consideration whereof should make thee more dutiful, and not encourage thee in a sinful course, yet mayest thou, by little and little, and by often falling, bring thyself into a better liking both of the wicked and of wickedness itself, whom thou oughtest to hate with a perfect hatred, and then God by just judgment cast thee into a sure sleep, that thy filthiness may be seen of men, and thou condemned, to the grief of the righteous, and scorned to the shame of the ungodly, and in the mean season, by provoking God's judgment, be spoiled of thy goodly ornaments, of thy godly desires, of religious thoughts, of zealous affections, of Christian communication, of holy endeavours, of assured persuasions of faith, of stedfast waitings through hope, of constant suffering by patience, and hearty rejoicings from love. In the perfect consummation of which things, because all happiness consisteth, beware, thou careless wretch, lest suddenly, by thy abominable filthiness, thou either for a time wholly deprive thyself of comfortable feeling of these things, or much diminish thy present graces and blessings received of the Holy Spirit, to the glory of God the Father. But why do I utter my voice, or strive to make a dead carcase move? Oh quicken thou me that art the fountain of life, and call thou out of heaven thy dwelling place, that my wandering soul may hear the voice of her shepherd, and follow thee whithersoever thou leadest; nay, of thy tender compassion take me up upon thy shoulders, and carry me gently into thy fold again; for thieves have stolen me away, and have bound my feet, so that I cannot go, and they watch for me until thou art gone, that they may carry me away quick from thy pastures. Oh do thou therefore presently deliver me, and give me thy helping hand; oh cast thou down by thy Spirit my raging lust, and by thy grace subdue my untamed affections. I am weak, O Lord, and unable to resist the force of my mighty adversary; send thy help from above, and save me out of the jaws of this cruel lion. Thou hast delivered me out of the mouth of hell: oh let not the gates thereof any more prevail against me; let me not any longer be occupied in ungodliness, lest my enemy triumph over me, saying in his malicious heart, There, there, so would I have it. Let this sin be far from me, O Lord, lest I should defile myself any more with this notorious wickedness; work therefore in my heart an utter detestation of it, that I may ever hereafter keep myself pure and unspotted for thy kingdom. Thou that art able to make of stones children to Abraham, mollify, I pray thee, my stony heart, that all manner of son-like affections may be imprinted therein; pluck up, O good Father, these roots of bitterness, that no unsavoury fruit may come of the tree, which thou by thine own hand hast planted. I desire, I look, I call, I cry for thy assistance, that I may conquer this unruly motion. O blessed Saviour, that has granted so many petitions on earth, to them that were careful for the body, fulfil, I pray thee, this my desire, not for health, nor strength, nor riches, nor honour, nor for food, nor apparel, but for thy heavenly grace and inspiration; yea, let me lose all those rather than be left in my sinful flesh, that I should be ruled any longer thereby. Mortify, good Father, in me the old body of sin, and give unto me a new body, purged from these dead works, to serve the living God; renew my spirit daily, that I may cast away these works of darkness; let it be enough, O merciful

Father, that my weakness in falling heretofore, hath been made known unto me, lest I should be too proud. Now let thy strength appear in putting this mine enemy under my feet, that thereby I may be bold to put my confidence in thee. Why should my body, made by thine hand, and my soul framed according to thy image, be given over as a prey into the hands of Satan? Deliver me, O Lord, from the snares of the hunter, and preserve me from the hand of mine enemy, who lieth in wait for my spiritual life, and laboureth my everlasting destruction; so shall I praise thee for thy great goodness, and magnify thy name for giving me conquest over my adversary that is too strong for me. To thee I fly for succour till this tempest be overpast; hide me I pray thee under thy shield and buckler, that none of the fiery darts of Satan take hold on me. Good Lord, for the love thou bearest unto mankind, for thy Son's sake, who hath taken our nature on him, grant that I may not be tempted above my strength, and that in all temptations I may fly unto thee as a horn of my salvation, yielding thee most humble and hearty thanks for that thou hast given me a desire to withstand my sinful flesh, which thy work I beseech thee for thy name's sake to perfect, and fully accomplish.

Mat. xxvi. 41, 'Watch and pray lest you enter into temptation; the spirit is willing, but the flesh is weak.'

ANOTHER ZEALOUS PRAYER.

ETERNAL GOD, almighty and most merciful, we thy unworthy servants, prostrate before thy throne of grace, do yield ourselves body and soul unto thee for all thy benefits, which thou from our birth hast heaped upon us, as though we had always done thy will, although we were occupied about vain things, never marked, never loved, never served, never thanked thee so heartily for them, as we esteem a mortal friend for the least courtesy. Therefore we come with shame and sorrow to confess our sins, not small but grievous, not a few but infinite, not past but present, not secret but presumptuous, against thy express word and will; against our own conscience, knowledge and liking, if any had done them, but ourselves. O Lord, if thou shouldst require but the least of them at our hands, Satan would challenge us for his, and we should never see thy face again, nor the heavens, nor the earth, nor all the goodness which thou hast prepared for man. What shall we do then, but appeal unto thy mercy, and humbly desire thy fatherly goodness, to extend that compassion towards us, which thy beloved Son our loving Saviour hath purchased, so mightily, so graciously, and so dearly for us? We believe and know that one drop of his blood is sufficient to heal our infirmities, pardon our iniquities, and supply our necessities; but without thy grace, our Light, our Strength, our Guide, we are able to do nothing but sin, as woful experience hath taught us too long, and the example of them which are void thereof, whose life is nothing else but the service of the world, the flesh, and the devil. Therefore, good Father, as thou in special favour hast appointed us to serve thee, likeas thou hast ordained all other creatures to serve us, so may it please thee to send down thy heavenly Spirit into our hearts, change our affections, subdue our reason, regenerate our wills, and purify our nature to this duty; so shall not thy benefits, nor thy chastisements, nor thy word return void, but accomplish that for which they were sent, until we be renewed to the image of thy Son. Good Lord, we beseech thee, look down, in the multitude of thy compassions, upon thy militant church, this sinful realm, thy gracious servant our dread sovereign, her honourable council, the civil magistrates, the painful ministers, the two universities, the people that sit in darkness, and all that bear thy cross. Gather us into one communion of thy truth, and give unto every man a spirit to his calling, that we being mindful of the account, and that we are called Christians, may firmly resolve, speedily begin, and continually persevere in doing and suffering thy holy will. Good Lord, bless and sanctify our meeting, that no temptation hinder me in speaking, nor them in hearing, but that thy word may be heard and spoken as the word of God, which is able to save our souls in that day. There is no cause, O God most just, why thou shouldest hear sinners which art displeased with sin, but for his sake which suffered for sin, and sinned not; in whose name we lift up our hearts, hands, and voices unto thee, praying as he hath taught us, Our Father which art, &c.

A MORNING PRAYER.

O Lord, prepare our hearts to prayer.

ETERNAL GOD, giver to them which want, comforter to them which suffer, and forgiver to them which repent, we have nothing to render thee but thine own. If we could give thee our bodies and souls, they should be saved by it, but thou wert never the richer for them. All is our duty, and all of us cannot perform it; therefore thy Son died, and thy Spirit descended, and thy angels guide, and thy ministers teach, to help the weakness of men. All things call upon us to call upon thee; and we are prostrate before thee, before we know how to worship thee; even since we rose we have tasted many of thy blessings, and thou hast begun to serve us before we begin to serve thee. Why shouldest thou bestow thy health, wealth, rest, and liberty upon us more than others? We can give no reason for it, but that thou art merciful. And if thou shouldest draw all back again, we have nothing to say but that thou art just. Our sins are so grievous and infinite, that we are fain to say with Judas, I have sinned, and there stop, because we cannot reckon them. All things else serve thee as they did at first; only men are the sinners in this world.

Our heart is a root of corruption, our eyes are the eyes of vanity, our ears are the ears of folly, our mouths are the mouths of deceit, our hands are the hands of iniquity, and every part doth dishonour thee, which would be glorified of thee. The understanding, which was given us to learn virtue, is apt now to apprehend nothing but sin; the will, which was given us to affect righteousness, is apt now to love nothing but wickedness; the memory, which was given us to remember good things, is apt now to keep nothing but evil things. There is no difference between us and the wicked. We have done more against thee this week than we have done for thee since we were born, and yet we have not resolved to amend; but this is the course of our whole life: first we sin, and then we pray thee to forgive it, and then to our sins again, as though we came to thee for leave to offend thee.

And that which should get pardon at thy hands for all the rest, that is, our prayer, is so full of toys and fancies, for want of faith and reverence, that when we have prayed, we had need to pray again, that thou wouldest forgive our prayers, because we think least of thee when we pray unto thee. What father but thou could suffer this contempt, and be contemned still? Yet, when we think upon thy Son, all our fear is turned into joy, because his righteousness for us is more than our wickedness against ourselves. Settle our faith in thy beloved, and it sufficeth for all our iniquities, necessities, and infirmities. Now, Lord, we go forth to fight against the world, the flesh, and the devil; and the weakest of our enemies is stronger than we. Therefore, we come unto thee, for thy

Holy Spirit to take our part, that is, to change our minds, and wills, and affections which we have corrupted ; to remove all the hindrances which let us to serve thee, and to direct all our thoughts, speeches, and actions to thy glory, as thou hast directed thy glory unto our salvation. Although we be sinners, O Lord, yet we are thine ; and therefore we beseech thee to separate our sins from us, which would separate us from thee, that we may be ready to every good, as we are to evil. Teach us to remember our sins, that thou mayest forget them ; and let our sorrow here prevent the sorrow to come. We were made like thee; let not flesh and blood turn the image of God to the image of Satan ; our foes are thy foes ; let not thine enemies prevail against thee, to take us from thee ; but make thy word unto us like the star which led unto Christ ; make thy benefits like the pillar which brought to the land of promise ; make thy cross like the messenger which compelled guests to the banquet, that we may walk before like examples, and alway look upon thy Son how he would speak and do, before we speak or do anything.

Keep us in that fear of thy majesty, that we may make conscience of all that we do, and that we may count no sin small, but leave our lying, and swearing, and surfeiting, and coveting, and boasting, and flaunting, and inordinate gaming, and wanton sporting, because they draw us to other sins, and are forbidden as straitly as others. Let not our hearts at any time be so dazzled, but that in all temptations we may discern between good and evil, between right and wrong, between truth and error ; and that we may judge of all things as they are, and not as they seem to be. Let our minds be always so occupied, that we may learn something of everything, and use all those creatures as means and helps prepared for us to serve thee. Let our affections grow so toward one another, that we may love thee as well for the prosperity of others as if it were our own. Let our faith and love and prayer be alway so ready to go unto thee for our help, that in sickness we may find patience, in prison we may find joy, in poverty we may find contentment, and in all troubles we may find hope. Turn all our joys to the joy of the Holy Ghost, and all our peace to the peace of conscience, and all our fears to the fear of sin ; that we may love righteousness with as great good will as ever we loved wickedness, and go before others in thankfulness towards thee, as far as thou goest in mercy towards us before them, taking all that thou sendest as a gift, and leaving our pleasures before they leave us ; that our time to come may be a repentance of the time past, thinking alway of the joys of heaven, the pains of hell, our own death, and the death of thy Son for us. Yet, Lord, let us speak once again; like Abraham, one thing more we will beg at thy hands; our resolutions are variable, and we cannot perform our promises to thee; therefore settle us in a constant form of obedience, that we may serve thee from this hour with those duties, which the world, the devil, and the flesh would have us defer until the point of death. Lord, we are unworthy to ask anything for ourselves; yet thy favour hath preferred us to be petitioners for others. Therefore, we beseech thee to hear us for them, and them for us, and thy Son for all. Bless the universal church with truth, with peace, and thy holy discipline. Strengthen all them which suffer for thy cause, and let them see thy Spirit of comfort coming towards them, as the angels came to thy Son when he was hungry.

Be merciful unto all those which lie in anguish of conscience for remorse of their sins; as thou hast made them examples, so teach us to take example by them, that we may look upon thy gospel to keep us from despair, and upon thy law to keep us from presumption. Prosper the armies which fight thy battles, and shew a difference between thy servants and thy enemies, as thou didst between the Israelites and the Egyptians, that they which serve thee not may come to thy service, seeing that no God doth bless besides thee. Make us thankful for our peace, whom thou hast set at liberty; while thou hast laid our dangers upon others, which mightest have laid their dangers upon us. And teach us to build thy church in our rest, as Solomon built thy temple in his peace. Have mercy upon this sinful land, which is sick of long prosperity; let not thy blessings rise up against us, but endue us with grace as thou hast with riches, that we may go before other nations in religion, as we go before them in plenty. Give us such hearts as thy servants should have, that thy will may be our will, that thy law may be our law, and that we may seek our kingdom in thy kingdom. Give unto our prince a princely heart, unto our counsellors the spirit of counsel, unto our judges the spirit of judgment, unto our ministers the spirit of doctrine, unto our people the spirit of obedience, that we may all retain the communion here, that we may enjoy the communion of saints hereafter.

Bless this family with thy grace and peace, that the rulers thereof may govern according to thy word, that the servants may obey like the servants of God, and that we may all be loved of thee. Now, Lord, we have commenced our suit, our understanding is weak, and our memory short, and we unworthy to pray to thee, more unworthy to receive the things which we pray for ; therefore we commend our prayers and ourselves unto thy mercy, in the name of thy beloved Son, our loving Saviour, whose righteousness pleads for our unrighteousness.

Our Father which art in heaven, &c.

A PRAYER FOR EVENING.

O Lord God, what shall we render unto thee for all thy benefits, which hast given thy Son for a ransom, thy Holy Spirit for a pledge, thy word for a guide, and reservest a kingdom for our perpetual inheritance ; of whose goodness we are created, of whose justice we are corrected, of whose mercy we are saved. Our sins strive with thy benefits, *which* are more. Let us count all creatures, and there be not so many of any kind as thy gifts, except our offences, which we return unto thee for them. Thou mightest have said before we were formed, Let them be monsters, or let them be infidels, or let them be beggars, or cripples, or bondslaves, so long as they live. But thou hast made us to the best likeness, and nursed us in the best religion, and placed us in the best land, that thousands would think themselves happy if they had but a piece of our happiness. Therefore, why should any serve thee more than we, which want nothing but thankfulness? Thou hast given us so many things, that we have scarce anything left to pray for, but that thou wouldest continue those benefits which thou hast bestowed already ; yet we covet as if we had nothing, and live as though we knew nothing. When we were children, we deferred till we were men ; now we are men, we defer until we be old men ; and when we be old men, we will defer until death. Thus we steal thy gifts, and do nothing for them ; yet we look for as much at thy hands as they which serve thee all their lives. The least of thy blessings is greater than all the courtesies of men ; and yet we are not so thankful to thee for all that we have, as we are to a friend for one good turn. We are ashamed of many sins in others, and yet we are not ashamed to commit the same sins ourselves, and worse than they. Yea, we have sinned so long almost, that we can do nothing else but sin, and occasion others to sin too, which would not sin but for us. If we do any evil, we do it cheerfully, and quickly, and easily ; but if we do any good, we do it faintly, and rudely, and slackly. When did we talk without vanity? when did

we give without hypocrisy ? When did we bargain without deceit ?
When did we reprove without envy ? When did we hear without
weariness ? When did we pray without tediousness ? Such is our
corruption, as though we were made to sin in deed, or in word, or
in thought. We have broken all thy commandments, that we
might see what good is in evil, which have felt nothing but guilt,
and shame, and expectation of judgment, while we might have had
peace of conscience, joy of heart, and all the graces which come
with thy Holy Spirit. Some have been won by the word, but we
would not suffer it to change us ; some have been reformed by the
cross, but we would not suffer it to purge us ; some have been
moved by thy benefits, but we would not suffer them to persuade
us ; nay, we have given consent to the devil, that we will abuse
all thy gifts so fast as they come. And therefore thy blessings
make us proud, thy riches covetous, thy peace wanton, thy meats
intemperate, thy mercy secure, and all thy benefits are weapons to
rebel against thee ; that if thou look into our hearts, thou mayest
say our religion is hypocrisy, our zeal envy, our wisdom policy, our
peace security, our life rebellion ; our devotion ends with our
prayers, and we live as though we had no souls to save.

What shall we answer for that which our conscience condemns ?
We are one day nearer to death since we rose, when we shall give
account how every day hath been spent, and how we have got
those things which others shall consume when we be gone. And
if thou shouldest ask us now what lust assuaged, what affection
qualified, what passion expelled, what sin repented, what good
performed, since we began to receive thy benefits this day ; we
must confess against ourselves, that all our works, words, and
thoughts have been the service of the world, the flesh, and the devil.
We have offended thee, and contemned thee all the day, and at
night we pray unto thee, Father, forgive us all our sins, which
have dishonoured thee, while thou didst serve us ; run from thee,
while thou didst call us ; and forgotten thee, whilst thou didst feed
us : so thou sparest us, so we sleep, and to-morrow we sin again.
This is the course of all our pilgrimage, to leave that which thou
commandest, and to do that which thou forbiddest. Therefore
thou mightest justly forsake us, as we forsake thee ; and condemn
us, whose conscience condemns ourselves : but who can measure
thy goodness, which givest all, and forgivest all ? Though we are
sinful, yet thou lovest us ; though we knock not, yet thou openest ;
though we ask not, yet thou givest. What should we have if we

did serve thee, which hast done all these things for thine enemies ! Therefore, thou which hast given us all things for our service, O Lord, give us a heart to serve thee, and let this be the hour of our conversion. Let not evil overcome good, let not thine enemy have his will; but give us strength to resist, patience to endure, and constancy to persevere unto the end.

Instruct us by thy word, guide us by thy Spirit, mollify us by thy grace, humble us by thy corrections, win us by thy benefits, reconcile our nature to thy will, and teach us to make profit of everything, that we may see thee in all things, and all things in thee ; and because, O most merciful Father, we walk between thy mercy and justice through many temptations, govern our steps with such discretion that the hope of mercy may prevent despair, and the fear of justice may keep us from presumption ; that in mirth we be not vain, in knowledge we be not proud, in zeal we be not bitter : but as the tree brings forth first leaves, then blossoms, and then fruit, so first we may bring forth good thoughts, then good speeches, and after a good life; to the honour of thy name, the good of thy children, and the salvation of our souls, remembering the time when we shall sleep in the grave, and the day when we shall awake to judgment. Now, the time is come, O Lord, which thou hast appointed for rest, and without thee we can neither wake nor sleep, which hast made the day and night, and rulest both ; therefore into thy hands we commend our souls and bodies that thou hast bought, that they may serve thee. Restore them, O Lord, to their first image, and keep them to thy service ; and resign us not to ourselves again, but finish thy work, that we may every day come nearer and nearer to thy kingdom, till we hate the way to hell as much as hell itself; and let every cogitation and speech and action be so many steps to heaven. For thy name's sake, for thy promise's sake, for thy Son's sake, O Lord, we lift up our hearts, hands, and voices unto thee in his name, which suffered for sin and sinned not.

Our Father which art in heaven, &c.

A PRAYER FOR A SICK MAN.

ALMIGHTY GOD and all-merciful Father, which art the physician of our bodies and souls, in thy hands are life and death. Thou bringest to the grave and pullest back again. We came into this world upon condition to forsake it whensoever thou wouldest call us; and now the summoners are come; thy fetters hold me, and none can loose me but he which bound me. I am sick in body and soul; but he hath strucken me which in judgment sheweth mercy. I deserved to die so soon as I came to life, but thou hast preserved me till now; and shall this mercy be in vain, as though we were preserved for nothing? Who can praise thee in the grave? I have done thee no service since I was born, but my goodness is to come; and shall I die before I begin to live? But, Lord, thou knowest what is best of all; and if thou convert me, I shall be converted in an hour; and as thou acceptest the will of David, as well as the act of Solomon, so thou wilt accept my desire to serve thee as well as if I did live to glorify thee. The spirit is willing, but the flesh is frail; and as I did live sinfully whensoever thy Spirit was from me, so I shall die unwillingly unless thy Spirit prepare me; therefore, dear Father, give me that mind which a sick man should have, and increase my patience with my pain, and call unto my remembrance all which I have heard, or read, or felt, or meditated, to strengthen me in this hour of my trial, that I, which never taught any good while I lived, may now teach others how to die, and to bear their sickness patiently. Apply unto me all the mercies and merits of thy beloved Son, as if he had died for me alone. Be not from me when the enemy comes, but when the tempter is busiest, let thy Spirit be busiest too; and if it please thee to loose me out of this prison, when I shall leave my earth to earth, let thine angels carry up my soul to heaven as they did Lazarus, and place me in one of those mansions which thy Son is gone to prepare for me. This is my Mediator which hath reconciled me and thee when thou didst abhor me for my sins; and thou didst send him from heaven to us, to shew that thou art bound to hear him for us; therefore in him I come unto thee, in him I call upon thee. O my Redeemer, my Preserver, and my Saviour, to thee be all praise, with thy Father and the Holy Spirit, for ever. Amen.

What shall stay me from my Father, my Brother, and my Comforter?

A COMFORTABLE SPEECH, TAKEN FROM A GODLY PREACHER LYING UPON HIS DEATHBED; WRITTEN FOR THE SICK.

I OWE to God a death, as his Son died for me. Ever since I was born, I have been sailing to this haven, and gathering patience to comfort this hour; therefore, shall I be one of those guests now that would not come to the banquet when they were invited? What hurt is in going to paradise? I shall lose nothing but the sense of evil, and anon I shall have greater joys than I feel pains; for my head is in heaven already, to assure me that my soul and body shall follow after. O death, where is thy sting? why should I fear that which I would not escape, because my chiefest happiness is behind, and I cannot have it unless I go unto it? I would go through hell to heaven; and therefore, if I march but through death, I suffer less than I would suffer for God. My pains do not dismay me, because I travail to bring forth eternal life; my sins do not fright me, because I have Christ my Redeemer; the Judge doth not astonish me, because the Judge's Son is my advocate; the devil amazes me not, because the angels pitch about me; the grave grieves me not, because it was my Lord's bed. Oh that God's mercy to me might move others to love him! for the less I can express it, the more it is. The prophets and apostles are my forerunners; every man is gone before me, or else he will follow after me. If it please God to receive me into heaven before them which have served him better, I owe more thankfulness to him. And because I have deferred my repentance till this hour, whereby my salvation is cut off, if I should die suddenly; lo, how my God, in his merciful providence to prevent my destruction, calls me by a lingering sickness, which stays till I be ready, and prepares me to my end, like a preacher, and makes me, by wholesome pains, weary of this beloved world, lest I should depart unwillingly, like them whose death is their damnation. So he loves me while he beats me, that his stripes are plasters to salve me; therefore, who shall love him, if I despise him? This is my whole office now, to strengthen my body with my heart, and to be contented as God hath appointed, until I can glorify him, or until he glorify me. If I live, I live to sacrifice; and if I die, I die a sacrifice; for his mercy is above mine iniquity. Therefore, if I should fear death, it were a sign that I had not faith nor hope, as I professed, but that I doubted of God's truth in his promise, whether he will forgive his penitent sinner or no. It is my Father, let him do what seemeth good in his sight. Come, Lord Jesus, for thy servant cometh ; I am willing, help my unwillingness.

Thus the faithful depart in another sort, with such peace and joy round about them, that all which see them, wish that their souls may follow theirs.

A LETTER WRITTEN TO ONE'S FRIEND IN HIS SICKNESS.

BELOVED, I marvel not that you have pain, for you are sick ; but I marvel that you cover it not for offence, because the wisdom of man is to bite in his grief, and always to shew more comfort in God than pain in suffering. Now God calleth to repetitions, to see whether you have learned more constancy than others. If sickness be sharp, make it not sharper with frowardness ; but know this is a great favour to us, when we die by sickness, which makes us ready for him that calleth us. Now you have nothing to think upon but God, and you cannot think upon him without joy ; your grief passeth, but your joy will never pass. Tell me, patient, how many stripes is heaven worth ? Is my friend only sick in the world, or his faith weaker than others ? You have always prayed, Thy will be done, and are you now offended that God's will is done? How hath the faithful man forgotten that all things, even death, turn to the best to them that love God ? Teach the happy, O Lord, to see his happiness through troubles. Every pain is a prevention of the pains of hell, and every ease in pain is a foretaste of the ease, and peace, and joys in heaven. Therefore, remember your own comforts to others before, and be not impatient when there is most need of patience ; but as you have ever taught us to live, so now give us an example to die, and deceive Satan, as Job did.

MORNING PRAYER.

O ETERNAL GOD and merciful Father, which art the light that no man can attain unto, and by thy marvellous lightness drivest away the darkness of the night and shadow of death, and by thy grace enlightenest all those that being in darkness come unto thee ; I thy unworthy servant do bless and praise thy most holy name for all the mercies and gracious benefits from time to time I have received from thee, and most humbly thank thee that thou hast vouchsafed me this favour, to pass this night in so quiet and comfortable rest, and hast brought me again to see and enjoy the light of the morning. And now I beseech thee, O Lord, of thine infinite goodness and mercy, by the merits of my blessed Saviour, that thy merciful compassion may this day be extended to me, that, being enlightened with thy grace, I may not be carried away by the power of darkness, to spend this day after the lusts and pleasures of my own corrupt mind; but that I may, with all conscience, follow thy Fatherly will, which thou hast revealed unto me in thy holy word. Increase in me, O Lord, all spiritual gifts and graces, and beat down in me all carnal and corrupt affections. Enable me by thy blessed Spirit, in some measure, both to withstand that which is evil, and to perform what is good and pleasing unto thee; and that neither by my own negligence, nor the power of any temptation, which either the world, the flesh, or the devil shall present unto me, I be driven away from a true faith, but may lay hold of those gracious promises that thou hast made unto me in Jesus Christ my Saviour. Dispel, O Lord, the thick mist and clouds of my sins, which corrupt my soul, and darken my understanding; and wash them away, I most humbly beseech thee, in the precious blood of thy Son's passion; that so I may be acknowledged for one of thine elect, when I shall appear before thy judgment-seat. Give me a will carefully to follow my vocation, and let thy blessing be upon me in the same. Bless me in my body, in my soul, and in whatsoever belongs unto me: lighten my mind, and inflame my heart with a love of those things that are good. And as my body, by thy power, is risen from sleep, so let my soul daily be raised from the slumber of sin and the darkness of this world, that so both together may enjoy that everlasting light which thou hast provided for thy saints, and purchased with the blood of thy dear Son our Saviour Jesus Christ, to whom with thee, O Father, and the blessed Spirit, be all honour and glory for evermore. Amen.

O LORD, PREPARE OUR HEARTS TO PRAYER.

O LORD GOD, our heavenly Father, we thy poor and wretched creatures give thee most humble and hearty thanks for our quiet and safe sleep, and for raising us up from the same. We beseech thee, for Jesus Christ's sake, to prosper us this day in our labour and travel, that it may be to the discharging of our duty in our vocations, principally to thy glory; next, to the profit of this church and commonwealth; and, last of all, to the benefit and content of our masters. Grant, dear Father, that we may cheerfully and conscionably do our business and labours, not as men-pleasers, but as serving thee our God, knowing thee to be the chief Master of us, and that thou seest and beholdest us with thy fatherly eyes, who hast promised reward to them that faithfully and truly walk in their vocation, and threatened everlasting death and damnation to them that deceitfully and wickedly do their works and labours. We beseech thee, O heavenly Father, to give us the strength of thy Spirit, that godly and gladly we may overcome our labours, and that the tediousness of that irksome labour which thou for our sins hast poured upon all mankind may seem to us more delectable and sweet. Fulfil now, O Lord, these our requests, for thy Son our Saviour's sake, in whose name we pray, as he himself hath taught us,

Our Father which art in heaven, &c.

EVENING PRAYER.

O ALMIGHTY and everlasting God, the Father of mercy and God of all consolation, that by thy merciful providence defendest all those that walk before thee, and put their trust in thee; I, poor and miserable sinner, unworthy of the least of thy favours, do yet presume, in the name and mediation of Jesus Christ, to present myself before thee, and to offer up this poor sacrifice of praise and thanksgiving unto thee; that thou hast nourished and preserved me by thy power, and hast guided and governed me by thy word and Spirit; and, as for all other thy blessings, so for that mercy that hath this day accompanied me, whereby I have both been preserved from many sins that the wickedness of my nature was inclined unto, and also delivered from many punishments that the sins that I have committed have deserved. I most humbly beseech thee, in the merits of Christ Jesus, to pardon and forgive me all my sins, which either in thought, word, or deed, I have this day, or any time heretofore, committed against thee; whether they be the sins of my youth or of my age, sins of omission or commission, whether wittingly or ignorantly committed ; good Lord, pardon them unto me, and let them not cause thee this night, as justly thou mayest do, to take vengeance of me ; but be merciful unto me, O Lord, in forgiving the evil I have committed, in supplying the good that I have omitted, in restoring me to that which I have lost, in healing my sores, in lightening my blindness, in cleansing my filthiness, and in altering the whole course of my corrupt mind ; that I may be diverted from that which is evil, and enabled to perform that which is agreeable to thy blessed will and word. And, Lord, as thou hast this day preserved and kept me in safety, so I most humbly beseech thee to protect me this night from all danger, both bodily and ghostly, and to give me such quiet and comfortable rest, as may enable me to walk on in that vocation wherein thou hast placed me, and that I may both be delivered from the darkness of this present night, and may also escape that everlasting darkness which thou hast provided for those that without repentance continue in their sins ; from which, good Lord, deliver me, and all those that belong unto thee ; and that for the merits of the death and passion of my blessed Saviour Jesus Christ, in whose name I continue my prayers for myself and thy whole church, saying, as he hath taught us, Our Father, &c.

MICRO-COSMO-GRAPHIA:

THE LITTLE WORLD'S DESCRIPTION;

OR,

THE MAP OF MAN,

FROM LATIN SAPPHICS OF THAT FAMOUS LATE PREACHER IN
LONDON, MR HENRY SMITH.

═══════════

TRANSLATED, AND DEDICATED

TO THE RIGHT HONOURABLE

HONORIA LADY HAŸ,

BY

JOSHUA SYLVESTER.

TO

THE RIGHT RIGHT HONOURABLE

HONORIA,

WIFE OF JAMES LORD HAY, SOLE DAUGHTER AND HEIR OF EDWARD LORD DENNY.

Equally bound, in humble gratitude,
    To two dear equals (to you equal dear);
    Unable, yet, with both at once to clear;
    Unwilling, yet, with either to be rude,
Fain would I crave to have my bond renewed
    For a more happy, or more hopeful year,
    When gracious heaven shall deign to set me free
    From old cold cares which keep my muse unmew'd;
Would you be pleased, madam, to interpose
    Your gentle breath, I would not doubt to speed;
    Such virtue hath your virtue still with those;
Therefore, in hope of your kind help, at need,
    This simple pledge, I offer at your feet,
    Altar of love, where both their vows do meet.

Your honourable virtue's humble votary,

JOSHUA SYLVESTER.

THE MAP OF MAN.

I SING not, but, in sighs abrupt,
Sob out the state of man, corrupt
  By the old serpent's baneful breath,
Whose strong contagion still extends
To every creature that descends
  From th' old little world of death.
Dread-dear Creator, new create
Thy creature ; Saviour, expiate
  This, and all our own addition :
O sacred Spirit, our spirits renew ;
Inform, reform, and tune me true,
  To condole our sad condition.
In earth, man wanders, pilgrim-wise,
Hopes, doubts, desires, faints, freezes, fries ;
  Crossed, tossed to and fro,
He turns, he winds, he finds no good ;
He aye complains that evil's flood,
  Far and wide, doth overflow.
His birth (in sin) begins in tears ;
His life is rife in pains and fears ;
  Will he, nill he, spoiling sport :
His death with groans, in doubtful case,
Sends him, God knows unto what place :
  Bless'd none rest but in the port.
The flesh against the spirit rebels,
The spirit again the flesh repels,
  Ever striving, never still :
And suddenly, while these contend,

Their common foe, the cursed fiend,
   Finds advantage both to kill.
Earth, stepdame-like, sharp rods doth yield
To scourge her sons : the sea is fill'd
   (Both above and under too)
With hideous horrors past report :
Th' air, whirling in tempestuous sort,
   Beats, and threats all to undo.
The country's rude, and foe to fame ;
The court, more brave, and more to blame,
   Painted faces, graces feign'd :
The city (there, Oh ! bad's the best),
Seat of deceit, and miser's nest ;
   Gold their god, ungodly gain'd.
Fair at the bar, stews at the stage ;
In wayfare thieves, in warfare rage ;
   Noise abroad, annoys at home ;
In churches, purchase, profanation,
Fiends seeming saints ; abomination :
   Everywhere, no fear of doom.
The throne's not given unto the just ;
The faithful is not put in trust ;
   Prophets are not held for true :
Nor loyal lov'd, nor learned grac'd,
Nor weary eas'd, nor worthy plac'd,
   Nor hath any here his due.
The impudent, the insolent,
The fool, the friend in compliment,
   And the sly, we see by proof,
Held eloquent, magnanimous,
Right pleasant, kind, ingenious,
   And the wealthy wise enough.
Reward is hard ; words are but wind :
Each art is long ; life short confin'd :
   Might makes right in every cause.
Physic is vile, and vilely us'd ;
Divinity disdain'd, abus'd ;
   Under foot men tread the laws.
The rich with rage, the poor with plaints,
With hate the wise, with scorn the saints,
   Evermore are curstly cross'd :
With painful toil the private man,

The nobler states with envy wan,
　　Without end are torn and toss'd.
If good, he fares no better for't;
If bad, no worse they him support;
　　Fortune serveth all alike:
Though she simper, though she smile,
Though she laugh outright awhile,
　　She is always slippery-sleek.
Who lately served, lords it now;
Who lately becked, now doth bow;
　　Valleys swell, and mountains sink:
Who lately flourish'd, now doth fade;
Who late was strong, now feeble made,
　　Feeding worms, in dust doth stink.
So, lowly rest; so, lofty rues,
Say that one might his fortune choose,
　　Under heav'n to have his will;
'Twould be a doubt among the wise,
Whether it better were to rise
　　To high state, or to sit still.
Phant'sy conceives, reason receives,
Passion repugns, and patience reaves.
　　What I wish, what I desire,
I see; and sense importunes so,
I covet, I commend it too:
　　Then again it doth retire.
Sense, whither now? 'tis grief to see
What flits so fast, so suddenly.
　　Reason, whither roams thy reach?
What hurts, were better still be hid,
And still unknown; O ill-bestid.
　　Poor in store, in wealth a wretch:
When fortune comes, she means our wrack;
And when she goes, she breaks our back;
　　Coming, going, all is one.
For, what she gives she takes away,
Unkind and blind, inconstant aye;
　　Frank to few, and firm to none.
Oft have I canvass'd, whether's case
Is worst, the fallen, or th' ever base;
　　Yet, scarce can I it decide.
The fall proves plainly for the first:

Want pleads, that ever want is worst;
Partial to their proper side.
It irks the fall'n to have been high,
Th' aye poor could wish he had been by,
Either other's state would glad.
If even in gladness sadness grow,
Were not I somewhat glad also,
How extreme should I be sad !
If care we take, it health impairs ;
If not, it takes us unawares,
Whether should we seek or shun ?
Whether (to pass unto the next)
The good or bad be most perplex'd,
Is another question.
The guilty suffers for his fault:
The guiltless doubts no less assault
By misfortune ; both desire
To live on earth, to draw this breath ;
Both fear to die ; and after death,
Torment of eternal fire.
Hence, slow day's labour wears us thin ;
Hence, lightly, nightly fears begin ;
Hence, rath rising, and late rest.
Hence, toughest storms, and roughest streams ;
Hence, griping cares, and ghastly dreams,
Waking, sleeping, do molest.
Winter 's too cold, summer 's too hot ;
Autumn too moist, which breeds the rot ;
All the hope is in the spring.
The lively spring is lovely fair ;
But if keen ice then chill the air,
Little pleasure doth it bring.
Seas drown the vales, the winds do heave
The hills to heav'n, the rocks they cleave ;
Bold ambition stands amaz'd,
Expecting where to build a fort
So strong and rampir'd in such sort,
That it never may be raz'd.
Peace is too drown'd in lust and sloth ;
War is too drunk with blood and wrath :
That too gaudy, this too grim.
Men's minds are all so delicate,

So soft and so effeminate,
 Small things, all things, grievous seem.
Either the head doth always ache,
Or palate slip, or palsy shake,
 Or our belly roars within;
Or else with choler we abound,
Or else with phlegm, or else unsound
 Tumour's humours scald our skin.
What dread of death, what greedy lust,
What surfeit, sloth, and deeds unjust,
 Daily plunge in perils rife;
What sword consumeth every hour,
And what the plague doth quick devour,
 Lengthens physic, shortens life.
Where's now Æneas? where's his sons?
Where's Hercules? where's Solomon?
 Where is David? where is Saul?
Where's Cyrus, Cæsar, and the rest?
Ah! he and they are all deceas'd.
 I must follow; so must all.
Hark! thou, whom most the people hails,
The wisest errs, the justest fails,
 Strongest limpeth now and then.
The humblest swells, the sober'st sips,
The holiest sins, the wariest slips:
 God is faultless; never man.
Too curious or too carelessly,
Too lavish or too slavishly,
 By the fool or by the knave,
Too cracking or too cravenly,
Too hateful or too gratefully,
 Haste or waste mars all we have.
Ambition's end is rule and reign,
Cruelties, conquest, guiles is gain,
 To grow rich by hook or crook.
Juggling and struggling, strife in all,
No triumph without fight will fall,
 Warless, none for peace may look.
We think, but never can intend,
Good thoughts well to begin, or end
 If perhaps they be begun.
Or, if we end them, never find

(However rare in any kind)
   Recompense when we have done.
Our heart it hath an inborn guest,
Will ill (it hight), it posteth press'd
   To the tongue, ill words to vent.
Desire, then, rushes to ill deeds ;
Vengeance anon the fact succeeds :
   Thus comes ill to punishment.
If safe this snake we choke or charm,
Within again we hug it warm,
   Daring, doubting, up and down ;
Till lust, as lighter, up doth surge,
And th' horror of the fearful scourge
   Fall as heavier to the ground.
Come, flesh, be frolic, take delight,
Let's revel now, 'twill once be night :
   Shall a little gout, or colic,
Or sudden qualm, or sullen care,
Or addle-fit of idle fear,
   Mar thy mirth ?   Come, flesh, be frolic.
What seeks we shun, what shuns we seek ;
What helps we loathe, what hurts we like ;
   Bird in hand we leave for bush.
For what we want we panting crave,
And loosely lavish what we have :
   Brag of that should make us blush.
With child with mirth, we bring forth scorn,
We bring up fury ; overborne,
   Mov'd and moving, either way.
Too sorry, or too merry—mad !
The happy man is never had
   While we wretches here do stay.
We reign and serve, we want and flow ;
We joy and mourn, we freeze and glow ;
   Vows we make and break together.
We build and batter, join and jar ;
We heap and scatter, make and mar ;
   And we flourish, and we wither.
We look to heaven, and leap to hell ;
Our hope and fear by turns rebel :
   Plunging down, or puffing up.
Please would we fame, but find demur ;

Please might we well, did will concur :
 Sloth doth stay, and lust doth stop.
So still we stand, and whine the while ;
Nought labour boots, nor love, nor wile :
 All is lost when 'tis too late.
Evils to th' evil and the good
Are daily sent ; and if withstood,
 We but faster foster fate.
I will at once give over quite,
Both to be wicked and upright—
 To do either right or wrong ;
For goods well gotten grow but thin,
Get hardly up, come slowly in ;
 And the ill-gotten last not long.
What shall I do ? If I forbear,
My causeless foe, I blush, I fear
 His despite and my disparage.
If to revenge me I resolve,
It satisfies, when I revolve,
 None's all faultless, in all carriage.
When I have spared, I wish t' have spoke ;
And when I speak, I would revoke—
 Better pleased t' have held my peace.
Would God I could, as wiser ones,
Both speak and hold my peace at once,
 So to live at quietness.
Dear mind, how dost thou ? Frail and sick,
My flesh implores thy succour, quick.
 Canst, Oh canst thou cure her grief ?
Oh deign, I prythee, then, with speed,
To help thy servant now at need—
 Send her reason for relief.
For faithful mind's firm resolution
Cures oftentimes th' ill constitution
 Of a body sick inclined.
But then the body, late deplor'd
For weak state, to health restored,
 Grows a burden to the mind.
O sin-bred hurt ! O inbred hell !
Nor full, nor fasting, never well—
 Never sound—what shall I say ?

Once all was well, and would be now
Better than ever, if that thou,
   Cursed sin, wert quite away.
But now, alas ! all mischief lies,
In ambush with all miseries,
   Man's confusion to conspire :
Desire and fear at once torment,
Fear is a tyrant, mal-content,
   And insatiate is desire.
Who fears ? who mourns ? who wants ? who wanders ?
Ah ! only men (will's ill-commanders),
   Man alone abounds therein.
Loud lamentations, lasting terrors,
Heart-wounding wants and wilful errors,
   Had not been, had man not been.
Here pestilence, there hunger's jaw,
Here drink, there duel, there the law,
   Snatches one or other hence.
Here cross, there care, or (better bless'd),
Who hap these haps to 'scape the best,
   Age devours without dispense.
Perpending this in mind perplex'd,
The miserable (envy vex'd),
   Cries, O beasts, O fowls, O fish !
You happy, harmless, stormless things,
Precise in nature's lessonings,
   Live you long ; you life may wish,
But, I think, better not be born ;
Or, born, hence quickly to return,
   To our mother's dusty lap ;
Than living, daily here to die,
In cares, and fears, and misery,
   By misheed, or by mishap.
While hunger gripes me gut and gall,
While burning thirst for drink doth call,
   While for cold I quake ; alas !
In languor long I linger on,
Oh happy those, whose woes, whose moan,
   Ridding quick doth quickly pass.
The stout, the coward, and the meek,
All skirmish under fortune like,
   Striking all with mischiefs aye ;

The stout repugns, the patient prays,
The hare-like coward runs his ways;
   Fortune differs not, but they.
Too peevish this, too pleasant that,
(Too fierce, or too effeminate),
   Golden mean can hardly stand
Betwixt these two extremes, upright,
'Tis worn so weak, and weigh'd so light;
   Error plays on either hand.
Wedlock, with wife and children clogs,
The single life, lust's heavier logs
   (Rare's the gift of continence).
The young man stalks, the old man stoops,
That over-dares, this ever droops;
   The infant crawls through impotence.
Masters tax servants, proud, slut, slow;
Servants churl master, mistress shrew;
   Either other's fault can find.
The daughter thinks her mother froward;
Mother her daughter deems untoward;
   Kit (they say) will after kind.
Princes do envy subjects' wealth;
Subjects do envy princes' health;
   Each doth envy others' good.
All, all do envy learning's honour
(If any be conferr'd upon her),
   Oh! oh wicked, wretched mood!
The soldier likes the rustic's calm,
The clown affects the soldier's palm;
   Thus doth envy inly fret her:
Our pastures parch, our herds be poor,
Our neighbour thrives in every store;
   Other's crop is ever better.
Fond lovers languish at their eyes;
The wrathful fosters and defies
   Frenzies, furies (wayward elves):
What need ye call for whip or scourge?
Their punishment what need we urge?
   Theirselves—errors scourge themselves.
Fear hunts the coward at the heel;
The cruel, still revenging steel;
   Ruin him that ruin seeks;

Heavy revenge on heinous crimes :
Yea, in the sin, the plague sometimes ;
  Heaven's just hand so justly strikes,
Sorrow and shame, for what is past ;
Care of the present, fear fore-cast
  Of the danger yet to come ;
Make all false pleasures shorter seem,
And sharpen too in pain extreme,
  Than even pain itself to some.
If I be merry, I am mad
(Say the severe) ; if sober-sad,
  Merry Greek me Meacock call.
Is't possible for any man
At once to please (do what he can)
  God, himself, the world, and all ?
Who greatness haughtily affects,
Who great things happily effects ;
  That is hated, this envied :
But hoping greatness, whoso haps
To fail, or fall in after-claps,
  Him the vulgar dare deride.
Virtue is vanquish'd by her foes.
Whose triumph even their forehead shews,
  'Tis a shame to be ashamed.
But shall I tell, and tell thee true,
Thy fate (the fruit that shall ensue
  Shameless shameful life untamed) ?
This fate then falls to be thine own,
Such shall thou reap as thou hast sown :
  Wages like thy work expect.
Who here their days in evil spend,
Shall suffer evils without end ;
  Such is Minos' doom direct.
Then swagger, stagger, spend, and spoil,
Steal, and conceal, and keep a coil ;
  Quickly shalt thou all forego :
Kill, conquer, triumph ; down again
Shalt thou be cast : bouze, beat, disdain ;
  Th' end's at hand, and comes not slow.
The wise bewail men's follies rife,
And fain would cure their vicious life
  With receipts of heav'nly skill :

But sin-sick fools (whatever prick
Benumb'd by custom) lethargic,
  Care not, fear not, feel no ill.
Who knoweth much, much ill he knows;
Who little recks, much good foregoes.
  Hence perplexed doubts he casts ;
What is great knowledge ? What so much
Of learning ? or of book-skill such ?
  But great blazes, and light blasts ?
While Plato, sportive, doth despise,
The sullen cynic's sloven guise :
  He, as fast (on th' other side)
Doth Plato's pomp as much condemn
And trample on : were both of them
  (Who can tell me ?) wise, or wide ?
Democritus, here, laughs a good :
Heraclitus, there, weeps a flood.
  Glad and sad would mend us fain :
But now, so stubborn-stiff is man,
That tears, nor tunes, nor aught else can
  Faults restore, nor fates restrain.
Sloth ne'er wanteth want for mate ;
Thrift, sweat and labour macerate ;
  Either in their issue languish :
So health is never without sin,
Nor sickness without pain within :
  Outward ache, or inward anguish.
Service is to the lofty mind
A curb, a spur to the abject hind ;
  Seldom or never stoops the will :
The vulgar voice, the common cry,
Is, Welcome, welcome liberty ;
  Good for good, but ill for ill.
A grief it is alone to be ;
But more, to have ill company :
  More or less (alas !) by this,
Appeareth plain, when all is done,
(As proof hath found) that under sun,
  Here's no full, no perfect bliss.
Who never yet himself could please,
What can content ? what use ? what ease ?
  What availeth wealth at will ?

Needy and naked here I live ;
To die, it doth me nothing grieve ;
 But to perish, and live still ;
I look to heaven, and there (alas !)
With fear I see my Judge's face,
 · Auditing my sums of sin.
I think of hell, and then I burn
Like Ætna, then to earth return,
 Cares and fears there never lin.
This feel I, thus I justly fare :
O man ! learn quickly, and have care,
 Sacred duties to observe.
This life is rife in troubles sore :
But yet (alas !) a million more,
 Our rebellion doth deserve.
Much like, or worse than former age,
The future's face we may presage :
 Better seldom comes, they say.
Now right, now wrong ; now good, now ill ;
Now fiend, now friend ; now God, now will,
 Seem to have alternate sway.
Nothing is gratis given nor got :
Each labours more or less (God wot),
 With the hand, or with the head.
None without art or virtue thrive ;
Nor art, nor virtue, all achieve :
 Only these, not always sped.
What should I seek or sue for much,
To live at rest ? Content is rich.
 Fortune often is too free,
And often kills where she's too kind :
But, had we once an equal mind,
 We should all contented be.
But every one is too secure,
In sunny days ; and in obscure,
 Too dejected in desire :
Hence, over-faint, or over-full ;
Too-pined, or too-plentiful,
 Fry we all with inward fire.
Now dust her dusty brood expects :
Come, earth to earth (of either sex).
 Pleasure trembles at her call,

Cries out of haste, complains of heaven :
But pain and sorrow (narrow driven)
   Are well pleased, and eas'd withal.
Who gives me grace to gush out tears,
And lends me space to pour forth prayers ;
   Yet, both seeming to neglect ?
'Tis God, the dreadful sinners' scourge ;
The gracious God, which oft doth purge
   Ills with pills, in his elect.
Behold me, thou that didst bestow
Thy Son on me ; forgive me, thou
   That didst suffer for my sin :
Assist and stay me evermore,
Thou, thou that here so oft before
   In my breast a guest hast been.
Regard us, Lord, unworthy though ;
Thy glory seek, thy mercy shew ;
   Enemies approach apace :
We fail, we fall, we cannot stand ;
Our foes will have the upper hand,
   But thou, help us with thy grace.
Witness myself that here lie slain,
But by thy touch reviv'd again ;
   Glad to live, to live to thee,
And yet desire to be dissolv'd
(When my due date shall be revolv'd)
   As more happy far for me.
Shew me the Holy Land, which flows
With milk and honey, saints' repose ;
   Train me in the new commerce,
In the new art of better life ;
Then farewell muses, farewell strife :
   In thy courts I will converse.
I cannot strike Apollo's string,
Study for heav'n, and timely ring
   Sacred Aaron's golden bell ;
Nor sing at once the Thespian songs,
And serve my country as belongs ;
   Therefore, muses, here farewell.

CERTAIN EPIGRAMS OF THE SAME MASTER H. S.

TRANSLATED, AND DEDICATED TO MY DEAR AFFECTED,

DUE RESPECTED,

DR HALL AND DR HILL.

I owe you each a larger sum,
Why bring I then to both a crumb?
To shew you both my shifts to live,
Even fain to borrow what I give.
But better so than blushless steal
Others' conceits, or debts conceal.
Till more my might, divide this mite,
A lark, they say, is worth a kite.
Some greater, greater things present,
Of lesser worth, or worser meant.
God measures not our work, but will:
Do you the like, and love me still.

J. S

1. OF A KING.

 1   2   3   4   5   6
Extirp, extol, know, keep, love, learn (from high)
 1   2   3   4   5   6
Bad, good, thyself, the law's path, peace, to die.

2. OF A LAWYER.

                  1   2   3
Live just (Justinian) still; shield, shun, suppress
           1   2   3
Good men's good cause, bribes, brawling peevishness.

3. Of a Physician.

He that can cure the sick, and keep the sound,
Shall be my leech, whether he kill or wound.

4. Of a Divine.

Know God; known, teach him ; as thou teachest, tread ;
So shall thy flock be as well taught as fed.

5. Of a Judge.

Both blind and lame I judge thee best to make,
Lest that thine eyes misgive, thy hands mis-take.

6. Of a Husbandman.

Good morrow bids the cock ; the owl bids good night ;
To country cares, I bid God speed them right.

7. Of a Captain.

In war and peace Christ is the sole commander,
To lead to God-ward ; follow still his standard.

8. Of all the Seven.

 1   2   3   4   5   6   7
So rule, plead, practise, preach, doom, delve, direct,
 1   2   3   4   5   6   7
Climes, causes, cures, CHRIST, crimes, turfs, troops select.

INDEXES.

INDEXES.

I. GENERAL INDEX.

Wicked, may hear, and study, and fast, and preach, and counsel, but cannot pray, i. 399.

Called in Scripture by all the names of the devil, ii. 20.

Take much more pains to do evil, than the righteous need to take for heaven, ii. 83.

When they cannot charge the godly with any serious crime, begin to grudge at their well-doing, ii. 151.

Widow, what is implied in the name, i. 30.

Wife, better to have none than a froward one, i. 12.

Two requisites in, godliness and fitness, i. 13.

Wives, their duties towards their husbands, i. 27 ; inferred from their names, *ib.*

Will of God, to know, is the first and best lesson of a Christian, i. 257.

Wine, not unknown before the flood, i. 297.

Wisdom, not found unless we apply our hearts to seek her, i. 285.

Without sobriety, does no good but evil, i. 471 ; rules for attaining, 476 ; marks of those who are wise above sobriety, 480.

Must be got betimes, as manna was gathered in the morning, ii. 85.

Wise, worldly, without the wisdom of God, commit some notorious foolishness in the sight of all men, ii. 190.

Wise men of the east, the first fruits of the Gentiles, ii. 195.

WISH, THE PILGRIM'S, i. 259.

Women, their honour is to bear children, and consequently to be married, i. 2.

Have many faults, i. 13.

Word and sacraments, the breasts wherewith our mother doth nurse us, i. 43.

Word, milk of, how to be desired, i. 490 : presently, 491 ; importunately, 492 ; continually, 493 ; compared to milk, because it is the only food of the faithful, as milk is of babes, 494 ; because it is not hard and intricate, but plain and easy to be conceived, 495 ; because it is sweet and comfortable to the soul, *ib.* ; how called *sincere* milk, 496.

Works, good, are the way by which, not the cause for which, we come to heaven, ii. 108.

World, an edge of bitterness put upon, to wean us from it, i. 238.

YOUNG MAN'S TASK, i. 215.

Young, should learn from the trials and experiences of others, i. 218.

The hope of the church, i. 228.

More zealous than the old, ii. 172.

Youth, the best time to sow the seed of virtue, i. 217.

The best season to seek God, ii. 84.

Zaccheus, his name signified *simple, pure, honest*, ii. 136 ; a man of little stature, but not of little wit, 140 ; before, a receiver of customs, now, of Christ, 149 ; his faith fruitful and lively, 155.

Zeal is the fire of the spirit, i. 130 ; should be temperate, *ib.*

Pleasing to God, ii. 89.

Zoroaster had knowledge of the coming of the Son of God, ii. 393.

II. TEXTS OF SERMONS.

III. OTHER TEXTS ILLUSTRATED.

FINIS.

Edinburgh:
Printed by John Greig and Son.